STUDY TEXT

Professional Paper 12

Management and Strategy

New in this June 1998 edition

- New case examples
- More on financial evaluation of proposed strategies
- Knowledge management
- Global branding
- Rearranged chapters on human resources management, and new material on performance management and organisational learning

FOR DECEMBER 1998 AND JUNE 1999 EXAMS

BPP Publishing
June 1998

First edition 1993
Sixth edition June 1998

ISBN 0 7517 0137 8 (Previous edition 0 7517 0077 0)

British Library Cataloguing-in-Publication Data
A catalogue record for this book
is available from the British Library

Published by

BPP Publishing Limited
Aldine House, Aldine Place
London W12 8AW

http://www.bpp.co.uk

We are grateful to the Association of Chartered Certified Accountants for permission to reproduce in this text the syllabus and teaching guide of which the Association holds the copyright. We are also grateful to the Association of Chartered Certified Accountants, the Chartered Institute of Management Accountants, the Association of Accounting Technicians and The Institute of Chartered Secretaries and Administrators for permission to reproduce past examination questions. The suggested solutions to past examination questions have been prepared by BPP Publishing Limited.

Printed in Great Britain by
Ashford Colour Press, Gosport, Hampshire

Contents

HOW TO USE THIS STUDY TEXT

Aims of this Study Text

To provide you with the knowledge and understanding, skills and applied techniques required for passing the exam

The Study Text has been written around the ACCA's Official Syllabus and the ACCA's Official 1998-9 Teaching Guide (reproduced below, and cross-referenced to where in the text each topic is covered).

- It is **comprehensive**. We do not omit sections of the syllabus as the examiner is liable to examine any angle of any part of the syllabus - and you do not want to be left high and dry.
- It is **up-to-date as at 1 June 1998**, which means that it more than fulfils the requirement for the December 1998 exams that students should be up-to-date as at 1 June 1998.
- And it is **on-target** - we do not include any material which is not examinable. You can therefore rely on the BPP Study Text as the stand-alone source of all your information for the exam, without worrying that any of the material is irrelevant.

To allow you to study in the way that best suits your learning style and the time you have available, by following your personal Study Plan (see below)

You may be studying at home on your own until the date of the exam, or you may be attending a full-time course. You may like to (and have time to) read every word, or you may prefer to (or only have time to) skim-read and devote the remainder of your time to question practice. Wherever you fall in the spectrum, you will find the BPP Study Text meets your needs in designing and following your personal Study Plan.

To tie in with the other components of the BPP Effective Study Package to ensure you have the best possible chance of passing the exam

Recommended period of use	Elements of BPP Effective Study Package
3-12 months before exam	**Study Text** Acquisition of knowledge, understanding, skills and applied techniques
↓	
1-6 months before exam	**Practice and Revision Kit** Tutorial Questions and helpful checklists of the key points lead you into each area. There are then numerous exam questions to try, graded by topic area, along with realistic suggested solutions prepared by BPP's own authors in the light of the Examiner's Reports. June 1999 examinees will find the 1999 edition of the Kit invaluable for bringing them up-to-date as at 1 December 1998, the cut-off date for the June 1999 examinable material
↓	
last minute - 3 months before exam	**Passcards** Short, memorable notes focused on what is most likely to come up in the exam you will be sitting

Settling down to study

By this stage in your career you are probably a very experienced learner and taker of exams. But have you ever thought about *how* you learn? Let's have a quick look at the key elements required for effective learning. You can then identify your learning style and go on to design your own approach to how you are going to study this text - your personal Study Plan.

Key element of learning	Using the BPP Study Text
Motivation	You can rely on the comprehensiveness and technical quality of BPP. You've chosen the right Study Text - so you're in pole position to pass your exam!
Clear objectives and standards	Do you want to be a prizewinner or simply achieve a moderate pass? Decide.
Feedback	Follow through the examples in this text and do the questions and the Quick Quizzes. Evaluate your efforts critically - how are you doing?
Study plan	You need to be honest about your progress to yourself - do not be over-confident, but don't be negative either. Make your Study Plan (see below) and try to stick to it. Focus on the short-term objectives - completing two chapters a night, say - but beware of losing sight of your study objectives
Practice	Use the Quick Quizzes and Chapter Roundups to refresh your memory regularly after you have completed your initial study of each chapter

These introductory pages let you see exactly what you are up against. However you study, you should:

- **read through the syllabus and teaching guide** - this will help you to identify areas you have already covered, perhaps at a lower level of detail, and areas that are totally new to you
- **study the examination paper section,** where we show you the format of the exam (how many and what kind of questions etc) and analyse all the papers set so far under the syllabus.

Key study steps

The following steps are, in our experience, the ideal way to study for professional exams. You can of course adapt it for your particular learning style (see below).

Tackle the chapters in the order you find them in the Study Text. Taking into account your individual learning style, follow these key study steps for each chapter.

Key study steps	Activity
Step 1 *Chapter topic list*	Study the list. Each numbered topic denotes a numbered section in the chapter
Step 2 *Introduction*	Read it through. It is designed to show you *why* the topics in the chapter need to be studied - how they lead on from previous topics, and how they lead into subsequent ones
Step 3 *Knowledge brought forward boxes*	In these we highlight information and techniques that it is assumed you have 'brought forward' with you from your earlier studies. If there are matters which have changed recently due to legislation etc then these topics are explained in full. Do not panic if you do not feel instantly comfortable with the content - it should come back to you as we develop the subject for this paper. If you are really unsure, we advise you to go back to your previous notes
Step 4 *Explanations*	Proceed methodically through the chapter, reading each section thoroughly and making sure you understand. Where a topic has been examined, we state the month and year of examination against the appropriate heading. You should pay particular attention to these topics.
Step 5 *Key terms* and *Exam focus points*	• **Key terms** can often earn you *easy marks* if you state them clearly and correctly in an appropriate exam answer (and they are indexed at the back of the text so you can check easily that you are on top of all of them when you come to revise) • **Exam focus points** give you a good idea of how the examiner tends to examine certain topics - and also pinpoint *easy marks*
Step 6 *Note taking*	Take brief notes if you wish, avoiding the temptation to copy out too much
Step 7 *Examples*	Follow each through to its solution very carefully
Step 8 *Case examples*	Study each one, and try if you can to add flesh to them from your own experience - they are designed to show how the topics you are studying come alive (and often come unstuck) in the real world
Step 9 *Questions*	Make a very good attempt at each one
Step 10 *Answers*	Check yours against ours, and make sure you understand any discrepancies
Step 11 *Chapter roundup*	Check through it very carefully, to make sure you have grasped the major points it is highlighting

Key study steps	Activity
Step 12 *Quick quiz*	When you are happy that you have covered the chapter, use the **Quick quiz** to check your recall of the topics covered. The answers are in the paragraphs in the chapter that we refer you to
Step 13 *Examination question(s)*	Either at this point, or later when you are thinking about revising, make a full attempt at the **Examination question(s)** suggested at the very end of the chapter. You can find these at the end of the Study Text, along with the **Answers** so you can see how you did. We highlight for you which ones are introductory, and which are of the full standard you would expect to find in an exam

Developing your personal Study Plan

Preparing a Study Plan (and sticking closely to it) is one of the key elements in learning success.

First you need to be aware of your style of learning. There are four typical learning styles. Consider yourself in the light of the following descriptions. and work out which you fit most closely. You can then plan to follow the key study steps in the sequence suggested.

Learning styles	Characteristics	Sequence of key study steps in the BPP Study Text
Theorist	Seeks to understand principles before applying them in practice	1, 2, 3, 4, 7, 8, 5, 9/10, 11, 12, 13 (6 continuous)
Reflector	Seeks to observe phenomena, thinks about them and then chooses to act	
Activist	Prefers to deal with practical, active problems; does not have much patience with theory	1, 2, 9/10 (read through), 7, 8, 5, 11, 3, 4, 9/10 (full attempt), 12, 13 (6 continuous)
Pragmatist	Prefers to study only if a direct link to practical problems can be seen; not interested in theory for its own sake	9/10 (read through), 2, 5, 7, 8, 11, 1, 3, 4, 9/10 (full attempt), 12, 13 (6 continuous)

Next you should complete the following checklist.

Am I motivated? (a) [ ]

Do I have an objective and a standard that I want to achieve? (b) [ ]

Am I a theorist, a reflector, an activist or a pragmatist? (c) [ ]

How much time do I have available per week, given: (d) [ ]

- the standard I have set myself
- the time I need to set aside later for work on the Practice and Revision Kit and Passcards
- the other exam(s) I am sitting, and (of course)
- practical matters such as work, travel, exercise, sleep and social life?

Now:

- take the time you have available per week for this Study Text (d), and multiply it by the number of weeks available to give (e). (e) [ ]
- divide (e) by the number of chapters to give (f) (f) [ ]
- set about studying each chapter in the time represented by (f), following the key study steps in the order suggested by your particular learning style.

This is your personal **Study Plan.**

Short of time?

Whatever your objectives, standards or style, you may find you simply do not have the time available to follow all the key study steps for each chapter, however you adapt them for your particular learning style. If this is the case, follow the Skim Study technique below (the icons in the Study Text will help you to do this).

Skim Study technique

Study the chapters in the order you find them in the Study Text. For each chapter, follow the key study steps 1-3, and then skim-read through step 4. Jump to step 11, and then go back to step 5. Follow through steps 7 and 8, and prepare outline Answers to Questions (steps 9/10). Try the Quick Quiz (step 12), following up any items you can't answer, then do a plan for the Examination Question (step 13), comparing it against our answers. You should probably still follow step 6 (note-taking), although you may decide simply to rely on the BPP Passcards for this.

Moving on...

However you study, when you are ready to embark on the practice and revision phase of the BPP Effective Study Package, you should still refer back to this study text:

- as a source of **reference** (you should find the list of key terms and the index particularly helpful for this)
- as a **refresher** (the Chapter Roundups and Quick Quizzes help you here)

And remember to keep careful hold of this Study Text when you move onto the next level of your exams - you will find it invaluable.

Help with case studies
Paper 12 bases all its questions on case studies offering either 25 or 50 marks. Here's how we help you.

Opening case study
The opening case study is an extended description of a fictitious company and covers all areas of the syllabus. We refer to it in self-contained sections throughout the Text. We have included it as a mental discipline - it is not in exam style or format, but is meant to get you thinking. Guidance as to how to use it is given in the beginning section of the opening case study on page 3.

Case examples
Throughout the text we describe what real companies do and how they illustrate, apply - or fail to apply - the theories discussed in the text.

Question practice
The exam question bank contains many exam-style case study questions, including three 50-mark case studies – these are compulsory in the exam.

Answering case study questions.
Students frequently have difficulty in answering this type of question because:

(a) It does not simply require a *description* of a topic.

(b) It requires knowledge and understanding of the *application* of an idea to a particular situation or problem

(c) It often involves more than one topic and an understanding of the *relationship* of several topics within a given problem.

Case studies test your ability to apply your knowledge in a practical way. They also test your approach to problem solving. The examiner wishes to see you have benefited by your studies in applying a coherent and practical analysis to a problem; that you are aware of the *range* of causes and possible solutions to any given problem; and that you have *identified* the causes of the problem before selecting any solution. The systematic approach to problem solving involves several stages in a carefully ordered sequence.

1	Define the problem
2	Identify the factors likely to be causing the problem
3	Collect and analyse the relevant facts
4	Identify the range of alternative courses of action likely to solve the problem
5	Examine the consequences of taking each action and their relative advantages and disadvantages
6	Select and implement the best course of action
7	Follow up to ensure your actions have solved the problem

First of all — You need to read the case *more than once*. Repeated readings enable you to grasp the main points easier than one laborious trawl. Skim read it first and review your choice of questions; then read it slowly and carefully, underlining key issues and/or personnel.

(a) What is going wrong?
What is your analysis of the situation?

(b) How would you help ....?
What other approaches could be tried?

Be sure you know the difference between these directions, but note that they frequently occur together, in which case your answer must cover *all* parts of the question.

Then — Re-read the case and make an *answer plan* relating the question to the factors you see in the case.

Step 1 — Start your answer with a clear definition of the problem. Ensure you have identified the problem and not simply its symptoms.

Step 2 — Identify and list the factors likely to be causing the problem. (There will often be 4 to 6 possible causes, so don't be satisfied with identifying a single cause.)

Step 3 — Demonstrate in your discussion how you could collect the relevant facts *before* attempting to solve the problem (for example by checking the records, and interviewing appropriate staff). Analyse the facts and identify the actual cause(s) of the problem.

Step 4 — Show, by writing down a list, that you are aware of the range of possible courses of action and the consequences of each.

Step 5 — Demonstrate in your answer that you would only select the appropriate course of action after analysing the relevant facts and information. Refer to any constraints which would affect your selection, such as limited resources and time, company rules and policies.

Step 6 — Show how you would implement your plan of action, say by counselling staff concerned, making arrangements for transfers, training and job changes.

Step 7 — Always show how you would follow up or check back to ensure your actions have in fact solved the problem.

ACCA OFFICIAL SYLLABUS

		Covered in Chapter
1	**Strategic management and business planning**	
(a)	Competitive advantage;	
(i)	its meaning in different markets and industries;	5, 17
(ii)	of nations and the implications of this for organisational success;	5
(iii)	the different approaches used by organisations and management in different countries and the lessons which can be applied to the UK;	5, 15
(iv)	the effect on organisations of working in an international environment, the key aspects of that environment and methods of entry into it.	5, 15
(b)	The future for nations, industries, organisations and the workforce (including management):	
(i)	scanning the environment of the organisation and the context in which it is set for changes, developments and opportunities;	5, 6
(ii)	forecasting trends and developments in relevant areas through the use of relevant quantitative and qualitative analysis;	5, 17
(iii)	future basing (ie anticipating long term prospects for the business and its likelihood of survival) and other scenario building techniques.	5, 7
(c)	Strategic management and business planning:	
(i)	the purpose of strategic management and business planning and the relationship between the two;	1, 2
(ii)	the methods which organisations use to plan for the future (including the role of information technology);	1,2, 3, 7
(iii)	the effects which the external environment may have on strategy and plans;	5, 6
(iv)	methods of gaining support and commitment for strategies;	1, 2, 8, 12
(v)	formulating and evaluating plans with an awareness of the various techniques available to managers;	1 ,3-7
(vi)	understanding and managing the risk of a proposed business plan for the plan itself and for all the aspects of business which it will influence;	8, 12
(vii)	reviewing strategy for the effect it will have on the organisation and the local and global community.	4, 5, 8
2	**Managing operations and services**	
(a)	Determining the work to be undertaken:	
(i)	estimating time and resources needed to undertake work;	9, 11, 13
(ii)	calculating the cost of services to be provided;	9, 11
(iii)	determining whether there are any reasons for the work being problematic or where contingencies are likely to occur.	11

	Covered in Chapter
(b) Planning resource allocation:	
(i) setting work objectives in line with organisational strategy so that the former contributes to the latter;	9, 10, 11
(ii) designing/modifying methods of achieving work objectives which are consistent with ethos, strategy, practices;	9, 10, 11
(iii) allocating available resources in an optimum way to achieve and exceed targets set;	9, 10, 11, 13
(iv) formulating and evaluating work plans including an awareness of assignment and allocation techniques;	9, 11, 13
(v) evaluating previous resource allocations to improve present performance;	9, 11, 13
(vi) the importance of time management	11, 13
(c) Monitoring and maintaining services:	
(i) the different concepts of quality;	16
(ii) monitoring and evaluating the implementation of work plans using methods which are consistent with organisational ethos and strategy, the concepts of quality;	9, 17
(iii) methods of assessing, analysing and interpreting information on service delivery and other non-financial targets, resource utilisation and costs.	9, 17
(d) Marketing:	
(i) the purpose and functioning of marketing and the different roles which it may play for the organisation;	14, 15
(ii) analysing market needs and identifying marketing opportunities and/or improvements in services;	14
(iii) obtaining a competitive advantage;	14, 15, 17
(iv) the impact of the global market.	6, 15

3 Human resources management

(a) Recruitment, selection, employment and dismissal:	
(i) the purpose of personnel specifications in the recruitment and selection of staff and the different forms which these may take;	18
(ii) identifying the competences and attributes required to meet and to develop the service as a whole through a number of different methods;	18
(iii) specifying personnel requirements in relation to the work to be undertaken, overall resources and the strategy, objectives and ethos of the organisation;	18
(iv) evaluating and determining the benefits and costs of additional/new personnel;	18
(v) identifying and evaluating suitable methods of recruitment;	18
(vi) the range of selection methods which are available, the different circumstances where they may be of use, their costs and benefits and best practice within each;	18
(vii) methods of motivating/supporting personnel within the work place;	19

	Covered in Chapter
(viii) staff appraisal and the assessment of personnel (including self) in relation to organisational direction, strategy, ethos, objectives and aims;	19
(ix) the legal and organisational policies and procedures regarding the warning and dismissal of personnel and the role of specialists/specialist departments in the process;	17, 21
(x) the role of employee groups and joint employer/employee groups/committees in promoting the welfare of personnel;	17, 18, 21
(xi) awareness of the legislation which affects recruitment, selection, employment and dismissal and the ways in which anti-discriminatory practice can be promoted;	21
(xii) the management of change - both organisational and personal.	12
(b) Human resources development:	
(i) the role which individual and team development can play in the growth and development of the organisation;	19
(ii) traditional versus progressive views regarding an organisation's human resources and their development;	18, 19
(iii) the relationship between human resource development and the structure and functioning of organisations;	18
(iv) the ways in which individuals and teams can be encouraged to grow and develop and the manner in which this can contribute to the organisation through career paths;	20
(v) the internal and external factors which may affect an individual's/team's development;	19
(vi) the different concepts and models of competence and the 'competent manager' and the ways in which these might enhance development;	19, 20
(vii) methods of encouraging and supporting development.	19, 20

4 Management of the working environment

(a) The main principles of current legislation in relation to the management of the working environment, and the ways in which these principles can be applied effectively.	21
(b) Monitoring, interpreting and applying good practice and legislation related to the work environment for the different needs of its users (such as staff and clients whether they are able bodied or with limited abilities).	21
(c) The role and purpose of health, safety and security requirements/procedures/guidelines.	21
(d) The roles and responsibilities in relation to the working environment and those within it and methods for improving practice.	21

		Covered in Chapter
5	**The accountant as an effective communicator**	
	The skills of communication which are necessary for effective accountants:	
(i)	seeking and clarifying information and views from others including reflecting back information and viewpoints to the giver;	13
(ii)	isolating the key aspects of information and summarising for others' use;	13
(iii)	presenting information clearly to others both orally and in writing;	13
(iv)	negotiating and agreeing with others;	13
(v)	promoting new ideas to others to gain their support;	13
(vi)	giving and receiving constructive criticism to improve future performance;	13, 20
(vii)	advising others in one's area of responsibility/expertise;	13, 20
(viii)	encouraging others to offer information, suggestions etc.	13, 20
6	**Strategic implications of information technology**	
	This section covers future developments of the system and the ways in which the user may monitor the latest best practice.	
(a)	Monitoring new developments/good practice in system design, operation, evaluation:	11
	(i) structured methods;	
	(ii) documentation;	
	(iii) testing and evaluation;	
	(iv) quality assurance.	
(b)	Sources and access to relevant specialist knowledge (eg computer programming):	9, 11, 16
	(i) accredited suppliers;	
	(ii) accredited contractors.	
(c)	Current good accounting practice and latest developments in accounting systems:	11
	(i) sources of information;	
	(ii) future developments.	
(d)	Information technology as a strategic resource including:	
	(i) criticality of information technology to the organisation in terms of funding, expenditure levels, strategic advantage;	3
	(ii) formulation, organisation and control of information strategy and activities;	3, 9
	(iii) responsibility accounting for information technology;	9, 11
	(iv) organisational positioning of the information systems department including centralisation versus decentralisation, information centres, end-user computing.	10

		Covered in Chapter
(e)	The management of information systems development, including:	
	(i) role, composition and significance of the steering committee;	11
	(ii) role of senior information technology management;	11
	(iii) criteria likely to influence project selection;	11
	(iv) use of project planning and control techniques;	11
	(v) information technology project appraisal.	11
(f)	Liaison between the information technology managers and the accountant to identify the needs of the organisation.	11

ACCA OFFICIAL 1998-1999 TEACHING GUIDE

This is the official 1998-1999 Teaching Guide, for the December 1998 and June 1999 exam.

Syllabus reference

Session 1 Introduction

BLOCK I - Strategic Management & Business Planning

Session 2 What is Strategy? – 1 1c(i)

Definitions of Strategy

- the different levels of strategy - corporate, business, operational, functional
- alternative definitions of strategy (eg: Hofer & Schendel, Ansoff, Andrews and, especially, Mintzberg)
- Drucker's analysis of and approach to making strategic decisions
- Johnson & Scholes' characteristics of strategic decisions
- gaining competitive advantage (Ohmae and Porter)

Session 3 What is Strategy? – 2

The Strategic Management Process

- define strategic management
- the purpose of strategic management and business planning, and the relationship between the two
- Mintzberg's strategy making in three modes - entrepreneurial, adaptive and planned
- "rational" models of strategic management
- "emergent strategy" and "crafting strategy"
- Japanese approach of "pursuing a vision"

Session 4 Building a Strategy 1c(ii)

Establishing Strategic Intent

- the importance of the mission statement
- characteristics of a good mission statement
- Mintzberg's definition of goals and objectives
- developing of goals and objectives
- the role of mission statement, goals and objectives in shaping a vision of the future

Strategic Options

- strategic options which an organisation might pursue
- implementing the strategies through internal or external growth

The Ideas of Professor Michael Porter

- the five forces model
- the meaning of "competitive advantage"
- generic strategies for gaining competitive advantage

Session 5 Some Strategic Planning Tools 1c(v)

Other Planning Tools

- product portfolio analysis (Boston Matrix etc)
- Ansoff's product/market growth vector
- Gap Analysis
- Life Cycle Analysis

Strategy Evaluation

- use of decision trees, ranking and scoring methods to formulate and evaluate strategy
- the impact of strategies on the organisation and the community
- linking strategies to possible scenarios

Analysing Risk

- sensitivity analysis using computer spreadsheets
- using risk analysis to assess uncertainty
- value of decision matrices in choosing alternative strategies
- importance of stakeholder and political risk analysis

Syllabus reference

Session 6 The Impact of Strategy on the Organisation 1c(vii)

Understanding the Organisation
- internal appraisal of the organisation
- Porter's value chain analysis
- influence of structure and systems on strategy

Organisation Culture
- the major influences on culture
- levels of culture
- the concept of excellence
- cultural influence on strategy
- identifying key strengths and weaknesses

BLOCK II - "No Man is an Island"

Session 7 The World in Which We Live 1a

The Global Environment
- key aspects of the international business environment
- the effect of an international environment on organisations
- alternative ways to enter foreign markets
- recent trends and developments in global business strategy

The Competitive Advantage of Nations
- Porter's determinants of national competitive advantage
- the implications for company strategy and national economics

The Impact of the Global Market
- national marketing and global marketing
- "global companies win out" Porter
- risks of global markets
- effects of cultural differences
- assessing opportunities and threats
- some key strategic issues

Session 8 The Business Environment 1b

Forecasting Trends and Developments
- role of forecasting in strategic decision making
- the techniques available
- the use of scenario building

Understanding the Environment
- key influences on the organisation
- effect of the external environment of corporate strategies and plans
- a framework for environmental analysis
- the concept of boundary management

Scanning and Monitoring the Environment
- identifying current and emerging changes
- the role of monitoring specific trends
- information sources

Syllabus reference

BLOCK III - Implementing Planning

Session 9 Building the Framework — 1c(ii)

A Framework for Strategy Implementation

- real work begins after strategies are formulated
- different skills needed for successful strategy
- implementation
- problems which can arise
- key implementation issues
- developing a framework

Matching Strategy with Structure

- different types of organisation structure
- effect of decentralised and centralised decision-making
- advantages and disadvantages
- Mintzberg's structural configurations
- influences on organisational design

Session 10 Operational Planning — 1c(vi)

Translating Strategic into Operational Plans

- the process by which strategic plans are translated into operating plans and policies
- the importance of active participation in the planning process
- a methodology for effective resource allocation
- budgets as tool for control

Planning at the Tactical/Operational Level

- simple aids to planning
- analysis of risk
- the role of computer packages

Session 11 Some Problems of Change — 1c(iv)

The Dynamics of Change

- why change is a challenge to management
- the role of force field analysis as a way of understanding change
- factors affecting an individual's responses to change
- why people may resist change

Managing Change

- ways of overcoming resistance
- key issues in successful change management
- how organisations can create readiness for change
- gaining support and commitment
- the role of the leader

The Change Process

- Lewin's 3-step model of change
- alternative models of change management
- implementing change through power politics
- a simple framework for the management of change

Strategy Review and Strategic Issue Management

- the importance of reviewing progress
- a framework for strategy review
- the importance of strategic issue management

Syllabus reference

BLOCK IV - Planning and the Individual

Session 12 Setting Employee Goals 2b(i), (ii), (iii), (iv)

Setting Work Objectives

- the role of individual work objectives in ensuring the achievement of the organisation's goals
- the hierarchy of objectives
- top down versus bottom up strategy setting
- management by objectives, its advantages and disadvantages
- setting objectives using Management by Objectives

Planning for the Achievement of Objectives

- setting priorities
- the role of policies and procedures
- formulating and evaluating work plans
- allocating available resources
- assessing and analysing resource allocation
- the importance of time management

Session 13 The Work to be Undertaken

Project Management 2a

- the project life cycle
- the objectives of project management 2b(v), (vi)
- breaking projects down into manageable units

Estimating Resource Requirements

- the importance of accurate estimates
- use of work breakdown structure to identify resource needs
- estimating direct and indirect costs
- why estimates may be inaccurate
- calculating total project costs

Planning the Timescale

- estimating the time needed
- Gantt charts, network analysis and critical path analysis
- use of resource histograms and resource smoothing
- parallel scheduling

Session 14/15 Marketing

The Role and Purpose of Marketing 2d

- the marketing concept
- the characteristics of a market oriented organisation
- marketing in not-for-profit organisations
- the main activities of the marketing function
- promoting the corporate image

Analysing Market Needs and Identifying Opportunities

- the objectives of market analysis
- a framework for analysing the market
- analysing buyer behaviour
- selection and control of distribution channels
- integration of pricing into the marketing activities
- market segmentation
- methods of consumer and market research
- developing new products and services

Syllabus reference

Session 16 Maintaining Services Pt1

The Concept of Quality 2c

- quality management (the ideas of Demming, Crosby, Juran, Feigenbaum, Ishikawa and Taguchi)
- the difference between "quality control" and "quality assurance"
- the role of standards (eg: BS5750/IS9000)
- total quality management

The Pursuit of Excellence

- the characteristics of a successful organisation (eg: Peters & Waterman, Goldsmith & Clutterbuck)
- the role of quality
- have we reached the end of sustainable excellence?

Session 17 Maintaining Services Pt2

Monitoring and Maintaining Quality 2c, d(iii)

- barriers to quality
- a total quality programme
- assessing the quality of services
- the role of quality audits, assessments and reviews
- continuous improvement

Pursuit of Competitive Advantage

- the strategic role of marketing
- sustainable competitive advantage
- gaining positional advantage
- sources of competitive advantage
- tactics of competitive advantage (defensive, offensive, flanking, market niches)

BLOCK V - Human Resource Management

Session 18 The Concept of Human Resource Management

An Overview of Human Resource Development 3b

- the role and purpose of Human Resource Management (HRM) and Human Resource Development
- the integration of HRM into strategic planning
- the main areas covered by a human resource plan and the formulation of personnel policies and procedures

The Task of Human Resource Development

- traditional views of human resources and their development compared with the more modern approach
- the relationship between human resource development and the structure and functioning of the organisation
- the role of individual and team development in the growth and development of the organisation
- the objectives, purpose and role of career management
- internal and external factors that might affect an individual's, or a team's, performance

Syllabus reference

Session 19 Recruitment and Selection

Recruitment 3a(i) - (vi)

- the process by which personnel requirements are determined
- different forms of employment
- the use of cost/benefit analysis in evaluating and determining the benefits of additional/new personnel
- the purpose of job and personnel specifications in the recruitment and selection of staff
- the different forms that personnel specifications can take
- suitable methods of recruitment

Selection

- the use of application forms and CVs as part of the selection process
- the role of the interview in the selection process and describe the different types of selection interviews
- the use of psychometric tests
- other methods of selection
- the usefulness of references

Session 20 Motivation, Appraisal & Discipline

Motivation 3a(vii), (viii)

- Schien's models of motivation
- the needs, expectancy and goal theories of motivation with reference to Maslow, Herzberg, McLelland, Vroom, Porter & Lawler, Latham and Locke
- methods of improving motivation

Appraisal

- the purposes of staff appraisal and the appraisal process
- outline the role of the assessment centre in assessing participants' competencies
- identify the importance of congruence between an organisation's appraisal system and its objectives, strategy and culture

Session 21 A Legal Framework

- contracts of employment, termination of employment, unfair dismissal, redundancy and maternity rights 3a(ix), (x), (xi)
- equal opportunities (eg: equal pay, sex discrimination, race relations)
- promotion of non-discrimination
- managers' responsibilities for developing good practice

BLOCK VI - Managing the Working Environment

Session 22 Legal Background

Legislation and the Working Environment 4

- the reasons for health, safety and security requirements
- outline the principal legislation affecting employers and employees
- how managers can keep up to date

Applying Good Practice

- the key elements of a health and safety programme
- the role of education and training
- the role of managers, supervisors, advisors etc
- essentials of a safety policy
- good housekeeping and prevention policies

Syllabus reference

Office Design
- the effect of environment on work performance
- different needs of various groups
- some guidelines for good design
- good office practice
- management responsibilities and the role of the office manager

BLOCK VII - Accountant as Communicator

Session 23 Gaining and Using Information

Seeking and Clarifying Information — 5(i) - (viii)
- the communication process both oral and written
- effective ways to gain information
- clarifying information
- good listening
- summarising information

Presentation and Persuasion
- presenting information in writing and verbally
- use of visual aids
- persuading others to your point of view

Negotiation
- different types of negotiating situation
- various stages of negotiation
- strategies and tactics
- effective negotiation skills

BLOCK VIII - Information Technology (IT)

Session 24 Evolution of IT Applications

Phases of Development — 6a, b, c
- the phases of development of information systems applications
- Nolan's six stages of evolution
- implications of the evolutionary process

The Importance of IT
- the criticality of IT spending
- use of McFarlan's Strategic Grid to analyse the importance of IT to a business
- the forces which drive an organisation round the Strategic Grid

Formulating an Information Systems Strategy
- why is it important?
- the elements of a strategy
- developing the strategy
- linking information systems planning to business goals
- liaison between IT managers and users
- the contribution of the accountant

Session 25 IT and Strategic Advantage

Using IT to Support Strategic Decision Making — 6d
- examples of strategic planning packages
- their limitations
- effect of IT on management processes in future

Using IT to Gain a Strategic Advantage
- IT as a strategic weapon
- how information technology permeates the value chain
- other frameworks to help identify options to use IT strategically

Syllabus reference

Session 26 Managing Information Systems

Deploying Information Systems Resources 5a(i) - (v)

- centralisation or decentralisation, the pressures for and against
- end user computing
- the role of the information centre
- factors influencing the positioning of IT resources

Information Systems Departments

- challenges facing Information Systems departments
- key issues facing department structure
- the role of the IT Director
- the role of steering committees

Session 27 Controlling IT

Control and Responsibility Accounting

- the main issues concerning control of IT
- measuring and evaluating the value of information systems
- the role of responsibility accounting
- the control architecture of responsibility accounting

Management of Information Systems Development

- a framework
- the steering committee, its role and composition
- the role of senior IT management
- project selection
- planning and controlling projects
- appraising IT

Session 28

A review of some of the major concepts

THE EXAMINATION PAPER

Assessment methods and format of the paper

	Number of marks
1 compulsory question of 50 marks	50
2 (out of 3) questions of 25 marks each	50
	100

Time allowed: 3 hours

Analysis of past examination papers

December 1997

Section A (Compulsory)

1 A UK based conglomerate has used acquisition as its main engine of growth. New directors have taken over. Evaluate growth strategies pursued so far; evaluate a particular acquisition; integrating the acquired company.

Section B

2 Choice of chief executives: inside or outside the firm. Strategy formulation

3 Competitive advantage of nations; risks and opportunities.

4 Job analysis and job description; recruitment policies.

June 1997

Section A

1 A medium sized holiday firm is losing money because of competitive pressures, yet needs to spend more. Discuss its current position, and how it can improve its existing business. Give an environmental appraisal, and select and justify a preferred strategic option.

Section B

2 Role of IT in business strategy

3 Vertical integration

4 Recruitment of professional staff

December 1996

Section A

1 A large computer firm (based on IBM) is facing the onslaught of technological change and low-cost competition. Assess financial and strategic position. Implications of abandoning a jobs-for-life policy.

Section B

2 Matrix organisation structure and co-ordination

3 Strategic marketing and competition

4 Approaches to quality management

June 1996

Section A

1 A non profit orientated arts organisation has recruited a new executive from the private sector to sort out a number of management and financial problems. Discuss stakeholders, strategic management processes and performance measurement indicators.

Section B

2 Time and stress management. Delegation

3 Marketing in a medium sized accountancy practice

4 Budgeting for IT. IT and the competitive forces

December 1995

Section A

1 A recently privatised bus company is seeking to develop a marketing orientation and to develop profit centres. Discuss training programmes, culture and marketing.

Section B

2 Introducing a staff appraisal scheme

3 Project management and information systems

4 Distinctive competences and critical success factors on entry to a new market sector

June 1995

Section A

1 A young graphic design company has grown significantly in the past ten years and is planning to go into the printing business, by acquisition. Discuss mission statements, risk, and acquisitions and mergers.

Section B

2 Strategic use of information technology in a food firm

3 Change management and stress

4 Modes of entry to overseas markets

December 1994

Section A

1 A specialist software house is considering its competitive strategy. Identify information requirements and relevant strategic models. Write a report identifying the strategic options suggesting, with reasons, the most suitable.

Section B

2 Justifying training expenditure: differences between HRM and personnel management

3 BS5750 certification in the context of a TQM programme

4 Setting objectives for obtaining information; report writing

June 1994

Section A (Compulsory question, 50 marks)

1 A firm of merchants, with a rather conservative image, is looking to recruit a human resources manager to ensure that the right personnel are hired and that they are trained to be responsive to customers. You are required to prepare notes for a presentation describing the role of HRM and the difficulties of introducing it to a culture which is resistant to change.

Section B (2 out of 3 questions, 25 marks each)

2 A company marketing financial services is moving offices. Describe the advantages and disadvantages of the proposed site, and any action to bring the office to an acceptable standard.

3 Describe the difference between marketing plans for non profit orientated organisations and marketing plans for profit making organisations. Outline the features of a marketing presentation.

4 Recruiting new people to the credit control department and providing them with computer training

Pilot paper

Section A (Compulsory question, 50 marks)

1 An engineering company with a reputation for quality but with declining profitability has 'lost its way' and needs a strategic plan. You are required to set out the characteristics of a strategic plan, describe some strategic planning tools and suggest how the company can build a strategy

Section B (2 out of 3 questions, 25 marks each)

2 The skills needed in a meeting set up to elicit information from a client

3 Information systems strategies: centralisation and decentralisation

4 Procedures and law relating to the dismissal of an employee

The ACCA provides the following further guidance on Paper 12: *Management and Strategy.*

This paper draws on the topics introduced in Paper 4 and examines them in greater detail. The paper looks at the theoretical background of management with the express purpose that the student will draw on this knowledge in order to improve his or her own management competence within his or her organisation. It aims to broaden the student's knowledge regarding management and organisations beyond that possible from working in one situation alone.

The objective of the Professional Stage

The main aim of the Professional Stage is to establish evidence of competence to practise as a professional accountant in private practice, public sector or in industry and commerce. This requires candidates to demonstrate not only that they have mastered the range of required knowledge, skills and techniques, but also that they are able to apply them in a managerial context.

By this stage, knowledge has to be fully integrated in the way it is used by professionals with a recognition of how the different subjects contribute to dealing with problems. This stage will present students with problems which test their skills and sensitivity in dealing with new contexts and unforeseen circumstances. In dealing with such situations, students will be expected to tailor solutions to previous problems appropriately and in a way which demonstrates their grasp of managerial skills.

Although emphasis will be given to practical issues, students will also be expected to criticise current practice and express views on developments in accounting. They will also be expected to show evidence of the necessary personal qualities and interpersonal skills required of the professional accountant.

Skills to be tested in the Professional Stage

Students should be able to demonstrate the ability to:

- draw on knowledge across all earlier papers studied;
- integrate that knowledge effectively and use it creatively in applying concepts and techniques;
- analyse and interpret data and information and present reasoned conclusions;

- diagnose and formulate appropriate solutions to problems which indicate commercial awareness;
- exercise judgement based on technical, political and commercial factors in developing and evaluating alternatives and in proposing solutions;
- adapt to new systems and circumstances;
- communicate analyses and conclusions effectively and with sensitivity for differing purposes and to contrasting audiences with due emphasis on social expectations

While the skills identified above will be tested directly by the questions set, in assessing the answers weight will be given to the students' ability to demonstrate a grasp of the following personal skills:

Interpersonal skills

Tact, sensitivity to political tensions and cultural differences, awareness of social, economic and political pressure, ability to influence

Management skills

Resource management: people, material, time and money, management of the client, management of change, in particular in technology, and contingency planning

Personal qualities

Persistence to pursue enquiries and probe responses, integrity, objectivity, independence and public responsibility

Aim of paper 12

To develop students' awareness that strategic decisions are the result of a trade off between various competing options, considered by an organisation's management. The paper explores the decision-making process; the need to weigh the arguments, make choices and realise that in most circumstances a single solution does not exist. Students will also appreciate the link between information technology (IT) and the effective management and the contribution of IT to the improvement of business performance.

On completion of this paper students should be able to:

- identify the principal ideas and concepts in the theory and practice of strategic management;
- assess the impact of environmental forces on organisation strategies and plans;
- understand the importance of linking information system development and management to business goals and needs;
- explain how information systems can be managed and developed;
- evaluate ways in which change may be managed successfully;
- plan projects and allocate resources in an optimum way;
- evaluate the strategic role of marketing;
- understand the managers' role and responsibilities in relation to the working environment;

- assess the importance of human resource development to organisations and identify methods of managing people effectively;
- improve communication skills as well as demonstrate the other skills expected at the Professional Stage.

Standard of the paper

The standard of the paper will be comparable to that required in the examinations for the final year of a three year UK honours degree course.

Prerequisite knowledge

Students need a sound understanding of the content of Paper 4 Organisational Framework and Paper 5 Information Analysis.

Paper 12 develops the coverage in Paper 4 Organisational Framework by:

- giving more emphasis to strategic management and business planning;
- extending the coverage of managing operations and services;
- examining the purpose and functioning of marketing in the organisation;
- providing a more in-depth review of human resource management;
- reinforcing the importance of communication;
- incorporating the main principles of legislation in relation to the management of the working environment.

Paper 12 builds on the knowledge of IT covered in Paper 5 Information Analysis by:

- reviewing and evaluating current best practice and latest developments in accounting systems;
- recognising the importance of IT as a strategic resource;
- covering, in more depth, the management of information system development.

Extent of integration

Management and IT are integrated in Paper 12 and students will be expected to appreciate the importance of linking information systems development and management to improve business performance.

Students need to be aware of the main principles of legislation in relation to the management of human resources and the working environment. However, questions will be set on principles and good practice and will not make specific reference to the UK legislation to ensure non UK students are not disadvantaged.

Questions will demand the application of quantitative techniques to solve problems of, for example, resource allocation and time management.

Students should also appreciate the link between Paper 12 and Paper 14 Financial Strategy in the areas of corporate decision making and business planning.

General note

Students are advised to read the 'Exam notes' published in the Students' Newsletter as these contain details of examinable legislation, changes in the syllabuses and other useful information for each examination session.

Opening case study
Brainworks plc

Opening case study

BRAINWORKS PLC

Chapter topic list

1 PROBLEMS WITH THIS PAPER

The syllabus for Paper 12 is:

- **Wide**: it covers corporate strategy, human resources management, marketing and IT.
- **Deep**: your understanding of the theory and models is tested by how well you **apply** them. Not only must you understand the jargon, you must be confident about **using** it.
- **Practical**: it is based on case studies and scenarios. Half the available marks are attached to a fifty-mark scenario. The remaining questions (a limited choice of 2 out of 3) are also in scenario format.
- **Unfamiliar in content**: you might have briefly covered some of the topics in Paper 4 The Organisational Framework and in Paper 5 Information Analysis, but the heart of the syllabus will be completely new to you.
- **Unfamiliar in approach**: accountancy students are often uncomfortable with the uncertainty, guesswork and judgement involved in this paper, but these reflect real life. There are no 'right' answers, unlike in some of the financial and management accounting papers. But:
  - Some answers are more **relevant** than others
  - Be **selective** in what you write in order to ensure your answers are relevant and to the point
  - You **apply models to situations** not **rules to problems**
  - **Argue your case**: the **quality of your reasoning** will earn you marks
  - Be **business-like**: this means answering in report or briefing paper format when asked to.

The syllabus is forward looking, as it is designed to prepare you for future management roles.

You cannot pass this paper by:

- **Repeating** what you have learned by rote
- **Waffling**: this is a 'wordy' imprecise subject, true, but you still need to be rigorous in how you approach it.

The big problem is the scenario element. You may be given two or more pages of information and a brief question about it.

Confidence in approaching scenarios can help you pass. Throughout this Study Text, we have tried to bring practical real-life case examples to the fore to illustrate the text or get you thinking about it.

The opening case study **Brainworks plc** is designed to familiarise you with scenario technique.

2 USING THE OPENING CASE STUDY

Brainworks plc is a **fictitious** company facing a number of issues relating to strategic choices and strategic management in approaching its products and markets. The market and environmental data have been developed for the case study: the case study does **not** purport to factual accuracy.

Brainworks plc is bolted on to each chapter in separate self-contained sections (so you are not forced to use it if you do not want to).

- In the **Introduction** box at the beginning of each chapter, you will find a number of questions relating to Brainworks plc relevant to the content of that chapter. Keep them in mind as you go through.
- At the end of the chapter, a section (**Brainworks plc update**) contains a few **brief** pointers as to how the chapter content relates to the questions raised about Brainworks plc in the chapter introduction. These are not answers to the questions, but are supposed to kick-start your thought processes. If you disagree - so much the better!

Brainworks plc is not an exam question, in style or standard, but a **learning aid** to help you develop some of the mental disciplines necessary to succeed in case study questions.

Brainworks plc does not fall in easy simple compartments; this is not its purpose.

For lecturers

- Brainworks plc might be useful in stimulating classroom discussion, either before or after you cover a topic. You might wish to pose additional questions on it, or develop your own material to explore some topic areas in more detail. Brainworks plc is open-ended and flexible.

For students, without classroom tuition

You can use Brainworks plc in a number of ways.

- Before you cover a topic to get you thinking.
- After you have covered a topic, to apply your learning.
- After you have completed the whole Study Text.
- During your revision, once you have mastered the technical material.
- In discussions with your fellow students.

A good way of getting to grips with case study material is to skim read it twice, and perhaps highlight key issues as you go along.

Feedback, please!

If you do make use of Brainworks plc, please let us know what you think of it. Your feedback will help us refine it for future students of this paper. Please send in your comments on any aspects of Brainworks plc on the customer feedback form at the end of this Study Text, with any other comments about BPP material that you may have.

3 BRAINWORKS PLC

History

Brainworks Holdings plc (BW) is one of the world's largest private employment agencies. Every day, it is responsible for sending over 1.5 million people to work. To put it in context, this is twice as many as are employed by General Motors, one of the world's largest car companies, and exceeds the population of some of the world's smaller countries.

Although BW is based in the UK, in 1985 it acquired **PeoplePower** of the US, for £500m. This had been financed by a leveraged buyout: BW borrowed to finance the takeover. £150m was borrowed from a consortium of banks, and is repayable in full in the year 2000. The remaining £350m was issued to investors as junk bonds with a 4% interest rate. According to the agreement with the banks, BW is allowed no other long-term borrowing, although it does have an overdraft facility of £40m.This is to cope with its occasionally volatile cash flows.

BW enjoyed rapid and spectacular growth in the UK before taking over **PeoplePower**.

(a) BW began in the 1960s supplying programmers and systems analysts to the IT industry. The rapid growth of the IT industry and the growth of the micro-computers and networking have created an almost inexhaustible demand for computer-literate personnel. Some of BW's employees end up training client staff as well as doing the jobs they were originally expected to do.

(b) Economic changes in the UK and the US in the 1980s and 1990s have shaken out the labour markets in those countries, and introduced long-term changes.

In the UK, in 1971 80% of males between 16 and 65 were in employment, but this is projected to fall to 70% by 2001. However, female participation in employment has increased from 44% in 1971 to over 55% projected for 2001.

Again in the UK, between 1987 and 1993, employment in manufacturing and construction fell by 18%, whereas service sector employment increased by 7%.

Many of the new service sector jobs are temporary or part-time positions. Many firms are employing a core full-time permanent workforce supplemented by a periphery of part-time workers, freelances or workers on temporary contracts.

(c) The US also has seen a decline in the manufacturing employment and a huge growth in the service sector. PeoplePower's main market was the provision of secretarial and other business services, although it had expanded aggressively into health care and nursing.

By 1997, despite one or two anxious moments in the 1990s recession, BW was the world's largest agency, with revenues of £4.5bn per year of which £3bn come from PeoplePower. Obviously, margins are more important than any statement of gross revenues. Typically, 85% of the revenue BW earns is accounted for by the salaries it pays its hire-workforce and by other salary-related deductions such as payroll taxes and National Insurance.

Organisation structure

BW is organised into a variety of divisions and subsidiaries, outlined in the diagram below. BW (UK) manages the firms operations in the UK.

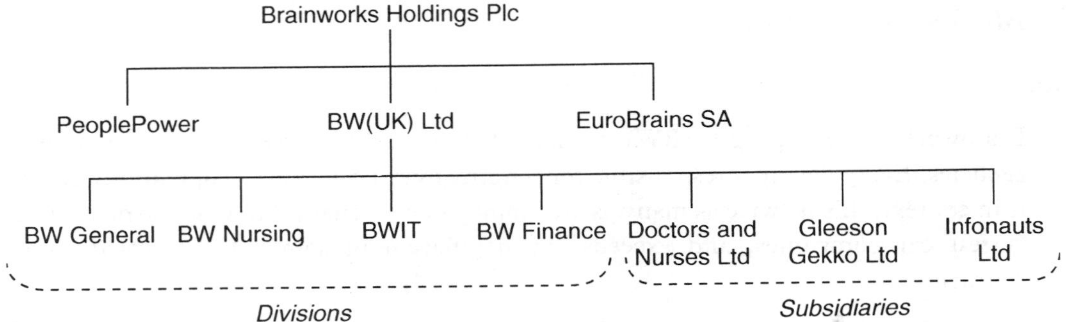

Supplying workers

Agency work

The market for temporary workers is very fragmented. There are hundreds of agencies. BW accounts for 8% of the world market. BW's nearest two competitors are two European companies: Diad, based in Switzerland, and Colec, based in France. These have recently announced a merger. Together, their combined revenues will amount to £4bn per year. Both have announced their intention to expand into the UK. They are starting to recruit for consultants.

The third largest European agency, Strand, is based in the Netherlands, and is making efforts to expand into Germany.

Another element of competition comes not from other agencies but from business service firms, which supply catering and cleaning services to firms. Agencies such as BW had previously supplied such workers.

However, to put the matter in context, in the USA, workers from agencies such as BW amounted to 2% of the US workforce, up from 1% in 1989. In the UK, this is slightly higher at 2.5%. In continental Europe, on average, whilst temporary work has been increasing, it currently accounts for only 1% of the workforce. This average conceals wide variations, however: in the Netherlands, 3% of all workers are employed by agencies.

The potential is probably much greater for agencies such as BW to expand. In France, for example, up to 20% of the workforce is employed on a temporary basis, but works directly for the companies concerned.

For temporary workers, BW (UK) has these divisions.

BW Nursing for health care staff
BW IT for information technology staff
BW Finance for temporary accounting and banking staff
BW General deals with everything, else, such as supplying secretaries, cleaners etc.

Recruitment for permanent positions

As well as providing temporary workers on specific assignments, BW acts as a recruitment agency to secure full time employees. Here, BW's activities are concentrated in the UK. BW(UK) operates through three subsidiaries.

(a) **Doctors and Nurses Ltd** - supplying health care professionals to NHS and private hospitals. This was acquired in 1983.

(b) **Gleeson Gekko Ltd** - supplying accounting and banking staff to the UK financial services sector.

(c) **Infonauts Ltd** - for IT specialists. In recent years, there has been a great demand from firms who wish to advertise on the Internet, and there has been a surge in demand for staff who are capable of designing and, as importantly, maintaining Internet **websites** which internet users can access.

In Europe, BW's operations are run by its subsidiary, **Eurobrains SA** which covers France, Germany, the Netherlands and Belgium and which mainly deals with financial services, although the firm intends to expand into IT services, in the manner of **Infonauts**.

Management, organisation and operations

BW has had a fairly turbulent management history. The architect of its purchase of **PeoplePower** was former chief executive and chairman Bill Begbie, who since 1996 has languished in prison as a result of an insider dealing prosecution. Announcing the takeover of PeoplePower, he said: 'My vision is to build BW into the biggest and best human resources agency in the world'.

The current chief executive is Willard Mann, from the US. Previously chief executive at PeoplePower, he was re-hired by BW's shareholders and bankers after Begbie's downfall. Willard Mann had fought BW's acquisition of PeoplePower, and has made no secret of his intention to split up the business: 'I am not convinced by the value of economies of scale in a business such as ours at an international level. If you grow too big, diseconomies set in. The whole thing is a distraction.'

The Board of Directors includes Willard Mann, a finance director, and a human resources director (for BW's own staff - or consultants as they are called).

Each BW subsidiary and division has its own board of directors. BW(UK) has the same team as the main board, with the addition of two marketing directors, who are responsible for communicating with BW's business customers and also with people who want to be taken on by the agency. However, the chairman of each subsidiary board is one of the directors of the BW. This arrangement has been set up to exercise central control to ensure that performance targets are met or exceeded.

Each of BW(UK)'s **subsidiaries** for permanent staff has its *own* network of offices dotted around its main markets. Doctors & Nurses, Gleeson Gekko and Infonauts each have a network of offices in the UK, although Gleeson Gekko is concentrated in London.

For the **temporary staff divisions** (Nursing, IT, Finance and General), BW(UK) has four hundred offices in the UK, and aims to be the natural choice for a variety of assignments. **All** of BW's temporary markets are dealt with from these offices. The average number of consultants in each office is eight. Bill Begbie made it a management policy that every office must have at least one representative from each 'temporary staff' division (Nursing, IT, Finance General).

Managing each office

BW(UK). In the UK, BW employs the services of 'consultants' in each office, who are responsible for placing applicants with jobs. Each consultant keeps his or her own file of temporary workers which he or she matches to the demands made by business clients.

PeoplePower has a similar set-up, except that it is not organised on an area basis: 'Americans don't mind moving around'. Instead, PeoplePower maintains **separate offices** for each main type of **business customer**. New York is central for financial staff, California for IT staff. PeoplePower invested very heavily in computer linkups. Willard Mann wants to install video-conferencing systems to interview potential contract workers, so that an IT specialist in Texas could be interviewed over the conferencing system by someone in, say, the San Francisco office.

Human resources

BW and its subsidiaries are obviously concerned for the human resources needs of their clients, but they have their own human resources to look after as well.

In the UK, BW's consultants are paid a low basic salary, but get a substantial commission and a flat fee of £100 every time an employee is placed. Consultants have a six month probation period. They are given some initial training by sitting in on interviews. At each office, the practice is for existing consultants to pass on one of their business clients to the new recruit. Each office has a manager who determines what these clients will be. Appraisals take place when convenient. Non performers are booted out fairly quickly.

PeoplePower on the other hand does not pay commission on each placement. Rather, each office has a profit target. Consultants get a bonus based on the total profit made by the office and PeoplePower as a whole. Appraisals take place every year. Each PeoplePower consultant is supposed to build up a 'personal competence' of unique knowledge, for example a type of employee or a market, for the firm as a whole.

Begbie had wanted to dismantle the US system, and replace it with something on the lines of the UK but the resistance was too high.

Each PeoplePower consultant is supposed to build up a good personal relationship with the companies he or she deals with, and is expected to phone up regularly even in the absence of any particular request to see if there are any unmet needs which PeoplePower could satisfy.

Management

Begbie liked to think of himself as a charismatic leader. He had himself photographed with leading politicians, and tried desperately to get his name mentioned in admiring terms in the business press. He actively courted management gurus.

'I see the firm has having essentially a family atmosphere,' he said, 'After all we are a people business. Everybody's contribution is valued. And I have an open door policy'. He regularly visited the local offices in the UK.

Willard Mann, on the other hand, is rather more dour. He pays few site visits, although speaks regularly to senior managers. He does, however, take a great interest in the profit targets of each of the main businesses, and takes cashflow especially seriously.

Mission and strategy

Begbie's vision was to build BW to the biggest and best temporary employment agency in the world, hence the purchase of PeoplePower. In line with his thinking, Begbie devised a mission statement for BW, which appears framed in every office of the company. The mission is as follows: 'BW's mission is simply this: to provide our clients with the right workers at the right time; to offer the right work to the temporary staff we hire out; to offer profits to our shareholders; and to satisfy our employees and the community'.

Willard Mann cannot be bothered with mission statements: 'especially with a firm as diverse as ours. Our staff need to be taken seriously, not preached at; anyhow, mission statements give too many hostages to fortune'.

Willard Mann states 'Our current corporate objective is to increase shareholder value, in whatever way, operational or organisational. The strategy? By increasing revenues through existing businesses, and by shaving costs where possible'. As Willard says, 'Employment law in most of Europe is a nightmare, and I've got enough trouble on my hands without expanding overseas'.

Possible changes

The financial results for 1997 have been disappointing. PeoplePower has been successful, but the BW(UK) and EuroBrains have not increased their profits significantly.

Indeed, confidential market research suggests that the adverse publicity regarding Begbie's fall has dented the trust placed in the business. More worrying, the research revealed that while business clients are fairly satisfied with BW's services, they are not loyal; and that jobseekers rate BW fairly low in comparison with other agencies. One competitor, for example, is known to send handwritten thankyou notes to contract staff who do particularly well for its clients. Other agencies offer the agency staff sickness benefits and even paid holidays. One of the comments on the market research report came from someone with a very negative image of BW: 'You claim to be a human resources firm. Well, your interviewer mis-spelt my name - irritating, but not a crime - expressed no interest in my experience, and told me I'd make a great secretary if I wore shorter skirts. And I'm a qualified systems analyst with a first class honours degree in Information Science! Call yourself professionals?'

BW (UK) has decided to install an information system to keep track of the pay of *all* the staff they sent to clients, in other words a centralised payroll system. BW (UK) has gone for a bespoke design, but implementing it has proved to be more expensive than planned. Half way through the project, Willard himself intervened to turn the system into an employee database which lists each employee's work experience and qualifications, as well as the clients the employee has worked with. Each consultant in every office will have a terminal and will be able to access every record. BW(UK)'s finance director had given the responsibility to the financial controller of BW(UK)'s southern region. The project is already 10% over budget, only half complete and the key systems analyst, hired on a temporary basis, has left to work elsewhere.

The marketing directors of BW(UK) have a number of worries.

(a) 'Some of our bigger business clients are getting fed up having to deal with local offices all the time. Sometimes they have to deal with several offices just to get a reasonable pool of applicants. Another problem is that some of the "temporary" work is becoming long-term for six months or so, to cope with changes in demand. They don't just want somebody to make tea for a week. It is also embarrassing and irritating that the consultants obviously compete with one another.'

(b) 'I'm also worried about Europe. Paris and Frankfurt are taking off as financial centres. Who knows? If the UK stays out of the single European currency, some of the City's work will end up going over the Channel.'

The finance director, who is also in charge of administration, makes the following suggestion.

'Why are we developing the information system ourselves when it could be outsourced? A facilities management firm will look after our IT requirements and we can hold them to a contract'.

Willard Mann decides to surprise them all.

'I felt that the original takeover of PeoplePower was misconceived, and quite honestly, I think we have negative synergy in this situation. So I vote we demerge. PeoplePower can retain its independence and BW(UK) and EuroBrains can go their own way in Europe. After all, it isn't as if we Americans benefit at all. The shareholders will do nicely out of a demerger: I don't think the share price reflects the value of the businesses as independent units. I've got a friendly merchant bank on side who'll do the job for us. Comments please by tomorrow evening, as I need to get to work on this.'

Part A
Strategic management

Chapter 1

STRATEGIC MANAGEMENT: THE TRADITIONAL APPROACH

	Chapter topic list	Syllabus reference
1	What is strategy?	1(c)(i)
2	Levels of strategy in an organisation	1(c)(i)
3	Making strategies: the rational model	1(c)(i), (ii)
4	For the rational model	1(c)(i), (ii)
5	Against the rational model	1(c)(i)
6	Brainworks plc update	

Introduction

This chapter outlines the framework of the book by describing the 'rational model' approach to strategic management. Once we have outlined what strategic management is, we see how it applies at different **levels** of business. We then describe the **process of planning** and outline the criticisms of this model. This is an important chapter, especially Section 3, as it offers a framework for this Study Text and is applicable to many exam questions.

Brainworks plc

1 What do you think is the role of strategic planning at Brainworks plc (BW)?

2 Do you think the distinction between corporate and business strategy is meaningful at BW?

1 WHAT IS STRATEGY?

1.1 To start off, read the case example below.

Case example

Hong Kong Telecom

Hongkong Telecom is a subsidiary of Cable & Wireless. The Chinese telecoms market is conservatively estimated to be worth more than £368 billion: only one in six Chinese households currently possesses a land-based phone line. The company has seen double-digit growth over the past three years in a highly competitive market, and is, according to chief executive Linus Chiang, "poised on the cusp of a reincarnation".

Competition

The company lost its domestic monopoly in 1995. "We were printing money," Cheung says. "Suddenly we were faced with competition and huge technological advances. We were good technically and technologically, but not in terms of service and efficiency."

"Rather than trying to fight off the competition by legalities and by making life more difficult for customers by forcing different dialling codes and so forth onto them, we have embraced competition and taken advantage of it. In the short term that approach is not helpful. But we are taking a long-term view and using competition as a driving force, an agent for change."

Culture and human resources

The key to success, he asserts, is 'attitude, a performance culture and a service culture'. Hongkong Telecom employees are judged against three key criteria: 'One, are you bold and decisive? Two, are you results-rather than activity-oriented? Three, are you effective – in other words, do you make things simple for internal and external audiences?'. There have been 2,500 voluntary redundancies over the past three years, and they are increasingly demanding on remaining managers. 'We are de-layering and fast-tracking and weeding out incompetence,' says Cheung.

Cheung introduced Operation Excel, a programme that focuses on revenue enhancement and cost control, and rewards initiative, performance, teamwork and results, as an antidote to the complacency bred by monopoly. The programme has helped effect transition to a dynamic performance culture.

There have been some novel initiatives. Cheung jokes that he is the Postmaster General as well as the CEO. 'I looked at the way we were distributing our four million telephone bills each month, and my boyhood newspaper delivery experience came in handy. I found we could achieve significant savings by utilising our employees to deliver some of our bills. Staff are able to make additional income too.' What's more, he has galvanised the entire workforce to sell mobile phones. And he leads by example, travelling business rather than first class on his frequent trips abroad.

Product/service innovation

Most significantly, the company has switched its focus from international direct dialling to other areas, including fixed line, mobile, and interactive services. They won the licence for video-on-demand and home shopping in November, and it is a world first, using complex technology to deliver laser disk quality movies, karaoke, gambling, computer games, TV shopping, etc. Accessible by anyone with a telephone and a TV set using a single controller, the service has the potential to reach Hong Kong's 1.5 million households over the next five years. Another innovation is Netvigator, an Internet access service launched into a marketplace of 80 competitors. To differentiate their offering, they focused on the customer interface, delivering useful, immediate information.

Competitive strategy

Hongkong Telecom's competitive differentiator is to respond to customer needs. Finance director David Prince explains: "In telecoms, competitors tend to start from price, because what we have are effectively commodity products. We are trying to bring more creativity in marketing and customer service to telecoms. We differentiate ourselves from the competition on quality rather than price, by providing a total package to suit individuals' lifestyles." When it lost its lead to Hutchison in the mobile phone market, Hongkong Telecom held its prices but improved its technology so that, for example, mobiles work in tunnels and underground trains.

Summary

Hongkong Telecom's long-term *objective* appears to be survival and growth in the face of competition.

This is achieved by strategies for *products and markets* which involve offering new products/services and, in future, exploiting the Chinese market. These products and services enable it to *differentiate* its offering.

The *functional strategy for human resources* involves delayering, changes to the promotions structure and new demands on managers.

KEY TERMS

Strategy: a course of action including the specification of resources required to meet a specific objective.

Tactics: the deployment of resources to execute an agreed strategy.

This definition will serve as a starting point, but we will revisit it later.

1.2 In the Hongkong Telecom case example above:

- The objective is survival and growth.
- The strategy is a changed approached to products and markets.
- The resources specified include the technological infrastructure and getting better performance out of existing personnel.

Strategy thus determines how objectives are achieved. There are many different ways of achieving objectives.

Question 1

How might a government's *objective* of reducing road traffic accidents be achieved?

Answer

Stricter policing; traffic calming; lower speed limits; tougher driving tests etc.

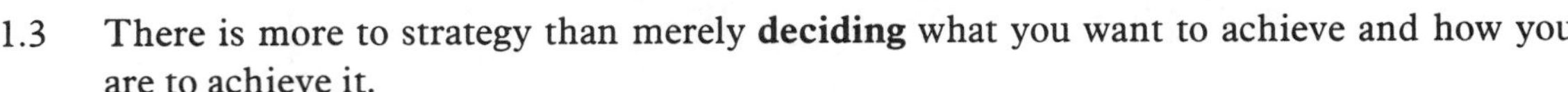

1.3 There is more to strategy than merely **deciding** what you want to achieve and how you are to achieve it.

KEY TERM

Strategic management: the development, implementation and control of agreed strategies.

1.4 Strategic management involves:

Phase	Application in Hong Kong telecom case example
Analysis	Discerning trends in the environment, looking at competitors
Choice	Deciding to innovate
Implementation	The *process* of changing the culture and organisation, and bringing the new products and services on-stream.
Control	After the strategies have been implemented, how successful have they been?

2 LEVELS OF STRATEGY IN AN ORGANISATION

2.1 Any level of the organisation can have objectives and devise strategies to achieve them. The strategic management process is multi-layered, as shown in the diagram below.

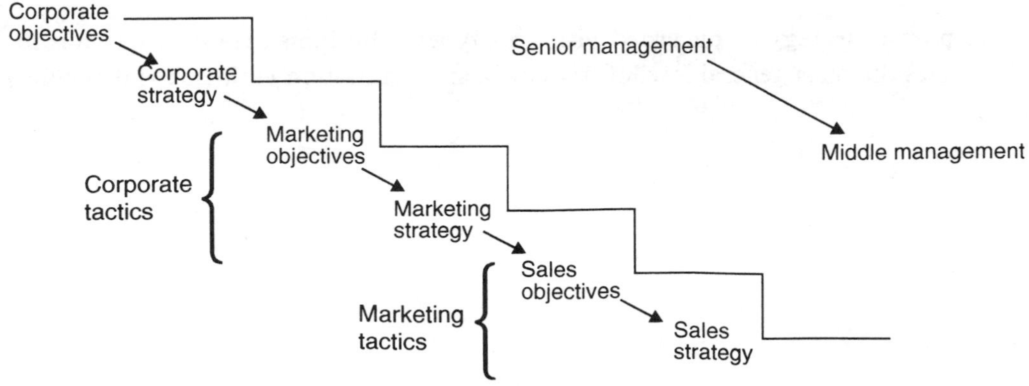

2.2 Hofer and Schendel refer to three levels of strategy.

- Corporate strategies
- Business strategies
- Operational and functional strategies, as in the diagram below

Levels of strategy

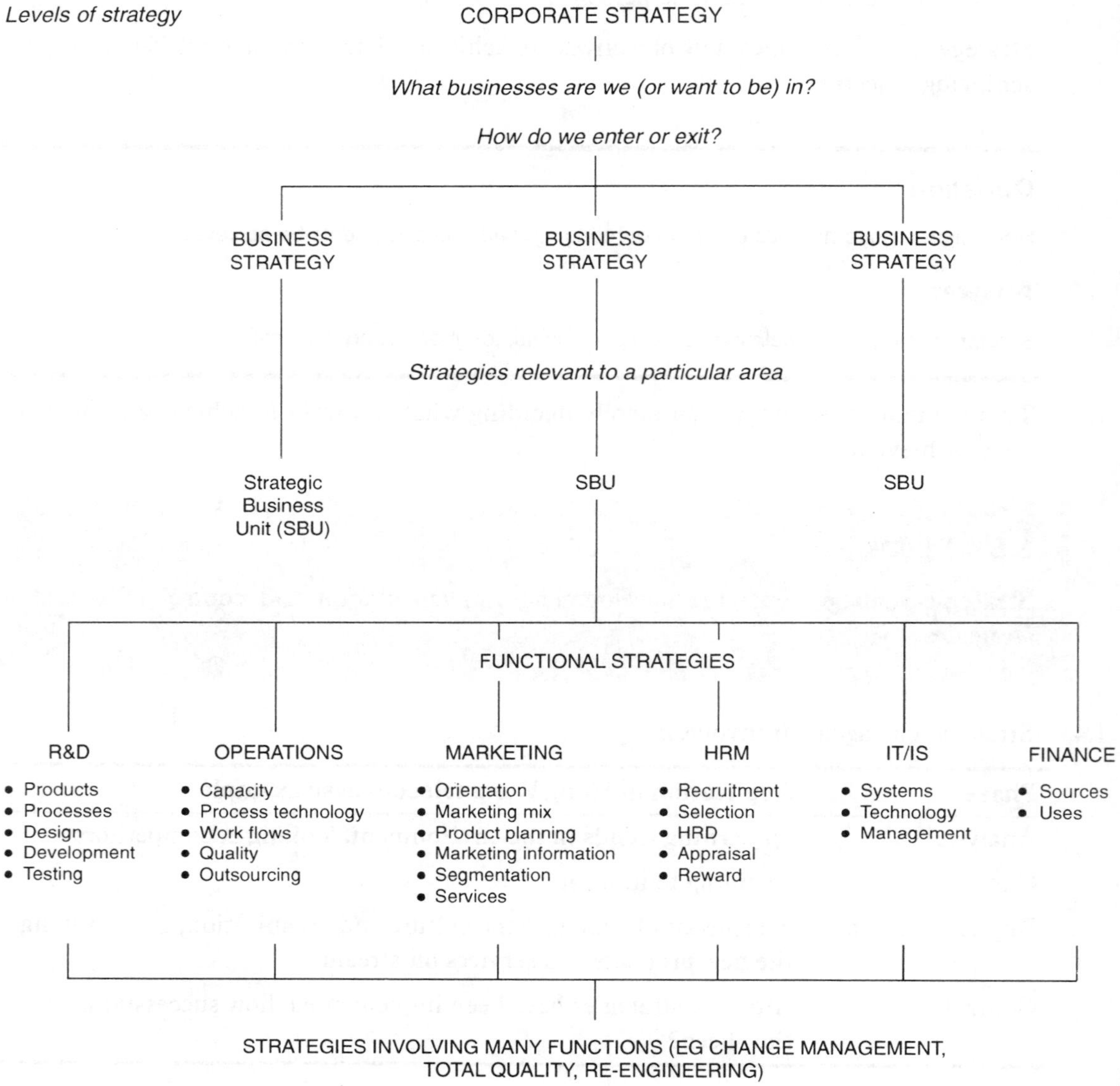

CORPORATE STRATEGY

What businesses are we (or want to be) in?

How do we enter or exit?

BUSINESS STRATEGY | BUSINESS STRATEGY | BUSINESS STRATEGY

Strategies relevant to a particular area

Strategic Business Unit (SBU) | SBU | SBU

FUNCTIONAL STRATEGIES

R&D	OPERATIONS	MARKETING	HRM	IT/IS	FINANCE
• Products • Processes • Design • Development • Testing	• Capacity • Process technology • Work flows • Quality • Outsourcing	• Orientation • Marketing mix • Product planning • Marketing information • Segmentation • Services	• Recruitment • Selection • HRD • Appraisal • Reward	• Systems • Technology • Management	• Sources • Uses

STRATEGIES INVOLVING MANY FUNCTIONS (EG CHANGE MANAGEMENT, TOTAL QUALITY, RE-ENGINEERING)

Corporate strategies

KEY TERM

Corporate strategy is concerned with what types of business the organisation is in. It 'denotes the most general level of strategy in an organisation' (Johnson and Scholes).

2.3 **Characteristics of corporate strategic decisions**

Characteristic	Comment
Scope of activities	What types of product
Environment	The organisation counters threats and exploits opportunities in the environment (customers, clients, competitors)
Capability	The organisation matches its activities to its resources: ie it does what it is able to do
Resources	Strategy involves choices about allocating or obtaining resources now and in future
Operations	Corporate strategies always affect operations
Values	The value systems of people in power influence them to understand the world in a certain way
Direction	Corporate strategy has a long-term impact on the direction of the organisation.
Complex	Corporate strategy is complex because it involves *uncertainty* about the future, *integrating* the operations of the organisation and *change*

(Mnemonic, using words in bold above: SECRets Of Value Directed Complexity)

2.4 Corporate strategy might involve diversifying into a new line of business or closing a business down. It might mean global expansion or contraction.

Business strategy

KEY TERM

Business strategy: how an organisation approaches a particular product market area.

2.5 This can involve decisions as to whether, in principle, a company should:

(a) Segment the market and specialise in particularly profitable areas.
(b) Compete by offering a wider range of products.

Case example

An example of a business strategy is the decision by Mercedes-Benz to expand its product range to include four wheel drive vehicles and smaller cars, culminating in the proposed merger with Chrysler.

2.6 Some large, diversified firms have separate **strategic business units** dealing with particular areas.

Functional/operational strategies

2.7 Functional/operational strategies deal with specialised areas of activity.

Functional area	Comment
Marketing	Marketing strategies involve devising products and services, pricing, promoting and distributing them, in order to satisfy customer needs at a profit. Marketing and corporate strategies are interrelated.
Production	A production strategy involves issues such as factory location, manufacturing techniques, outsourcing etc.
Finance	Finance strategies involve ensuring that the firm has enough financial resources to fund its other strategies by identifying sources of finance and using them effectively. Pricing decisions are both marketing and finance issues.
Human resources management (HRM)	The objective of any human resources strategy is to secure personnel of the right skills in the right quantity at the right time, and to ensure that they have the right skills and values to promote the firm's overall goals.
Information systems	A firm's information systems are becoming increasingly important, as an item of expenditure, as administrative support and as a tool for competitive strength. Not all information technology applications are strategic, and the strategic value of IT will vary from case to case.
R&D	New products and techniques.

Question 2

Ganymede Ltd is a company selling widgets. The finance director says: 'We plan to issue more shares to raise money for new plant capacity - we don't want loan finance - which will enable us to compete better in the vital and growing widget markets of Latin America. After all, we've promised the shareholders 5% profit growth this year, and trading is tough.'

Identify the corporate, business and functional strategies in the above statement.

Answer

The corporate objective is profit growth. The corporate strategy is the decision that this will be achieved by entering new markets, rather than producing new products. The business strategy suggests that those markets include Latin America. The operational or functional strategy involves the decision to invest in new plant (the production function) which is to be financed by shares rather than loans (the finance function).

2.8 Section summary

- Corporate strategies are for the organisation as a whole.
- Business, operational and functional strategies flow from the corporate strategy.

3 MAKING STRATEGIES: THE RATIONAL MODEL 6/97

3.1 For this and the next chapter, we discuss different approaches to making strategies.

3.2 In this section we outline the **rational model** which forms the structure for the rest of the text. First, a case example as to how it applies in practice.

Case example

Goold and Quinn (in *Strategic Control*) cite Ciba-Geigy, a Swiss-based global firm with chemicals and pharmaceuticals businesses, as an example of formal strategic control and planning processes.

(a) Strategic planning starts with the identification of strategic business sectors, in other words, areas of activity where there are identifiable markets and where profit, management and resources are largely independent of the other sectors.

(b) Strategic plans containing:

(i) Long term objectives
(ii) Key strategies
(iii) Funds requirements

are drawn up, based on a 'comprehensive analysis of market attractiveness', competitors etc.

(c) At corporate level, these plans are reviewed. Head office examines all the different plans, and, with a 7-10 year planning horizon, the total risk, profitability, cash flow and resource requirements are assessed. Business sectors are allocated specific targets and funds.

KEY TERM

Planning: 'the establishment of objectives and the formulation, evaluation and selection of the policies, strategies, tactics and action required to achieve these objectives. Planning comprises long-term/strategic planning, and short-term operations planning.'

3.3 Strategic plans are generally:

- Documented (written down).
- The result of a formal, systematised process with a start and end point.
- Determined or endorsed by senior managers, with little direct involvement from operational managers, although they may be consulted.

3.4 The diagram on the next page outlines the process of strategic planning. At each stage, the process involves the use of various techniques, tools and **models** (described later in this text) to make sense of the situation. You will be expected to show familiarity with these models in your answers to exam questions.

Exam focus point

In his comments on candidates' performance in the December 1997 exam, the examiner stated that 'candidates should:

- Only use models which are appropriate to the setting, and ... relate them to the case material.
- Avoid being over-theoretical
- Answer the questions which were asked not what they would like them to be
- Make an effort to carry out a controlled financial analysis in question 1 so as to evaluate strategies and recommend new ones.

3.5 Below we describe briefly the purpose of each stage, but they are covered in more detail in later chapters.

Strategic planning model

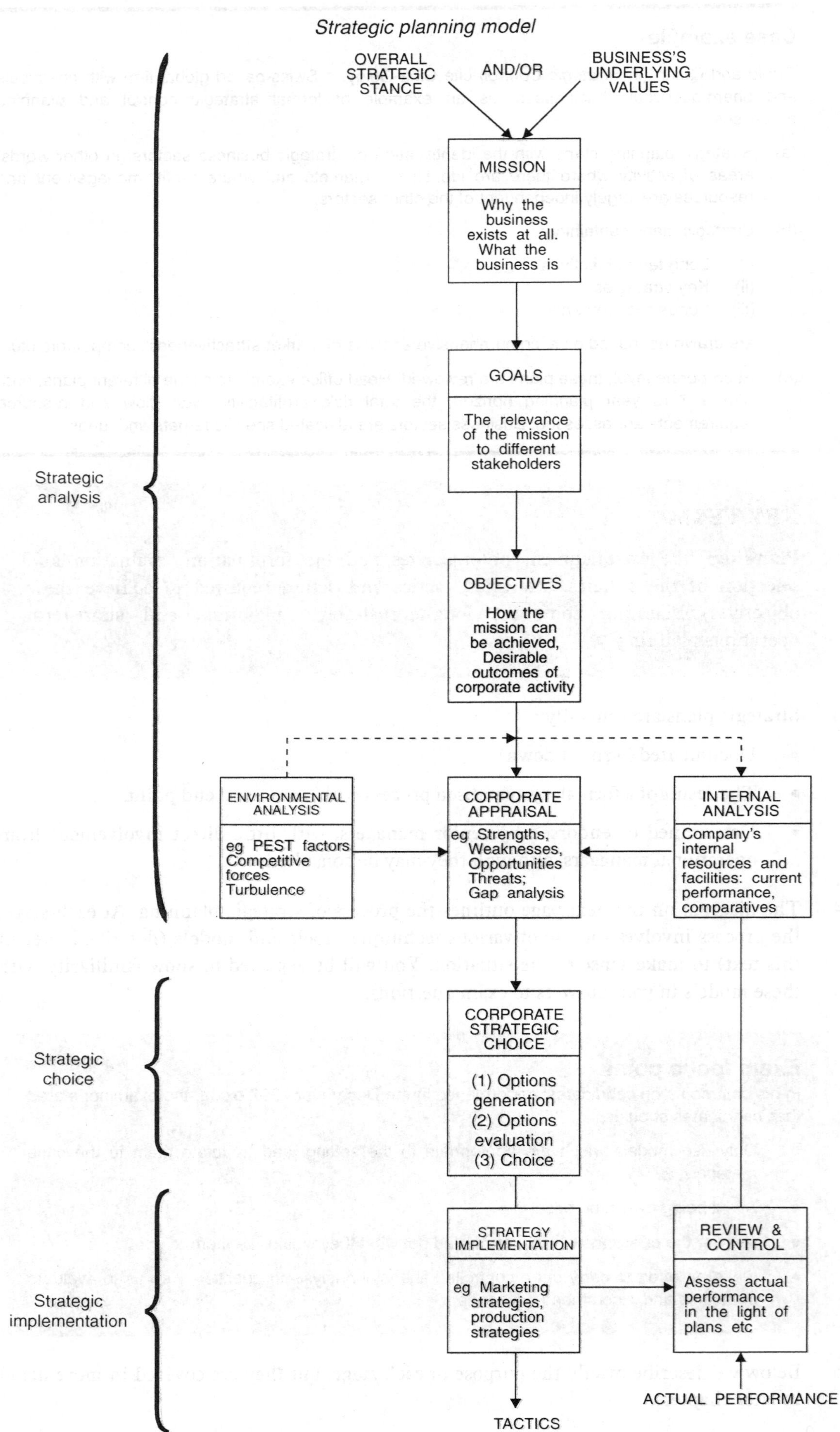

3.6 **Strategic analysis**

	Stage	Comment	Key tools, models, techniques
Step 1	Mission	Mission denotes values, the business's rationale for existing	• Mission statement
Step 2	Goals	Interprets the mission to different stakeholders	• Stakeholder analysis
Step 3	Objectives	Quantified embodiments of mission	• Measures such as profitability, time scale, deadlines
Step 4	Environmental analysis	Identify opportunities and threats	• PEST analysis • Porter's 5 force analysis; 'diamond' (competitive advantage of nations) • Scenario building
Step 5	Position audit or situation analysis	Identify strengths and weaknesses Firm's **current** resources, products, customers, systems, structure, results, efficiency, effectiveness	• Resource audit • Distinctive competence • Value chain • Product life cycle • Boston (BCG) matrix • Marketing audit For IT: • Nolan's stage model • McFarlan's grid • Awareness frameworks
Step 6	Corporate appraisal	Combines Steps 4 and 5	• SWOT analysis charts
Step 7	Gap analysis	Compares outcomes of Step 6 with Step 3	• Gap analysis

3.7 **Strategic choice**

Stage	Comment	Key tools, models, techniques
Strategic options generation	Come up with new ideas: • How to compete (competitive advantage)	• Value chain analysis • Scenario building • Porter's generic strategic choices
	• Where to compete	• Ansoff's growth vector
	• Method of growth	• Acquisition vs organic growth

Stage	Comment	Key tools, models, techniques
Strategic options evaluation	Normally, each strategy has to be evaluated on the basis of • Acceptability • Suitability • Feasibility • Environmental fit	• Stakeholder analysis • Risk analysis • Decision-making tools such as decision trees, matrices, ranking and scoring methods • Financial measures (eg ROCE, DCF) For IT: Opportunity Frameworks

3.8 **Implementation and functional strategies**

Stage	Comment	Key tools, models, techniques
Resource planning	Deploying the resources to achieve the strategy	• Critical success factors • Outsourcing
Operations plans		• Activity schedules • Budgets • Project management • For IT, systems development methodologies
Organisation structure and culture	Designing the organisation to implement the strategy	• Mintzberg's five element model • Departmentation
Change	Implement changes	• Force field analysis • Unfreeze-change-refreeze • Negotiation
Functional strategies	HRM	• Personnel planning • Motivation (eg Maslow) • Appraisal schemes
	Production	• TQM
	Marketing	• Marketing information systems • Marketing mix • Segmentation • Product life cycle (again)

3.9 **Control**

Stage	Comment	Key tools, models, techniques
Control	Review performance and amend	• Critical success factors • Balanced scorecard
	Performance indicators	• Marketing information system • Budgets

3.10 Don't worry - all these will be described in the appropriate chapter in the text. You can use these tables as checklists. Many of the models can be used in all phases of the strategic management process.

3.11 Contents of a strategic plan

Context

- Results of environmental appraisal
- Results of position audit

Long-term plan

- Mission statement
- Long-term objectives (eg market share, volume sales, position in industry)
- Critical success factors

The year ahead

- Annual goals
- Major strategic projects (eg new organisation structure, IT systems etc)

Implementation

- Schedules
- Budgets
- Performance measures

Exam focus point

A 50-mark case study set in June 1997 covered the strategic analysis and choice stages (paras 3.6, 3.7 above) of the process.

3.12 Section summary

- According to the rational model, strategic management is a process of analysis, choice, implementation and control.
- Strategic plans are documents indicating what is to be done in the year ahead and further into the future.

4 FOR THE RATIONAL MODEL 6/96

4.1 Assumptions of the rational model

(a) **'Top down'**. Senior managers, or planning departments, 'think great thoughts'. The results of their deliberations are documented in a plan, and are refined into greater and greater detail.

(b) **Corporate first**. Strategies for the organisation as a whole are developed prior to strategies for individual business units or functions.

(c) **Breakdown**. Strategic planning can be broken down into its subcomponents, in the same way as manual work can be.

(d) **Objective evaluation**. Strategies are evaluated objectively on their merits, unclouded by bias.

Ansoff: objectives

4.2 Ansoff, who is closely associated with the rational model, suggests that businesses pursue objectives.

- Economic (eg return on investment and subsidiary objectives such as market share)
- Social (eg to satisfy other stakeholders)
- Environmental (to cope with change)

4.3 Organisations need to follow the rational model because:

- The future is uncertain: **partial ignorance**.
- Conventional investment appraisal techniques (DCF) cannot deal with the uncertainties of product market decisions.
- A well thought-out strategy provides consistency in what the organisation does: a **common thread.**

A few words about these issues.

Partial ignorance

4.4 Ansoff distinguishes two types of decision.

- Standard **operating procedures** (eg operating a piece of equipment) in which all the variables are known.
- **Strategic decisions,** in which variables are not known.

4.5 Strategic decisions are taken in conditions of partial ignorance. Consequently, strategies are the '**decision rules** and guidelines which guide the process of development', in the lack of any more certain information. In other words, the purpose of the elaborate stages of the rational model is to identify and eliminate the uncertainties surrounding the organisation.

4.6 Setting objectives and strategies to achieve them enables the firm to take decisions as to what to do in particular cases.

Case example

The extent of the Windfall Tax on the privatised utilities was a cause of uncertainty. Before May 1st 1997 the uncertainty lay in whether it would be levied at all, as it depended on a Labour victory.

Between May 1st and July 2nd 1997 the uncertainty was the rate it would be levied, and which industries would be hit.

Strategy as a common thread

4.7 Ansoff says that a strategy provides a business with a **common thread.** An oil company might describe itself as being in the 'energy' business. As it basically deals with the extraction of energy from below the ground, it could expand into natural gas.

- A conglomerate might make a wide diversity of products (eg valves, underwear). The common thread is not the actual products or markets, but that the products are made with **simple technology** and the **markets are mature.**
- On the other hand, a common thread might be the products that are made (eg **motor cars,** in all shapes and sizes).

- Customers can be a common thread: gas companies now sell electricity.
- Synergy describes complementary between new and existing activities (ie 'two plus two equals five').

Case example

Arguably, the Automobile Association pursues synergy. Positioning itself as the fourth emergency service, not only does it deal with car emergencies, but offers an emergency plumbing and electrician service for its members.

Drucker

4.8 **Risk.** According to Drucker, a strategy can involve a **conscious** choice as to:

- **The business**: what the organisation intends to do in the environment and how it is to respond to opportunities or threats.
- The **degree of risk** it faces: all strategies, because they are made in conditions of partial ignorance, involve a risk. Strategic planning cannot avoid risk, but it can avoid unnecessary risk.
- The **long-term**: Drucker suggests that decisions taken *now* have implications for the *future*.
- **Resource development**: this involves decisions as to organisation structure, outsourcing and investment.

4.9 According to Drucker, strategic planning is something organisations **should** do. Strategic planning is:

(a) The continuous process of making **present risk-taking decisions systematically** and with greatest knowledge of their future effect: discovering the new things that need to be done and when.

(b) **Organising systematically the efforts** needed to carry out these decisions, ie ensuring that everything 'degenerates into work'. The aim of strategic planning is action **now**, and its realisation in **processes** and **behaviour.**

(c) '**Measuring the results** of these decisions ... through organised, systematic feedback'.

4.10 The emphasis on doing things in a **systematic way** naturally leads to the importance planning, deciding what things to do, the order in which they are done, and when they should be done.

4.11 Formal strategic planning is a process that can take several months, and might even be the responsibility of a separate department.

Case example

Oil firms typically have long lead times between:

(a) Deciding to invest in a new field
(b) Bringing the investment on stream so that it can earn money.

Oil firms have to think 20 years ahead, in order to:

(a) Maintain supplies in future, a constant round of exploitation

(b) Keep in business at present.

Some oil firms are investing in renewable energy sources such as solar power, because they assume that pressure to reduce CO_2 emissions (for which petrol usage is responsible) will hit demand.

4.12 Advantages of a formal system of strategic planning

Advantages	Comment
Identifies risks	Strategic planning helps in managing these risks.
Forces managers to think	Strategic planning can encourage creativity and initiative by tapping the ideas of the management team.
Forces decision-making	Companies cannot remain static - they have to cope with changes in the environment. A strategic plan helps to chart the future possible areas where the company may be involved and draws attention to the need to keep on changing and adapting, not just to 'stand still' and survive.
Better control	Management control can be better exercised if targets are explicit.
Enforces consistency at all levels	Long-term, medium-term and short-term objectives, plans and controls can be made consistent with one another. Otherwise, strategies can be rendered ineffective by budgeting systems with performance measures which have no strategic content.
Public knowledge	*Drucker* has argued that an entrepreneur who builds a long-lasting business has 'a theory of the business' which informs his or her business decisions. In large organisations, that the theory of the business has to become public knowledge, as decisions cannot be taken only by one person. As Drucker says 'business enterprise ... requires that entrepreneurship be systemised, spelled out as a discipline and organised as work'.
Time horizon	Some plans are needed for the long term.
Co-ordinates	Activities of different business functions need to be directed towards a common goal.
Clarifies objectives	Managers are forced to define what they want to achieve.
Allocates responsibility	A plan shows people where they fit in.

Case example

The UK *defence industry* faces lower government spending and greater competition as contracts are put out to open tender. There is greater competition in export markets. Having failed to diversify into civil areas, companies are changing the way they work.

Planning

A number of assumptions can be made about the environment and customer demands.

(a) Military needs are for mobile and flexible forces.

(b) For economic reasons, reliability and maintainability are desired.

(c) There should be military applications of civilian technology.

(d) The Ministry of Defence has also tightened up on procurement, replacing cost-plus contracts with competitive tenders.

Defence firms are undertaking strategic management. All firms are concerned with cash flow and productivity. *Strategic planning departments* have been set up to provide necessary inputs and analyses. The planners emphasise the threat from arms manufacturers in Russia, Germany and Japan. Analysts have identified that improvements in productivity and quality, to ensure the systems work, are of key importance.

Marketing Business (October 1996) highlighted the fact that UK arms firms are adopting marketing concerns and customer focus - leading to increased sales. There are moves to consolidate the European defence industry, into a few larger firms.

Description or prescription?

4.13 A fault line that runs through much of the literature on strategy making is the difference between:

- **De**scribing what businesses **actually do,** and
- **Pre**scription, which tells businesses what they **ought to do.**

4.14 Planning appears like 'common sense'; when it fails in practice, it is assumed that this is because people did not follow the rational model 'well enough'. But there are more powerful criticisms, which we outline below.

Exam focus point

The 50-mark case study in June 1996 covered the introduction of the rational model to a non-profit making organisation, facing the resource constraints of reduced central government funding.

4.15 Section summary

- The rational model forces people to think in a systematic way, in conditions of partial ignorance.
- It ensures consistency and control by publicly outlining what the business should do, and by ensuring departmental resources are marshalled to the corporate plan.

5 AGAINST THE RATIONAL MODEL

5.1 Criticisms of the rational model concern how it has worked in **practice,** and more fundamental problems of **theory.** Many of these criticisms were made by Henry Minztberg.

5.2 **Criticisms of strategic planning in practice**

Problem	Comments
Practical failure	Empirical studies have not proved that formal **planning** processes ('the delineation of steps, the application of checklists and techniques') contribute to success.
Routine and regular	Strategic planning occurs often in an **annual cycle.** But a firm 'cannot allow itself to wait every year for the month of February to address its problems.'
Reduces initiative	Formal planning discourages **strategic thinking.** Once a plan is locked in place, people are unwilling to question it. Obsession with particular performance indicators mean that managers focus on fulfilling the plan rather than concentrating on developments in the environment.

Problem	Comments
Internal politics	The assumption of 'objectivity' in evaluation ignores political battles between different managers and departments.
Exaggerates power	Managers are not all-knowing, and there are limits to the extent to which they can control the behaviour of the organisation.

5.3 Criticism of the rational model in theory

Mintzberg identified some fundamental fallacies of the planning model. These are the first four in the table below. The fifth is derived from John Kay.

Criticism	Comment
Formalisation	Strategy formation is a job which, like bricklaying, can be analysed into its component parts. But 'we have no evidence that any of the strategic planning systems - no matter how elaborate - succeeded in capturing (let alone improving on) the messy informal processes by which strategies really do get developed.'
Detachment: divorcing planning from operations	Managers manage by using 'remote' control. Senior managers at the top 'think great thoughts' while others scurry beneath them. This implies that managers do not really need day to day knowledge of the product or market. But strategic thinking is necessary to detect the strategic messages **within** the nitty gritty of operations (eg like finding gold dust in a stream). Information from the environment is picked up most acutely at operational level.
Formulation precedes implementation	A strategy is planned - then it is implemented. But **defining** strengths and weaknesses is actually very difficult in advance of **testing** them. 'The detached assessment of strengths and weaknesses may be unreliable, all bound up with aspirations, wishes and hopes'. Discovering strengths and weaknesses is a **learning process**. Implementing a strategy is necessary for learning - to see if it works. Where learning is needed, where the future is uncertain, strategic thinking cannot be divorced from implementation.
Predetermination	Planning assumes that the environment can be forecast, and that its future behaviours can be controlled, by a strategy planned in advanced and delivered on schedule. In conditions of stability, forecasting and extrapolation make sense. But forecasting cannot cope with discontinuities (eg war). In many cases forecasting functions as 'comforting magic'.
The military analogy	The rational model is often illustrated by an army. Its objective is to beat the enemy; the strategy describes how. This analogy is easy to grasp, but it may not be particularly relevant to business organisations. Their objectives are more complex and perhaps more ill-defined than an army's. They compete with other organisations for customers. They are less able to **command** resources than an army. Their employees want the organisation (and their jobs in it) to remain in permanent existence.

Where do we go from here?

5.4 Mintzberg's critique has not been fully accepted. Although the idea that planning is the **only** means by which strategies can be **made** is flawed, planning does have many uses, if carried out sensibly.

- It can force people to **think**.
- It can **publicise** strategic decisions.
- It can help **direct** activities in some cases
- It can **focus debate**. But these are supporting roles; they cannot fully account for the making of strategy itself.

Exam focus point

There rational model is a useful way of analysing the information in a case study. Be sensitive to Mintzberg's perhaps exaggerated critique, but for exam purposes the rational model will help you understand the question and, where appropriate, structure your answer.

5.5 Section summary

- The rational model has not conspicuously succeeded in practice.
- There are theoretical problems with the assumptions of formalisation, detachment and predetermination.

6 BRAINWORKS PLC UPDATE

Questions can be found in the Introduction box at the beginning of this Chapter.

6.1 *Question 1.* We are not told directly of formal planning processes, but clearly the rational model is employed, on the surface at least. Begbie outlined a mission statement, even though Willard thinks it is a waste of time. The firm is currently reviewing its position. However, it is difficult to get an idea as to where BW(UK)'s management think BW(UK) is going. They are reacting rather than thinking ahead.

6.2 *Question 2.* BW is hardly a united business, so it is hard to find any 'corporate strategy' for BW as a whole, independent of the units within it, other than the decision to demerge.

Question 3

As a conclusion to this chapter, we will bring together all of the points covered in an example, in the context of a non profit orientated organisation.

An Institution of Higher Education is concerned at a falling trend in applications. Outline the steps should it take to develop a strategy to halt this trend.

Answer

Step 1: Analysis

Find out the reasons for the falling trend in applications.

(a) The courses are no longer attractive to students, because their content or quality is not up to the standard expected by them.

(b) Other institutions of higher education, with a higher academic status, are beginning to offer similar courses.

(c) The qualifications students obtain are no longer sufficient to guarantee graduates a job at the end of the course.

(d) The costs of the course are now so high that they deter applicants.

(e) The size of the target market is falling.

Step 2: Objective

The Institution's objective is assumed to be to improve the appeal of its courses, and so to increase applications by a targeted quantity.

Step 3: Strategy

Develop a strategy to improve the situation, as far as possible as it has the power to do so (for example the costs of courses might be controlled by government, not by the Institution itself).

(a) New or improved courses might be designed. Student needs should be investigated.

   (i) What sort of courses do they need? Both the structure of the courses (full time, block release, day release etc) and academic content should be reviewed.

   (ii) What quality of teaching (and teaching equipment) is required? If existing staff are unable to teach the subjects required, some re-planning or re-training of manpower will be necessary.

   The product should be capable of satisfying student needs before it can be sold.

(b) If qualifications are no longer sufficient to guarantee graduates a job, the needs of *potential employers* should also be investigated. Courses should be designed so as to produce graduates whom employers would prefer to recruit in preference to other people with different qualifications, or even with no qualifications at all.

Step 4: More detailed planning

(a) Design courses to suit customer needs better.
(b) Allocate resources to a campaign to attract applicants (eg communications).

Step 5: Control

Any strategy should have a quantified target (for example to raise applications by x% per annum for the next five years) and there should be some procedure or control mechanism whereby actual results are monitored, compared against the strategic plan, and evaluated.

Chapter roundup

- **Strategy** is a course of action, specifying the resources required, to achieve an objective. There are many levels of strategy in an organisation.
  - **Corporate**: the general direction of the whole organisation
  - **Business**: what the organisation, or its strategic business units, does in an organisation.
  - **Operational/functional**: specific strategies for different departments of the business.
- According to the rational model, strategy is about the achievement of goals and objectives. Strategy-making is a process with the following steps.
  - **Mission, goals and objectives**. An organisation's mission answers the question 'what business are we in?' Goals and objectives determine what the business should achieve if it is to satisfy its mission.
  - **Analysis of the environment** of the organisation and its internal position
  - **Generation of alternative options** to satisfy objectives
  - **Choice of preferred option**, based on rational and objective criteria of evaluation
- The rational model implies that strategies are best generated from the **top down**. It provides a **common thread** and enables decisions to be taken in conditions of **partial ignorance** (Ansoff), where **risk** (Drucker) is inevitable.
- The rational model might work in **stable environments**, and for certain kinds of organisations, but there are practical and theoretical problems in asserting that a planning process is the only or best way of generating strategy.
- Criticisms include:
  - Its failure in practice
  - Over reliance on **formalisation, detachment** and **predetermination**
  - It assumes firms can know what their strengths are before testing them

Quick quiz

1 What is strategic management? (see para 1.3, 1.4)

2 List the characteristics of corporate strategic decisions. (2.3)

3 Distinguish between corporate and functional strategy. (2.3, 2.7)

4 What are the stages in the rational model of strategic planning? (3.6 - 3.9)

5 What types of strategy are outlined in the strategy generation process? (3.7)

6 What are the bases of strategic choice? (3.7)

7 What objectives characterise business? (4.2)

8 Why do Ansoff and Drucker support the rational model? (4.4 - 4.9)

9 List the advantages of planning? (4.12)

10 What are the practical drawbacks to the rational model? (5.2)

11 What might be the *real* use of planning in strategic management? (5.4)

Question to try	Level	Marks	Time
1	Introductory	n/a	30 mins
2	Exam standard	25	45 mins

Chapter 2

OTHER MODELS OF STRATEGIC MANAGEMENT

Chapter topic list		Syllabus reference
1	The need for new models	1(c)(i), (ii)
2	Patterns and competences: Andrews	1(c)(i), (ii)
3	Emergent strategies and how to craft them: Mintzberg	1(c)(i), (ii)
4	A behavioural approach?	1(c)(i), (ii)
5	Incrementalism	1(c)(i), (ii)
6	Strategic thinking and vision	1(c)(i), (ii)
7	Competition, environmental fit and trade-offs	1(c)(i), (ii)
8	Mintzberg's 5 Ps	1(c)(i), (ii)
9	Brainworks plc update	

Introduction

This chapter contains some alternative approaches to the rational model. The **incrementalist model** suggests that small scale adjustments are preferred to wholesale reviews. Both the incrementalists and **Johnson and Scholes** recognise the political and **behavioural context.** Mintzberg's **emergent strategies** model suggests that some strategies develop by accident, and strategic management involves shaping or **crafting** these developments. Ohmae and Porter describe strategy in **competitive** terms - but unlike Porter, Ohmae assumes that **strategic thinking** is a matter of intuition rather than rational analysis. The final section of this chapter describes the many uses of the concept of strategy, as an 'integrative concept'.

Brainworks plc

1 How do you think strategy has actually been developed in Brainworks plc over the years?

2 Do you think strategic decisions could be taken in a better way?

3 What functional decisions do you think will have a strategic impact?

4 Do you think 'vision' and intuition are needed at Brainworks plc?

1 THE NEED FOR NEW MODELS

1.1 The case example below puts into a radically different perspective the issues raised in the previous chapter. It will show why the 'common sense' rational model cannot *always* be trusted.

Case example

Honda

Honda is now one of the leading manufacturers of motorbikes. The company is credited with identifying and targeting an untapped market for small 50cc bikes in the US, which enabled it to expand, trounce European competition and severely damage indigenous US bike manufacturers. By 1965, Honda had 63% of the US market. But this occurred by accident.

On entering the US market, Honda's **planned strategy** was to compete with the larger European and US bikes of 250ccs and over. These bikes had a defined market, and were sold through dedicated motorbike dealerships. Disaster struck when Honda's larger machines developed faults - they had not been designed for the hard wear and tear imposed by US motorcyclists. Honda had to recall the larger machines.

Honda had made little effort to sell its small 50 cc motorbikes - its staff rode them on errands around Los Angeles. Sports goods shops and ordinary bicycle and department stores had expressed an interest, but Honda did not want to confuse its image in its 'target' market of men who bought the larger bikes.

The faults in Honda's larger machines meant that reluctantly, Honda had no alternative to sell the small 50cc bikes just to raise money. They proved very popular with people who would never have bought motorbikes before. Eventually the company adopted this new market with enthusiasm with the slogan: 'You meet the nicest people on a Honda'.

The strategy had **emerged**, against managers' conscious intentions, but they eventually responded to the new situation.

2 PATTERNS AND COMPETENCES: ANDREWS

Andrews: strategies are patterns of management decisions

2.1 Unlike Ansoff, Andrews does not accept the validity of separating objectives from the strategies designed to achieve them.

KEY TERM

For Andrews, **corporate strategy** is: 'the *pattern* of decisions in a company that determines and reveals its objectives, purposes, or goals, that produces the principal policies and plans for achieving those goals, and defines the range of business the company is to pursue, the kind of economic and human organisation it is or intends to be, and the nature of the economic and non economic contribution it intends to make to its shareholders, employees, customers and communities'.

2.2 Strategy arises out of the **general management process** whereby **senior** managers direct and control the business. Strategy is still senior management's concern.

- This general management process generate **consistent** decisions. For example, a firm's managers may prefer certain types of market opportunities (eg low risk) than others.
- Separating 'objectives' from the strategies to achieve them 'leads to narrow and mechanical conceptions of strategic management and endless logic-chopping'.

Case example

Philips

'Philips, Europe's largest consumer electronics group, is to limit the extent to which it stakes its future on product breakthroughs - aiming for predictability in growth rather than seeking rewards in expensive and risky innovations.

The company - in earlier years inventor both of the compact disk and the failed V2000 video system - came close to bankruptcy in 1991 but recovered to achieve record net profits of Fl 2.52bn ($1.33bn)four years later before sliding back into a Fl 590m loss last year.

Mr Boonstra, new president for the company adds, 'Again and again we have proved vulnerable to market fluctuations, to the trade cycle, to success or lack of success with a particular product. 'We then put all our faith in a new invention, a new product, as if it is some magic wand that will solve all our problems with the market, the competition and price erosion. And if it fails to live up to its promise, we suffer setbacks. We are now seeking to break out of this cycle of all-or-nothing offensives. Under Mr Boonstra's cuts a number of projects from the Timmer era have been abandoned.' (*Financial Times*, 25 March 1997)

In other words, Mr Boonstra is recognising that the **pattern of decision making** the firm had employed was no longer relevant or useful.

Strategy is the exploitation of competences

KEY TERM

The **distinctive competence** of an organisation is what it does well, uniquely, or better than rivals. Andrews says that, for a relatively undifferentiated product like cement, the ability of a maker to 'run a truck fleet more effectively' than its competitors will give it competitive strengths (if, for example, it can satisfy orders quickly).

2.3 Strategic opportunities must be related to the firm's resources. A strategic approach involves identifying a firm's **competences**. 'Members of organisations develop judgements about what they think the company can do well - its core of competence.' These competences may derive from:

(a) **Experience** in making and marketing a product or service.
(b) The talents and potential of individuals in the organisation.
(c) The **quality of co-ordination**.

3 EMERGENT STRATEGIES AND HOW TO CRAFT THEM: MINTZBERG 12/97

Exam focus point

This topic was explicitly examined in December 1997, when 11 marks in a section B question were available for you to 'indicate under what circumstances strategy formulation should be initiated by senior managers or by middle/operational managers'. The examiner was disappointed that few candidates knew about emergent strategies (below) or incrementalism (Section 5). This is surprising as both topics are explicitly mentioned in the ACCA's teaching guide and have been covered in previous editions of this BPP Study Text.

This only goes to show that you *cannot* skate over topics you feel uncomfortable with because they are difficult, counter-intuitive or theoretical.

3.1 In the Honda case example at the beginning of this chapter, we mentioned that the planned strategy of selling large bikes had to give way to a strategy which had emerged by accident, almost. Henry Mintzberg develops this theme further.

3.2 **Emergent strategies** do not arise out of conscious strategic planning, but from a number of ad hoc choices, perhaps made lower down the hierarchy. They may not initially be recognised as being of strategic importance. Emergent strategies develop out of **patterns of behaviour,** in contrast to planned strategies or senior management decisions which are imposed from above. An exercise will make the point clearer.

Question 1

Aldebaran Ltd is a public relations agency founded by an entrepreneur, Estella Grande, who has employed various talented individuals from other agencies to set up in business. Estella Grande wants Aldebaran Ltd to become the largest public relations agency in North London. Management consultants, in a planning document, have suggested 'growth by acquisition'. In other words, Aldebaran should buy up the other public relations agencies in the area. These would be retained as semi-independent business units, as the Aldebaran Ltd group could benefit from the goodwill of the newly acquired agencies. When Estella presents these ideas to the Board there is general consensus with one significant exception. Livia Strange, the marketing director, is horrified. 'How am I going to sell this to my staff? Ever since we've been in business, we've won business by undercutting and slagging off the competition. My team have a whole culture based on it. I give them champagne if they pinch a high value client. Why acquire these new businesses - why not stick to pinching their clients instead?'

What is the source of the conflict?

Answer

Livia Strange's department has generated its own pattern of competitive behaviour. It is an emergent strategy. It conflicts directly with the planned strategy proposed by the consultants. This little case history also makes the additional point that strategies are not only about numbers, targets and grand plans, but about the organisational cultures influencing a person's behaviour.

Deliberate and emergent strategies

3.3 The diagram below should help explain the point.

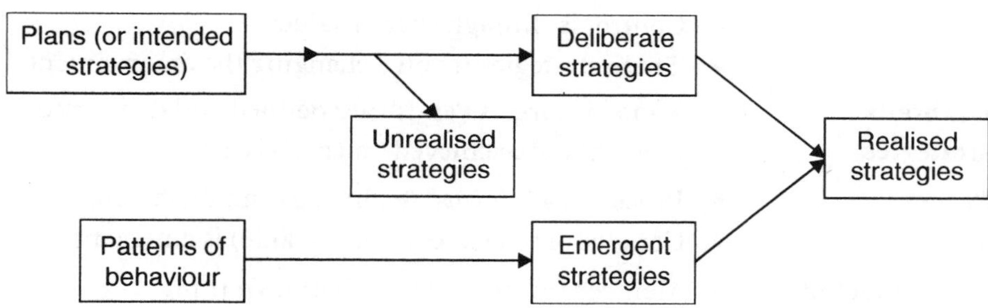

(a) **Intended strategies** are plans. Those plans or aspects of plans which are actually realised are called **deliberate strategies.**

(b) **Emergent strategies** are those which develop out of patterns of behaviour.

3.4 The task of **strategic management** is to control and shape these emergent strategies as they develop.

Case example

BPP began life as a training company. Lecturers had to prepare course material. This was offered for sale in a bookshop in the BPP building. Owing to the demand, BPP began offering its material to other colleges, in the UK and world-wide. BPP Publishing, which began as a small offshoot of BPP's training activities, is now a leading publisher in the market for targeted study material for the examinations of several professional bodies. It is unlikely that this development was anticipated when the course material was first prepared.

3.5 No realised strategy will be *wholly* deliberate or *wholly* emergent. The line between deliberate and emergent elements within each strategy will be in part influenced by organisation structure and culture.

Implicit or explicit strategies

3.6 We already mentioned the fact that entrepreneurs have a theory of the business which they may or may not document.

- Implicit strategies are 'in the boss's head'
- Explicit strategies are properly documented

Some plans are more explicit than others.

3.7 With these in mind, Mintzberg identified eight styles of strategic management.

Style	Comment
Planned strategies	• Precise intentions • Explicit intentions (ie written down, documented) • Imposed by central leadership • Large number of controls • Maximises predictability
Entrepreneurial strategies	• Intended strategy derives from the vision of strong leadership • Not always explicit
Ideological strategies	• Intended strategy is the collective vision of the organisation's members • Control is through shared values • These strategies involve changing the environment
Umbrella strategies	• Strategic targets ('ends') are defined and deliberate • How they are achieved ('means') is emergent
Process strategies	• Processes are formal (eg hiring) and deliberate • Content of strategies (what is done) is emergent
Disconnected strategies	• Members of subunits 'do their own thing' • Strategies are emergent for the whole organisation, deliberate for subunits
Consensus strategies	• Groups in the organisation converge on common patterns of activity
Imposed strategies	• Strategy is imposed by the environment (eg a strong customer) - which pre-empts the organisation's own choice

Question 2

Using the categories in 3.7 above, decide what sort of strategy you think is described in the following scenarios.

(a) The Early Morning TV company was formed to broadcast in the two hours each morning before breakfast TV. The company is owned by its five hosts and presenters, as an equal partnership. They sell advertising time. Their broadcasting strategy is 'a mission to explain'. Individual presenters appear on a different morning each week.

(b) Terry's Textiles is a company selling standard grey socks. It has one major customer, the huge retailer Charles Herbert. Charles Herbert has recently decided to install electronic data interchange and just in time systems. Terry's Textiles would not normally consider adopting these innovations, but Charles Herbert has offered to pay some of the cost.

Answer

(a) This could be an ideological strategy as the broadcasting strategy is not heavily defined. On the other hand, as the presenters find their feet it could end up as a consensus strategy.

(b) Imposed strategy.

Crafting emergent strategies

3.8 Managers cannot simply let emerging strategies take over. Why?

- **Direction.** The emergent strategy may be inappropriate for the long-term direction of the organisation and may have to be corrected.
- **Resources.** It may have future implications for resource use elsewhere: in most organisations, different parts of the business compete for resources.
- Managers might wish to build on the strategy by **actively devoting more resources** to it.

3.9 Mintzberg uses the metaphor of **crafting strategy** to help understand the idea. As opposed to senior managers deciding everything advance from the vantage point of an ivory tower, the idea of strategy as a **craft** evokes an idea of 'skill, dedication, perfection, through mastery of detail'. Forming a strategy and implementing it are 'fluid processes of **learning** through which creative strategies evolve', rather like, according to Mintzberg, shaping the clay on a potter's wheel.

3.10 Separating 'thinking' and 'doing' has the following result.

(a) A **purely deliberate strategy prevents learning** (once the formulators have stopped formulating). For example it is hard with deliberate strategies to 'learn from mistakes', or stumble by accident into strategic growth.

(b) A **purely emergent strategy defies control.** It may in fact be a bad strategy, dysfunctional for the organisation's future health.

3.11 Deliberate strategies introduce strategic change as a sort of quantum leap in some organisations. In this case, a firm undergoes only a few strategic changes in a short period but these are very dramatic.

Case example

In other organisations, however, strategic change can be *haphazard.* Mintzberg mentions the example of the Canadian National Film Board. This used to make short documentaries but ended up by chance with a feature film. This forced it to learn the marketing of such films, and so it eventually became much more involved in feature length productions than before - 'strategy by accident'.

3.12 The strategist must be able to **recognise** patterns and to manage the process by which emergent strategies are created. In other words, the strategist must be able to **find strategies** as well as **invent them**.

How to craft strategy

3.13 Mintzberg lists these activities in crafting strategy.

Activity	Comment
Manage stability	• Most of the time, managers should be implementing the strategies, not planning them. • Obsessions with change are dysfunctional. Knowing *when* to change is more important. You cannot *assume* perpetual environmental turbulence. • Formal planning is the detailed working out of the agreed strategy.
Detect discontinuity	• Environments do not change regularly, nor are they always turbulent, though managers should be on the lookout for changes. *Some* small environmental changes are more significant for the long term than others, though guessing which these are is a problem. ○ Technological developments: **Hoffmann-LaRoche** began as a small firm making dyes. It acquired the patents to vitamins when no one else wanted them. It is now an industry leader. ○ International developments: spotting international trends which are important to the organisation (which markets are likely to grow and so forth) must be supplemented by assessments of commercial and political risks.
Know the business	• An intimate feel for the business has to include an awareness and understanding of operations.
Manage patterns	• Detect emerging patterns and to help them take shape. Some emergent strategies must be uprooted, others nurtured.
Reconciling change and continuity	• 'Crafting strategy .... requires a natural synthesis of the future, present and past.' Obsessions with change and/or continuity can be counterproductive.

3.14 Section summary

- Strategy can emerge from patterns of behaviour, perhaps at operational level.
- Managers have to craft emergent strategies, accepting some and giving them resources, and rejecting others.
- An organisation's realised strategy will be a mix of emergent and intended strategies.

Question 3

Britannia Hospital has just appointed a new director, Florian Vole, imported from the private sector, where he had run 'Hanky House' a niche retail operation specialising in handkerchiefs and fashion accessories. The recession put the business into receivership, but Mr Vole was sought out to inject his private sector expertise in running a public sector institution. He calls a meeting of the hospitals senior managerial, medical and nursing staffs. 'What the public sector has been missing too long is vision, and when you're eyeball-to-eyeball with change, it's vision that you need, not planning documents and statistics. We need to be nimble and quick to adapt to our customer's ever changing needs. That is our strategy!'

What do think of Florian Vole's approach?

Answer

Mr Vole hasn't quite made the transition from the fashion industry, where desire for silk handkerchiefs is relatively fickle, to an institution like Britannia Hospital. Here planning is necessary. Resources must be obtained to cope with future needs. 'Customer needs' are likely to be fairly basic (ie security, comfort, medical attention, stimulation). However, in the actual delivery of care and services, Florian Vole has a point: experimentation with new care techniques might improve the hospital's service to its patients.

4 A BEHAVIOURAL APPROACH?

4.1 A criticism of the rational model is that it ignores the fact that strategists are human beings and **strategy formation reflects the internal politics** of the organisation.

4.2 Johnson and Scholes' state that 'strategy needs to be understood as an outcome of the social, political and cultural processes of management in organisation'. Johnson and Scholes describe the following phases in the strategic decision-making process.

Step 1. **Problem awareness**

- Internal results, customer responses or environmental changes can make **individuals** aware of a problem.
- A **trigger** alerts the **formal** information system to the problem, so that organisational activity takes over from the individual's consideration of the problem.

Step 2. **Problem diagnosis.** Managers try to analyse and get to the root of the problem. Information may be used to rationalise, rather than challenge, management's existing view of the situation. **Formal analysis** in practice plays a little role.

Step 3. **Solution development.** Some possible solutions are developed and one is selected.

- **Memory search**: solutions which worked in the past.
- **Passive search**: wait for a solution to suggest itself.

Solutions begin with a vague idea, which is further refined and explored by internal discussion.

Step 4. **Solution selection**

- **Eliminate unacceptable plans.** This screening process involves bargaining, diplomacy and judgement rather than formal evaluation according to the business case. ('Unacceptable' might mean 'unacceptable' in terms of organisational politics, rather than in terms of business sense.)
- **Endorsements.** Many strategic decisions **originate from management subsystems,** which senior managers authorise. Junior managers might filter strategic information, or ignore certain options, to protect themselves.

4.3 Johnson and Scholes are less averse to planning than Mintzberg, but instead of assuming a rational objectivity, they anchor plans in the behaviour of the organisation and the people in it.

5 INCREMENTALISM

Bounded rationality

5.1 Herbert Simon was aware that the rational model could not readily be realised in practice. In practice, managers are limited by time, by the information they have and by their own skills, habits and reflexes. In real life:

- The manager **does not optimise** (ie get the best possible solution).
- Instead **the manager satisfices.** The manager carries on searching until he or she finds an option which appears tolerably satisfactory, and adopts it, even though it may be less than perfect. This approach Simon characterised as **bounded rationality**.

Lindblom's alternative approach - incrementalism

5.2 Lindblom suggests that in the real world:

(a) Strategic managers do **not** evaluate all the possible options open to them in a given situation, but choose between few alternatives.

(b) Strategy making involves **small scale extensions** of past policy - incrementalism - rather than radical shifts following a comprehensive rational analysis.

(c) Strategy making necessitates accommodation or compromises with interested groups through political bargaining - a process Lindblom described as **partisan mutual adjustment**.

5.3 **Advantages**

Lindblom thought his incremental model was to be *preferred* to the rational model.

- Strategy making involving small scale extensions of past practices avoids major errors.
- It is more likely to be acceptable, because consultation, compromise and accommodation are built into the process.
- Comprehensive rational planning is impossible, and likely to result in disaster if actively pursued.

5.4 **Disadvantages**

- Incrementalism does not work where radical new approaches are needed, and it has a built-in conservative bias. Forward planning does have a role.
- Even as a descriptive model of the public sector, it does not always fit. Some changes do not seem incremental, but involve dramatic shifts.
- Incrementalism ignores the influence of corporate culture, as it filters out unacceptable choices.
- It might only apply to a stable environment.

Question 4

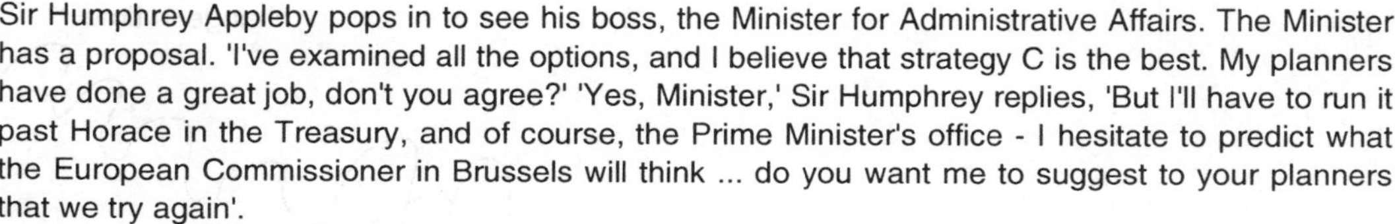

Sir Humphrey Appleby pops in to see his boss, the Minister for Administrative Affairs. The Minister has a proposal. 'I've examined all the options, and I believe that strategy C is the best. My planners have done a great job, don't you agree?' 'Yes, Minister,' Sir Humphrey replies, 'But I'll have to run it past Horace in the Treasury, and of course, the Prime Minister's office - I hesitate to predict what the European Commissioner in Brussels will think ... do you want me to suggest to your planners that we try again'.

What models of strategic planning and management are discussed here?

Answer

The Minister is a planner: he's describing the rational model. Sir Humphrey is advocating the partisan mutual adjustment model. See Paragraph 5.6(c) for details.

A middle way? Logical incrementalism

5.5 Strategy is best described as a **learning process**. It is impossible to predict the long-term consequences of decisions made in situations of crisis or change. So, managers deliberately keep their decisions small scale.

KEY TERM

Logical incrementalism: managers have a vague notion as to where the organisation should go, but strategies should be tested in small steps, simply because there is too much uncertainty about actual outcomes.

5.6 Logical incrementalism has the best of both worlds.

- The broad outlines of a strategy are developed by an in-depth review.
- There is still practical scope for day-to-day incremental decision making.

Contrasts

5.7 The implications of rationality and incrementalism can be expressed in diagrammatic form.

(a) *Rational planning model*

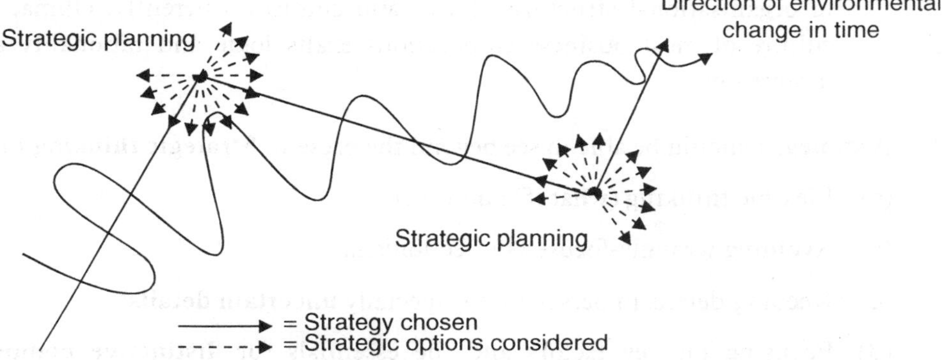

The dangers of the rational model are that the environment may change too quickly for the planning processes to react. All directions are considered, however.

(b) *Incremental model*

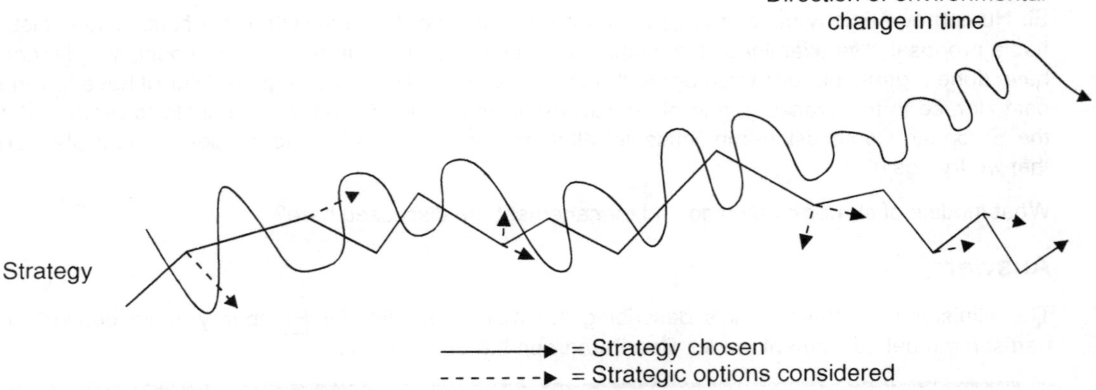

Incremental change may not be enough as the number of strategic options considered may be insufficiently radical to cope with environmental shift.

5.8 Section summary

- Managers do not take optimal (ie the best) decisions but satisfactory ones (decisions which will 'do').
- Managers do not pursue the whole rational model, but take small-scale decisions, building on what has gone before (incrementalism).

6 STRATEGIC THINKING AND VISION

Strategic thinking as an intuitive process

6.1 Kenichi Ohmae (in *The Mind of the Strategist*) argues that **formal strategic planning processes have withered strategic thinking.** Strategy is essentially a creative process.

- **Successful strategists** 'have an idiosyncratic **mode of thinking** in which company, customers and competition merge in a dynamic interaction out of which a comprehensive set of objectives and plans for action eventually crystallises'.
- My message ... is that successful business strategies result not from rigorous analysis but from a **particular state of mind**'.
- For Ohmae, the challenge to strategic management is to try to reproduce this ability in organisational structures, forms and cultures. Currently, Ohmae says that 'the culture of most business corporations exalts logic and rationality as opposed to innovation.

6.2 A strategist should be able to see beyond the present. **Strategic thinking** involves:

(a) Flexible thinking (what if? questions).

(b) Avoiding wrongly-focused perfectionism.

(c) Keeping details in perspective (especially **uncertain details**).

(d) Focusing on key factors and the essentials (or **distinctive competences**) of a business.

6.3 **How successful strategic thinking operates**

(a) **Ask the right question**. Find a **solution to a problem** rather than a **remedy to a symptom**. (Analogy: painkillers reduce a headache, they do not go to the underlying problem which may be poorly made spectacles, bad lighting or whatever.)

(b) **Observe the problems.**

(c) **Group** problems together by a process of **abstraction** (eg brainstorming) to see what they have in common (the **key factors**).

Ohmae gives an example from an organisation's personnel system.

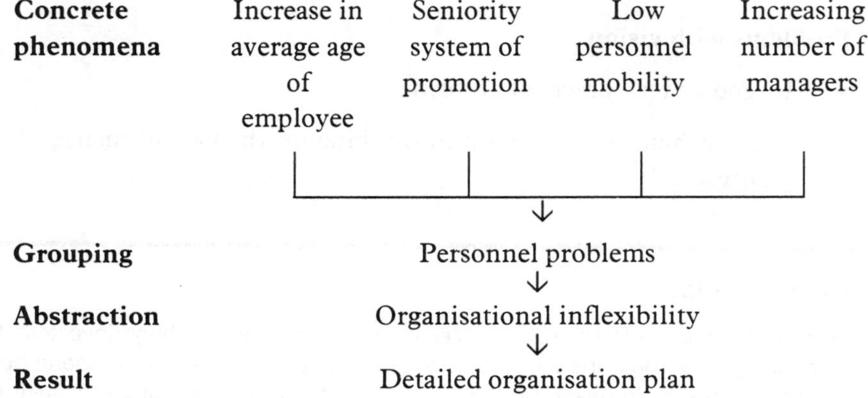

Vision

6.4 A strategic thinker should have a **vision** of:

(a) What the business *is* now.
(b) What it *could* be in an ideal world.
(c) What the ideal world would be like.

Case example

At the moment there is a debate in the computer industry about the future of the PC. The head of *Oracle* believes that the PC is dead and will be replaced by the *Network Computer,* which will download software from the internet, rather than storing it on a hard disk.

The 'vision' is of a world full of Network Computers, simpler to use than the PC. In some respects this vision is self-serving, as publicising it will encourage other firms in the industry to follow suit.

6.5 A vision gives a general sense of direction to the company, even if there is not too much attention to detail. A vision, it is hoped, enables **flexibility** to exist in the context of a guiding idea. 'Like the North Star, a manager's vision is not a goal. Rather, it is the orientation point that guides the company in a specific direction. A vision should be clear. The vision of Apple Computers, in the early days of the PC industry was to "democratise the computer"'. (Hinterhuber and Popp)

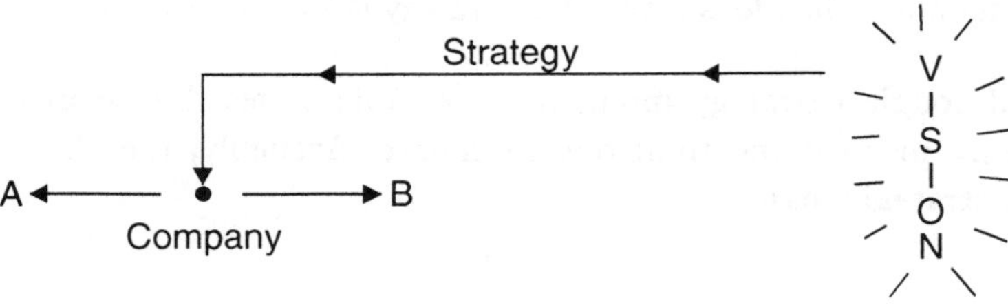

A company with two choices would move to 'B' rather than 'A'. The strategy draws on the vision. A vision might provide the 'boundaries' (in Simon's description of bounded rationality) for the firm's direction.

6.6 Nebulous concepts of vision, by its nature undefined, seem to take us a long way from strategy and planning as discussed in Chapter 1. We began with a simple process of strategic management: problem identification, analysis, solution. We end up with processes of observation and abstraction, guided by a creative insight into vision.

6.7 **Problems with vision**

- It ignores real, practical problems
- It can degenerate into wishful thinking on the part of managers, blinding them to reality.

Case example

General Motors in the US had a collective vision, resulting in huge investment in automation and technology to become the *21st Century Corporation*. Whereas its European operations have been notably successful in beating off the Japanese, the American parent, despite its huge investment stumbled in the face of Japanese and US domestic competition for a while in the 1980s, although the company has now improved.

Exam focus point

Vision was part of a question in June 1996.

7 COMPETITION, ENVIRONMENTAL FIT AND TRADE-OFFS

Environmental fit

7.1 For *Hofer and Schendel*, a strategy secures a **fit with the environment**. Success flows from this fit.

(a) The environment is a key factor in the behaviour of any organisation, as organisations derive their **inputs** from it and distribute their **outputs** to it. The environment has a variety of influences over the organisation.

(b) **Fit or suitability** suggests that 'organisations are successful when they intentionally achieve internal harmony and external adaptation to their environment. Managers should use analytical techniques to identify the relationship between the organisation's internal capability and competences, and the external outputs. In very basic terms, the need for the fit is identified by the SWOT analysis and strategies are undertaken to secure the fit.'

(c) Hofer and Schendel suggest that strategy is a mediating force.

7.2 Thus, although a strategy might be acceptable or feasible **in principle**, this does not necessarily make it the right one to choose. Arguably, the choice of strategy should follow a **strategic logic**.

KEY TERM

According to Stacey (*Strategic Management and Organisational Dynamics*), **strategic logic** is 'that a proposed sequence of actions is:

(a) Consistently related to the objectives of the organisation on the one hand; and

(b) Matches the organisation's capability (including its structure, control systems and culture) to its environment.

The idea is that all the pieces of the strategic puzzle should fit together in a predetermined manner.

Competition

7.3 Most businesses face competitors. According to Ohmae, what counts is performance in **relative terms**. 'A good business strategy' (says Ohmae in his book *The Mind of a Strategist*) then is 'one by which a firm can gain significant ground on its competitors at an acceptable cost' , shaping the environment rather than merely reacting to it. Here's how.

Method	Comment
Re-adjust current resources	Identify the key factors for success (or distinctive competence) and concentrate resources on these activities.
Relative superiority	A *relative* advantage can still be achieved by exploiting the competitors' actual or potential weaknesses.
Challenge assumptions	Challenge the accepted assumptions of doing business in a particular market (eg telephone banking challenges the need for branch networks in banks).
Degrees of freedom	Finding new ways of exploit markets (eg by segmentation, product/service differentiation etc).

7.4 In all cases, direct competition on the competitors' own turf is avoided. Successful strategy is the interplay of three Cs: **customers**, **competitors** and the **corporation**. This Ohmae calls the **strategic triangle**.

7.5 Michael **Porter** defines strategy in similar competitive terms.

KEY TERM

Competitive strategy is 'the taking of offensive or defensive actions to create a defendable position within an industry ... and ... a superior return on investment'.

We will encounter Porter in later chapters.

7.6 Porter (Harvard Business Review, Nov - Dec 1996) highlights the importance of taking a competitive viewpoint. Porter suggests that over the past twenty years, firms have been learning to play to a new set of rules: benchmarking, outsourcing and the nurture of a few basic core competences. **The assumption is that rivals can easily copy any position, and so many companies are competing destructively** with each other in a state of **hyper-competition**. 'The root of the problem is the **failure to distinguish operational effectiveness and strategy** ... Management tools [eg TQM, business process re-engineering] have taken the place of strategy. As managers push to improve on *all* fronts, they move further away from viable competitive positions'.

7.7 **Creating a sustainable strategic position**

Task	Comment
Operational effectiveness is not the same as strategy	Organisational effectiveness involves doing the **same** things better than other firms. Managers' use of TQM is geared towards operational effectiveness - improvements here can be imitated.
Strategy rests on unique activities	Competitive strategy is about being **different** ... choosing to perform activities differently or to perform different activities than rivals.'
A sustainable strategic position requires trade-offs	• Trade-offs limit what a company does. Trade-offs occur: o When activities are not compatible (eg an airline can offer a cheap no-meals service, or offer meals; doing both results in inefficiencies). o Where there will be inconsistencies in image and reputation. o Where an activity is over or underdesigned for its use (eg overqualified staff in menial positions).
Strategy is about combining activities, and the way in which its activities fit and reinforce one another:	• This is hard to imitate. (Operational effectiveness is about being good at *individual* activities.)
Strategy is about choices, not blindly imitating competitors	Of course, many firms operate inefficiently, and so can benefit by improving operational effectiveness, but those at productivity frontier need to make choices and trade-offs. 'Caught up in the race for operational effectiveness, many managers simply do not understand the need to have a strategy.' Conventional wisdom within the industry is often strong, homogenising competition.

7.8 There is a difference of emphasis between the work of Ohmae and Porter.

(a) Porter's work implies that **explicit analysis** of strategy and position is necessary for strategic decision making, although he is not so interested in the *process* of strategic decision making as in the *outcome* of strategic choices.

(b) Ohmae believes strategic decision-making is more subjective and 'intuitive'. Analysis is an aid, not the key, to strategy.

7.9 Ohmae and Porter assume that:

(a) The **survival** of a business is impossible without a **competitive strategy**.
(b) The **actual strategy** chosen will be **unique** to the organisation.
(c) The market place is sometimes like a **battlefield**.

7.10 Section summary

- For businesses, strategy must address competitors.
- The best strategies are distinctive, not imitations of what other firms do.
- Strategy is not the same as operational effectiveness.
- Strategy is about choices: including choices of what **not** to do.

8 MINTZBERG'S 5 P'S

8.1 Henry Mintzberg's overview of the work of many writers on strategy suggests five ways in which the term strategy is used. A strategy can be a:

- **Plan**
- **Ploy**
- **Pattern**
- **Position**
- **Perspective**

Strategy as plan

8.2 In this definition a strategy is a 'consciously intended course of action'. See Chapter 1.

Strategy as ploy

8.3 A 'ploy' is a manoeuvre in a competitive game (Ohmae or Porter). For example a firm might add unnecessary plant capacity. The intention is not to produce the goods but to **discourage a competitor** from entering the market. The strategy is not the plant-building but the deterrence. (See Chapter 17.)

Strategy as pattern

8.4 We discussed this earlier in this chapter the context of Andrews and Mintzberg's ideas of emergent strategies.

Strategy as position

8.5 This relates to **environmental fit**, and the relationships (competitive or co-operative) with other organisations. A position might be a distinctive niche, whereby the firm makes distinctive products or services or exploits a distinct competence.

Strategy as perspective

8.6 Finally, Mintzberg mentions that strategy can construct a unique way of looking at the world, of interpreting information from it and judging its opportunities and choices.

(a) As such, it can refer to **organisation culture**. 'Strategy in this respect is to organisation as personality is to the individual'. Selznick described it as 'commitments to ways of acting and responding'. Different organisations with different strategic perspectives might respond to the same environmental stimulus in different ways.

(b) Here is a simplistic caricature to make this point. The culture of Country A holds that all violence against human life is evil, even in self defence. The culture of Country B places high status on prowess in battle. How will each respond when invaded by Country C, which is more powerful than either of them?

- Country A is more likely to negotiate or even capitulate.

- Country B's army will fight to the last, and will be less scrupulous about loss of life.

8.7 These 5P's are not mutually exclusive. In fact they complement each other. In the right circumstances, any of the definitions will be the most apt. There is no hierarchy in which one comes before the other. A perspective can give rise to a plan: but the process of planning can result in an alteration of perspective.

Question 5

Here are some issues of strategy. Which of Mintzberg's categories (plan, position, ploy, perspective, pattern) do you think they fit into?

(a) The general manager of the Beardsley Hospital prepares a strategy. To minimise the time doctors spend walking from place to place she has rearranged the hospital so that services are clustered around patients. She has the resources so that this change will be phased in over three years, firstly Ophthalmology, secondly Oncology, thirdly Paediatrics, and so on.

(b) Two market traders sell fruit and vegetables. One decides to specialise in exotic fruits, as he feels there are enough well-off and/or experimentally minded people in his area to make it worth his while.

Answer

(a) This is probably strategy as *plan.* A document is being prepared by senior management.

(b) This is strategy as *position.* The market trader specialising in exotic fruit is trying to carve himself a niche.

---

9 BRAINWORKS PLC UPDATE

Questions can be found in the Introduction box at the beginning of this Chapter.

9.1 *Question 1.* BW has exhibited several modes of strategy-making. Begbie had a deliberate strategy of expansion, but it is not clear the extent to which this is explicitly documented. The same could be true of Willard Mann's approach, despite his different personality. The nearest thing it approximates to is perhaps an **entrepreneurial** strategy, which is becoming **disconnected.**

9.2 *Question 2.* BW is facing a variety of problems - and so there might be a case for a consistent stock-taking exercise according to the rational model. It appears that strategies are not emerging, not are they being developed, to cope with the environmental shift towards 'longer-term' temporary work.

9.3 *Question 3.* The financing decisions will be a strategic problem. If the company does 'demerge', how will the debt be allocated among the successful companies?

9.4 *Question 4.* Begbie was a visionary of sorts, but it is not clear that this is what BW needs right now. Although Willard Mann needs to consider matters other than the numbers, he is only really interested in PeoplePower, and the case study describes **nobody** with an idea of where BW(UK) is heading or where it should be. In short, strategic management at BW is a mess.

Chapter roundup

- According to Andrews, strategy is a **pattern of management decisions**, which emanates from the formal management structure of the organisation.
- Some thinkers argue that the rational approach is a hopelessly inaccurate description of how strategic planning actually occurs. Lindblom proposes an **incremental approach**, the centrepiece of which is the concept of partisan mutual adjustment, by which changes are implemented slowly after a process of negotiation. Logical incrementalism is a development from this.
- Johnson and Scholes suggest an approach which follows a similar outline to the rational model, but which accounts for the **'political' and cultural influences on managers.**
- The rational approach also fails to identify **emergent strategies**, or allow for them, according to Mintzberg. Operations level can be a source of strategic change. Emergent strategies arise out of **patterns of behaviour**. They are not the result of the conscious intentions of senior managers. They have to be shaped or **crafted**. **Realised strategies** include intended and emergent strategies.
- Approaches to strategic management differ in the extent to which they are **deliberate or emergent**, and the extent to which they are **explicit.**
- Ohmae argues that it is not always possible to make strategic decisions only through rigorous analysis: successful **strategic thinking** involves a **creative and intuitive** approach to the business.
- Both Porter and Ohmae see business strategy is **competitive terms.** Competitive **advantage is always relative** to competition.
- Porter asserts that many businesses, concentrating on improving operational effectiveness, have lost sight of the fact that strategy is **unique,** it involves making **trade-offs, choices** and **combining activities.**
- A **vision** can guide a firm's strategic choices, but it can impede an assessment of strategic realities.
- Mintzberg suggests that 'strategy' is used to mean **plan**, a **ploy**, a **pattern**, a **position** and a **perspective**.

Quick quiz

1 What do you understand by 'pattern' of decisions? (see paras 2.1, 3.2)

2 What is the problem of separately identifying objectives and strategies? (2.2)

3 What is a distinctive competence? (2.3)

4 Distinguish between deliberate strategies and emergent strategies (3.3)

5 Distinguish between ideological strategies and consensus strategies. (3.7)

6 How does Mintzberg suggest strategy is crafted? (3.13)

7 According to Johnson and Scholes, what happens in 'problem diagnosis'? (4.2)

8 What is meant by optimising, satisficing, and bounded rationality? (5.1)

9 What is the partisan mutual adjustment model? (5.2)

10 What are the problems with incrementalism? (5.4)

11 What is Ohmae's view of the origin of successful strategy? (6.1)

12 Describe Ohmae's view of the operation of strategic thinking. (6.3)

13 What is environmental fit? (7.1)

14 What are the three sides of the strategic triangle? (7.4)

15 What does Porter believe constitutes a sustainable strategic position? (7.7)

16 What are the five meanings of strategy, according to Mintzberg? (8.1)

Question to try	Level	Marks	Time
3	Introductory	n/a	30 mins

Chapter 3

STRATEGIC MANAGEMENT AND INFORMATION TECHNOLOGY

Chapter topic list		Syllabus reference
1	**Emergent strategies for IT**	**6(c)(i), 6(d)**
2	**The case for planning**	**6(d)(I)**
3	**Brainworks plc update**	

Introduction

Information technology affects all areas of a business. It is potentially so important that it is far more than a simple operational strategy. IT requires strategic management of its own, but there are special considerations. Arguably, IT shows some of the pitfalls of purely **emergent strategies**, and there are strong justifications for using the rational **planning** model in many areas. Throughout this text, you will see how IT can be integral to corporate, business and functional strategies. This is why we introduce it here.

Brainworks plc

1 What stage, if any, of Nolan's model does BW (UK) and PeoplePower occupy?

1 EMERGENT STRATEGIES FOR IT

1.1 Few organisations have adopted IT overnight. Mostly, this has been an evolutionary process whereby technological changes have opened up new possibilities for IT.

1.2 Richard Nolan's **stage hypothesis,** outlined below, attempts to model how organisations have adopted IT.

Stage 1 Initiation

1.3 The firm begins its involvement with IT.

(a) **Applications**. The objective is to discover to identify suitable applications (eg **payroll**), and to **save money** on clerical processing. There are a number of separate IT applications, sometimes called **islands of automation**: they carry out restricted, defined tasks, with no connections between them.

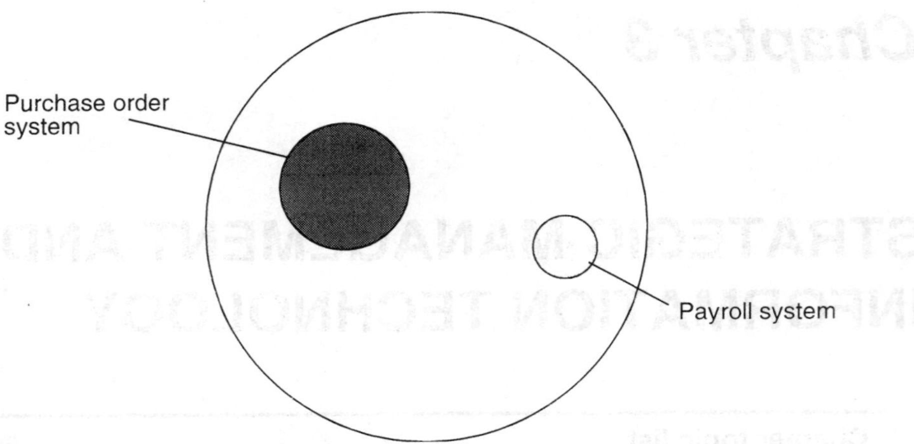

(b) **Organisation:** data processing is a separate department, for technical experts.

(c) **Control:** there are computer controls, but few management controls and little planning.

(d) **Users** have little involvement.

Step 2 Contagion

1.4 The use of IT spreads.

(a) **Applications**. Many more applications are developed, but a lot of time is spent updating old ones. This is a period of unplanned, haphazard growth.

(b) **Organisation**. The IS department is still centralised, but end-users begin to influence what it does. Programmers become more sensitive to user needs.

(c) **Controls** are still very lax. IT is a corporate overhead, and budgetary control over IT expenditure is limited. Furthermore, there are few checks over requests for more applications.

(d) **User awareness.** Users are enthusiastic about IT, but have little understanding as to its benefits and drawbacks.

Stage 3 Control

1.5 The excesses of the contagion stage (too many applications not providing value for money, overspend) lead to tight management controls.

(a) **Applications**. There are restrictions on the development of new systems; existing applications are consolidated. Users might feel frustrated.

(b) **Organisation**. The IT function is properly organised and headed by a manager, who has to justify expenditure, just as is the case with other departments.

(c) **Control**. Financial, quality and other controls (eg steering committees) are introduced over projects and purchases. User departments begin to be charged for the IT resource, as a way of controlling costs. However, controls are mainly exercised in and over the IT department.

(d) **Users** begin to understand IT.

Step 4 Integration

1.6 The role of IT in the business and the controls over it are greatly clarified. **IT begins to be considered as integral to business issues.**

(a) **Applications** begin to cross the boundaries of each business function (eg integrating sales order processing and stock control). However, data is often duplicated, so there is an attempt to integrate information and accounting systems. A **management information system** enables managers to get information about many of the firm's activities from a database.

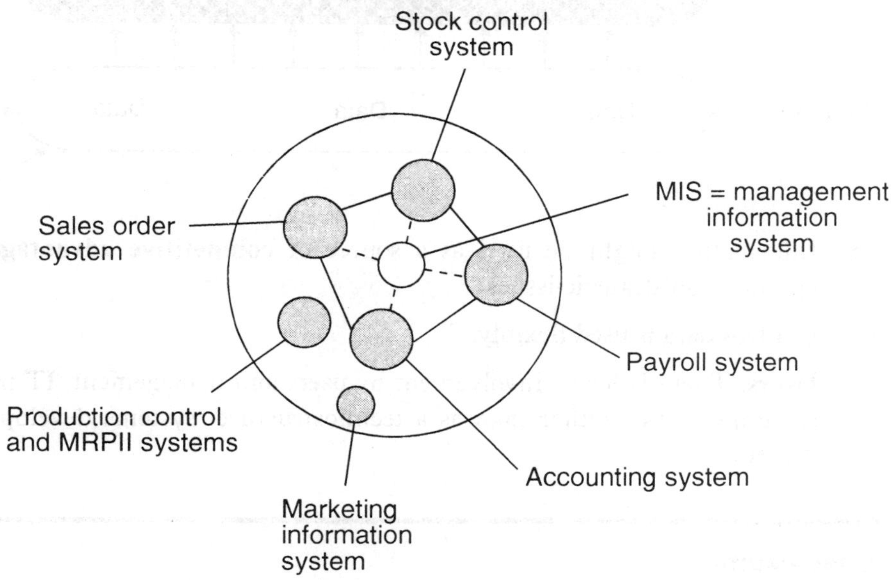

(b) **Organisation:** perhaps a higher profile for IT?

(c) **Controls.** More planning is introduced to IT.

(d) **User involvement** in policy and project management increases.

Step 5 Data administration

1.7 The organisation gains confidence in managing IT. Information is seen as a resource. **Information requirements, not the technology** which supports it, is the focus of management attention.

(a) **Applications.** The organisation seeks to develop a single integrated database serving organisational needs, and applications are devised to use the database.

(b) **Organisation**. A database administrator is appointed.

(c) **Control**. 'Data' rather than the systems which process it, is the subject of control. To avoid duplication, data definitions, coding systems, file layouts etc are standardised.

(d) **Users** become more accountable themselves for the integrity and correct use of information.

Step 6 Maturity

1.8 **Information flows reflect the real life requirements of the organisation.** An organisation's information systems and databases become a sort of mirror in which the workings of the organisation can be scrutinised, modelled and analysed, in a way that was not possible before.

(a) **Applications.** In theory, then, data about all the organisation's activities find their way into an information system, which can be interrogated in a variety of ways. If the information is analysed with sufficient rigour it may be possible to discover those areas in the organisation's **value chain** (see Chapter 6) where savings can be made or advantages delivered. Zuboff refers to this as the '**textualisation of work**'.

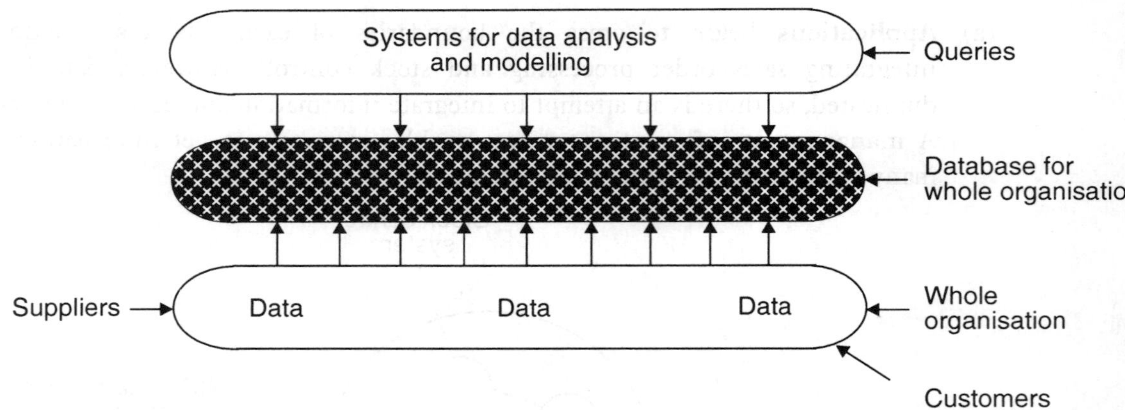

(b) Information might be used as a source of **competitive advantage**. There is an emphasis on strategic issues.

(c) **Control data** is used flexibly.

(d) **Users.** There is heavy involvement by users and management. IT professionals act as **support staff** rather than as a technostructure: systems developments are user driven.

Case example

The South Bank Arts Centre in London has used *Concentrics*, a system which covers 'everything from space allocation to the timely supply of fireworks for a performance of Tchaikovsky's 1812 Overture'.

At the same time, the planning system is used as a marketing tool. Customer details are entered into the system, so that the firm can tailor its direct mailshots, and thus save money on advertising.

The accounting system is also to be integrated with the other systems to enable 'open access to the accounting system to non-financial departments, giving them responsibility for their own budgeting and report writing'.

The electronic diary and scheduling system will streamline the production process. The aim is to control overheads so as to maintain artistic budgets.

1.9 Value of the stage hypothesis

- **Diagnostic:** managers might be able to make sense of IT's current position in the organisation and where it might be headed.
- **Prescriptive:** it suggests remedies which IT managers in the business can prescribe to correct any problems.

1.10 Problems with the stage hypothesis

- **Dated.** First developed in 1974, it preceded PCs, Windows 95, networks, the Internet, client/server architecture and office e-mail.
- **Linearity.** Some organisation's use of IT have the characteristics of a number of the stages.
- **Size.** IT is much cheaper than before, and so the management issues do not really arise for many of the smaller businesses running a PC. Many firms are able to run word processing, spreadsheet and bookkeeping very cheaply

1.11 Key lessons of the stage hypothesis

- IT is a **management problem**
- **Users** are empowered by IT

1.12 The stage model was 'born for the DP era'. (DP stands for data processing.) Earl describes the differences between the DP era and the IT era as follows.

		DP	IT
(a)	Money spent on IT is	... a cost	... an investment
(b)	The role of IT in business is	... support	... critical
(c)	IT applications are	... tactical	... strategic
(d)	The economic context of IT is	... neutral	... welcoming
(e)	IT's social impact is	... limited	... pervasive
(f)	Technologies	... computing	... multiple
(g)	Management of IT	... delegated	... leadership

Question 1

Take your company. What stage of IT use do you think it occupies? Is your firm in the DP era or the IT era?

1.13 The future management problems of IT will be no longer, perhaps, be those of control and cost-efficiency (as IT is cheap) but of :

- Configuring IT at those places in the value chain (see Chapter 6) where it can deal with weaknesses and enhance competitive performance.
- Ensuring that the firm manages the risks of IT appropriately.

IT and emergent strategies

1.14 Nolan's stage hypothesis described what was essentially an **emergent strategy**.

- IT was adopted by departments according to their operational needs without any real idea of what wider overall implications there might be.
- Organisations ended up with a number of different IT systems which may or may not have been compatible.

1.15 With IT, more than with other functional strategies, a crafting strategy approach is not always entirely appropriate.

- Issues of **systems compatibility and design are at the heart of the overall value** of the system to an organisation.
- **Conscious planning**, not crafting strategies after the event, is necessary to ensure that IT's potential is maximised and that pitfalls are avoided.
- The trend has to be **greater user involvement.**

1.16 **Reconciling** the need for top-down IT planning with the need for 'bottom-up' user involvement is the subject of Section 2.

1.17 Section summary

- Nolan described six stages of IT use: initiation, contagion, control, integration, data administration, and maturity.
- The stage model might be old-fashioned, but it is a useful diagnostic tool.
- Purely emergent strategies do not suit IT, but user involvement is necessary and desirable.

2 THE CASE FOR PLANNING 6/97

Case example

The Millennium Bomb

When many old computer programs were written, few people anticipated they would still be in use by the year 2000; but they are still here, patched up and modified.

Sadly, at one time, computer memory was a scarce resource, and so programmers saved 'space' by limiting the digits used to contain the date. Many old computer programmes are unable to cope with the change of year from 1999 to 2000 as they assume that going from 99 to 00 means changing from 1999 to 1900, not 2000. *For some systems, every line of computer code has to be examined.* Implications are these.

(a) A *rectification cost* of £31bn is given as the estimate for the *UK as a whole*.

(b) *Individual companies*

  (i) Resources which could have been spent on new products or marketing programmes, say, will be spent on curing this problem.

  (ii) There is possibility of severe disruption to the activities of *service organisations* which use IT extensively, such as transportation (eg timetabling) and the NHS.

  (iii) Organisational functions and systems with direct customer contact (eg the accounts department) might also be adversely affected.

  (iv) Not only information systems are affected, but also factory machinery and so on.

The government has suggested that most firms seriously *underestimate* the severity of the situation. The costs are large and potentially disastrous.

2.1 With this sobering example in mind, it is easy to understand why managers should pay proper attention to IT.

2.2 **The case for a planned strategy for IT**

- **Costs.**
- IT is **critical** to the success of many organisations.
- IT is a **strategic weapon** for competitive advantage can come from IT
- The economic or industry **context** can compel IT.
- IT affects all levels of **management**.
- IT means a revolution in the way **information** is created, and presented to management.
- Many **stakeholders,** internal and external, are involved.
- **Technical** issues are important.
- **Effective management** can make a real difference to effective IT use.

(Mnemonic, using words in bold: Costs are Critical in a Strategic Context; Managers Inform Stakeholders of Technical Effectiveness.)

Costs

2.3 **IT is a high cost activity.** Key issues are:

- The total amount spent on IT.
- How much is spent on other areas of the business.

- How well the funds are spent.
- The time-lag between the expenditure and the benefits received.
- The difficulty of quantifying the benefits.
- Firms with highly automated manufacturing systems have a high proportion of fixed costs and lower variable labour costs. This affects risk.

Criticality

2.4 **IT is critical to the success** of the some organisations.

- **IT has brought some industries into being**. For example, it is unlikely that global financial markets would have developed the range and sophistication of financial instruments, and the possibility for trading at any time of day, without IT.
- **Security**. Banks and other firms go to extraordinary lengths to protect themselves from a breakdown in their current systems. A failure of computer systems to work would result in a failure of some organisations to function at all. (On the other hand, many organisations are not dependent on IT.)

Strategic weapon

2.5 IT can be used as a strategic weapon to:

(a) Gain competitive advantage for the organisation.

(b) Improve productivity and performance (eg in design and manufacturing).

(c) Alter the management and organisational structure of the business (eg electronic mail, telecommuting).

(d) Develop new businesses (eg Reuters created an electronic market place where subscribers could trade via Reuter terminals).

Economic/industry context

2.6 IT is an **enabling technology**, and can produce dramatic changes in individual businesses and whole industries, especially where there are other major forces for change. Just under 50% of UK companies in a recent DTI survey use the internet.

Case example

The Internet has implications for the structure and strategies of some industries. Take telecommunications. The telephone tariff system is 'fundamentally a fixed cost system, but we pay for it on the basis of a variable - mainly voice minutes. What is more, where the charges are levied bears no relation to where the costs occur'.

The Internet threatens to undermine this. Access to the Internet is normally charged at *local* call rates. It is now possible to hold conversations over the Internet, which 'will undermine the "price per distance" business model' which allows telephone companies to charge more for long distance calls. The quality of the connection is currently low, but not for much longer.

Levels of management

2.7 IT permeates the different layers of management, as a routine feature of office life and a facility for everyone to use.

(a) Senior managers can see more precisely what goes on at operational level.

(b) Operational management can be empowered by IT (eg expert systems) to take decisions, which computers can support.

(c) **Delayering**. IT renders redundant the information processing role of middle managers.

(d) Use of IT requires so-called **intellective** skills, the ability to analyse and manipulate abstract data. These used to be management's concern.

(e) Email systems and diary planning systems enable managers to **co-ordinate** their activities better. 63% of UK companies in a recent survey by the DTI use email.

Management information

2.8 IT affects:

- The **quantity** of management information. Anecdotal evidence suggests that some managers suffer from information overload (especially with email).
- The **flexibility** and scope of management information (expert systems, databases).
- **Costing systems.** These must change to reflect the changed cost structure attendant on heavily-automated processes (eg ABC).

Stakeholders

2.9 Stakeholders are interested in an organisation's use of IT.

(a) **Customers and suppliers** have preferences as to how IT should be used (eg electronic data interchange).

(b) **Governments:** copyright, data protection, security.

(c) **IT manufacturers** pioneer the development and use of new technology. Users need to make their voices heard so that they can influence what manufacturers do.

(d) **Consumers** (eg in testing IT-based products such as teleshopping using ATMs). Both their expectations of IT and their willingness to use it are important for its success.

(e) **Employees** and internal users (as IT affects work practices).

Technical issues

2.10 A strategic view of IT must take detailed **technical issues** into account. Ignoring the technology-based choices in IT is rather like ignoring interest rates when you are borrowing money. (Two UK building societies abandoned a merger because of incompatibility between their computer systems.)

2.11 The **security** of IT-based systems can be compromised by **technological** as well as management failures. Some organisations, especially those whose IT systems are important or critical, have to be concerned with security issues (hence some banks have fault-tolerant systems).

Case example

It is now possible to make payment over the Internet, but banks and credit card companies are still worried about possible fraud. However, solutions are being developed – but hackers always seem to be able to crack any encryption technology developed.

The importance of management

2.12 Success or failure in implementing IT depends on the systems themselves and the management effort behind them. IT will fail if:

(a) It is used to tackle the wrong problem (ie the use of IT has not been thought through in the wider organisational context). Often those applications which are **easiest to computerise** are chosen in preference to those which are **most important**.

(b) Senior management are not interested in and do not appreciate the significance of IT based choices.

(c) Users are ignored in design and development.

(d) No attention is given to behavioural factors in design and operation.

2.13 IT requires proper planning and management attention, because IT can affect the long-term performance of the enterprise in many ways.

Case example

An example of the importance of the wider organisational processes for the success of information technology is provided by the *Taurus project.*

This was a project, funded by various institutions in the City of London and managed by the Stock Exchange, to computerise certain aspects of share trading and *registration.* There was an existing computer system, Talisman, but for various reasons it was regarded as being no longer suitable.

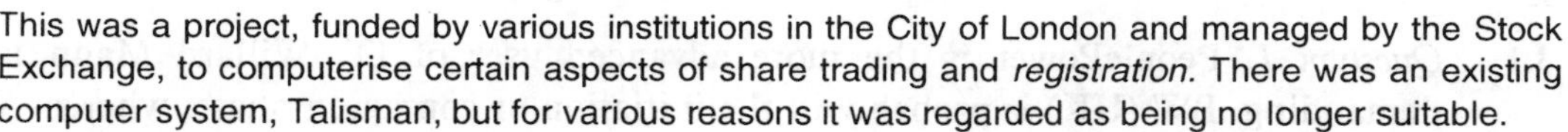

(a) A new system was felt to be necessary because of large trading volumes in *shares* expected after the Big Bang.

(b) Stock markets and bourses elsewhere in Europe use computerised settlement systems. These are giving increasing competition to London as a financial centre.

However, the plans to develop a computer system failed, at a substantial cost to City institutions and damage to London's reputation as a financial centre. What went wrong? There was nothing inherently impossible about the task: automated settlement has been achieved in other financial centres. A number of reasons were suggested.

(a) Poor project management with inadequate control.

(b) The system was designed to *replicate* existing structures. Rather than use *one* central database, it was decided to use a system of separate but linked databases. Not to do so would have taken away business (and profits) from *share registrar* companies. The design was made unnecessarily complex in order to cater for all the vested interests. This then is an instance of the neutralisation of technology's possible benefits by wider social and organisational choices.

Reconciling planning and emergent strategies

2.14 That said, it is short-sighted to go back to a planning model that ignores the value and **creativity** of emergent strategies.

- Opportunities for the use of IT cannot always be identified in advance.

- Creative thinking needs to be encouraged.
- There should be many inputs as possible to the planning process.
- Users are becoming more powerful, as this becomes technologically possible.

2.15 According to Earl, many successful IT developments have been:

- **User-driven**, with the active support of superiors in user departments.
- **Evolutionary developments** of existing approaches, rather than revolutionary change.
- Developed outside the **information system function.**
- **Marketed extensively** throughout the organisation and to customers.
- Developed in **consultation with customers.**

ATM, home banking

2.16 Indeed, IT departments are now enabled, within the framework of the plan, to offer user-friendly systems to help users devise their own applications.

Exam focus point

A June 1997 question highlighted the importance of IT by suggesting that it is 'far too important to be left only to computer specialists'.

2.17 Section summary

- Planning for IT is important because of cost, criticality, potential strategic importance and **technical** issues.
- **Relying on** planning alone fails to exploit the value of emergent strategies.

3 BRAINWORKS PLC UPDATE

Questions can be found in the Introduction box at the beginning of this Chapter.

3.1 *Question 1*. PeoplePower is the more advanced user of IT. Willard Mann is fairly demanding. BW (UK) is probably in the initiation or contagion phase, whereas Willard Mann wishes to vastly enhance the scope of information systems at BW. Clearly there are management problems.

Chapter roundup

- **Information technology** links computers with communications.
- Information technology's growth in power has left some organisations struggling to catch up. New managerial problems have arisen, especially as IT has spread. Over-optimism gave way to control, and more cautious assessments of the benefits of IT. Nolan's **stage hypothesis** describes this history.
- IT is of **strategic importance** owing to its **cost**, its **critical** role to the success of some organisations, its potential as a **strategic weapon** and its effect on all **management levels**. Organisations need to assess both existing and future uses of IT.
- Management approaches to IT have veered between excessive planning and the chaos resulting from emergent strategies.

Quick quiz

1. What is Nolan's stage hypothesis? (see paras 1.2-1.8)
2. Distinguish between the DP era and IT era (1.12)
3. Why is a purely crafting strategy not entirely suitable for IT? (1.15)
4. Why should IT be planned? (2.2)
5. How does IT affect management? (2.7)
6. Why are detailed *technological* issues important in an IT strategy? (2.10 - 2.11)
7. Why is relying on top-down planning inappropriate to IT? (2.14)

Question to try	Level	Marks	Time
4	Introductory	n/a	30 mins

Part B

Strategic analysis and planning

Chapter 4

MISSION, GOALS AND OBJECTIVES

	Chapter topic list	Syllabus reference
1	Mission	1(c) (ii), (iv), (v)
2	Goals and objectives: introduction	1(c)(ii), (iv)
3	Commercial goals and objectives	1(c)(ii), (iv)
4	Stakeholders' goals and objectives	1(c)(ii), (iv)
5	Subverting mission	1(c)(ii), (iv)
6	Brainworks plc update	

Introduction

In theory, an organisation's **mission** - why it exists in society at all - is the guiding idea behind the organisation's activities. **Goals and objectives** are devised to fulfil the mission. Some, but not all, are quantified and so are easily measurable. Goals and objectives also interpret the organisation's mission to a number of different client groups or **stakeholders**, all of whom have an interest in what the organisation does. Mission can be easily subverted, or is given only lip service.

Brainworks plc

1. Comment on BW's mission statement. Why do you think Willard Mann thinks it is a waste of time?
2. Do you think the concept of strategic intent will be useful for BW?
3. What goals/objectives do you think are driving BW? How explicit are they? Is mission being subverted?

1 MISSION 6/95

KEY TERM

Mission 'describes the organisation's basic function in society, in terms of the products and services it produces for its clients' (Mintzberg).

Case example

'The Co-op'

The Co-operative movement is a good example of the role of mission. The Co-operative Wholesale Society and Co-operative Retail Society are business organisations, but their mission is not simply profit.

Rather, being owned by their suppliers/customers rather than external shareholders, they have always, since the foundation, had a wider social concern.

The Co-op has been criticised by some analysts on the grounds that it is insufficiently profitable, certainly in comparison with supermarket chains such as Tescos.

The Co-op has explicit social objectives. In some cases it will retain stores which, although too small to be as profitable as a large supermarket, provide an important social function in the communities which host them.

Of course, the Co-op's performance as a retailer can be improved, but judging it on the conventional basis of profitability ignores its social objectives.

Elements of mission

1.1 **Purpose**

Why does the company exist, or why do its managers and employees feel it exists?

(a) To create wealth for shareholders?

(b) To satisfy the needs of all stakeholders (including employees, society at large, for example)?

(c) To reach some higher goal ('the advancement to society' and so forth)?

1.2 **Strategy**. Mission provides the commercial logic for the company, and so defines:

(a) The business the company is in, and the products/services it offers.
(b) The competences by which it hopes to prosper, and its way of competing.

1.3 **Policies and standards of behaviour**

The mission needs to be converted into everyday performance. For example, a service firm that wishes to be the best in its market must aim for standards of service, in all its operations, which are at least as good as those offered by its competitors. In service businesses, this includes simple matters such as politeness to customers, speed at which phone calls are answered and so forth.

1.4 **Values**

Mission is a 'cultural glue that enables the organisation to function as a unity'. Values relate to the organisation's culture and are the basic, perhaps unstated, beliefs of the people who work in the organisation. (Mintzberg defines values as ideology, in other words a means of control through shared beliefs.)

(a) Values can include **principles of business**:

(i) Commitment to suppliers and staff
(ii) Social policy eg on non-discrimination or ecology
(iii) Commitments to customers

(b) **Loyalty and commitment**. A sense of mission may inspire employees to sacrifice their own personal interests for the good of the whole. This however has to be reciprocated by company loyalty to its staff (eg long-term staff retention).

(c) **Guidance for behaviour**. A sense of mission helps create a work environment where there is a sense of **common purpose**.

1.5 A sense of mission within an organisation requires that the values of the business as a **collective entity** are in tune with the **personal values** of the individuals working for it. In conflicts of ethics, clashes between organisational and personal values are hard to resolve if someone's principles disagree with what the organisation wants.

1.6 For there to be a strong, motivating sense of mission, the four elements above must be mutually reinforcing.

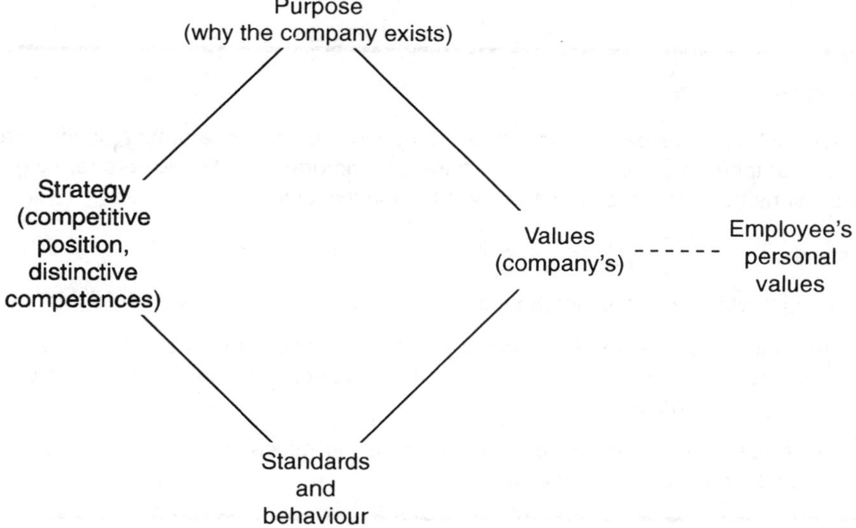

Case examples

- The most obvious example is a religious organisation where an individual's faith and organisational teaching and purpose are the same.
- Sometimes employees can have a sense of mission even where there is chaos in management. For example, a doctor's dedication to his or her patients may be strong despite poor management, say, by the health authority or hospital trust.

The importance of mission

1.7 Although hard to quantify (and hence, from an accountant's viewpoint, of dubious value) mission is taken seriously by many firms.

(a) Values and feelings are integral elements of **consumers' buying decisions,** as evidenced by advertising, branding and market research. Therefore, there is no reason to exclude these matters from a company's decision-making processes further up the line. Customers not only ask 'What do you sell?' but 'What do you stand for?'

(b) A respect for quantifiable information is part of the professional culture and training of the accountant; other people have different values and priorities.

(c) Studies into organisational behaviour suggest that employees are **motivated** by more than money. A sense of mission and values can help to motivate employees.

(d) Many firms take mission seriously in strategic management.

Case example

Some writers believe there is an empirical relationship between strong *corporate values* and profitability.

The *Financial Times* reported (22 February 1993) the result of research by the Digital Equipment Corporation into a sample of 429 company executives.

(a) 80% of the sample have a formal mission statement.

(b) 80% believed mission contributes to profitability,

(c) 75% believe they have a responsibility to implement the mission statement.

(d) *Only* 6% admitted, openly, that corporate values make *little* difference in practice, although 30% believed that 'values' should be subordinated to commercial gain in case of conflict.

Question 1

'Whistle blowers' are people who give information to the government or the press about those activities of their employers which they think are immoral. Whistle blowers rarely gain in financial or career terms from doing so. What motives do you think they have?

Answer

Assuming pecuniary gain is not the main reason, a whistle blower's motives might be as follows.

(a) An employee's sense of mission (eg to the patients, in the case of NHS whistle blowers) may be stronger than mere loyalty to management if the whistle blower disagrees with management decisions.

(b) An employee's code of professional ethics (eg ethical guidelines for accountants) may take precedence over corporate culture.

Mission, vision and strategic intent

1.8 We have encountered vision earlier. A vision is a view of the organisation's (or indeed the industry's future) state. A mission can connect a strategy to a vision.

1.9 **Differences between mission and vision**

(a) Mission is about the here and now, whereas vision refers to the future.

(b) A vision which is too vague will fail to motivate, whereas a mission is designed to motivate.

(c) A vision, when achieved, might lose motivating power, unless it can be reinvented.

1.10 **Strategic intent** is similar to the 'strategy' concept of mission as outlined in paragraph 1.2. Strategic intent, as defined by *Hamel and Prahalad*, involves:

(a) The desire to attain a particular leadership position in the future.

(b) Communicating the *value* of the target as the main motivating factor to employees.

(c) A guide to resource allocation for the attainment of the target.

1.11 Campbell, Young and Devine consider that this concept fails because it does not take note of the fact that people are motivated by *current* values and activities. To **use strategic intent** as a means of motivating employees **presupposes that the workforce is already motivated** and committed to the company.

1.12 To summarise:

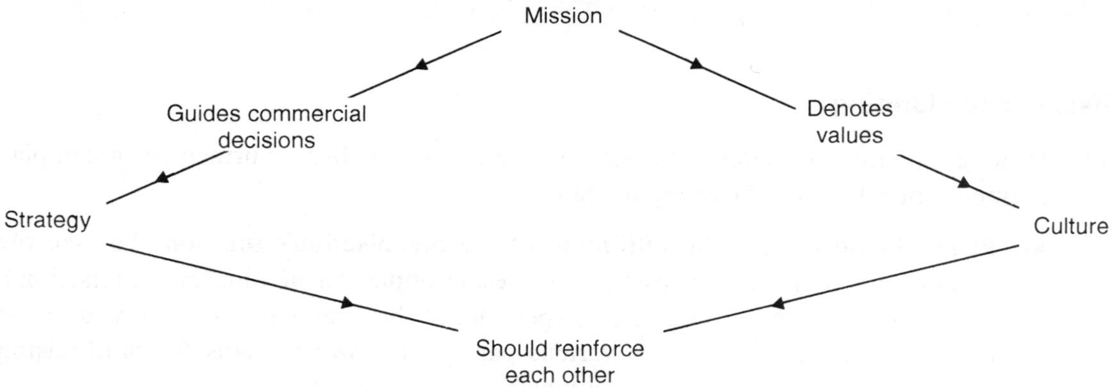

Mission statements

1.13 **Mission statements** are formal statements of an organisation's mission. They might be reproduced in a number of places (eg at the front of an organisation's annual report, on publicity material, in the chairman's office, in communal work areas etc). There is no standard format, but they should be:

(a) Brief - easy to understand and remember.
(b) Flexible - to accommodate change.
(c) Distinctive - to make the firm stand out.

Case examples

The following statements were taken from annual reports of the organisations concerned. Are they 'mission statements'? If so, are they any good?

(a) **Glaxo** 'is an integrated research-based group of companies whose corporate purpose is to create, discover, develop, manufacture and market throughout the world, safe, effective medicines of the highest quality which will bring benefit to patients through improved longevity and quality of life, and to society through economic value.'

(b) **IBM (UK)**: 'We shall increase the pace of change. Market-driven quality is our aim. It means listening and responding more sensitively to our customers. It means eliminating defects and errors, speeding up all our processes, measuring everything we do against a common standard, and it means involving employees totally in our aims'.

(c) **Matsushita**: 'the duty of the manufacturer is to serve the foundation of man's happiness by making man's life affluent with an inexpensive and inexhaustible supply of life's necessities.'

(d) The **Guinness Group:** Guinness plc is one of the world's leading drinks companies, producing and marketing an unrivalled portfolio of international best-selling brands, such as Johnnie Walker, Bell's and Dewar's Scotch whiskies, Gordon's and Tanqueray gins, and Guinness stout itself - the world's most distinctive beer. The strategy is to focus resources on the development of the Group's alcoholic drinks businesses. The objectives are to provide superior long-term financial returns for shareholders, to create a working environment in which people can perform to their fullest potential and to be recognised as one of the world's leading consumer brand development companies.

(e) **The British Film Institute.** 'The BFI is the UK national agency with responsibility for encouraging and conserving the arts of film and television. Our aim is to ensure that the many audiences in the UK are offered access to the widest possible choice of cinema and television, so that their enjoyment is enhanced through a deeper understanding of the history and potential of these vital and popular art forms.'

Exam focus point

In June 1995 you were asked to assess whether 'To win' is suitable as a mission statement.

Mission and planning

1.14 Although the mission statement might be seen as a set of abstract principles, it can play an important **role in the planning process**.

(a) **Plans should outline the fulfilment of the organisation's mission**. To take the example of a religious organisation (the best example of a 'missionary organisation'), the mission of 'spreading the gospel' might be embodied in plans to send individuals as missionaries to various parts of the world, plans for fund-raising activities, or even targets for the numbers of new converts.

(b) **Evaluation and screening**. Mission also acts as a yardstick by which plans are judged.

(i) Take the example of a financial services organisation which runs a number of 'ethical' investment funds. 'Ethical' investment funds exclude from their investment portfolios shares in firms involved in alcohol, tobacco and armaments. Therefore, if a new fund manager proposed as part of an investment strategy to invest in shares of a diversified company involved in several product market areas, the company would be examined to see if its activities included those which the investment fund considered 'unethical'. The investment strategy would be assessed with reference to the investment fund's mission.

(ii) Mission helps to ensure consistency in decisions.

(c) **Implementation**. Mission also affects the implementation of a planned strategy, in terms of:

(i) The ways in which the firm carries out its business.
(ii) The culture of the organisation.

In other words, mission can be embodied in the policies and behaviour standards of the firm.

1.15 Section summary

Mission:

- Provides a focus for strategic decisions.
- Creates values to guide discretionary decision-taking.
- Replaces national or divisional subcultures with a corporate culture.
- Communicates the nature of the organisation to insiders and outsiders

2 GOALS AND OBJECTIVES: INTRODUCTION

2.1 From the mission, goals are derived.

KEY TERM

Goals are *'the intentions behind decisions or actions*, the states of mind that drive individuals or collectives of individuals called organisations to do what they do.' Mintzberg (*Power In and Around Organisations*)

(a) **Operational goals** can be expressed as **objectives**. Mintzberg says that an objective is a goal expressed in a form by which its attainment can be **measured**. Here is an example.

   (i) Mission: deliver a quality service

   (ii) Goal: enhance manufacturing quality

   (iii) Objectives: over the next twelve months, reduce the number of defects to 1 part per million

(b) **Non-operational goals** or **aims** on the other hand cannot be expressed as objectives. Mintzberg quotes the example of a university, whose goal might be to 'seek truth'. This cannot really be expressed as a quantified objective. To 'increase truth by 5% this year' does not make a great deal of sense.

2.2 Objectives should meet the SMART criteria. They should be:

- Specific
- Measurable
- Attainable — acronym SMART
- Results-orientated
- Time-bounded

2.3 However, not all goals, as we have seen, can be measured, or can ever be attained completely. **Customer satisfaction** is a goal, but satisfying customers and ensuring that they remain satisfied is a **continuous process** that does not stop when one target has been reached.

2.4 **Features of goals and objectives in organisations**

(a) **Goal congruence** (ie goals should be consistent with each other).

   (i) **Across all departments.** There should be **horizontal** consistency. In other words, the goals set for different parts of the organisation should be consistent with each other.

   (ii) **At all levels.** Objectives should be consistent **vertically**, in other words at all levels in the organisation.

   (iii) **Over time.** Objectives should be consistent with each other over the **same time span**.

(b) An objective should **identify the beneficiaries** as well as the nature and size of the benefit.

2.5 **Types of goal**

Goal	Comment
Ideological goals	These goals focus on the organisation's mission. They are shared sets of beliefs and values.
Formal goals	Imposed by a dominant individual or group (eg shareholders). People work to attain these goals, as a means to their personal goals. (In other words, you do what your boss tells you to in order to earn a wage to support your family etc.)
Shared personal goals	Individuals reach a consensus about what they want out of an organisation (eg a group of academics who decide they want to pursue research).

Goal	Comment
System goals	Derive from the organisation's existence as an organisation, independent of mission. More about this in Section 5 of this chapter.

2.6 **Section summary**

- Goals can be objectives (quantified and SMART) or aims (not quantified).
- There should be goal congruence. There are many different levels of goal which people work towards.

3 COMMERCIAL GOALS AND OBJECTIVES

3.1 Objectives are normally quantified statements of what the organisation actually intends to achieve over a period of time.

3.2 **Uses of objectives**

- Objectives **orientate the activities** of the organisation towards the fulfilment of the organisation's mission, in theory if not always in practice
- In business organisations, a paramount consideration is **profitability**. The mission of a business, whether this is stated or not, must be to carry on its activities at a profit.
- Objectives can also be used as standards **for measuring the performance** of the organisation and departments in it.

Corporate and unit objectives

3.3 **Corporate objectives** concern the firm as **a whole**, for example:

- Profitability
- Market share
- Growth
- Cash flow
- Return on capital employed
- Risk
- Customer satisfaction
- Quality
- Industrial relations
- Added value
- Earnings per share

3.4 Similar objectives can be developed for each **strategic business unit (SBU)** (An SBU is a part of the company that for all intents and purposes has its own distinct products, markets and assets.)

3.5 **Unit objectives** are objectives that are specific to individual units of an organisation. Some examples are as follows.

(a) **Commercial**

(i) Increase the number of customers by x% (an objective of a sales department).

(ii) Reduce the number of rejects by 50% (an objective of a production department).

(iii) Produce monthly reports more quickly, within 5 working days of the end of each month (an objective of the management accounting department).

(b) **Public sector**

(i) Introduce x% more places at nursery schools (an objective of a borough education department).

(ii) Respond more quickly to calls (an objective of a local police station, fire department or hospital ambulance service).

(c) **General**

(i) Resources (eg finding cheaper sources of raw materials, reducing borrowing costs, 'hiring top-quality college graduates').

(ii) Market (eg market share, market standing).

(iii) Employee development (eg training, promotion, safety).

(iv) Innovation in products or processes (eg 3M's policy is that a set percentage of revenue each year should be derived from new products).

(v) Productivity (the amount of output from resource inputs).

(vi) Technology.

Primary and secondary objectives

3.6 Some objectives are more important than others. There is a **primary corporate objective** (restricted by certain constraints on corporate activity) and other **secondary objectives** which are strategic objectives which should combine to ensure the achievement of the primary corporate objective.

(a) For example, if a company sets itself an objective of growth in profits, as its primary objective, it will then have to develop strategies by which this primary objective can be achieved.

(b) Secondary objectives might then be concerned with sales growth, continual technological innovation, customer service, product quality, efficient resource management (eg labour productivity) or reducing the company's reliance on debt capital etc.

Trade-off between objectives

3.7 When there are several key objectives, some might be achieved only **at the expense of others**. For example, a company's objective of achieving good profits and profit growth might have adverse consequences for the cash flow of the business, or the quality of the firm's products.

3.8 There will be a **trade-off** between objectives when strategies are formulated, and a choice will have to be made. For example, there might be a choice between the following two options.

Option A 15% sales growth, 10% profit growth, a £2 million negative cash flow and reduced product quality and customer satisfaction.

Option B 8% sales growth, 5% profit growth, a £500,000 surplus cash flow, and maintenance of high product quality/customer satisfaction.

If the firm chose option B in preference to option A, it would be trading off sales growth and profit growth for better cash flow, product quality and customer satisfaction. The long-term effect of reduced quality has not been considered.

Long-term and short-term objectives

3.9 Objectives may be long-term and short-term.

(a) A company that is suffering from a recession in its core industries and making losses in the short term might continue to have a primary objective in the long term of achieving a steady growth in earnings or profits, but in the short term, its primary objective might switch to survival.

(b) Secondary objectives will range from short-term to long-term. Planners will formulate secondary objectives within the guidelines set by the primary objective, after selecting strategies for achieving the primary objective.

3.10 EXAMPLE

A company's primary objective might be to increase its earnings per share from 30p to 50p in the next five years.

(a) **Strategies** for achieving the objective might be selected to include the following.

- Increasing profitability in the next twelve months by cutting expenditure.
- Increasing export sales over the next three years.
- Developing a successful new product for the domestic market within five years.

(b) **Secondary objectives** might then be re-assessed to include the following.

- The objective of improving manpower productivity by 10% within twelve months.
- Improving customer service in export markets with the objective of doubling the number of overseas sales outlets in selected countries within the next three years.
- Investing more in product-market research and development, with the objective of bringing at least three new products to the market within five years.

Case example

On Easter Sunday 1997, the UK saw the launch of a new commercial TV station, Channel 5 (C5). The following objectives are relevant.

(a) *Primary objectives* - profit for its various shareholders. C5 is a commercial station, unlike Channel 4 which has distinct public service objectives in its charter.

(b) *Secondary objectives*

C5 sells advertising time. The rates it can charge are often determined by audience share. To satisfy advertisers C5, has to have *audience share objectives.*

(c) These audience share objectives affect various operational aspects of the business.

(i) *Coverage.* C5 had to ensure that enough of the population can receive C5 - some parts of the country are still not covered.

(ii) *Availability.* Before the launch, many people's video recorders had to be *retuned*: up to 11m households were believed to be affected by interference from the new station. Retuning problems delayed the initial launch of the channel. This was a *short term*, but critical, *operational objective.*

(iii) *Programming.* Finally, audience share targets set priorities for programming. C5 has positioned itself as 'modern mainstream' against ITV.

Conflict between goals

3.11 **Dealing with conflicts between different types of goals**

(a) **Rational evaluation** according to financial criteria.

(b) **Bargaining**. Managers with different goals will compete and will form alliances with other managers to achieve their goals.

(c) **Satisficing**. Organisations do not aim to maximise performance in one area if this leads to poor performance elsewhere. Rather they will accept satisfactory, if not excellent, performance in a number of areas.

(d) **Sequential attention**. Goals are dealt with one by one, as it were, in a sequence.

(e) **Priority setting**. Certain goals get priority over others. This is determined by senior managers, but there are quite complicated systems to link goals and strategies according to certain criteria.

3.12 Section summary

- Primary objectives for a business are essential financial.
- Secondary objectives suggest the primary objectives.
- In practice, objectives conflict (eg over the long and short term) and a variety of methods are used to establish which are most important.

4 STAKEHOLDERS' GOALS AND OBJECTIVES 6/96

Case example

Hoechst

(From the *Financial Times*, 13 March 1997).

'Shares in Hoechst, the world's largest drugs and chemicals group, tumbled 8 per cent yesterday after the German company revealed it had abandoned plans to seek a separate listing for its pharmaceuticals business. It also revealed fourth-quarter results well below expectations.

Pharmaceutical companies are traditionally more profitable than chemicals companies, and their shares usually attract a higher rating. For conglomerates spanning both activities, the value of the drugs business tends to be disproportionately diminished by the chemicals arm.

Last year Hoechst said a public offering for MHR, its drugs business, was a priority and hinted at a listing this year. However, Mr Jürgen Dormann, chairman, said yesterday the group no longer planned to list HMR. Meanwhile, the group is accelerating its exit from chemicals.

The Lex column commented: 'Hoechst's U-turn is astounding. The group's rationale for the new strategy is sketchy. It argues borrowings have fallen faster than planned, so an HMR flotation is no longer a financial necessity - but debt will rise in 1997. Hoechst also makes much of keeping full control of drugs and linking it with its other life science businesses. But two of these, agrochemicals and diagnostics, are themselves joint ventures. This about-face seems to have more to do with *management's desire to keep on running the more attractive pharmaceutical business* than with anything else'. (BPP italics)

4.1 Johnson and Scholes (*Exploring Corporate Strategy*) argue that although 'economic' objectives are an important influence on strategy formulation, 'strategies tend to evolve in organisations within a cultural and political system'

Stakeholders

KEY TERM

Stakeholders: groups or individuals whose interests are directly affected by the activities of a firm or organisation

4.2 Here are some stakeholder groups.

Stakeholder group	Members
• Internal stakeholders	Employees, management
• Connected	Shareholders, customers, suppliers, lenders
• External	The government, local government, the public

4.3 Stakeholder groups can exert influence on strategy. The greater the power of a stakeholder group, the greater its influence will be.

4.4 Each stakeholder group has different expectations about what it wants, and the expectations of the various groups will conflict.

Case example

The high speed link

As a piece of unfinished business after the building of the Channel Tunnel, there was supposed to be a high speed rail link between Dover and London for the Eurostar trains. (Currently, they have to slow down as soon as they reach England because they have to share lines with commuter traffic.) A high speed link would cut journey times by 35 minutes.

The Conservative government wanted the link to be built by the private sector, the preferred company being *London and Continental Railways* (LCR). Revenues from Eurostar, however, were disappointing, and LCR could not raise the money from bankers.

The UK government, a stakeholder in the transport infrastructure, was keen for the link to be built, as indeed was the French government. However, it refused to fork out the £1.7bn required just to bail out LCR.

Eventually, in July 1998, an innovative arrangement was adopted. The UK government guaranteed various loans, in return for 35% of pre-tax profits after 2020. Railtrack will manage the project, which will be split into two sections. It is hoped that, when it eventually arrives at Stratford, east London, it will provide jobs for the local community and lead to the area's renewal.

Finally, the Eurostar rail service will be taken over by a consortium of other transport operators, British Airways, National Express and others. BA plan a rail service between Heathrow Airport and continental Europe. *Virgin*, another contender, is to complain to the competition authorities in Brussels.

4.5 There are two approaches to stakeholder theory for profit-orientated business organisations.

Strong view	**Weak view**
Each stakeholder in the business has a legitimate claim on management attention. Management's job is to balance stakeholder demands.	Satisfying stakeholders such as customers *is* a good thing - but only because it enables the business to satisfy its primary purpose, the long term growth in owner wealth.

4.6 **Problems with the strong stakeholder view**

(a) Managers who are accountable to everyone are, in fact, accountable to none.

(b) Managers decide on the 'balance' between different stakeholders - they will invariably favour their own interests.

(c) It confuses a stakeholder's interest in a firm with a person's citizenship of a state.

(d) People have interests, but this does not give them rights.

Stakeholders' objectives

4.7 Here is a checklist of stakeholders' objectives. It is not comprehensive.

(a) **Employees and managers**

(i) Job security (over and above legal protection)
(ii) Good conditions of work (above minimum safety standards)
(iv) Job satisfaction
(v) Career development and relevant training

(b) **Customers**

(i) Products of a certain quality at a reasonable price
(ii) Products that should last a certain number of years
(iii) A product or service that meets customer needs.

(c) **For suppliers**: to offer regular orders in return for reliable delivery and good service.

(d) **For shareholders**: to provide an appropriate return.

(e) **For society as a whole**

(i) Control pollution
(ii) Financial assistance to charities, sports and community activities
(iii) Co-operate with government authorities in identifying and preventing health hazards in the products sold.

We return to stakeholder analysis Chapter 8.

Case example

British Airways publicity once indicated the following corporate goals.

(a) Safety and security
(b) Strong and consistent financial performance
(c) Global reach
(d) Superior services
(e) Good value for money
(f) Healthy working environment
(g) Good neighbourliness

'Overall, our aim is to be the best and most successful company in the airline industry.'

(1) BA's success is measured according to its standing in comparison with *other* airlines. BA was one of the industry's few profit-makers shortly after the Gulf War: although it may not top all league tables, quality of service has improved massively. It has operated effectively over a large number of its goals, in comparison with competitors.

(2) BA has also achieved consistent performance over a variety of its goals. Had it plunged into loss, there would be some doubts about its effectiveness.

Exam focus point

The case study in the exam does not always describe a profit-orientated business, and managers might be affected by different stakeholder influences. Identifying the:

- objectives, and
- power

of different stakeholder groups will help you to determine the priorities of the organisation and the likely constraints on what it does.

4.8 Section summary

- Stakeholders have an 'interest' in an organisation, but it is debatable whether they have rights over it.
- Stakeholders pursue their own goals.

5 SUBVERTING MISSION

5.1 Problems with mission

Problem	Comment
Ignored in practice	The inherent danger of mission is that it will not be implemented. Mintzberg writes 'organisations, too, can have trouble operationalising their lofty goals, with the result that their *official* goals - what they claim to be their goals - often do not correspond with the end they actually seem to pursue'.
Public relations	Sometimes, of course, mission is merely for public consumption, not for internal decision making.
'Post hoc'	Missions are sometimes 'fictions produced by an organisation to account for, explain, or *rationalise* its existence to particular audiences'. In other words, mission does not drive the organisation, but what the organisation actually does is assumed to be a mission.
Too full of generalisations	'Best', 'quality', 'major': is just a wish list.

5.2 System goals (see paragraph 2.5) are those which organisations as **systems** pursue. These goals have a habit of subverting mission, by making mission subordinate to them. System goals include the following.

Goal	Comment
Survival	Individuals benefit from the organisation's existence (as their employer, for their social life), irrespective of what the organisation actually does. There is a strong incentive for an organisation to survive simply because it keeps its managers in work.
Efficiency	This is the greatest benefit for a given cost. However, an organisation can be **efficient** (doing things well) as opposed to being **effective** (doing the right things). Efficiency takes precedence over effectiveness because it means doing more of the same, and does not require consideration of other stakeholders.

Goal	Comment
Control	Organisations try 'to exercise some control over their own environments'. Examples of control are vertical integration (eg to control supply), diversification (to reduce uncertainty).
Growth, sometimes	**Managers** benefit directly from growth, in terms of salaries and status. 'Growth is the natural goal of the manager' as it reduces vulnerability to the environment and other organisations.

These goals are interrelated: growth can bring efficiency. Of course, growth often does benefit shareholders and fulfils the mission, but not always.

5.3 **Enforcing mission**

(a) **Formal imposition.** Powerful persons or groups with power within or outside the organisation (eg the owner) can impose their idea of the mission on others.

(b) **Shared values.** A professional organisation (eg a hospital) might pursue mission as part of the professional ethics of the organisation's members.

(c) **Value system and culture.** The organisation with a strong ideology (eg a religious sect) has a strong sense of mission.

5.4 Section summary

- Mission can be ignored or treated as PR.
- Mission can be subverted by systems goals.

6 BRAINWORKS PLC UPDATE

Questions can be found in the Introduction Box at the beginning of this Chapter.

6.1 *Question 1.* BW's existing mission statement seems fairly vacuous. It describes the business and identifies what BW has to do. However, the mission seems to be completely disregarded in practice; no wonder Willard is sceptical.

6.2 *Question 2.* Strategic intent will be useful for BW, in competitive terms. Currently the company is focused on its shareholders - but there is little data as to how it should react to the **competition** it now faces from Daid and Colec.

6.3 *Question 3.* As well as explicit profit targets, you could argue that the firm has been driven by some of its managers' **personal** goals: Begbie's dishonesty and egomania; and Willard's desire to put the clock back and reverse the takeover, which he opposed in the first place.

Chapter roundup

- **Mission** describes an organisation's **purpose** (ie its **basic function in society**). Mission directs strategy, embodies values, and influences policies and standards of behaviour.
- Mission may be embodied in a **mission statement**, which should be brief, flexible and distinctive.
- The mission has to be translated into actual business practice. According to the rational model, this is achieved by **goals** covering all areas of the business and most, if not all, stakeholder groups.
- People use the words **goal and objective interchangeably**, it is useful to keep in mind the difference between those goals which can be expressed as **objectives** (quantitative and SMART) and **aims**, which are not quantitative.
- An organisation has many goals and objectives. A business has **profitability** or **return** as an overriding goal. However each **stakeholder group** has its own expectations of the business. Managers have to satisfy stakeholders, but this depends on the power different stakeholders have.
- **Systems** goals are those which the organisation's existence as an organisation encourages it to pursue. They are independent of the organisation's basic mission. **Survival** and **growth** are examples. Managers, as a stakeholder group, are capable of **subverting the organisation's mission**, as they have day to day control. Technical experts (eg work study analysts) are less concerned with *mission* than exercising their specialisation for whoever is interested. They have less interest in the survival of the organisation than do line managers.

Quick quiz

1. What is the role of mission in organisations? (see paras 1.1 - 1.4)
2. What do you understand by 'strategic intent'? (1.10)
3. What should characterise a mission statement? (1.13)
4. What is the distinction sometimes drawn between aims and objectives? (2.1)
5. What types of goals do people pursue in organisations? (2.5)
6. Draw up a list of corporate objectives of a business. (3.3)
7. What are the ways of dealing with goal conflict? (3.11)
8. Draw up a list of stakeholders. (4.2)
9. What sort of expectations might employees have of a business? (4.7)
10. Why is survival a 'systems' goal? (5.2)

Question to try	Level	Marks	Time
5	Introductory	n/a	30 mins

Chapter 5

ENVIRONMENTAL ANALYSIS

Introduction

The aim of environmental analysis is to review the environment for **Opportunities** and **Threats**, and to secure environmental fit. An organisation has many interchanges with its environment. It draws inputs from it and outputs goods and services to it. The environment is a major **source of uncertainty**.

An organisation is affected by **general environmental trends** usefully summarised in the **PEST** model. Issues relating specifically to its particular industry reflect the **competitive environment**, and we discuss **Porter's five forces model** as a way of analysing it. We also discuss **globalisation** - the result of free trade in goods and services - and the challenges this offers organisations. Porter believes that a *nation's* infrastructure of physical and human resources and the relationship between its industries, can influence the **global competitive** effectiveness of its industries. The process of environmental analysis is complex, so we discuss how it can be made easier through the use of modelling techniques such as **scenario building.**

Brainworks plc

1 How dynamic and how complex do you think BW's environment is?

2 Do you think globalisation is relevant to BW?

3 Do you think BW has responded to social change?

Case example

BSE

The importance of environmental factors of many kinds is demonstrated by the scare over BSE in beef and the emergence of a similar disease, CJD, in humans.

(a) Before the scare, beef consumption in the UK was already in decline, as a result of changing eating habits (a social and cultural factor).

(b) Government policy since World War II has been to make the UK self-sufficient in food - a political factor. The government and the institutions of the European Union are heavily involved in agriculture. The dispute became a political issue between the UK and the EU. The UK had the highest number of reported cases, but there were rumours that countries in continental Europe were under-reporting.

(c) A ban on the sale of UK beef has an affect on the economic environment of other firms - McDonald's, for example, responded to customer concern by importing beef. It has since lifted this ban.

(d) Feeding animal protein to cattle, which eat grass in the wild, was a technological development, as are growth hormones etc.

Clearly the BSE scare was feared but unexpected. How were the various industries affected?

(a) Farms - culling of cows, some compensation from the European Union. So-called 'organic' farmers, who do not use intensive feeding technology, might see an opening in the market in the long term.

(b) Abattoirs. Typically, these have high fixed costs, and operate on low margins. In the short term, they benefited from culling cattle.

(c) Food processors - some cheaper meats are no longer accessible for processing.

(d) Restaurants and retailers - customers switched to alternative meats in the short term.

Since the shock has died down, demand for prime cuts of beef has recovered, although this is not true of mince. Furthermore, McDonald's has decided to use British beef again. Such sudden shocks are fairly rare for most firms, but the case does illustrate very clearly how 'the environment' can never been taken for granted.

In 1998, however, over two years into the crisis, exports from mainland Britain into continental Europe are still prohibited, although beef from Northern Ireland is exempt from the ban.

1 THE GENERAL ENVIRONMENT

1.1 'The environment' of an organisation is everything outside its boundaries. As organisations are social systems they have a variety of relationships with the environment as outlined in the diagram below.

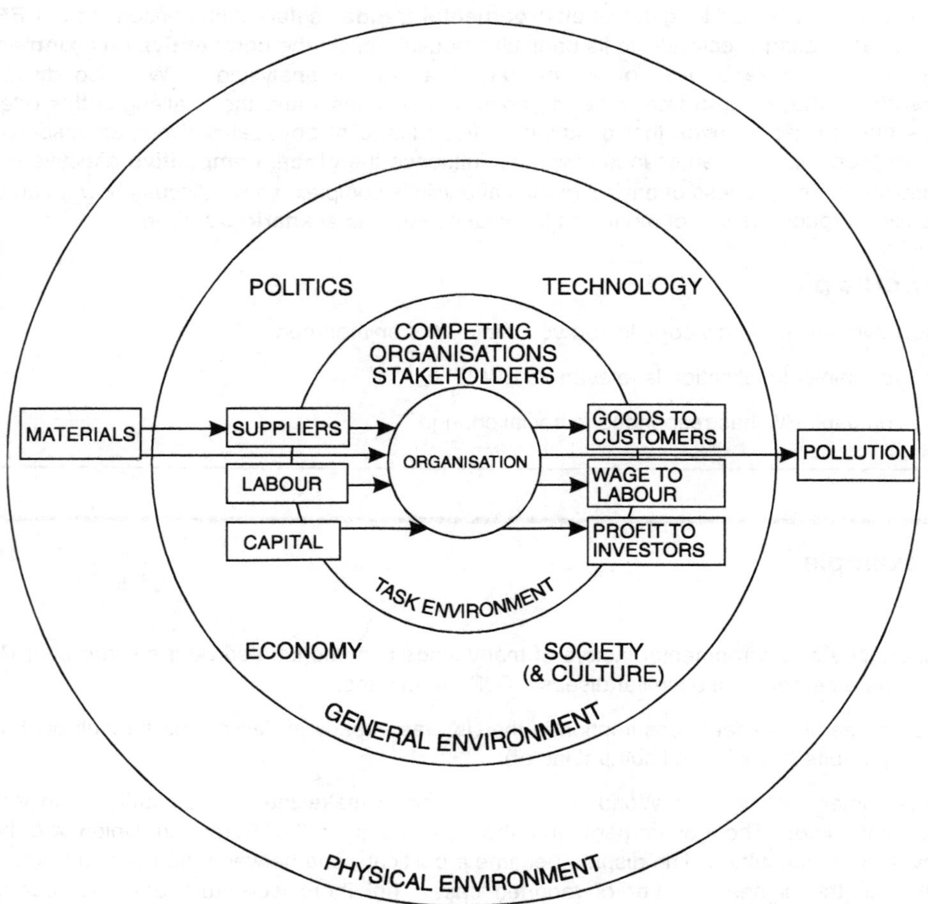

1.2 As you can see:

(a) The task (or micro or near) environment is of immediate concern, and is uniquely configured for each organisation: no organisation has a network of suppliers, customers, competitors or stakeholders identical to another's.

(b) The general (or macro or far) environment relates to factors in the environment affecting all organisations.

- Political-legal factors
- Economic factors
- Social and cultural factors
- Technological factors

(PEST)

Exam focus points

(1) The PEST model is a useful checklist for general environmental factors - in the real world they are all interlinked, of course.

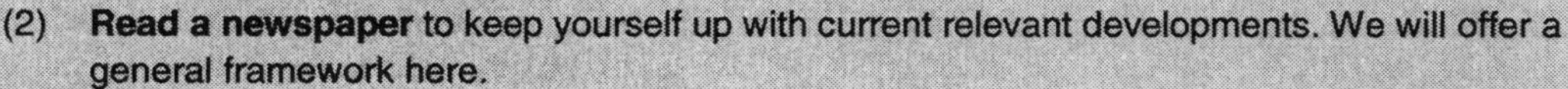

(2) **Read a newspaper** to keep yourself up with current relevant developments. We will offer a general framework here.

The political and legal environment

1.3 We will outline in **general** terms some key issues to keep in mind. Laws come from common law, parliamentary legislation and government regulations derived from it, and obligations under EU membership and other treaties.

1.4 **Legal factors affecting all companies**

Factor	Example
General legal framework: contract, tort, agency	Basic ways of doing business; negligence proceedings
Criminal law	Theft (eg of documents in Lanica's failed bid for the Co-op); insider dealing; bribery; deception
Company law	Directors and their duties; reporting requirements; takeover proceedings; shareholders' rights; insolvency
Employment law	Trade Union recognition; Social Chapter provisions; possible minimum wage; unfair dismissal; redundancy; maternity; Equal Opportunities
Health and Safety	Fire precautions; safety procedures
Data protection	Use of information about employees and customers
Marketing and sales	Laws to protect consumers (eg refunds and replacement, 'cooling off' period after credit agreements); what is or isn't allowed in advertising
Environment	Pollution control; waste disposal
Tax law	Corporation tax payment; Collection of income tax (PAYE) and National Insurance contributions; VAT

1.5 Some legal and regulatory factors affect **particular industries**, if the public interest is served. For example, electricity, gas, telecommunications, water and rail transport are subject to **regulators** (Offer, Ofgas, Oftel, Ofwat, Ofrail) who have influence over:

- Competition and market access
- Pricing policy (can restrict price increase)

1.6 This is because either:

- The industries are, effectively, monopolies.
- Large sums of public money are involved (eg in subsidies to rail companies).

Case example

Gas deregulation

Government policy. Gas used to be a state monopoly. The industry was privatised as one company, British Gas. Slowly, the UK gas market has been opened to competition: now about 20 suppliers compete with British Gas.

Regulators. Ofgas regulates the gas industry. Ofgas has introduced a Code of Conduct requiring gas suppliers to train sales agents, allow for a cooling off period and so on.

Contracts. British Gas is vulnerable to competitors because of its prices. When it was privatised, it inherited 'take or pay contracts' requiring it to buy gas at a specific price from gas producers. Since that time, gas prices have fallen, and competitors have been able to benefit from this.

New markets. Government policy has also deregulated the electricity market, so that companies such as British Gas can now sell electricity.

1.7 **Anticipating changes in the law**

- The governing party's election **manifesto** is a guide to its political priorities, even if these are not implemented immediately.
- The government often publishes advance information about its plans (**green paper** or **white paper**) for consultation purposes.
- The **EU's single market programme** indicates future changes in the law.

Case example

- The Labour Party indicated in its election manifesto that trade unions would have greater recognition rights. These have now been fleshed out.

Political risk and political change

1.8 The political environment is not simply limited to legal factors. Government policy affects the whole **economy**, and governments are responsible for enforcing and creating a **stable framework** in which business can be done. A report by the World Bank indicated that the quality of **government policy is important in providing the right**:

- **Physical infrastructure** (eg transport).
- **Social infrastructure** (education, a welfare safety net, law enforcement).
- **Market infrastructure** (enforceable contracts, policing corruption).

1.9 However, it is **political change** which complicates the planning activities of many firms. Here is a checklist for case study use.

Factor	Example
Possibility of political change	• Dissatisfaction with low prices at which utilities were sold to private sector
Likely nature of impact	• Windfall tax
Consequences	• How much will be paid
Coping strategies	• Cash flow planning
Influence on decision making	• Lobbying - BT said that, being no longer a monopoly, it should be excluded.

Political risk

1.10 The political risk in a decision is the risk that political factors will invalidate the strategy and perhaps severely damage the firm. Examples are:

- Wars.
- Expropriation ('rationalisation') of business assets by overseas governments.
- Other forms of political influence in local decision making.
- Local political chaos making business difficult.

1.11 A **political risk checklist** was outlined by Jeannet and Hennessey. Companies should ask the following six questions.

1. How **stable** is the host country's political system?
2. How **strong** is the host government's commitment to specific rules of the game, such as ownership or contractual rights, given its ideology and power position?
3. How **long** is the government likely to remain in **power**?
4. If the present government is **succeeded**, how would the specific rules of the game change?
5. What would be the effects of any expected **changes** in the specific rules of the game?
6. In light of those effects, what **decisions and actions should be taken now**?

There are many sources of data. The *Economist Intelligence Unit* offers assessment of risk. Management consultants can also be contacted.

1.12 Another example of how matters can change is given below.

Case example

Indonesia was perceived as an Asian 'tiger' economy, providing an attractive environment to British businesses and investors. The country was run autocratically and a system of 'crony capitalism' (where lucrative monopolies were given to members of the President's family) developed. Late in 1997, the exchange rate of Indonesia's currency the rupiah fell dramatically as investors fled: Indonesia's largest companies are heavily indebted, but this debt is denominated in UK dollars. At time of writing, over 100 people have been killed in riots, there has been widespread looting, and the Foreign Office is advising British nationals to leave. Democratic legitimacy reduces political risk as it can accommodate change.

On 23 May 1998, the Financial Times reported that the new Indonesian government had cancelled – or put on hold – contracts with Thames Water and Lyonnaise Des Eaux for unspecified reasons relating to the old regime. By early June, the Thames contract was apparently reinstated. The Indonesian government has, effectively, assumed the currency risk of the indebted companies. Watch out for more news.

The economic environment

1.13 The economic environment is an important influence at local and national level.

Factor	Impact
Overall growth or fall in Gross Domestic Product	Increased/decreased demand for goods (eg dishwashers) and services (holidays).
Local economic trends	Type of industry in the area. Office/factory rents. Labour rates House prices.
National economic trends:	
• Inflation	Low in most countries; distorts business decisions; wage inflation compensates for price inflation
• Interest rates	How much it costs to borrow money affects **cash flow**. Some businesses carry a high level of debt. How much customers can afford to spend is also affected as rises in interest rates affect people's mortgage payments.
• Tax levels	Corporation tax affects how much firms can invest or return to shareholders. Income tax and VAT affect how much consumers have to spend, hence demand.
• Government spending	Suppliers to the government (eg construction firms) are affected by spending.
• The business cycle	Economic activity is always punctuated by periods of growth followed by decline, simply because of the nature of trade. The UK economy has been characterised by periods of 'boom' and 'bust'. Government policy can cause, exacerbate or mitigate such trends, but cannot abolish the business cycle. (Industries which prosper when others are declining are called *counter-cyclical* industries.)

1.14 The **forecast state of the economy** will influence the planning process for organisations which operate within it. In times of boom and increased demand and consumption, the overall planning problem will be to **identify** the demand. Conversely, in times of recession, the emphasis will be on cost-effectiveness, continuing profitability, survival and competition.

1.15 **Key issues for the UK economy**

(a) The **service sector** accounts for most output. Services include activities such as restaurants, tourism, nursing, education, management consultancy, computer consulting, banking and finance. Manufacturing is still important, especially in exports, but it employs fewer and fewer people (20% of the labour force in 1995, accounting for 25% of GDP).

(b) The **housing market** is a key factor for people in the UK. Most houses are owner-occupied, and most people's wealth is tied up in their homes. UK borrowers generally borrow at variable rates of interest, so are vulnerable to changes in interest rates.

(c) **Tax and welfare.** Although headline rates of tax have fallen, people have to spend more on private insurance schemes for health or pensions. The government aims to target welfare provision on the needy and to reduce overall welfare spending by getting people into work.

(d) *Productivity*. An economy cannot grow faster than the underlying growth in productivity, without risking inflation. UK manufacturing productivity is still lower than that of its main competitors, but in services, the UK is relatively efficient.

1.16 **Impact of international factors**

Factor	Impact
Exchange rates	Cost of imports, selling prices and value of exports; cost of hedging against fluctuations
Characteristics of overseas markets. Different rates of economic growth and prosperity, tax etc.	Desirable overseas markets (demand) or sources of supply.
Capital, flows and trade	Investment opportunities, free trade, cost of exporting

These are covered in detail later in this chapter.

Case examples

In 1997, the volume of global merchandise trade grew by 9.5%, over three times more than world output, not untypical of the period since 1950.

The growth in trade has affected the *logistics industry (transport, warehouse, etc)* (worth US $130bn of which £31.6bn is outsourced). Total logistics expenditure in the EU is likely to rise from £130bn in 1996 to $155bn in 2001.

The major problem is congestion. The EU is planning ECU 350bn on trans-European networks (road, rail and air links) with possible extensions into Eastern Europe. Despite the single market, goods are still being held up at national borders.

The social environment - social ... may be fairly stable

Demography

KEY TERM

Demography is the study of population and population trends

1.17 The following demographic factors are important to organisational planners.

changes in age profile ; location ; wealth ; culture

the sum total of the beliefs, knowledge, attitudes of mind & customs to which people are exposed in their social conditioning

Factor	Comment
Growth	The rate of growth or decline in a national population and in regional populations.
Age	Changes in the age distribution of the population. In the UK, there will be an increasing proportion of the national population over retirement age. In developing countries there are very large numbers of young people.
Geography	The concentration of population into certain geographical areas.
Ethnicity	A population might contain groups with different ethnic origins from the majority. In the UK, about 5% come from ethnic minorities, although most of these live in London and the South East.
Household and family structure	A household is the basic social unit and its size might be determined by the number of children, whether elderly parents live at home etc. In the UK, there has been an *increase* in single-person households and lone parent families.
Social structure	The population of a society can be broken down into a number of subgroups, with different attitudes and access to economic resources. Social class, however, is hard to measure (as people's subjective perceptions vary).
Employment	In part, this is related to changes in the workplace. Many people believe that there is a move to a casual flexible workforce; factories will have a group of **core employees**, supplemented by a group of insecure **peripheral employees**, on part time or temporary contracts, working as and when required. Some research indicates a 'two-tier' society split between '**work-rich**' (with two wage-earners) and '**work-poor**'. However, despite some claims, **most employees are in permanent, full-time employment.**
Wealth	Rising standards of living lead to increased demand for certain types of consumer good. This is why developing countries are attractive as markets.

1.18 **Implications of demographic change**

(a) **Changes in patterns of demand**: an ageing population suggests increased demand for health care services: a 'young' growing population has a growing demand for schools, housing and work.

(b) **Location of demand**: people are moving to the suburbs and small towns.

(c) **Recruitment policies**: there are relatively fewer young people so firms will have to recruit from less familiar sources of labour.

(d) **Wealth and tax.**

Culture

KEY TERM

Culture is used by sociologists and anthropologists to encompass 'the sum total of the beliefs, knowledge, attitudes of mind and customs to which people are exposed in their social conditioning.'

1.19 Through contact with a particular culture, individuals learn a language, acquire values and learn habits of behaviour and thought.

(a) **Beliefs and values.** Beliefs are what we feel to be the case on the basis of objective and subjective information (eg people can believe the world is round or flat). *Values* are beliefs which are relatively enduring, relatively general and fairly widely accepted as a guide to culturally appropriate behaviour. Beliefs shape attitudes and so create tendencies for individuals and societies to behave in certain ways.

(b) **Customs:** modes of behaviour which represent culturally accepted ways of behaving in response to given situations.

(c) **Artefacts:** all the physical tools designed by human beings for their physical and psychological well-being: works of art, technology, products.

(d) **Rituals.** A ritual is a type of activity which takes on symbolic meaning, consisting of a fixed sequence of behaviour repeated over time.

The learning and sharing of culture is made possible by *language* (both written and spoken, verbal *and* non-verbal).

1.20 **Underlying characteristics of culture**

(a) **Purposeful.** Culture offers order, direction and guidance in all phases of human problem solving.

(b) **Learned.** Cultural values are 'transferred' in institutions (the family, school and church) and through on-going social interaction and mass media exposure in adulthood.

(c) **Shared.** A belief or practice must be common to a significant proportion of a society or group before it can be defined as a cultural characteristic.

(d) **Cumulative.** Culture is 'handed down' to each new generation. There is a strong traditional/historical element to many aspects of culture (eg classical music).

(e) **Dynamic.** Cultures adapt to changes in society: eg technological breakthrough, population shifts, exposure to other cultures.

Case example

Islamic banking

Islamic banking is a powerful example of the importance of culture in an economy. The Koran abjures the charging of interest, which is usury. However whilst interest is banned, profits are allowed. A problem is that there is no standard interpretation of the sharia law regarding this. Products promoted by Islamic banks include:

(a) Leasing (the Islamic Bank TII arranged leases for seven Kuwait Airways aircraft)
(b) Trade finance
(c) Commodities trading

The earlier Islamic banks offered current accounts only, but depositors now ask for shares in the bank profits. To tap this market, Citibank, the US bank, opened an Islamic banking subsidiary in Bahrain.

1.21 Knowledge of the culture of a society is clearly of value to businesses in a number of ways.

(a) **Marketers** can adapt their products accordingly, and be fairly sure of a sizeable market. This is particularly important in export markets.

(b) **Human resource managers** may need to tackle cultural differences in recruitment. For example, some ethnic minorities have a different body language from the majority, which may be hard for some interviewers to interpret.

1.22 Culture in a society can be divided into **subcultures** reflecting social differences. Most people participate in several of them.

Subculture	Comment
Class	People from different social classes might have different values reflecting their position of society.
Ethnic background	Some ethnic groups can still be considered a distinct cultural group.
Religion	Religion and ethnicity are related.
Geography or region	Distinct regional differences might be brought about by the *past* effects of physical geography (socio-economic differences etc). Speech accents most noticeably differ.
Age	Age subcultures vary according to the period in which individuals were socialised to an extent, because of the great shifts in social values and customs in this century. ('Youth culture'; the 'generation gap' etc).
Sex	Some products are targeted directly to women or to men. The gay community, also, might be considered a subculture in its own right.
Work	Different organisations have different corporate cultures, in that the shared values of one workplace may be different from another.

Case example

Consider the case of a young French employee of *Eurodisney*.

(a) The employee speaks the French language - part of the national culture - and has participated in the French education system etc.

(b) As a youth, the employee might, in his or her spare time, participate in various 'youth culture' activities. Music and fashion are emblematic of youth culture.

(c) As an employee of Eurodisney, the employee will have to participate in the corporate culture, which is based on American standards of service with a high priority put on friendliness to customers.

1.23 Cultural change might have to be planned for. There has been a revolution in attitudes to female employment, despite the well-publicised problems of discrimination that still remain.

Question 1

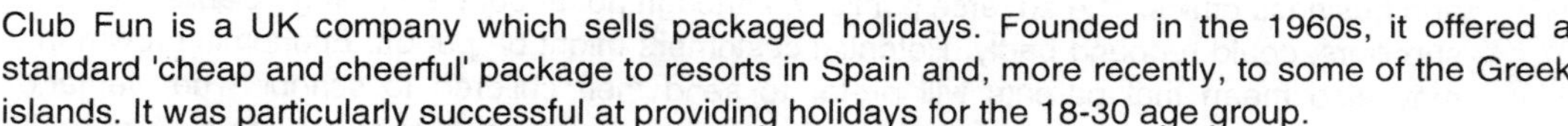

Club Fun is a UK company which sells packaged holidays. Founded in the 1960s, it offered a standard 'cheap and cheerful' package to resorts in Spain and, more recently, to some of the Greek islands. It was particularly successful at providing holidays for the 18-30 age group.

What do you think the implications are for Club Fun of the following developments?

(a) A fall in the number of school leavers.
(b) The fact that young people are more likely now than in the 1960s to go into higher education.
(c) Holiday programmes on TV which feature a much greater variety of locations.
(d) Greater disposable income among the 18-30 age group.

Answer

The firm's market is shrinking. There is an absolute fall in the number of school leavers. Moreover, it is possible that the increasing proportion of school leavers going to higher education will mean there will be fewer who can afford Club Fun's packages. That said, a higher disposable income in the population at large might compensate for this trend. People might be encouraged to try destinations other than Club Fun's traditional resorts if these other destinations are publicised on television.

Business ethics

1.24 The conduct of an organisation, its management and employees will be measured against **ethical standards** by the customers, suppliers and other members of the public with whom they deal.

1.25 **Types of ethical problem a manager may meet with in practice**

(a) **Production practices.** Attempts to increase profitability by cutting costs may lead to dangerous working conditions, inadequate safety standards in products or reprehensible practices (eg child labour). This is a problem for firms which outsource production to low-cost factories overseas.

(b) **Gifts.** There is a fine line to be drawn between gifts, accepted as part of a way of doing business, and bribes.

(c) **Social responsibility**: companies are being held to account for pollution and human rights issues.

(d) **Competitive behaviour.** There is a distinction between competing aggressively and competing unethically and illegally.

Question 2

The Heritage Carpet Company is a London-based retailer which imports carpets from Turkey, Iran and India. The company was founded by two Europeans who travelled independently through these countries in the 1970s. The company is the sole customer for carpets made in a number of villages in each of the source countries. The carpets are hand woven. Indeed, they are so finely woven that the process requires that children be used to do the weaving, thanks to their small fingers. The company believes that it is preserving a 'craft', and the directors believe that this is a justifiable social objective. Recently a UK television company has reported unfavourably on child exploitation in the carpet weaving industry. There were reports of children working twelve hour shifts in poorly lit sheds and cramped conditions, with consequent deterioration in eyesight, muscular disorders and a complete absence of education. The examples cited bear no relation to the Heritage Carpet Company's suppliers although children are used in the labour force, but there has been a spate of media attention. The regions in which the Heritage Carpet Company's supplier villages are found are soon expected to enjoy rapid economic growth.

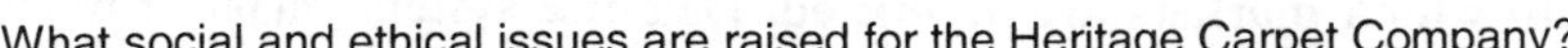

What social and ethical issues are raised for the Heritage Carpet Company?

Answer

Many. This is a case partly about boundary management and partly about enlightened self-interest and business ethics. The adverse publicity, although not about the Heritage Carpet Company's own suppliers, could rebound badly. Potential customers might be put off. Economic growth in the area may also mean that parents will prefer to send their children to school. The Heritage Carpet Company as well as promoting itself as preserving a craft could reinvest some of its profits in the villages (eg by funding a school), by enforcing limits on the hours children worked. It could also pay a decent wage. It could advertise this in a 'code of ethics' so that customers are reassured that the children are not simply being exploited. Alternatively, it could not import child-made carpets at all. (This policy, however, would be unlikely to help communities in which child labour is an economic necessity.)

Technological factors

1.26 Technology refers to:

(a) **Apparatus or equipment:** eg a TV camera.

(b) **Technique:** eg how to use the TV camera to best effect, perhaps in conjunction with other equipment such as lights.

(c) **Organisation:** eg the grouping of camera-operators into teams, to work on a particular project.

1.27 **Technology contributes to overall economic growth.** The **production possibility curve** describes the total production in an economy. Technology can increase total output, by enabling:

(a) Gains in productivity (more output per units of input);
(b) Reduced costs (eg transportation technology, preservatives).
(c) New types of product.

1.28 **Effects of technological change on organisations**

(a) **The type of products or services that are made and sold.**

Case example

The development of the transistor made valve radios obsolete. Japanese firms were thus able easily to enter the consumer electronics market, where they are now key competitors. Japanese firms had no previous investment in valve radio production.

(b) **The way in which products are made** (eg robots, new raw materials).

(c) **The way in which services are provided.**

Case examples

Mail order/Internet

(a) Companies selling easily transportable goods - for instance, books and CDs - can offer much greater consumer choice and are enjoying considerable success.

(b) The financial sector is rapidly going electronic - call centres are now essential to stay in business, PC banking is on the way, and the Internet and interactive TV are starting to feature in business plans.

(d) **The way in which markets are identified.** Database systems make it much easier to analyse the market place.

(e) **The way in which firms are managed.** IT encourages 'delayering' of organisational hierarchies, homeworking, and better communication.

(f) **The means and extent of communications with external clients.**

1.29 The impact of *recent* technological change also has potentially important social consequences, which in turn have an impact on business.

(a) **Homeworking.** Whereas people were once collected together to work in factories, home working will become more important.

(b) **Intellective skills.** Certain sorts of skill, related to interpretation of data and information processes, are likely to become more valued than manual or physical skills.

(c) **Services.** Technology increases manufacturing productivity, releasing human resources for service jobs. These jobs require **greater interpersonal skills** (eg in dealing with customers).

The physical environment: ecology

1.30 The importance of physical environmental conditions

(a) **Resource inputs**. Managing physical resources successfully (eg oil companies, mining companies) is a good source of profits.

(b) **Logistics.** The physical environment presents logistical problems or opportunities to organisations. Proximity to road and rail links can be a reason for siting a warehouse in a particular area.

(c) **Government.** The physical environment is under the control of other organisations.

(i) Local authority town planning departments can influence where a building and necessary infrastructure can be sited. Zoning regulations prohibit the siting of commercial developments in some residential districts. An example is the increases in numbers of out of town supermarkets, but further developments are being curtailed.

(ii) Governments can set regulations about some of the organisation's environmental interactions.

(d) **Disasters.** In some countries, the physical environment can pose a major 'threat' to organisations. The example of the earthquake in Kobe, Japan, springs to mind.

An interrelationship between environmental factors: ecological issues and strategic planning

1.31 Issues relating to the effect of an organisation's activities on the physical environment (which, to avoid confusion, we shall refer to as 'ecology'), have come to the fore in recent years for a number of reasons.

(a) The **entry into decision-making** or political roles of the generation which grew up in the **1960s**.

(b) **Growth in prosperity** might have encouraged people to feel that 'quality of life' is more than just material production and consumption.

(c) Expansion of **media coverage** (eg of famines, global warming) has fuelled public anxiety.

(d) **Disasters** (eg Chernobyl, forest fires in Asia) have aroused public attention.

(e) **Greater scientific knowledge.** For example, it became known only recently that it was possible to measure the hole in the ozone layer and to assess its causes.

1.32 How issues of ecology will impinge on business

- **Consumer demand** for products which appear to be ecologically friendly.
- Demand for **less pollution** from industry.
- Greater **regulation** by government and the EU.
- **Polluter pays.** Demand that businesses be charged with the external cost of their activities.
- Possible requirements to conduct **ecology audits**.
- Opportunities to develop **products and technologies** which are ecologically friendly.

1.33 The consumer demand for products which claim ecological soundness has waxed and waned, with initial enthusiasm replaced by cynicism as to 'green' claims.

(a) **Marketing.** Companies such as *Body Shop* have exploited ecological friendliness as a marketing tool.

(b) **Bad publicity.** Perhaps companies have more to fear from the impact of bad publicity (relating to their environmental practices) than they have to benefit from positive ecological messages as such. An example from the USA is the consumer campaign to boycott tuna produced by companies whose methods of fishing endanger the lives of dolphins.

(c) **Lifestyles.** There may be a limit to which consumers are prepared to alter their lifestyles for the sake of ecological correctness.

(d) Consumers may be **imperfectly educated** about ecological issues. (For example, much recycled paper has simply replaced paper produced from trees from properly managed (ie sustainably developed) forests.) In short, some companies may have to 'educate' consumers as to the relative ecological impact of their products.

1.34 As far as pollution goes, there has been a longish history on ecological legislation and it is likely that governments will take an increased interest in this area. Companies might have to face a variety of measures designed to deal with the pollution.

(a) **Government taxes and fees**. A **Landfill Tax** was introduced in the UK from October 1996. Companies can improve their waste handling.

(b) **Government regulations**. Fines might be imposed for persistent breach of pollution guidelines, and pollution might be monitored by government inspectors. The UK government has stated **targets** for **recycling** and reducing **carbon dioxide emissions**.

(c) **Tradable pollution permits** (USA). Every year, the government issues pollution permits to relevant firms for a certain price. These permits can be sold. It might be cheaper for a company to reduce its pollution than do nothing, as the cost could be recouped by the revenue gained by selling the permit. There is talk about introducing this scheme globally.

(d) **Commercial opportunities.** Companies can benefit from the commercial opportunities proposed by the new concern for ecological issues. Chemicals companies have been able to benefit from the development of safe alternatives to CFC gases.

(e) Finally, a firm can **relocate** its activities to a country where ecological standards are less strict, or have a lower priority in relation to other economic and social objectives, such as economic growth.

Case example

A battle is looming between the EU and the US on the issue of genetically-modified crops. These crops are modified to be resistant to certain pesticides – enabling spraying of pesticides to get rid of pests. US consumers do not mind. EU consumers are very suspicious, having had their fill of food scares recently. Environmentalists are worried that the genes can mutate and that hard-to-kill hybrids might be released into the environment.

Exam focus point

You might need to use environmental analysis later in the strategic planning process, when discussing strategic options, as in the June 1997 case.

1.35 Section summary

- Use PEST as a checklist.
- Not all environmental factors are equally relevant to all firms at all times.

2 COMPETITIVE FORCES 29/10/98

2.1 In discussing competition Porter (*Competitive Strategy*) distinguishes between factors which characterise the nature of competition:

(a) **In one industry compared with another** (eg in the chemicals industry compared with the clothing retail industry) and make one industry as a whole potentially more profitable than another (ie yielding a bigger return on investment).

(b) **Within a particular industry.** These relate to the competitive strategies that individual firms might select.

2.2 Five **competitive forces** influence the state of competition in an industry, which collectively determine the profit (ie long-run return on capital) potential of the industry as a whole. **Learn them.**

(a) The threat of **new entrants** to the industry.
(b) The threat of **substitute** products or services.
(c) The bargaining power of **customers**.
(d) The bargaining power of **suppliers**.
(e) The **rivalry** amongst current competitors in the industry.

The threat of new entrants (and barriers to entry to keep them out)

2.3 A new entrant into an industry will bring extra capacity and more competition. The strength of this threat is likely to vary from industry to industry, depending on:

(a) The strength of the **barriers to entry**. Barriers to entry discourage new entrants.
(b) The likely **response of existing competitors** to the new entrant.

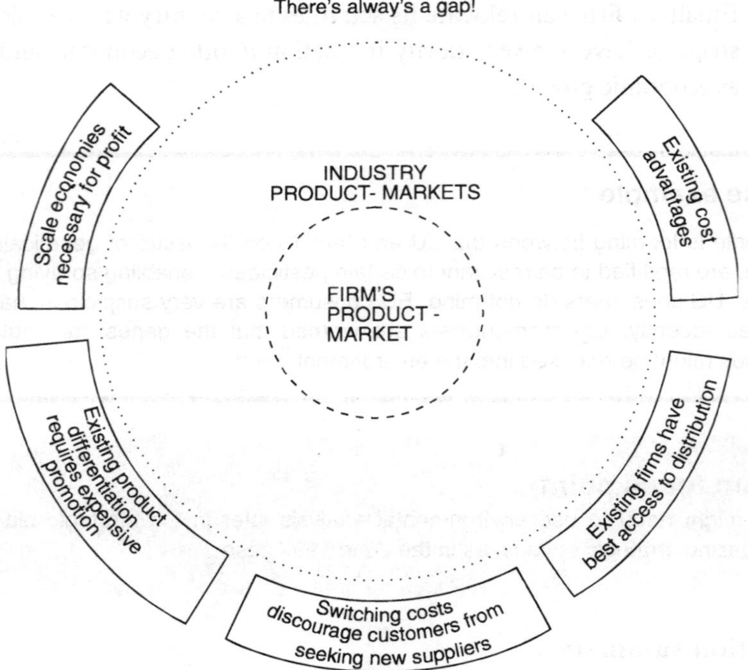

2.4 Barriers to entry

(a) **Scale economies**. High fixed costs often imply a high breakeven point, and a high breakeven point depends on a large volume of sales. If the market as a whole is not growing, the new entrant has to capture a large slice of the market from existing competitors. This is expensive (although Japanese companies have done this in some cases).

(b) **Product differentiation**. Existing firms in an industry may have built up a good brand image and strong customer loyalty over a long period of time. A few firms may promote a large number of brands to crowd out the competition.

Case example

The *UK detergent industry*

Complete newcomers (eg Ecover) had to go for niches or unusual distribution channels at first. New entrants would have to spend heavily to overcome the existing brand loyalties and to build up a brand image of their own. These high 'start-up' losses might deter would-be competitors.

(c) **Capital requirements**. When capital investment requirements are high, the barrier against new entrants will be strong, particularly when the investment would possibly be high-risk.

Case example

Telecommunications

The capital requirements for entering the telecommunications business are falling. Although many telecommunications firms had invested in optical fibre networks for trunk (eg long-distance calls), the final connection to the household was a practical monopoly for BT owing to the expense. TV Cable companies have slowly dented this. Furthermore, IONICA seeks to provide 'local loop' connections by radio rather than by copper wire.

(d) **Switching costs**. Switching costs refer to the costs (time, money, convenience) that a customer would have to incur by switching from one supplier's products to another's. Although it might cost a **consumer** nothing to switch from one brand of frozen peas to another, the potential costs for the **retailer or distributor** might be high.

(e) **Access to distribution channels.** Distribution channels carry a manufacturer's products to the end-buyer. New distribution channels are difficult to establish, and existing distribution channels hard to gain access to.

(f) **Cost advantages of existing producers, independent of economies of scale** include:

- Patent rights.
- Experience and know-how (the learning curve).
- Government subsidies and regulations
- Favoured access to raw materials.

Case example

Japanese firms

A little while ago, it was assumed that, following the success of Japanese firms worldwide in motor vehicles (Nissan, Honda, Toyota) and consumer electronics (eg Sony, JVC, Matsushita), *no* Western companies were safe from Japanese competition. Kao (household goods), Suntory (drinks), Nomura (banking and securities) were seen as successors to firms such as Procter and Gamble, Heineken etc.

This has not happened: for example, Japanese pharmaceutical firms, such as Green Cross, have not achieved the world domination (anticipated in 1982). US and European firms are still dominant in this industry.

Perhaps cars and consumer electronics are the exception rather than the rule. The reason for this might be distribution. Normally, outsiders do not find it easy to break into established distribution patterns. However, distribution channels in cars and consumer electronics offered outsiders an easy way in.

(a) The *car industry* is vertically integrated, with a network of exclusive dealerships. Given *time* and *money*, the Japanese firms could simply build their own dealerships and run them as they liked, with the help of local partners. This barrier to entry was not inherently *complex*.

(b) *Consumer electronics*

(i) In the early years, the consumer electronics market was driven by *technology*, so innovative firms such as Sony and Matsushita could overcome distribution weaknesses with innovative products, as they had plenty to invest. This lowered entry barriers.

(ii) Falling prices changed the distribution of hifi goods from small specialist shops to large cut-price outlets, such as *Comet*. Newcomers to a market are the natural allies of such new outlets: existing suppliers prefer to shun 'discount' retailers to protect margins in their current distribution networks.

Japanese firms have *not* established dominant positions in:

(a) Healthcare, where national pharmaceuticals wholesalers are active as 'gatekeepers'
(b) Household products, where there are strong supermarket chains
(c) Cosmetics, where department stores and specialist shops offer a wide choice.

2.5 Entry barriers might be **lowered** by:

- Changes in the environment
- Technological changes
- Novel distribution channels for products or services

Exam focus point

Barriers to entry featured in December 1995, when a carpet manufacturing company was considering an entry to retailing.

The threat from substitute products

2.6 A **substitute product** is a good/service produced by **another industry** which satisfies the same customer needs.

Case example

The Channel Tunnel

Passengers have several ways of getting to London to Paris, and the pricing policies of the various industries transporting them there reflects this.

(a) 'Le Shuttle' carries cars in the Channel Tunnel. Its main competitors come from the *ferry* companies, offering a substitute service. Therefore, you will find that Le Shuttle sets its prices with reference to ferry company prices, and vice versa.

(b) Eurostar is the rail service from London to Paris/Brussels. Its main competitors are not the ferry companies but the *airlines.* Prices on the London-Paris air routes fell with the commencement of Eurostar services, and some airlines have curtailed the number of flights they offer.

The bargaining power of customers

2.7 Customers want better quality products and services at a lower price. Satisfying this want might force down the profitability of suppliers in the industry. Just how strong the position of customers will be depends on:

(a) How much the **customer buys.**

(b) How **critical** the product is to the customer's own business

(c) **Switching costs (ie the cost of switching supplier).**

(d) Whether the products are **standard items** (hence easily copied) or specialised.

(e) The **customer's own profitability:** a customer who makes low profits will be forced to insist on low prices from suppliers.

(f) Customer's **ability to bypass** the supplier or might take over the supplier.

(g) The **skills** of the customer **purchasing staff,** or the price-awareness of consumers.

(h) When **product quality** is important to the customer, the customer is less likely to be price-sensitive, and so the industry might be more profitable as a consequence.

Case example

For example, although the Ministry of Defence may wish to keep control over defence spending, it is likely as a customer to be more concerned that the products it purchases perform satisfactorily than with getting the lowest price possible for everything it buys.

The bargaining power of suppliers

2.8 Suppliers can exert pressure for higher prices. The ability of suppliers to get higher prices depends on:

(a) Whether there are just **one or two dominant suppliers** to the industry, able to charge monopoly or oligopoly prices.

(b) The threat of **new entrants** or substitute products to the **supplier's industry**.

(c) Whether the suppliers have **other customers** outside the industry, and do not rely on the industry for the majority of their sales.

(d) The **importance of the supplier's product** to the customer's business.

(e) Whether the supplier has a **differentiated product** which buyers need to obtain.

(f) Whether **switching costs** for customers would be high.

Case example

The *computer industry* provides an example of the changing power of customers and suppliers. Until the advent of PCs, the computer industry was dominated by a small number of suppliers, led by IBM and followed by companies like Burroughs, Sperry and Data General. Equipment and software supplied by each manufacturer was generally incompatible with that made by a competitor. The computer firms were able to 'lock in' their customers, as switching costs were so high. Customers could not mix and match, and so competition as to price was largely irrelevant when it came to system upgrades.

This all changed with the PC. But now, Microsoft is accused of forcing PC manufacturers installing Windows software to include its internet browser, too. This is felt to be anti-competitive, although Microsoft argues that customers, who gain an operating system of enhanced functionality, only benefit.

The rivalry amongst current competitors in the industry

2.9 The **intensity of competitive rivalry** within an industry will affect the profitability of the industry as a whole. Competitive actions might take the form of price competition, advertising battles, sales promotion campaigns, introducing new products for the market, improving after sales service or providing guarantees or warranties. Competition can:

(a) Stimulate demand, expanding the market.

(b) Leave demand unchanged, in which case individual competitors will make less money, unless they are able to cut costs.

2.10 The intensity of competition will depend on the following factors.

(a) **Market growth**. Rivalry is intensified when firms are competing for a greater market share in a total market where growth is slow or stagnant.

(b) **Cost structure**. High fixed costs are a tempt for to compete on price, as in the short run *any* contribution from sales is better than none at all.

(c) **Switching**. Suppliers will compete if buyers switch easily (eg Coke vs Pepsi).

(d) **Capacity**. A supplier might need to achieve a substantial increase in output *capacity*, in order to obtain reductions in unit costs.

(e) **Uncertainty**. When one firm is not sure what another is up to, there is a tendency to respond to the uncertainty by formulating a more competitive strategy.

(f) **Strategic importance.** If success is a prime strategic objective, firms will be likely to act very competitively to meet their targets.

(g) **Exit barriers** make it difficult for an existing supplier to leave the industry.

(i) Fixed assets with a low **break-up value** (eg there may be no other use for them, or they may be old).

(ii) The cost of **redundancy payments** to employees.

(iii) If the firm is a division or subsidiary of a larger enterprise, the **effect of withdrawal on the other operations** within the group.

(iv) The **reluctance of managers** to admit defeat, their loyalty to employees and their fear for their own jobs.

(v) **Government pressures** on major employers not to shut down operations, especially when competition comes from foreign producers rather than other domestic producers.

Case examples

- The *car industry* is a major employer, but there is widespread global overcapacity. Governments (eg in France, regarding Renault) try to prevent closures.
- *Package holidays.* Travel firms arrange hotels a year in advance based on forecast demand. If they over-estimate, they have empty rooms to fill, hence the discounts and special deals frequently offered late in the season, which reduce profits.

Question 3

The *tea industry* is characterised by oversupply, with a surplus of about 80,000 tonnes a year. Tea estates 'swallow capital, and the return is not as attractive as in industries such as technology or services'. Tea cannot be stockpiled, unlike coffee, keeping for two years at most. Tea is *auctioned* in London and prices are the same in absolute terms as they were 15 years ago. Tea is produced in Africa and India, Sri Lanka and China. Because of the huge capital investment involved, the most recent investments have been quasi-governmental, such as those by the Commonwealth Development Corporation in ailing estates in East Africa. There is no simple demarcation between buyers and sellers. Tea-bag manufacturers own their own estates, as well as buying in tea from outside sources.

In 1997 tea prices were described in India at least as being 'exceptionally firm ... The shortage and high prices of coffee have also raised demand for tea which remains the cheapest of all beverages in spite of the recent rise in prices. Demand from Russia, Poland, Iran and Iraq are expected to rise.

(a) Carry out a five forces analysis.

(b) Thinking ahead, suggest a possible marketing strategy for a tea-grower with a number of estates which has traditionally sold its tea at auction.

Answer

(a) Here are some ideas. Barriers to entry are high. There are plenty of substitute products (coffee), competitive rivalry is high because of the difficulty of stockpiling products. Customer bargaining power is high, but supplier power is low: all it needs is capital, the right sort of land and labour.

(b) *Williamson and Magor* has begun to switch from selling tea at auction to consumer marketing. The firm is aiming to build up its own brand image in the UK and Germany, by offering - by mail order - unblended, specialist teas from its Indian estates. It advertised via Barclays Premier Card magazine; replies were used to set up a customer database. When the company's Earl Grey tea was recommended on BBC2's *Food and Drink,* these existing customers were targeted with a letter and a sample.

The impact of information technology on the competitive forces

Case example

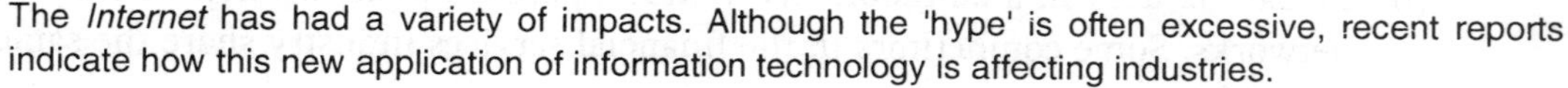

The *Internet* has had a variety of impacts. Although the 'hype' is often excessive, recent reports indicate how this new application of information technology is affecting industries.

In March 1996, the Financial Times reported that German companies were losing lucrative niche markets because the *Internet* made it easier for customers to compare prices from other suppliers by obtaining other information over the Internet. High prices made German retailers vulnerable in an age when 'a shopper with a credit card and computer could sit at home and could order from around the world'. The Internet has *increased competition.* The Internet is a competitive weapon. Tesco's home shopping service is supported by internet technology.

2.11 **Barriers to entry** and IT

(a) **IT can raise entry barriers** by increasing economies of scale, raising the capital cost of entry (by requiring a similar investment in IT) or effectively colonising distribution channels by tying customers and suppliers into the supply chain or distribution chain.

(b) **IT can surmount entry barriers**. An example is the use of telephone banking, which sometimes obviates the need to establish a branch network.

2.12 **Bargaining power of suppliers** and IT

(a) **Increasing the number of** accessible **suppliers.** Supplier power in the past can derive from various factors such as geographical proximity and the fact that the organisation requires goods of a certain standard in a certain time. IT enhances supplier information available to customers.

(b) **Closer supplier relationships.** Suppliers' power can be *shared*. CAD can be used to design components in tandem with suppliers. Such relationships might be developed with a few key suppliers. The supplier and the organisation both benefit from performance improvement, but the relations are closer.

(c) **Switching costs.** Suppliers can be integrated with the firm's administrative operations, by a system of electronic data interchange.

2.13 **Bargaining power of customers.** IT can 'lock customers in'.

(a) **IT can raise switching costs.**

(b) **Customer information systems** can enable a thorough analysis of marketing information so that products and services can be tailored to the needs of certain segments.

2.14 **Substitutes.** In many respects, **IT itself is 'the substitute product'**. Here are some examples.

(a) Video-conferencing systems might substitute for air transport in providing a means by which managers from all over the world can get together in a meeting.

(b) IT is the basis for new leisure activities (eg computer games) which substitute for TV or other pursuits.

(c) E-mail might substitute for some postal deliveries.

2.15 **IT and the state of competitive rivalry.**

(a) IT can be used in support of a firm's **competitive** strategy of cost leadership, differentiation or focus. These are discussed later in this text.

(b) IT can be used in a **collaborative** venture, perhaps to set up new communications networks. Some competitors in the financial services industry share the same ATM network.

Exam focus point

10 marks were available in a June 1996 question about the impact of IT on the competitive forces relevant to a supermarket.

2.16 Section summary

- The competitive environment of a firm is characterised by five forces: barriers to entry, substitute products, suppliers, customers and the intensity of competition.
- IT has implications for all these forces.

3 GLOBAL FACTORS

Case example

Indian software

Software is conventionally thought to be a high-tech product made in wealthy 'First World' countries. However, India has a flourishing software industry.

Infosys is a firm based in Bangalore in southern India: 'An engineer at Infosys .... presses a computer key in Bangalore .... and his machine connects directly with the computer centre of the Holiday Inn hotel chain 12,000 miles away in the US ..... Thanks to satellite technology, engineers in Bangalore can communicate almost instantaneously with counterparts in the US, Europe and Japan ... Many foreign high-tech companies believe India's engineers are hard to beat because they speak English, the language of international high-tech trade and are trained at some of the best universities in the developing world .... monthly wages for programmers in India are just $225 (£158) compared with $600 in Singapore and $2,500 in the US.'

A report in the *Economist* (23/3/1996) suggests that India's software industry, having notched up sales of $1.4bn in 1995, is growing at 40% pa. However it still only supplies 0.5% of the world market.

3.1 International business conditions are having an increasingly significant impact on organisations.

(a) They affect the nature of the industry.

(b) They affect the various positions of different countries, the size and wealth of their markets and the prosperity and efficiency of their productive bases.

(c) They affect the management, by governments or international institutions, of the framework in which business is done.

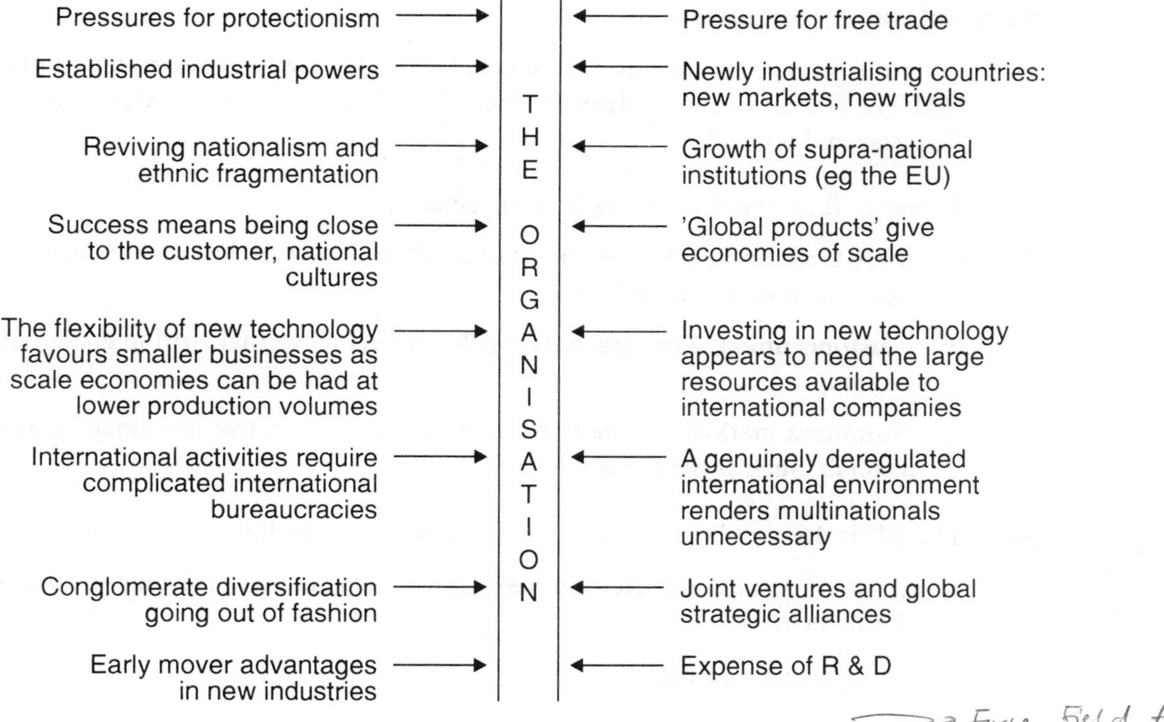

3.2 The theory of **comparative advantage** suggests that **free trade** is the best way to promote global economic growth, and by implication domestic prosperity. In other words, people should be free to buy and sell goods and services anywhere in the world.

3.3 Despite the theory of comparative advantage, many countries have limited or controlled their trading activities, with varying success.

(a) **Import substitution**. Countries sought to build up domestic industries to replace the need for imports. This has failed.

(b) **Export-led growth**. Countries promoted economic growth by exporting. Japan is the most successful example of export-led growth. This has been conspicuously successful.

3.4 **Protectionist measures to restrict competition** from overseas producers, for whatever reasons, include:

(a) **Quotas** on the number of items that can be imported (eg Japanese cars).

(b) **Import bans** (eg Brazil prohibited the import of cheap US-made computers).

(c) **Restrictions** on foreign ownership of certain industries (eg defence).

(d) **Tariffs**.

(e) **Abuse of** quality control and technical **standards**.

3.5 Business people and politicians have had an ambivalent attitude in the past towards this issue.

(a) Protectionist policies give the businesses the benefit of a cosy domestic market. Their inefficiencies are not penalised, and customers pay higher prices.

(b) Free trade is more often supported by businesses which import components or which need to export to be profitable. In recent years, the argument has been going in the favour of freer trade and governments have taken a number of steps to promote it.

Regional trading organisations

3.6 Countries in various regions have entered into closer economic arrangements such as NAFTA (USA, Canada, Mexico), the EU, Mercosur (Brazil, Argentina, Uruguay, Paraguay and now Chile).

3.7 There are three types of free trade arrangements.

(a) **Free trade area:** free movements of goods and services, but restrictions retained on movement of labour and capital.

(b) **Customs union:** a free trade area with a common external tariff to goods outside the union.

(c) **'Common market'**: all the features of (a) and (b) plus free movement of labour and capital, much as the EU is now.

3.8 The **EU** is the world's largest single market, but is unusual in that it features:

- A common political decision-making process (Council of Ministers, Commission, Parliament).
- Soon, a single currency.

3.9 The EU single market programme has involved areas as diverse as harmonising technical standards, opening up areas such as telecommunications to competition, consumer protection, mutual recognition of professional qualifications and so on. Much work remains to be done.

Case example

Aviation in the EU

On April 2 1997, the European Union completed the liberalisation of its aviation market. From that day, European airlines saw the removal of the last restrictions on their operations, leaving them free to operate domestic services in countries other than their own. In the past, air transport (including level of fares and services) had been heavily regulated, as many governments chose to support the 'national' airline. The UK was one of the first to privatise air transport. The final stage allows airlines to set their own fares or services within the EU, subject to predatory pricing restrictions.

In 1996 there were 156 carriers offering scheduled services, compared with 99 in 1986. Small airlines, such as Ryanair, EasyJet and Virgin Express have all introduced low cost flights between a range of EU countries.

However, fares for many European routes are still higher than the equivalent distances in the US. In part this is because airports are still publicly owned, in the main, and landing 'slots' (periods of time available for take off and landing) are hard to come by.

3.10 Before getting carried away by notions that the world is splitting irretrievably into three trading blocks, remember that:

- There is increasingly free movement of capital between the world's major financial centres.
- Global trade is becoming liberalised (see below), after the 1993 GATT agreement.
- Some of the world's markets offering the greatest potential for growth (eg India and China) are not part of a 'trading block'.
- New technology, such as the Internet, makes it harder to police trade barriers in some areas.

3.11 Also bear in mind that 'protectionist' measures are not the only barrier to entry. Differences in:

- Tax regimes
- Wage levels
- Infrastructure
- Language and culture
- Skills levels
- Prosperity

still exist.

International trade liberalisation: the WTO

3.12 Since 1945, the major industrial, and now the developing, countries have sought to increase trade. The fall of communism, and the failure of state control of trade have added to the pressure for free trade. In 1997, merchandise trade grow by 9.5%, three times the growth in world output.

3.13 The WTO was formed in 1995 as successor to the former General Agreement on Tariffs and Trade (GATT). The GATT was originally signed by 23 countries in 1947 as an attempt to promote free trade (its membership increased to 128 countries). The aims of GATT were to:

(a) Reduce existing barriers to free trade.
(b) Eliminate discrimination in international trade.
(c) Prevent the growth of protectionism.

3.14 GATT succeeded in reducing world tariffs substantially, after a series of 'rounds' of negotiation, in the 1960s and 1970s, culminating in December 1993, with a very ambitious programme for the liberalisation of world trade, including agriculture, financial services, patent and copyright etc. It was estimated at the time that the opening up of markets for agricultural and industrial goods following the 1993 GATT accord would add around US$200-300 billion to world income by the year 2002.

3.15 Ratification of the agreement by member governments followed during 1994. The new World Trade Organisation (WTO) was set up in 1995 to enforce the agreement. Important facts to keep in mind about the WTO are these.

(a) **The WTO has dispute resolution powers.** Aggrieved countries can take matters up with the WTO if they cannot be resolved bilaterally.

Case example

Costa Rica asked the WTO to rule against the USA's barriers to Costa Rica's exports of men's underwear to the US. Costa Rica won the case.

(b) **Membership** of the WTO requires **adherence to certain conditions** regarding competition in the home market etc. Consequently, certain countries such as China have yet to be admitted.

(c) **Membership rules are slightly less onerous for 'developing countries'**, which can maintain some protectionist measures, but this is a matter of dispute.

Case example

Telecommunications liberalisation

February 1997 saw a WTO-sponsored deal on telecommunications liberalisation world wide. (The following extracts are from a Financial Times report, 19 March 1997.)

'In Geneva, some 69 countries representing about 90 per cent of the world's $600bn telecoms services business agreed - with varying levels of commitment - to open their markets to competition, to allow foreigners to take stakes in domestic telecoms companies and to put in place fair trading legislation.

(a) The telecoms services covered by the agreement include voice telephony, data transmission, telex, telegraph, facsimile, private leased circuits, fixed and mobile satellite systems, cellular telephony, mobile data services and paging.

(b) The most important participants - the US, the European Union, Canada and Japan - led the way. But the list of signatories also encompasses much of the developing world: Brazil, Colombia, the Philippines, India and Pakistan were among those making bigger commitments to liberalisation than ever before.'

Developing countries hope to benefit from investment: telecommunications can be an important stimulus to economic growth.

(c) Customers, the big operators, manufacturers and world trade are all expected to benefit from the pact.'

  (i) The average cost of international calls could fall by 80 per cent over the next few years.

  (ii) There could be a $1,000bn boost to the world economy over the next decade as a consequence of the pact.

(d) 'In the short term, there will inevitably be losers, too. State-owned operators currently enjoying monopoly profits will suffer from the onset of competition and from declining prices. National economies will benefit.'

The agreement provides a common regulatory framework and underpins many of the changes evidence in the industry. Some countries are not used to liberalisation, however.

A global market?

3.16 Some writers assert that, with the WTO, free movement of capital, the world has now become a **global market**, or a **'borderless world'**: this implies that 'national economies and cultures are dissolving before the great flows of trade, finance and information ... unconstrained global markets for capital and goods allow companies to allocate resources to maximise benefits for consumers'. (Paul Hirst, *Globaloney*, Prospect Magazine, February 1996).

3.17 Despite the real gains in liberalisation 'globalisation' in this full-blooded form is **not an accurate description** of the reality facing most businesses. The existence of global markets should not be taken for granted in terms of all products and services, or indeed in all territories.

(a) **Depends on the industry.** Some services are still subject to **managed trade** (eg some countries prohibit firms from other countries from selling insurance) and there are some services which by their very nature can never be exported (eg haircuts etc are resolutely 'local').

(b) There is **unlikely ever to be a global market for labour,** given the disparity in skills between different countries, and restrictions on immigration. Companies can best respond by relocating, but this is perhaps not always a viable commercial option.

(c) **Depends on the market**

- **Upmarket luxury goods** may not be required or afforded by people in developing nations: whilst there is competition, it is limited to certain locations.
- Some goods can be sold almost anywhere, but to limited degrees. Television sets are consumer durables in some countries, but still luxury or relatively expensive items in other ones.

3.18 Some goods, such as oil, are needed almost everywhere: arguably, the oil industry is truly global. There are relatively few companies serving the aerospace market, so this is also 'global' in a way.

Case example

Financial markets

Two reports in the Economist 16 May 1998 indicate the extent to which globalisation is affecting a number of industries.

(a) Most of the banks operating in the City of London are non-UK owned. Tokyo, now embarking on financial services deregulation, will go the same way: 'Foreign firms show every sign of cleaning up; only two years ago foreign firms accounted for less than a quarter of the turnover on Tokyo's stock exchange. Now this is almost a third. Foreign firms offer more research. Japanese firms face stiff competition from foreign firms with cleaner images and better fund managers. 'Fund managers have their sights on managing Japan's huge pool of pension money.'

(b) American firms are moving into the market for UK domestic savings. Merill Lynch is to open six regional offices in the UK. 'Britain has all the usual attractions such as an ageing population and a government keen to promote private savings.'

3.19 **Effect of 'globalisation' on the firm**

- Lower barriers to entry, hence incoming competition.
- Opportunities to compete abroad via exports.
- Opportunities to invest abroad.
- Opportunities to raise finance from overseas sources of capital.

Question 4

Identify some of the PEST factors affecting a firm as it seeks to trade overseas.

Answer

Political factors: political conditions in individual overseas markets or sources of supply, relationships between governments and the activities of supra-national institutions (eg EU regulations on product standards).

Economic factors

(a) The overall level of economic activity and prosperity.

(b) The relative levels of inflation in the domestic and overseas market (as inflation affects your prices).

(c) The exchange rate, regarding its level and volatility

Social and cultural factors

(a) Cultural practices, the different levels of education and literacy, religious belief and practices, and the role of women.

(b) The media and distribution systems in overseas markets. Countries have very variable rates of newspaper readership.

(c) The differences of ways of doing business (eg it is reputed that Japanese companies are concerned to avoid excessive legalism).

(d) To what extent should the product be adapted to local tastes?

(e) Different ethical views.

(f) How are local operations to be managed? Expensive expatriate staff to ensure central control? Local managers to ensure flexibility?

Technological factors

(a) The degree to which a firm can imitate the technology of its competitors.

(b) A firm's access to domestic and overseas patents.

(c) Intellectual property protection (eg copyright, patents), which varies in different countries.

(d) Technology transfer requirements (some countries regard investments from overseas companies as learning opportunities and require the investing company to share some of its technology).

(e) The relative cost of technology compared to labour.

Global or boundary-less corporations

3.20 Some argue there is an increasing number of 'stateless corporations', whose activities transcend national boundaries, and whose personnel come from any country.

(a) **Multinationals**

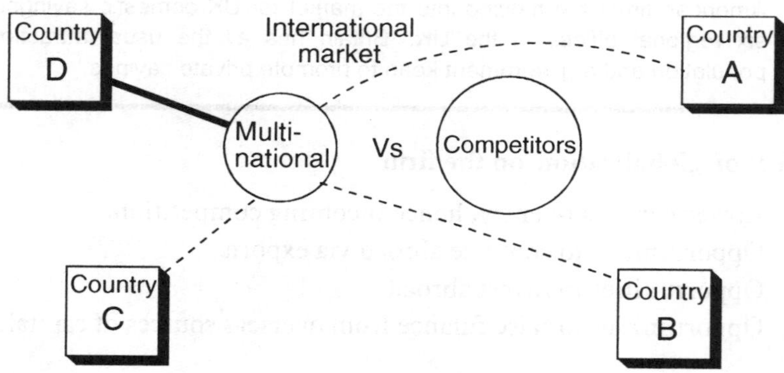

= strong links (eg R&D, `home base' head office, strategic decision making)

- - - - - = weak links (subsidiaries)

In this case the links between the company and countries C, B and A are likely to be severed before that with D which is the home country.

(b) **Global**

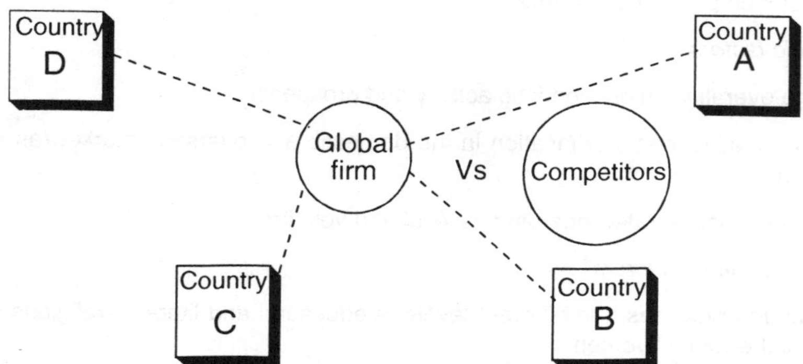

The global corporation can shift between countries.

3.21 This theory has some attractive evidence, particularly in a relatively open economy like that of the UK, which is host to a number of multinational corporations and has attracted a fair degree of inward investment.

3.22 **Do these stateless corporations really exist?** Against Reich's view the following objections have been raised (by Yao-Su Hue and John Cantwell).

(a) **Workforce.** Most multinationals, other than those based in small nations, have less than half of their employees abroad.

(b) **Ownership and control of multinationals remain restricted.** Few so-called global companies are currently quoted on more than two stock markets, but more and more are seeking a listing in a number of financial markets.

(c) **Top management is rarely as multinational in composition** as the firm's activities. (A foreigner is rarely seen on the Tokyo-based board of a Japanese multinational.)

(d) National residence and status is important for **tax reasons**.

(e) **R&D.** The bulk of a typical multinational's research and development is generally done in the home country, where strategic decisions are made. But this is changing, especially as R & D is sometimes subcontracted.

(f) Where **capital is limited**, 'global' companies stick to the home market rather than developing overseas ones.

(g) Finally, profits from a global company must be **remitted somewhere.**

3.23 **Do multinationals have to be big?**

(a) Open markets and common standards now make it easier for small firms to sell products worldwide, as these barriers are lower.

(b) Cheaper technology (eg IT). When technology was expensive only big firms could afford. Many technological benefits are now available to small firms.

(c) Capital markets are now open to smaller companies.

3.24 Section summary

- Free trade is increasing.
- Globalisation applies to some, but not all industries and markets.
- Few genuinely boundary-less corporations exist, even if the trend is in that direction.

4 THE COMPETITIVE ADVANTAGE OF NATIONS 12/97

Exam focus point

In December 1997 15 marks were available for describing Porter's 'diamond' (see 4.8 below). Despite the topic being covered in this BPP Study Text and being clearly indicated in the teaching guide few answer were able to cite this framework.

4.1 Michael Porter's *The Competitive Advantage Of Nations,* suggests that some nations' industries succeed more than others in terms of international competition. UK leadership in some industries (eg ship-building) has been overtaken (by Japan and Korea).

4.2 Porter does **not believe that countries or nations as such are competitive**, but he asks:

(a) 'Why does a **nation become the home base** for successful international competitors in an industry?'

(b) 'Why are firms based in a particular nation able to create and **sustain competitive advantage** against the world's best competitors in a particular field?'

(c) 'Why is **one nation** often the home for **so many of an industry's world leaders**?'

4.3 Porter believes that national origin influences an individual firm's competitive stance especially in international markets. Porter 'seeks to isolate the national attributes that foster competitive advantage in an industry'.

4.4 'National' competitiveness in an industry cannot be reduced to:

(a) Macroeconomics (budget deficits, interest rates).

(b) Cheap labour (it is better to be able to compete in spite of high wage costs).

(c) Natural resources (Japan imports most of its raw materials, Russia has them in abundance).

(d) Government policy of export promotion (although influential in some cases).

(e) Management practices (eg once derided US styles of management have produced many successful industries such as software).

4.5 The original explanation for **national** success was the theory of **comparative advantage**. This held that relative factor costs in countries (eg the fact that some raw materials are cheaper in country A than in country B, but others are cheaper in B than A) determined the appropriateness of particular economic activities in relation to other countries. (In other words, *countries* should monopolise in what they are best at in relation to other countries.)

4.6 Porter argues that **industries which require high technology and highly skilled employees** are less affected than low technology industries by the relative costs of their inputs of raw materials and basic labour as determined by the national endowment of factors. The reasons are as follows.

(a) **Technological change gives firms the power to by-pass constraints on resources** (such as shortages of labour) and can **nullify the advantages of other firms** elsewhere (if you can do something more efficiently).

(b) **Most companies have easy access to resources, through global free trade.** Firms do not depend on their home country's endowment of a resource to become competitive. For example, BP was a successful multinational long before North Sea Oil. BP's competitive success has nothing to do with the UK's national endowment of oil.

(c) **Competing on price is of fleeting benefit** anyway, as it is only of short term advantage.

4.7 **Comparative advantage** is too **general a concept** to explain the success of **individual companies and industries**. If high technology and global markets allow firms to circumvent (or ignore) the constraints (or advantages) of their home country's endowment of raw materials, cheap labour, access to capital and so forth, how can they be successful internationally?

so what are the factors of success?

4.8 Porter identifies determinants of national competitive which are outlined in the diagram below. Porter refers to this as the **diamond.**

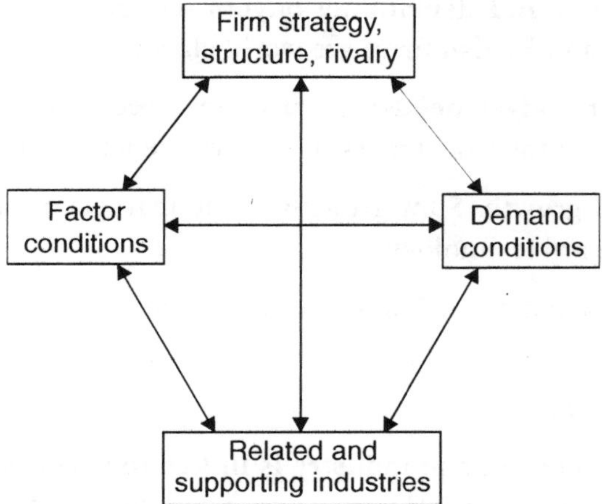

Analysing the 'diamond'

Factor conditions

4.9 **Factor conditions** are a country's particular endowment of inputs (eg raw materials, land, capital, infrastructure) to production.

(a) Human resources (skills, price, motivation, industrial relations).

(b) Physical resources (land, minerals, climate, location relative to other nations).

(c) Knowledge (scientific and technical know-how, educational institutions).

(d) Capital (ie amounts available for investment, how it is deployed - eg government investment, equity shares, loans, savings rates).

(e) Infrastructure (transport, communications, housing).

4.10 Porter distinguishes between:

(a) **Basic factors:** natural resources, climate, semiskilled and unskilled labour, and seed capital. Basic factors are passively inherited, or at best their creation involves little private or social investment. Basic factors are **unsustainable** as a source of national competitive advantage. The wages of unskilled workers in industrial countries are undermined by even lower wages elsewhere.

(b) **Advanced factors** include modern digital communications, highly educated personnel (eg computer scientists), research laboratories and so forth. They are necessary to achieve high order competitive advantages such as differentiated products and proprietary production technology.

4.11 **An abundance of factors is not enough.** It is the efficiency with which they are deployed that matters. The former USSR has an abundance of natural resources and a fairly well educated workforce, but was an economic catastrophe.

Demand conditions: the home market

4.12 The **home market determines how firms perceive, interpret and respond to buyer needs.** This information puts pressure on firms to innovate and provides a launch pad for global ambitions.

(a) There are **no 'cultural' impediments** to communication.

(b) The **segmentation** of the home market shapes a firm's priorities: companies will be successful globally in segments which are similar to the home market.

(c) **Sophisticated and demanding buyers** set standards. ('The British are known for gardening, and British firms are world class in garden tools'.)

(d) **Anticipatory buyer needs:** if consumer needs are expressed in the home market earlier than in the world market, the firm benefits from 'experience'.

(e) The **rate of growth**. Slow growing home markets do not encourage the adoption of 'state of the art' technology.

(f) **Early saturation** of the home market will encourage a firm to export.

Related and supporting industries

4.13 **Competitive success in one industry is linked to success in related industries**. Porter cites the Italian footwear industry as an example, as Italy has related success in other leather goods industries. Domestic suppliers are preferable to foreign suppliers, as 'proximity of managerial and technical personnel, along with cultural similarity, tends to facilitate free and open information' flow at an early stage.

Firm strategy, structure and rivalry

4.14 **Structure**. National cultural factors create certain tendencies to orientate business-people to certain industries.

(a) Many Italian firms are family run businesses. They are leaders in industries where economies of scale are modest. Italian firms pursue focus strategies.

(b) German firms, according to Porter, have a strong showing in 'industries with a high technical content.'

4.15 **Strategy.** Industries have different **time horizons**, funding needs and so forth.

(a) **National capital markets** set different goals for performance. In some countries, banks are the main source of capital. Banks have a different set of priorities than equity shareholders.

(b) When an industry faces difficult times, a nation's industries **can either innovate within the industry**, to sustain competitive position or **shift resources from one industry to another** (eg diversification). Porter argues that diversification is a way of avoiding risk, rather than enhancing productivity.

4.16 **The state of domestic rivalry** has 'a profound role to play in innovation and the ultimate prospects for international success'. Even in small countries such as Switzerland and Sweden, successful industries were composed of strong local rivals. (Strategies which aim to nurture single 'national champions' have often failed.)

4.17 Domestic rivalry is important because:

- There can be no special pleading about 'unfair' foreign competition.
- With little domestic rivalry, firms are happy to rely on the home market.
- Tough domestic rivals teach a firm about competitive success.
- Domestic rivalry forces firms to compete on grounds other than basic factors.
- Each rival can try a different strategic approach.

Influencing the 'diamond'

4.18 A country's diamond is always vulnerable to change or mismanagement.

4.19 Governments can influence the determinants in the diamond by:

(a) Altering demand conditions (eg as a buyer).

(b) Implementing policies towards education and capital markets, in other words, altering the supply conditions of advanced factors.

(c) Promoting competition (eg through anti-trust legislation).

Interactions between the determinants

4.20 The factors in the 'diamond' are interrelated. Each factor can affect the behaviour of the others and competitive advantage rarely rests on only one element of the diamond.

(a) **Related industries** affect **demand conditions** for an industry. An example from the context of international marketing is 'piggy-back' exporting in which an exporting company also exports some of the products of related industries.

(b) **Domestic rivalry** can encourage the **creation of more specialised supplier industries.**

4.21 Porter says that a nation's competitive industries are **clustered**. A cluster is a linking of industries through relationships which are either vertical (buyer-supplier) or horizontal (common customers, technology, skills). For example, 'Sweden is competitive in pulp and paper and in wood handling machinery'.

4.22 A cluster means that a nation is successful in the following ways.

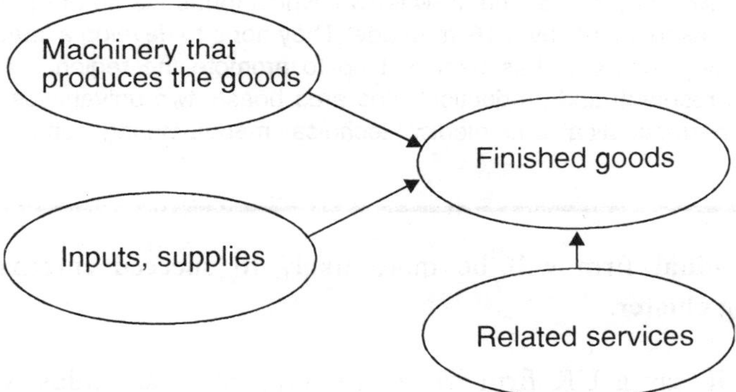

4.23 Porter believes clustering to be a key to national competitive advantage, even though within a country the industry may be clustered in a particular area. This is common to all types of industries.

(a) The Italian ceramic tile industry is clustered in Sassuolo.
(b) The UK merchant banking industry is largely based in London.
(c) American information technology companies are clustered in Silicon Valley.

4.24 **How does a country create a diamond of competitive advantage?**

(a) Factors of production provide the seed corn. A large endowment of easily mined iron ore would suggest metal-working industries.

(b) Related and supporting industries can also be a foundation, if the competences within them can be configured in a new way.

(c) Extraordinary demand in the *home market* based on national peculiarities and conditions can set the demand conditions determinant in the diamond.

4.25 Being first to establish a diamond in a particular industry can raise barriers to entry for others. Moreover, even when a cluster disappears (eg if an important factor in the industry is low-cost production, this can be relocated elsewhere) some of the 'high value added' elements of it can be retained in the original country.

Losing competitive advantage

4.26 As industries evolve, losses of competitive advantage can also be sustained. National competitive advantage is lost when the factors in the diamond are no longer self supporting.

(a) **Factor deterioration.** If factors such as infrastructure and human resources are not created and upgraded (eg through effective education), competitive advantage will fade.

(b) **Local demand conditions** fall out of synchronisation with **global demands** if consumers become less demanding.

(c) **Reinforcing clusters might unwind** if industry relocates.

(d) **Firm rivalry is limited.** Britain, Porter believes, has a small number of relatively large companies, rather than a thriving Mittestand (medium-sized businesses) as exists in Germany. Merging rather than competing was the preferred choice.

Case example

The Swedish and Danish governments are co-operating to form a 'Medicon valley', comprising the areas either side of the Oresund, a waterway which forms the border between them. The Oresund is due to be linked shortly by a 16km bridge. They hope to develop a 'medical industrial complex'. A Medicon Valley Academy has been set up to promote the region 'as a centre of medical and biotechnical research and production'. The area boasts two universities, three university hospitals and forty pharmaceutical and medical-technical manufacturing companies.' (*Financial Times,* 4 April 1997)

4.27 The **individual** firm will be more likely to succeed internationally if there is a **supporting cluster.**

4.28 However, if, say a UK firm wishes to compete in an industry in which there is no national competitive advantage, it can take a number of steps to succeed.

(a) **Compete in the most challenging market,** to emulate domestic rivalry and to obtain information. If a firm can compete successfully in such a market, even if this only means carving out a small niche, it holds well for its success.

(b) **Spread research and development** activities to countries where there is an established research base or industry cluster already.

(c) Be prepared to **invest heavily in innovation**.

(d) **Invest in human resources,** both in the firm and the industry as a whole. This might mean investing in training programmes.

(e) **Look out for new technologies** which will change the rules of the industry. The UK with its large efficient research base should have some creative ideas.

(f) **Collaborate with foreign companies.** American motor companies, successfully learned 'Japanese' production techniques.

(g) **Supply overseas companies**. Japanese car plants in the UK have encouraged greater quality in UK components suppliers. Inward investment provides important **learning opportunities** for domestic companies.

(h) **Source components from overseas.** In the UK crystal glass industry, many firms buy crystal glass from the Czech Republic, and do the cutting and design work themselves. Conversely, firms can sell more abroad.

(i) **Exert pressure on politicians** and opinion formers to create better conditions for the 'diamond' to develop (eg in education).

4.29 Does Porter's analysis describe a generally applicable law, which will be relevant to all times, or is it only a 'snapshot' of a particular time?

(a) **Clustering**. Regional trading blocks might make these ideas out of date. The lowering of trade barriers can mean that a 'cluster' might cover several countries.

(b) **IT and communications**. There is less reason for a geographic concentration of certain industries, especially knowledge-based ones, as communications shrink distances. Porter's book was written before the widespread commercial expansion of the Internet.

(c) Multinational companies might become **less influenced by their national origins in future** even though few genuinely global firms exist at present.

(d) **Inward investment**. The UK car industry is substantial, and its output in 1998 is higher than it was ten years before, but hardly any of the industry is now owned by British investors (Reliant Robin). To what extent is it a 'cluster'? Many foreign companies have invested in the UK. A large number of component firms supply them and small specialist engineering firms provide high value consulting advice.

(e) A large number of firms are **relocating** from high-cost countries to countries with lower costs.

(f) Porter was writing when the rise of Asian economies seemed unstoppable and Europe was written off as a sufferer of Eruo-sclerosis. Also, the environment of world trade is now freer.

(g) No-one can realistically predict the 'industries of the future'.

4.30 Section summary

- Porter suggests an industry's national origin is important for its competitive success.
- In the long term advanced factors are more significant than basic factors.
- The diamond includes factor endowments, related and supporting industries, home demand and domestic rivalry.
- Industries are clustered.

5 ENVIRONMENTAL ANALYSIS: INFORMATION AND MODELS

Environmental analysis

5.1 Johnson and Scholes suggest that a firm should conduct an **audit of environmental influences.** This will identify the environmental factors which have had a significant influence on the organisation's development or performance in the past.

5.2 Strategic decisions are made in partial ignorance, as we have seen, because the environment is uncertain. Uncertainty relates to the **complexity and dynamism** of the environment.

(a) **Complexity** arises from:

(i) The **variety of influences** faced by the organisation. The more open an organisation is, the greater the variety of influences. The greater the number of markets the organisation operates in, the greater the number of influences to which it is subject.

(ii) The amount of **knowledge** necessary. All businesses need to have knowledge of the tax system, for example, but only pharmaceuticals businesses need to know about mandatory testing procedures for new drugs.

(iii) The **interconnectedness** of environmental influences. Importing and exporting companies are sensitive to exchange rates, which themselves are sensitive to interest rates. Interest rates then influence a company's borrowing costs.

(b) **Dynamism**. Stable environments are unchanging. Dynamic environments are in a state of change. The computer market is a dynamic market because of the rate of technological change.

Question 5

Analyse the environments of the two situations below according to the criteria in paragraph 5.2.

(a) A new product has just been introduced to a market segment. It is proving popular. As it is based on a unique technology, barriers to entry are high. The product will not be sold outside this market segment.

(b) A group of scientists has recently been guaranteed, by an EU research sponsoring body, funds for the next ten years to investigate new technologies in the construction industry, such as 'smart materials' (which respond automatically to weather and light conditions). This is a multi-disciplinary project with possible benefits for the construction industry. A number of building firms have also guaranteed funds.

Answer

(a) The environment is *simple*, as the product is only being sold in one market. The environment is *dynamic*, as the product is still at the introduction stage and demand might be predicted to increase dramatically.

(b) The environment is complex, but stable. The knowledge required is uncertain, but funds are guaranteed for ten years.

5.3 It is not always easy to detect which environmental factors will be relevant in future.

(a) Ansoff suggested that strategic signals from the environment can be detected through a sequence, as follows.

Step 1 Managers have a 'sense of turbulence'.
Step 2 The cause is identified.
Step 3 The cause becomes concrete enough to describe and then assess.
Step 4 Responses are identified and costed.

(b) Mintzberg argues that the sequence above is a waste of time. After all, every customer is a potential 'signal' of environmental change and no system is capable of detecting those signals which are more significant than others.

system nervousness

Strategic intelligence

> **KEY TERM**
>
> **Strategic intelligence**, according to Donald Marchand, is defined as 'what a company needs to know about its business environment to enable it to anticipate change and design appropriate strategies that will create business value for customers and be profitable in new markets and new industries in the future'.

5.4 **Many firms' intelligence gathering procedures reflect the organisation structure.** Each function of the organisation collected information relevant to its own concerns, without any wider 'corporate viewpoint'.

(a) A separate strategic planning department collects data on trends.
(b) The marketing department identifies customers' needs.
(c) The R&D department identifies new technology.
(d) The production department suggests process innovation.

5.5 A corporate strategy concerns the **whole** organisation. There are dangers in planning the gathering of strategic information on a departmental or functional basis.

(a) The data collected reflects the **restricted functional view**, not the overall corporate view.
(b) There are inevitable **gaps and blind-spots** in the information collected.
(c) Until recently (with the arrival of e-mail and intra-net applications) **sharing information** across functional departments **has been very difficult**.

5.6 **Why information should be shared**

(a) Not all strategic knowledge or decision-making capacity resides at the top of the firm.
(b) Sharing encourages 'a **diversity of interpretations** and views about the future'. For example, the marketing department may realise the commercial significance of new technology that may have escaped R&D.
(c) As companies delayer and lose management levels, the **organisation hierarchy** which used to distribute information is **less effective** at this task.

5.7 A model of the process of creating strategic intelligence is outlined below.

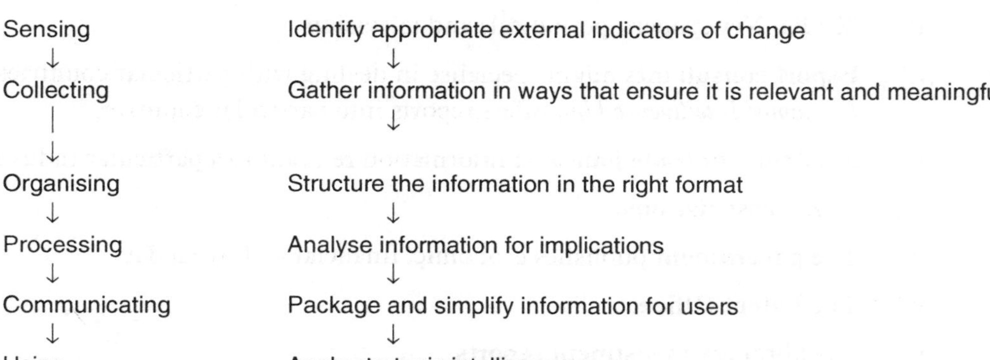

It is easy to be overwhelmed by the volume and variety of relevant environmental information on offer. The temptation to ignore it completely is understandable, especially as managers are often more concerned with short-term issues relating to immediate production. Much environmental information cannot be easily quantified, and so is therefore harder to assimilate into decision making systems.

5.8 **Key dimensions of strategic intelligence**

Dimension	Comment
Information culture	What is the role of information in the organisation? Is it only distributed on a 'need to know basis' or do people have to give specific reasons for secrecy?
Future orientation	Is the focus on *specific* decisions and trade-offs, or a *general* attitude of enquiry?
The structure of information flows	Is communication vertical (up and down the hierarchy), or horizontal?
Processing strategic intelligence	Are 'professional' strategists delegated to this task or is it everybody's concern?
Scope	Is strategic intelligence dealt with by senior management only, or is it dispersed throughout the organisation?
Time horizon	Short-termist or orientated towards the long term?
The role of IT	Many firms are using IT to enhance communication across business functions.
Organisational 'memory'	Do managers keep in mind the lessons of past successes or failures?

Sources of strategic intelligence

5.9 (a) **Internal sources and sources relatively close to the company**

(i) **Sales forces** obtain customer and competitor information.

(ii) **Market research**. Although generally this deals with specific issues, it can indicate general environmental concerns (eg consumers' worries).

(iii) The **management information system** may generate information about the environment, although its main focus is internal.

(iv) Many **departmental plans** contain environmental data which can be used for other purposes.

(b) **External sources of environmental data**

(i) **Media**. Newspapers, periodicals and television.

(ii) **Export consultants** might specialise in dealing with particular countries. The *Economist Intelligence Unit* offers reports into particular countries.

(iii) **Academic or trade journals:** information relevant to a particular industry.

(iv) **Trade associations.**

(v) The **government** publishes economic, financial and social data.

(vi) The **Patent Office.**

(vii) Stockbrokers' **investment reports.**

(viii) Specialist **consultancy firms** (eg CACI) provide information.

(ix) The **Internet.**

5.10 It is now possible to access large volumes of generally available information through **databases** held by public bodies and businesses.

(a) Some **newspapers** offer computerised access to old editions, with search facilities looking for information on particular companies or issues (eg FTPROFILE).

(b) **Public databases** are also available for inspection (eg on-line legal database, JUSTIS).

(c) **Dun and Bradstreet** provide general business information. *AC Neilsen* operate on-line information regarding products and market share.

(d) The **Internet** is a source of data either through services offered by on-line service providers or via general surfing.

Forecasts

5.11 Forecasting attempts to reduce the uncertainty managers face. In **simple/static conditions the past is a relatively good guide** to the future. Techniques are:

(a) **Time series analysis.** Data for a number of months/years is obtained and analysed. The aim of time series analysis is to identify:

(i) Seasonal and other cyclical fluctuations

(ii) Long term underlying trends.

An example of the use of this approach is the UK's monthly unemployment statistics which show a 'headline figure' and the 'underlying trend'.

(b) **Regression analysis** is a quantitative technique to check any underlying correlations between two variables (eg sales of ice cream and the weather). Remember that the relationship between two variables may only hold between certain values. (You would expect ice cream consumption to rise as the temperature becomes hotter, but there is probably a maximum number of ice creams an individual can consume in a day, no matter how hot it is.)

5.12 **Dynamic/complex conditions**

- **Future developments:** the past is not a reliable guide.
- Techniques such as **scenario building** are useful as they can propose a number of possible futures.
- **Complex environments** require techniques to reduce the effects of complexity on organisational structure and decision-making.

Technological forecasting

5.13 Technological change is a source of uncertainty, but can be countered by:

- Ensuring that employees are kept up to date with relevant developments.
- The **Delphi model:** A panel of experts offers views on the probability, over a future time period, of various forecast occurrences such as inventions, breakthroughs or regulatory changes.

Econometric models for medium-term forecasting

5.14 Econometrics is the study of economic variables and their interrelationships, using computer models. Short-term or medium-term econometric models might be used for forecasting. This method of forecasting depends on:

(a) The firm's ability to identify key 'indicators' of change, in advance of the change actually occurring. **Leading indicators** are indicators which change *before* market demand changes. For example, a sudden increase in the birth rate would be an indicator of future demand for children's clothes. Similarly, a fall in retail sales would be an indicator to manufacturers that demand from retailers for their products will soon fall.

(b) The ability to predict the span of time between a change in the indicator and a change in market demand. Change in an indicator is especially useful for demand forecasting when they reach their highest or lowest points (when an increase turns into a decline or vice versa).

Scenario building

5.15 Because the environment is so complex, it is easy to become overwhelmed by the many factors. Firms therefore try to model the future and the technique is *scenario building*.

KEY TERM

A scenario is 'an internally consistent view of what the future might turn out to be'.

(a) Macro-scenarios deal with the environment as a whole.

(b) Industry scenarios narrow the focus to the competitive conditions in particular industries.

Macro scenarios

5.16 **Macro scenarios** use macro-economic or political factors, creating alternative views of the future environment (eg global economic growth, political changes, interest rates). Macro scenarios developed because the activities of oil and resource companies (which are global and at one time were heavily influenced by political factors) needed techniques to deal with uncertainties.

Case example

The *Guardian* (28 August 1995) identified three macro scenarios for the UK economy, as outlined in a study by Cash, Hughes and Hawthorn. In particular they contrast the UK's future in manufacturing and services (eg media, banking). The authors outline three possible scenarios.

(a) *Base projection*: 'Britain is stuck on a low growth path, with unemployment remaining at about 2m'. This might be because the UK sucks in imports at a greater rate than it exports, and exports of financial and miscellaneous services are not enough to make up the gap.

(b) '*Super-serv*' scenario. This assumes that the UK's trend in manufacturing remains the same, but that the volume of financial and miscellaneous service exports doubles. If this occurs, unemployment would fall, by 2003, to 1 million. By that year UK exports of such services would exceed the US's.

(c) '*Fast-man*'. This assumes that businesses reinvest in manufacturing, so that manufactured exports rise by 14% more than the base projection, leading to a small manufacturing surplus in 2003.

These scenarios are based on a 5.5% annual growth in world trade. The article does not indicate whether one scenario more probable than the others.

Industry scenarios

5.17 Porter believes that the most appropriate use for scenario analysis is if it is restricted to an industry. An **industry scenario** is an internally consistent view of an industry's future structure. It is not a forecast, but a possibility.

5.18 A set of industry scenarios is selected to reflect a range of possible futures. The **entire range**, not the most *likely* 'future', is used to design a competitive strategy. The process is as follows.

Scenario Building
- pessimistic
- optimistic
- most likely

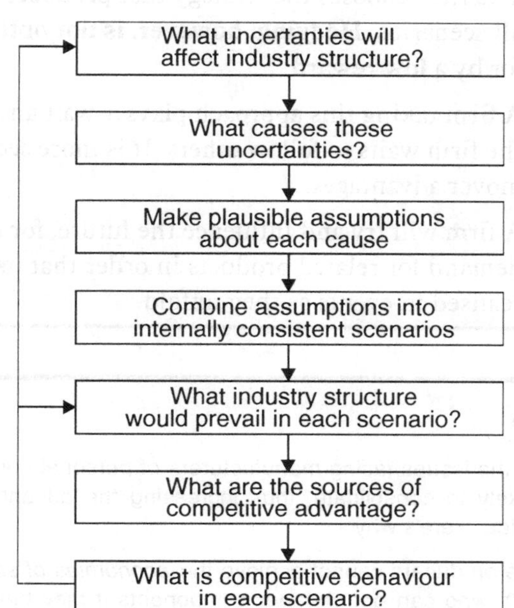

5.19 Each scenario is based on **assumptions** about certain **variables.** These variables should be assessed for:

(a) The degree of **uncertainty** in the variable
(b) Its potential **impact** on industry structure
(c) **Managerial beliefs** about its importance
(d) The **practicality** of the assumptions (ie avoid implausible assumptions)
(e) The **consistency** of assumptions

5.20 An analysis of the scenario involves:

(a) Determining the future industry structure
(b) Developing the implications of the scenario for industry attractiveness
(c) Identifying implications for competitive advantage

5.21 The future industry structures identified in each scenario will affect competitive behaviour in different ways. A scenario might highlight the probability of price competition and downward pressure on prices: some competitors will be better able than others to cope with this.

5.22 **Using scenarios to formulate competitive strategy**

(a) A strategy built in response to only **one scenario is risky,** whereas one supposed to cope with them **all might be expensive.**

(b) Choosing scenarios as a basis for decisions about competitive strategy.

Approach	Comment
Assume the most probable	This appears to be common sense, but this choice puts too much faith in the scenario process and guesswork. A less probable scenario may be one whose **failure** to occur would have the **worst** consequences for the firm.
Hope for the best	A firm designs a strategy based on the scenario most attractive to the firm: wishful thinking.
Hedge	The firm chooses the strategy that produces **satisfactory** results under **all** scenarios. **Hedging, however, is not optimal**. The **low risk** is paid for by a **low reward**.
Flexibility	A firm taking this approach plays a 'wait and see' game. This means that the firm waits to follow others. It is more secure, but sacrifices first-mover advantages.
Influence	A firm will try and influence the future, for example by influencing demand for related products in order that its favoured scenario will be realised in events as they unfold.

Case example

Here are some of the issues facing manufacturers of personal computers over the next few years. The industry is likely to consolidate, thus increasing the advantage of the biggest brand name computer companies. Here's why.

(a) Small volume producers cannot achieve the *economies of scale* enjoyed by Dell and Hewlett Packard (HP), who can get cheaper components if they buy in bulk. Smaller manufacturers cannot then compete on price.

(b) Bigger manufacturers can insist on JIT supply, thereby lowering storage costs. They can form close ties with suppliers to get early access, to innovatory technology

(c) *Usage*. Intel chips not only power individual computers but are at the heart of many *networks*. They now power workstations. Smaller manufacturers cannot really compete in this market.

(d) There is a new segment of low-cost machines for use at hom. This now accounts for 25% of the US market (in 1997). Prices will fall further thus encouraging first time buyers, and so expanding the total size of the market.

(e) Distribution channels favour larger producers. Internet sale of PCs favour firms with flexible logistics. Dell pioneered the 'build to order method'.

Currently, the largest makers, Compaq and IBM are feeling 'squeezed' by Dell and HP. In the 'second tier, Apples, NEC and AST have lost ground. In Europe, ICL and Olivetti have pulled out of the PC market. There are still hundreds of very small PC makers accounting for 25% of world sales, either reaching specialist or local markets. Their survival depends on offering 'high-touch' service, responding in a quicker or more flexible way to the bigger and more remote suppliers.

For consumers, the prospect is less choice but lower prices.

IT and the industry

5.23 **How important for the industry is change in information technology?** This can significantly affect the assumptions underlying a particular scenario but is hard to analyse.

Awareness frameworks

5.24 **Awareness frameworks** help executives assess the general impact of developments IT on the industry and on business. They can be used in environmental scanning and in scenario. These in turn can be classified into:

(a) Refocus frameworks.
(b) Impact models.
(c) Scoping models (see Chapter 7, as they have other uses).

5.25 **Refocus frameworks** exist to 'help change mind-sets', in other words they challenge people's basic assumptions about the use and value of IT.

(a) **Transformational change**. Can IT change the way business is done to secure competitive advantage?

(b) **Incremental change**. Should the company use IT to improve access to the market place, or use it to improve the firm's existing operations?

	Market place	*Internal operations*
Transformational/ significant change		
Incremental change to traditional products and processes		

5.26 **Impact models** asses the likely effect of IT on the industry, the firm and its strategy.

Impact	**IT effect**
Industry	Fundamental change to the industry
Firm	Influences the competitive forces
Strategy	Influences firm's competitive strategy

5.27 A **fundamental change** in the industry includes a technology that dramatically changes its cost profile or entry barriers. Technology can raise or lower the level at which scale economies can be achieved.

Case example

The death of the book?

For many years, people have speculated that IT would lead to the death of print media. For example, *Encyclopaedia Britannica* announced in 1998 that it was going to put its entire output on CD-ROM and no longer publish the huge multi-volumed encyclopaedia for which it is known.

Yet companies such as Dorling Kindersley produce both books and CD-ROMS. BPP Publishing's Autumn 1998 range of CD-ROMs for ACCA students will not replace the Study Texts. They will encourage self-testing and enable the user to drill down to greater levels of detail if an answer is wrong. CD-ROMs cannot easily be used on public transport and, for many leaning activities, the sequential approach of a text is better.

5.28 Section summary

- Environmental uncertainty is caused by dynamism and complexity.
- Strategic intelligence should be shared.

- Scenarios and other techniques can be used to model the future. Various models of IT use can be applied.

6 BRAINWORKS PLC UPDATE

Questions can be found in the Introduction box at the beginning of this Chapter.

6.1 *Question 1*. Is the labour market changing *fast*? No - the timescales are fairly long. However, BW's services are a derived demand, and so the environment is therefore complex.

6.2 *Question 2*. Globalisation *is* relevant for certain of BW's businesses. Willard is wrong to say that national markets are the only things that are important. In Europe, there are no legal impediments to the free movement of labour. In some industries, such as computing, people may move from country to country. Finally BW(UK) can benefit from PeoplePower's experience in the US.

6.3 *Question 3*. BW has grown on the back of social change, so it has responded successfully in the past. However, it is less clear whether it is able to cope with the supposed new labour market structure. And certainly, given the complaint read out at the meeting, some of its professional specialists have yet to come to terms with elementary cultural changes in the labour market.

Chapter roundup

- The **organisation's environment** is a source of **uncertainty**, depending on how **complex** or **dynamic** it is. General factors (PEST) affect all organisations.
- The **physical** environment is important for logistical reasons, as a source of resources, and because of increasing regulation.
- The **economic** environment affects firms at national and international level, both in the *general* level of economic activity and in particular variables (eg exchange rates).
- The **law** impinges on organisations, defining what they can or cannot do. **Political change** is a source of environmental uncertainty.
- The **social and cultural** environment features long-term social trends and people's beliefs and attitudes (eg concern with ecological issues).
- The **competitive environment** is structured by five forces: **barriers to entry; substitute products**; the bargaining power of **customers**; the bargaining power of **suppliers**; **competitive rivalry**.
- The international business environment has been in a state of tension between pressures for **free trade** and protectionism. Free trade is winning, but globalisation brings its own problems.
- A result of free trade is that domestic **markets are less protected** than previously. Protected home markets are no longer secure, but there are **new opportunities** in foreign markets.
- Porter argues that the national origin of a company can be a factor in its competitive advantage. A country's advantage in an industry is gained from the way it manages the **'diamond'** ie the relationship between **factor endowments** (resources, human skills etc), **competition** in the home market, the **demand in the home market** and **related and supporting industries**.
- Some argue that there is now a single **global market**. This is true of some goods and services (eg aircraft engines) but less so of others. **Global corporations** are supposed to act independently of national considerations. Trade liberalisation and reduced technology costs might favour small businesses in the global market place.
- There are many sources of environmental information. Analysing this information, much of which is not quantitative, is no easy task especially if it is not shared. **Scenarios** are models of the future. They can be developed for the world as a whole or for particular industries in it.

Quick quiz

1 What is the significance of the law? (see para 1.4)

2 How would you assess political risk? (1.11)

3 What are the economic influences on an organisation? (1.13)

4 Identify two social factors in strategic planning (1.17, 1.19)

5 What is the possible importance of technological change? (1.28)

6 In what ways will issues related to ecology affect an organisation's business practices? (1.31)

7 What are the five competitive forces? (2.2)

8 List some barriers to entry. (2.4)

9 How does IT affect barriers to entry? (2.11)

10 List some of the trends in the international business environment. (3.1)

11 What are the four factors determining a country's competitive advantage in an industry? (4.8)

12 What is a cluster? (4.21 - 4.23)

13 What factors give rise to complexity in an organisation's environment? (5.1)

14 List some sources of environmental data (5.9)

15 What are the problems in using past trends as a prediction of future behaviour? (5.11)

16 How would you go about creating an industry scenario? (5.18)

Question to try	Level	Marks	Time
6	Exam standard	25	45 mins

Notes

Chapter 6

POSITION AUDIT

Chapter topic list		Syllabus reference
1	**The position audit**	**1(c)(vii)**
2	**Resources and limiting factors**	**1(c)(vii)**
3	**Converting resources: the value chain**	**1(c)(vii)**
4	**Outputs: the product portfolio**	**1(c)(v)**
5	**Organisation structure**	**1(c)(vii)**
6	**Organisation culture**	**1(c)(vii)**
7	**Use of IT**	**6(d)(i)(ii), 6(f)**
8	**The customer base**	**1(c)(vii)**
9	**Brainworks plc update**	

Introduction

In this chapter we examine some of the key aspects of the organisation's current **position**. A **resource audit** identifies any gaps in resources and limiting factors on organisational activity. **Value chain** analysis identifies how the business adds value to the resources it obtains, and how it deploys these resources to satisfy customers. A **competence** is a skill which the organisation has which can ensure a 'fit' between the environment and the organisation's capability. The internal appraisal should identify **strengths and weaknesses**.

We then review the organisation's current outputs, its **product portfolio.**

Organisation structure and culture are also strategic issues. Structure describes how the organisation controls its work, and culture describes the 'mind-set' of managers and staff.

IT is potentially of strategic importance and **McFarlan's** grid is a useful model for assessing its current and future significance.

The purpose of all this activity is the customer, and a review of the **customer base** should identify trends and developments.

Brainworks plc

1 What would you identify as the dominant culture or cultures at BW? What problems arise from this?

2 Does BW *as a whole* have a distinctive competence?

3 What are the main limiting factors over BW's activities?

1 THE POSITION AUDIT 12/96

KEY TERM

Position audit is:

Part of the planning process which examines the current state of the entity in respect of:

(a) resources of tangible and intangible **assets** and finance;
(b) products, brands and markets;
(c) operating systems such as production and distribution;
(d) internal organisation;
(e) current results;
(f) returns to stockholders.

Exam focus point

The December 1996 50 mark case study dealt mainly with the position audit. You had to analyse past developments in the firm's strategic and financial position and assess why management had failed to respond.

2 RESOURCES AND LIMITING FACTORS

2.1 A **resource audit** is a review of the organisation's:

Resource	Example
Material inputs	Source. Suppliers. Waste. New materials. Cost. Availability. Future provision
Human resources	Number. Skills. Wage costs. Proportion of total costs. Efficiency. Labour turnover. Industrial relations
Management	Size. Skills. Loyalty. Career progression. Structure.
Fixed assets	Age. Condition. Utilisation rate. Value. Replacement. Technologically up-to-date? Cost.
Working capital	Credit and turnover periods. Cash surpluses/ deficits.
Finance	Short-term and long term. Gearing levels.
Intangible assets	Patents. Goodwill. Brands.
Organisation	Culture and structure.
Knowledge	Ability to generate and disseminate ideas. Innovation.

2.2 **Resources are of no value unless they are organised into systems,** and so a resource audit should go on to consider how well or how badly resources have been utilised, and whether the organisation's systems are effective and efficient.

Limiting factors

2.3 Every organisation operates under resource **constraints**.

KEY TERM

A limiting factor or **key factor** is 'a factor which at any time or over a period may limit the activity of an entity, often one where there is shortage or difficulty of supply.'

Examples

- A shortage of production capacity
- A limited number of key personnel, such as salespeople with technical knowledge
- A restricted distribution network
- Too few managers with knowledge about finance, or overseas markets
- Inadequate research design resources to develop new products or services
- A poor system of strategic intelligence
- Lack of money
- A lack of staff who are adequately trained

2.4 Once the limiting factor has been identified, the planners should:

- In the short term, make best use of the resources available.
- Try to reduce the limitation in the long term.

Resource use

2.5 Resource use is concerned with the efficiency with which resources are used, and the effectiveness of their use in achieving the planning objectives of the business. The two key words here are efficiency and effectiveness.

KEY TERMS

(a) **Efficiency** as 'how well the resources have been utilised irrespective of the purpose for which they have been employed'.

(b) **Effectiveness** as: 'whether the resources have been deployed in the best possible way'.

Case example

A key resource is 'capital'. British and US firms have been accused of not making enough capital investment, in comparison with businesses in the Tiger economies. But investment has to be productive: much of the late 1980s investment boom in Japan has resulted in massive over-capacity. Other investment capital has been wasted in speculative property development.

American firms score highly on *capital productivity*. In other words, they get the best return from the capital invested.

Distinctive competences

2.6 To recap from Chapter 1, a strategic approach involves identifying a firm's **competences**. 'Members of organisations develop judgements about what they think the company can do well - its core competence.' These competences may derive from:

(a) **Experience** in making and marketing a product or service
(b) The talents and potential of individuals in the organisation
(c) The **quality of co-ordination.**

2.7 The **distinctive competence** of an organisation is what it does well, or better, than its rivals. Andrews says that, for a relatively undifferentiated product like cement, the ability of a maker to 'run a truck fleet more effectively' than its competitors will give it competitive strengths (if, for example, it can satisfy orders quickly).

Case examples

(a) A **technological core competence**. Sony had a core competence of miniaturisation, which enabled it to develop personal stereos. Canon had a core competence based around optics and miniaturisation: it manufactures 84% of laser printer engines.

(b) A **core competence is also possible in services**. For example, GPS in France was the first French company to offer one-hour photograph development. It now offers a one-hour spectacle service. The core competence is in 'one hour' processing, whether it be of a film or a lens prescription.

2.8 (a) Some competences are necessary to stay in business at all. For a restaurant, catering is a core competence; for a manufacturing firm it is not.

(b) A distinctive competence is something which *competitors* find hard to copy, for whatever reasons. This is what makes it distinctive. The competence might be:

(i) Complex technically.

(ii) Hard to copy, if involves complex interrelationships between various business functions *within* the organisation.

(iii) Hard to define, if it results experience, corporate culture etc.

(c) As with all management jargon, some business people use the term to describe almost everything the organisation does.

2.9 The strategic purpose of the distinctive competence is that the organisation deploys it to secure a 'fit' with the environment.

Comparisons

2.10 The resource audit can be combined with a **comparative analysis** of other firms.

(a) Anticipated and past performance can be compared.

(b) A company's performance in relation to its competitors and industry **norms** can be assessed.

(c) **Industry best practice** can be used as a yardstick.

(i) **Competitor profiles:** analysis of the performance of key competitors.

(ii) **Benchmarking.** Benchmarks are goals of performance which an organisation wishes to achieve in particular value activities. A benchmark for quality would be so many reject parts per million. This is to identify best practice and so achieve it. (Benchmarking is covered in depth in Chapter 17.)

Exam focus point

Competences featured in December 1995, in connection with critical success factors (see Chapter 9).

2.11 Section summary

- A resource audit covers the organisation's material, financial, human and intangible resources.
- Limiting factors are constraints over what the organisation can do.
- A distinctive competence is the deployment of resources in a unique way.

3 CONVERTING RESOURCES: THE VALUE CHAIN

3.1 The **value chain** model of corporate activities, developed by Michael Porter, offers a bird's eye view of the firm and what it does. Competitive advantage, says Porter, arises out of the way in which firms organise and perform **activities**. (In other words, this describes *how* an organisation uses its inputs and transforms them into the outputs that customers to pay for.)

Activities

KEY TERM

Activities are the means by which a firm creates value in its products. (They are sometimes referred to as **value activities**.)

3.2 Activities incur costs, and, in combination with other activities, provide a product or service which earns revenue. 'Firms create value for their buyers by performing these activities.'

3.3 EXAMPLE

Let us explain this point by using the example of a **restaurant**. A restaurant's activities can be divided into buying food, cooking it, and serving it (to customers). There is no reason, in theory, why the customers should not do all these things themselves, at home. The customer however, is not only prepared to **pay for someone else** to do all this but also **pays more than the cost of** the resources (food, wages etc). The ultimate value a firm creates is measured by the amount customers are willing to pay for its products or services above the cost of carrying out value activities. A firm is profitable if the realised value to customers exceeds the collective cost of performing the activities.

(a) Customers **'purchase' value**, which they measure by comparing a firm's products and services with similar offerings by competitors.

(b) The business **'creates' value** by carrying out its activities either more efficiently than other businesses, or combine them in such a way as to provide a unique product or service.

Question 1

Outline different ways in which the restaurant can 'create' value.

Answer

Here are some ideas.

(a) It can become more efficient, by automating the production of food, as in a fast food chain.

(b) The chef can develop commercial relationships with growers, so he or she can obtain the best quality fresh produce.

(c) The chef can specialise in a particular type of cuisine (eg Nepalese, Korean).

(d) The restaurant can be sumptuously decorated for those customers who value 'atmosphere' and a sense of occasion, in addition to a restaurant's purely gastronomic pleasures.

(e) The restaurant can serve a particular type of customer (eg celebrities).

Each of these options is a way of organising the activities of buying, cooking and serving food in a way that customers or chosen customers will value.

3.4 Porter (in *Competitive Advantage*) grouped the various activities of an organisation into a **value chain**. Here is a diagram.

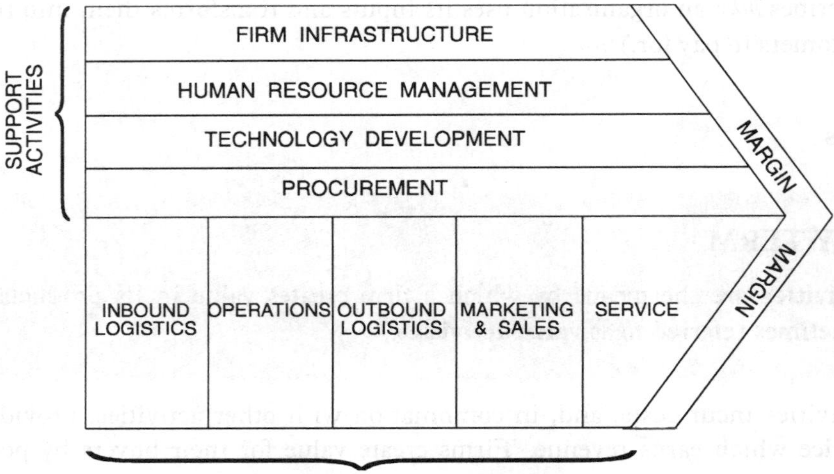

The **margin** is the excess the customer is prepared to **pay** over the **cost** to the firm of obtaining resource inputs and providing value activities.

Activity

3.5 **Primary activities** are directly related to production, sales, marketing, delivery and service.

	Comment
Inbound logistics	Receiving, handling and storing inputs to the production system (ie warehousing, transport, stock control etc).
Operations	Convert resource inputs into a final product. Resource inputs are not only materials. 'People' are a 'resource' especially in service industries.
Outbound logistics	Storing the product and its distribution to customers: packaging, warehousing, testing etc.
Marketing and sales	Informing customers about the product, persuading them to buy it, and enabling them to do so: advertising, promotion etc.
After sales service	Installing products, repairing them, upgrading them, providing spare parts and so forth.

3.6 **Support activities** provide purchased inputs, human resources, technology and infrastructural functions to support the primary activities.

Activity	Comment
Procurement	Acquire the resource inputs to the primary activities (eg purchase of materials, subcomponents equipment).
Technology development	Product design, improving processes and/or resource utilisation.
Human resource management	Recruiting, training, developing and rewarding people.
Management planning	Planning, finance, quality control: Porter believes they are crucially important to an organisation's strategic capability in all primary activities.

3.7 **Linkages** connect the activities of the value chain.

(a) **Activities in the value chain affect one another**. For example, more costly product design or better quality production, might reduce the need for after-sales service.

(b) **Linkages require co-ordination**. For example, Just In Time requires smooth functioning of operations, outbound logistics and service activities such as installation.

Value system

3.8 A company's value chain is not bounded by a company's borders. Activities that add value do not stop at the organisation's **boundaries**. For example, when a restaurant serves a meal, the quality of the ingredients - although they are chosen by the cook - is determined by the grower. The grower has added value, and the grower's success in growing produce of good quality is as important to the customer's ultimate satisfaction as the skills of the chef. A firm's value chain is connected to what Porter calls a **value system**.

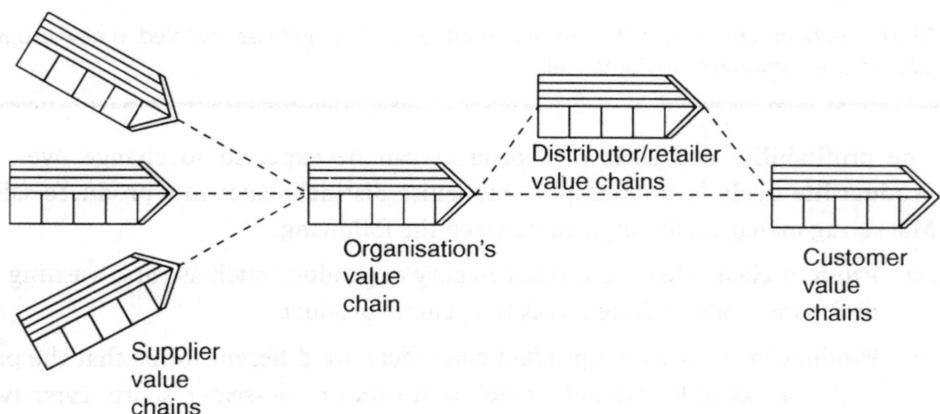

3.9 **Using the value chain.** A firm can secure competitive advantage by:

- Inventing new or better ways to do activities
- Combining activities in new or better ways
- Managing the linkages in its own value chain
- Managing the linkages in the value system

Question 2

Sana Sounds is a small record company. Representatives from Sana Sounds scour music clubs for new bands to promote. Once a band has signed a contract (with Sana Sounds) it makes a recording. The recording process is subcontracted to one of a number of recording studio firms which Sana Sounds uses regularly. (At the moment Sana Sounds is not large enough to invest in its own equipment and studios.) Sana Sounds also subcontracts the production of records and CDs to a number of manufacturing companies. Sana Sounds then distributes the disks to selected stores, and engages in any promotional activities required.

What would you say were the activities in Sana Sounds' *value chain?*

Answer

Sana Sounds is involved in the record industry from start to finish. Although recording and CD manufacture are contracted out to external suppliers, this makes no difference to the fact that these activities are part of Sana Sounds' own value chain. Sana Sounds earns its money by managing the whole set of activities. If the company grows then perhaps it will acquire its own recording studios. A *value chain of activities* is not the same as an *organisation's business functions*.

3.10 Section summary

- The value chain models how activities can be deployed to add value for the customer.
- Value chains are part of a value system.
- Firms can benefit by performing activities in a unique way and/or exploiting linkages.

4 OUTPUTS: THE PRODUCT PORTFOLIO

The product life cycle

4.1 Many firms make a number of different products or services. Each product or service has its own financial, marketing and risk characteristics. The combination of products or services influences the attractiveness and profitability of the firm.

Case example

Glaxo has for many years produced *Zantac* an anti-ulcer drug. Patents expire after a defined period.

Glaxo has been anticipating this development for a while and has invested in new drugs to provide income when returns from Zantac fall.

4.2 The profitability and sales of a product can be expected to change over time. The **product life cycle** is an attempt to recognise distinct stages in a product's sales history. Marketing managers distinguish between the following.

(a) **Product class:** this is a broad category of product, such as cars, washing machines, newspapers, also referred to as the generic product.

(b) **Product form:** within a product class there are different forms that the product can take, for example five-door hatchback cars or two-seater sports cars; twin tub or front loading automatic washing machines; national daily newspapers or weekly local papers etc.

(c) **Brand.** The particular type of the product form (for example Ford Escort, Vauxhall Astra; Financial Times, Daily Mail, Sun etc). This is sometimes referred to as *brand,* but we must be careful how we use this word.

4.3 The product life cycle applies in differing degrees to each of the three cases. A product-class (eg cars) may have a long maturity stage, and a particular make or brand *might* have an erratic life cycle (eg Rolls Royce) or not. Product forms however tend to conform to the 'classic' life cycle pattern, commonly described by a curve as follows.

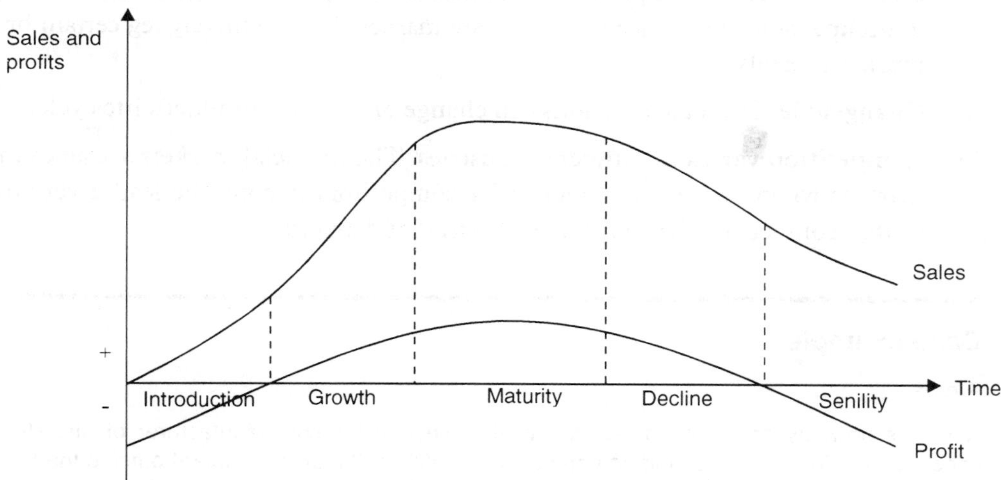

4.4 **Introduction**

- A new product takes time to find acceptance by would-be purchasers and there is a slow growth in sales. Unit costs are high because of low output and expensive sales promotion.
- There may be early teething troubles with production technology.
- The product for the time being is a loss-maker.

4.5 **Growth**

- If the new product gains market acceptance, sales will eventually rise more sharply and the product will start to make profits.
- Competitors are attracted. As sales and production rise, unit costs fall.

4.6 **Maturity.** The rate of sales growth slows down and the product reaches a period of maturity which is probably the longest period of a successful product's life. Most products on the market will be at the mature stage of their life. Profits are good.

4.7 **Decline**. Some products reach a stage of decline which may be slow or fast. Eventually, sales will begin to decline so that there is over-capacity of production in the industry. Severe competition occurs, profits fall and some producers leave the market. The remaining producers seek means of prolonging the product life by modifying it and searching for new market segments. Many producers are reluctant to leave the market, although some inevitably do because of falling profits.

The relevance of the product life cycle to strategic planning

4.8 In reviewing outputs, planners should assess, if possible:

(a) The **stage of its life cycle** that any product has reached.

(b) The **product's remaining life**, ie how much longer the product will be able to contribute significantly to profits.

(c) How **urgent is the need to innovate**, to develop new and improved products in time?

Difficulties of the product life cycle concept

4.9 (a) **Recognition**. How can managers recognise where a product stands in its life cycle?

(b) **Not always true.** The traditional S-shaped curve of a product life cycle does not always occur in practice. Some products have no maturity phase, and go straight from growth to decline. Some never decline if they are marketed competitively (eg certain brands of breakfast cereals).

(c) **Changeable**. Strategic decisions can change or extend a product's life cycle.

(d) **Competition varies** in different industries. The financial markets are an example of markets where there is a tendency for competitors to copy the leader very quickly, so that competition has built up well *ahead* of demand.

Case example

Airbus

Airbus is now, by some measures, the world's second largest manufacturer of aircraft - it is a consortium of four partners, and commands about 30% of the airliner market outside the EU. Airbus has launched a range of aircraft which compete with Boeing in every sector of the market, save the jumbo 747.

Airbus is expected to be very profitable. 'It has a relatively modern range of aircraft in an industry with product life cycles of 25 years or more.'

Airbus is seeking to compete with the Boeing 747 perhaps by finding new partners in Asia to build a new 'super-jumbo'. The 'carrot' Airbus offers to potential partners is that it will be able to introduce new technology.

Portfolio planning: the Boston Matrix

4.10 **Portfolio planning** analyses the current position of an organisation's products in their markets, and the state of growth or decline in each of those markets. Several matrices have been developed over the years to analyse market share, market growth and market position.

KEY TERM

Market share: 'One entity's sale of a product or service in a specified market expressed as a percentage of total sales by all entities offering that product or service.'

Market share, market growth and cash generation: the Boston classification

4.11 The **Boston Consulting Group** (BCG) developed a matrix, based on empirical research, which classifies a company's products in terms of potential cash generation and cash expenditure requirements.

		Market share	
		High	*Low*
Market growth	*High*	Stars	Question marks
	Low	Cash cows	Dogs

4.12 This growth/share matrix for the classification of products into cash cows, cash dogs, rising stars and question marks is known as the **Boston classification** (or the **Boston Matrix**).

(a) **Stars** are products with a high share of a high growth market. In the short term, these require capital expenditure in excess of the cash they generate, in order to maintain their market position, but promise high returns in the future.

(b) In due course, stars will become **cash cows**, with a high share of a low-growth market. Cash cows need very little capital expenditure and generate high levels of cash income. Cash cows generate high cash returns, which can be used to finance the stars.

(c) **Question marks** are products in a high-growth market, but where they have a low market share. Do the products justify considerable capital expenditure in the hope of increasing their market share, or should they be allowed to 'die' quietly as they are squeezed out of the expanding market by rival products? Because considerable expenditure would be needed to turn a question mark into a star by building up market share, question marks will usually be poor cash generators and show a negative cash flow.

(d) **Dogs** are products with a low share of a low growth market. They may be ex-cash cows that have now fallen on hard times. Dogs should be allowed to die, or should be killed off. Although they will show only a modest net cash outflow, or even a modest net cash inflow, they are 'cash traps' which tie up funds and provide a poor return on investment, and not enough to achieve the organisation's target rate of return.

There are also **infants** (ie products in an early stage of development), **warhorses** (ie products that have been cash cows in the past, and are still making good sales and earning good profits even now) and even **cash dogs**, which are dogs still generating cash.

Question 1

The marketing manager of Juicy Drinks Ltd has invited you in for a chat. Juicy Drinks Ltd provides fruit juices to a number of supermarket chains, which sell them under their own label. 'We've got a large number of products, of course. Our freshly squeezed orange juice is doing fine - it sells in huge quantities. Although margins are low, we have sufficient economies of scale to do very nicely in this market. We've got advanced production and bottling equipment and long term contracts with some major growers. No problems there. We also sell freshly squeezed pomegranate juice: customers loved it in the tests, but producing the stuff at the right price is a major hassle: all the seeds get in the way. We hope it will be a winner, once we get the production right and start converting customers to it. After all the market for exotic fruit juices generally is expanding fast.'

What sort of products, according to the Boston classification, are described here?

Answer

(a) Orange juice is a cash cow

(b) Pomegranate juice is a question mark, which the company wants to turn into a star.

Case example

Unilever and Nestlé

Unilever and Nestlé, two FMCG (fast moving consumer goods) giants, reappraised their strategies in 1996.

'Persuading Chinese farmers to buy detergents and residents of Arctic Russia to spend money on instant coffee is no mean feat for Unilever and Nestlé, two of the world's largest consumer goods producers. But reviving turnover and profits in the mature markets of north-west Europe and North America is proving just as tough. Satiated consumers ignore the welter of marketing messages. Dubious about brands, they seek value for money in retailers' own-label products.

(*Financial Times*, September 11, 1996)

Both firms have introduced new management structures.

- Leaner and more autonomous management.
- Innovation in products and marketing.

Both firms own a large number of different businesses. Both firms have access to **cash cows**. (Nestlé is blessed with a prodigious cash generator - instant coffee. For Unilever, margarine plays a similar but less lucrative role.) The firms are taking different approaches to dealing with diversity.

Unilever intends to focus on core product categories. Unilever says it know what it wanted to do but did not always succeed. **'Star'** categories such as ice cream and cosmetics were identified, but sometimes they were denied sufficient financial and human resources. 'The strategy was there but the execution wasn't,' says Mr Tabaksblat.

Unilever has introduced a new analytical tool to assess its businesses. Unilever will reduce its huge portfolio by 'harvesting' some products (taking profits but reinvesting little), and selling or closing others. The group has already disposed of its processed meats and mass-market cosmetics businesses in the past 18 months.

With fewer businesses, Unilever can pour more financial, technical and human resources into those that remain. It can also concentrate its efforts on emerging markets. Two years ago Unilever said it planned to have 30% of its turnover from emerging markets by 2000. This goal has now been achieved.

The focus on new markets has had a profound effect on *research and development*. In the past, a handful of big development centres created products for mature markets which were then passed on to emerging markets. Over the past few years, however, Unilever has set up a network of more than 50 centres to meet regional needs. The Latin American region, for example, is now producing 'stunning levels of innovation', Mr FitzGerald says. Some new products are also flowing to mature markets. Within six months of Unilever Thailand having a big hit with Organics shampoos, the range was in production in Europe.

Nestlé's approach is slightly different, but it has already restructured its activities. Nestlé believes that all it needs to do is to get more products into more markets. The firm aims to double turnover every ten years - some two thirds of this will be *organic growth*, 'reversing the ratio off the late 1980's'. Unlike Unilever, it will dispose of fewer business and will 'hold onto a long tail of minor products ... if they are profitable.' Nestlé has spent aggressively to become the world's largest bottler of mineral water.

Exam focus point

It is possible to apply the portfolio approach to a firm in several different businesses, as indeed was the case in December 1997. The firm in the case study operated in a low-tech industry but was considering entering a high-tech business. In a diversified business, each business has different cash characteristics in a similar way to products in a portfolio – but we discuss diversification as a strategy in Chapter 7.

4.13 Section summary

- Most organisations offer several products/services. These have different financial and marketing needs.
- Existing products generate cash for investment in newer products, which will in turn generate cash in future.

5 ORGANISATION STRUCTURE

5.1 Organisation structure determines how work is allocated, directed and controlled, in order to achieve the goals of the organisation.

Co-ordinating tasks

5.2 Mintzberg suggests **five methods of co-ordination.**

(a) **Mutual adjustment.** 'Work rests in the hands of the doers' who co-ordinate work by informal communication. This is used for the **most simple** work and the **most complicated**: simple because it is an obvious mechanism for small groups (eg two canoeists); complex, as in some tasks it is impossible to plan ahead. For example, thousands of specialists may not know what needs to be done on a research project if the outcome is uncertain. Because they cannot predict in advance what will be discovered, they will adjust their activities in the light of new information.

(b) **Direct supervision.** One person is responsible for co-ordinating the work of others. This person issues instructions and monitors performance.

(c) **Standardisation of work processes.** The contents of work are 'specified or programmed' (eg standard procedures for carrying out an audit).

(d) **Standardisation of outputs.** Outputs in this instance can mean a set level of profits (or level of performance) but the work process itself is not designed or programmed.

(e) **Standardisation by skills and knowledge.** The kind of knowledge and training required to perform the work is specified. For example, doctors are trained in the necessary skills before being let loose on patients.

5.3 The relative **complexity of the work affects the chosen method of co-ordination.**

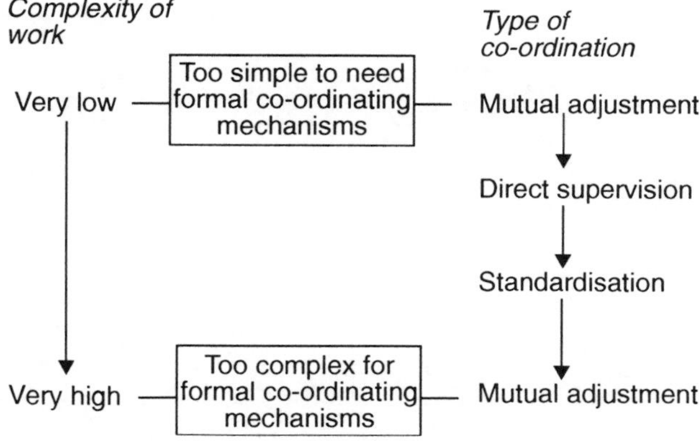

Components of organisation structure and systems: Mintzberg's analysis

5.4 The **organisation structure** embodies mechanisms for co-ordinating work.

5.5 An organisation is a 'social arrangement for the controlled performance of collective goals' (Buchanan and Huczynski). Mintzberg believes that any organisation is based on the following principles.

- **Job specialisation** (the number of tasks in a given job, the division of labour).
- **Behaviour formalisation** (in other words, the standardisation of work processes).
- **Training** (to enforce work standardisation).
- **Indoctrination** of employees (in the organisation's culture).
- Unit **grouping** (eg organisation by function, geographical area, or product).
- Unit **size** (eg span of control).
- **Planning and control systems.**
- **Liaison** and **communication** devices (networks, committees, matrix structures).

5.6 These principles can be embodied in an organisation in a number of ways. Mintzberg identifies five component parts.

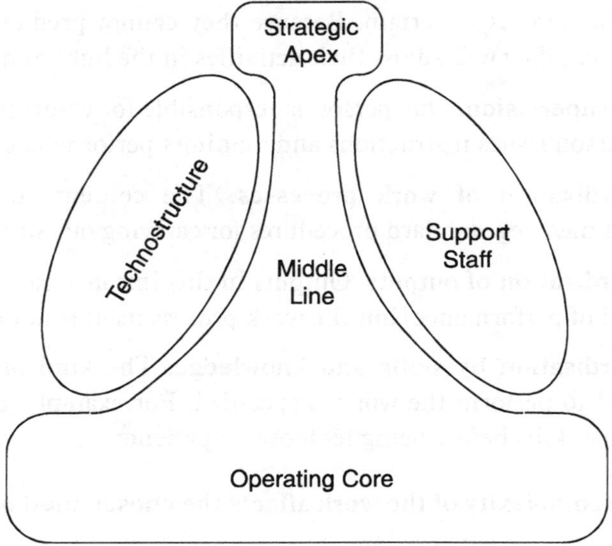

Component	Comment
Operating core	People directly involved in production (ie in securing inputs and processing them into outputs and distributing those outputs), perhaps the **primary activities** of the value chain.
Strategic apex	Owner, board of directors. Ensures that the organisation follows its mission and serves the needs of its owners. Its job is supervision, control, boundary management and strategy.
Middle line	People in this area administer the work done. The chain of formal authority runs from senior managers at the apex through middle managers to front line supervisors at the operating core. It converts the wishes of the strategic apex into the work of the operating core.
Technostructure	Administrators and planners **standardise work**. Work-study analysts (eg engineers) standardise work processes by analysing and determining the most efficient method of doing a job. Planners (eg quality staff, accountants) standardise outputs. Personnel analysts standardise skills by arranging for training programmes.
Support staff	Ancillary services such as public relations, legal counsel, the cafeteria do not plan or standardise production. They function independently of the operating core.

5.7 These elements are linked in five ways.

(a) **Organisation hierarchy** (see below).

(b) **Flow of regulated activity**. Inputs are processed into outputs. The activities in the value chain are controlled and linked.

(c) **Informal communications** supplement or bypass the formal communication system.

(d) **System of work constellations**. Groups of people, permanent or temporary, work on distinct tasks. For example, the members of the accounts department work together. Some constellations are temporary: for example, in producing a set of annual financial statements, people from the finance department (for the numbers), the sales department (for detailed statistics) and public relations (for presentation) need to be involved.

(e) **Ad hoc decision processes.** A decision process involves recognising a problem, diagnosing its causes, finding a solution and implementing it. For any one decision, these activities occur in a number of different places in the organisation. For example, customer care personnel might first hear of a problem with faulty goods, but the decisions as to how to prevent the problem happening again will be taken in by the production department.

Influence of components

5.8 **Coalitions** of individuals 'may occur within departments, geographical locations, different levels in the hierarchy, different age groups'. Such groups might manipulate the direction it takes.

5.9 Each component has its own **preferred co-ordination mechanism** which we will discuss in Chapter 10.

Hierarchy and span of control

5.10 **Organisation structure** can influence managers' preferences for certain strategic choices. For example, an organisation which is very decentralised, and in which units actively compete with each other, may not take well to a strategy involving co-operation. Even where a competitive element is absent, people's loyalty might be to their group, section or subsidiary as opposed to the organisation as a whole. This will determine the strategic options likely to be favoured and implemented.

5.11 Formal organisation structure offers:

- A **division of labour** and a source of authority.
- Planned **divisions of responsibility.**
- **Power centres** which control its efforts.
- **Substitution of personnel** (ie the position of Financial Controller does not disappear when the current occupant resigns).
- The ability to **combine personnel** in different ways.

5.12 The formal organisation structure:

- **Groups work** and workers into logically-related and balanced positions.
- **Defines** and **delegates responsibility.**
- Establishes **relationships** between positions.

5.13 The existing organisation structure is worth reviewing because it:

(a) Can **help or hinder the mission** and effectiveness of the organisation.

(b) Might have to be **changed**, which takes time.

(c) Shapes the **deployment of value activities** and the management of the **linkages** between them.

(d) **Channels and filters information** from markets and personnel.

(e) **Is the arena for various political manoeuvrings** by management and other interested groups (especially in the partisan mutual adjustment model).

(f) **Denotes the organisation's existing priorities** (whether deliberate or emergent strategies).

5.14 The **scalar chain** (or chain of command) describes the organisation hierarchy, from the most junior to the most senior. A long scalar chain has many levels: in other words there are many ranks between the most junior and the senior (eg trainee, technician, assistant accountant, senior accountant, assistant financial controller, financial controller etc). A short scalar chain has fewer levels.

5.15 The **span of control** (unit size) refers to the number of subordinates working for a manager in the level immediately below the manager.

5.16 A **tall organisation** has a large number of management levels and probably small spans of control.

- These are 'unfashionable' as they are held to be cumbersome and inflexible. People think they slow down communications and responsiveness to the market, and stifle initiative.
- They offer more secure **promotion paths.**

5.17 **Flat organisations** (few management levels) are becoming more popular, as they are supposed to be more flexible and responsive. Flat organisations are made possible by:

- Information technology, reducing the information processing function of middle management.
- Giving front line employees more responsibility (empowerment).

5.18 **Delayering** is the removal of management layers. Many large organisations have shed large numbers of managerial staff in this way. We will come back to this in Chapter 10.

Authority and the technostructure

5.19 **Authority is the right** to do something, whereas **power relates to the ability** to exercise authority. (Authority is normally derived from position in the hierarchy.)

- **Line authority** reflects a manager's direct authority over a subordinate.
- **Staff authority** is the right to give advice and is normally exercised by one department over another.
- **Functional authority** is staff authority exercised through procedures which managers in other departments have to follow. The personnel department sets down recruitment procedures; the finance department lays down expenditure authorisation procedures.

5.20 Often, **members of the technostructure seek to expand their area of control** and expertise for reasons not necessarily connected with the organisation's well being (eg acquiring a costly 'state of the art' computer system when this is not needed).

5.21 However, **managers in the middle line might ignore necessary controls** or ignore the productivity enhancements that the technostructure might suggest.

Power

5.22 Charles Handy (*Understanding Organisations*) identified six types of power from different sources, and we have added a seventh.

(a) **Physical** or coercive **power** (ie force) is absent from most organisations most of the time, although disciplinary procedures offer non-physical coercion.

(b) **Resource power:** is the control over resources which are **valued** by the individual or group to be influenced.

(i) Senior managers can grant promotion or pay increases to subordinates.

(ii) The relative importance of different resources changes over time. For example, the marketing department is 'powerful' if the firm's strategy rests on the development of new markets.

(c) **Position power** is associated with a particular job in the **organisation hierarchy** which gives superiors formal **authority** over subordinates. Position power has certain 'hidden' benefits.

(i) Access to information.
(ii) Contact with other 'powerful' individuals in the organisation.
(iii) The right to organise conditions of work and ways of decision-making.

(d) **Expert power** belongs to an individual because of his or her **acknowledged expertise**. Many technostructure jobs in an organisation (eg computer systems analysts) rely on expert power.

(e) **Personal power** or **charisma** is related to the individual's force of personality, ability to inspire loyalty etc.

(f) **Negative power** is the use of disruptive attitudes and behaviour to stop things from happening. The obvious example is strike action. A manager might refuse to co-operate with his/her colleagues, if an agreed policy adversely affects his/her position.

(g) **Information** is a crucial strategic resource.

(i) **Manipulation**. Withholding information or distorting it can be an important way for subordinates to influence strategy. The advent of *executive information systems*, however, might make managers less dependent on information from subordinates.

(ii) **Environmental knowledge**. Financial and marketing personnel have greater knowledge of, and control over, an organisation's relationship with the external environment. This is important when the environment is hostile.

The informal organisation

5.23 The **informal organisation** refers to work and social relationships that exist outside the formal organisation structure.

- Certain individuals might have a **significant influence** outside of their formal authority (eg if one of the directors gets on well with the MD).
- An inefficient formal organisation structure might force employees to rely on the informal organisation to get work done.

5.24 The informal organisation depends on individual personalities and, unlike the formal organisation structure, is affected when someone leaves.

5.25 **Significance of organisation structure**. Organisation structure influences strategy formation because:

- **Different 'coalitions'** in the organisation have their own agendas to promote and sources of power.
- Structure and **culture are closely related** and culture influences how managers interpret the world.
- **Implementing a strategy sometimes requires a change to the structure** (see Chapter 10.)

5.26 Section summary

- Organisation structure directs communication and deploys resources in order to co-ordinate work.
- Each component (apex, technostructure, operating core, middle line, support staff) prefers to co-ordinate work in a different way.
- Organisation hierarchy outlines formal authority, but there are other sources of power within the organisation which influence what it can do.

6 ORGANISATION CULTURE

6.1 We encountered culture in Chapter 5: it is the 'sum total of the beliefs, knowledge, attitudes of mind and customs to which people are exposed in their social conditioning'.

6.2 An organisation culture may be shared by people in an organisation because they work for it. They assume the ways of behaving and interpreting the world that are accepted in the organisation.

6.3 **Components of organisation culture**

Component	Comment
Practices	Rituals and ceremonies, whether formal or informal (Christmas party, Awards)
Relationship between superiors/ subordinates	Are bosses approachable?
Communications	Stories (eg about the early days of the company), symbols
Physical artefacts	Office layout and décor, which govern communications, formality
Common language	Employees at EuroDisney are the 'cast', customers are 'guests'
Values	'Quality is more important than price.' 'We will always be ethical'.
'The recipe'	Managers have certain basic assumptions as to how work should be done and how strategic threats should be countered.

Case example

Dress code

To get an idea of how a culture operates, we can consider a company's dress code, that is the type of clothes deemed appropriate for office or business use.

(a) Microsoft - apparently men are not expected to wear suits, and people can dress more or less as they please. But Mircrosoft is not a 'relaxed' place to work.

(b) One of the most elaborate dress codes, and the problems it caused was BT's (as described by John Kay, *Financial Times*, 12 January 1996).

   (i) After privatisation, senior employees were told to adopt 'suitable business dress'. People complained that they did not know what this meant, so the firm promulgated a *dress code.* Senior male employees were to wear smart suits, collared shirts and ties.

   (ii) Somebody came in wearing a red suit: 'undeniably smart, but it was the smartness of a night club rather than a boardroom'. The dress code was amended to specify *colour* (not red) and *brightness* (dark blues: OK; bright blues: not OK).

   (iii) Ties were a more intractable problem, given the enormous variety. 'A clearance procedure seemed the best answer. Anyone who bought a new tie could submit it to the dress code department which had 42 days to rule on whether or not it was suitable business dress' ... but of course this depended on 'the suit and the shirt that went with it'.

   (iv) This raised the issue of an appeal mechanism, but letting the dress code department be 'judge and jury in implementing regulations it had devised ... violated natural justice'.

   (v) Therefore a small group of senior directors and an independent fashion adviser 'would hear complaints from employees who felt their ties had been unreasonably rejected'.

   (vi) To cope with the probe of changing fashion, 'a well-known fashion designer agreed to chair a standing working party to advise the company on fashion trends'.

(vii) 'By this time, the dress code extended to 50 pages, largely impenetrable ... Knowledge of its contents was confined to the dress department which by this time consisted of 20 people, mostly lawyers, the union representative who negotiated over it, and a few cranks ...'

New management felt they had two options. Supply a uniform or reissue the instruction to wear business dress. They did the latter. If anybody was in doubt, they could ask the dress regulator.

6.4 **Characteristics of culture**

Characteristic	Comment
Exclusive	Organisation culture reinforces the organisation's sense of identity, but can suppress important information inconsistent with the culture.
Group	A culture is shared: it sets criteria by which people are judged.
Coherent	The assumptions of a culture should reinforce each other.
Consistent over time	A culture gives its participants a sense of continuity.
Consequences	The group's or the individual's actions follow on from the culture.
Supportive	Some activities are justified and supported if they fit in with the culture.
Pattern	The way in which a member of staff treats a customer might reflect the way a member of staff is treated by his or her supervisor.
Offer solutions to dilemmas	Culture helps people decide how to act on particular problems (eg cost vs quality).
Cultures can learn	Cultures can change over time.

6.5 To sum up:

KEY TERM

Culture: 'Culture comes from within people and it is put together by them to reward the capacities they have in common. Culture gives continuity and identity to the group. It balances contrasting contributions and operates as a self-steering system which learns from feedback. It works as a pattern of information and can greatly facilitate the exchange of understanding. The values within a culture are more or less harmonious.' (Charles Hampden-Turner)

6.6 **Influences on culture**

(a) **The organisation's founder.** A strong set of values and assumptions is set up by the organisation's founder, and even after he or she has retired, these values have their own momentum.

(b) **The organisation's history.**

(i) The way an organisation works reflects the era when it was founded. Farming, for example, sometimes has a craft element to it.

(ii) The effect of history is seen in by stories, rituals and symbolic behaviour. They legitimise how people behave and suggest priorities for attention.

(c) **Recruitment**. An organisation with a strong culture recruits employees and managers who naturally conform to it. In other words the *selection process* maintains the culture or creates the culture by selecting people 'who fit in'.

(d) **Leadership and management style**. Managers lead by example whether they like it or not.

(e) **Structure and systems** have consequences for culture - see below.

(f) **Mission:** are people focused on the mission or not.

(g) **Superior/subordinate relationships:** formal or information; degree of delegation.

(h) **Relationships between staff:** competitive or collaborative - this is clearly influenced by whether teams or individuals are rewarded.

Case example

A few years ago, British Airways opened a new aircraft maintenance hangar in Bristol, on the principles of Japanese-style management (as reported by the *Financial Times*). 'BMAC was careful in who it chose to work at the plant. It was wary of mechanics accustomed to sloppy work in local car repair garages and wanted people who already had a flexible approach to their work. Many of the staff recruited had never worked on aircraft before.

The management ideas include flexible working, identical uniforms for workers and a single canteen etc.

Culture and structure

6.7 The relationship between an organisation's culture and its structure and systems is very close, in that culture reinforces patterns of individual behaviour which are also controlled by the structure.

6.8 Handy notes four types of culture, each named after a Greek god. No one culture is better than another: it depends on circumstances.

- **Zeus (power culture).** This is based on **personalities**, particularly the dynamic entrepreneur at the centre. Little formalisation, few rules.
- **Apollo (role culture, bureaucracy).** People do what is expected of **their position**, no more. Work is proceduralised and routine. High formalisation, with a presumption of logic and rationality, are features of bureaucracy. (The case example of BT's dress code suggests a culture of Apollo at the time.)
- **Athena (task culture).** There are few dominant leaders, and work is best characterised by a succession of projects. **Team identity** and **individual creativity** are important. Performance is judged by results: experience and talent, not length of service, are rewarded.
- **Dionysus (existential culture).** The organisation exists to support the individuals within it, who promote their careers. Barristers' chambers are an example. Also some agencies (eg modelling, literary agencies) might share features of this culture, as they are promoting 'star performers'.

6.9 Handy suggests that most organisations contain a mixture of at least two of these types.

- **Different people are suited to different cultures.**

- **Different cultures are suited to different jobs:** not all work is most efficiently managed on a project basis, as in a task culture.

6.10 The descriptions above interrelate four different strands and there is a 'best fit' between them:

(a) The individual
(b) The type of the work the organisation does
(c) The culture of the organisation
(d) The environment

Case example

Handy cites a pharmaceutical company which at one time had subcontracted all its manufacturing until turnover and cost considerations justified a factory of its own. The company hired nine talented individuals to design and run the factory. Result:

(a) The *design team* ran on a task culture, with a democratic/consultative leadership style, using project teams for certain problems. This was successful while the factory was being built.

(b) After its opening, the factory, staffed by 400, was run on similar lines. There were numerous problems. Every problem was treated as a project, and the workforce resented being asked to help sort out 'management' problems. In the end, the factory was run in a slightly more autocratic way. Handy states that this is a classic case of an *Athenian* culture to create a factory being superseded by an *Apollonian* culture to run it. Different cultures suit different businesses.

6.11 Corporate culture is almost the air people breathe at work. Its assumptions and prejudices are barely noticed, and it can vitally affect the effectiveness of the organisation.

Question 4

Ascribe each of the following statements to one of Handy's four corporate cultures.

People are controlled and influenced by:

(a) the personal exercise of rewards, punishments or charisma;

(b) the impersonal exercise of economic and political power to enforce procedures and standards of performance;

(c) communication and discussion of task requirements leading to appropriate action, motivated by personal commitment, to achieve the goal;

(d) intrinsic interest and enjoyment in the activities to be done, and/or concern and caring for the needs of the other people involved.

Answer

(a) Zeus
(b) Apollo
(c) Athena
(d) Dionysus

6.12 Corporate culture is particularly important for service businesses. In the past 20 years, many organisations have actively sought to change their cultures.

Culture and strategy

6.13 Because culture is a collection of shared beliefs and practices, it is thus an important filter of information and an interpreter of it, as suggested in the diagrams below. Culture might be embedded in the assumptions of the strategic planners.

(a) **Ignoring culture**

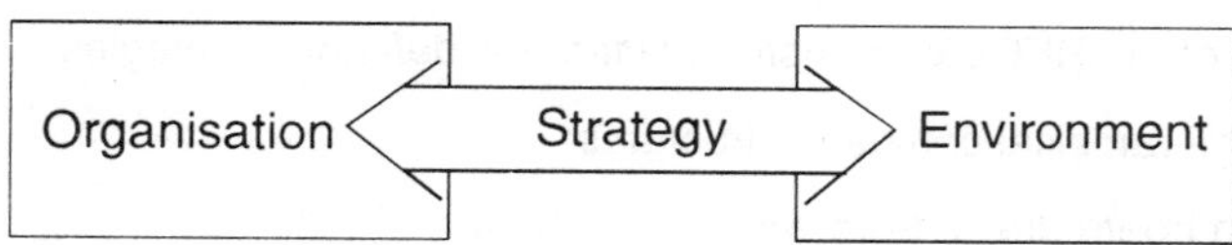

(b) **Including culture**

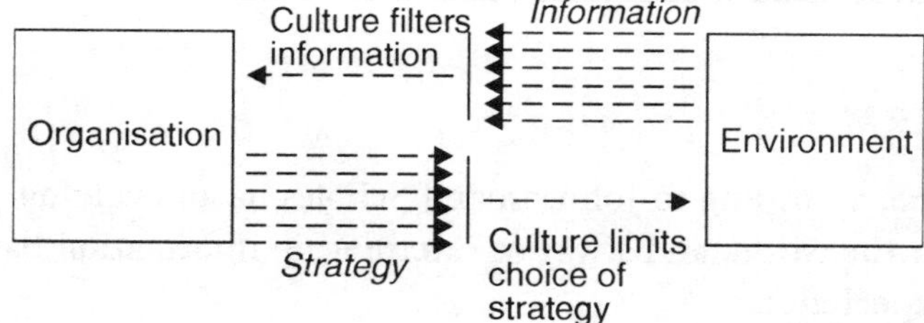

Culture filters and reconfigures environmental information. At the same time culture **filters out a number of strategic choices**. For example, a firm might have a cultural predisposition against embarking on risky ventures. Another culture might have an ingrained 'Buy British' approach. Finally, if culture is embodied in **behaviour**, existing behaviour may make a strategy incompatible with the culture and so impossible to implement.

6.14 Miles and Snow analyse three strategic cultures, and a fourth 'non-strategic' culture.

(a) **Defenders**. Firms with this culture like low risks, secure markets, and tried and trusted solutions. These companies have cultures whose stories and rituals reflect historical continuity and consensus. Decision-taking is relatively formalised. (There is a stress on 'doing things right' ie efficiency.) Personnel are drawn from within the industry.

(b) **Prospectors** are organisations where the dominant beliefs are more to do with results (doing the right things ie effectiveness). They seek to expand and to move into new areas.

(c) **Analysers** try to balance risk and profits. They use a core of stable products and markets as a source of earnings like prospectors, but move into innovative areas that prospectors have opened up. Analysers follow change, but do not initiate it.

(d) **Reactors**, unlike the three above, do not have viable strategies. Arguably, they do not have a strategy, either deliberate or emergent, at all, unless it is simply to carry on living from hand to mouth, muddling through.

Case example

Electricity

Miles and Snow's analysis was applied to the responses by the regional electricity companies (RECs) to takeover bids outlined in autumn 1995. (The RECs are responsible for supply and distribution of electricity.) As at October 1995, seven of the 12 RECs in England and Wales had received takeover bids.

At privatisation they 'shared a common heritage and hence ... greater similarities than would be found in more well-established private sector market places'.

(a) Eastern Group 'embraced' the possibility of an alliance with Hanson, even though it was the biggest REC. Eastern exhibits the characteristics of a 'prospector'. Its chief executive is 'non-REC' 'with a North American corporate pedigree and a greater interest in activities outside the traditional REC field'.

(b) Norweb and Midlands were 'cautious prospectors' which allow significant degrees of decentralisation, and a 'willingness to bring in executives with experience external to the industry'. They countenance 'strategic alliances'.

(c) Many of the RECs 'demonstrated classical defender strategies'. These featured:

   (i) hierarchical company structures;

   (ii) a board drawn from *within* the industry;

   (iii) incremental growth, rather than more rapid growth by entering new business areas; little enthusiasm for diversification.

KEY TERM

The **recipe,** according to Johnson and Scholes, is an evolving set of beliefs, a way of looking at the world, and a way of interpreting information based on **management's shared experience.**

6.15 Although the **environment poses strategic questions,** it is **people who make sense of it** and devise strategies. Whilst the recipe provides cultural coherence it can impede strategic renewal. If the corporate strategy is failing, a company will:

Step 1 Place tighter *controls* over implementation (eg give tougher performance targets to sales staff); but if *this* fails ...

Step 2 Develop a new strategy (eg sell in a new market); but if this fails as well ...

Step 3 Only now will the company abandon the recipe (eg realise that the product is obsolete).

Question 5

Jarvis Tools Ltd makes machine tools for a variety of industries. Until now, it has had a captive market, but it is now facing competition from a Korean machine tool company. The threat is *growing* but at the moment Jarvis is in a good position. The tools are customised. They require a high degree of accuracy, so customers have to wait a fairly long time for the product, although Jarvis is recognised as being a leader in both innovation and quality. The firm historically has made all of its subcomponents in house. The company was founded by Fred Jarvis, an engineer. Every year an award is given for 'Major Contribution to the Craft of Machine Tooling at Jarvis' to a favoured or 'excellent' worker. Management consultants have suggested three alternatives for dealing with the competition.

(a) Speed up product design and development, perhaps by subcontracting some components to outside firms.

(b) Engage in a joint venture or marketing agreement with the Korean company, so that the Korean company will be directed to market segments that Jarvis does not serve.

(c) Achieve a BS EN ISO 9000 (formerly BS5750) certification as soon as possible.

Which of the strategies do you think Jarvis Tools Ltd would adopt, if corporate *culture* were the *determining* factor?

Answer

Strategy (c), the gaining of BS EN ISO 9000 certification, is the likeliest strategic option, though perhaps not the best. The company's traditions of *craftsmanship* (eg the annual award) would appear to highlight quality issues as ones in which managers already have an interest.

Subcontracting would be unthinkable, if it is an assumption of the corporate culture that outsiders cannot be trusted. The culture would predispose the company to doing 'more of the same'. The company would not realise that its production delays *could* be a competitive weakness: timeliness is not high on its list of priorities.

6.16 Peter Drucker (*The Theory of the Business, Harvard Business Review*, September-October 1994) argues that many companies fail because managers' **theory of the business** no longer works.

- A theory of the business contains the assumptions (about markets, technology etc) that 'shape any organisation's behaviour, dictate its decisions about what to do and what not to do, and define what an organisation considers meaningful results'.
- A valid theory of the business is based on realistic assumptions about environment, mission and core competences. The assumptions in all three areas must **fit reality,** must be understood throughout the organisation and must be tested.

Excellence

Exam focus point

No question will ask you to rattle off the characteristics of excellence. Indeed, the theory is a little out of date but it is still in the Teaching Guide and you can apply it to the companies in the case study.

6.17 In their book *In Search of Excellence* (1982), Peters and Waterman designated certain companies as excellent because those companies:

(a) Over a 20 year period had given an above average return on investment.
(b) Had a reputation for innovation.

6.18 Peters and Waterman identified eight attributes of excellence. Many of them relate to corporate culture, with the implication that with a strong culture, success will follow.

(a) **A bias for action** is preferred to analysis.

(b) **Closeness to customers.** Excellent firms do not just sell products, they also provide customer satisfaction.

(c) **Autonomy and entrepreneurship.**

(d) **Productivity through people**. Employees are a source of quality and product and process improvement.

(e) **Hands-on, value driven**. There is a commitment to shared corporate values. The core content of the dominant beliefs is narrow in scope.

(f) **Stick to the knitting**. Excellent companies do not embark on a strategy of conglomerate diversification.

(g) **Simplicity.** Excellent companies are not over-complicated, and the head office staff is *small*.

(h) **Simultaneous loose-tight properties**. Autonomy is shifted downwards. However, centralising tendencies are based on results for quality and service. These values are enforced.

6.19 Peters and Waterman found that the '**dominance and coherence of culture' was an essential feature of the 'excellent'** companies they observed. A 'handful of guiding values' was more powerful than manuals, rule books, norms and controls formally imposed (and resisted). They commented: 'If companies do not have strong notions of themselves, as reflected in their values, stories, myths and legends, people's only security comes from where they live on the organisation chart.' Such values should be part of the organisation's mission.

6.20 **Excellence theories have been criticised,** and Tom Peters has almost disowned the concept. Key problems are:

- Many 'excellent' companies have stumbled.
- It concentrates on operational issues rather than long term strategy.
- Strong cultures can impede necessary change.
- It proposes that there is 'one best way' to succeed.

6.21 Excellence does not appear to involve any long-term strategic thinking, other than as a by-product of 'sticking to the knitting' and keeping 'close to customers' and sharing 'core values'. IBM was close to its customers because customers had no alternative: IBM had control of a proprietary and expensive technology. Furthermore, in *Disruptive Technologies: Catching the Wave* (Joseph Bower and Clayton Christensen, *Harvard Business Review*, January-February 1995), the authors assert that keeping 'close to your customers' can have disadvantages: 'an industry's leaders are rarely in the forefront of commercialising new technologies that do not initially meet the functional demands of mainstream customers'. In other words, new technologies are developed and take established industry leaders unawares, as they cannot predict the demand for it in existing (rather than future) markets.

6.22 Section summary

- Culture enables managers to interpret information (the recipe) and dictates their responses to environmental challenge.
- Culture is an important component of operational effectiveness.
- Culture is related to structure.

7 USE OF IT **6/95**

7.1 Information technology adds a few more complications to strategic decision making.

(a) The niceties of IT are **not always appreciated by senior executives** yet technical issues in IT can be of strategic importance (eg compatibility of software, data processing capacity, 'functionality' of software).

(b) **IT can be used to create new types of business,** none of which meets a pre-existent demand. As an analogy, there could be no 'demand' for recorded music until technology made it possible. Some new technologies require that a demand is created for them.

(c) **IT can be used in existing businesses,** as we shall see, yet IT's capacity is increasing all the time. It is a 'moving target' for planners.

7.2 Most important, however, is an informed and critical appraisal of a firm's use of IT.

Internal appraisal: existing and future IT uses: McFarlan's grid

7.3 IT functions in four possible ways in an organisation. **McFarlan** analysed these in a grid, as follows.

		Strategic impact of application development portfolio (ie future systems)	
		Low	*High*
Strategic impact of existing systems	*Low*	Support	Turnround
	High	Factory	Strategic

7.4 **Support role**

Information systems have **little relevance to a firm's existing or future** success.

(a) IT thus requires below average investment and little management attention.

(b) Earl quotes the example of a cement manufacturing company. IT might be used to speed up administration and to make occasional improvements to the manufacturing process. (*Note*. We are discussing *information* technology, not any technology.) It is not vital or critical to the manufacture or distribution of cement.

7.5 **Factory role**

Existing IT applications are important. However, future IT developments are not anticipated to be relevant. Earl mentions a steel works, with an existing on-line real-time system for controlling production. It is **production** technology, not **information** technology, that will be most important.

7.6 **Strategic role**

Existing and future developments are at the heart of the company's future success. In fact, the business **operation depends on IT**: without IT it would not exist at all. Many finance/service companies depend on computers, telecommunications and databases.

7.7 **Turnround role**

Existing IT is not important, but **future developments** are likely to **have a significant impact.** In this case, IT is becoming *more* important. Its role and profile in the organisation is being enhanced. An example would be a firm which moved its computer system from back operation (eg administration) to front operation (providing the service).

7.8 **Moving round the grid.** A firm can be pushed by three forces.

(a) The fit between IT's potential and the firm's strategy (and resources).

(b) The strategic choices actually made by management about IT in the past.

(c) The firm's environment. For example, competitors might exploit IT and the firm might have to copy them.

Question 6

Readyware Clothes makes clothes. IT spending has been strictly controlled, and IT is used mainly for accounting, processing sales orders, and printing invoices. One of its major customers, Keaton and Lamarque, has sent the firm the following letter: 'It has always been our intention to source most of our clothes for sale from domestic suppliers - we've always valued speed and responsiveness. We have recently, however, received interesting offers from a supplier in Hong Kong who has offered a wider ranging flexibility in design with new production technology. Can you offer anything similar? At the least, we would advise you to automate your sales order processing system so it can become interlinked with our purchasing systems for greater responsiveness'.

(a) In view of the original IT configuration, what square on the grid did the company find itself in?

(b) If the company's management made a decision to introduce the new ordering systems and the new production technology, what square on the grid would it occupy?

(c) What forces were driving it round the grid, if any?

Answer

(a) Support

(b) Turnround (the new ordering system was becoming critical to keep the customer)

(c) The main forces driving it round were:

(i) the competitive environment (the overseas producer, and the customer's demand);
(ii) the management decision to respond to this by using an IT-based strategy.

IT's potential and business strategy

7.9 The fit between IT's potential and the firm's strategy and resources is difficult to assess.

(a) Non-specialist managers might have an **exaggerated idea of the benefits IT** can bring. If IT requires major changes to business practice, organisational impediments to such changes can impede its effectiveness.

(b) The firm's **strategy may have to change in response to technological advances** adopted by competitors. Management therefore has to second-guess competitors.

(c) **Changes in IT capacities and costs may rapidly change the potential fit** between a firm's strategy and its IT resources.

Management's strategic choices

7.10 Management's own wider strategic choices can have important consequences.

(a) **Business strategy**. Let us assume that a company wishes to cut costs, and that manufacturing **domestically** with **current technology** is becoming too expensive.

(i) Apart from automating its existing production processes to drive down costs, the company can use IT as a marketing and design tool (as well as examining other areas of the value chain where costs can be saved or products/services enhanced).

(ii) Alternatively, the company can move to a foreign country with lower labour costs, perhaps even **downgrading** its technological skills in the process, if it is convinced that low labour costs are essential and that IT is less important.

(b) **Past IT decisions**. Management might have chosen a particular technology *in the past* which limits its ability to change. Changing to a new system might involve more effort than management can provide. Firms with mainframes might stick with that technology (even though they might not have chosen mainframes if starting from scratch).

(c) **Planning failures**. Management's early failure to make such choices might have resulted in an **emergent strategy** for IT being adopted in some departments.

Exam focus point

You could have used McFarlan's grid in a June 1995 question involving a food company - you had to indicate the strategic position of IT.

7.11 Section summary

- IT can have a support, factory, strategic or turnround role depending on the industry.
- Management choices and environmental developments can change the role of IT.

8 THE CUSTOMER BASE

8.1 A **marketing audit** involves a review of an organisation's products and markets, the marketing environment, and its marketing system and operations. The profitability of each product and each market should be assessed, and the costs of different marketing activities established.

8.2 **Information obtained about markets**

(a) **Size of the customer base**. Does the organisation sell to a large number of small customers or a small number of big customers?

(b) **Size of individual orders**. The organisation might sell its products in many small orders, or it might have large individual orders. Delivery costs can be compared with order sizes.

(c) **Sales revenue and profitability.** The performance of individual products can be compared, perhaps as follows:

Product group	*Sales revenue*		*Contribution to profits*	
	£'000	% of total	£'000	% of total
B	7,500	35.7	2,500	55.6
E	2,000	9.5	1,200	26.7
C	4,500	21.4	450	10.0
A	5,000	23.8	250	5.6
D	2,000	9.5	100	2.2
	21,000	100.0%	4,500	100.0%

An imbalance between sales and profits over various product ranges can be potentially dangerous. In the figures above, product group A accounts for 23.8% of turnover but only 5.6% of total contribution, and product group D accounts for 9.5% of turnover but only 2.2% of total contribution.

(d) **Segments.** An analysis of sales and profitability into export markets and domestic markets.

(e) **Market share.** Estimated share of the market obtained by each product group.

(f) **Growth.** Sales growth and contribution growth over the previous four years or so, for each product group.

(g) Whether the **demand** for certain products is **growing, stable or likely to decline.**

(h) Whether **demand is price sensitive** or not.

(i) Whether there is a growing tendency for the market to become **fragmented**, with more specialist and 'custom-made' products.

8.3 **Information about current marketing activities.**

- Comparative pricing

- Advertising effectiveness
- Effectiveness of distribution network
- Attitudes to the product, in comparison with competitors

(Marketing is examined in depth in later chapters.)

Customers

8.4 Many firms - especially in business-to-business markets - sell to a relatively small number of customers. **Key customer analysis** calls for six main areas of investigation.

(a) **Key customer identity.** Name of each key customer. Location. Status in market. Products they make and sell. Size of firm (capital employed, turnover, number of employees).

(b) **Customer history**

(i) First purchase date.

(ii) Who makes the buying decision in the customer's organisation?

(iii) What is the average order size, by product?

(iv) What is the regularity/ periodicity of the order, by product?

(v) What is the trend in size of orders?

(vi) What is the motive in purchasing?

(vii) What is the extent of the customer's knowledge of the firm's products and of competitors' products?

(viii) On what basis does the customer reorder? How is the useful life of the product judged?

(ix) Were there any lost or cancelled orders? For what reason?

(c) **Relationship of customer to product**

(i) Are the products purchased to be resold? If not, for what purpose are they bought?

(ii) Do the products form part of the customer's service/product?

(d) **Relationship of customer to potential market**

(i) What is the size of the customer in relation to the total end-market?

(ii) Is the customer likely to expand, or not? Diversify? Integrate?

(e) **Customer attitudes and behaviour**

(i) What interpersonal factors exist which could affect sales by the firm and by competitors?

(ii) Does the customer also buy competitors' products?

(iii) To what extent may purchases be postponed?

(iv) What emotional factors exist in buying decisions?

(f) **The financial performance of the customer**

How successful is the customer in his own markets? Similar analysis can be carried out as on competitors.

(g) **The profitability of selling to the customer**

This is an important part of key customer analysis, and must provide answers to questions such as the following.

(i) What profit/contribution is the organisation making on sales to the customer, after discounts and selling and delivery costs?

(ii) What would be the financial consequences of losing the customer?

(iii) Is the customer buying in order sizes that are unprofitable to supply?

(iv) What is return on investment in plant used? (This will require valuation of the plant and equipment involved in supplying each customer. The valuation might be at historical book value or current cost.)

(v) What is the level of inventory required specifically to supply these customers?

(vi) Are there any other specific costs involved in supplying this customer, eg technical and test facilities, R & D facilities, special design staff?

(vii) What is the ratio of net contribution per customer to total investment on both a historic and replacement cost basis?

Such an evaluation would be a part of research into potential market opportunities. Smaller customers should not be ignored and there should be a similar analysis of the organisation's other customers, although a separate analysis for each individual customer may not be worthwhile, and customers may be grouped - ie on the basis of order sizes or another such characteristic (ie geographical basis).

8.5 **Not all customers are as important as others**. The checklist below can help identify the most important.

Strategic importance evaluation guide	*High*	*Medium*	*Low*	*N/A*
1 Fit between customer's needs and our capabilities, at present and potentially.				
2 Ability to serve customer compared with our major competitors, at present and potentially.				
3 'Health' of customer's industry, current and forecast.				
4 'Health' of the customer, current and forecast.				
5 Customer's growth prospects, current and forecast.				
6 What can we learn from this customer?				
7 Can the customer help us attract others?				
8 Relative *significance:* how important is the customer compared *with other* customers?				
9 What is the *profitability* of serving the customer?				

9 BRAINWORKS PLC UPDATE

Questions can be found in the Introduction box at the beginning of this chapter.

9.1 *Question 1.* Begbie talked the language of Dionysus, with the emphasis on a family atmosphere. The UK firm appears to retain the existential culture, to a degree, as each consultant works independently. The US office has more of a task culture: there is no competition between consultants for clients.

9.2 *Question 2*. BW has a competence, but it is shared by others. In the UK, BW is not noticeably better than its competitors, so it is hardly distinctive. PeoplePower addresses the issue by trying to develop expertise in particular markets.

9.3 *Question 3*. The main limiting factor is the employment market, and the number and skill of the consultants that BW employs.

Chapter roundup

- A **position audit** reviews the organisation's current position.
- **Resource audits** identify physical human and material resources and how they are deployed into a **distinctive competence**, something it does uniquely well.
- The **value chain** describes those activities of the organisation which add value to purchased inputs. Primary activities are involved in the production of goods and services. Support activities provide necessary assistance. **Linkages** are the relationships between activities. Managing the value chain, which includes relationships with outside suppliers, can be a source of strategic advantage.
- The **product life cycle** concept holds that products have a life cycle, and that a product demonstrates different characteristics of profit and investment at each stage in its life cycle. The life cycle concept is a model, not a prediction. (Not all products pass through each stage of the life cycle.) It enables a firm to examine its portfolio of goods and services as a whole.
- The **Boston classification** classifies products in terms of their capacity for growth within the market and the market's capacity for growth as a whole. A firm should have a balanced **portfolio of products**.
- **Organisation structure** indicates how value activities are **co-ordinated** within the organisation. Organisations are characterised by formal division of labour, **hierarchies** of authority (scalar chains) and networks of **authority** and power. There are five components.
- The organisation structure influences strategy, as it is one of the ways in which power is deployed and **information** communicated.
- **Culture** is relevant to strategy. While strong cultures can enhance performance, they tend to exclude information inconsistent with their underlying assumptions. Strong cultures can reduce flexibility. Culture can determine the type of people employed and the basic assumptions of which the organisation is based. It is related to organisation structure.
- In developing a strategy for information systems, a firm needs to be aware of its current and future strategic role. **McFarlan's** grid describes four possible roles as **support, factory, turnround** and **strategic**.
- A **marketing audit** renews the customer base and effectiveness of marketing operations.

Quick quiz

1 What is a limiting factor? (see para 2.3)

2 What is a competence? (2.7)

3 What is the significance of the value chain? (3.3, 3.9)

4 Distinguish between product class, product form and brand. (4.2)

5 List the stages of the product life cycle. (4.4 - 4.7)

6 What are the problems with the product life cycle. (4.9)

7 What are stars, cash cows, question marks, and dogs? (4.11)

8 Describe the five component parts of the organisation. (5.6)

9 What is meant by scalar chain? (5.14)

10 Distinguish position power from expert power. (5.22)

11 What are the major influences on an organisation's culture? (6.6)

12 What are analysers and reactors? (6.14)

13 List the characteristics of supposedly 'excellent' companies. (6.18)

14 Draw McFarlan's grid and explain what it means (7.3 - 7.7)

15 How can management's past strategic choices influence whether a firm shifts to a different square on McFarlan's grid? (7.10)

16 What information might be gained from a marketing audit? (8.1)

17 What is key customer analysis? (8.4)

Question to try	Level	Marks	Time
7	Exam standard	25	45 mins
8	Exam standard	25	45 mins

Chapter 7

STRATEGIC OPTIONS GENERATION

Introduction

Once the internal and external analyses are complete, the next task is to develop strategies. **SWOT analysis** is a way of identifying the extent to which an organisation has managed to obtain a fit with the environment: it identifies internal **strengths** and **weaknesses**, and external **opportunities** and **threats**. Strategies are developed to exploit strengths and opportunities, and to mitigate threats and weaknesses. **Gap analysis** is a technique of quantifying the extent to which new strategic projects are necessary. We can identify three basic strategic decisions.

How you compete: competitive strategy. Taking the **industry scenario** into account, it should be possible to identify the best way of competing. The value chain, which we encountered earlier, can be used here.

Where you compete. This decision relates to the products sold and the markets they are sold in: Ansoff's model.

Method of growth. This decision relates to whether a firm grows by its own efforts (organic growth) or acquires other businesses (acquisition).

The strategic options suggested are then evaluated, according to the firm's chosen criteria. Some of the techniques for analysis and evaluation are covered in Chapter 7.

The syllabus covers the use of **strategic planning software,** although no question has been set as yet. How do you think it accord with some of the ideas about making strategies outlined in Chapters 1 and 2?

Brainworks plc

1 Do you agree that Willard Mann is right to demerge the UK and US business? What arguments can you marshall to disagree with his view?

2 Is diversification a suitable strategy for BW?

3 What is the value of applying Porter's generic strategy concepts to BW?

1 CORPORATE APPRAISAL (SWOT ANALYSIS)

Case example

'*CWC to hang up on Mercury (Financial Times*, 25 April 1997)

The biggest challenge yet to British Telecommunications' dominance of the UK telecoms market will emerge next week, when Cable & Wireless Communications lists on the London and New York stock markets.

The company will have, at a stroke, a 10 per cent share of the £21bn fixed and mobile UK telephony market - against BT's 67 per cent - serving more than 1m customers. The group will also have about 600,000 television customers. CWC will be by far the largest of the cable companies, being five times the size by market capitalisation of its closest rival, Telewest.

While it trails behind BT's 20m domestic customers by a long way, CWC's unfinished cable network will eventually pass 6m homes. However, the network will take two years to complete and require £2.3bn further expenditure. There is also the possibility of other cable companies merging with CWC, either through acquisition or partnership. Another possibility is the addition of One-2-One, Mercury's part-owned mobile telecoms business, sometime in the future.

CWC has taken the highly risky step of abandoning its existing brands, including the well-known Mercury identity, in favour of establishing the name 'Cable and Wireless'.

Another aspect bolstering CWC's challenge to BT is its digital broadband fibre optic network. With telecoms demand being increasingly driven by non-voice traffic, such as data and the Internet, the superior capacity of a broadband network will stand it in good stead. In particular, its ability to deliver a range of multimedia services like home shopping, Internet access and banking is an advantage.

CWC's management is also being seen as a positive factor in the group's future development.

The mediocre performance of the cable industry is shown by penetration rates - the number of people taking a service out of those able to receive cable - hovering about 20 per cent and churn rates - customers failing to renew subscriptions - above 30 per cent. If people have not subscribed to the services of Nynex, Bell or Videotron, with telephone prices below those of BT's and a host of satellite channels, why should they take up an offer from CWC?

"Better customer service, better marketing, more choice and more competitive prices," says Mr Wallace. There is also the threat posed by BSkyB, the satellite operator, which his due to launch its own digital satellite service later this year. "We have a fantastic opportunity here," says Mr Wallace. "We have the resources, the skills and the service. Now we need to deliver." '

By April 1998, however, CWC had scrapped its central marketing department, whilst retaining the consumer marketing department. Central marketing controlled brand advertising. Consumer marketing controlled the marketing of mass products, such as cable and telecoms.

1.1 The purpose of **corporate appraisal** (SWOT analysis) is to **combine** the assessment of the environment and the analysis of the organisation's internal resources and capabilities.

KEY TERM

Corporate appraisal: 'a critical assessment of the strengths and weaknesses, opportunities and threats in relation to the internal and environmental factors affecting the entity in order to establish its condition prior to the preparation of a long-term plan.'

1.2 A **strengths and weaknesses** analysis expresses which areas of the business have:

(a) Strengths that should be exploited
(b) Weaknesses which should be improved

It therefore covers the results of the position audit.

1.3 **Opportunities.**

(a) What opportunities exist in the business environment?
(b) Their inherent profit-making potential.
(c) The organisation's ability to exploit the worthwhile opportunities.

1.4 **Threats**

(a) What threats might arise?
(b) How will competitors be affected?
(c) How will the company be affected?

The opportunities and threats might arise from the PEST and competitive factors.

Bringing them together

1.5 The internal and external appraisals will be brought together, and perhaps shown in cruciform chart.

1.6 EXAMPLE

STRENGTHS	WEAKNESSES
£10 million of capital available	Heavy reliance on a small number of customers
Production expertise and appropriate marketing skills	Limited product range, with no new products and expected market decline. Small marketing organisation.
THREATS	**OPPORTUNITIES**
A major competitor has already entered the new market	Government tax incentives for new investment.
	Growing demand in a new market, although customers so far relatively small in number.

The company is in imminent danger of losing its existing markets and must diversify its products and/or markets. The new market opportunity exists to be exploited, and since the number of customers is currently small, the relatively small size of the existing marketing force would not be an immediate hindrance. A strategic plan could be developed to buy new equipment and use existing production and marketing to enter the new market, with a view to rapid expansion. Careful planning of manpower, equipment, facilities, research and development would be required and there would be an objective to meet the threat of competition so as to obtain a substantial share of a growing market. The cost of entry at this early stage of market development should not be unacceptably high.

1.7 The SWOT technique can also be used for specific areas of strategy such as IT and marketing.

1.8 Effective SWOT analysis does not simply require a categorisation of information, it also requires some **evaluation of the relative importance** of the various factors under consideration.

- These features are only of relevance if they are **perceived to exist by the consumers.** Listing corporate features that internal personnel regard as strengths/weaknesses is of little relevance if they are not perceived as such by the organisation's consumers.
- In the same vein, threats and opportunities are conditions presented by the external environment and they should be independent of the firm.

1.9 The SWOT can now be used guiding strategy formulation. The two major options are as follows.

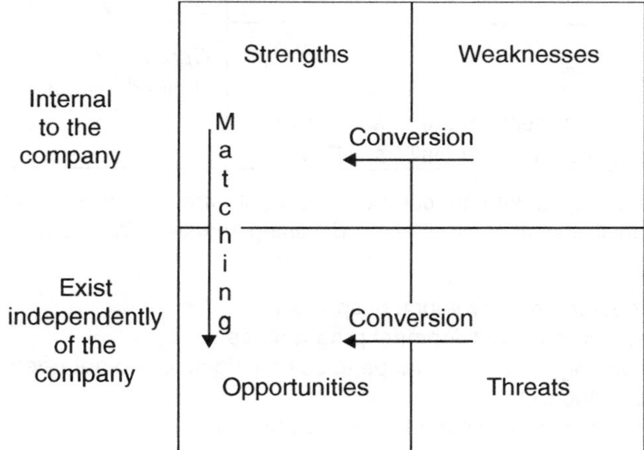

(a) **Matching**

This entails finding, where possible, a match between the strengths of the organisation and the opportunities presented by the market. Strengths which do not match any available opportunity are of limited use while opportunities which do not have any matching strengths are of little immediate value.

(b) **Conversion**

This requires the development of strategies which will convert weaknesses into strengths in order to take advantage of some particular opportunity, or converting threats into opportunities which can then be matched by existing strengths.

Question 1

Hall Faull Downes Ltd has been in business for 25 years, during which time profits have risen by an average of 3% per annum, although there have been peaks and troughs in profitability due to the ups and downs of trade in the customers' industry. The increase in profits until five years ago was the result of increasing sales in a buoyant market, but more recently, the total market has become somewhat smaller and Hall Faull Downes has only increased sales and profits as a result of improving its market share.

The company produces components for manufacturers in the engineering industry.

In recent years, the company has developed many new products and currently has 40 items in its range compared to 24 only five years ago. Over the same five year period, the number of customers has fallen from 20 to nine, two of whom together account for 60% of the company's sales.

Give your appraisal of the company's future, and suggest what it is probably doing wrong.

Answer

A general interpretation of the facts as given might be sketched as follows.

(a) Objectives: the company has no declared objectives. Profits have risen by 3% per annum in the past, which has failed to keep pace with inflation but may have been a satisfactory rate of increase in the current conditions of the industry. Even so, stronger growth is indicated in the future.

(b)

Strengths	*Weaknesses*
Many new products developed. Marketing success in increasing market share	Products may be reaching the end of their life and entering decline. New product life cycles may be shorter. Reduction in customers. Excessive reliance on a few customers. Doubtful whether profit record is satisfactory.
Threats Possible decline in the end-product. Smaller end-product market will restrict future sales prospects for Hall Faull Downes.	*Opportunities* None identified.

(c) Strengths: the growth in company sales in the last five years has been as a result of increasing the market share in a declining market. This success may be the result of the following.

(i) Research and development spending.
(ii) Good product development programmes.
(iii) Extending the product range to suit changing customer needs.
(iv) Marketing skills.
(v) Long-term supply contracts with customers.
(vi) Cheap pricing policy.
(vii) Product quality and reliable service.

(d) Weaknesses:

(i) The products may be custom-made for customers so that they provide little or no opportunity for market development.

(ii) Products might have a shorter life cycle than in the past, in view of the declining total market demand.

(iii) Excessive reliance on two major customers leaves the company exposed to the dangers of losing their custom.

(e) Threats: there may be a decline in the end-market for the customers' product so that the customer demands for the company's own products will also fall.

(f) Opportunities: no opportunities have been identified, but in view of the situation as described, new strategies for the longer term would appear to be essential.

(g) Conclusions: the company does not appear to be planning beyond the short-term, or is reacting to the business environment in a piecemeal fashion. A strategic planning programme should be introduced.

(h) Recommendations: the company must look for new opportunities in the longer-term.

(i) In the short term, current strengths must be exploited to continue to increase market share in existing markets and product development programmes should also continue.

(ii) In the longer term, the company must diversify into new markets or into new products and new markets. Diversification opportunities should be sought with a view to exploiting any competitive advantage or synergy that might be achievable.

(iii) The company should use its strengths (whether in R & D, production skills or marketing expertise) in exploiting any identifiable opportunities.

(iv) Objectives need to be quantified in order to assess the extent to which new long-term strategies are required.

2 GAP ANALYSIS

KEY TERM

(a) **Forecasting:** 'the identification of relevant factors and quantification of this effect on an entity as a basis for planning'.

(b) **Projection.** A projection is an expected future trend obtained by extrapolation. It differs from a forecast in that it is principally concerned with quantitative factors whereas a forecast includes judgements. **Extrapolation** is a technique of determining a projection by statistical means.

(c) **Gap analysis** is the comparison of an entity's ultimate objective with the sum of projections and already planned projects.

2.1 Gap analysis compares:

(a) The organisation's **targets** for achievement over the planning period; with

(b) What would the organisation be **expected to achieve** if it carried on in the current way with the same products and selling to the same markets. This is called an **F_0 forecast.**

This difference is the 'gap'. New strategies will then have to be developed which will close this gap, so that the organisation can expect to achieve its targets over the planning period.

A forecast or projection based on existing performance: F_0 forecasts

2.2 For example, if the company sells ten products in eight markets, produces them with a certain quantity and type of machinery in one factory, has a gearing structure of 30% etc, a forecast will be prepared, covering the corporate planning period, on the assumption that none of these items is changed.

2.3 **Preparing an F_0 forecast**

- The analysis of revenues, costs (eg fixed, variable and unit) and volumes.
- Projections into the future based on past trends.
- Identifying other factors affecting profits and return (eg external factors).
- Finalising the forecast.

Comparing the F_0 forecast with objectives determines the size of the task facing the company if it wishes to achieve its target profits.

Errors in the forecast

2.4 Forecasts can never be completely accurate - they might be misleading in cases of environmental turbulence. But in stable environments, they are valid, if adjusted for error. Errors can be accounted for by:

(a) Estimating **likely variations**: for example, 'in 1999 the forecast profit is £5 million with possible variations of plus or minus £2 million'.

(b) Providing a **probability distribution** for profits: for example, 'in 1999 there is a 20% chance that profits will exceed £7 million, a 50% chance that they will exceed £5 million and an 80% chance that they will exceed £2½ million. Minimum profits in 1999 will be £2 million'.

2.5 The gap could be filled by new product-market growth strategies.

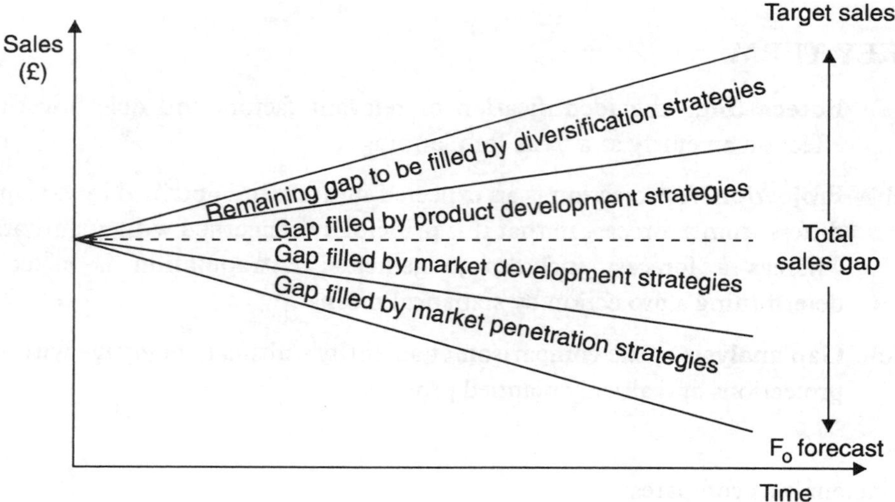

Question 2

Gap analysis can be used to model a variety of factors in addition to sales and profit. How do you think you could use gap analysis for manpower?

Answer

(a) The F_0 forecast would start with current manpower levels, and would be projected into the future assuming natural wastage, no training and no new appointments.

(b) The organisation would have to assess its needs in terms of manpower *numbers* and *skills*.

(c) Strategies to fill the gap would include recruitment and training programmes.

3 COMPETITIVE STRATEGY: HOW TO COMPETE 12/94, 12/97

Exam focus point

The December 1996 exam asked about competitive stance, and also the product-market growth strategies discussed in Section 5.

3.1 Competitive advantage is anything which gives one organisation an edge over its rivals in the products it sells or the services it offers.

3.2 Porter argues that a firm should adopt a competitive strategy which is intended to achieve some form of competitive advantage for the firm.

KEY TERM

Competitive strategy means 'taking offensive or defensive actions to create a dependable position in an industry, to cope successfully with ... competitive forces and thereby yield a superior return on investment for the firm. Firms have discovered many different approaches to this end, and the best strategy for a given firm is ultimately a unique construction reflecting its particular circumstances'. (Porter)

The choice of competitive strategy

3.3 Porter believes there are three *generic strategies* for competitive advantage.

KEY TERM

(a) **Cost leadership** means being the lowest cost producer in the industry as a whole.

(b) **Differentiation** is the exploitation of a product or service which the *industry as a whole* believes to be unique.

(c) **Focus** involves a restriction of activities to only part of the market (a segment) through:

   (i) Providing goods and/or services at lower cost to that segment (**cost-focus**);

   (ii) Providing a differentiated product or service to that segment (**differentiation-focus**)

3.4 **Cost leadership and differentiation are industry-wide strategies. Focus involves segmentation** but involves pursuing, **within the segment only**, a strategy of cost leadership or differentiation.

Cost leadership

3.5 A cost leadership strategy seeks to achieve the position of lowest-cost producer in the **industry as a whole.** By producing at the lowest cost, the manufacturer can compete on price with every other producer in the industry, and earn the higher unit profits, if the manufacturer so chooses.

3.6 **How to achieve overall cost leadership**

(a) Set up production facilities to obtain **economies of scale**.

(b) Use the **latest technology** to reduce costs and/or enhance productivity (or use cheap labour if available).

(c) In high technology industries, and in industries depending on labour skills for product design and production methods, exploit the **learning curve effect**. By producing more items than any other competitor, a firm can benefit more from the learning curve, and achieve lower average costs.

(d) Concentrate on **improving productivity**.

(e) **Minimise overhead costs**.

(f) **Get favourable access to sources of supply**.

(g) **Relocate to cheaper areas**

Case example

Large out-of-town stores specialising in one particular category of product are able to secure cost leadership by economies of scale over other retailers. Such shops have been called **category killers**, an example of which is PC World.

Differentiation

3.7 A differentiation strategy assumes that competitive advantage can be gained through **particular characteristics** of a firm's products. Products may be categorised as:

(a) **Breakthrough products** offer a radical performance advantage over competition, perhaps at a drastically lower price (eg float glass, developed by *Pilkington*).

(b) **Improved products** are not radically different from their competition but are obviously superior in terms of better performance at a competitive price (eg microchips).

(c) **Competitive products** derive their appeal from a particular compromise of cost and performance. For example, cars are not all sold at rock-bottom prices, nor do they all provide immaculate comfort and performance. They compete with each other by trying to offer a more attractive compromise than rival models.

3.8 **How to differentiate.**

(a) **Build up a brand image** (eg Pepsi's 'blue' cans are supposed to offer different 'psychic benefits' to Coke's).

(b) **Give the product special features** to make it stand out (eg Russell Hobbs' Millennium kettle incorporated a new kind of element, which boils water faster).

(c) **Exploit other activities of the value chain** (see Section 4 below).

Case example

Daewoo

Daewoo Cars in the UK has cleverly differentiated its product offering from its competitors'. As cars, Daewoo vehicles are based on Vauxhall so there are few technical innovations. Daewoo did a marketing research exercise, and decided to address other issues relating to car purchase and usage.

Its advertisements are concerned less with the car, than with:

(a) The fact that its salespeople are not paid by commission;
(b) Daewoo's offer to service the cars itself and provide a courtesy car while it does so.

Although other car adverts, such as Rover's, seek to promote a relationship with the customer, Daewoo's goes further than most.

Of course, not everybody would respond to such concerns and so service is the basis of differentiation.

3.9 Advantages and disadvantages of industry-wide strategies

Advantages	*Cost leadership*	*Differentiation*
New entrants	Economies of scale raise entry barriers	Brand loyalty and perceived uniqueness are entry barriers
Substitutes	Firm is not so vulnerable as its less cost-effective competitors to the threat of substitutes	Customer loyalty is a weapon against substitutes
Customers	Customers cannot drive down prices further than the next most efficient competitor	Customers have no comparable alternative
Suppliers	Flexibility to deal with cost increases	Higher margins can offset vulnerability to supplier price rises
Industry rivalry	Firm remains profitable when rivals go under through excessive price competition	Brand loyalty should lower price sensitivity

Disadvantages

Cost leadership	*Differentiation*
Technological change will require capital investment, or make production cheaper for competitors	Sooner or later, customers become price sensitive
Competitors can learn via imitation	Customers may no longer need the differentiating factor
Cost concerns ignore product design or marketing issues	
Increase in input costs can reduce price advantages	Imitation narrows differentiation

Focus (or niche) strategy

3.10 In a focus strategy, a firm concentrates its attention on one or more particular segments or niches of the market, and does not try to serve the entire market with a single product.

Case example

A good example of a niche strategy is that adopted by the makers of *Sibelius 7*, a computer system for composers of music.

Contrary to most other developments in software, *Sibelius 7* requires dedicated hardware to work effectively: it cannot be run on a PC or Mac with a soundcard. Users of the software have to buy hardware too.

(a) **A cost-focus strategy:** aim to be a cost leader for a particular segment. This type of strategy is often found in the printing, clothes manufacture and car repair industries.

(b) A **differentiation-focus strategy:** pursue differentiation for a chosen segment. Luxury goods are the prime example of such a strategy.

3.11 **Advantages**

(a) A niche is more secure and a firm can insulate itself from competition.
(b) The firm does not spread itself too thinly.

3.12 **Drawbacks of a focus strategy**

(a) The firm sacrifices economies of scale which would be gained by serving a wider market.

(b) Competitors can move into the segment, with increased resources (eg the Japanese moved into the US luxury car market, to compete with Mercedes and BMW).

(c) The segment's needs may eventually become less distinct from the main market.

Which strategy?

3.13 Although there is a risk with any of the generic strategies, Porter argues that a firm *must* pursue one of them. A **stuck-in-the-middle** strategy is almost certain to make only low profits. 'This firm lacks the market share, capital investment and resolve to play the low-cost game, the industry-wide differentiation necessary to obviate the need for a low-cost position, or the focus to create differentiation or a low-cost position in a more limited sphere.'

Question 3

The managing director of Hermes Telecommunications plc is interested in corporate strategy. Hermes has invested a great deal of money in establishing a network which competes with that of Telecom UK, a recently privatised utility. Initially Hermes concentrated its efforts on business customers in the South East of England, especially the City of London, where it offered a lower cost service to that supplied by Telecom UK. Recently, Hermes has approached the residential market (ie domestic telephone users) offering a lower cost service on long-distance calls. Technological developments have resulted in the possibility of a cheap mobile telecommunication network, using microwave radio links. The franchise for this service has been awarded to Gerbil phone, which is installing transmitters in town centres and stations etc.

What issues of competitive strategy have been raised in the above scenario, particularly in relation to Hermes Telecommunications plc?

Answer

(a) Arguably, Hermes initially pursued a cost-focus strategy, by targeting the business segment.

(b) It seems to be moving into a cost leadership strategy over the whole market although its competitive offer, in terms of lower costs for local calls, is incomplete.

(c) The barriers to entry to the market have been lowered by the new technology. Gerbil phone might pick up a significant amount of business.

3.14 In practice, it is rarely simple to draw hard and fast distinctions between the generic strategies as these are conceptual problems underlying them.

(a) **Problems with 'cost leadership'**

(i) **Internal focus.** Cost refers to internal measures, rather than the market demand. It can be used to gain market share: but it is the **market share which is important,** not cost leadership as such.

(ii) **Only one firm.** If cost leadership applies cross the whole industry, only one firm will pursue this strategy successfully.

(iii) **Higher margins can be used for differentiation.** Having low costs does *not* mean you have to charge lower prices or compete on price. A cost leader can choose to 'invest higher margins in R & D or marketing'. Being a cost leader arguably gives producers more freedom to choose *other* competitive strategies.

(b) **Problems with differentiation.** Porter assumes that a differentiated product will always be sold at a *higher price*.

(i) However, a **differentiated product** may be sold at the same price as competing products in order to **increase market share.**

(ii) **Choice of competitor.** Differentiation from whom? Who are the competitors? Do they serve other market segments? Do they compete on the same basis?

(iii) **Source of differentiation.** This can include **all** aspects of the firm's offer, not only the product. Restaurants aim to create an atmosphere or 'ambience', as well as serving food of good quality.

3.15 **Focus** probably has fewer conceptual difficulties, as it ties in very neatly with ideas of market segmentation. In practice most companies pursue this strategy to some extent, by designing products/services to meet the needs of particular target markets.

3.16 'Stuck-in-the-middle' is therefore what many companies actually pursue quite successfully. Any number of strategies can be pursued, with different approaches to **price** and the **perceived added value** (ie the differentiation factor) in the eyes of the customer.

3.17 Section summary

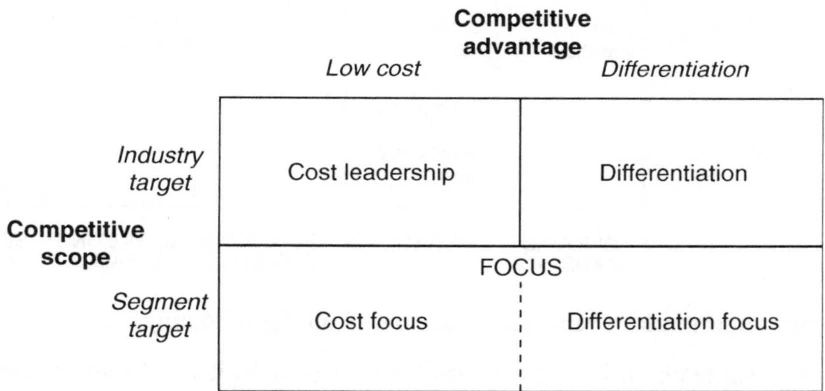

4 USING THE VALUE CHAIN AND IT IN COMPETITIVE STRATEGY

4.1 The value chain can be used to design a competitive strategy, by deploying the various activities strategically. The examples below are based on two supermarket chains, one concentrating on low prices, the other differentiated on quality and service. See if you can tell which is which.

(a)

	INBOUND LOGISTICS	OPERATIONS	OUTBOUND LOGISTICS	MARKETING & SALES	SERVICE
Firm infrastructure	Central control of operations and credit control				
Human resource management	Recruitment of mature staff	Client care training	Flexible staff to help with packing		
Technology development		Recipe research	Electronic point of sale	Consumer research & tests	Itemised bills
Procurement	Own label products	Prime retail positions		Adverts in quality magazines & poster sites	
	Dedicated refrigerated transport	In store food halls Modern store design Open front refrigerators Tight control of sell-by dates	Collect by car service	No price discounts on food past sell-by dates	No quibble refunds

(b)

	INBOUND LOGISTICS	OPERATIONS	OUTBOUND LOGISTICS	MARKETING & SALES	SERVICE
Firm infrastructure	Minimum corporate HQ				
Human resource management		De-skilled store-ops	Dismissal for checkout error		
Technology development	Comuterised warehousing		Checkouts simple		
Procurement	Branded only purchases big discounts	Low cost sites			Use of concessions
	Bulk warehousing	Limited range Price points Basic store design		Low price promotion Local focus	Nil

4.2 The two supermarkets represented are based on the following.

(a) The value chain in 4.1(a) is similar to that of Lidle, a 'discount' supermarket chain which sells on price, pursuing a cost leadership, or perhaps more accurately, a cost-focus strategy. This can be seen in the limited product range and its low-cost sites.

(b) The value chain in 4.1(b) is based on Marks and Spencer foods, which seeks to differentiate on quality and service. Hence the 'no quibble' refunds, the use of prime retail sites, and customer care training.

(c) You can probably think of other innovations such as loyalty cards and *home delivery*.

Strategies for IT: the value chain

4.3 IT can be used at each stage in the value chain.

4.4 **Operations.** IT can be used to **automate and improve physical tasks** in the operating core. It also **provides information** about operational processes.

(a) **Process control.** Computer systems enable better measurement and tighter control over production processes.

(b) **Machine tool control.** Machine tools can be automated and their movements made more precise (eg **direct numerical control** is where the computer is linked directly to the machine tool).

(c) **Robots** can automate some procedures.

(d) **Computer integrated manufacturing** integrates all aspects of an organisation's manufacturing activities. 'IT cannot solve basic organisational problems, but the essence is the use of the IT to provide integration through communication effectiveness and efficiency'.

4.5 **Inbound and outbound logistics**

(a) **Warehousing.** *Parcelforce* uses IT to track the progress of different parcels through the system.

(b) Create **virtual warehouses** of stock actually held at **suppliers**. For example an organisation with several outlets might have each connected to a system which indicates the total amount of stock available at different sites.

Case example

Amazon Books

Amazon is the world's most successful internet bookstore. It is based near America's main book wholesalers. It does not have a warehouse of its own.

(c) Planning procedures to schedule production such as MRPII.

4.6 **Marketing and services**

(a) **Internet websites** can be used as an advertising medium and to gather information about customers.

(b) **Customer databases** enable firms to monitor consumers' buying habits and to identify new segments.

(c) Supermarkets use **EPOS** systems to give them a precise hour-by-hour idea of how products are selling to enable speedy ordering and replenishments.

Case example

Tesco is piloting its Internet Superstore. IT can be combined with home delivery. The customer goes to Tesco's website, accesses the Internet Superstore, builds up a 'shopping list' by selecting items from a product database, and then selects a time and date for delivery.

4.7 **Support**

(a) **Procurement.** IT can automate some purchasing decisions and save paperwork if the organisation's purchase systems are linked directly to the sales order systems of its suppliers (eg by electronic data interchange).

(b) **Technology development.** *Computer automated design (CAD)* enables design modification and simulation, saving money.

(c) **Human resources** applications in the office include the maintenance of a **skills database**, staff planning (eg using network analysis), computer based training, time attendance systems, payroll systems and pension systems.

HR applications include homeworking, now that powerful PCs the Internet and ISDN are affordable.

Other frameworks for assessing IT

4.8 Earl describes a number of other frameworks for assessing IT's potential strategic benefits.

Opportunity frameworks

4.9 **Opportunity frameworks** are analytical tools designed to assess whether a firm has the opportunity of strategic advantage in a particular area. They are designed to bring out the relevance of IT to business strategies.

(a) **Systems analysis frameworks** consider the **whole** systems base of the organisation. They include the **value chain,** discussed earlier.

(b) **Applications search tools**

(c) **Technology fitting frameworks**

4.10 **Applications search tools** probe a particular business area (eg marketing section) to see whether IT would be useful.

Case example

Ives and Learmouth developed a **customer resource lifecycle** which identifies the lifecycle of how a customer acquires a product or service. It investigates the links between the suppliers and the customers. The phases of the life cycle are as follows.

Step 1 **Requirements**. What exactly does the customer require, and how much?

Step 2 **Acquisition**. How does the customer get hold of the resource? From whom? How and when does the customer order and pay? How does the customer test the product for acceptability?

Step 3 **Stewardship**. How does the customer look after the product or service? How is the resource repaired and enhanced?

Step 4 **Retirement**. Return or disposal of the product, and the relevant accounting treatment.

The firm's activities and the possible use of IT in each of these phases can then be examined.

Case example

Thomson Holidays introduced an IT based reservation system which provided both holiday information and the facility to make reservations. This was installed in agents' offices. It succeeded because:

(a) agents used Thomson's services a great deal already, and so the system could be employed for existing uses;

(b) it provided up-to-date details for people booking at the 'last minute', so it offered product differentiation.

4.11 **Technology fitting frameworks.** Instead of fitting the technology to the business use, this works the other way around. Technology is an opportunity, which can be *exploited* and for which a business use might be found: the firm has to think of *creative ways* of doing so.

4.12 **Scoping models** respond to the difficulty in assessing how information can be exploited for competitive advantage. Porter and Miller produced an **information intensity matrix** which analyses the **amount of information** in the:

(a) **Product itself** (eg oil has a low information content, a newspaper has a high information content). Where this is high (eg a newspaper) IT can be used to process or present it more effectively. For example, many newspapers have Internet websites.

(b) **Value chain** (low in the case of a cement maker making a simple product in bulk in a simple process, high in the case of a complex, technologically sophisticated product such as aircraft). Where information content in the value chain is high, IT can result in radical changes to business processes to ensure that the linkages in the value chain are managed effectively.

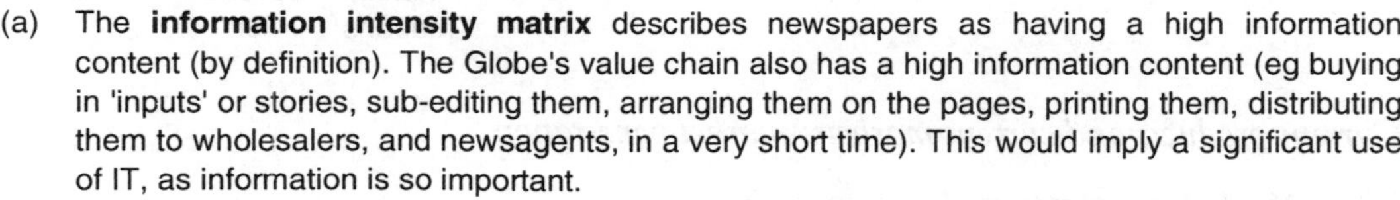

		Information in product	
		Low	*High*
Information in value chain	*Low*	Cement maker	
	High	Oil (refined)	Newspaper

Question 4

The management of the *Globe*, a national daily newspaper in the UK, is considering the introduction of radically new technology to enhance its internal processes and the services it gives its distributors and readers. The management wishes to encourage researchers and business planners to access its archive of historical data.

Can you think of any possible IT applications? What framework could be used to analyse the suitability of these ideas? Use the models suggested in this and the previous chapter.

Answer

This exercise tries to get you to apply some of these models to a 'knowledge based industry', newspaper publishing. Here are some suggestions.

(a) The **information intensity matrix** describes newspapers as having a high information content (by definition). The Globe's value chain also has a high information content (eg buying in 'inputs' or stories, sub-editing them, arranging them on the pages, printing them, distributing them to wholesalers, and newsagents, in a very short time). This would imply a significant use of IT, as information is so important.

(b) **Applications search tools** are also useful, as they can identify the possible uses of information technology.

  (i) What do distributors actually want (eg speed of delivery)?

  (ii) What do customers require (eg better graphics in maps and visual presentation)?

  (iii) New distribution systems (eg by fax).

  (iv) Using IT to create a database of archive material which can be accessed over the telecommunications network.

  (v) Store data on CD ROM.

(c) Futuristically, technology might be used to supplement print-based newspapers. Some writers argue that customers will be able to 'dial up' the stories they are interested in, which will be distributed over a communications network. Some newspapers are already exploring such a service.

5 PRODUCT-MARKET STRATEGY: DIRECTION OF GROWTH (ANSOFF) 6/97, 12/97

KEY TERM

Product-market mix is a short hand term for the **products/services** a firm sells (or a service which a public sector organisation provides) and the **markets** it sells them to.

Product-market mix: Ansoff's growth vector

5.1 Ansoff drew up a **growth vector matrix**, describing a combination of a firm's activities in current and new markets, with existing and new products.

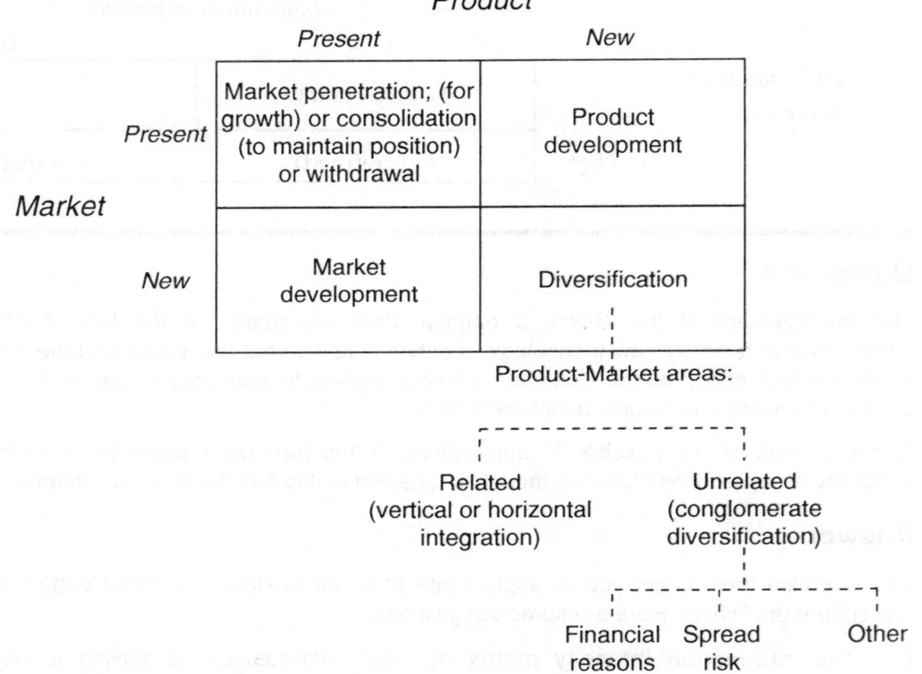

Current products and current markets: market penetration

5.2 **Market penetration.** The firm seeks to:

(a) **Maintain or to increase its share** of current markets with current products, eg through competitive pricing, advertising, sales promotion

(b) Secure dominance of growth markets

(c) Restructure a mature market by driving out competitors

(d) Increase usage by existing customers (eg airmiles, loyalty cards)

Present products and new markets: market development

5.3 **Market development** in which the firm seeks new markets for its current products, firm's products or services are a strength a new markets are a service opportunity or that the company is currently restricted in the markets it sells to. Ways of developing markets include:

(a) **New geographical areas** and export markets (eg a radio station building a new transmitter to reach a new audience).

(b) **Different package sizes** for food and other domestic items so that both those who buy in bulk and those who buy in small quantities are catered for.

(c) **New distribution channels** to attract new customers (eg organic food sold in supermarkets not just specialist shops

(d) **Differential pricing policies** to attract different types of customer and create **new market segments**. For example, travel companies have developed a market for cheap long-stay winter breaks in warmer countries for retired couples.

New products and present markets: product development

5.4 Product development is the launch of new products to existing markets.

(a) **Advantages**

(i) Product development forces competitors to innovate.

(ii) Newcomers to the market might be discouraged.

(b) The **drawbacks** include the expense and the risk.

Case example

Over the next few years, the UK will be saturated with huge number of TV channels as a result of digital TV. This gives the opportunity to enhance the services TV can provide, including 'new video on demand (NVOD – multiple showings of a film on different channels, starting 15 minutes apart).

New products: new markets (diversification)

5.5 **Diversification** occurs when a company decides to make **new products for new markets**. It should have a clear idea about what it expects to gain from diversification. There are two types of diversification, related and unrelated diversification.

(a) **Growth.** New products and new markets should be selected which offer prospects for growth which the existing product-market mix does not.

(b) **Investing surplus** funds not required for other expansion needs: but the funds could be returned to shareholders.

(c) The firm's strengths match the opportunity if:

(i) Outstanding new products have been developed by the firm's research and development department

(ii) The profit opportunities from diversification are high.

Related diversification

KEY TERM

Related diversification is 'development beyond the present *product market*, but still within the broad confines of the industry ... [it] ... therefore builds on the assets or activities which the firm has developed' (Johnson and Scholes). It takes the form of vertical or horizontal integration.

5.6 **Horizontal integration** refers to 'development into activities which are competitive with or directly **complementary** to a company's present activities. Sony, for example, started to compete in computer games.

5.7 **Vertical integration** occurs when a company becomes its own:

(a) **Supplier** of raw materials, components or services (**backward vertical integration**). For example, backward integration would occur where a milk producer acquires its own dairy farms rather than buying raw milk from independent farmers; or

(b) **Distributor** or sales agent (**forward vertical integration**), for example: where a manufacturer of synthetic yarn begins to produce shirts from the yarn instead of selling it to other shirt manufacturers.

5.8 **Advantages of vertical integration**

(a) A **secure supply of components** or raw materials with more control. Supplier bargaining power is reduced.

(b) **Strengthen the relationships** and contacts of the manufacturer with the 'final consumer' of the product.

(c) Win a share of the **higher profits**.

(d) Pursue a **differentiation strategy** more effectively.

(e) Raise **barriers to entry**.

5.9 **Disadvantages of vertical integration**

(a) **Overconcentration.** A company places 'more eggs in the same end-market basket' (Ansoff). Such a policy is fairly inflexible, more sensitive to instabilities and increases the firm's dependence on a particular aspect of economic demand.

(b) The firm **fails to benefit from any economies of scale or technical advances** in the industry into which it has diversified. This is why, in the publishing industry, most printing is subcontracted to specialist printing firms, who can work machinery to capacity by doing work for many firms.

Case examples

(a) **Horizontal integration**. Since water and electricity distribution were privatised in the UK, there have been a number of changes. Regional water companies have purchased **regional electricity distribution** firms. For example, *Norweb* has been bought by *North West Water*. Although the businesses are very different, they have a very similar customer base, and cost savings can be achieved by shared billing, accounts management etc.

(b) **Vertical integration**. Before privatisation, the UK electricity industry was a state-owned monopoly, vertically integrated from power generation to distribution. Privatisation effectively split up these two businesses, to introduce competition in power generation, so that the regional distribution companies could buy from a number of suppliers. However, the power distribution companies sought to buy a regional distribution company, giving them a captive market: National Power was set to buy Southern Electric, but the bid was blocked by the government on the grounds that it would inhibit competition.

Exam focus point

The June 1997 paper described a clothing manufacturer which was considering going into retailing, by buying a small chain of shops. You had to evaluate the pros and cons of such a move. Some manufacturers, such as Laura Ashley and Benetton, have followed this approach, with varying success.

Unrelated diversification

KEY TERM

Unrelated or conglomerate diversification 'is development beyond the present *industry* into products/ markets which, at face value, may bear no close relation to the present product/market.'

5.10 Conglomerate diversification is now very unfashionable. However, it has been a key strategy for companies in Asia, particularly South Korea.

5.11 **Advantages of conglomerate diversification**

(a) **Risk-spreading.** Entering new products into new markets offers protection against the failure of current products and markets.

(b) **High profit opportunities**. An improvement of the **overall profitability and flexibility** of the firm through acquisition in industries which have better economic characteristics than those of the acquiring firms.

(c) **Escape** from the present business. For example, Reed International moved away from paper production and into publishing.

(d) **Better access to capital** markets.

(f) **No other way to grow.** Expansion along existing lines might create a monopoly and lead to government investigations and control. Diversifications offer the chance of growth without creating a monopoly.

(g) **Use surplus cash.**

(h) **Exploit under-utilised resources.**

(i) **Obtain cash,** or other financial advantages (such as accumulated tax losses).

(j) **Use a company's image and reputation** in one market to develop into another where corporate image and reputation could be vital ingredients for success.

5.12 **Disadvantages of conglomerate diversification**

(a) The **dilution of shareholders' earnings** if diversification is into growth industries with high P/E ratios.

(b) **Lack of a common identity and purpose** in a conglomerate organisation. A conglomerate will only be successful if it has a high quality of management and financial ability at central headquarters, where the diverse operations are brought together.

(c) **Failure in one of the businesses will drag down the rest**, as it will eat up resources. *British Aerospace* was severely damaged by the effect of a downturn in the property market on its property subsidiary, *Arlington Securities*.

(d) **Lack of management experience** in the business area. *Japanese steel companies* have diversified into areas completely unrelated to steel such as personal computers, with limited success.

(e) **No good for shareholders.** Shareholders can spread risk quite easily, simply by buying a diverse portfolio of shares. They do not need management to do it for them.

Diversification and synergy

5.13 **Synergy** is the 2 + 2 = 5 effect, where a firm looks for **combined results** that reflect a better rate of return than would be achieved by the same resources used independently as separate operations. Synergy is used to justify the diversification.

5.14 **Obtaining synergy**

(a) **Marketing synergy:** use of common marketing facilities such as distribution channels, sales staff and administration, and warehousing. For example the AA offers loans to customers as well as breakdown services.

(b) **Operating synergy:** arises from the better use of operational facilities and personnel, bulk purchasing, a greater spread of fixed costs whereby the firms competence can be transferred to making new products. For example, although there is very little in common between sausages and ice cream, both depend on a core competence of *refrigeration*.

(c) **Investment synergy:** the joint use of plant, common raw material stocks, transfer of research and development from one product to another - ie from the wider use of a common investment in fixed assets, working capital or research.

(d) **Management synergy:** the advantage to be gained where management skills concerning current operations are easily transferred to new operations because of the similarity of problems in the two industries.

Exam focus point

'Synergy' can be applied to many aspects of a firm's activities. Marketing synergy appeared in December 1997 for 5 marks. Effectively, an acquirer wished to use the 'brand' of the firm it had acquired elsewhere within the group to boost sales and margins *worldwide*. We discuss international marketing in Chapter 15.

Case example

Pearson has four main businesses: consumer publishing (Penguin), TV production (Thames, Grundy), educational publishing (Addison Wesley, Longman and Simon & Schuster) and information (Financial Times, Economist). It is likely (at time of writing) that Pearson will focus its activities by disposing of its TV interests in order to concentrate on education. With the purchase of Simon & Schuster, Pearson now the biggest educational publisher in the world. There is some synergy between the publishing companies and Pearson's newspaper interests (eg FT).

5.15 Synergy is probably difficult to achieve in practice when one company takes over another. All too often, the expectations of synergy that help to justify a business combination fail to materialise.

Case example

For the merger of two computer companies Burroughs and Sperry into Unisys was justified by the fact that there were synergies between them. However, two incompatible ranges of computer were manufactured for some time afterwards.

Certainly, making sure that synergy is achieved calls for good management. Synergy is probably more discussed in takeover bids than actually implemented.

Question 4

A large organisation in road transport operates nationwide in general haulage. This field has become very competitive and with the recent down-turn in trade, has become only marginally profitable. It has been suggested that the strategic structure of the company should be widened to include other aspects of physical distribution so that the maximum synergy would be obtained from that type of diversification.

(a) Name three activities which might fit into the suggested new strategic structure, explaining each one briefly.

(b) Explain how each of these activities could be incorporated into the existing structure.

(c) State the advantages and disadvantages of such diversification.

Answer

The first step in a suggested solution is to think of how a company operating nationwide in general road haulage might diversify, with some synergistic benefits. Perhaps you thought of the following.

(a) Moving from nationwide haulage to international haulage.

(b) Moving from general haulage to 'speciality' types of haulage, perhaps haulage of large items of plant and machinery, or computer equipment.

(c) Providing a despatch service for small items (although this too is a very competitive business).

(d) Hiring smaller vehicles to customers for 'self-drive'.

(e) Moving into warehousing.

Only three suggestions are required by the question. You may have thought of different ideas to those in the list. You should appreciate however, that the principles of diversification need to be applied in a specific situation and there are no obvious ready-made and off-the-peg answers to such problems.

(a) To move from nationwide to international haulage, the company might be able to use its existing contacts with customers to develop an international trade. Existing administration and depot facilities in the UK could be used. Drivers should be available who are willing to work abroad, and the scope for making reasonable profits should exist. However, international road haulage might involve the company in the purchase of new vehicles (eg road haulage in Europe often involves the carriage of containerised products on large purpose-built vehicles). Since international haulage takes longer, vehicles will be tied up in jobs for several days, and a substantial investment might be required to develop the business. In addition, in the event of breakdowns, a network of overseas garage service arrangements will have to be created. It might take some time before business builds up sufficiently to become profitable.

(b) The same broad considerations apply to speciality types of haulage. Existing depot facilities could be used and existing customer contacts might be developed. However, expertise in specialist work will have to be 'brought in' as well as developed within the company and special vehicles might need to be bought. Business might take some time to build up and if the initial investment is high, there could be substantial early losses.

In the same way, you should be able to consider the other means of diversification suggested earlier in the solution. Although items (a) and (b) above do not cover all of the following items, the factors which need to be considered in a policy of diversification are as follows.

(a) Potential synergy.

(b) The size of the initial investments.

(c) The potential for growth and profits.

(d) Facilities required.

(e) Manpower required and expertise needed.

(f) The difficulties in building up customer contacts.

(g) Contingency planning: what happens if things do not go as well as expected? What is the worst possible outcome?

(h) Risk.

(i) To what extent are the products and services new, and to what extent are the markets new?

Withdrawal

5.16 It might be the right decision, to cease producing a product and/or to pull out of a market completely. This is a hard decision for managers to take if they have invested time and money of if the decision involves redundancies.

5.17 **Exit barriers** make this difficult.

(a) Cost barriers include redundancy costs, the difficulty of selling assets.

(b) Managers might fail to grasp the principles of opportunity costing ('we've spent all this money, so we must go on').

(c) Political barriers include government attitudes. Defence is an example.

(d) Marketing considerations may delay withdrawal. A product might be a 'loss-leader' for others, or might contribute to the company's reputation for its breadth of coverage.

(e) Psychology. Managers hate to admit failure, and there might be a desire to avoid a 'bloodletting'. Furthermore, people might wrongly assume that carrying on is a low risk strategy.

5.18 **Reasons for exit**

(a) The **company's business** may be in buying firms, selling their assets and improving their performance, and then selling them at a profit.

(b) **Resource limitations** mean that less profitable businesses have to be abandoned. A business might be sold to a competitor, or occasionally to management (as a buy-out).

(c) A company may be forced to quit, because of **insolvency**.

(d) **Change of competitive strategy**. In the microprocessor industry, many American firms have left high-volume DRAM chips to Asian firms so as to concentrate on high value added niche products.

(e) **Decline in attractiveness of the market.**

(f) **Funds can earn more elsewhere.**

Case examples

Pearson has sold a number of businesses, including Mindscape a software publisher.

5.19 Section summary

Product-market strategy can be:

- Penetration: same products, same markets
- Product development: new products, same markets
- Market development: same products, new markets
- Diversification: new products, new markets
- Withdrawal
- Any combination of the above, depending on the product portfolio

6 METHOD OF GROWTH

6.1 **Growth** can involve:

(a) **Building up new businesses** from scratch and developing them (sometimes called organic growth);

(b) **Acquiring** already existing businesses from their current owners via the purchase of a controlling interest in another company.

(c) A **merger** is the joining of two or more separate companies to form a single company.

(d) Spreading the costs and risks (**joint ventures** or other forms of **co-operation**).

Companies may expand or diversify by developing their own internal resources, but they are also likely to consider growth through acquisitions or mergers.

6.2 **The purpose of acquisitions**

(a) **Marketing advantages**

(i) Buy in a new product range

(ii) Buy a market presence (especially true if acquiring a company with overseas offices and contacts that can be utilised by the parent company)

(iii) Unify sales departments or to rationalise distribution and advertising

(iv) Eliminate competition or to protect an existing market

(b) **Production advantages**

(i) Gain a higher utilisation of production facilities and reap economies of scale by larger machine runs

(ii) 'Buy in' technology and skills

(iii) Obtain greater production capacity

(iv) Safeguard future supplies of raw materials

(v) Improve purchasing by buying in bulk.

(c) **Finance and management**

(i) Buy a high quality management team, which exists in the acquired company

(ii) Obtain cash resources where the acquired company is very liquid

(iii) Gain undervalued assets or surplus assets that can be sold off ('asset stripping')

(iv) Obtain tax advantages (eg purchase of a tax loss company).

(d) **Risk-spreading**

(e) **Independence**. A company threatened by a take-over might take over another company, just to make itself bigger and so a more expensive 'target' for the predator company.

(f) **Overcome barriers to entry.**

6.3 Many acquisitions **do** have a logic, and the **acquired company can be improved** with the extra resources and better management. Furthermore, much of the criticisms of **takeovers** has been directed more against the notion of **conglomerate diversification** as a strategy rather than takeover as a **method of growth**.

Case example

Amersham/Nycomed

It does not take X-ray vision to spot the commercial sense in Amersham International's merger with Norway's Nycomed. The enlarged group will be the world's largest supplier of diagnostic imaging agents - which enhance X-rays and medical scans - with 30 per cent of a £3bn market. The fit, in products, technology and geography, is excellent. And the group is promising annual cost savings of £40m within three years. Amersham's timing looks impeccable. Its shares have jumped a fifth since it announced a merger with the biotech division of Pharmacia & Upjohn three weeks ago, while Nycomed's have been woeful performers. As a result, Amersham's shareholders will get 50 per cent of the new group, although their company if contributing less than 40 per cent of the profits. At yesterday's prices, Amersham is valued at around 19 times forecast 1997 earnings and Nycomed only 14 times.

That does not mean it is a bad deal for the Norwegians. Relief that Nycomed has found another partner, two years after its failed merger attempt with Ivax of the US and despite a poor record since, sent the shares up 23 per cent yesterday.

Investors will also want reassurance that price pressure in US contrast media, the source of Nycomed's problems, is stabilising. And the potential of Nycomed's new ultrasound technology is still unclear. But a rating of 16 times estimated 1998 earnings does not look expensive for a rapidly growing healthcare company.

(*Financial Times,* 2 July 1997)

6.4 **Problems with acquisitions and mergers**

(a) **Cost**. They might be too expensive, especially if resisted by the directors of the target company. Proposed acquisitions might be referred to the government under the terms of anti-monopoly legislation.

(b) **Customers** of the target company might resent a sudden takeover and consider going to other suppliers for their goods.

(c) **Incompatibility**. In general, the problems of assimilating new products, customers, suppliers, markets, employees and different systems of operating might create 'indigestion' and management overload in the acquiring company. A proposed merger between two UK financial institutions was called off because of incompatible information systems.

(d) **Asymmetric information**. John Kay suggests that the 'acquisitions' market for companies is rarely efficient.

(i) The existing management 'always knows more about what is for sale than the potential purchaser. ... Successful bidders are often only the people who were willing to pay too much - that is the reason why their bid succeeds'.

(ii) 'At the same time, good buys may be ignored, because there is no potential purchaser confident that he really is making a good buy.'

(e) **Driven by the personal goals** of the acquiring company's managers, as a form of sport, perhaps.

(f) **Corporate financiers and banks** have a stake in the acquisitions process as they can charge fees for advice.

(g) **Poor success record of acquisitions.** Takeovers benefit the shareholders of the acquired company often more than the acquirer. According to the Economist Intelligence Unit, there is a consensus that fewer than half all acquisitions are successful.

(h) **Firms rarely take into account non-financial factors.** A survey by London Business School examining 40 acquisitions (in the UK and USA) revealed some major flaws.

(i) All acquirers conducted financial audits, but only 37% conducted anything approaching a management audit: despite detailed audits of equipment, property, finances etc, few bothered with people.

(ii) Some major problems of implementation relate to **human resources and personnel issues** such as morale, performance assessment and culture. Especially in service industries and 'knowledge-based' or creative businesses, many of the firm's assets are effectively the staff. If key managers or personnel leave, the business will suffer.

Case example

A classic example of an acquisition gone wrong was the purchase, by Midland Bank, of *Crocker Bank*, an American bank. Midland allowed Crocker's management a fair degree of autonomy. Very shortly after the purchase, it emerged that Crocker was riddled with bad debts, largely as a result of property lending.

This failed acquisition proved very expensive. Perhaps the end-result is that Midland, at one time in the 1930s the biggest bank in the world, is now a subsidiary of the Hong Kong and Shanghai Banking corporation.

Exam focus point

The June 1995 exam asked you to advise a company contemplating a takeover, using lessons from other firms.

Organic growth

6.5 Organic growth (sometimes referred to as internal development) is the primary method of growth for many organisations, for a number of reasons. Organic growth is achieved through the development of internal resources.

6.6 **Reasons for pursuing organic growth**

(a) **Learning.** The process of developing a new product gives the firm the best understanding of the market and the product.

(b) **Innovation.** It might be the only sensible way to pursue genuine technological innovations, and exploit them. (Compact disk technology was developed by Philips and Sony, which earns royalties from other manufacturers licensed to use it.)

(c) There is **no suitable target for acquisition.**

(d) Organic growth can be **planned more meticulously** and offers little disruption.

(e) It is often **more convenient** for managers, as organic growth can be financed easily from the company's current cash flows, without having to raise extra money on the stock market (eg to fund an acquisition).

(f) The **same style of management and corporate culture** can be maintained.

(g) **Hidden or unforeseen losses are less likely** with organic growth than with acquisitions.

(h) **Economies of scale** can be achieved from more **efficient use of central head office** functions such as finance, purchasing, personnel, management services etc.

6.7 **Problems with organic growth**

(a) **Time** - sometimes it takes a long time to climb a **learning curve**.

(b) **Barriers to entry** (eg distribution networks) are harder to overcome: for example a brand image may be built up from scratch.

(c) The firm will have to **acquire the resources independently.**

(d) Organic growth may be **too slow for the dynamics of the market**.

6.8 Organic growth is probably ideal for market penetration, and suitable for product or market development, but it might be a problem with extensive diversification projects.

Joint ventures, alliances and franchising

6.9 Short of mergers and takeovers, there are other ways by which companies can co-operate.

6.10 **Consortia:** organisations co-operate on specific business prospects.

Case example

Airbus is an example, a consortium including British Aerospace, Dasa, Aerospatiale and Casa (of Spain). However, it does have an unusual financial structure, and there are moves to turn it into a normal company.

6.11 **Joint ventures:** Two firms (or more) join forces for manufacturing, financial and marketing purposes and each has a share in both the equity and the management of the business.

(a) **Share funds**. As the capital outlay is shared, joint ventures are especially attractive to smaller or risk-averse firms, or where very expensive new technologies are being researched and developed (such is the civil aerospace industry).

(b) **Cut risk**. A joint venture can reduce the risk of government intervention if a local firm is involved (eg Club Mediterranée pays much attention to this factor).

(c) Participating enterprises **benefit from all sources of profit**.

(d) **Close control** over marketing and other operations.

(e) Overseas, a joint venture with an indigenous firm provides **local knowledge, quickly**.

(f) **Synergies**. One firm's production expertise can be supplemented by the other's marketing and distribution facility.

(g) **Learning.** Alliances can also be a 'learning' exercise in which each partner tries to learn as much as possible from the other.

(h) **Technology**. New technology offers many uncertainties and many opportunities. Such alliances provide funds for expensive research projects, spreading risk.

(i) **The alliance itself can generate innovations**

(j) The alliance can involve **'testing' the firm's core competence** in different conditions, which can suggest ways to improve it

6.12 **Disadvantages of joint ventures**

(a) Conflicts of interest between the different parties.

(b) Disagreements may arise over profit shares, amounts invested, the management of the joint venture, and the marketing strategy.

(c) One partner may wish to withdraw from the arrangement.

Case example

e.g.

SGS-Thompson's semiconductor manufacturing facility in Shenzhen, China (cost US$110m) was a joint venture. There were many problems, including the unsuitable site, selected by the Chinese partner. By 1996, according to The Economist, 'morale was at rock bottom and the partners did not trust each other'. "Vendors were ripping us off, the government was robbing us blink, key employees were on the take." The situation has now improved.

Other arrangements

6.13 A **licensing agreement** is a commercial contract whereby the licenser gives something of value to the licensee in exchange for certain performances and payments.

(a) The licenser may provide:

- (i) Rights to produce a patented product or use a patented production process.
- (ii) Manufacturing know-how (unpatented).
- (iii) Technical advice and assistance.
- (iv) Marketing advice and assistance.
- (v) Rights to use a trademark, brand etc.

(b) The licenser receives a royalty.

(c) Production is higher with no investment.

(d) The licensee might eventually become a competitor.

(e) The supply of essential materials, components, plant.

6.14 **Subcontracting** is also a type of 'alliance'. Co-operative arrangements also feature in supply chain management, JIT and quality programmes.

6.15 **Franchising** is a method of expanding the business on less capital than would otherwise be possible. For suitable businesses, it is an **alternative business strategy to raising extra capital** for growth. Franchisers include Budget Rent-a-car, Dyno-rod, Express Dairy, Holiday Inn, Kall-Kwik Printing, KFC, Prontaprint, Sketchley Cleaners, Body Shop and even McDonald's.

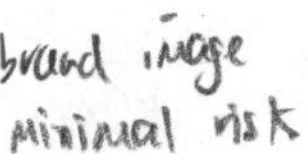

(a) The **franchiser** offers its:

(i) Name, and any goodwill associated with it

(ii) Systems and business methods.

(iii) Support services, such as advertising, training, help with site decoration etc.

(b) The **franchisee:**

(i) Provides capital, personal involvement and local market knowledge.

(ii) Pays the franchiser, in one way or another, for being granted these rights, and also the other support services.

(iii) Has responsibility for the day-to-day running, and for the ultimate profitability, of his own franchise.

6.16 **Disadvantages of franchising**

- The **search for competent candidates** is both costly and time consuming where the franchiser requires many outlets (eg McDonald's in the UK).

- **Control** over franchisees (McDonald's franchisees in New York recently refused to co-operate in a marketing campaign).

The virtual firm

6.17 An extreme example of an alliance is the so-called **virtual firm**. A virtual firm is created out of a **network of alliances** and subcontracting arrangements: it is as if most of the activities in a particular value chain are conducted by different firms, even though the process is loosely co-ordinated by one of them. It is outsourcing taken to its greatest extent.

6.18 For example, assume you manufacture small toys. You could in theory **outsource**:

(a) The design to a consultancy
(b) Manufacturing to a subcontractor in a low-cost country
(c) Delivery arrangements to a specialist logistics firm
(d) Debt collection to a bank (factoring)
(e) Filing, tax returns, bookkeeping to an accountancy firm.

6.19 Virtual corporations effectively put market forces in all linkages of the value chain - this has the advantage of creating *incentives* for suppliers, perhaps to take risks to produce a better product, but can lead to a loss of control.

6.20 Section summary

- Acquisitions enable swift growth but there are often management problems.
- Organic growth is sometimes too slow, as the firm has to climb a learning curve.

Remember that acquisitions and organic growth can be used for any of the product-market strategies outlined in Section 5.

7 USING SOFTWARE IN GENERATING STRATEGIES

Strategic planning packages

7.1 A variety of software packages exist to help with strategic planning. Some are commercially available, while others have been developed by larger businesses in house, or by management consultants. We discuss them here, as they use environmental and position audit data to suggest strategies.

Business Insight

7.2 **Business Insight** is an American package costing around £250. It is an **expert system** designed to collect information from the user about the business and its marketing strategy and offer a variety of analyses of the data that has been input.

7.3 The system is built on **rules** that draw on concepts put forward by management and marketing experts such as Porter and Kotler.

7.4 Data is input under a series of headings such as 'Market Definition', 'Competition', 'Suppliers', 'Financials', each of which has series of sub-headings. Market Definition, for instance is designed mainly to elicit information about prospective customers under four headings.

Market Definition

1. **The Environment**
2. **Prospect Characteristics**
3. **Prospect Objectives**
4 **Prospect's purchase decision**

7.5 Each sub-heading has a series of further sub-headings.

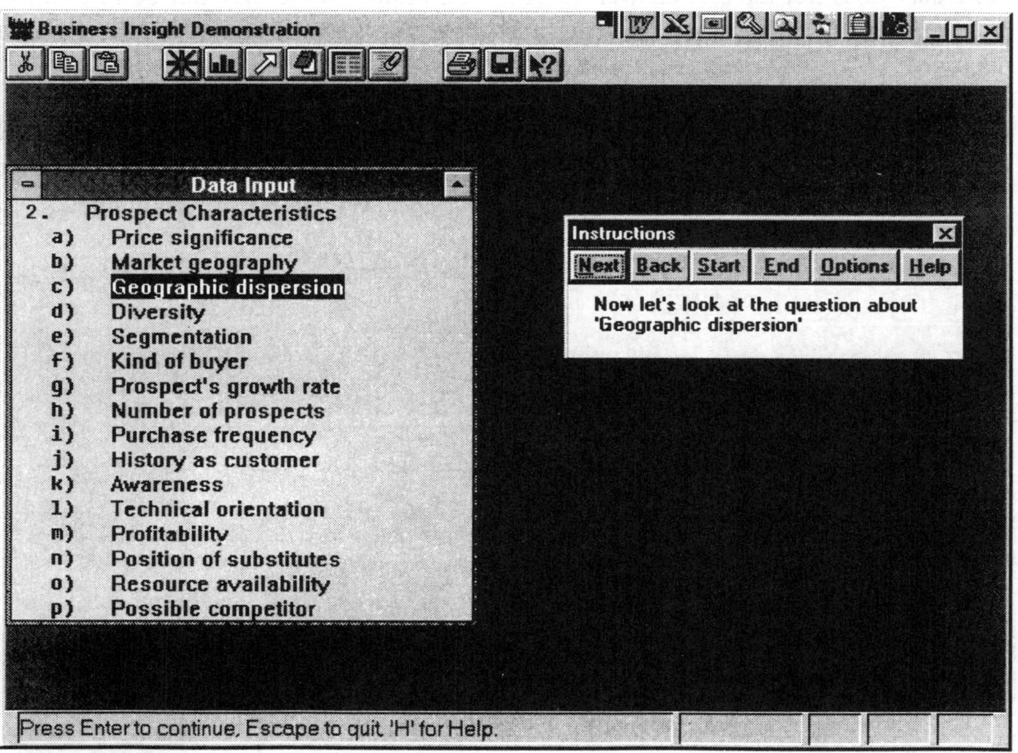

7.6 If you were to click on, say, Geographical Dispersion, you would be presented with a question, as follows.

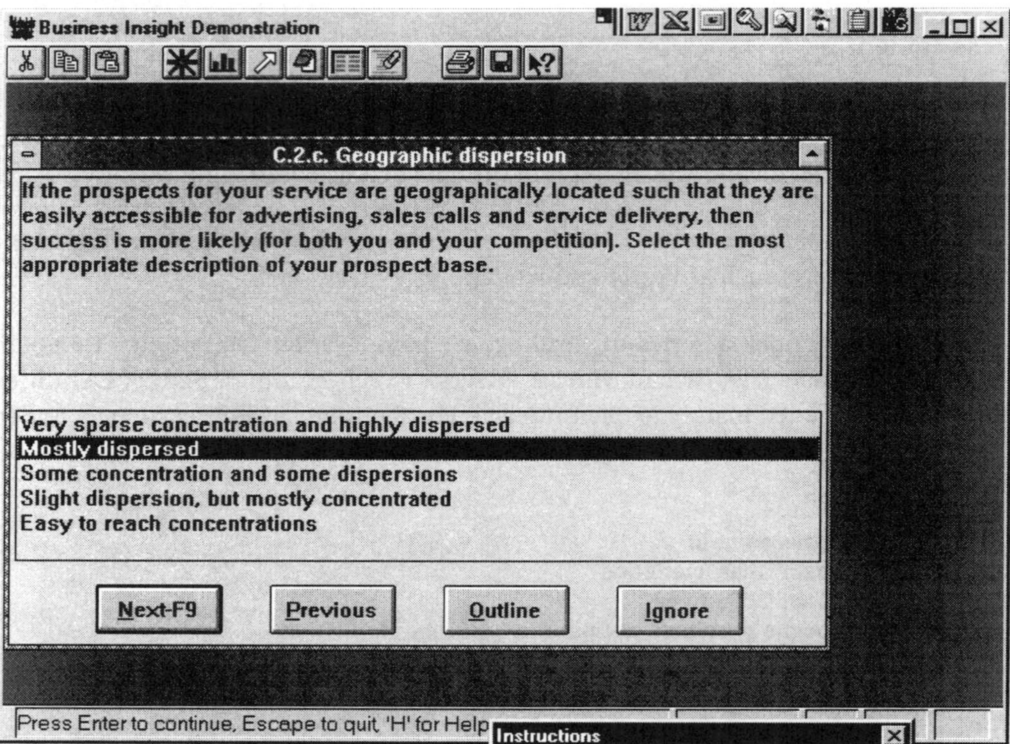

7.7 The user does not have to answer all of the questions (some may not be relevant or the answer may not be known at present), and the answers can be changed later if conditions change.

7.8 Once as much data as possible has been input, the system can analyse it and produce output in a variety of forms. In the illustration below, for example, the package rates a **focus strategy** as the one most likely to be successful for a particular company.

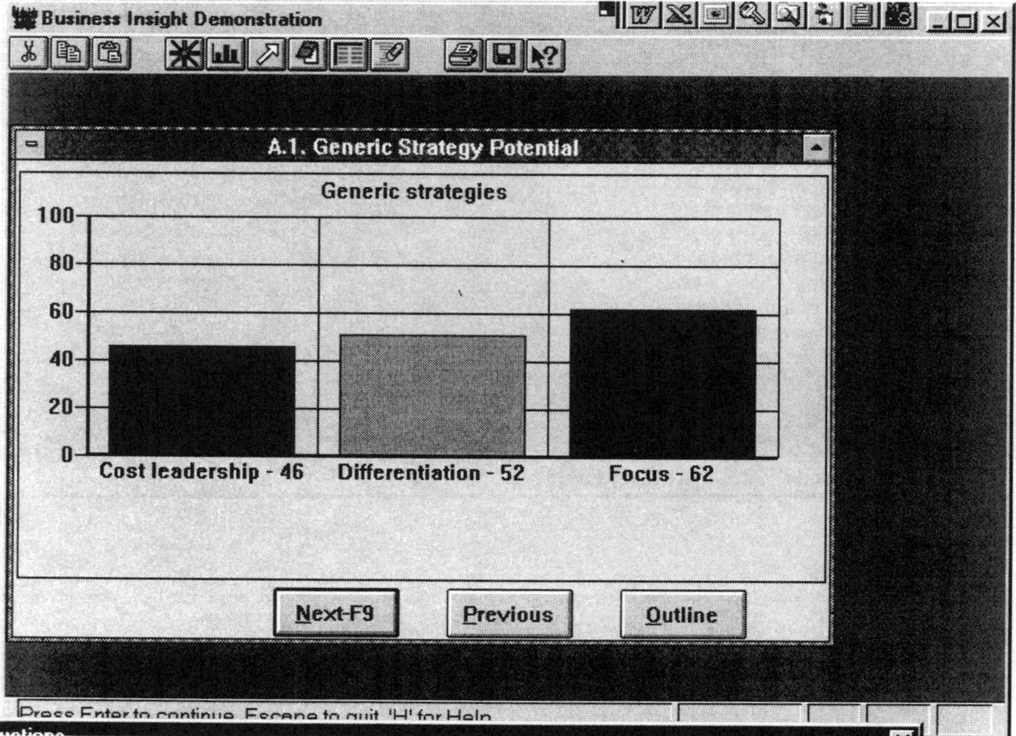

7.9 Here it indicates that the company's offering is under-priced.

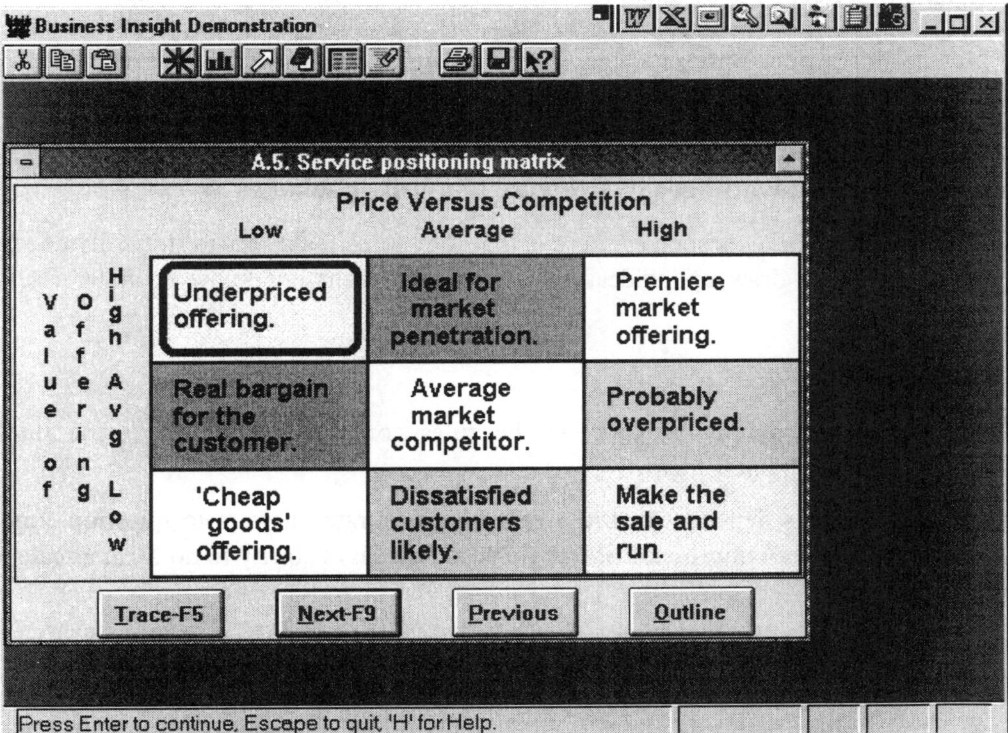

7.10 The package produces a series of 'Observations', generated by comparing the input data with the rules in the system. For example one observation might be that the business could 'expect very strong competitive rivalry', and it would be possible to trace this comment back to the data inputs that gave rise to it.

7.11 The package also rates the business in terms of critical success factors. One such factor is **profit potential**, based on Porter's **five forces** model, which we discussed in Chapter 5.

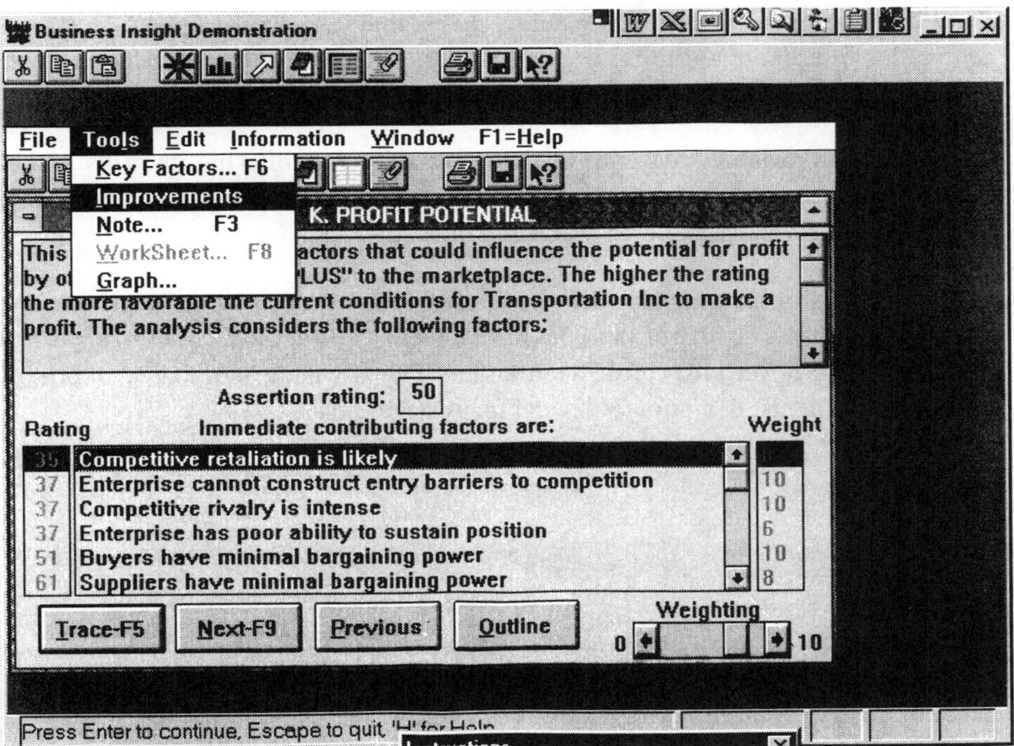

7.12 Clicking on 'Improvements', here, would bring up a series of suggestions as to the **actions** that needed to be taken to achieve a higher profit potential rating.

7.13 This is not a once-only exercise. The package allows the user to save a number of different strategies and has a facility for **comparing** one with another.

Advantages and disadvantages of strategic planning packages

7.14 The **advantage** of tools such as these is that they force managers to think about strategic issues, and they draw upon ideas that managers might not know about or realise the relevance of.

7.15 **Disadvantages**

(a) A package is only as good as the rules contained within it; some might be invalidated by new ideas.

(b) The analysis depends on the user giving accurate answers to questions, many of which are very impressionistic ('rate your business's ability to do X on a scale of 1 to 10').

(c) Brilliant new ideas are often born because their inventor has the ability to break away from conventional thinking.

(d) Any of the failings of the 'rational model' apply to this approach in that it is oversystematised: go back to Chapter 1 to refresh your memory.

8 BRAINWORKS PLC UPDATE

Questions can be fond in the Introduction box at the beginning of this chapter.

8.1 *Question 1.* Willard Mann does not believe there are any synergies from the merger of PeoplePower with Brainworks - he explicitly says that he does not see any economies of scale. However, you could argue that in certain key markets - such as financial services - there are real opportunities for synergy, given that London and New York are both centres for international capital trading. BW and PeoplePower could share information and give their business clients a more internationally diverse choice of candidates.

8.2 *Question 2.* BW probably does not need to diversify - it is offering its skills to a heavily segmented market, and there is probably still scope for expansion. However, one or two ideas for new services are offered at the end of chapter 13.

8.3 *Question 3.* It is in hard to know how to apply Porter's model. Business clients are more concerned with the quality of candidates than fees. Anyhow, BW does not appear to have thought of any novel ideas of differentiation. The US firm is probably offering better quality to its clients. BW pursues several focus strategies.

Chapter roundup

- The **SWOT analysis** combines the results of the environmental analysis and the internal appraisal into one framework for assessing the firm's current and future strategic fit, or lack of it, with the environment. It is an analysis of the organisation's strengths and weaknesses, and the opportunities and threats offered by the environment.
- **Gap analysis** quantifies what a firm must do to reach its objectives. Any gap between the firm's objectives and the forecast results of continuing with other activities must be met somehow.
- **Competitive strategy** involves a choice between being the lowest cost producer (**cost leadership**), making the product different or apparently different from competitors' products in some way (**differentiation**) or specialising on a segment of the market (**focus**, by addressing that segment by a strategy of cost leadership or differentiation).
- **Porter** believes that a firm *must* choose one of these or be **stuck-in-the-middle**.
- The value chain can be used as a tool to devise competitive strategies. IT can support the value chain.
- **Product-market** strategies involve determining which products should be sold in which markets, by market penetration, market development, product development and diversification.
- Some firms like to diversify their activities into related areas.
- Vertical integration is when a firm carries out more activities in the value system.
- Horizontal integration is expansion into similar areas.
- Conglomerate diversification is expansion into unrelated businesses. Diversification is assumed to be risky.
- The **method of growth** can vary.
    - Companies can grow **organically**, building up their own products and developing their own market.
    - On the other hand they may choose to acquire these ready-made by buying other companies. **Acquisition** is often an easy way of diversification. Acquisitions are risky because of the incompatibility of different companies.
    - Many firms grow by other means, such as joint ventures or franchising.
- Software can be used to support strategic planning decisions but its underlying risks and assumptions should be tested.

Quick quiz

1 Define corporate appraisal. (see para 1.1)

2 What are the major options in using SWOT to guide strategy formulation? (1.9)

3 What is gap analysis? (2.1)

4 List three generic strategies for competitive advantage. (3.3)

5 What is required for a successful cost leadership strategy? (3.6)

6 How do you differentiate? (3.8)

7 What are the drawbacks of a focus strategy? (3.12)

8 What is meant by stuck-in-the-middle? (3.13)

9 How might the value chain be used in strategy formulation? (4.1, 4.3)

10 Draw Ansoff's growth vector diagram. (5.1)

11 What are the disadvantages of vertical integration? (5.9)

12 What are the disadvantages of conglomerate diversification? (5.12)

13 What is synergy? (5.13)

14 Why might firm contemplate making acquisitions? (6.2)

15 Describe joint ventures. (6.11)

16 What is the virtual firm? (6.17)

17 What are the pros and cons of strategic planning software? (7.14, 7.15)

Exam questions tend to cover many elements of the strategic management process, hence the 25-mark case study, typical of Section B questions, and your first 50 mark case study, in the list below.

Question to try	Level	Marks	Time
9	Exam standard	25	45 mins
10	Exam standard	50	90 mins

Chapter 8

STRATEGIC OPTIONS EVALUATION

Chapter topic list		Syllabus reference
1	Evaluation	1(c)(v)
2	Financial evaluation: an example	1(c)(v)
3	Ranking costs and benefits	1(c)(v)
4	Risk and uncertainty	1(c)(v)
5	Stakeholders	1(c)(v)
6	Brainworks plc update	

Introduction

The techniques in this chapter aim to show how in some cases, a systematic and rational approach to evaluating and company strategic options can be achieved. Financial evaluation appears in the exam regularly, so we show you an example of some of the issues involved.

A number of techniques enable decision-making in conditions of partial ignorance to be quantified. **Decision trees** enable the different expected values of different options to be compared. **Decision matrices** enable management's basic optimism or pessimism to be taken into account. **Sensitivity analysis** demonstrates the extent to which an outcome will change if inputs to the situation change.

Finally, the views of **stakeholders** need to be taken into account: a strategy affects different stakeholders in different ways.

Brainworks plc

1 Who are the key stakeholders in the demerger decision?

1 EVALUATION 12/97

Exam focus point

In December 1997, you had to evaluate the growth strategies the firm in the case study had pursued to date. Always make use of the financial data provided in the case, but don't be dominated by it.

1.1 According to the rational model, individual strategies have to be *evaluated*, according to a number of criteria, before a strategy or a mixture of strategies is chosen. Three criteria are suitability, feasibility and acceptability.

Suitability

1.2 **Suitability** relates to the **strategic logic** of the strategy. The strategy should fit the situation of the firm. Does it:

- **Exploit** company strengths and distinctive **competences**?
- Rectify company **weaknesses**?
- **Neutralise** or deflect environmental **threats**?
- Help the firm to seize **opportunities**?
- **Satisfy the goals** of organisation?
- **Fill the gap** identified by gap analysis?
- Generate/maintain **competitive advantage**?
- Involve an acceptable level of **risk**?
- Suit the **politics** and corporate **culture**?

Feasibility

1.3 **Feasibility** asks whether the strategy can in fact be implemented. In other words, does the firm have:

(a) Enough **money**?
(b) The **ability** to deliver the goods/services specified in the strategy?
(c) The ability to deal with the likely **responses that competitors** will make?
(d) Access to **technology, materials and resources**?
(e) Enough **time** to implement the strategy?

1.4 Strategies which do not make use of the existing competences, and which therefore call for new competences to be acquired, might not be feasible because:

(a) Acquiring competences via organic growth takes time.

(b) If a takeover is therefore necessary, its disadvantages may outweigh the advantages.

(c) Time must be allowed for new organisational and communication patterns to develop and operate freely, and for personal abilities and relationships to mature.

Acceptability (to stakeholders)

1.5 **The acceptability** of a strategy relates to people's expectation of it. It is here that stakeholder analysis can be brought in. More about stakeholders in Section 4 below.

(a) **Financial considerations**. Strategies will be evaluated by considering how far they contribute to meeting the dominant objective of increasing shareholder wealth.

- Return on investment
- Profits
- Growth
- EPS
- Cash flow
- Price/Earnings
- Market capitalisation (ie value of shares on the stockmarket)

(b) **Customers** may object to a strategy if it means reducing service, but on the other hand they may have no choice.

(c) **Banks** are interested in the implications for cash resources, debt levels etc.

(d) **Government**. A strategy involving a takeover may be prohibited under monopolies and mergers legislation.

(e) **The public**. Similarly, the environmental impact may cause key stakeholders to withhold consent - out of town superstores are now frowned upon by national and local government.

(f) **Risk**. Different shareholders have different attitudes to risk. A strategy which changed the risk/return profile, for whatever reason, may not be acceptable.

1.6 Of course, not all stakeholders are equally important or have 'rights' to be considered.

Case example

Coca-Cola

In the 1980s, *Coca-Cola* decided to change its flavour to compete with Pepsi. Market research, taster tests and so forth elicited favourable responses to the change, and so after this evaluation exercise the new formulation was introduced. A small group of consumers vociferously opposed the change; and this opposition spread suddenly and rapidly like an epidemic, forcing Coca-Cola to re-introduce the old formula.

Apparently some consumers perceived Coke to symbolise 'American values', and changing the formula appeared to be an assault on them.

Other consumers, who had initially favoured the product, turned against it, for reasons that could not be predicted by market researchers. This exemplifies:

(a) The limitations of planning

(b) The seemingly random behaviour of the environment (as it became fashionable *not* to drink the new formula)

(c) The way in which small causes (a few disaffected Coke-drinkers) can generate major consequences

(d) The limitations to organisational gathering of information and strategic evaluation.

1.7 Section summary

Strategy is evaluated according to:

- Suitability to the firm and its position
- Feasibility, (the firm's capability to implement the strategy)
- Acceptability to key stakeholders

2 FINANCIAL EVALUATION: AN EXAMPLE

Exam focus point

In answering case study questions, you may be given financial (eg profit) data which you may be expected to use. By this stage in your studies you should be fully confident about basic profit and cash flow calculations - they won't be all that technically demanding in Paper 12.

2.1 Needless to say, strategies are evaluated in their impact on future profits, but this is not a precise science. By now, however, you should feel able to use profit and DCF analysis, so answer the Question below.

Question 1

T plc is a well-established company providing telecommunications services both nationally and internationally. Its business has been concerned with telephone calls, the provision of telephone lines and equipment, and private telecommunication networks. T plc has supplemented these services recently by offering mobile phones, which is an expanding market world-wide.

The company maintains a diverse customer base, including residential users, multi-national companies, government agencies and public sector organisations. The company handles approximately 100 million calls each working day, and employs nearly 140,000 personnel.

Strategic development

The Chairman of T plc stated within the latest Annual Report that there are three main areas in which the company aims to develop in order to remain in a world leader in the telecommunications market. He believes that the three main growth areas reflect the evolving nature of the telecommunications market, and will provide scope for development.

The areas in which development is planned are:

(1) Expansion of the telecommunications business in the national and overseas markets, both by the company acting on its own and through partnership arrangements with other suppliers.

(2) Diversification into television and multi-media services, providing the hardware to permit telephone shopping from home and broadcasting services.

(3) Extension of the joint ventures and strategic alliances which have already been established with companies in North America, Europe, India and the Far East.

The Chairman explained that the company is intent on becoming a world leader in communications. This will be achieved through maintaining its focus on long-term development by improving its services to customers, developing high-quality up-to-date products and being innovative, flexible and market-driven. His aim is to deliver a world-class service at competitive cost.

Financial information

Comparative statistics showing extracts from the company's financial performance in its national telecommunications market over the last two years are as follows:

	Last year	*Previous year*
	£ million	£ million
Turnover	16,613	15,997
Profit before interest and tax	3,323	2,876
Capital employed	22,150	21,300

The company estimates its cost of capital to be approximately 11%.

The Chairman expressed satisfaction with the increase in turnover and stated that cost efficiencies were now being generated following completion of a staff reduction programme. This would assist the company in achieving a target return on capital employed (ROCE) in this market of 20% over the next three years.

Business opportunities

The Chief Executive of T plc has stated that the major opportunities for the company lie in the following areas:

- encouraging greater use of the telephone;
- provision of advanced services, and research and development into new technology, including the Internet and systems integration;
- the increasing freedom from government control of world-wide telecommunication services.

An extensive television and poster advertising campaign has been used by the company. This was in order to penetrate further the residential market by encouraging greater use of the telephone with varying charging incentives being offered to residential customers.

To further the objective of increasing long-term shareholder value, the company is actively considering investment of £200 million in each of the next three years in new technology and quality improvements in its national market. Because of its specialist technical nature, the investment is not expected to have any residual value at the end of the three-year period.

Following the investment, the directors of T plc believe that its rate of profit before interest and tax to turnover in its national telecommunications market will remain constant. This rate will be at the same level as last year for each of the three years of the investment.

Markets and competition

The company is currently experiencing an erosion of its market share and faces increasingly strong competition in the mobile phone market. While T plc is the leader in its national market, with an

85% share of the telecommunications business, it has experienced a reduced demand for the supply of residential lines in the last five years as competition has increased.

The market for the supply of equipment in the national telecommunications market is perceived to be static. The investment of £200 million in each of the next three years is estimated to increase T plc's share of this market to a level of 95%. The full improvement of 10% is expected to be received by T plc next year and its market share will then remain at this level for the full three-year period. It is anticipated that unless further investment is made after the three-year period, T plc's market share will revert to its current level as a consequence of the expected competitive response.

Industry regulation

The government has established an industry regulatory organisation to promote competition and deter anti-competitive behaviour.

As a result of the activities of the regulator and aggressive pricing strategies, it is anticipated that charges to customers will remain constant for the full three-year period of the new investment.

All cash flows can be assumed to occur at the end of the year to which they relate. The cash flows and discount rate are in real terms.

Required

(a) Evaluate and comment on T plc's proposed investment in new technology and quality improvements in its national telecommunications market.

Assume that variable costs are 80% of the incremental revenue, and that fixed costs will not increase. Ignore working capital.

(b) Assess to what extent the investment in new technology and quality improvements in T plc's national telecommunications market contributes towards the closure of the company's planning gap in respect of its target ROCE.

Note: You may assume that the entire capital investment is written off at the end of the three-year period.

(c) Recommend a strategy which T plc could employ to close the planning gap and achieve the strategic development aims identified by the Chairman.

Answer

(a) T's proposed investment in technological improvements

Using DCF

Investment outflows Size of investment: £200m per year for three years, or a total in cash terms of £600m. Using discount tables, the discount factor for three years at 11% (cost of capital) of 2.444 gives a present value of these cash outflows of £488.8m

Revenue inflows. The assumption is that market share will increase from 85% to 95%. Currently, turnover, for 85% of the market is £16,613m. This will increase to £18,567m (£16,613 × 95/85), in other words an inflow of £1,954m pa or, applying the discount rate, £4,767m over three years.

Variable costs, according to the question, are 80% of the incremental revenue. This amounts to £1,954m × 80% = £1,563.2m or, applying the discount factor, £3,814.2m, over three years.

Net present value

	£m
Size of investment, NPV	(488.8)
Revenues	4,767.0
Variable costs	(3,814.2)
Net present value	464.0m

Using ROCE

Whilst in cashflow terms, the scheme is a good one, being higher than T's cost of capital, T actually measures its performance in terms of return on investment, with a target ROI of 20%

The investment is £200m per year, and annual revenues less variable costs increase by £391m (ie £1,954m less £1,563m). However, we must question whether the investment can be separated from the firm's other capital employed. In year 1 for example, total profit will be £3,323m plus £391m = £3,714m. For the sake of argument, as a percentage of capital employed (£22,150m) this amounts to 16.7%, an improvement on last year but not as high as target. (It is interesting that capital employed for last year was £850m more than the previous year, whereas the profit was only £447m higher – does this imply new capital was brought in?)

All these figures go to show is that the firm's targets are varied. The investment, whilst perfectly beneficial in cash terms, does not reflect the target ROCE even though it goes towards it.

Shareholders' objectives

It is slightly surprising that no objectives have been set for the share price or other performance indicators such as earnings per share, which are couched in terms more relevant to the investment community.

(b) *Closing the planning gap*

The chairman hopes to achieve a target ROCE of 20%. On capital employed of £22,150, this suggests a *target annual profit* of £22,150 × 20% of £4,430m. In other words, annual profit will have to increase by £1,107m (£4,430m less £3,323m currently). The new investment, providing £391m per annum (£1,954m uncleared revenue × 20%, ie variable costs are 80%) amounts to 35% of the planning gap. Additional profit of £716m is needed to close the planning gap.

The calculation ignores the following issues.

(i) The risk of regulatory response
(ii) Competitor reaction
(iii) The need for expenditure to maintain market share.

(c) *Strategies to close the planning gap*

> *Tutorial note.* Ideas for suitable strategies are flagged throughout the question, and you could have happily built on your answer to (d). But remember that this part of the question does not address market share objectives or innovation objectives but is directly focused on increasing reported ROCE and hence profit over the next three years. Any strategies you suggest must, whatever else they do, be profitable and not require huge investments no matter how large the 'long-term' benefits will be.

To close the planning gap, T has to generate annual profits (in addition to the £391m already generated) of £716m. Furthermore, because the gap is expressed as ROCE, any new investment might affect the capital employed figure. Projects will be chosen which offer the highest possible return.

(i) *More cost cutting*? To chose the remaining gap, T could cut its costs further by approximately 5% (being £716m /(£16,613m - £3,323m). A 1% cut in costs would achieve savings of £143m. The Chairman wants T 'to deliver a world-class service at competitive cost' and, indeed, cost-cutting is specifically mentioned in the question: 'cost efficiencies were now being generated following completion of a successful staff reduction programme. This would assist the company in achieving a target return on capital employed in this market of 20% over the next three years)'. However, we are not given data as to the scale of the cost efficiencies.

(ii) *Penetration (domestic)*. T cannot simply increase its prices to raise revenue as its prices are regulated. The number of subscribers is likely to fall to competitors. T can encourage customers to make more use of the phone, simply to generate revenue, for the same level of fixed costs. (Friends and Family discounts are an example.) As argued earlier, attention to penetration strategies is necessary.

Penetration (overseas markets) This is a big opportunity – but this must not be achieved at the expense of a massive investment, which would decrease return on capital in the next three years, and take time to generate profits. It thus seems likely that T should concentrate its efforts on where it can best add value, in alliance with local firms. Such strategic alliance should generate revenue but with little pressure on costs or investments.

(iii) *Market development*

T already operates in a number of overseas markets. New markets can include *new overseas markets* or *new consumer markets*. T is already aiming to build a genuinely global presence, and so might be able to take advantage of opportunities in Latin America or Africa. Such investments need to be handled carefully. T does not need to install a fixed line network and can 'leapfrog' over older or intermediate technologies.

A genuinely global market is, in a way, a new market. Exploiting this global market with a *suitable alliance*, is also possible, firstly because of an increase in *telecommunications traffic*, and secondly because of world trade liberalisation in services. A potential problem is that prices will almost certainly fall, so T has to position itself to get revenue from increased volume or offer higher value-added services such as network management.

However, from the chairman's point of view, such *alliances can take time to develop*. They are also subject to heavy regulatory pressure. Whether they will be able to develop the increased revenue is open to question.

(iv) *Product development*. The chairman has already indicated new services, such as home shopping and *internet services*. The internet can be a source of revenue growth, simply because of the use of telecommunications traffic which can be charged to users. T can also gain more of the potential revenue by acting as a service provider (like AOL or Compuserve) in its own right. As the internet becomes more of a consumer than a specialist service, T's brand name should stand it in good stead.

(v) *Diversification* is, classically, the *highest risk strategy* which may offer the highest rewards providing it is related as opposed to conglomerate diversification. The chairman has not mentioned smaller scale initiatives – T after all has a huge subscriber base, and could use it to collect bills for other companies via the phone bill. T will never be a content provider for the multimedia groups it serves; others will do just as well, but as owner of the hardware and the communications system it stands to profit from the increased traffic.

Summary

Most of the chairman's suggestions offer the prospect of significant wealth – but they seem to be *long-term investments* rather than the focus on the relatively short-term profit and ROCE targets which the chairman is concerned with. Cost cutting and market penetration, in the UK and overseas, is the best way to deliver the targets.

3 RANKING COSTS AND BENEFITS

3.1 A strategy can be assessed on how it achieves the organisation's objectives, but some **objectives may conflict** and the choice may not be clear cut.

3.2 The approaches below compare strategies according to the way they support some objectives rather than others, or those whose benefits cannot be quantified easily.

Ranking and scoring

3.3 **Ranking and scoring methods** best illustrated by means of a simple example. The **objectives are weighted** in relative **importance** (eg minimising competitive threats may be more important than other objectives). We assume for the example below that the strategic options cannot be realistically combined.

Objectives *Strategic option*	*Growth in profit by over 10%*	*Reduce dependence on suppliers*	*Minimise competitive threats*	*Score*	*Rank*
Do nothing	X	X	X	-	
Cut costs by subcontracting	✓	X	X	4	3rd
Expand product range	✓	X	✓	9	1st
Offer discounts to customers for fixed term contract	X	X	✓	5	2nd
Objective weighting	4	3	5		

In the above example, expanding the product range would be chosen as the firm believes it will enhance profits and minimise competitive threats.

3.4 In many cases, the strategies may not be mutually exclusive, or it might be possible to implement all the strategic options above (other than doing nothing). However the example indicates:

(a) The relative importance given to different commercial objectives
(b) The assessment of a strategy as to how well it conforms with them

Cost/benefit analysis

3.5 **Cost/benefit analysis** (CBA) is a strategy evaluation technique often used in the public sector, where many of the costs and benefits of a project are **intangible** and where market forces do not capture all costs and benefits.

(a) The project and its overall objectives are defined.

(b) It is not always easy to put a value on **social costs**. For example, a new road might result in excessive noise for local residents. They can be asked how much, in principle, they would be able and prepared to pay to move to a quieter dwelling. This gives a very rough estimate of the value of tranquillity. Financial costs are easy to assess.

(c) The **net benefits** for the project are estimated, if possible. A road might reduce journey times, and so save money. These are compared with costs, and the project is appraised by discounted cash flow (NPV and IRR) or cost/benefit ratios.

3.6 Private sector companies might be interested in CBA because:

(a) CBA can be applied **internally** (eg assessing an information systems project).

(b) **It can help them negotiate with public sector officials**. For example, large building projects require permission from the local authority. Local government officials sometimes insist on certain social benefits to be included in a project, so that some of the potential 'nuisance costs' can be covered.

4 RISK AND UNCERTAINTY 6/95

4.1 Strategies, by definition, deal with future events: the future cannot be predicted. Forecasts can, as we have seen, be wrong and there is a possibility that losses will result.

4.2 We can make a distinction between **risk** and **uncertainty**, but often the terms are used **interchangeably**.

KEY TERM

(a) **Risk** is sometimes used to describe situations where outcomes are not known, but their **probabilities** can be estimated. (This is the underlying principle behind insurance.)

(b) **Uncertainty** is present when the outcome cannot be predicted or assigned probabilities. (Many insurance policies exclude 'war damage, riots and civil commotion'.)

Types of risk and uncertainty

4.3

Risk	Comment
Physical risk	Earthquakes, fire, flooding, and equipment breakdown. In the long-term, climatic changes: global warming, drought (relevant to water firms).
Economic risk	Assumptions about the economic environment might turn out to be wrong. Not even the government forecasts are perfect.
Financial risk	A strategy might be regarded 'risky' if: (i) It results in increased borrowings (and increased gearing). (ii) The cash flows from the business are volatile. (iii) There is a need for significant capital expenditure with uncertain or volatile future returns. (iv) The strategy alters investors' perceptions thereby increasing their required rate of return.
Business risk	Lowering of entry barriers (eg new technology); changes in customer/supplier industries leading to changed relative power; new competitors and factors internal to the firm (eg its culture or technical systems); or management misunderstanding of core competences.
Political risk	Nationalisation, sanctions, civil war, political instability, can all have an impact on the business.

Exam focus point

The June 1995 exam asked you to apply the list of risks above to the company outlined in the 50-mark case.

Adjusting for risk

4.4 A firm might require that all investments make a return of, say, 5%. This can be adjusted for risk.

(a) **Return**. The target return could be raised to compensate for the risk.

(b) **Payback**. To protect cash flows, it might be made a condition of all new investment projects that the project should pay back within a certain period of time, say three to four years.

(c) **Finance**. It might be determined that the investment should be financed under strict conditions (eg only from profits).

Risk appraisal in strategy evaluation

4.5 Planners try to **quantify the risk**, so as to compare the estimated riskiness of different strategies.

(a) '**Rule of thumb**' methods might express a range of values from worst possible result to best possible result with a best estimate lying between these two extremes.

(b) **Basic probability theory** expresses the likelihood of a forecast result occurring. This would evaluate the data given by informing the decision-maker that there is, for example, a 50% probability that the best estimate will be achieved, a 25% chance that the worst result will occur and a 25% chance that the best possible result will occur. This evaluation of risk might help the executive to decide between alternative strategies, each with its own risk profile.

(c) One way of measuring the dispersion or '**spread of values**' with different possible outcomes from a decision is to calculate a **standard deviation** of the expected value (EV) of profit. The higher the standard deviation, the higher the risk, as the EV is more volatile.

Exam focus point

The syllabus requires you to have some knowledge of the techniques used in decision theory. You should be familiar with them from Paper 9. You will not be asked to use them in the exam, but you should refer to them when necessary.

Knowledge brought forward

You need to know where or when these might be applied, but it is inconceivable that in this paper you would be asked a numerical question on decision trees etc.

Decision theory

The problems posed by the existence of uncertainty in decision making lie mainly in the measurement and description of possible outcomes.

Point estimates

- Where uncertainty exists, any single point estimate which is made for a variable is no more than a typical value of that variable and so it may not be borne out by events
- Hence *accurate* forecasts of revenues and costs become difficult to make

Information overload

A further difficulty lies in the challenge to *present information* in such a way that the recipient, who will make the decision, receives enough knowledge concerning the effect of uncertainty on the range of possible outcomes without being overloaded by information.

Attitude to risk

- A *risk seeker* is someone who is interested in the best outcomes no matter how small the chance they may occur
- A decision maker is *risk neutral* if he is concerned with what will be the most likely outcome
- A *risk averse* decision maker acts on the assumption that the worst outcome might occur

Decision-making techniques

The existence of uncertainty does not alter the fundamentals of decision making: there is still a need for correct decision definition and the correct incremental approach to valuation using opportunity costs and so on, but the measurement of relevant amounts becomes more difficult.

Conservative estimates

- Outcomes are estimated in a conservative manner in order to provide a built-in safety factor
- However, this method fails to give explicit consideration to a range of outcomes
- By concentrating only on conservative figures, it may also fail to consider the *most likely* outcomes

Three-point estimates

- Data are provided for the most likely, for pessimistic and for optimistic outcomes and hence the method provides information on the range of outcomes

Expected values

- Single point estimates are derived using the probabilities of the various possible outcomes
- Outcomes are weighted by probabilities and so the range of outcomes is given consideration but is not shown in the figure derived

Uncertainty: calculations

In an uncertain situation it may be possible to identify different possible outcomes and analyse them in various ways.

Expected values

- If contribution might be £10,000, £20,000 or £30,000, with respective probabilities of 0.3, 0.5 and 0.2, the expected value of contribution is:

	£
10,000 × 0.3	3,000
20,000 × 0.5	10,000
30,000 × 0.2	6,000
Expected value	19,000

- There may be further additional *conditions*, for example there may be only a 75% chance of making one of these three positive contributions and a 25% chance of a negative contribution of £10,000, in which case the expected value is (£19,000 (calculated as above) × 0.75) + (£(10,000) × 0.25) = £14,250 – £2,500 = £11,750 .
- A decision tree may help you to sort out the various possibilities (see below).

Payoff tables: decision matrices

- Draw up a decision matrix or *payoff table* and make decisions based on attitude to risk using criteria such as the following
    - *Maximax*: maximise the maximum contribution
    - *Minimin*: minimise the minimum costs or losses
    - *Maximin*: maximise the minimum profit
    - *Minimax*: minimise the maximum costs or losses
- Here is a type of payoff table that illustrates the different contributions that might be earned depending on the action taken in anticipation of the future and on what actually happens

- Here are two payoff tables for two separate decisions.

		Profits					*Costs*	
		Actions					*Actions*	
	A	*B*	*C*			*D*	*E*	*F*
	I 100	80	60		IV	40	50	60
Circumstances	II 90	120	85	*Circumstances*	V	70	80	25
	III –20	10	40		VI	20	30	30
Max profit	100	120	85	*Min cost*		20	30	25
Min profit	–20	10	40	*Max cost*		70	80	60

  - For the first decision, action B would be chosen using *maximax* and action (using maximin).
  - For the second decision, action D would be chosen using minimin and F using minimax.

  If both profits and losses could occur, just treat losses as negative profits and apply the maximin criterion.

Decision trees

A decision tree is a diagram which illustrates the choices and possible outcomes of a decision. All the possible choices that can be made are shown as branches on the tree and all the possible outcomes of each choice are also shown as subsidiary branches.

Drawing decision trees

It is conventional to draw decision trees from left to right and to use symbols to distinguish between points at which decisions must be made (a square) and points at which the outcome of a particular alternative is uncertain (a circle).

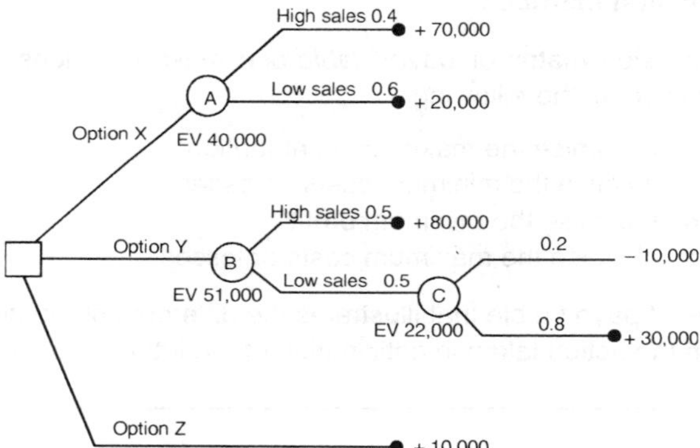

- The diagram depicts a decision in which it is necessary to choose between three options, X, Y and Z.
  - If option X is chosen, there are two possible outcomes
  - If option Y is chosen, there are three possible outcomes
  - If option Z is chosen, the outcome is certain

The figure at the end of each branch of the tree represents the result of choosing a certain option and of a certain outcome occurring: if option X is chosen and outcome A is high sales, this will result in profit (or sales, or contribution or extra costs etc) of £70,000.

The figure written along each branch represents the probability of a certain outcome occurring. There is a 40% chance that sales will be high if option X is chosen.

Evaluation

The evaluation of the decision tree is done by 'rolling' back from right to left and calculating the expected value of each possible outcome, taking account of its probability.

4.6 **Decision matrices** are useful in strategic planning because:

(a) They can be applied in scenario analysis - remember that scenario analysis identifies alternative futures, one of the elements of a decision matrix.

(b) They embody managerial attitudes to risk - arguably maximax and minimin 'hope for the best' whereas maximin and minimax 'expect the worst'. They take account of managers' basic assumptions in a systematic way.

4.7 The **role of decision trees in strategic planning** is to assess which choices are mutually exclusive, and to try to give them some quantitative value. As such they are useful in:

(a) Clarifying strategic decisions when they are complex.
(b) Using risk (in probability terms) as an input to quantifying the decision options.
(c) Ranking the relative costs and benefits of the options.

4.8 That said, many of the options in a decision may not be mutually exclusive, and the decision tree may inhibit a creative approach to a problem by assuming that they are. Finally, it is often easy to forget that an **expected value is only useful for comparative purposes**, taking probability into account. It is **not a prediction** of an actual outcome. (If you toss a coin, there is a 50:50 chance of it turning heads; but in any one throw it will be either heads or tails, not a bit of both.)

Sensitivity analysis

4.9 Ansoff suggests that decision theory is of limited relevance in measuring risk, and **sensitivity analysis** should be used in preference. This involves:

- **Identifying each variable factor** in the calculation
- **Assessing the effect on the result** if the variable was amended by x% up or down.

4.10 This will highlight those variables which are most likely to have a significant effect on the final result. This helps managers identify which strategies are the riskiest, as certain environmental variables might lead to great volatility in returns.

4.11 Sensitivity analysis involves asking 'what if?' questions, and so it can be used for strategic planning. By changing the value of different variables in the model, a number of different **scenarios** for the future will be produced.

4.12 EXAMPLE

Wage increases can be altered to 10% from 5%; demand for a product can be reduced from 100,000 to 80,000, the introduction of new processing equipment can be deferred by six months, on the revised assumption that there will be delays, and so on. Sensitivity analysis can be formalised by identifying key variables in the model and then changing the value of each, perhaps in progressive steps. For example, wage costs might be increased in steps by 5%, 7½%, 10%, 12½% and 15% and the effect on profits and cash flows under each of these five wage cost assumptions can be tested.

4.13 In this way, a full picture would emerge of how the achievement of planning targets would be affected by different values for each key variable. **Once the most critical variables have been established**, management then can:

(a) **Apply the most stringent controls** to the most critical variables.

(b) **Alter the plans** so that the most critical variables are no longer as critical. For example, if a car manufacturing company's marketing management are planning to stop producing an old model of car and switch production resources to an entirely new model, sensitivity analysis might show that its profitability will be critically dependent on the speed with which the new model gains acceptance in the market.

(c) **Choose a lower-risk plan**. For example, if a London-based company has the choice of expanding its operations into either the rest of the UK or into France and the Low Countries, it might find that Continental operations would offer prospects of bigger profits, but the risk of failure might be bigger too and so it might opt to expand in the UK instead.

4.14 Section summary

- There are many types of risk.
- Risk can be accounted for by raising the return.
- Decision trees, matrices and sensitivity analysis are all used to model risk, by incorporating probability assessments and management assumptions.

5 STAKEHOLDERS

5.1 The evaluation techniques discussed assume that managers are:

(a) **Free to choose** organisational objectives.
(b) **Able to** implement them **autonomously**.

5.2 Sometimes stakeholders, have sufficient power to influence management's choice of strategy. There are two aspects of stakeholder risk. The risk that:

(a) The strategic option **poses to the interests** of the different stakeholders.

(b) **Stakeholders will respond** in such a way as to reduce the attractiveness of the proposed strategy.

5.3 There are three broad types of stakeholder in an organisation, as we have seen.

(a) Internal stakeholders (employees, management).
(b) Connected stakeholders (shareholders, customers, suppliers, financiers).
(c) External stakeholders (the community, government, pressure groups).

5.4 **Stakeholder risks**

Stakeholder	Interests to defend	Response risk
Internal: managers and employees (eg restructuring, relocation)	• Jobs/careers • Money • Promotion • Benefits • Satisfaction	• Pursuit of 'systems goals' (see Chapter 4) rather than shareholder interests • Industrial action • Negative power to impede implementation • Refusal to relocate • Resignation
Connected		
Shareholders (corporate strategy)	• Increase in shareholder wealth, measured by profitability, P/E ratios, market capitalisation, dividends and yield • Risk	• Sell shares (eg to predator) or boot out management

Stakeholder	Interests to defend	Response risk
Bankers (cash flows)	• Security of loan • Adherence to loan agreements	• Denial of credit • Higher interest charges • Receivership
Suppliers (purchase strategy)	• Profitable sales • Payment for goods • Long-term relationship	• Refusal of credit • Court action • Wind down relationships
Customers (product market strategy)	• Goods as promised • Future benefits	• Buy elsewhere • Sue
External		
Government	• Jobs, training, tax	• Tax increases • Regulation • Legal action
Interest/pressure groups	• Pollution • Rights • Other	• Publicity • Direct action • Sabotage • Pressure on government

5.5 How stakeholders relate to the management of the company depends very much on what **type of stakeholder** they are - internal, connected or external - and on the **level in the management hierarchy** at which they are able to apply pressure. Clearly a company's management will respond differently to the demands of, say, its shareholders and the community at large.

5.6 The way in which the relationship between company and stakeholders is conducted is a function of the parties' **relative bargaining strength** and the philosophy underlying **each party's objectives.** This can be shown by means of a spectrum.

Stakeholders' bargaining strength	Weak					Strong
Company's conduct of relationship	Command/ dictated by company	Consultation and consideration of stakeholders' views	Negotiation	Participation and acceptance of stakeholders' views	Democratic voting by stakeholders	Command/ dictated by stakeholders

5.7 **Conflict** between stakeholders is characterised in the relationship between managers and shareholders. The relationship can run into trouble when the managers' decisions focus on maintaining the corporation as a vehicle for their managerial skills while the shareholders wish to see radical changes so as to enhance their dividend stream and increase the value of their shares.

5.8 Clearly, each stakeholder group considers itself in some way a 'client' of the organisation, thus broadening the debate about organisation effectiveness. Indeed, the organisation might be seen as a **system of power relations** between different interest groups.

5.9 In *Power In and Around Organisations*, Mintzberg identifies groups that not only have an **interest** in an organisation but **power** over it.

The external coalition

- Owners (who hold legal title)
- Associates (suppliers, customers, trading partners)
- Employee associations (unions, professional bodies)
- Public (government, media)

The internal coalition

- The chief executive and board at the strategic apex
- Line managers
- Operators
- The technostructure
- Support staff
- Ideology (ie 'culture')

5.10 Each of these groups has three basic choices.

- **Loyalty**. They can do as they are told.
- **Exit**. For example by selling their shares, or getting a new job.
- **Voice**. They can stay and try to change the system. Those who choose **voice** are those who can, to varying degrees, influence the organisation. Influence implies a degree of power and willingness to exercise it.

5.11 Mintzberg believes that the **relationship between the coalitions and their relative power** affect the organisation's behaviour. We have already seen that organisations have **system goals**, but here are some more points to ponder.

(a) The role of **ideology** (or culture) is a force for stability. 'Past precedents' create a momentum that is difficult to arrest.

(b) **Control systems** also act as a 'set of techniques to enforce precedents'. (A budget is supposed to control behaviour for a fixed period.)

(c) **Slack resources** are excess surpluses (of cash, labour) which the organisation can use to **buy off** those stakeholders who want the organisation to change its goals.

(d) The **chief executive** is a force for stability, as a lot of the job involves reconciling the needs of the various coalitions.

(e) **Equilibrium** is often a preferred option for the power groups in the organisation. However environmental forces can create major changes.

5.12 Existing **structures and systems** can **channel stakeholder influence** because:

(a) They are the **location of power**, giving groups of people varying degrees of influence over strategic choices.

(b) They are **conduits of information**, which shape strategic decisions.

(c) They **limit choices** or give some options priority over others. These may be physical or ethical constraints over what is possible.

(d) They **embody culture**.

(e) They **determine the successful implementation** of strategy.

(f) The **firm has different degrees of dependency** on various stakeholder groups. A company with a cash flow crisis will be more beholden to its bankers than one with regular cash surpluses.

Question 1

Ticket and Budget International is a large multinational firm of accountants. The firm provides audit services, tax services, and consultancy services for its many clients. The firm has a strong Technical Department which designs standardised audit procedures. The firm has just employed a marketing manager. The marketing manager regards an audit as a 'product', part of the entire marketing mix including price (audit fees), place (usually on the client's premises) and promotion (advertising in professional journals) The marketing manager is held in high regard by the firm's senior partner. The marketing director and the senior partner have unveiled a new strategic plan, drawn up in conditions of secrecy, which involves a tie-up with an advertising agency. The firm will be a 'one-stop shop' for business services and advice to management on any subject. Each client, or 'customer' will have a dedicated team of auditors, consultants and advertising executives. Obviously, a member of staff will be a member of a number of different teams.

The firm has recently settled a number of expensive law suits for negligence (which it has, of course, 'contested vigorously') out of court, without admitting liability. The Technical Department is conducting a thorough review of the firm's audit procedures.

In the light of what we have covered in this section, what do you think will be the organisational and stakeholder influences on the proposed strategy?

Answer

Accountants have divided loyalties - to their firm, and to their profession.

The Technical Department will almost certainly resist such a change, as the proposals devalue audit to being one of many business services to management. An audit is undertaken for the benefit of shareholders, not the company management. The Technical Department (the firm's technostructure) is also powerful as enforcement of the standards it will suggest should reduce professional negligence costs. The technostructure will thus exert a powerful influence over the strategy and business practices. External influences include *professional associations* (eg the ACCA) which have a technostructural influence on the profession as a whole. The marketing manager may also be misled as to the degree to which *customers* want a 'one-stop shop' for accounting and advertising services. Perhaps he is overestimating the power of this factor in the external coalition.

This exercise also covers some of the issues discussed in Chapter 6.

5.13 Different stakeholders will have their own views as to strategy. As some stakeholders have *negative power,* in other words power to impede or disrupt the decision, their likely response might be considered. Note that this would be expected in the light of the *partisan mutual adjustment model* of decision making.

6 BRAINWORKS PLC UPDATE

Questions can be found in the Introduction box at the beginning of this chapter.

6.1 *Question 1.* The firm's **bankers and investment advisers** have a stake in the demerger decision - they will be able to make fat fees from them. It is hard to see the **employees** being upset by the demerger. Perhaps **PeoplePower's staff** would welcome the decision, so that they do not have to report to London. Shareholders should benefit, if value is 'unlocked'.

Chapter roundup

- Strategies are evaluated according to their **suitability** to the firm's situation, their **feasibility** in terms of resources and competences and their **acceptability** to key stakeholders groups (eg shareholders).
- **Management** can use a number of **analytical techniques** to assess a firm's current situation, to suggest plans for the future, and to evaluate the viability of different strategic options. None of these techniques should be considered as anything other than 'tools to think with'. All aim to clarify strategic decision making by simplifying it.
- Much strategy evaluation is involved with reducing the **risk** of a particular course of action, or assessing what that risk is. **Risk** is classified as business, financial, economic, political and physical.
- **Ranking and scoring** methods enable the strategist to give weights to certain objectives, and to score a strategy or set of strategies accordingly.
- **Decision matrices** enable the organisation to develop a coherent approach to dealing with projects (ie to maximise potential profits or minimise losses).
- Risk can sometimes be quantified, using **probability theory.** The standard deviation of a number of outcomes is a measure of risk.
- **Decision trees** are used to map a number of mutually exclusive alternatives and determine some value for them, taking probability into account.
- **Sensitivity analysis** is a way of analysing the degree to which a strategy is vulnerable to changes in certain variables.
- Different **stakeholder groups** have different assessment of the risk a strategy poses to their interests. Some are able to exercise power over management.

Quick quiz

1 What three criteria are used to evaluate strategies? (see para 1.1)

2 Why do organisations use ranking and scoring methods? (3.1)

3 List five types of risk and uncertainty. (4.3)

4 What adjustments might a firm make for risk? (4.4)

5 Why should decision trees be used with caution by strategists? (4.8)

6 What is sensitivity analysis? (4.9)

7 What is meant by 'voice'? (5.10)

8 How do existing structures and systems channel stakeholder influence? (5.11)

Question to try	Level	Marks	Time
11	Exam-standard	50	90 mins

Part C
Implementing strategies

Chapter 9

IMPLEMENTATION

Chapter topic list

Introduction

This chapter covers the process of putting the corporate strategy into practice. **Resources** have to be deployed - and the use of **critical success factors** indicates what needs to be done, by identifying key **tasks. MBO** also aims to integrate the business a whole with the activities of individual managers at **operations level.**

We also focus on the specific needs of the **information resource** in strategies for **systems, technology and management,** all with the aim of **integrating IT and business objectives.**

Brainworks plc

1 Draw up some critical success factors for BW(UK)

2 Should BW outsource its information systems function?

1 SETTING OBJECTIVES FOR DEPARTMENTS AND MANAGERS: MBO

1.1 Formulating strategic plans is one thing: implementing them is quite another.

(a) We have seen in looking at Mintzberg's analysis that **not all intended strategies are implemented**. Those that are (deliberate strategies) frequently cross over with emergent strategies. Emergent strategies develop as they are implemented, so perhaps it would not be correct to talk about an implementation stage at all.

(b) It is impossible to plan for every eventuality. Some **decisions of strategic importance may not be anticipated** in the strategic plan.

(c) Implementation often involves **adjusting the plan** in the light of changed conditions.

(d) An organisation has to ensure how its resources are deployed at:

(i) Corporate level (between different businesses).

(ii) Unit level (between functions, departments and so forth).

(e) Decisions at operations level may be taken without any consideration of their overall strategic implications. A sudden cutback or delay in investment in a new technology for the sake of financial reporting, say, may have a damaging impact on the strategy. So, resource allocation is sometimes a strategic issue.

1.2 **EXAMPLE**

(a) A company wishes to expand into a new market. That is its strategic decision.

(b) In practice, this means that individual sales personnel have to persuade a host of new customers to buy the product. The strategy is made real by the work of many individuals, sometimes in isolation, sometimes in small teams, sometimes in large organisational formations.

Management by objectives

KEY TERM

Management by objectives (MBO) is a scheme of planning and control which cooridnates:

(a) Short-term plans with longer-term plans and goals

(b) The plans (and commitment) of junior with senior management

(c) The efforts of different departments.

1.3 **Achieving organisational goals**

(a) **Direction**. Each job is directed towards the same organisational goals. Each managerial job must be focused on the success of the business as a whole, not just one part of it.

(b) **Target**. Each manager's targeted performance must be derived from targets of achievement for the organisation as a whole.

(c) **Performance measurement**. A manager's results must be measured in terms of his or her contribution to the business as a whole.

(d) **Each manager must know** what his or her targets of performance are.

1.4 Consequently, to ensure co-ordination, the various functional objectives must be interlocked:

(a) **Vertically** from top to bottom of the business.

(b) **Horizontally**, for example, the objectives of the production function must be linked with those of sales, warehousing, purchasing, R & D etc.

(c) **Over time**. Short-term objectives can be regarded as intermediate milestones on the road towards long-term objectives.

1.5 The hierarchy of objectives which emerges is this.

STRATEGIC PLANS (LONGER-TERM)

|

TACTICAL PLANS
(Shorter-term, for product
market development,
resource development,
operations and organisation)

|

UNIT, OR
DEPARTMENTAL PLANS

|

INDIVIDUAL MANAGERS' OBJECTIVES

1.6 Two different approaches are:

(a) **Top-down management** Senior managers (perhaps the managing director) can tell managers what to do and set up control procedures.

(b) **Bottom-up management**. The contribution and motivation of each manager in the business can be developed by involving him or her in the planning process.

Advocates of MBO argue that managers will only be committed to their objectives if they are **allowed to assume responsibility** for setting their own objectives for their unit of the business. Higher management should, however, reserve the right to approve or disapprove the manager's proposed objectives.

Setting unit objectives for departments: Steps 1 to 4

1.7 **Unit objectives** are required for all departments.

Step 1 They must be set first of all in terms of primary targets, relating to:

- Profitability
- Level of activity, or turnover
- Achievement of production schedules and delivery dates
- The quality of output or services
- Safety
- Efficiency in the use of resources (labour, productivity, material usage)
- Plant utilisation; ... and so on.

Step 2 For each of these primary targets, secondary targets (or sub-targets) will be set.

- Profitability: the contribution required from each individual product, and the method of fixed overhead allocation.
- Quality of output: the acceptable level of rejected units at inspection should be specified for each type of work and product, the acceptable standards of workmanship identified, target requirements for after-sales service and customer complaints might be set out.

Step 3 **Identify which individual managers** within the unit are in a position to influence the achievement of each of them.

Step 4 Top management will then make a **unit improvement plan** for each unit of the business, setting out specifically the objectives for improvement, the performance standards and the time scale. Although many of these plans will be given a one-year duration so as to fit within a scheme of budgetary control, some aspects may be longer-term. Each unit improvement plan must be approved by the senior manager with overall responsibility for the unit.

Setting key results: Steps 5 to 7

1.8

Step 5 The unit improvement plan is then broken down into a series of **key results** and **performance standards** required from the various individual managers within the unit. For example, the key results of an information systems manager might be as given below.

ITEM	KEY RESULT
Service to users	To ensure that users get regular software upgrades, with appropriate helplines and training.
Use of resources and efficiency levels	The time when users cannot use the network must not exceed 5%.
Costs	The cost per operating hour must not exceed £60.
Quality	Queries from users must be responded to within ten minutes.

Step 6 A personal **job improvement plan** should be agreed with each manager, which will make a quantifiable and measurable contribution to achievement of the plans for the department, branch or company as a whole, within specified time periods.

Step 7 A systematic **performance review** of each manager's results is also necessary.

- A performance review must be a formal and disciplined review of the results achieved by each manager, carried out regularly on pre-determined dates. Performance standards in key results areas provide the means of comparison for actual results achieved.
- Failure to achieve satisfactory results should initiate control action first by the manager, with prompting from his or her superior.

1.9 Top management should ensure that:

(a) **Unit objectives** are **consistent** with **each other** and with overall **corporate objectives**.

(b) The approach deals with **common areas** of improvement, not just the job of the individual manager.

(c) Managers know which objectives/improvement schemes take priority.

(d) Every key area of business performance is the responsibility of one manager, and that there are **no gaps where control is non-existent.**

(e) There is **no unnecessary duplication** of control work by more than one manager.

1.10 Senior managers should provide conditions which will help managers to achieve their key results and job improvement plans.

(a) There must be an efficient and effective **management information system** to provide feedback of results. Each manager should be given the information needed to control his or her own performance.

(b) There must be an **organisation structure** which provides managers with sufficient flexibility and freedom of action.

(c) There should be a sense of 'team spirit and corporate purpose' within the organisation.

1.11 **Advantages of MBO**

(a) Better planning and control, therefore better management.

(b) **Clarification of operational goals** within the framework of a long-term plan.

(c) It **converts strategic plans** into **management action** plans and budgets.

(d) It **co-ordinates individual management targets** into the overall scheme, so managers knows what is expected of them.

(e) It **commits** individual managers to their targets.

(f) It encourages better **communication** and co-ordination within the organisation.

(g) It helps to **identify the need for change** in organisational goals or individual managers and provides a system for making such changes.

1.12 **Disadvantages of MBO**

(a) It is not as effective as it should be if strategic plans have not been properly established; MBO should be used within the structure of an overall corporate planning system.

(b) Some targets may be **long-term** whereas managers may prefer **short-term** targets and tangible results. If a person expects to be transferred to a different job after, say, two years, he or she will not be satisfied with targets for a three or four year period.

(c) There is a danger of **inflexibility**, ie individual objectives, once set, are not changed because the overall plan is rigidly adhered to. There must be flexibility and a willingness to accept amended objectives in the light of changing circumstances.

(d) It can be a **time-consuming exercise** which might not justify the benefit achieved.

(e) It might call for a significant **change** in the attitudes of senior managers, the style of leadership and the organisation structure if it is to function effectively as a system.

(f) It requires considerable **inter-personal** skills by managers throughout the organisation.

(g) It might **overstress the need for individual achievements at the expense of teamwork.**

Question 1

The Griswold Cutlery Company is an old established firm, selling high quality stainless steel cutlery to markets in the UK, France and Germany. It is based in Sheffield. The managing director, Mr Paul Griswold, great grandson of the firm's founder, has just taken over from his father, Matthew Griswold. Matthew Griswold was a manager of the old school. As the boss, he liked to exert power and employees were afraid to disagree with him. He encouraged strict conformance to company procedures: 'rules are rules, they are there to be followed, and I don't like changing them'. Paul Griswold wants to introduce MBO. Do you think this will be an easy task?

Answer

The company's existing culture does not appear to be one in which MBO could flourish. MBO requires that subordinates are relatively independent in negotiating with the boss and that the boss is willing to delegate. Neither of these conditions seems to be present in this company.

1.13 MBO is now thought to be a bit **dated**, especially as its key insights are **absorbed into general management practice.** MBO implies an **organisation hierarchy**.

(a) This presupposes the **rational model** of management.

(b) It **empowers managers**, but still implies the existence of many management **layers**, between the strategic apex and the operating core.

(c) It **assumes that objectives** are not in conflict, or that they **can be reconciled easily.**

(d) It assumes that there is **no high 'power-distance'**, in other words that it is possible for senior and junior managers to co-operate as if they were equals.

1.4 Section summary

- MBO aims to interlock corporate and unit objectives, and to the objectives of individual managers with the achievement of the plan.
- It specifies unit improvement plans, job improvement plans and key results.

2 RESOURCE PLANS

2.1 Corporations live in a world where some resources are more limited than others. A strategy requires decisions as to how resources should be deployed.

Resource planning at corporate level

2.2 The strategic plan, overall, might require a total change in the organisation's resources. There are two variables to be considered here.

(a) **Degree of change**. Will the organisation need more or fewer resources of personnel, capital (for investment purposes) and so forth?

(b) **Extent of central direction.** Will these resources be **allocated** by:

- The corporate centre?
- According to the requests and decisions of the operating units themselves? In this case, how far is the allocation decided by a political process or by 'objective' criteria?

2.3 **Four methods for allocating resources**

		Change	
		Low	*High*
Central direction	*Low*	**Bargaining** between departments or SBUs	**Competition** between units
	High	**Formula** (eg increase all depts by 5%)	Planners **impose** priorities

- Scarcity of key resources leads to higher central control.
- Resource allocation decisions, and hence the strategies that underlie them, are constrained by the **existing distribution** of resources and power.

Resource planing at operational level

2.4 **Resource planning** involves planning the resources (and identifying potential resources) of the undertaking in order that the defined and agreed corporate objectives may be achieved. At operational level the stages in resource planning are as follows.

Step 1 **Resource identification.** What resources will be **needed** to implement the strategy? All the required resources should be identified - manufacturing resources, manpower, R & D, finance, marketing mix etc.

Step 2 **Fit with existing resources.** An assessment must be made of whether:

- The required resources are **already** in place.
- Any **new** resources that are needed can be developed from existing resources.
- There will have to be some **changes** to existing resources in order to implement the strategy.

Step 3 **Fit between required resources.** An assessment must also be made, how these new resources can be properly integrated with current resources. For example, increasing output might require more people *and* more machines, and extra resources might be needed for training.

2.5 The situation might be explained more simply by means of a Venn diagram.

Some strategies can be met from existing resources, new resources, or a mixture of existing and new resources in tandem, but the objectives and strategies which cannot be met will have to be deferred until a later time, or abandoned altogether.

Preparing resource plans

Planning issues: critical success factors

2.6 Resource plans can be prepared in detail, providing organisations know what they need to achieve.

KEY TERMS

(a) **Critical success factors** *(CSFs)* 'are those factors on which the strategy is fundamentally dependent for its success'.

(b) **Key tasks** are what must be done to ensure each critical success factor is satisfied.

(c) **Priorities** indicate the order in which tasks are completed.

2.7 **EXAMPLE**

- Some CSFs are generic to the whole industry, others to a particular firm. The critical success factor to run a successful **mail order business** is speedy delivery.
- A CSF of a **parcel delivery service** is that it **must be quicker than the normal post.**
- Underpinning critical success factors are **key tasks.** If *customer care* is a CSF, then a key task, and hence a measure of performance, would include responding to enquires within a given time period. There may be a number of key tasks - but some might be more important than others, or must come first in a sequence.

Question 2

Draw up a list of four critical success factors for the strategy of the organisation for which you work.

2.8 **EXAMPLE**

CSFs can be used to **translate strategic objectives** into performance targets and tactical plans. Here is an example.

(a) Dogger Bank plc's business objective is increased profits.

(b) The strategy for increased profits is to increase revenue per customer.

(c) Increasing revenue per customer might not be possible unless customers buy other services from the bank (eg insurance).

(i) The **critical success factor** will be the number of extra services sold to each customer.

(ii) A **key task** might involve developing a customer database so that the firm can target customers within information about other services more effectively.

2.9 Some CSFs which cover both financial and non-financial criteria are outlined below.

Sphere of activity	*Critical factors*
Marketing	Sales volume Market share Gross margins
Production	Capacity utilisation Quality standards
Logistics	Capacity utilisation Level of service

Some criteria which are regularly used in choosing between alternative plans for specific aspects of marketing are outlined below.

Activity	*CSF*
New product development	Trial rate Repurchase rate
Sales programmes	Contribution by region, salesperson Controllable margin as percentage of sales Number of new accounts Travel costs
Advertising programmes	Awareness levels Attribute ratings Cost levels
Pricing programmes	Price relative to industry average Price elasticity of demand
Distribution programmes	Number of distributors carrying the product

Components of the resource plan

2.10 CSFs give some idea of the resources that are needed. For example, if the key task in Paragraph 2.8 is the development of a customer database, then the resources needed might include the services of a systems analyst, hardware etc.

2.11 The resource plan might use the following tools.

(a) **Budgets** (see section 6 below)

(b) **Plans** for obtaining and using human resources, such as recruitment and selection and training.

(c) **Network analysis,** indicating how resources will be deployed in a particular sequence. This is especially relevant for 'one-off' projects.

2.12 The **accountant** has an obvious role in resource planning. Resources in any organisation are scarce, and there will be a whole host of ideas or projects competing for resources. There may not be resources for them all, so the accountant will be involved in selecting those which make the most efficient use of resources available. The price of resources is expressed in financial terms, so measures such as contribution per unit of limiting factor might be useful.

Outsourcing

KEY TERM

Outsourcing: sub-contracting work to external suppliers, for example producing a subcomponent or providing a service. (Many firms pay a computer bureau to run their payroll for them.)

2.13 **Key issues in outsourcing**

(a) **Resource usage.** When a company makes products in-house it is tying up resources which could be used for other more profitable purposes (ie there is an opportunity cost).

(b) **Supplier commitment.** If a company cannot produce all the output it needs in-house, it will be *forced* to use external suppliers to some extent. This might oblige the company to offer a supply contract to a supplier which guarantees a minimum supply quantity over a period of time.

(c) **Control**. In-house production might be easier to control in terms of product quality and the reliability of delivery. Certainly, the supplier has its own objectives.

(d) **Quality assurance**. External suppliers need to be reliable in terms of product quality and reliability of delivery times, and alternative sources of supply should be sought, in case one supplier becomes too unreliable or too expensive. One way of vetting suppliers is to check to see if they have BS EN ISO 9000 certification.

(e) **Compulsion**. Certain areas of the public sector are required to consider outsourcing.

(f) **Vulnerability**. If the outsourcing arrangement goes wrong a firm can suffer if it loses the expertise.

(g) **Contract compliance**. The outsourcing arrangement requires strict attention to contracts. This *can* be a source of operational inflexibility, if the contract has to be laboriously renegotiated when circumstances change.

(h) **Expertise.** Outsourcers can offer more expertise.

Case example

Parts distribution

Rover Cars had a long-standing arrangement with Unipart – the components and logistics group – whereby Unipart distributed parts for Rover cars.

Early in 1998, BMW, Rover's owner, decided to take back control of the parts division. BMW wanted strategic control of its parts distribution and the profits stream stemming from it. Rover now has to set up its own distribution infrastructure.

Unipart has expanded into other components businesses, working for Jaguar, Volkswagen and Daihatsu. It has parts distribution contracts with non-car firms such as Hewlett-Packard, various railway companies. It is also working with the UK government's buying agency to improve services and goods supply chains.

Facilities management: outsourcing IT

2.14 Rather than maintain a computing department, some organisations choose to contract out their computer operations to a private company, which might be paid a fee to provide a service.

- A computer bureau is an **external** service.
- **Facilities management** (FM) companies operate **within** the organisation. The FM company must work to a contract and will bear any losses.

2.15 FM companies are contracted to take over part or all of an organisation's computing facilities. Facilities management can range from:

(a) Project management assistance, to
(b) Complete control of systems development, to
(c) Running an organisation's entire computing function.

2.16 **Advantages of facilities management**

(a) A small organisation may have substantial IT requirements, but may not have the staff, management time or expertise.

(b) Facilities management is an effective form of **cost control**, as there is a **contract** where services are specified in advance for a fixed price. If the facilities management supplier is inefficient, the extra costs will not be borne by the 'host' organisation.

(c) A facilities management company has **economies of scale**. If two organisations employ the same FM company, the FM company's research into new products or technologies can be shared between its clients.

(d) Similarly, FM companies can employ staff with specific **expertise** which can be shared between several clients. FM is a way of coping with the skills shortage widely felt to be a feature of the IS labour market.

2.17 **Disadvantages**

(a) **Key role of information.** Unlike office cleaning or catering, an organisation's computing and information services are too important to be contracted out.

(b) **Different objectives. Technologies which play a strategic role** in an organisation's success cannot be handed over to outsiders.

(c) **The FM company has strategic objectives of its own**, which are different from (though probably not conflicting with) the strategic objectives of the host. An IS function run by an FM company will be even more separate from the overall business functions than an organisation's own IS department.

(d) **No going back.** Once an organisation has handed over its computing to an FM company, it is locked in to the arrangement. The decision is very difficult to reverse. Should the FM company supply unsatisfactory levels of service, then the effort and expense an organisation would have to incur to rebuild its own computing function and expertise would be enormous.

(e) **IT awareness.** The use of FM does not encourage a proper awareness of the potential costs and benefits of IT amongst managers '...many managers naturally lean towards FM because they are technophobic and frightened by their jargon-spouting DP departments. The result is that they opt for the easy if short-sighted route'.

2.18 Section summary

- At corporate level resources are allocated by bargaining, imposition, competition or a formula, depending on changes in resource requirement and the strength of the corporate centre.
- At operational level, resource needs can be estimated by identifying critical success factors and key tasks underpinning them.

3 OPERATIONS PLANS

KEY TERM

Operations plans are 'the fully detailed specifications by which individuals are expected to carry out the predetermined cycles of operations to meet sectional objectives.'

3.1 Operations plans are made for marketing, production, distribution and finance, IT systems etc. They are **interrelated**.

- The **marketing plan** will detail expected selling quantities, and timings, advertising expenditure sales force activities. (Marketing is covered in detail later in this text.)
- From the estimates of selling quantities, the required **production plan** can be formulated, stating what needs to be produced and at what cost, to match the volume and diversity of products that marketing expects to sell. The production programmes should include cost estimates (allowing for inflation) for direct materials, labour, energy and any other major expenditures, as well as overhead recovery.

3.2 There are potential 'snags' in co-ordinating the efforts of the marketing and production departments to produce an optimal plan.

(a) **Marketing staff** are occasionally **over-optimistic** about what they can sell, and so might ask for too much production. This will result in excess stocks.

(b) **Inefficiencies in manufacture** might give rise to unnecessarily high costs, thereby denying the marketing function the chance to sell at a profit the goods for which there is demand at a given price.

(c) Many small companies fail through **over hasty expansion** or **over trading**, for example by:

- **Pursuing volume sales as opposed to profitable sales** (ie selling a lot, at low and unsustainable margins). A large firm might see this as an investment in market share, but for a small firm without sufficient backing or resources, this can be a strategy for disaster.
- **Getting one large order, and forsaking others** if a firm gets one very large order, from a large company, it might product only to meet that order, and so it might forsake other sales. A diverse customer base may be a better guarantee of long term success.

Operations planning issues

The manufacturing plan

3.3

MANUFACTURING PLAN

1 Objectives: level of output to be attained: related to the corporate and marketing objectives.

2 Situation analysis: summary of the manufacturing function's strengths and weaknesses, eg:

(a) potential down-time on faulty machines;

(b) probability of delays in the delivery and installation of new equipment.

3 Environmental forecast: a statement of how environmental factors might affect the performance of the manufacturing function. Apart from delays in the delivery of plant or raw materials by suppliers, other factors might include strikes in supplier organisations or other organisations (eg transport strikes), the poaching of skilled employees by competitors, supply shortages etc.

4 Summary outline of the manufacturing plan: this gives general details of the plan of action, units to be produced, etc. The manufacturing plan should be related to the overall corporate plan, and the marketing plan.

5 Details of quality targets.

6 Detailed plans of action: this is an area of major planning effort and is the most detailed part of the functional plan.

7 Contingency plans.

8 Resources required to carry out the plan.

Capacity planning

3.4 **Matching capacity with demand**

(a) **Demand matching** attempts to match demand with production runs for the same **quantity**. This strategy may involve high-cost short production runs, but this is arguably a feature of **just-in-time** inventory control systems.

(b) **Operation smoothing** gears production to average demand, but requires the holding of considerable levels of finished goods inventory when demand is seasonally low. This may not be possible with perishable goods or fashion products, and certainly not with services.

3.5 **Increase capacity**. If there is an expected growth in sales over the planning period, plans should be made to *increase capacity* using methods such as:

(a) Obtaining more factory space, equipment and employees.
(b) Introducing high-volume labour-saving equipment in the existing factory space.
(c) Planning to sub-contract some production work to outside suppliers.

3.6 Whenever there is an addition to capacity, there is likely to be a period of time during which actual demand is less than the new capacity, and so there are idle resources.

3.7 **Cutting capacity**. If a surplus in capacity is expected, planners will have the task of suggesting how the unwanted capacity should be got rid of.

(a) Reducing capacity at each manufacturing plant by making employees redundant and selling off plant and equipment. A target of reducing the labour force by, say, 10% pa for four years might be set.

(b) Selling off unwanted capacity to another company, or to a management buyout.

(c) Part time working.

3.8 Capacity decisions can be painful ones, particularly in declining industries. Coal, steel, shipbuilding and the railways have all been faced with excess capacity for long periods. The coal industry's capacity has been cut relentlessly.

Standardisation of products and components

3.9 Many firms use standard components. The possible advantages arising from the adoption of a standard product and component parts are these.

- It permits 'flow type' production with **long production runs** and reduced unit costs.
- The **production method is uniform.**
- **Design and tooling is simpler** because it relates to a single production method.
- Unit costs may be further reduced by discounts on the **large purchase quantities.**
- **Less training** is needed.
- **Design staff are less pressurised.**
- **Standard processes** mean that production management is now simpler.
- **Lower costs of inspection** will be incurred.
- **Production** may well be **faster.**
- **Lower levels of inventory** may be needed.
- The components are **tried and tested.**
- **Stock control is simpler** (less variety).
- An **improved spare parts service** should be available.
- Since suppliers' costs will be cheaper, **prices should be lower** to customers.
- There should be **more suppliers** willing to produce the standard items.

Case example

VW and Audi cars share many of the same parts even though the cars are very different.

Physical distribution management

3.10 **Physical distribution management** is concerned with the physical transportation and warehousing of products.

- Transportation: type (eg cars, ships), size etc
- Materials handling in storerooms and warehouses
- Packaging
- Warehousing procedures
- Inventory levels and stock control
- The location of warehouses
- Order processing

3.11 Rising costs of freight, warehousing and stockholding, however, have forced attention towards physical distribution systems, and have stimulated the question as to how far distribution factors should influence marketing decisions, and how carefully should distribution activities be co-ordinated and integrated.

3.12 If a company is seeking to build or acquire a new warehouse, it must seek a general area and then a specific site in that area.

(a) Selecting the area will depend on its market potential.

(b) The choice of site *within* an area will depend on:

- Sites available
- Delivery and collection arrangements.
- Local transport facilities (road, rail, etc)
- Future development in the area.
- Tenure (lease or a freehold).
- Geographical position.
- Size in relation to market potential.

4 THE INFORMATION RESOURCE

Types of information

4.1 Information is a key business resource. Drucker suggests the executive's tool kit has four **types of information**.

(a) **Foundation information** (eg profitability, cash flow) is only useful insofar that, if abnormal, it tells us something is wrong.

(b) **Productivity information** is exemplified by traditional measures of productivity. Such information is only slowly being developed for *knowledge* and *service* work.

(c) **Competence information:** competence is the ability 'to do something others cannot do at all or find difficult to do even poorly'. A firm should meticulously analyse what it does best (eg it might find unexpected uses for its products, which it can exploit).

(d) **Resource-allocation information** tells us how resources are used.

4.2 These four kinds of information relate to **tactics** and the **current business. For strategy** organised information about the **environment** is necessary: 'at least half the important new technologies that have transformed an industry in the past 50 years came from outside the industry itself'. Such information is unpredictable, informal or unstructured.

Levels of information

4.3 We can categorise information as strategic, tactical and operational.

4.4 EXAMPLE

In a **finance subsystem:**

- The **operational level** would deal with cash receipts and payments, bank reconciliations and so forth.
- The **tactical level** would deal with cash flow forecasts and working capital management.

- **Strategic level** financial issues are likely to be integrated with the organisation's commercial strategy, but may relate to the most appropriate source of finance (eg long-term debt, or equity).

4.5 The type of information at each level can be seen in the table below.

	Inputs	*Process*	*Outputs*
Strategic	Plans, competitor information, overall market information	Summarise Investigate Compare Forecast	Key ratios, ad hoc market analysis, strategic plans
Management/tactical	Historical and budget data	Compare Classify Summarise	Variance analyses Exception reports
Operational	Customer orders, Programmed stock control levels, cash receipts/payments	Update files Output reports	Updated file listings, invoices

Types of information system

4.6 These information requirements can be met, to a greater or lesser degree, by a firm's information systems.

Transaction processing systems

4.7 Transaction processing systems (TPS) are used at operational level for routine processing of data items and transactions. They provide the raw material for management information systems (MIS).

- Process: updating master files using transactions files
- Examples: ledgers, stock, payroll, order processing.

Management information systems

KEY TERM

Management information system: 'a system to convert data from internal and external sources into information and to communicate that information, in an appropriate form, to managers at all levels in all functions to enable them to make timely and effective decisions for planning, directing and controlling the activities for which they are responsible'. (Lucey).

4.8 An MIS cannot deal with:

- Qualitative data/information
- Informal information: Many managers express preference for 'grapevine' in information gathering
- Unprogrammed information

Decision support systems

4.9 These are a type of MIS which deal with semi-structured problems.

(a) **Features:**

- User-friendly
- Flexible
- Analytical capabilities
- Do not make decisions, but support decision maker

(b) **Components:**

- **Language module** for communication with user
- **Problem processing** module for analysis
- **Knowledge module** providing data storage

The best known and most widely used example of a DSS is the **spreadsheet**.

Expert systems

4.10 An expert system does make decisions. Its advantages include a learning ability, span of knowledge and use of 'fuzzy logic' to overcome gaps. An expert system is used in specific applications, including:

- Oil and mineral industries
- Credit approval in banking

4.11 Specific components of an expert system are as follows.

- **Knowledge base:** a collection of facts and rules.
- **Knowledge acquisition program:** captures data to add to knowledge base.
- **Inferencing engine:** processes rules and establishes which apply.
- **Explanation program:** provides the user interface.

Executive information systems

4.12 An executive information systems (EIS) is a system which provides information to senior management. It is designed to be very easy to use. Features are:

- Provides summary level data from organisation's MIS/TPS
- Allows executive to 'drill down'
- Flexible data manipulation facilities
- Graphics for user-friendly presentation
- Template system for pro-forma/consistent reports

Question 3

What do you consider is the importance of some of the management information systems discussed above for organisation hierarchy?

Answer

(a) Expert systems bring the power of expertise to the desk. Say a person wants a loan from a bank. An expert system can be used for credit scoring, so the request will not have to be directed back to a superior.

(b) Executive information systems mean that senior management can focus easily on operations so the middle management function of information processing might disappear.

All in all, this points to 'delayering' of management hierarchies, but counterbalanced by the creation of new jobs in information management.

4.13 Section summary

- Different types of information are needed at different levels.
- Information systems aim to provide them.

5 PLANNING THE INFORMATION RESOURCE 6/97

Exam focus point

A June 1997 question asked you to identify the benefit of integrating strategic planning with the supporting technological infrastructure.

Integrating IT and business objectives

5.1 A firm's IT strategy should support the overall strategy of the business.

5.2 IT *can* be considered a functional strategy, in other words a preserve of the data processing department, but IT might also be viewed as an aspect of corporate strategy: The strategy for information systems deals with the deployment of a crucial resource throughout the *whole* business.

5.3 A representation of IT strategy development is given in the diagram which follows.

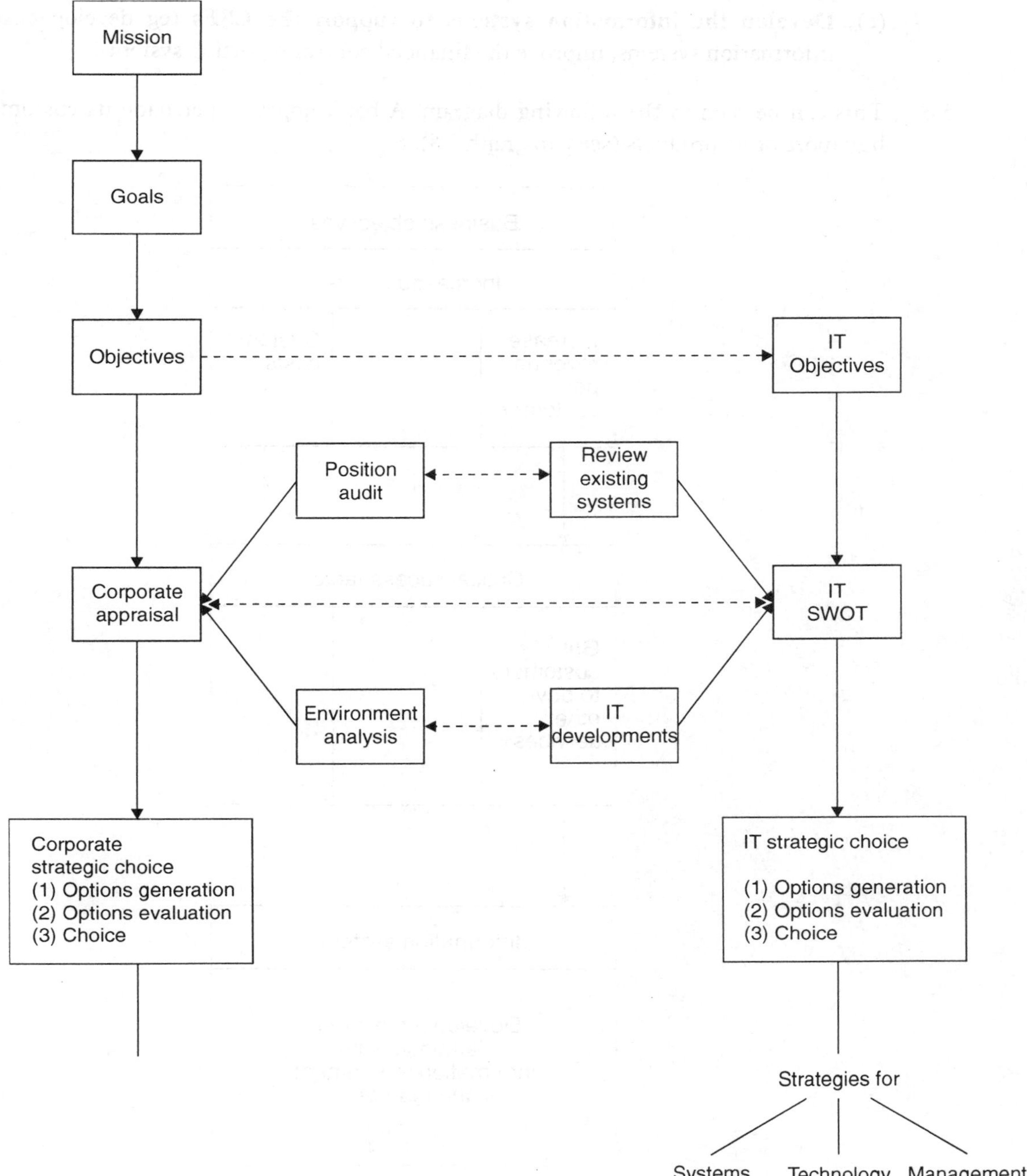

Business objectives and IT resources

5.4 The **identification of business needs** and the information technology framework to satisfy them is at the **heart of a strategy for information systems** and information technology. This is not always feasible, especially if an organisation's use of IT has grown in a haphazard fashion, and the purpose of the strategy is to impose some sort of order on an already chaotic situation.

5.5 **Critical success factors** (CSFs) can translate business into IT objectives. We have already discussed them in the preparation of resource plans.

(a) **Define business objectives** (eg raise earnings per share, develop new businesses).

(b) **Identify the CSFs** whose success is necessary for the organisation to flourish (eg new markets, new products, core activities).

(c) **Develop the information systems to support the CSFs** (eg develop customer information systems, improve the financial control reporting system).

5.6 This can be seen in the following diagram. A bank hopes to persuade its customers to buy more of its products (see paragraph 2.8).

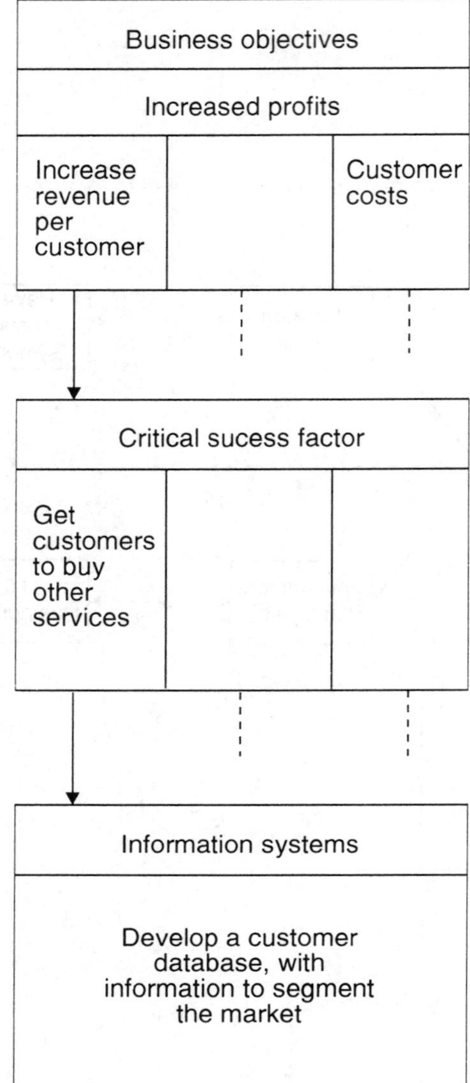

5.7 The identification of business needs, as you can see from the above diagram, is a top-down exercise. The usefulness of critical success factors (CSFs) is that they function as linking pins between IT and business planning even without a formal business strategy. Don't think, however, that going from a critical success factor to the relevant information strategy is easy.

Plans for information systems

5.8 An organisation might draw up a **strategic information systems plan.** An information strategy for an organisation can be said to cover three areas: systems, technology, management.

KEY TERM

The **information systems strategy** is the 'long-term directional plan...seen to be business-led, demand-oriented and concerned to exploit IT either to support business strategies or create new strategic options'.

5.9 The **information systems** strategy therefore deals with the integration of an organisation's information requirements and information systems planning with its long-term overall goals (customer service etc). The IS strategy deals with:

- **What applications should** be developed.
- **Where resources** should be deployed.

5.10 We can draw another grid, which suggests what we can do with our systems once we have reviewed them.

Business value \ Technical quality	Low	High
Low	Divest system	Reassess system
High	Renew/upgrade the system	Maintain and enhance system

(a) **Technical quality** refers to the cost, reliability, speed and functionality of the system.

(b) **Business value** refers to the value of the system and the ease with which it can be used. This can be measured by the intensity of usage.

5.11 **Information technology strategy** follows on from the IS strategy above.

(a) It deals with the **technologies** of:

- Computing
- Communications
- Data
- Application systems.

(b) This provides a **framework** for the analysis and design of the **technological infrastructure** of an organisation. For example, this might involve guidelines for makes of computers and software purchased (eg must support Windows 98) and so forth. This strategy basically indicates how the information systems strategies will be implemented.

5.12 **Information management strategy** is the basic approach an organisation has to the management of its information systems, including:

- Planning information systems developments.
- Organisational management of information systems (eg the role of the information director).
- Control (eg cost control).
- Technology (eg systems development methodologies).

Question 4

Babbage and Newman plc is a company with an established base of IT applications. The finance department has a fully computerised accounting system. The marketing department has developed a primitive customer modelling package. The production department does not need IT.

The Finance Director is in charge of IT at Babbage and Newman. He proposes in the annual corporate budget a 10% increase in IT expenditure based on last year, for the relevant departments. This will enable system upgrades.

Comment.

Answer

There is no strategy at all. The Finance Director regards IT as a cost. Moreover the IT 'strategy' is directed to enhancing its existing base (eg in the accounts department) rather than areas where it might prove competitively valuable (eg in marketing).

5.13 Section summary

The relationship between the three elements is summarised in the table below.

	Information systems strategy	*Information management strategy*	*Information technology strategy*
Subject	What?	Context?	How?
Basis	Divisional/product-market	Organisational	Processes/activities
Orientation	Demand (for applications)	Relationships (between people)	Supply (of technology)
Focus	Business (product - market)	Management	Technology (new developments, designs etc)

6 BUDGETS AND STRATEGIC MANAGEMENT

6.1 How budgetary control can help strategic management

Objective	Comment
Strategic direction	Operations and resource plans, and hence budgets, should be derived from business strategies.
Resource allocation	Resources should be allocated according to the required outputs. Budgets should be directed towards achieving CSFs.
Continuous improvement	Firms should always seek to improve their performance in relation to customer needs, industry best practice and competitors. Budgets should support continuous improvement.
Goal congruence	'Managers must understand the effect of their decisions on the work processes beyond their departmental boundaries'.
Add value	The time spent on budgetary activities should be worth more than its cost.

Cost reductions	When an organisation's targets include improved productivity, or restoring profitability, cost reductions are likely to be a crucial short-term target. The budget will be the planning mechanism.
Targets and responsibilities	Budgets will set targets for divisions, departments, and sub-sections of departments. Individual managers should be aware of what their personal targets are.

6.2 **Typical application of budgets**

Budget	Comment
Capital budgets	Reflect cash flows for different projects, capital rationing decisions, funding methods
Working capital	Stock, debtor and creditor levels
Departmental budgets	This will clearly implement the allocation of financial resources between departments
Consolidated budgets	These enable planning of resource use as a whole

6.3 The budget **should be properly related to the strategic plan**. Although many budgets are prepared for one year, the factors which should influence the **budget period** are as follows.

(a) Strategic plans have a **planning horizon** in excess of one year.

(b) **Implementation**. The long time required to purchase or erect new buildings, to move a company to a different location etc explain why the planning horizon for capital budgets is usually several years.

(c) **Resources**. A distinction can be made between long-term planning and short-term budgeting according to the 'fixed' or 'variable' nature of the resources of the business. In the *long-term*, all resources are variable in quantity, but in the *short-term*, although some resources are variable, others are fixed.

(d) **Error**. All budgets involve some element of forecasting and guesswork, since future events cannot be quantified with accuracy. The more distant the planning horizon, the greater the uncertainty and the wider the margin of error will be.

(e) The **greater the rate of change** that is likely in the future, the **nearer the planning horizon** should be.

6.4 **Problems with budgets**

(a) **Traditional budgets are based on the structure of the organisation**, with **responsibility centres** of different kinds representing where budgetary control is exercised. However, recent developments such as TQM and business process re-engineering **require mangers to think in terms of processes**, with the customer at the end of them, not of a *static* organisation structure.

(b) **Incremental.** At its worst, the traditional budgeting process commences with management setting a revenue forecast and financial targets. Departmental budgets are then prepared based on last year's costs and year-to-date actuals, 'plus or minus a bit'.

(c) Most budgets are prepared over a **one-year period** to enable managers to plan and control financial results for the purposes of the annual accounts. There is a need for management to satisfy shareholders that their company is achieving good results, and for this reason, the arbitrary one-year financial period is usually selected for budgeting. It is not necessarily relevant to the business strategy.

Case examples

A small number of companies have gone so far as to abolish 'budgeting' as traditionally practised.

(a) IKEA took the move in 1992 of abolishing its internal budgets. Its chief executive is reported in *The Economist* (November 1994) to have said, 'We realised that our business planning system was getting too heavy; we can use the time saved for doing other things better.'

(b) Volvo has dropped its once-a-year traditional budgeting process and introduced a new 'concurrent' planning process. This has a permanent focus on objectives and uses key performance indicators, rolling forecasting and short- and long-term scorecards.

6.5 **Participation in the budgeting process**

Exam focus point

Many students *assume* that participating in decision making inevitably improves standards of performance - but don't repeat this uncritically.

'Participation can mean almost anything to anyone.' There might be a sharp difference of views between management and employees as to what *participation* should actually involve.

6.6 **Conventional wisdom** about participation and the implementation of decisions is that when individuals participate in decision making, they will be **more satisfied** with their job and colleagues and they will be **more productive**, there will be **fewer communication problems,** and when circumstances change, the individuals can **adapt more quickly**, and more readily to adjust their plans accordingly.

6.7 Hopwood **questioned the wisdom** of generalising research findings. The degree of participation required to achieve a better implementation of decisions will depend on circumstances. Participation certainly **appears to raise morale**, but it is by **no means clear that it also improves productivity and performance.**

6.8 The **acceptance** of decisions can be improved with participation, but what about the **quality of decisions**?

(a) Groups tend to opt for decisions with **higher payoffs but greater risks** than individual decision-takers. However, greater risk-taking does not necessarily mean better decisions.

(b) The degree of participation which is most likely to produce the best quality of decisions will **vary according to circumstances**, depending, for example, on what the decisions are about and who would be affected by them, the fundamental department in which the decisions are taken (eg personnel decisions lend themselves more readily to participation than finance or production decisions), the number of subordinates involved and their capabilities and the experience of the senior manager.

(c) 'It is simply naive to think that participative approaches are *always* more effective than more authoritarian styles of management or vice versa.

6.9 Section summary

- Budgets are generally prepared for the short term to allocate resources.
- They should be sensitive to the strategic plan.
- Participation *can* improve the acceptance and quality of decisions, depending on circumstances.

7 INFORMATION SYSTEMS COST CONTROL 6/96

7.1 Information systems are a major cost. Firms with separate IS departments need to collect and budget for these costs somehow.

Information technology costs as a corporate overhead

7.2 IT is treated as a general administrative expense or corporate overhead, and is *not* allocated to user departments.

(a) **Advantages**

(i) Simple and cheap to administer.

(ii) It encourages innovation and experimentation by the information systems department, which user departments might be unwilling to pay for.

(iii) Little conflict, over costs at least, between the IS department and user departments.

(b) **Disadvantages**

(i) The IS department has little day-to-day incentive to control costs or use available resources efficiently.

(ii) It does not encourage responsible use of the IS resource by **user departments**, who do not have the cost information to prioritise their requirements.

(iii) If decisions regarding IS resources are taken at senior level in the organisation, there is still ample scope for internal politicking, if funds are limited

IS department costs charged to users

7.3 As information systems support a wide variety of functions in an organisation, and information systems incur significant capital and revenue costs, it is not surprising that many organisations should seek to develop costing systems so that **user departments pay for their use of the information technology resource.**

Information technology charged out on a cost basis

7.4 **Pricing** computer services might:

(a) **Allocate scarce computing resources** according to economic efficiency
(b) **Regulate overall demand** for computing services within an organisation.

7.5 A **cost based chargeout system** means that users are charged a proportion of the costs of the IS department. Cost based chargeout systems should motivate users to employ computer resources efficiently by reflecting actual use. The following measures can help the fulfilment of this objective.

(a) **Chargeout rates should be based on a tangible service** to which the user can relate such as cost per:

- Transaction processed.
- Page.
- Hour of programmer's and/or analyst's time.

(b) **Standard costing systems** should be used, so that:

(i) User depaftments are not penalised for inefficiencies in the IS department.

(ii) The IS department is not penalised for variances caused by user departments' increased usage.

(iii) User departments are not charged with those long term fixed costs of the IS department itself (eg its building), over which they have no control.

7.6 **The advantages and disadvantages of the cost based chargeout system**

(a) **Advantages**

(i) Simplicity.

(ii) It motivates user departments to consider the costs of their usage of IT services and to regulate them efficiently.

(iii) Many other costing systems in the organisation are based on responsibility accounting.

(b) **Disadvantages**

(i) Unless precautions are taken, inefficiencies in the IS department are merely passed on to users.

(ii) Although simple in concept, it is complex in practice.

(iii) It is often difficult to determine an appropriate cost unit on which to base the chargeout system.

(iv) Users are faced, effectively, with a monopoly supplier.

Market-based chargeout methods

7.7 The IS department sets its own prices and charges for its services to make a **profit**. This is only workable in a situation where there is an **external market** for the same services.

(a) **Advantages**

(i) External standards of service and price are available.
(ii) It supposedly encourages an entrepreneurial attitude.
(iii) Prices are negotiable.

(b) **Disadvantages**

(i) No comparable and/or efficient markets outside the organisation where services of the type and intensity that users require can be purchased.

(ii) It is difficult to implement where common or shared resources are concerned.

(iii) It may not be in the organisation's strategic interest for user departments to buy from outsiders: the IS department's fixed costs still have to be covered, and there may result an under-use of resources available within the organisation.

7.8 **Successful use of market-based chargeout methods**

(a) **Routine and structured services are appropriate** for this treatment, as market prices can be used as a guideline. For example, payroll processing is often undertaken by a computer bureau, which may do the work more cheaply than a firm's IS department. The task is well defined, and there is a definite external market for the services.

(b) External supply or purchase should **sometimes be forbidden** (eg from a direct competitor, or where organisational security needs may be compromised).

(c) It should **fit in with the organisation's overall IS strategy.**

IT costs incurred by user departments

7.9 **End-user computing** might result in departments spending quite large sums of money on information systems, without these sums being separately identified in their budgets.

- Many **individual items** of IT (such as PCs, the odd new software package, a bit of networking software) do not, on their own, represent a large expense. Much IT expenditure may not appear even as a capital item. It is quite easy to 'lose' IT costs in the department's operating expenditure budgets.
- **In aggregate**, however, the amounts spent by departments on IT might be quite considerable, and yet the organisation may, because of the dispersed nature of the purchase decisions, miss out on bulk discounts. Some of the economies of scale in systems management may therefore be lost.

7.10 **Procedures to control IT expenditure at department level**

(a) **Purchases** of all IT equipment to be subject to **review and approval** by the IS department or information centre.

(b) Each department should **budget separately for IT based costs**. The budget will be agreed with the IS department in advance.

(c) A person in each functional department should be made specifically **responsible** for that department's IT expenditure.

Selling information systems expertise to cut costs?

7.11 One way of reducing IS costs is for firms to sell their IS expertise to outsiders. Two examples of this are:

- Turning the IS department into a consultancy or FM firm in its own right
- The sale of software or systems developed in-house.

7.12 **Advantages**

- It adds commercial credibility to the company that made it.
- It can turn competitors into followers by establishing an IT infrastructure.
- It can set standards for the industry, thus enabling the supplying company to dictate how the market functions, by setting standards and procedures.

7.13 The **disadvantage** is the possible loss of competitive advantage, if this unique competence is available to be shared.

Question 5

What do you think the significance of value chain analysis should be to decisions to contract out certain computer functions to facilities management companies?

Answer

A value chain identifies those activities where value is added. IS would be contracted out if the IS function of the organisation is not relevant to the organisation's distinctive competence. In some organisations IT might be a primary activity, or even part of the product or service itself. In others it might merely be secondary, and better managed by a different specialist firm, which offers scale economies and specialist expertise.

7.14 Section summary

The cost of the IT resource can be:

- Absorbed as a general overhead.
- Allocated to users if their key tasks need IT resources.

8 CONTINGENCIES AND CONTINGENCY PLANS

KEY TERM

Contingencies are uncontrollable events which are not provided for in the main corporate plan.

8.1 Where contingencies are known about, **contingency plans** should be prepared in advance to deal with the situation if and when it arises. Such plans might be prepared in detail, or in outline only, depending on the likelihood that the contingency will become a reality.

8.2 EXAMPLE

A company which exports or imports goods will be susceptible to fluctuations in foreign exchange rates. Although the risks of foreign exchange exposure can be reduced, by matching assets and liabilities in each currency the company deals in, and in the short term by means of forward exchange contracts, the company will almost certainly be unable to eliminate foreign exchange risks over its longer-term corporate planning period.

Contingency plans can be prepared to deal with adverse exchange rate movements, by speculating how far rates might alter and calculating the implications of various degrees of change. If the company's products are to remain competitive in their markets, 'trigger points' will need to be identified, and contingency plans drawn up containing outline instructions about what will need to be done if the exchange rate passes above or below a certain trigger point.

8.3 Other contingencies can be dealt with by:

- Insurance (eg fire etc).
- Backup facilities (eg in the case of computer failure).

9 IMPLEMENTING PLANS

9.1 Implementation of plans requires three tasks.

(a) **Document the responsibilities** of divisions, departments and individual managers.

(b) **Prepare responsibility charts** for managers at divisional, departmental and subordinate levels.

(c) **Prepare activity schedules** for managers at divisional, departmental and subordinate levels.

This process is sketched out in the diagram below.

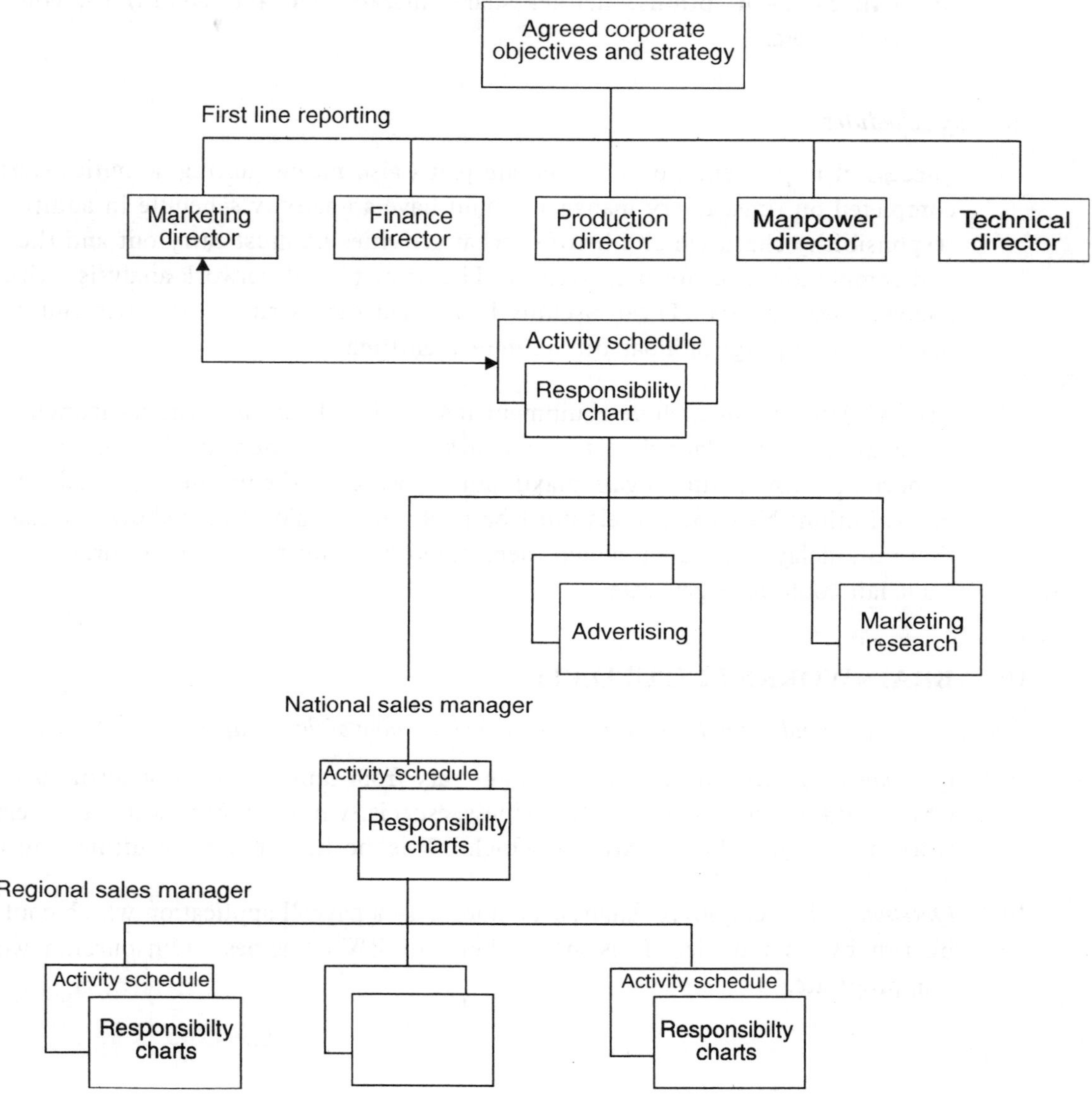

9.2 **Responsibility charts** can be drawn up for management at all levels in the organisation, including the board of directors. They show the control points that indicate what needs to be achieved and how to recognise when things are going wrong. For each manager, a responsibility chart will indicate the following.

(a) The manager's major objective.
(b) The manager's general programme for achieving that objective.
(c) Sub-objectives.
(d) Critical assumptions underlying the objectives and the programme.

9.3 EXAMPLE

The responsibility chart for the *marketing director* might be drawn up along the following lines.

(a) **Major objective and general programme:** to achieve a targeted level of sales, by means of selling existing well-established products, by breaking into some new markets and by a new product launch.

(b) **Sub-objectives:** details of the timing of the product launch; details and timing of promotions, advertising campaigns etc.

(c) **Critical assumptions:** market share, market size and conditions, competitors' activity etc.

Activity schedules

9.4 Successful implementation of corporate plans also means getting activities started and completed on time. Every manager should have an activity schedule in addition to his responsibility chart, which identifies what activities he must carry out and the start up and completion dates for each activity. The principles of network analysis (critical path analysis: see Chapter 11) can usefully be applied here. Critical activities and dates and permissible slippage or 'float' times can be identified.

9.5 Critical dates might include equipment installation dates and product launch dates. In some markets, the launch date for a new product or new model can be extremely important, with an aim to gain maximum exposure for the product at a major trade fair or exhibition. New car models must be ready for a major motor show, for example. If there is a delay in product launch there might be a substantial loss of orders which the trade fair could have generated.

10 BRAINWORKS PLC UPDATE

Questions can be found in the Introduction box at the beginning of this Chapter.

10.1 *Question 1*. Critical success factors might vary from unit to unit. For business clients, a CSF would be the level of repeat business, especially in temporary work. For permanent work, a CSF might be the extent to which BW is the 'first choice' recruitment agency.

10.2 *Question 2*. The employee database is more than a payroll application which could easily be run by an outsider. It is at the heart of BW's business. Outsourcing would be inappropriate.

Chapter roundup

- The planning of **resources** requires consideration of three central issues: **current resource needs**, whether these needs are satisfied by **existing resources**, and **future resources** required. The various activities of the value chain can be examined to see if there is a fit between these elements. The mode of resource allocation depends on the degree of **central direction** of the organisation and the **change** to which it is subjected.
- **Critical success factors** can be used to determine where resources should be allocated.
- **Operations planning** is detailed planning for strategy implementation and control, in marketing, production and distribution for example. Capacity can be planned by demand matching, operation smoothing and subcontracting. Supply has to be planned to ensure reliable sources. Distribution planning should help minimise inconvenience to customers in the receipt of the firm's products.
- **Budgets** are statements in financial terms of the necessary resources for a plan. Contingency plans would be drawn up to mobilise resources in case of crises or matters not working out as anticipated.
- **Information systems** are a resource for managers. DSS facilitate management decisions and EIS enable management to access a firm's data in any easy way.
- Strategies are required for **systems** (what information is needed), **technology** (how information is provided) and **management**.
- IT costing is problematic because it is not always easy to design appropriate chargeout methods. The aim should be to control costs and promote efficient use in user departments.

Quick quiz

1 List the pros and cons of MBO (see paras 1.11, 1.12)
2 What are the issues of resource planning? (2.4)
3 What are critical success factors? (2.6, 2.9)
4 What is outsourcing? (2.13) Is it appropriate for IT? (2.16, 2.17)
5 What is operations planning? (3.1)
6 What are the advantages of standardisation? (3.9)
7 List some aspects of physical distribution. (3.10)
8 What types of information do managers need? (4.1)
9 What are the components of an organisation's strategy for the use of information? (5.8)
10 What are the objectives of budgets if they are to support strategic management? (6.1)
11 What are three ways of dealing with information systems costs? (7.2, 7.4, 7.7)
12 Distinguish between responsibility charts (9.2) and activity schedules. (9.4)

Question to try	Level	Marks	Time
12	Exam standard	25	45 mins
13	Exam standard	25	45 mins

Chapter 10

ORGANISATION STRUCTURES

Chapter topic list		Syllabus reference
1	Strategy and structure	1(c)(ii)
2	Structural configurations	2(b)(ii)
3	Centralisation and decentralisation	2(b)(ii)
4	Departmentation	2(b)(ii)
5	Organising information systems activities	6(d)(iv), 6(e)(ii)
6	Brainworks plc update	

Introduction

The relationship between organisation structure and strategy has been touched upon, but in this chapter we see how, ultimately, **organisation structure can be led by the type of strategy** and work processes adopted. A key influence in the environment. Revisit Chapter 5 to remind yourself of what is meant by environmental uncertainty (simple/stable/complex/dynamic).

Five organisation **configurations** are described. These are models which describe how work is co-ordinated in an organisation, and indicate the influences that the various component parts of the organisation have on its structure. The pros and cons of **centralisation and decentralisation** are then discussed, with the choices for organisation hierarchy.

For IT, the key issue is to manage users so that their autonomy does not lead to practices inappropriate to the wider organisation.

Brainworks plc

1 What structural configuration is used by BW(UK)?

2 What do you think of the company's approach to managing information systems?

Case example

The UK's National Health Service has suffered a number of reorganisations in the past few years, with a variety of objectives.

(a) An 'internal market' was introduced in 1991: hospitals became self-governing trusts and regional health authorities and some general practitioners (fundholders) bought services from them: the purchaser/provider split. The objective was to cut costs and improve efficiency.

This created a 'two-tier' service, and there was a huge increase in management costs. Competition, which was meant to increase efficiency and quality, reduced co-operation between hospitals.

(b) The current government intends to end the internal market but retain the purchaser/provider split.

General practitioners will *have* to co-operate. (They did not *have* to become fundholders). Care will be purchased by 'primary care groups' (PCGs) in a region, representing GPs, nurses, social services and so on, covering about 100,000 people. Some (PCGs) will merely advise the health authority; others will be in charge of the budget.

1 STRATEGY AND STRUCTURE

Influences on organisation structure

1.1 Organisational structure refers to how work is co-ordinated, how decisions are taken, how people are organised into departments etc. Below we summarise the possible influences on organisation structure.

Influence	Comment
Age	• The older the organisation, the more formalised its behaviour. Work is repeated, so is more easily formalised and standardised. • Organisation structure reflects the age of the **industry**'s foundation.
Size and growth	The larger the organisation: the **more elaborate** its structure will be, the larger the average size of the units within it, the more formalised its behaviour (for consistency).
Tasks	The complexity of the task (eg milking cows, designing drugs) affects the structure of the organisation.
Co-ordination	Mutual adjustment, direct supervision and standardisation all have consequences for organisation structure.
Skills of managers and workers	Can people be left alone to do the job, or do they require close supervision?
Job design	Are jobs broken down into discrete activities?
Geographic dispersion	An organisation with several sites will have a different organisation structure from one located in one place.
Fashion	Bureaucracies are deeply unfashionable, but they are often the best at doing certain kinds of work. Indeed, **Burns and Stalker**, who developed the concept of organic and mechanistic organisations held that neither type of organisation had any intrinsic merits, as the key variables were **product-markets** and **technology**.
Control	The more an organisation is subject to **external control** (eg by government, holding company) the more centralised and formalised its structure. The power needs of organisational members (to control others, or at least to control their own working conditions) can lead to centralisation.
Technology	• The stronger the technical system (ie the technology) the more formalised the work, and the more bureaucratic the structure of the operating core. • The more sophisticated the technology, the more elaborate and professional the support staff will be (eg specialists who understand it). • **Information technology** has a profound effect on organisation structure, especially with regard to delayering.
Environment and markets	See below
Strategy	See below

(Mnemonic, using initial words in bold above: Ageing Shabby Trains Convey Shiftworkers, Job-seekers, Graduates and First-time Commuters To Evening Schools.)

Lawrence and Lorsch: diversity, uniformity and the environment

1.2 The **contingency approach** suggests that the ideal structure of an organisation will vary in type according to the organisation's particular situation.

1.3 Lawrence and Lorsch suggested that the structure which is actually selected is likely to be a 'compromise' between pressures which pull in opposite directions, to **diversity** and to **uniformity**. (These cover technical matters such as procedures, but also matters such as managers' psychological outlook, similarity of personality and so on.)

- **Uniformity:** most parts of the organisation are managed in a similar way.
- **Diversity:** there are different management practices in different departments.

1.4 **Pressures for uniformity**

Pressure	Comment
Stability	The organisation can grow to such a size as to take advantage of economies of scale (discounts for large purchases etc). This advantage is maximised if the firm makes use of standardised rules and procedures, which are indicators of uniformity.
Need for centralised control	Where the organisation is large, centralised control may only be effected by having standardised rules and procedures or a common organisation culture.
Personnel	A large organisation with a low-skilled workforce will find that uniformity (rules, procedures etc) will enable more to be produced. Set procedures also allow specialised skills, once developed, to be of benefit to the whole organisation.
Technology	Similar technologies generate similar organisation structures.
Public responsibility	Detailed rules and procedures enable the firm to cope with strict environmental constraints.

1.5 **Pressures for diversity**

- Differences in regional characteristics, markets, customers or products.
- Differences in the technology used in various aspects of the organisation's work.
- The greater readiness of individuals to identify with smaller work groups than with an entire organisation.
- The desire of subordinates to have more authority (for 'decentralisation').

1.6 Organisations with **high diversity** needed **integration devices** - committees, liaison groups etc - to co-ordinate their activities properly.

1.7 Lawrence and Lorsch carried out research into the influence of the **environment** on diversity and uniformity.

(a) **Different industries** (namely plastics, food and containers). The best structures were:

	Plastics	*Industry foods*	*Containers*
Environmental uncertainty	High	Moderate	Low
Degree of differentiation	High	Moderate	Low

(b) **Different business functions** (marketing, production, R&D)

The degree of *environmental uncertainty* was found to differ between the divisions. Production experienced the lowest degree of environmental uncertainty; R&D experienced the highest. As one would therefore expect, production was the most structured of the three departments, with R&D being the least structured.

	R&D	*Marketing*	*Production*
Environmental uncertainty	High	Moderate	Low
Formality	Low	High	High
Time horizon	Long	Short	Short

Strategy and structure

1.8 Organisations develop strategies to cope with changed environmental conditions. To what extent does organisation **structure follow strategy**? *Chandler* endeavoured to find out by conducting a detailed historical study of four US businesses. His conclusions were that:

(a) Any changes in organisation structure were related to the organisation's method of growth.

(b) The method of growth reflected changes in the US economy, especially demand.

(c) Re-organisations were influenced by current management fashions.

1.9 Chandler identified **three levels of administrative activity**.

(a) The **general office** allocates resources to the **divisions,** responsible for a product line or sales region.

(b) The **divisional central office** administers **departments,** responsible, say, for manufacture and sales.

(c) **Departmental offices** manage **field units** (individual factories).

1.10 These levels arose out of the development of business strategies, such as geographical expansion. The businesses were responding to the threat of losing markets and the development of new markets.

(a) **Geographic expansion** calls for **departmental offices** to be set up to administer the **new field units**.

(b) **Vertical integration** requires a central office and multi-departmental structure.

(c) **Diversification** requires a general office to administer **divisions** operating in different industries.

1.11 Section summary

- There are many contingent influences on organisation structure.
- Two important influences are environmental uncertainty and business strategy.

2 STRUCTURAL CONFIGURATIONS

2.1 Mintzberg's theory of organisational **configuration** describes how both formal structure and power relationships exist in organisations. To recap, there are five main components.

- The **strategic apex** directs strategy.
- The **operating core** contains those people directly involved in production.
- The **middle line** converts the wishes of the strategic apex into the work of the operating core.
- The **technostructure** standardises the work.
- **Support staff** provide ancillary services such as public relations or legal counsel.

2.2 Mintzberg suggests that there are five ideal 'types' of organisation, each of which configures the five components above in a significantly different way. Each component of the organisation has its own dynamic, which leads to a distinct type of organisation.

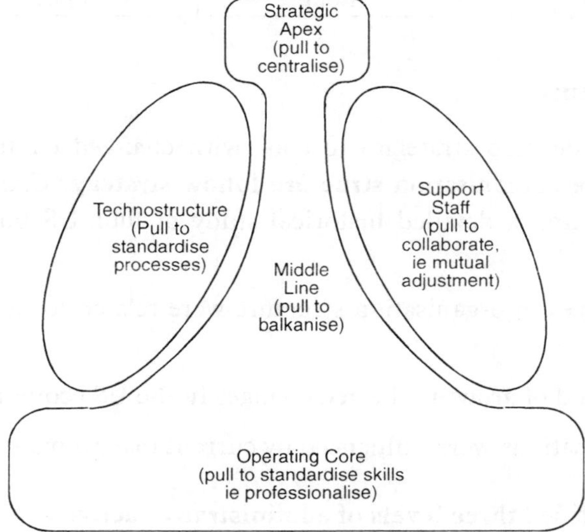

The simple structure

KEY TERM

The **strategic apex** wishes to retain control over decision-making, and so exercises what Mintzberg describes as a **pull to centralise**, hence the **simple structure**.

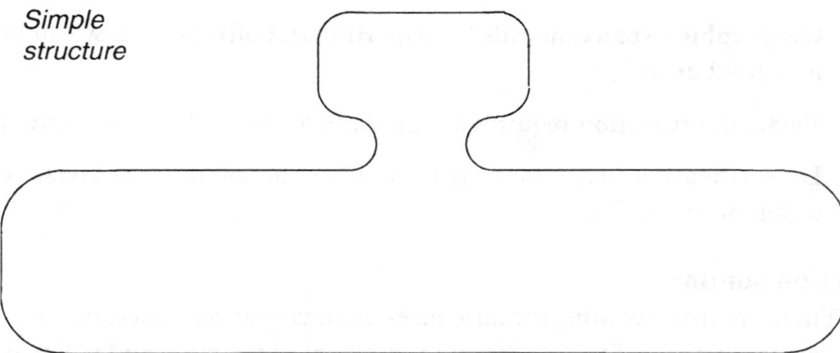

2.3 **Key issues**

(a) **Typical examples:** the simple structure is characteristic of small, young organisations dominated by a single entrepreneur or management team.

(i) If it grows, it might encounter a crisis of leadership. Informal controls may not be sufficient.

(ii) Strategies might be made on the basis of the manager's hunches - a **visionary** style?

(iii) The firm might be dominated by personalities, symptomatic of a **power culture** perhaps.

(iv) The simple structure is **risky** as it depends on the expertise of one person. Such an organisation might be prone to **succession crises**. Who takes over if the boss dies? This problem is often encountered in family businesses.

(v) **Centralisation** reflects management's full knowledge of the operating core and its processes but senior managers might intervene too much.

(b) **Environment:** simple but dynamic.

(c) **Co-ordination is achieved by direct supervision**. It has a wide control span, no middle line (implying minimal hierarchy) and no technostructure (implying little formalisation or standardisation of behaviour). It is thus flexible.

The machine bureaucracy

KEY TERM

The **technostructure** exerts a **pull to standardise of processes**. It thus creates a **machine bureaucracy**.

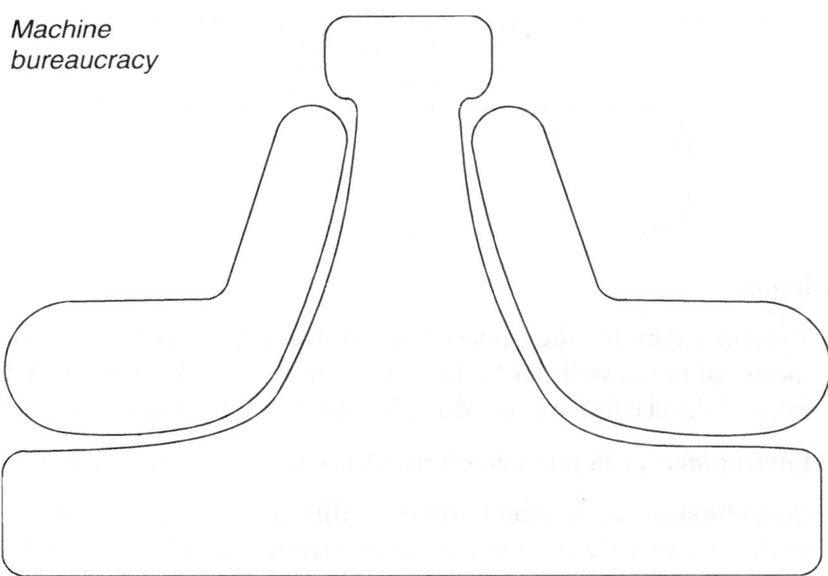

2.4 **Key issues**

(a) **Typical example:** any bureaucracy, working on a sophisticated and well-tuned set of rules and procedures. Everybody knows their place. Work is routine. Machine bureaucracies are associated with routine technical systems.

(b) **Environment:** simple and stable. The machine bureaucracy is the most efficient structure for integrating sets of simple and repetitive tasks.

(c) **Co-ordination** is by **standardisation of the work processes** of the operating core. Direct supervision by the apex is limited as work standardisation ensures co-ordination. The middle line ensures that the standards designed by the technostructure are adhered to.

(d) There is a strong emphasis on the **division of labour** and in **particular on control. Uncertainty has to be eliminated** eg by vertical integration. Outsourcing would not be favoured.

(e) **Formal communication** is most important. Authority is **hierarchical**.

(f) **Problems**

(i) Machine bureaucracies **cannot adapt**: they are designed for specialised purposes. They are driven by performance, not problem solving.

(ii) **Conflict** is rife between different departments, between line and staff, and between operating core and management.

The professional bureaucracy

KEY TERM

The **operating core** oversees a **pull to standardise skills.** The operating core seeks to minimise the influence of *all* administrators (mainly the middle line and technostructure) over the work they do. This is called the **professional bureaucracy.**

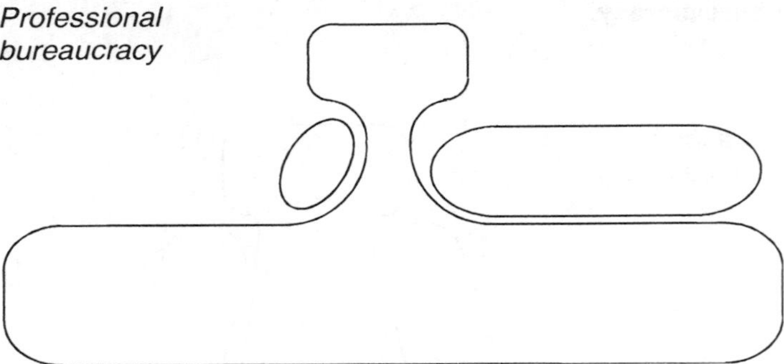

2.5 Key issues

(a) **Typical example**: the professional bureaucracy hires trained specialists who are socialised in the skills and values of the profession. A school is an example: *teachers*' work in the classroom is not directly supervised, but teachers are trained outside.

(b) **Environment:** complex and stable. (A teacher faces a new class every year.)

(c) **Co-ordination** is by **standardising skills** (eg at teacher training colleges). Most work processes are too complex to be precisely standardised by a technostructure. For example, doctors have a diagnostic role.

(d) Power tends to be based on expertise, not formal position in the hierarchy.

(e) Professionals **control their own work, and seek collective**, perhaps democratic **control** over the administrative **decisions which affect them**. There might be two 'organisation hierarchies'.

(i) Bottom-up for the operating core doing the work.

(ii) Top-down for the administration staff, who also manage much of the organisation's boundary.

(f) **Problems**

(i) The professional bureaucracy cannot always cope with any variations of standards, as control is exercised through training.

(ii) If the environment is fast moving, it can be slow to react.

Question 1

How would a machine bureaucracy and a professional bureaucracy ensure that accounting transactions are correctly posted?

Answer

The machine bureaucracy would devise very precise procedures and rule-books telling untrained clerks exactly what to do in any situation.

The professional bureaucracy would employ trained and perhaps qualified accounts staff, whose professional training would give them the expertise to make the right decision.

(4) The divisional form

KEY TERM

The **middle line** seeks as much autonomy for itself as possible. It exerts a **pull to balkanise**. The result is the **divisional form.**

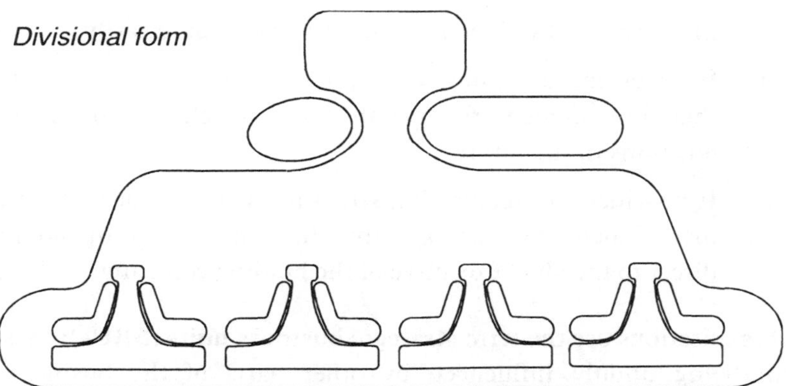
Divisional form

2.6 **Key issues**

(a) **Typical example:** any business with autonomous regions or product divisions, each with its own revenues, expenditures, investment programmes.

(b) **Environment.** The effects if limited because each division is monitored by its objective performance towards a **single integrated set of goals** set by the **strategic apex**, each division is individually configured as a machine bureaucracy. Each division is partly insulated from environmental pressures and faces less uncertainty than if it were an independent company.

(c) **Co-ordination** is by **standardisation of outputs** - but such 'outputs' are normally performance measures such as profit targets, set by the strategic apex.

(d) **Communication** between divisions and head office is restricted, formal and related to performance standards. Influence is maintained by headquarters' power to hire and fire the managers who are supposed to run each division.

(e) Divisionalisation is a function of organisation **size**, in numbers and in product-market activities.

(f) **Problems** with the divisional form.

(i) A division is partly **insulated from shareholders** and from **capital markets**, which ultimately reward performance.

(ii) It 'piggybacks on the machine bureaucracy in a single stable environment, and may feel drawn back to that form'.

(iii) The economic advantages it offers over independent organisations 'reflect fundamental **inefficiencies in capital markets**'. (In other words, different product-market divisions might function better as independent companies.)

(iv) Headquarters management at the strategic apex have a tendency to **usurp divisional profits** (eg by management charges, cross-subsidies and unfair transfer price systems).

(v) In some businesses, it is impossible to identify completely independent products or markets.

(vi) Divisionalisation is only possible at a fairly **senior management level**, because there is a limit to how much independence in the division of work can be arranged.

(vii) It is a **halfway house**, relying on **personal control over performance by senior managers** and **enforcing cross-subsidisation**.

(g) Divisionalisation does have some **advantages**.

(i) It focuses the attention of management below 'top level' on business performance and results.

(ii) Management by objectives can be applied more easily.

(iii) It gives more authority to junior managers early in their careers, and therefore provides them with work, which grooms them for more senior positions in the future.

(iv) It provides an organisation structure which reduces the number of levels of management. The top executives in each federal unit should be able to report direct to the chief executive of the holding company.

2.7 Some organisations use the term **strategic business units (SBUs):** these can stand alone, without being unduly influenced by other parts of the business. For each SBU, independent strategic decisions can be made about expansion, market share, cost structure, pricing, innovation, R & D etc. Within the organisation structure, each SBU should stand as a major investment centre. Each SBU **might be constituted as a separate legal entity (a subsidiary)** for each division. This makes **ownership** easy to transfer or share (in a joint venture).

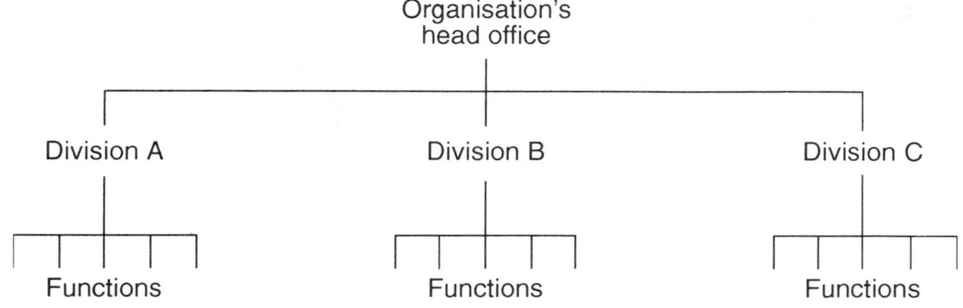

Case example

RACAL spun off its Vodafone subsidiary.

2.8 **'Successful' divisionalisation.**

(a) It must have **properly delegated authority**, but strong 'control' should be retained at centre by head office.

(b) A decentralised unit must be **large enough** to support the quantity and quality of management it needs.

(c) Each decentralised unit must have a **potential for growth** in its own area of operations.

(d) There should be **scope and challenge** in the job for the management of the decentralised unit.

(e) Different divisions should treat each other as **independent companies**.

The adhocracy

KEY TERM

The **adhocracy** does not rely on standardisation to co-ordinate its activities, yet it is much more complex than the simple structure. The **support staff** exert a pull towards *collaboration*.

Adhocracy

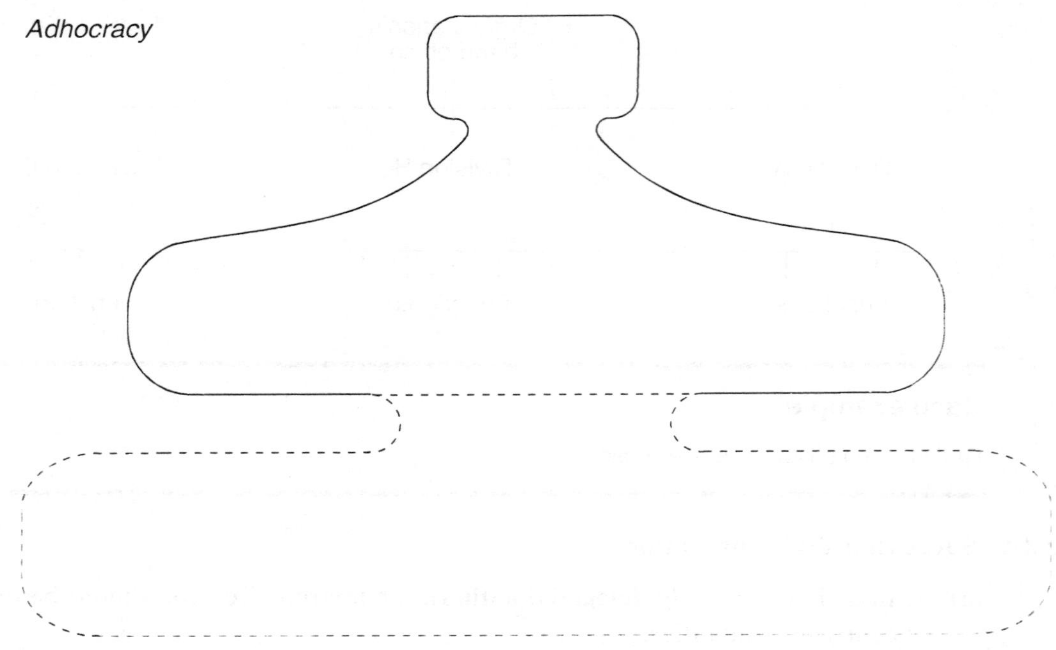

2.9 **Key issues**

(a) **Typical examples.** Specialists are deployed in **market-based project teams** which group together and disperse as and when a project arises and ends. A film production company employs director, actors, camera people, set designers etc. There is little formalisation of behaviour.

(b) **Environment**. The adhocracy is positioned in a **dynamic and complex** environment.

(c) **Co-ordination** is informal, by **mutual adjustment**. (The adhocracy relies on the expertise of its members, but **not through standardised skills**.)

(d) **Evolution**. The adhocracy is driven to bureaucratise itself as it ages. The organisation will **eventually specialise in what it does best**, driving it to more stable environmental conditions and predictable work processes, leading perhaps to a professional bureaucracy.

(e) Decision-making power depends on the type of decision and the situation in which it is made, rather than level in hierarchy. 'No-one ... monopolises the power to innovate'.

(f) **Strategy** is hard to determine in the adhocracy. It depends partly on the projects that come along (like a film studio). The strategic apex does not **formulate strategies**, but is engaged in battles over strategic **choices** (eg which films shall we make?) and liaisons with outside parties.

(g) **Problems of adhocracies**

   (i) The adhocracy is an **ambiguous environment** for work. This elicits complex human responses, as many people dislike ambiguity.

   (ii) The adhocracy is **not suitable for standardised work:** it is a custom producer.

   (iii) It has a **high cost of communication**, and workloads are unbalanced.

2.10 **Types of adhocracy**

(a) The **operating adhocracy** seeks to **innovate** to serve its **clients**, whereas the professional bureaucracy seeks perfection. (Mintzberg uses an analogy of a theatre company. An adhocratic theatre company produces new plays. A professional bureaucratic one would seek to produce ever more perfect renditions of Shakespeare.)

(b) The **administrative adhocracy** innovates to serve its own convenience. The operating core is split off, frequently subcontracted or automated, or even forms a separate organisation. The support staff are important, a central pool of expert talent from which project teams are drawn.

2.11 Mintzberg mentions one other co-ordinating factor: **mission**. A **missionary organisation** is one welded together by ideology or culture. There is job rotation, standardisation of values (norms) and little **external** control (eg like a religious sect).

2.12 **Section summary**

Mintzberg's theory of structural configuration covers many issues, over and above formal organisation structure.

(a) The type of work the organisation does (customised or standardised).
(b) The complexity of the tasks (simple or complex).
(c) The environment (stable or dynamic).

Configuration	**Co-ordination mechanism**	**Key part**	**Environment**	**Possible characteristics**
Simple	Direct supervision	Strategic apex	Simple/dynamic (even hostile)	Small, young, centralised, personality-driven.
Machine bureaucracy	Standardised work processes	Techno-structure	Simple/stable	Old, large, rule-bound, specialised
Professional bureaucracy	Standardised skills	Operating core	Complex/stable	Decentralised, emphasis on training
Divisional form	Standardised outputs	Middle line	Varies; each division is shielded to a degree	Old, large, divisions are quasi-autonomous, decentralised, bureaucratic
Adhocracy	Mutual adjustment	Support staff	Complex/ dynamic	High automation

Question 2

Which organisation configurations are suggested in the following cases?

(a) Creation Ltd provides public relations services to clients. It is run by five partners, with a staff of copy editors, designers, party-throwers and people with contacts in the press. Clients contact one of the partners who assembles a team to solve the client's problem, though the partner does not direct the solution.

(b) The St Imelda Hospital is involved in providing physiotherapy to accident victims. It recruits trained physiotherapists, each of whom is allocated a patient. The hospital does not determine exactly what sort of treatments should be used.

Answer

(a) Adhocracy
(b) Professional bureaucracy

3 CENTRALISATION AND DECENTRALISATION

3.1 Centralisation and decentralisation refer to where decisions are taken in an organisation.

(a) **Geography**. Some decisions might have to be referred back to a head office which controls what goes on, even if they are relatively trivial.

(b) **Management layer**. Some decisions might have to be referred upwards in the hierarchy. In other words, the firm does not practise delegation.

KEY TERMS

(a) **Centralisation** means a greater degree of central control.

(b) **Decentralisation** means a greater degree of delegated authority to regions or sub-units.

3.2 **Advantages of centralisation**

Advantage	Comment
Control	Senior management can exercise greater control over the activities of the organisation and co-ordinate their subordinates or sub-units more easily.
Standardisation	With central control, procedures can be standardised throughout the organisation. (In other words, it can lead to a machine bureaucracy.)
Corporate view	Senior managers can make decisions from the point of view of the organisation as a whole, whereas subordinates would tend to make decisions from the point of view of their own department or section.
Balance of power	Centralised control enables an organisation to maintain a balance between different functions or departments.
Experience counts	Senior managers ought to be more experienced and skilful in making decisions. In theory at least, centralised decisions by senior people should be better in 'quality' than decentralised decisions by less experienced subordinates.
Lower overheads	Centralised management will often be cheaper in terms of managerial overheads. When authority is delegated, there is often a duplication of management effort (and a corresponding increase in staff numbers) at lower levels of hierarchy.
Leadership	In times of *crisis*, the organisation may need strong leadership by a central group of senior managers.

3.3 **Advantages of decentralisation**

Advantage	Comment
Workload	It reduces the stress and burdens of senior management.
Job	It provides subordinates with greater job satisfaction by giving them more say in making decisions which affect their work.
Local knowledge	Subordinates may have a better knowledge than senior management of 'local' conditions affecting their area of work.
Flexibility and speed	Delegation should allow greater flexibility and a quicker response to changing conditions. If problems do not have to be referred up a scalar chain of command to senior managers for a decision, decision-making will be quicker. Since decisions are quicker, they are also more adaptable, and easier to change in the light of unforeseen circumstances which may arise.
Training	By allowing delegated authority to subordinates, management at middle and junior levels are 'groomed' for eventual senior management positions, because they are given the necessary experience of decision-making. Delegation is therefore important for management development and succession planning.
Control	By establishing appropriate sub-units or profit centres to which authority is delegated, the system of control within the organisation might actually be improved. Targets for performance by each profit centre can be established, actual results monitored against targets and control action taken by appropriate subordinates with the necessary authority; the subordinates would then be held accountable and responsible for their results, and areas of efficiency or inefficiency within the organisation would be more easily identified and remedied. However, Mintzberg pointed out some of the flaws in this argument.

3.4 **Contingency approach.** Centralisation suits some functions more than others. Central functions might include the *public relations* department.

- The **research and development function** might be centralised into a single unit, as a resource for each division.
- Sales departments might be decentralised on a terroritial basis.
- We will discuss the issue in the context of IT later in this chapter.

Centralisation and strategic planning

3.5 Goold and Campbell categorised three types of strategic planning organisation, according to whether:

- Decisions are made at the centre or by subsidiaries
- How the centre measures and controls the performance of subsidiaries.

3.6 They identified three management styles.

(a) **Strategic planners** (such as Cadbury-Schweppes) have a small number of core businesses. Head office plays a big part in making the strategic planning decisions for all its businesses, and subsidiaries are required to implement these global plans.

(b) **Strategic controllers** tend to be diversified. Headquarters are remote. Strategic planning involves:

(i) The issue of general guidelines from head office, on group objectives and background economic assumptions and indicating 'crucial problems' for each subsidiary.

(ii) Each subsidiary then formulates its own detailed strategic plans.

(iii) These plans are reviewed and approved by head office.

The success of this sort of a planning organisation depends on how good the top management at head office are in perceiving the crucial questions for each subsidiary, and ensuring that the subsidiary's plans give a satisfactory answer to them.

(c) **Financial controllers** (such as GEC and Tarmac) are groups where most strategic decisions are made by the subsidiaries without head office interference. Head office exercises control over subsidiaries according to results - ie financial performance and success or failure in achieving financial targets.

Question 3

XYZ has over 500 profit centres (ranging from baggage handling equipment to stockings) and revenues of £7bn. Head office staff amount to 47. Each profit centre must provide the following.

(a) The *annual profit plan*. This is agreed in detail every year, after close negotiation. It is regarded as a commitment to a preordained level of performance.

(b) A *monthly management report*, which is extremely detailed (17 pages). Working capital is outlined in detail. Provisions (the easiest way to manipulate accounts) are highlighted.

Is XYZ a strategic planner, a strategic controller or a financial controller?

Answer

Financial controller.

3.7 Influences on the choice of planning organisation

(a) Highly diversified groups are much more difficult to control from the centre, and a **financial controller** system would probably be suitable.

(b) When **big capital investments** are planned, head office should be involved in the decision.

(c) When **cash flow** is tight, other strategies must be sacrificed to the paramount concern for short term survival and attention to cash flow.

(d) Organisations in a single industry which is fairly stable would perhaps be more efficiently managed by a hierarchical, centralised management system, structured perhaps on a functional basis (production, marketing etc).

(e) Top management might prefer one approach.

3.8 Section summary

- Centralisation offers control and standardisation.
- Differentiation offers local knowledge.
- This applies also the strategic planning processes.

4 DEPARTMENTATION

4.1 An organisation changes as it grows in size.

(a) **Economies of scale** may call for the establishment of departments of specialist or experts (eg research and development, management scientists etc).

(b) More **levels in the organisation hierarchy** create problems of delegation of authority and control.

(c) **Specialist support teams** (eg service and maintenance, quality control, corporate planning, organisation and methods, data processing etc) are created to ease the burdens and complexities of line management.

(d) Separate groups and **departments** continue to be formed as specialisation extends; new problems of communication and co-ordination (or integration) now arise.

KEY TERM

The creation of departments is known as **departmentation.**

4.2 Different patterns of departmentation are possible, and the pattern selected will depend on the individual circumstances of the organisation.

4.3 **Geographic area (or territory)**

Some authority is retained at Head Office (organised, perhaps, on a functional basis) but day-to-day service operations are handled on a territorial basis. Within many sales departments, the sales staff are organised territorially.

(a) **Advantages**

- Better and quicker local decision making at the point of contact between the organisation (eg a salesman) and its customers.
- Cheaper to establish area factories/offices (eg costs of transportation and travelling may be reduced).

(b) **Disadvantages**

- The duplication of management effort.
- Diversity of approach.

4.4 **By function**

Functional organisation accommodates the division of work into specialist areas. (In other words, below the strategic apex there is a finance department, and sales department, a production department)

(a) **Advantages**

- Concentrates expertise
- Economies of scale
- Suits firms with few product ranges and not too many markets

(b) **Disadvantages**

- Co-ordination problems between functions.
- It is organisation by work speciality rather than customer or product (which ultimately drive a business).

4.5 **By product/brand**

(a) Some organisations group activities on the basis of products or product lines. Some functional departmentation remains (eg manufacturing, distribution, marketing and sales) but a divisional manager is given responsibility for the product or product line, with authority over personnel of different functions.

(i) **Advantages**

(1) Individual managers can be held accountable for the **profitability** of individual products.

(2) **Specialisation** can be developed. For example, service engineers who specialise in a single product should also provide a better after sales service.

(3) The different functional activities and efforts required to make and sell each product can be co-ordinated and integrated by the divisional/product manager.

(ii) **Disadvantage** is that it increases the overhead costs and managerial complexity of the organisation.

(b) **By brand**. Large organisations may produce a number of different brands of the same basic product, such as washing powder or toothpaste. A brand manager is responsible for the brand.

4.6 **By customer or market segment**. A manufacturing organisation may sell goods through wholesalers, export agents and by direct mail. It may therefore organise its sales, marketing and distribution functions on the basis of types of customer, or market segment. Departmentation by customer is commonly associated with sales departments and selling effort, but it might also be used by a jobbing or contracting firm where a team of managers may be given the responsibility of liaising with major customers (eg discussing specifications and completion dates, quality of work, progress chasing etc).

Case example

TLG, a lighting equipment maker based in Hertfordshire, has abandoned 'its country-by-country managerial structure and adopted a pan-European system of managing its business by product categories' (*Financial Times*, 21 February 1997). This comes at the end of a period of evolutionary change and development in the market.

(a) 'Five years ago it was very difficult to develop a product for five different countries in Europe. But now, in our business, the characteristics of our products and the installation habits are converging.'

TLG - which started with vertically-integrated operations in each geographical market - has gradually recognised the need to develop a common approach across Europe.

(b) In 1991 the group introduced a 'matrix' system of management, by which regional executives took on pan-European responsibilities.

(c) Early last year the group decided this system did not go far enough towards Europe-wide integration. Many of its customers - wholesalers and retailers - were themselves becoming pan-European and telling their suppliers they wanted to deal with one company throughout Europe.'

The company decided to review its operations, and asked Ernst and Young for advice.

(a) Functional structure (ie with a separate manufacturing director, technical director etc) was rejected because production methods differed so greatly across the product range.

(b) Instead, the firm rationalised its product range and adopted product divisionalisation.

'The group set up three 'centres of excellence' in Europe, based around its core lighting product: indoor commercial, indoor architectural and outdoor lighting. Each division is headed by a managing director with Europe-wide responsibilities. The group has also appointed a European commercial director to manage and develop the existing salesforces. "The selling operations are still country-based because we want the point of contact with our customers to remain on the same basis as it was previously."

Divisional managers are beginning to see the benefits of the new organisation. Terry Smith, director of the indoor commercial division, says the new system makes its easier for the group to transfer its best manufacturing and design practices across Europe and between divisions.

4.7 In practice many organisations are *hybrid*. The R&D and finance department, say, might be functionally organised, but production and marketing might be organised by brand.

Sharing control: matrix and project organisation

Case example

Matrix management first developed in the 1950s in the USA in the aerospace industry. Lockheed-California, the aircraft manufacturers, were organised in a functional hierarchy. Customers were unable to find a manager in Lockheed to whom they could take their problems and queries about their particular orders, and Lockheed found it necessary to employ 'project expediters' as customer liaison officials. From this developed 'project co-ordinators', responsible for co-ordinating line managers' efforts to solve a customer's problems. Up to this point, these new officials had no functional responsibilities. Due to increasingly heavy customer demands, Lockheed eventually created 'programmer managers', with authority for project budgets and programme design and scheduling. These managers therefore had functional authority and responsibilities.

4.8 **Project organisation**

(a) Projects require a diversity of skills, drawn from different business functions. (Technical term: **multi-functional project teams**). Projects have a **finite life span**, so the arrangement is **temporary**.

(b) Authority is thus shared between **project managers** and the heads of the functional departments. Functional department heads are responsible for the organisation of each department, but project managers are responsible for all aspects of the project itself. An employee might expect to receive directions/commands from a project co-ordinator as well as from the functional head.

4.9 A **matrix organisation** is a permanent arrangement. For example a **geographical structure** can be **superimposed** on top of a **functional departmental structure** in a **matrix**. An individual may be a member of the finance function but may also report to a regional or country director.

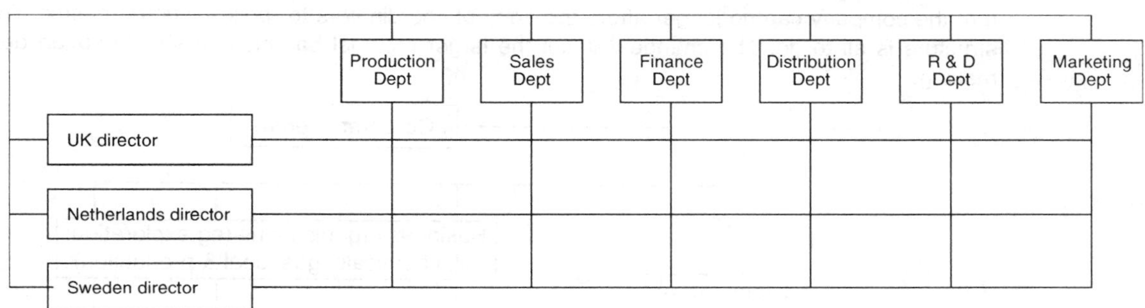

The product managers may each have their own marketing team, in which case the marketing department itself would be small or non-existent.

4.10 **Advantages of a matrix structure**

(a) **Greater flexibility** in responding to environmental influences

(b) Dual authority **prevents the dominance of one viewpoint** over decisions.

(c) They allocate responsibility for **end-results.** A product manager is responsible for product profitability, a project leader is responsible for ensuring that the task is completed, and a study course leader has direct responsibility for the provision of a complete efficient and effective course to students.

(d) They provide for **inter-disciplinary co-**operation and a mixing of skills and expertise.

(e) They motivate employees to work harder and more efficiently by providing them with greater participation in planning and control decisions.

4.11 **Disadvantages of matrix organisation**

(a) **Conflicts** between functional managers and product/project managers.
(b) **Reporting to two bosses** (or more) can be stressful.
(c) **Costly** - co-ordination mechanisms are expensive.

Case example

The example below suggests the varying pressures underlying the structure of a business on a worldwide scale.

Shell

For historical reasons, Shell had a complicated matrix structure Shell announced the end of its old matrix organisation.. Each country or region had its own operating companies.

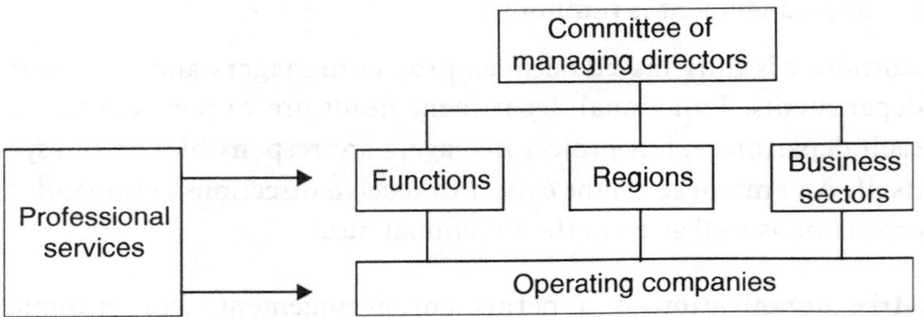

A given operating company could be defined by geography, or business sector for example. The structure was very elaborate and required the support of large groups of executives, representing 'national or regional units, business sections (or divisions) and functions such as finance. It is felt that the company can no longer afford the army of coordinators to "police" such a matrix'. This old structure is all to go. The change will 'cut the larger regional baronies'. It should speed decision making.

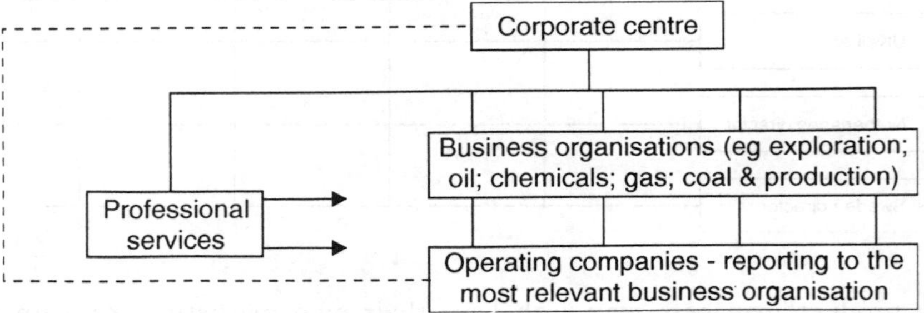

The operating companies are unchanged, so a local basis is maintained and the operating companies still have a link to the corporate centre.

Current issues

Delayering

4.12 **Flat organisations** are becoming more common with the current fashion for delayering, in other words reducing the number of tiers between the highest and lowest levels.

(a) **Information technology** has reduced the information and processing tasks of middle management.

(b) Modern management theories aim to '**empower**' the workforce to take decisions.

(c) Delayering has gone hand in hand with a trend towards **downsizing** whereby large numbers of managers and staff have been made redundant. In theory, this is supposed to make organisations 'leaner' and more flexible. Often, however, it is a simple **short-term cost cutting exercise** with no fundamental improvement to the business, as no resources or capacity are available for future growth. The Economist termed this **corporate anorexia.**

Management problems of outsourcing

4.13 Outsourcing has been adopted by many organisations, and it has implications for scalar chain and span of control. Let us take the simple example of office cleaning.

(a) **Reporting.** In the past the office cleaners would have been recruited by the firm, and they would probably have reported to the person in charge of maintaining the physical structure of the building, who would have reported to an administration manager.

(b) With outsourcing arrangements, the **chain of command is effectively broken**. The firm has a contract with the external supplier, and therefore has no direct management control over the cleaning staff.

(c) Someone has to **manage and monitor the contract**, to ensure that the firm supplying cleaning services keeps to the precise terms of the contract. For matters such a cleaning and catering the issues are very clear cut. However, government departments and local governments outsource a substantial proportion of their services and so contract management becomes a major management task.

(d) **Disputes can easily end up in court**. The firm cannot discipline the supplier's employee for poor quality work. Managers save money, and gain expertise, but perhaps at the expense of operational flexibility.

4.14 Paradoxically outsourcing can make operational management **less** flexible.

4.15 Section summary

- There are many ways of grouping people into departments; most organisations combine several of them.
- Matrix and project organisation exist to co-ordinate activities - for the customers' benefit - across departmental lines.

5 ORGANISING INFORMATION SYSTEMS ACTIVITIES

5.1 In Chapter 3, we described how computerisation had evolved over time. This was reflected in the management structure. Key **management** issues arising from technological changes are:

- The integration of computing and telecommunications technology.

- Centralised transaction processing has given way to **end-user computing.**
- De facto **standards** (Windows) have overtaken proprietary operating systems in many cases.
- IT requires **strategic management**, because of its cost, criticality to the organisation's operations and its capacity to promote competitive advantage.

5.2 **Organisations have responded** to these trends by:

(a) **Raising the level of IT staff**, sometimes to the extent of appointing **information directors.**

(b) Setting up **information centres** to aid users to develop their own applications.

(c) Developing overall **strategies** for information systems (similar in concept to sales strategies etc).

(d) Setting **standards** for hardware and software acquisition.

(e) **Increasing resources** devoted to information systems security.

The information director

5.3 The **information director** (ID) should be a member of the Board of Directors, or occupy a position of similar executive seniority.

- The ID raises IT issues at Board level.
- The ID brings business issues to bear on the activities of IT personnel.

5.4 A successful information director needs:

(a) General management ability
(b) Understanding of how the organisation operates
(c) Good technical expertise in developing and running information systems.

5.5 **The role of the information director**

Role	Comment
Integrating	Ensuring the organisation's acquisition and use of IT fits in with the goals of the organisation.
Controlling	Ensure that *users* operate IT for the benefit of the organisation; this covers: • Technical standards (eg only buy from one supplier) • Software standards (eg only use Excel for spreadsheet applications) • Establishment of *corporate* as opposed to *departmental* databases • Providing an information systems service function.

Role	Comment
Designing	The information director may be responsible for the overall design of an organisation's information systems. This responsibility is likely to be delegated on a day to day basis.
Liaison	Liaison between information systems professionals and the rest of the organisation, eg *technical assistance*, discussions with users as to their needs, advice on the impact of information systems on organisational structure, working environment and so forth.
Environmental scanning	This is essential for a strategic perspective. IT affects ways of doing business, supplier-customer relationships etc. The information director will seek to dovetail these types of facility into the organisation's overall commercial strategy. The legal environment is also complex: data protection legislation, the vexed status of copyright on the Internet, virus problems and so on.

5.6 **Problems facing the information director**

(a) Shortages of skilled staff.

(b) Backlogs in application development caused by (a) above, and also the fact that much programming time is spent repairing old applications rather than developing new ones.

(c) Ensuring continued expansion.

The information systems department

5.7 While the Information Director reports at board level, performing an overall guidance and propaganda role, the number of management responsibilities relating to information systems are quite large. These responsibilities may not be the remit of a single individual, as the personnel structure will vary from organisation to organisation.

5.8 **Responsibilities entailed in information systems management**

Role	Comment
Administration	This includes the secretarial work, accounting, and library services of the information function. These support services are likely to be provided by other business functions. The IS manager's administrative responsibilities include budgeting (for capital and revenue expenditure) and personnel selection, training and welfare.
Strategic control and planning	IS plans should be tied into the overall business plan of the organisation. Planning activities include development of procedures and standards for guidance of staff (eg choice of systems development methodologies and control) and assigning development work to subordinates, and liaising with users to assess their needs.
Information systems development	This includes systems design, programming and so forth. The IS manager is likely to be a member of any steering committee for a project and will probably be instrumental in the choice of a project manager.

Role	Comment
User support	This is the development and operation of applications. Information systems personnel can aid users to develop their own applications. Also, they can provide advice, help lines, and other services. (This is the role of the Information Centre.)
Service management computer operations and data centres	Currently, these contain complex and powerful systems, and are similar in function to the old style computer centres. The IS manager will review the operation of services provided to user departments.
Network management	Ensure that networks are secure, with protection from viruses, operational (enough capacity on the file server) and that appropriate confidentiality (eg through passwords, user profiles restricting access to certain files) is maintained, new users are added, there are adequate connections etc.

5.9 The position of the information systems function within an organisation has changed over time.

(a) **Early days.** The data processing function was put under the control of the **predominant user** usually the finance department.

(b) Then, as technology usage began to spread, a **separate DP department** was developed. The DP department was tight-knit, specialised, and carried out all of an organisation's processing activities.

(c) **End-user computing** has changed the role of the central department producing information systems. However, it is not wise to regard a central department as a thing of the past for two reasons.

(i) Some **central control is needed** to ensure compatibility between different departments.

(ii) **User departments** are probably **incapable** of designing and implementing **large, complicated** and expensive systems **which cut across departmental or functional boundaries.**

Information systems development personnel

5.10 **Systems and programming manager**

(a) Project management of IT projects (see Chapter 11).
(b) Maintenance and updating of existing systems.
(c) liaising between the systems analysis team and the programming team.
(d) Arranging technical training and helping with staff recruitment.
(e) Controlling the work of the information systems development.

5.11 **The tasks of the systems analyst**

(a) **Systems analysis.** Analysing current systems and discovering user objectives.
(b) **Systems design** - Design a system that will achieve these requirements.
(c) **Systems specification.** Specify the system in detail.
(d) **Systems testing.**
(e) **Keeping the system** under review.

5.12 **Programmers** take over from the systems analysts and have the task of writing the programs and, whereas necessary maintaining programmes, upgrading programmer and debugging them.

5.13 The systems analysts and programmers are also responsible for preparing full documentation of the system and each program in the system.

Service management personnel

5.14 **Operations manager**

The operations manager is in charge of the activities of the computer or data centre (eg firms with large centralised mainframes, super-computers or those using an extensive client server network).

(a) Providing a computer operations service to user departments

(b) Ensuring that the firm has enough resources to meet the demands for information processing.

(c) Arrange for adequate maintenance of the hardware.

(d) Provide adequate security, for example in monitoring virus infections.

(e) Deal with errors and downtime.

(f) Ensuring users are adequately connected to the network.

(g) Ensuring the proper operation of the file server.

5.15 In addition, a firm might have a file librarian or a database manager.

End-user computing

KEY TERM

End-user computing: 'the direct, hands-on use of computers by users - not indirect use through systems professionals or the data processing staff. End-users include executives, managers, professional staff, secretaries, office workers, salespeople and others' (Sprague and McNurlin *Information Systems Management in Practice*).

5.16 End-user computing has been fuelled by:

- The introduction of PCs and networking to user departments.
- User-friendly software (eg Windows).
- Greater awareness of computers and what they can do.
- The applications backlog: most information systems departments do not have the resources to cope with all the demands for new applications pressed on them.

Question 4

List some uses of IT by end-users.

Answer

The uses of computers by end-users include:

- Accounting and calculating (eg spreadsheets)
- Writing (word processing)

- Search and retrieval of information (interrogating a database)
- Aiding communications (computer networks, electronic mail)
- Presentation of information (graphics)
- Planning, scheduling and monitoring (project management)
- Personal organisation (electronic diary facilities)
- Routine transaction processing
- Learning and education (computer based training)
- End-user programming (developing new programs)
- Decision support.

5.17 **Management issues related to end-user computing**

(a) Responsibility for the **development of applications**: user departments or the IS department?

(b) **Duplication of effort**. Development of similar applications in different departments can occur, duplicating programming effort.

(c) **Security** may be a problem if access to the system is easy to obtain.

5.18 **Advantages of user-developed systems**

(a) Relieves shortage of systems development personnel.

(b) Eliminates the problem of information requirements determination by information systems personnel.

(c) Transfers the information system implementation process to users.

5.19 **Disadvantages of user developed systems**

(a) The elimination of the separation of the functions of user and analyst.

(b) The limits on user ability to identify correct and complete requirements for an application.

(c) Lack of user knowledge and acceptance of application quality assurance procedures for development and operation.

(d) Unstable user systems.

(e) The dangers of private information systems.

(f) The possibility of undesirable information behaviour.

5.20 An approach to dealing with these problems is the **information centre**, which enables a proper convergence of intended strategies and emergent strategies in the use of IT, and is described below.

The information centre

KEY TERM

An **information centre** (IC) is a small unit of staff with a good technical awareness of computer systems, whose task is to provide a support function to computer users within the organisation.

5.21 ICs are useful in organisations which use distributed processing systems or PCs quite heavily, and so have many 'non-technical' people in charge of hardware, files and software scattered throughout the organisation.

5.22 **Services offered by an information centre**

Service	Comment
Help Desk	Ensures that staff time is spent on their real work rather than on IT problems. Help may be via the telephone, site visits, or e-mail. Common problems and their solutions can be posted on a bulletin board for all to read
Remote diagnostic software	Enables staff in the IC to 'take control' of a computer whose user is having problems and sort out the problem for them.
Response	The help desk needs sufficient **staff and technical expertise** to respond quickly to problems with hardware or software.
Contacts and relationships with suppliers	Ensures that they fulfil their maintenance obligations and their maintenance staff are quickly on site when needed.
Maintain a record of problems	To identify those that occur most often.
Training	**Training software** can be developed or purchased and made available over a network from a central server.
Modifying the system	If the problem is with the **system itself**, a solution is found, either by modifying the system or by investment in appropriate hardware or software. The IC can also consider the viability of **suggestions for improvements** to the system and brings these into effect, where possible, for all users who stand to benefit.
Standards	The IC is also likely to be responsible for setting, and for encouraging users to conform to common **standards** for **hardware** (all of the equipment used in the organisation is compatible), **software** (information generated by one department can easily be shared with and worked upon by other departments), **programming** (applications developed by users are efficient and secure) and **data** (ie certain conventions such as the format of file names should be followed throughout the organisation. to facilitate sharing and storage and retrieval of information by as many users as possible).
Security	**Backup** files (eg on the file server), **procedures** for company-wide use, or distributing **anti-virus software**.
Applications development	Technical guidance to the developers to encourage **comprehensible** and **documented** user-developed programs, which can be used throughout the organisation.

Question 5

Radical Chains plc is a large publishing conglomerate, which produces academic and popular magazines for well defined market segments. The company has been taken over and is under new management. An information director has just been appointed. The former senior management had not really worried about IT. There are three incompatible desk-top publishing systems used for layout. Furthermore, a number of different word processing packages are used. This means that, in some cases, temporary staff acquainted with one of the packages have to be brought in when some of the permanent employees have little to do. The journalists produce copy for several magazines. Most journalists only learn one WP package, and copy sometimes has to be retyped. What should the information director do?

Answer

Obviously, you wouldn't plan for this situation. But before rushing in with standards, do a cost/benefit analysis: the three DTP systems might have important differences between them, which indicate why they have been chosen for particular titles. The cost of temps may not be too great, if the benefits of maintaining three systems are taken into account..

That said, it is likely that a degree of standardisation would make matters better.

(a) Chose one DTP package and one WP package for all future IT projects. The other two might be phased out.

(b) Train journalists and typists in the other two packages, so that there are fewer skill shortages at any particular time.

Centralisation versus decentralisation of IT

5.23 Technological changes have shifted the balance of power over processing from the information systems department to user departments. The issues of **centralisation** and **decentralisation** relate both to **technical matters** and **managerial issues.**

Issue	Comment
Data management	Decentralisation can result in a riot of minor applications, with subtly different definitions of data reducing the ability to compare like with like or use for generating information. This might mean that the organisation's data resource as a whole is insufficiently transparent.
Hardware	Compatibility is less of a problem than in the past, if only because 'Windows' has become a *de facto* standard.
Software	If, say, two departments set up their own databases using different software, this would inhibit sharing data, or require complex programs.
Security	Networked PCs are less secure than mainframes. (However they are much more flexible to use.)
Cost	Networks of PCs are not always cheaper than central servers (mainframes). This is because the cost of 'add-ons', maintenance and so forth for PCs are much greater than that for mainframes.
Corporate vs functional	Looking at the **value chain** means considering the organisation as a **whole**. A decentralised approach to IT applications can result in IT being reduced to functional control: potentially revolutionary applications for reconfiguring **business processes** will not be identified.
Organisation structure	The degree of centralisation is not only influenced by technical issues, but by organisation structure. An organisation which is decentralised for most strategic issues will probably have a decentralised approach to IT.

Case example

An example of the tension between centralisation and decentralisation is provided by *knowledge management*. This involves making the best possible use of information from outside, and ideas and information generated from within the firm. Knowledge must be shared, as we have seen in the context of strategic intelligence. Knowledge management is a discipline dealing with *how* knowledge is collected and disseminated within the organisation. Companies with heavy R & D expenditure need to be aware of their *intellectual capital.* Companies keep information on customers, the market and other areas of strategic intelligence.

Technology is an *enabler*, not the driver.

Glaxo Wellcome (*Information Week* 13 –26 May 1998)

(a) The goals of the business drive knowledge management
(b) Three key issues
    (i) Content of 'knowledge'.
    (ii) Culture of the firm.
    (iii) Underpinning technology enabling distribution of knowledge.

Glaxo Wellcome has an 'Information Policies and Standards' group, which focuses on helping the business to manage its information effectively, decides what *information to keep*, and how to *categorise* it (personal, corporate, departmental, groups and projects.'

Glaxo Wellcome has also developed the use of the intra-net.

(a) *Content.* The firm does not have single 'content manger' to look after what goes *into* the intra-net. This is the responsibility of a number of groups, who bring in published information and make it visible on the intranet.
(b) *Use.* There is an *intranet management centre* which focuses less on content than on making the technology *easy to use.*

The firm's knowledge management needs require the integration of internal and external information.

5.24 Section summary

- IT needs consideration at board level.
- End-user computing gives power to end users.
- The role of DP department has evolved from *running* an organisation's IT applications to supporting and guiding end-users. The information centre performs this role.

6 BRAINWORKS PLC UPDATE

Questions can be found in the Introduction box at the beginning of this chapter.

6.1 *Question 1.* BW has some of the characteristics of a professional bureaucracy.

6.2 *Question 2.* Currently IT is run ineffectively by the finance department. If it is to have a radical impact then it ought to be considered at board level. Willard Mann obviously has some idea of its potential. Another management issue is that no mention is made of the Data Protection Act.

Chapter roundup

- Mintzberg identifies five possible structural configurations. Each derives from the desire of its constituent parts to pull the organisation in its direction. There is an argument that structure ultimately derives from business strategy.
- A **simple structure** is dominated by strategic apex, closely related to an operating core.
- A **machine bureaucracy** exercises control by standardising processes.
- A **professional bureaucracy** exercises control by standardising skills.
- A **divisonalised form** involves the delegation of authority to middle line managers, who are governed by the strategic apex via a variety of techniques (eg financial control, or detailed planning or strategic control).
- An **adhocracy** is project orientated: people with a variety of skills disperse and regroup around a number of clients or projects.
- **Centralisation** of authority is a feature of many kinds of organisation. Centralisation enables standardisation and control, but constricts flexibility and responsiveness.
- **Departmentation** methods include grouping people by geography, function, product/brand or customer.
- **Matrix management** is a way of sharing authority.
- Information systems pose unique management problems of co-ordination, direction and cost.
- The **information director** is responsible for ensuring that IT issues are discussed at Board level and for developing the strategy.
- **Information centres** give advice and support to users and maintain standards. They enable a convergence of intended and emergent strategies in the use of IT.
- The **information systems department** is involved in administration, strategic control of IT, development of IS user support and service management.
- Some **central control** is necessary to ensure that the organisation as a whole benefits from IT.

Quick quiz

1. What influences organisation structure? (see para 1.1)
2. What is the origin of the simple structure? (2.3)
3. What sort of configuration is normally created by the technostructure? (2.4)
4. Give examples of professional bureaucracies. (2.5)
5. What are the problems of divisionalisation? (2.6)
6. What form does an adhocracy lapse into? (2.9)
7. Distinguish between operating and administrative adhocracies (2.10)
8. Distinguish between strategic planners, strategic controllers and financial controllers. (3.6)
9. What are the advantages and disadvantages of matrix structures? (4.10, 4.11)
10. What co-ordination and management problems result from outsourcing? (4.13)
11. How have organisations responded to the growing connection between computing and telecommunications technologies? (5.2)
12. Describe the role of the information director. (5.5)
13. What are the functions of the information systems department? (5.8)
14. Define end-user computing. (5.16)
15. What is an information centre? (5.21)
16. What are the issues involved in decentralised information systems? (5.23)

Question to try	Level	Marks	Time
14	Exam standard	25	45 mins

Chapter 11

PROJECT MANAGEMENT

	Chapter topic list	Syllabus reference
1	**What is project management?**	**2(a), 2(b)(i) - (vi)**
2	**Planning and resourcing techniques**	**2(a), 2(b)(i) - (vi)**
3	**Project planning tools**	**2(a), 2(b)(i) - (vi)**
4	**Management implications of project management techniques**	**2(a), 2(b)(i) - (vi)**
5	**Information systems projects**	**6(e)**
6	**Brainworks plc update**	

Introduction

Project management is a fairly well contained topic in the syllabus. The difference between project planning and other parts of planning is that a **project is not a repetitive activity**. That said, it encapsulates on a small scale many issues of planning and management, including the details of resource allocation.

For **information systems**, their technical complexity and the specialist expertise needed should not detract from the fact that they are developed for **users**, whose involvement in every stage of the systems design process is essential. There is always a temptation for systems analysts in the technostructure to develop technically perfect systems, whereas the user needs something less advanced. Systems development **methodologies** and prototyping are two ways by which the user can be drawn into the development process.

Brainworks plc

1. Identify situations in which project management techniques might come in useful for BW.
2. Comment on BW(UK)'s management of information systems projects.

1 WHAT IS PROJECT MANAGEMENT?

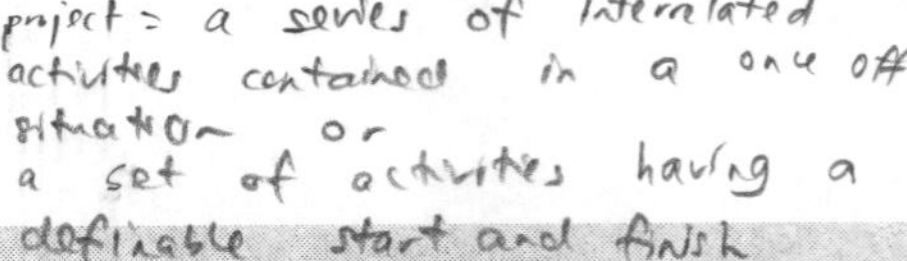

KEY TERM

A **project** is 'an undertaking that has a beginning and an end and is carried out to meet established goals within cost, schedule and quality objectives' (Haynes, *Project Management*).

1.1 Characteristics of projects

(a) Specific start and end points.
(b) Well-defined objectives.
(c) The project endeavour is to a degree unique and not repetitious.
(d) The project usually contains costs and time schedules.
(e) A project cuts across many organisational and functional boundaries.

1.2 **Examples of projects**

Project	Comment
Building and construction	The construction of the Channel Tunnel was a project, which ended when the tunnel was opened for normal service. The project involved raising finance, planning the digging, laying tracks etc.
Manufacturing	Projects can be a feature of job production. For example, the manufacture of an oil rig, normally to precise specifications, involves co-ordinating a large number of separate activities. This will cease when the rig is finished.
Management	Development of an information system, and the mounting of a major trade exhibition.
Research and development	• Some research projects (such as the international project for mapping the human genome) have definite objectives, even though, if you are breaking new ground, it is not always possible to keep to a strict timetable. • Some research activities are open-ended however, and some projects will suggest themselves from the results of particular aspects of research.

1.3 All projects involve, according to Dennis Lock, the 'projection of ideas and activities into new endeavours. No project can ever be exactly the same as anything which has gone before.' The steps and tasks leading to completion can never be described accurately in advance.

Unique features of project management

KEY TERM

Project management is directed at an end. It is not directed at maintaining or improving a continuous activity. It thus has a limited objective within a limited time span. According to Lock, 'the job of **project management** is to foresee as many dangers as possible, and to plan, organise and control activities so that they are avoided.'

1.4 **Special management problems with projects**

Problem	Comment
Teambuilding	The work is carried out by a team of people usually assembled for one project, who must be able to communicate effectively and immediately with each other.
Expected problems	There can be many novel **expected** problems, each one of which should be resolved by careful design and planning prior to commencement of work.

Problem	Comment
Unexpected problems	There can be many novel **unexpected** problems, particularly with a project working at the limits of existing and new technologies. There should be mechanisms within the project to enable these problems to be resolved during the time span of the project without detriment to the objective, the cost or the time span.
Delayed benefit	There is normally no benefit until the work is finished. The 'lead in' time to this can cause a strain on the eventual recipient who feels deprived until the benefit is achieved (even though in many cases it is a major improvement on existing activities) and who is also faced with increasing expenditure for no immediate benefit.
Specialists	Contributions made by specialists are of differing importance at each stage. Assembling a team working towards the one objective is made difficult due to the tendency of specialists to regard their contribution as always being more important than other people's and not understanding the inter-relationship between their various specialities in the context of the project.
Stakeholders	If the project involves several parties with different interests in the outcome, there might be disputes between them.

Case examples

(a) In the private sector, the *Channel Tunnel* cost a lot more than originally supposed, and there were many public disputes between Eurotunnel plc and the construction companies.

(b) Keep an eye on the *Millennium Dome*: a dome larger than Trafalgar Square is to be built on decontaminated land in Greenwich. It has to be completed to specification and on time for 31 December 1999.

1.5 Why projects go wrong

Reason	Comment
Unproven technology	Estimating the project duration can be difficult when it involves new technology or existing technology at its limits.
Over-optimism	Costs are often wildly underestimated by optimistic designers particularly with new technology.
Changing client specifications	Clients who are vague as to what they want or who continually change their mind make it impossible to adhere to the planned duration and cost - a problem with IT projects.
Control	Project management teams often fail to exercise control under changing circumstances.
'Politics'	When a project goes wrong in terms of time and money, the project management team and various contractors make optimistic comments. The client is committed politically to its completion, so it becomes difficult to cancel as nobody dares make the decision.

Reason	Comment
Deadlines	The project manager accepts an unrealistic deadline for having the system up and running. The timescale is fixed too early on in the planning process: the user's idea of when the system would be needed is taken as the deadline, before sufficient consideration is given to the realism of this timescale.
Planning	Poor or non-existent planning is a recipe for disaster. Unattainable deadlines might be promised.
Project managers are technicians not managers	A special problem with IT projects: the technical ability of IS staff is no guarantee of management skill. Often, however, the only promotion path available is to a management role.
Control is non-existent	No performance reviews.
Poor timetabling and resourcing	It is no use being presented on day 1 with a team of programmers, when there is systems analysis and design work to do.
Lack of senior management support	Especially with IT projects, a *management sponsor* from higher up in the organisation is needed to argue the project's case to senior management, or even to the steering committee. During the project implementation itself, the management sponsor lends prestige and authority to the project. The management sponsor can be useful in sorting out disputes between the project managers and users.

1.6 **Successful projects are many, and include:**

- The world of commercial property development when experienced teams can be assembled and the project is subject to the strict control of market forces.
- The construction at London's Waterloo station of a terminus for Channel Tunnel trains: the building was complete some time before the commencement of Channel Tunnel passenger services.
- The recent landing of an unmanned space craft on Mars.
- Most launches of new products.

The objectives of project management

1.7 The objectives, broadly speaking, of project management arise out of the deficiencies in para 1.5.

Objective	Comment
Quality	The end result should conform to the proper specification. In other words, the result should achieve what the project was supposed to do.
Budget	The project should be completed without exceeding authorised expenditure.
Timescale	The progress of the project must follow the planned process, so that the 'result' is ready for use at the agreed date. As time is money, proper time management can help contain costs.

The project life cycle

1.8 A typical project has a **project life cycle.**

- Conceiving and defining the project
- Planning the project
- Carrying out the plan (project implementation) and control
- Completing and evaluating the project

Conceiving and defining the project

1.9 A project often arises out of a perceived problem or opportunity. However, it is often not clear precisely what the problem is.

Step 1 **Analyse the problem.** The project team should study, discuss and analyse the project, from a number of different aspects (eg technical, financial). Defining the problem or opportunity the project is supposed to address is a necessary step to a solution.

Step 2 **Write the project definition.** Defining the project is an iterative process. In other words, there will be several stages, with each definition being more detailed and refined than before. The project might be defined in a:

- Contract
- Product specification
- Customer's specification

Step 3 **State the final objective of the project.** This clarifies what the project is trying to achieve (eg a sales system).

Step 4 **List the success criteria for a project.** These are the project's *basic* requirements and perhaps desirable enhancements. For the Channel Tunnel to be considered a 'success', the tunnel had to link the UK and France. If this was not done, the project would be a *total* failure. Other factors add to the value of the project (eg the rail/road combination). These can be analysed into **must objectives** and **want objectives.**

Step 5 **Alternative strategies** to find the best way to reach the project objective. Brainstorming sessions might be useful here.

Step 6 **Evaluate alternatives.** These alternatives are evaluated on the basis of technical and practical feasibility.

Step 7 **Assess the chosen strategy:** more detailed review and testing is carried out.

(i) A feasibility study examines the technical and financial aspects of the project, costing its critical assumptions and exposing possible flaws or unrealistic expectations.

(ii) Marketing might include detailed market research or even using a test market.

(iii) Other ways of testing are *pilot testing* or *simulation.*

Planning the project

1.10 A **project plan** aims to ensure that the project objective is achieved within the objectives of quality, cost and time. This involves three steps, once the basic project objective and the underlying activities have been agreed.

Step 1 **Break the project down into manageable units.** As a simple example, if your objective is to cook a dinner party for your friends, you will break down this task into preparing the starter, the main course, and then the dessert. If you were a stickler for planning, you could break these down further into detailed tasks (chop onions, peel potatoes). This is sometimes called establishing a **work breakdown structure** (see paragraphs 2.5 to 2.8 below).

Step 2 **For each unit, estimate the resources needed** (in materials, money and time).

Step 3 **Schedule and plan resource requirements and timings of each sub-unit. Gantt charts, network analysis** and so forth are ways by which this can be achieved. **Costing** is also part of the project planning stage.

Carrying out the plan: implementation and control

1.11 The project implementation stage is when the plans are put into action. Frequently a project is directed by a **project manager** (see 1.16 below).

Step 1 **Review progress** to see that standards, outlined in the project specifications, are maintained.

(i) **Control point, identification charts** indicate the sort of things that might go wrong, and the action taken to rectify them.

(ii) **Project control charts** use budget and schedule plans to give a status report on progress (eg cumulative time and cost) so that variances can be calculated.

Step 2 **Monitor performance**, by:

- Inspection
- Progress reviews (at regular stages)
- Quality testing
- Financial audit

Step 3 **Take corrective action.** Falling behind schedule, because of some circumstance unforeseen at the planning stage, might require the rescheduling of the project or a change in resource configuration. If the project is over budget, cost savings can be found, or alternatively, more funds might be available from the client.

Completing and evaluating the project: post-audit

1.12 Finally, the project must be delivered to the customer, of course after final testing and review. Note that 'delivery' might include preparation of subsidiary matters such as instruction manuals.

1.13 **Project evaluation** asks two questions.

(a) **Did the end result of the project meet the client's expectations?**

For example in a construction project, does the building represent what the client wanted? This question includes considerations of:

- The actual design and construction of the end product
- The timetable achieved: was the project achieved on time?
- The cost: was the project more or less within budget?

(b) **Was the management of the project as successful as it might have been, or were there bottlenecks or problems?**

Reviewing the management of the project can identify:

(i) Problems that might occur on future projects with similar characteristics

(ii) The performance of the team individually and as a group.

In other words, any project is an opportunity to learn how to manage future projects more effectively.

The role of the project manager

1.14 The project manager has resources of time, money and staff. These have to be co-ordinated effectively. The project manager's duties are summarised below.

Duty	Comment
Outline planning	Project planning (eg targets, sequencing) • Developing project targets such as overall costs or timescale needed (eg project should take 20 weeks). • Dividing the project into activities (eg analysis, programming, testing), and placing these activities into the right sequence, often a complicated task if overlapping. • Developing a framework for the procedures and structures, manage the project (eg decide, in principle, to have weekly team meetings, performance reviews etc).
Detailed planning	Work breakdown structure, resource requirements, network analysis for scheduling.
Teambuilding	The project manager has to meld the various people into an effective team.
Communication	The project manager must let superiors know what is going on, and ensure that members of the project team are properly briefed.
Co-ordinating project activities	Between the project team and users, and other external parties (eg suppliers of hardware and software).
Monitoring and control	The project manager should estimate the causes for each departure from the standard, and take corrective measures.
Problem-resolution	Even with the best planning, unforeseen problems may arise, and it falls upon the project manager to sort them out, or to delegate the responsibility for so doing to a subordinate.
Quality control	This is a problematic issue, as there is often a short-sighted trade-off between getting the project out on time and the project's quality.

1.15 Section summary

- A project is not a continued activity.
- Project objectives are quality, time and budget.
- Each project has a life cycle.
- Projects fail because of poor planning, poor management, political problems and vague or changing client specifications.
- Most projects are run by a project manager.

Exam focus point

The December 1995 exam offered 15 marks on project management, in the context of a recently privatised bus firm changing over to new systems.

2 PLANNING AND RESOURCING TECHNIQUES 6/95

2.1 Dennis Lock writes that 'an accurate estimate of project costs provides a proper basis for management control.'

(a) **Ball-park estimates** are made before a project starts. These are very rough indeed and might be accurate to within 25%.

(b) **Comparative estimates** are made if the project under consideration has some similarities with previous ones. Accuracy will depend, of course, on how similar the project is to the projects it is compared with. Lock suggests that it is possible to be accurate to within 15%.

(c) **Feasibility estimates** (probably accurate to within 10%) arise from preliminary aspects of the design. Building companies use feasibility estimates.

(d) **Definitive estimates** (accurate to within 5%) are only made when *all* the design work has been done.

2.2 Any *estimate* must be accompanied by a proviso detailing its expected *accuracy*.

(a) It is unreasonable to expect exact accuracy, but the project manager should be able to keep within estimates, particularly for projects with

- No 'margin of safety'
- Tight profit margins.

(b) Estimates can be improved by:

- Learning from past mistakes.
- Ensuring sufficient design information.
- Ensuring as detailed a specification as possible from the customer.
- Properly analysing the job into its constituent units, especially where labour costs are concerned.

Question 1

Springfield Builders has agreed to do some building work at Gowley House, a stately home in Hertfordshire. Springfield Builders are charging the owners of Gowley House the sum of £10,000. They estimate that the job will cost them £8,000, plus an estimated profit of £2,000. What would be the effect on profit of cost estimating errors of:

(a) +/- 5%
(b) +/- 10%
(c) +/- 20%

Answer

(a) An error of +/- 5% would mean that the profit would be increased or reduced by £400 (ie 5% × £8,000) in other words 20%.

(b) A 10% error would increase or reduce profits by £800 which is 40% of the profit.

(c) A 20% error would increase or decrease profits by £1,600 or 80% of profit.

Work breakdown structure (WBS)

KEY TERM

Work breakdown structure is the analysis of the work of a project into different units or tasks.

WBS:

(a) Identifies the work that must be done in the project.

(b) Determines the resources required.

(c) Sequences the work done, so that resources can be allocated in the most convenient way.

2.3 For example, *wiring* a house can be sub-divided into connecting the mains, fitting light sockets and power points etc. Dealing with the foundations involves digging, filling, area marking, damp proofing and disposal of soil.

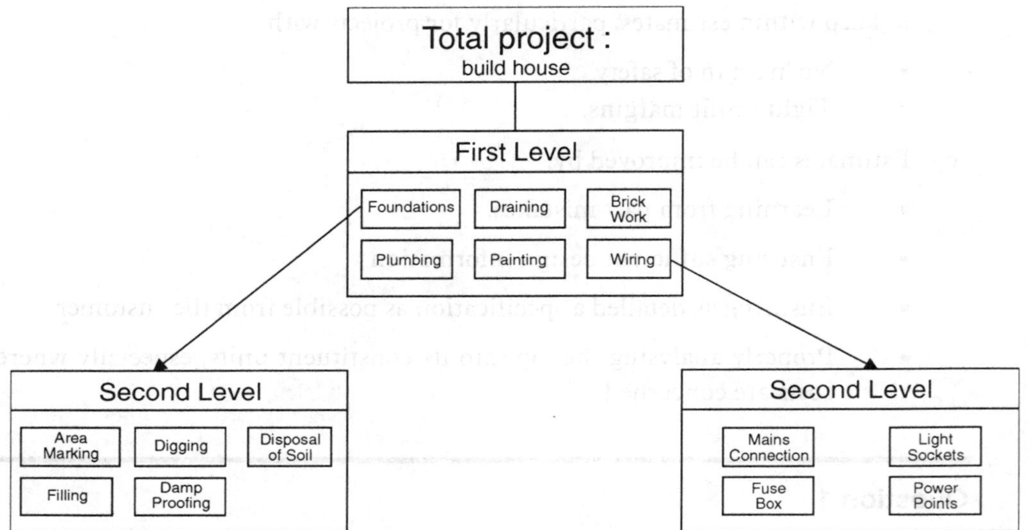

The process of work breakdown continues until the smallest possible sub-unit is reached. Digging the foundations for example would be analysed so that the number of labour hours needed, and hence the cost, could be determined.

2.4 Lock recommends giving each sub-unit of work a code number to enable resources to be obtained and the work to be planned.

Question 2

Draw up a work breakdown structure for moving into a new house.

Cost estimation

2.5 **Use of WBS in devising estimates.**

(a) From the WBS it is possible to 'compile a complete **list of every item** that is going to attract expenditure.'

(b) **Checklists** can be used to ensure that all factors (technical, legal, planning) can be taken into account.

(c) **Estimation forms** can be designed to be based on the work breakdown structure, so that by each work unit number, there are columns for labour, materials and so forth.

2.6 **Costs** should be analysed into:

(a) **Direct costs** of a project include labour, raw materials and sub-components.

(b) **Overhead costs** include heating, lighting and so forth, and can be fixed and/or variable. Overhead allocation can be difficult in some project environments, as a large element of the project costs might be fixed or sunk. (For example, a building company is unlikely to buy a brand new crane for every house it builds. An element of a crane's depreciation charge might be charged to a project.)

(c) **In-house costs** and **subcontracted** costs.

2.7 Collating the various costs identified with each unit of the work breakdown structure:

(a) Provides a useful cost analysis for various business functions.

(b) Assists cost control.

(c) Provides evidence, in any dispute with the client, that the costs are reasonable. (**Technical cost investigations** occur when the client sends technical cost officers to examine the books. The right to do so might be incorporated in the original contract.)

2.8 **Labour time estimates**

A project manager relies on the *personal* opinions of the individuals in each department as to the time it would take to do a job.

(a) 'Estimates for any work will **more frequently be understated than overstated**'.

(i) Many people are **eager to please** the project manager.

(ii) People do **not** learn to estimate better. (In some companies, a rule of thumb is to add 50% on to the estimated time given by production or design staff.)

(b) On occasions when people's estimates are **over-pessimistic**, a cause might be a desire to **inflate departmental budgets**.

(c) Finally, some estimators are **inconsistent**. This is worst of all.

2.9 A formula can be used to estimate the time of a particular activity for project planning purposes.

t_0 = the most optimistic duration
t_m = the most likely duration
t_p = the most pessimistic duration

In this case, which uses a *normal distribution*, the formula is as follows

$$t_e \text{ (ie estimated time)} = \frac{t_o + 4t_m + t_p}{6}$$

Not every project can be planned in this way.

2.10 **Materials estimates**

(a) **Total materials cost**. Design engineers should prepare provisional lists of materials required for each task. The purchasing department should provide some idea of the costs.

(b) **Lead times for receipt**. Failure to receive materials on time can result in unexpected delay.

(c) Estimating problems arise out:

(i) **Contingencies**. Projects can be delayed because of design errors, production mistakes, material and component failures. An allowance is sometimes built in. This contingency allowance can be estimated by reviewing problems in previous projects.

(ii) Additional work can be included in the contract price on a 'provisional basis'.

(iii) **Increases in prices** will increase costs over the contract's life. This might also be built into the contract.

2.11 **Section summary**

- A project should be broken down into its constituent tasks (work breakdown structure).
- Cost, labour and materials estimates can be obtained, sometimes with difficulty, for each task.

3 PROJECT PLANNING TOOLS

3.1 The project manager thus needs to **schedule the activities** or tasks in the most efficient way given:

(a) The **dependency** of some activities on others. In other words, job B may need to be done before job C. For example, the foundations of a house are *always* laid before the roof is constructed.

(b) **Constraints on resources.** Some resources will not be available at the ideal time or at the lowest price (eg overtime payments). For example, a computer project manager may have to compete with other project managers for the availability of certain skilled staff.

3.2 The project manager will have been given a broad-brush time estimation for any activity. For this you need:

(a) The **duration** of each sub-unit of work.

(b) The **earliest time** work in a particular unit must be started.

(c) The **latest time** it must be started.

Gantt charts

3.3 A simple plan for a project is based on a *bar line chart*. This is sometimes called a *Gantt chart*.

(a) It can be used as a *progress control chart* with the lower section of each bar being completed as the activity is undertaken.

(b) A delay in a particular piece of work and its 'knock on' effect on other work can be shown in a *linked bar chart*. This shows the links between an activity and preceding activities which have to be completed before this particular activity can start.

3.4 Here is an example.

No.	DESCRIPTION OF WORK OR ACTIVITY	TIME (DAYS)													
		1	2	3	4	5	6	7	8	9	10	11	12	13	14
1	Excavate for foundations and services (drainage)	■	■												
2	Concrete foundations			■	■										
3	Build walls and soakaways for drainage					■	■	■	■						
4	Construct roof									■	■				
5	Fit garage doors									■					
6	Provide services (electric)											■			
7	Plaster												■		
8	Decorate													■	■

- **Advantage:** easy to understand
- **Disadvantage:** limited when dealing with large complex projects in that they can only display a restricted amount of information and the links between activities are fairly crude.

3.5 To overcome these problems we use a more sophisticated technique known as network analysis.

Critical path analysis (CPA or network analysis)

3.6 Network analysis is a project planning technique which aims to map the activities in a particular project, and the relationship between them. CPA describes the **sequence** of activities, and how long they are going to take. These diagrams are drawn left to right.

(a) **Events** (1 and 2) are represented by circles. Activities (eg A) connect events.

(b) The **critical path** is represented by drawing an extra line or a thicker line between the activities on the path. It is the **minimum amount of time** that the project will take.

(c) It is the convention to note the earliest start date of any activity in the *top* right hand corner of the circle.

(d) We can then work *backwards* identifying the *latest* dates when activities have to start. These we insert in the bottom right quarter of the circle.

3.7 A completed network diagram would be as follows. The **critical path** is AEG. Note the **float time** of five days for Activity F. Activity F can begin any time between days 4 and 9, thus giving the project manager a degree of flexibility.

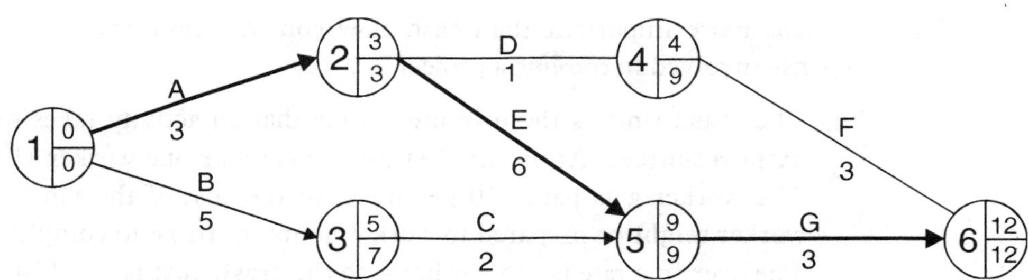

Resource histograms

3.8 If all activities are started as soon as possible, the labour requirements can be shown on a bar chart. Bar charts such as these are sometimes called **resource histograms.**

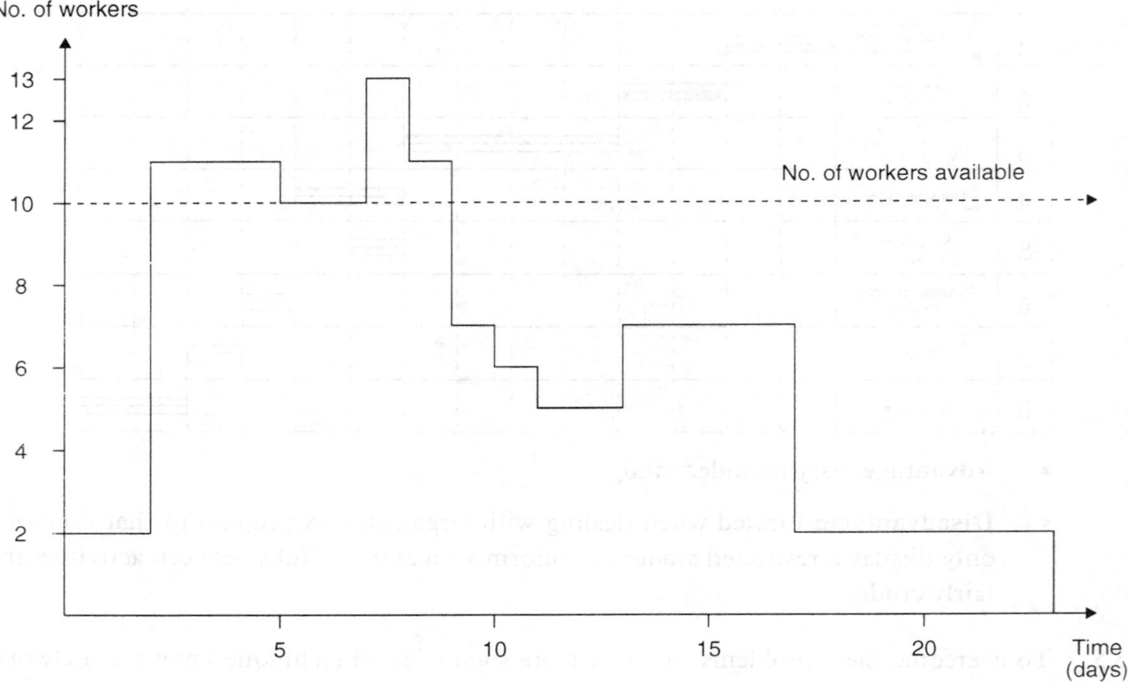

3.9 The number of workers required on the seventh day is 13. Can we re-schedule the non-critical activities to eliminate any excessive requirement? The various floats show whether we can move any activity.

3.10 We might be able to re-arrange activities so that we can make use of the workers available from day 9 onwards.

Float times and costs

3.11 **Float time,** as we have seen, is slack time.

(a) Total float on a job is the time available (earliest start date to latest finish date) *less* time needed for the job. If, for example, job A's earliest start time was day 7 and its latest end time was day 17, and the job needed four days, total float would be:

$(17 - 7) - 4 = 6$ days

(b) **Free float** is the delay possible in an activity on the assumption that all preceding jobs start as early as possible and all subsequent jobs also start at the earliest time.

(c) **Independent float** is the delay possible if all preceding jobs have finished as late as possible, and all succeeding jobs have started as early as possible.

3.12 Perhaps more important than cash flow consideration are the total expense and the expense involved in *crashing* a project.

(a) The **crash time** is the **minimum** time that an activity takes to be completed with **extra resources**. At its simplest job X may take one worker $1^1/_2$ days, say 12 hours. The worker gets paid £10 per hour, so the cost of the job is £120. However, the worker might be prepared to work 4 hours overtime to complete the job in one day. The overtime rate is £15 per hour, so the **crash cost** is $(8 \times £10) + (4 \times £15) = £140$.

(**Crash time** is never more than normal time; **crash cost** is never less than normal cost.)

(b) Crashing also has the affect of changing the critical path as extra resources can change the activity's duration.

3.13 It is possible therefore to draw up *two* sets of estimates identifying the cost:

- Without crashing
- With crashing

Criticisms of critical path/network analysis

3.14 The critical path method is an invaluable aid to planning and scheduling but it does have certain drawbacks.

(a) It is **not always possible to devise an effective WBS for a project.**

(b) **It assumes an essentially linear and sequential relationship** between activities: in other words it assumes that once Activity A is finished, Activity B proceeds, and that Activity B has no impact on Activity A. Consequently, it is not very good at coping with the possibility of **feedback** or iteration (in other words, the result of an activity later in the sequence may be relevant to an earlier activity).

(c) There are inevitable **problems in estimation**. Where the project is completely new, the planning process may be conducted in conditions of relative ignorance.

(d) **Costs are based only on labour hours**, and all the problems relating to absorption of indirect overheads apply. Labour hours may only be a small proportion of the money involved in the project.

(e) Although network analysis plans the use of resources of labour and finance, it **does not appear to develop plans for contingencies, other than crashing time**. This is not so much a criticism of network analysis in itself, as the reflection that the project manager must take other considerations into account: planning involves more than scheduling. For example, the manager might have a contingency source of computer support in case of computer breakdown.

(f) CPA **assumes a trade-off between time and cost** - but this does not really hold where a substantial portion of the cost is **indirect overheads** or where the direct labour proportion of the total cost of limited.

4 MANAGEMENT IMPLICATIONS OF PROJECT MANAGEMENT TECHNIQUES

4.1 Network analysis is a means of finding the best way to schedule activities, by highlighting the interrelationships between them. Central to the ideas are that work is broken down into units which can be analysed **independently** of each other.

Parallel engineering

4.2 Certain companies have taken this approach to product development. **Parallel engineering techniques** aim to speed the time taken to get a product to market. Once the overall idea of a design is agreed, individual development teams go ahead on **different aspects** of the project, in designing both the product and the production process and machinery.

Management by objectives (MBO)

4.3 Network planning analysis facilitates MBO because:

(a) A project's goals are clearly defined.
(b) It is possible to measure results.
(c) A manager's effort is directed towards achieving goals most efficiently.

Management by exception

4.4 Network planning facilitates management by exception, in which management attention is concentrated on items which deviate from plans. 'Critical operations usually make up about 20% of the project activities that can affect the overall progress'. Project management techniques enable management by exception by identifying, from the outset, those activities which might delay the others.

5 INFORMATION SYSTEMS PROJECTS

5.1 Many of the project management issues described so far apply to information systems. Indeed, historically, one of the problems with information systems projects has been poor specification in planning. The systems rewrites involved in the Millennium Bomb (see Chapter 3) could have been avoided with better planning.

The steering committee: overview

5.2 If the organisation introduces new computer systems regularly, it might set up a steering committee

(a) **Membership**

(i) The information director, or a senior IS staff member.
(ii) An accountant for technical financial advice relating to costs and benefits.
(iii) Senior user management.

(b) **Responsibilities**

(i) Assisting with formation of strategies for information systems.

(ii) Authorising systems development projects.

(iii) Reviewing the progress of individual development projects.

(iv) In an organisation which has a continuing programme of new information systems projects:

- Assessing the contribution of each project to the long term corporate objectives of the organisation.

- Ranking projects in order of priority and assigning resources to the most important projects first.

- Taking decisions to defer projects when insufficient resources are available.

(c) The steering committee will only meet occasionally, and the detailed study of individual projects should be made the task of a feasibility study team for each project which will report its findings and recommendations to the steering committee.

Project selection criteria

5.3 In many cases, there might not be the resources for every desirable information system to be implemented. In short there has to be an exercise of **project selection**. This can be reduced to a number of basic questions.

(a) Does the project accord with the **organisation's information strategy** and **business objectives**?

(b) If so, is it **technically feasible** with the available hardware, software and personnel?

(c) Is it **economically viable**?

Even if the answer to all three questions is YES, the project may still not go ahead, as it might be of a lower priority than other projects.

5.4 These questions are generally answered in the **feasibility study**.

Factor	Comment
Cost effectiveness	A system which appears to give large benefits in terms of costs saved and/or benefits received should obviously be given a high priority.
Staff availability	Does the new system would call for the recruitment of specialised and possibly 'expensive' new staff?
Systems complexity	The least complex systems should normally be developed first because they could be brought on-line fairly quickly.
Long term benefits	A company's resources are limited, so the systems which give the greatest long-term benefit should get priority. There may be other ways of dealing with short-term, possibly one off, requirements.
Future compatibility	If the new systems are eventually to operate on an integrated basis, the initial choice should perhaps be for the system which incorporates the most aspects of the new total system in order that subsequent developments can be more readily achieved.
Technological obsolescence	Are the company's needs are likely to change within the near future? There is no point buying a system which will not be able to cope.
Environment	Depending on the size and type of computer configuration, are the buildings, cabling, spaces etc sufficient?

5.5 In this section we describe some approaches to the successful planning and management of information systems.

Systems development lifecycle (SDLC)

5.6 The SDLC is a disciplined approach to systems upgrades intended to ensure the system meets the needs of the organisation without any waste of time and money. Many organisations adopted this approach.

5.7 There are six stages, although in practice the first three may overlap, and so may the fourth and fifth. These are outlined in the diagram and table below.

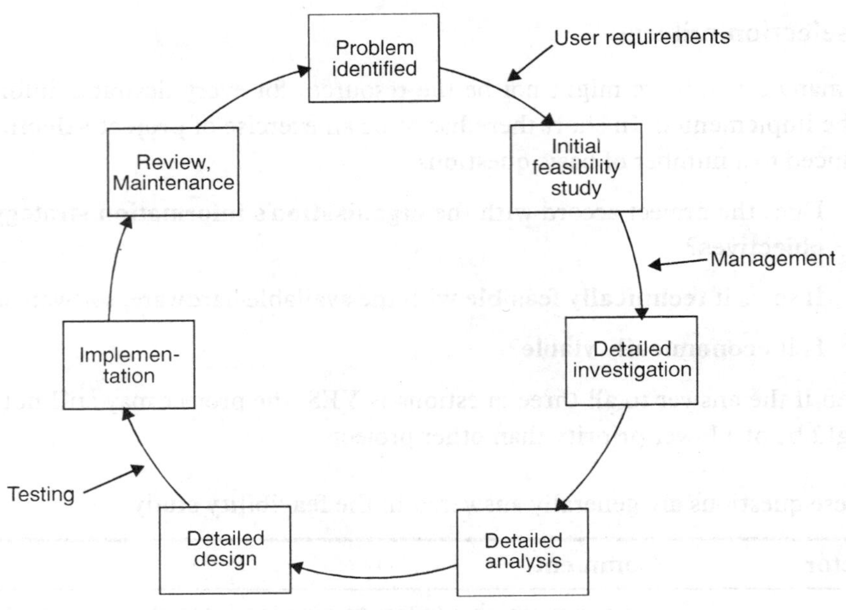

SYSTEMS DEVELOPMENT LIFE CYCLE	
Feasibility study	Briefly review the existing system Identify possible alternative solutions
Systems investigation	Obtain details of current requirements and user needs such as data volumes, processing cycles and timescales Identify current problems and restrictions
Systems analysis	Consider why current methods are used and identify better alternatives
Systems design	Determine what inputs, processing and storage facilities are necessary to produce the outputs required Consider matters such as program design, file design and security Prepare a detailed specification of the new system.
Systems implementation	Write or acquire software, test it, convert files, install hardware and start running the new system
Review and maintenance	Ensure that the new system meets current objectives, and that it continues to do so

Criticisms of the systems development life cycle approach

5.8 Its main advantage was it discouraged an immediate rush into detailed programming, but it has a number of drawbacks.

Drawback	Comment
Ignores management	While it was efficient at automating operational areas within easily defined processing requirements, such as payroll, the information needs of middle and senior management were ignored. Computerisation was a means of speeding up high-volume routine transaction processing, not providing information for decision-making.
No radical rethink of current operations	Computer systems were often modelled after the manual systems they were replacing.

Drawback	Comment
Systems go out of date and are inflexible	An organisation's processing requirements change and a lot of time can be spent updating old computer programs.
User requirements were poorly defined	Much systems design is based around what the user, at an **early stage** in the development of a system, has specified as to what output is required. A simple **change** in user requirements costs over 20 times as much to rectify after **acceptance testing** than after the **design phase**.
Dissatisfied users	New systems rarely lived up to users' expectations. Even with packaged software, users may be disappointed.
Documentation	Much system documentation was highly technical, more of a technical manual than a guide for the user. Problems could also occur, if inadequately documented modifications led to 'bugs' elsewhere in the system.
Systems not complete	Many routine transaction processing systems could not cope with unusual situations, and so some complicated processing was still performed manually.
Applications backlog	Time overruns means that systems take a long time to develop. The applications backlog is the systems in the pipeline whose development has been delayed. One of the causes is the time spent to maintain old systems. In some cases over 60% of time spent by the programming section of a IS department will be spent on maintenance.

Methodologies

5.9 Information **systems development methodologies** were developed to overcome the problems outlined above.

KEY TERM

A **systems development methodology** is 'a collection of procedures, techniques, tools and documentation aids which will help systems developers in their efforts to implement a new information system. A methodology will consist of phases, themselves consisting of sub-phases, which will guide the systems developers in their choice of techniques that might be appropriate at each stage of the project and also help them plan, manage and control information systems projects.' (Avison and Fitzgerald).

Structured systems analysis and design methodology (SSADM)

5.10 Structured methods are an approach to systems analysis and design which:

(a) Emphasises the **logical design** of a system (eg what types of data item there are, the relationships between them, what processing operations they undergo and so on) **before physical implementation** (eg before programs are written, hardware specified).

(b) Proceeds from the **general to the particular** via a series of modules, stages and steps (so the system as a whole is designed before individual applications or programs).

(c) **Documents** the process in a standard way using techniques such as dataflow diagrams, with **evidenced user involvement**.

5.11 SSADM is a widely used methodology. SSADM:

(a) Describes **how** a system is to be developed.

(b) Reduces development into stages, and each stage contains a number of steps. The work done in one stage is refined and developed in the next.

(c) Checks itself, and can be **tailored** to a number of applications.

5.12 The structure of SSADM (version 4) is outlined below.

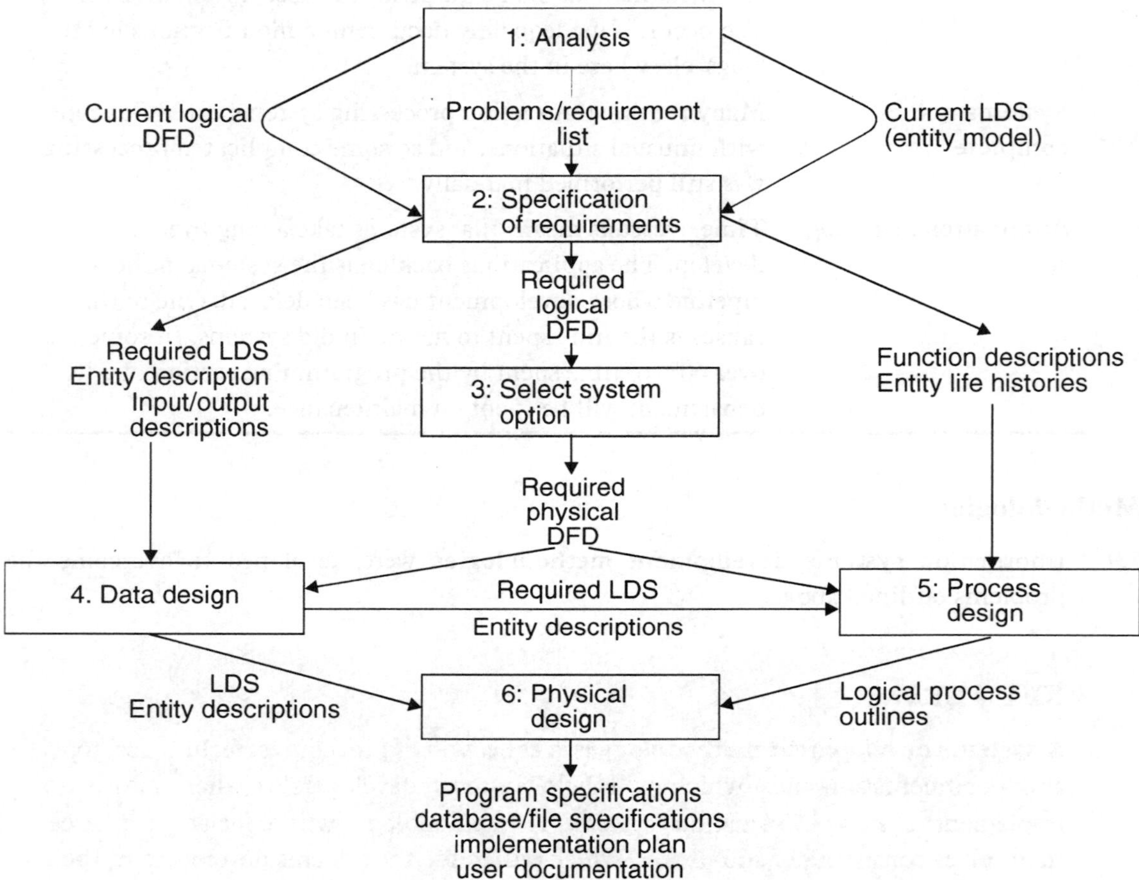

Stage 0: Feasibility study

5.13 This stage, although not mandatory in many SSADM projects, is to examine the 'case' for undertaking a particular project in terms of its technical feasibility and cost/benefit, as described above. This stage is divided into four steps.

(a) **Prepare for the feasibility study**, taking a preliminary view and setting out plans for the rest of the study.

(b) **Define the problem,** where a problem (some deficiency in the system as it is now running, or an anticipated future deficiency) is identified. Information about it is gathered and the new requirements are set out in a Problem Definition Statement.

(c) **Select feasibility options:** a series of options are identified for solving, or at least coping with the problems defined. Each potential project identified will have an outline specification and will be costed.

(d) **Write the feasibility study report**, which should also contain costings for the next phase.

Stage 1: Investigation of current environment

5.14 The **current system** is investigated, described, analysed and **documented** using the techniques of observation, questionnaires, document description forms and so forth. Some of the work may have been done already during the feasibility study. A result of this stage is a **problems/requirements** list or **requirements catalogue**.

(a) **Problems** could be encountered over a range of areas, including data input, poor controls, volumes higher than the system can cope with, poor user interface, slow response times and inflexibility in processing.

(b) **Requirements** can in fact be solutions to the problems identified in the current system, but could also imply a completely new way of doing things, (for example replacing batch by on-line processing). Users are invited to describe what:

- They want a system to do
- Items of data are required for it to deal with
- Information is required.

Stage 2: Business system options

5.15 This involves the specification of the requirements of the new system, where what users actually require is laid down in detail. Any solution offered must satisfy these requirements.

(a) There will normally be a number of possible solutions and those considered the best will be put forward to users as Business System Options.

(b) Users are then asked to make a choice.

Stage 3: Requirements specification

5.16 The team takes the results of the previous stage, and arrives at a **requirements specification**.

(a) The chosen option is defined more precisely.

(b) Specifications for **input and output** (eg on screen) from the chosen system are prepared.

(c) A **relational data analysis** (normalisation) is performed on the input and output descriptions to identify any data items that might not have been noticed, or drawn in enough detail, in the existing logical data structure.

Stage 4: Technical system options

5.17 Users are asked to make *choices* concerning the means by which they would like the system to be implemented: there might be a number of ways of implementing a system physically. These can include:

(a) Hardware configuration (for example client/server, networked PCs).
(b) Software (use of a DBMS or a conventional file structure).

Stage 5: Logical design

5.18 Data and file structures for the entire new system are designed. The input to this stage are the descriptions of input and output from stage 3, and functions and processes that act upon or use data items are specified. This stage includes the development of output formats, and specifying the type of **dialogue** that users will have with the system, to ensure that it is consistent with what has been prepared so far.

Stage 6: Physical design

5.19 Physical design involves the following tasks.

(a) Initial physical design (obtaining the design rules from the chosen DBMS, and applying them to the logical data design drawn up in the previous stages).

(b) Further define the processing required (eg consider audit, security and control).

(c) Program specifications detail exactly what a program is to achieve.

(d) Program specifications are assessed for their performance when implemented.

(e) File and database specifications are designed in detail.

(f) Operating instructions are drawn up (user documentation).

Question 3

At what stage (if any) in a SSADM-led project might the following recent developments be considered?

(a) A new type of computer currently in development is the so-called Network computer (NC). The main driving force behind this is the Oracle software company, which is the second largest in the world after Microsoft. The NC is intended to be used for similar purposes to the PC, but unlike a PC it does not have a hard disk: its applications are downloaded when needed from a public network such as the Internet or an organisation's own 'Intranet'.

The thinking behind this is that PCs are too complex and they give users far more computing power than they really need. For example, e-mail and word-processing do not require desktop processing power or huge storage space. A number of manufacturers such as IBM and Sun Microsystems plan to build computing devices such as screen phones, NC televisions and desktop computers.

(b) Java is a programming system developed in 1995 by Sun Microsystems. Many people believe it will fundamentally change the software industry as we know it by blurring the distinctions between different kinds of computers. Java software runs on a non-existent computer called a Java Virtual Machine or JVM, and any computer can be programmed to make it behave like a JVM.

Answer

The NC (if it takes off as a business solution) might well be one of the options offered at Stage 2.

Java has implications for both Stage 2 and Stage 4.

Data-driven methodologies

5.20 Whilst structured analysis emphasises processes, which are broken down into logically defined segments of a system, other approaches to system design emphasise the *data* used by a system. Even if applications change, the data already collected may still be relevant. This, in many respects, is the approach behind *database* design.

CASE tools

5.21 **CASE tools** automate document production and ensure automation of some of the design operation.

5.22 **Features and facilities** include:

- Diagramming facilities for use with a mouse
- Creation of data dictionary
- Access controls
- Checking facilities to ensure consistency and adherence to rules/standards
- Prototyping facilities

5.23 **Advantages of using CASE tools**

- Diagramming and revision are made easier.
- Accuracy and consistency of diagrams are improved.
- Prototyping is simplified and speeded up.
- Blocks of code can be re-used.

Prototyping

5.24 Prototyping helps programmers write application programs quickly. The programmer can check with the users whether the prototype meets their needs and amend it quickly if necessary.

(a) **Advantages**

- A mock-up can be demonstrated before time and money has been committed to build the system in full.
- Gives users chance to respond before development is complete.
- Allows quicker program development.
- Ensures a common approach to and understanding of design by all parties.

(b) **Disadvantages**

- Some prototyping tools are inefficient and generate excessive program code.
- It does not produce suitable documentation.

System justification

5.25 A new system should not be recommended unless it can be justified. The justification for a new system would have to come from:

(a) An evaluation of the costs and benefits of the proposed system (complicated by the fact that many of the system cost elements are poorly defined and that benefits can often be highly qualitative and subjective in nature).

(b) Other performance criteria.

Costs

5.26 These may be tangible or intangible.

'Tangible' costs

Type	Description
Capital items	• Equipment (hardware and software): processors; storage devices; printers; communications equipment • Installation costs: air-conditioning, partitioning, furniture
Development items	• Software creation • Third party staff costs • Production of documentation • Staff recruitment/training • Systems implementation • Redundancy costs
Operating (running) costs	• Additional staff • Consumables/stationery • Maintenance • Accommodation and occupancy • Insurance

5.27 **Intangible costs**

Type	Description
Switching costs	• Reduced efficiency • Staff discontent
Locking-in costs	Choice of one supplier may bar use of others, even where more cost efficient (compatibility)
Opportunity costs	Loss of other IT projects

5.28 **Benefits**

(a) Tangible benefits are economically quantifiable.

- Lower stock levels (increased efficiency)
- Lower staff costs (cost savings)
- Higher output (improved efficiency)

(b) Intangible benefits are difficult to quantify but may be the reason a system is developed

- Competitive advantage
- Improved staff morale
- Improved customer service
- Improved management decision making

5.29 Section summary

- Information systems projects require proper planning.
- A steering committee gives overall approval.
- A feasibility study gives an in-depth examination of a new system.
- Methodologies such as SSADM ensure users are involved and that the system is properly documented.
- New systems must pay their way but it is often hard to quantify their benefits.

6 BRAINWORKS PLC UPDATE

Questions can be found in the Introduction box at the beginning of the chapter.

6.1 *Question 1*. Project management techniques will be useful in:

(a) The proposed demerger, as a great deal of work will have to be co-ordinated.
(b) Implementing the new information system.

6.2 *Question 2*. Clearly, the employee database development is an example of a project that is failing. Proper objectives perhaps were not defined and the 'client' specification changed halfway through, from being a payroll system to a more complex exercise. No wonder the analyst left.

Chapter roundup

- A **project** is an undertaking with a defined beginning and end, directed towards the achievement of a specified goal (eg building a house).
- **Project management** always involves dealing with the unexpected. Each project is in some respects new.
- The **objectives** of project management are to ensure that the end product conforms with customer specification and is produced on time and within budget.
- The **project life cycle** can be broken down into the stages of project definition, planning, implementation, completion and review.
- **Estimating** is always hazardous. Relatively small estimating errors can dent profits significantly.
- **Work breakdown structure** is the analysis of work into tasks. This can be used to estimate costs (by defining the resources needed for each task), and to schedule activities by determining which activities depend on which.
- **Project planning tools** include **network analysis**, **Gantt charts** and **resource histograms.**
- **Information development projects** require the same sort of control techniques as any other project. Obtaining **accurate user specifications** at the early stage is very important, as the cost of late design changes is enormous.
- The **steering committee** is responsible for overseeing the success of individual projects, and selecting projects for approval. IT projects often require a **management sponsor**.
- **Criteria for selecting a project** for development include: conformance with the organisation's strategy, cost effectiveness, staff availability, systems complexity, long-term benefits, technological issues.
- The **systems development life cycle**, and other methodologies such as **SSADM**, were developed to bring order to the system development process.

Quick quiz

1. Define 'project'. (see para 1.1)
2. What are the distinctive problems of project management? (1.4)
3. What is involved in project definition? (1.9)
4. What four different types of estimate can be given? (2.1)
5. What is work breakdown structure? (2.3)
6. What is technical cost investigation? (2.7)
7. What is a Gantt Chart? (3.3)
8. What are the problems with CPA? (3.14)
9. What are the responsibilities of a steering committee? (5.2)
10. List the criteria for selecting an information systems development projects. (5.4)
11. List the phases of the systems development life cycle. (5.7)
12. What is the applications backlog? (5.8)
13. What is an information systems methodology? (5.9)
14. List the phases of SSADM. (5.12)
15. What are the costs of a new system? (5.26, 5.27)

Question to try	Level	Marks	Time
15	Exam standard	25	45 mins

Chapter 12

CONFLICT AND CHANGE

Introduction

This chapter deals with change in the organisation and the often difficult task of implementing it. Change gives rise to **conflict**. We look at conflict as a social process, between **groups** in the organisation and within **individuals**. Various **interest groups** in a conflict are likely to have different perspectives on the nature of the situation and the issues that create it. **Force field analysis** identifies the relative strength and weaknesses of opposing forces. The section on **negotiation** describes techniques for avoiding conflict, where change cannot simply by imposed.

Brainworks plc

1. To what extent has conflict been managed successfully in BW?
2. What changes might be needed?
3. Will Willard Mann find it easy to push through the demerger?
4. Assuming the employee database is built, what implementation problems can you foresee?

1 WHAT IS CHANGE?

1.1 Change, in the context of organisation and management, can relate to:

(a) The environment.
(b) The products the organisation makes or the services it provides.
(c) How products are made, or who makes them.
(d) Management and working relationships.
(e) Organisation structure or size (growth).

1.2 Buckley and Perkins (1984) made a distinction, although it is not used by many writers, between:

(a) Change, which is gradual and small
(b) Transformation, which is change on a significant scale.

TRANSFORMATION

Organisational	*In the way the system operates*	*In employee consciousness*
Major changes in job definitions, reporting lines (lines of authority) etc	Major changes in communication patterns, working relationships and processes	Major changes in the way that things are viewed, involving shifts in attitudes, beliefs and myths

1.3 All but the smallest changes need careful planning. Major organisational changes should usually originate during the corporate planning process. You will recall from the earlier chapter on corporate planning that the first stages in corporate planning are to:

(a) Establish the organisation's major objectives
(b) Carry out an analysis of the strengths and weaknesses of the organisation, and of the opportunities and threats in its environment.

Case example

William Grant and Sons

People Management (September 1996) described how whisky distiller William Grant and Sons called on Jack Black, a 'business preacher', to help a workforce struggling to come to terms with a major **change programme**.

Whisky producers like to emphasise **tradition** in their advertising: the centuries old recipes, the oak casks, the rural landscape around the distillery, the company's colourful founding fathers and their forelock-tugging workers.

William Grant and Sons, the Scottish distiller, in the last three years has put itself through a major programme of change. Until then, the image of tradition would have been nearer the truth. As David Nisbet, HR director at William Grants, puts it: 'We were benignly autocratic and paternalistic. Now we are team-based and non-hierarchical, but getting from one to the other proved difficult'.

The journey started with a **physical move** by the bottling plant and administrative headquarters from Paisley, west Glasgow, to Motherwell, east of the city.

At the same time, the company **derecognised most of its unions**, retaining a purely representational agreement with one union at each site.

Meanwhile, the whole workforce was being organised into **teams** of between three and 30 people each.

In short, it was the **'big bang'** approach to the management of change. For the restrained, Calvinist culture that predominated among the workforce, it was a little too much to absorb. To many people, quality circles were infra dig.

Nisbet recalls: 'It was like pulling teeth. They sat round in these meetings and nothing happened. They weren't contributing'. What was needed was a massive injection of enthusiasm, an overnight **culture change**. It came from a Scottish consultant who has been making a name for himself over recent years as a kind of business preacher, a saver of commercial souls and the slayer of cynicism. Jack Black has been described as a cross between Billy Connolly and Billy Graham. It may seem strange that his 'mental fitness programme' could have enthused a workforce in a part of the world where the statement 'it's quite nice' is the ultimate accolade.

Black's programme, Mindstore, synthesises the ideas of many others - including Tony Buzan's mind-mapping techniques, neurolinguistic programming and the theories of Napoleon Hill, one of the first people to analyse leadership qualities - and delivers then in a humorous, chalk-and-talk style, interspersed with paper exercises which each participant does on their lap.

Since Mindstore, according to Nisbet, everyone in the organisation has been looking at their objective-setting. Each team has set three 'Smart goals' and is now moving to what they call 'Winner's goals'.

Initially, the **managers** took the course: then about a third of employees, from all levels, chose to go on it. But a drawback soon became apparent: 'some people still didn't have a positive **attitude to change** and didn't want to go on the course. They were finding it very difficult when their colleagues were coming back from it all fired up, positive and full of enthusiasm. They felt it put more pressure on them, and they were becoming more stressed and fearful.'

This manifested itself as absenteeism and an increase in visit to the occupational health department. The HR director made the decision to make it compulsory to attend Mindstore, despite the fact that 'the only way to really get it into the company culture is to make it mandatory'.

'You tend to find that when a company gives the workforce "stretching" goals, they usually do that in an environment of fear, so people don't buy it. But if you train the people concerned to understand all this, which is what we do, they will set bigger goals than management would ever come up with.'

---

2 CONFLICT IN ORGANISATIONS

2.1 Conflict can result from attempts at change, which inevitably alters the balance of power between different stakeholder groups.

2.2 The existence of conflict in organisations might be considered inevitable or unnatural, depending on your viewpoint.

The 'happy family' view: conflict is unnatural

2.3 The happy family view presents organisations as:

(a) **Co-operative structures**, designed to achieve agreed common objectives, with no systematic conflict of interest.

(b) **Harmonious environments**, where conflicts are **exceptional** and arise from:

- Misunderstandings;
- Personality factors;
- The expectations of inflexible employees;
- Factors outside the organisation and its control.

2.4 This kind of view is common in managerial literature, which attempts to come up with training and motivational techniques for dealing with conflicts which arise in what are seen as potentially 'conflict-free' organisations. Conflict is thus blamed on bad management, lack of leadership, poor communication, or 'bloody-mindedness' on the part of individuals or interest groups that impinge on the organisation. The theory is that a strong culture, good two-way communication, co-operation and motivational leadership will 'eliminate' conflict.

The conflict view

2.5 In contrast, some see organisations as **arenas** for conflict on individual and group levels.

(a) Members battle for limited resources, status, rewards and professional values.

(b) Organisational politics involve constant struggles for control, and choices of structure, technology and organisational goals are part of this process. Individual and organisational interests will not always coincide.

(c) The Marxist view suggests that organisational conflict is part of an inevitable struggle, as long as some (the capitalist class) own and control the means of production, and others who produce the wealth (the proletariat) do not.

The 'evolutionary' view

2.6 This view regards conflict as a means of **maintaining the status quo**, as a useful basis for **evolutionary change**.

- **Conflict** keeps the organisation **sensitive to the need to change**, while reinforcing its essential framework of control.
- The **legitimate pursuit of competing interests** can balance and preserve social and organisational arrangements.

2.7 This '**constructive conflict**' view may perhaps be the most useful for managers and administrators of organisations, as it neither:

(a) Attempts to dodge the issues of conflict, which is an observable fact of life in most organisations; nor

(b) Seeks to pull down existing organisational structures altogether.

2.8 Conflict *can* be highly desirable. Hunt suggests that conflict is constructive, when its effect is to:

- Introduce different **solutions** to problems.
- **Define power relationships** more clearly.
- Encourage **creativity** and the testing of ideas.
- **Focus attention** on individual contributions.
- **Bring emotions** out into the open.
- **Release hostile feelings** that have been, or may be, repressed otherwise.

2.9 **Conflict can also be destructive**. It may:

- **Distract attention** from the task.
- **Polarise** views and 'dislocate' the group.
- Subvert **objectives** in favour of secondary goals.
- Encourage **defensive** or 'spoiling' behaviour.
- Force the group to **disintegrate.**
- Stimulate emotional, **win-lose conflicts,** ie hostility.

Case example

Tjosvold and Deerner researched conflict in different contexts. They allocated to 66 student volunteers the roles of foremen and workers at an assembly plant, with a scenario of conflict over job rotation schemes. Foremen were against, workers for.

One group was told that the organisational norm was to 'avoid controversy'; another was told that the norm was 'co-operative controversy', *trying* to agree; a third was told that groups were out to win any arguments that arose, 'competitive controversy'. The students were offered rewards for complying with their given norms. Their decisions, and attitudes to the discussions, were then monitored.

(a) Where controversy was avoided, the foremen's views dominated.

(b) Competitive controversy brought no agreement - but brought out feelings of hostility and suspicion.

(c) Co-operative controversy brought out differences in an atmosphere of curiosity, trust and openness: the decisions reached seemed to integrate the views of both parties.

But can real managers and workers be motivated to comply with useful organisational 'norms' in this way?

2.10 **Conflicts of interest** may exist throughout the organisation - or even for a single individual. There may be conflicts of interest between local management of a branch or subsidiary and the organisation as a whole.

- Sales and production departments in a manufacturing firm (over scheduling, product variation)
- Trade unions and management.

2.11 **Interest groups** such as trade unions tend to wield greater power in conflict situations than their members as individuals. Trade Unions are organisations whose purpose it is to promote their members' interests. (Strike action has to be preceded by a ballot.)

2.12 Section summary

Three views of conflict are that it is:

- Unnatural
- Inevitable
- Necessary for the organisation to change

3 CHANGE AND THE INDIVIDUAL

3.1 Effect of change on individuals

(a) There may be **physiological changes** in a person's life, both as the natural product of development, maturation and ageing, and as the result of external factors (a change in the pattern of shift-working).

(b) **Circumstantial changes** - living in a new house, establishing new relationships, working to new routines - will involve letting go of things, and learning new ways of doing things.

(c) Change affects individuals **psychologically.**

(i) **Disorientation** before new circumstances have been assimilated. A new set of models may have to be confronted, if the change involves a new roles set, new 'milieu', new relationships.

(ii) **Uncertainty** may lead to **insecurity**, especially acute in changes involving work (staying in employment) and/or fast acclimatisation (a short learning curve may lead to feelings of incapacity).

(iii) New expectations, challenges and pressures may generate **role stress** in which an individual feels discomfort in the role he or she plays.

(iv) **Powerlessness**. Change can be particularly threatening if it is perceived as an outside force or agent against which the individual is powerless.

Resistance to change at work

3.2 Resisting change means attempting to preserve the existing state of affairs against pressure to alter it. Despite the possibly traumatic effects of change most people do *not* in fact resist it on these grounds alone. Many people long for change, and have a wealth of ideas about how it should be achieved.

3.3 **Sources of resistance to change**

(a) **Attitudes or beliefs**, perhaps arising from cultural, religious or class influences (for example resistance to changes in the law on Sunday trading).

(b) **Loyalty to a group and its norms**, perhaps with an accompanying rejection of other groups or 'outsiders'.

(c) **Habit or past norms**. This can be a strong source of clinging to old ways, whether out of security needs, respect for tradition, or the belief that 'you can't teach an old dog new tricks' (for example resistance to the introduction of new technology).

(d) **Politics** - in the sense of resisting changes that might weaken the power base of the individual or group or strengthen a rival's position. Changes involving increased delegation may be strongly resisted by senior management, for example.

(e) **The way in which any change** is put forward and implemented.

(f) **Personality**.

3.4 **Immediate causes of resistance in any particular situation**

(a) **Self-interest:** if the status quo is perceived to be comfortable, or advantageous to the individual or the group.

(b) **Misunderstanding and distrust:** if the reasons for, or the nature and consequences of, the change have not been made clear. This aggravates uncertainty and suspicion about the perceived threat.

(c) **Contradictory assessments:** people might disagree over the likely costs and benefits of the change.

(d) **Low tolerance of change itself:** differences in tolerance of ambiguity, uncertainty, challenge to self-concept etc.

3.5 **Reactions to proposed change**

(a) **Acceptance** whether enthusiastic espousal, co-operation, grudging co-operation or resignation.

(b) **Indifference:** usually where the change does not directly affect the individual evidence is apathy, lack of interest, inaction.

(c) **Passive resistance:** refusal to learn, working to rule; pleas of ignorance or defensiveness; procrastination.

(d) **Active resistance:** deliberate 'spoiling', go-slows, deliberate errors, sabotage, absenteeism or strikes.

Technological change and the working environment

3.6 The consequences of **technological changes** are particularly felt in the world of work.

(a) Unskilled and **semi-skilled jobs** will be automated.

(b) **Degrading of old skills**. New skills will be needed, and there will be more pressure on managers to provide training or re-training for staff.

(c) As equipment becomes simpler to use, there could be opportunities for **greater flexibility** in manning, with one worker able to carry out more varied tasks. In manufacturing, there may be more continuous shift work working (24 hours a day).

(d) Since more jobs will be **part-time**, there will be less need for full-time employees. More work will be sub-contracted, and full-time jobs axed.

(e) Better communications systems, portable computers etc reduce the need for people to work together in an office. There will be more **working at home.**

(f) Working at home is likely to speed up the progression towards 'sub-contracting', and some managers might become self-employed **consultants** with a 'main client' (their erstwhile employer) and a number of smaller clients who are picked up as the individual gradually markets his services more widely.

(g) Improved information systems should help managers to **plan and control** work more effectively.

(h) Better information systems open up opportunities for more **centralisation** of decision making by top management and a reduced need for **middle managers**.

3.7 Areas of concern

Issue	Comment
Job security	Employees might think that the new system will put them out of a if it reduces the need for human intervention. The threat of being out of work would unsettle the entire office staff.
Status loss	A new system might result in a loss of status for the individual or department concerned.
Promotions	A new system might damage **career prospects** by reducing the opportunities for promotion (eg if it reduces the requirement for staff in middle management and supervisory grades).
Social change in the office	New systems might disrupt the established 'social system' of the office. Individuals who are used to working together might be separated into different groups, and individuals used to working on their own might be expected to join a group.
Bewilderment	It is easy for individuals to be confused and bewildered by change.
Fear of depersonalisation	Staff may resent losing the ability to introduce the 'human touch' to the work they do.

Case example

E-mail

Reports in the papers suggest that e-mail enhances informal communications, so much so that use of e-mail for items not directly related to work is a matter for disciplinary procedures.

Other reports are that e-mail is used to *avoid* personal communications - people have been bullied and even 'sacked' by e-mail.

3.8 Section summary

People resist change because of:

- Psychological reasons
- Worries about job security and uncertainty.

Often, however, people welcome change.

4 MODELS OF THE CHANGE PROCESS 6/95

4.1 A systematic approach should be established, for planning and implementing changes. Here is a model.

Step

1 Determine need or desire for change in a particular area.

2 Prepare a tentative plan.
- Brainstorming sessions a good idea, since alternatives for change should be considered (Lippitt 1981)

3 Analyse probable reactions to the change

4 Make a final decision from the choice of alternative options
- Decision taken either by group problem-solving (participative) or by manager on his own (coercive)

5 Establish a timetable for change
- 'Coerced' changes can probably be implemented faster, without time for discussions.
- Speed of implementation that is achievable will depend on the likely reactions of the people affected (all in favour, half in favour, all against etc).
- Identify those in favour of the change, and perhaps set up a pilot programme involving them. Talk with the others who resist the change.

6 Communicate the plan for change
- This is really a continuous process, beginning at Step 1 and going through to Step 7.

7 Implement the change. Review the change.
- Continuous evaluation and modifications

The change process

4.2 In the words of John Hunt (*Managing People at Work*): 'Learning also involves re-learning - not merely learning something new but trying to unlearn what is already known.' This is, in a nutshell, the thinking behind Lewin/Schein's three stage approach to changing human behaviour, which may be depicted as follows.

UNFREEZE existing behaviour → Attitudinal/ behavioural change → REFREEZE new behaviour

Step 1 **Unfreeze** is the most difficult (and in many cases neglected) stage of the process, concerned mainly with 'selling' the change, with giving individuals or groups a **motive** for changing their attitudes, values, behaviour, systems or structures.

(a) If the need for change is immediate, clear and necessary for the survival of the individual or group (for example change in reaction to an organisation crisis), the unfreeze stage will be greatly accelerated. Routine changes may be harder to 'sell' if they are perceived to be unimportant and not survival-based.

(b) Culture change (see Section 9 below) is perhaps hardest of all, especially if it involves basic assumptions. Unfreezing processes need:

- A trigger (eg a crisis).
- Someone to challenge and expose the existing behaviour pattern.
- The involvement of outsiders.
- Alterations to power structure.

Step 2 **Change** is mainly concerned with identifying what the new, desirable behaviour should be, communicating it and encouraging individuals and groups to adopt it. The new ideas must be shown to work.

Step 3 **Refreeze** is the final stage, implying consolidation or reinforcement of the new behaviour. Positive reinforcement (praise, reward etc.) or negative reinforcement (sanctions applied to those who deviate from the new behaviour) may be used.

Case example

In a Harvard Business Review article (November – December 1997), Pascale, Milleman and Groga described change at *Shell Malaysia*. Its new chairman, who arrived in 1992, found an overstaffed organisation, facing declining revenues and increased competition, and offering poorer standards. The functional departments quarrelled a great deal but the culture did not encourage outright confrontation. Their way of dealing with impasses was 'smooth and avoid'.

'For more than a year, Knight (the new chief executive) tried to achieve authentic alignment among his eight-person executive team. Somehow the goal always eluded his grasp. In exasperation, he scheduled an event to which all 260 of Shell's mid-level and senior mangers were invited. At this unusual gathering:

(a) Knight proposed two new strategic changes.

(b) Managers were asked to deal with the issues in groups and come up with a response.

(c) Most lower level managers agreed with the plans, despite the fact they realised that their operating practices would have to change.

(d) This isolated the 'obstructionist' senior managers, one of whom was fired – 'a firing heard round the world'.

Strategies for change management

4.3 Peter Honey (quoted by Robinson in *Managing after the Superlatives*) suggests that each of the causes of change identified below can be dealt with in a different way.

Cause	How to deal with it
Parochial self-interest	**Negotiation** (eg offer incentives to those resisting on grounds of self-interest).
Misunderstanding	is best dealt with by **educating and reassuring** people. Lack of trust is harder to counter: trust has to be earned.
Different viewpoints of the situation	Change can be promoted through participation and by **involving potential resisters**. Where change initiators *depend* on resisters or do not have all the information, this technique is especially important.
Low tolerance of change	Force the change through and then **support** the new behaviours it requires. In short, people have to be encouraged (by carrot and stick methods) to adopt the new methods. An example is discrimination legislation, which is supported by councils to promote equal opportunities.

4.4 Peter Honey devised a simple diagram which combines the degree of involvement required of change resisters with that required of the change initiators.

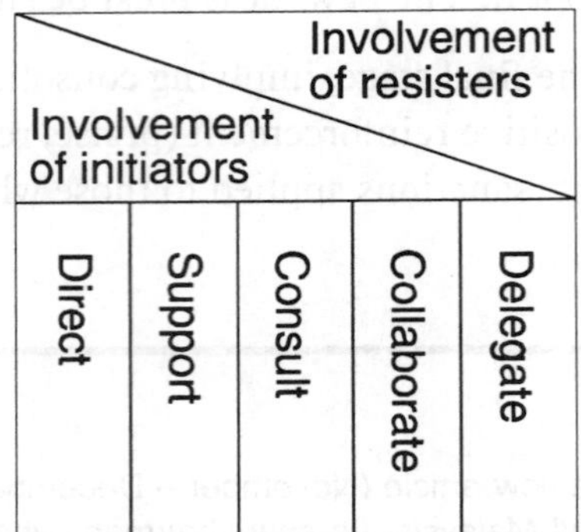

(a) **Direct:** this is equivalent to a 'tells' leadership style. The initiator decides and explains the change.

(b) **Support:** the leader decides the changes and has to be actively involved in supporting them.

(c) **Consult:** the leader invites ideas from subordinates to solve the problem.

(d) **Collaborate:** the change is jointly decided.

(e) **Delegate:** the decision, within certain boundaries, is taken by subordinates.

Champion of change model: the role of the change agent

4.5 The **champion of change model** recognises the importance of change being led by a **change agent**, who may be an individual or occasionally a group.

Step 1 **Senior management** decide in broad terms what is to be done.

Step 2 They appoint a **change agent** to drive it through. Senior management must:

- Support the change agent, if the change provokes conflict between the agent and interest groups in the organisation.
- Review and monitor the progress of the change.
- Endorse and approve the changes, and they ensure that they are publicised.

Step 3 The change agent has to **win the support of functional and operational managers,** who have to introduce and enforce the changes in their own departments. The champion of change has to provide advice and information, as well as evidence that the old ways are no longer acceptable.

Step 4 The change agent **galvanises managers into action** and gives them any necessary support. The managers ensure that the changes are implemented operationally, in the field. Where changes involve, say, a new approach to customer care, it is the workers who are responsible for ensuring the effectiveness of the change process.

It is only after change has been implemented at operational level that the change agent's role becomes of little importance.

4.6 New information systems developments often need management support and a management sponsor.

Exam focus point

Implementing a series of redundancies in the context of a factory reorganisation featured in the June 1995 exam.

4.7 Section summary

- Most changes require that the old ways are consciously abandoned (unfreeze - change - refreeze).
- Some changes require the active support of a change agent, as inertia is common.

5 FORCE FIELD ANALYSIS

5.1 Current organisational practices and interest groups can embody a powerful inertia holding up the change process.

5.2 Kurt Lewin developed a simple technique of visualising the change process called **force field analysis.** In any group or organisational situation there is an interplay of driving and restraining forces. The balance between them keeps things as they are. The example below describes a public sector organisation whose management are introducing a performance review system.

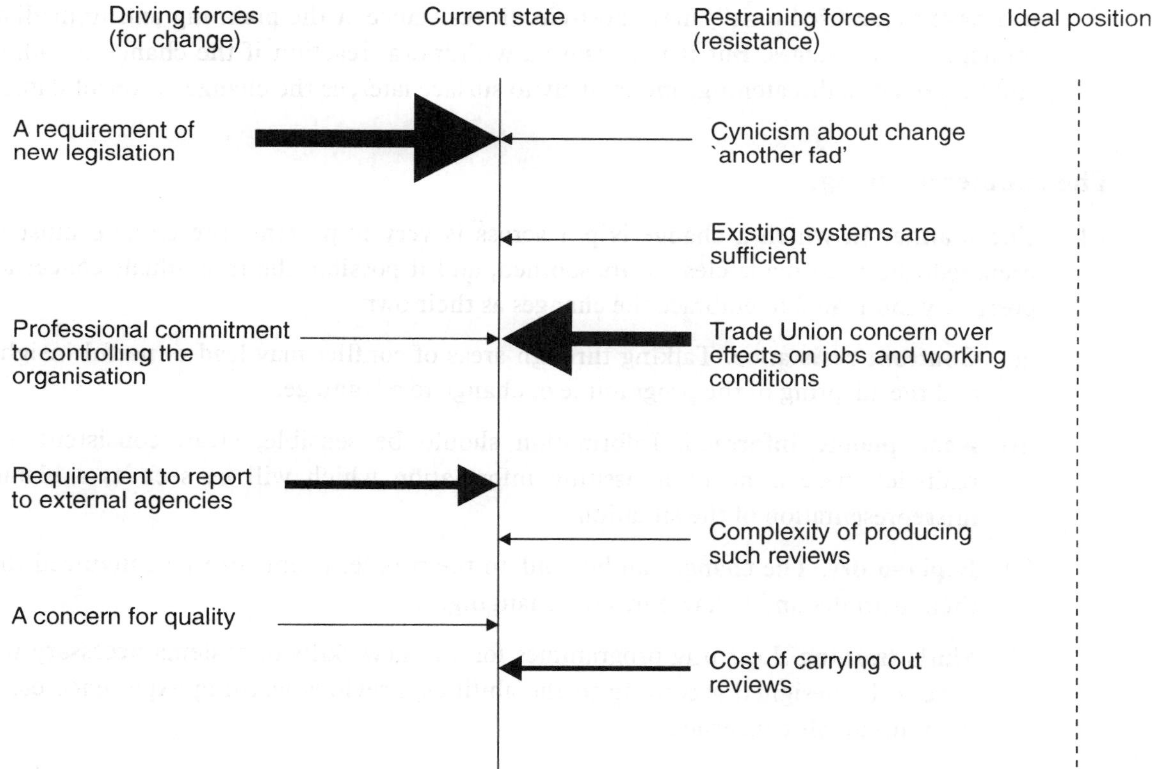

5.3 Forces can be impersonal (eg a new law, new technology), personal (the commitment of a new leader), institutional (trade union), or environmental (competitors). Lines of varying thickness to represent the probable strength of different forces.

5.4 The force field model suggests two ways of dealing with change.

(a) Strengthening driving forces. People associated with the driving forces can be co-opted to 'educate opponents'.

(b) Weakening the opposing forces by:

(i) Persuasion (eg getting endorsement by a supposedly neutral consultant, although vested interests will have to be addressed directly).

(ii) Concessions - buying people off.

(iii) Involving people in diagnosing problem situations (eg in quality circles) wins over 'hearts and minds'.

(iv) Coercion.

6 OVERCOMING RESISTANCE TO CHANGE

6.1 When dealing with resistance to change, managers should consider the changes:

- Pace
- Manner
- Scope

Pace of change

6.2 The more gradual the change, the **more time** is available for questions to be asked, reassurances to be given and retraining (where necessary) embarked upon. Many **information systems** are implemented slowly, eg via pilot testing, to iron out bugs and let staff become acclimatised to the new system.

6.3 Presenting the individual concerned with a **fait accompli** ('Let's get it over with - they'll just have to get used to it!') may short-circuit resistance at the planning and immediate implementation stages. But it may cause a withdrawal reaction if the change is radical and perceived as threatening, and is likely to surface later, as the change is consolidated.

The manner of change

6.4 The **manner** in which a change is put across is very important: the climate must be prepared, the need made clear, fears soothed, and if possible the individuals concerned positively motivated to embrace the changes as their own.

(a) **Confront resistance.** Talking through areas of conflict may lead to useful insights and the adapting of the programme of change to advantage.

(b) **Keep people informed.** Information should be sensible, clear, consistent and realistic: there is no point issuing information which will be seen as a blatant misrepresentation of the situation.

(c) **Explanatory.** The change can be 'sold' to the people: people can be convinced that their attitudes and behaviours *need* changing.

(d) **Skills training.** Learning programmes for any new skills or systems necessary will have to be designed according to the abilities, previous learning experience etc of the individuals concerned.

(e) **Empathy**. 'Putting yourself in the shoes of the other person' and getting to know the people involved in and affected by changes enables their reactions to be anticipated.

(f) The degree to which **consultation or participation** will be possible (or genuine) will depend on management's attitude towards the competence and trustworthiness of its workforce.

When to start participation	*How participation is achieved in practice*
(a) From the beginning, discuss ideas. Gradually, acceptable ideas will emerge.	The desire of the manager for participation must be genuine. It won't work if' participation is something the top orders the middle to do from the bottom'. (Kanter 1983)
(b) Make tentative plans for change, and then start to discuss them with subordinates.	1. Ask for input of ideas.
(c) Decide to make a change and then try to sell the idea to subordinates.	2. Seriously consider input and evaluate it objectively.
Approaches (a) or (b) are preferred for 'real' participation.	3. Use good ideas.
	4. Reject bad ideas.
	5. Give credit/rewards to providers of good ideas.
	6. Convince the providers of bad ideas that their ideas were bad.

Coercion

6.5 Explicit or implicit **coercion**, that is, **autocratic** or **unilateral** imposition of change. It can be effective given certain conditions, for example where:

(a) Behavioural change or **compliance** is all that is required, and where resistance in attitudes can have no significantly detrimental effect on performance.

(b) The **balance of power** is heavily weighted in favour of the change agent.

(c) The **prevailing culture** is one of acceptance of dictatorial change, and there is little expectation of anything else.

Scope of change

6.6 The **scope of change** should also be carefully reviewed.

(a) **Total transformation** will create greater insecurity - but also greater excitement, if the organisation has the kind of innovative culture that can stand it - than moderate innovation.

(b) There may be **hidden changes** to take into account: a change in technology may necessitate changes in work methods, which may in turn result in the breaking up of work groups.

(c) Management should be aware of **how many different aspects** of their employees' lives they are proposing to alter - and therefore on how many fronts they are likely to encounter resistance.

Question 1

Watch out for examples of organisations undergoing change in the press and see how it is being handled. Technological change, takeovers, new conditions of work and relocations are amongst the many examples you may see reported.

Also, note carefully how your own organisation handles changes, or mishandles them. Are you, or any of your colleagues, inclined to resist change?

Question 2

Why might participation be necessary in *information systems development*?

Answer

User department employees should be encouraged to participate fully in the design of the system, when the system is a tailor-made one. Participation should be genuine.

(a) Their suggestions about problems with the existing system should be fully discussed.
(b) The systems analyst's ideas for a new system should be discussed with them.
(c) Their suggestions for features in the new system should be welcomed.
(d) They know more about their jobs - and what they need - than the analyst.
(e) Their contribution is important in specifying the outputs required of the system.

Case example

The famous research by *Coch and French* into resistance to change in a pyjama factory provides evidence in favour of consultation. The company faced resistance to frequent changes to jobs and work methods necessitated by the product and production method development. This resistance showed in pay complaints, absenteeism and leaving, low efficiency (despite financial incentives), restriction of output and hostility to management. The main problem was that changes and transfers led to loss of status and earnings, through reduced efficiency ratings.

Coch and French designed an experiment in which changes were introduced in three production groups with different levels of participation.

(a) The *non-participative group* was informed about the change but not involved in the decision-making. Resistance was immediate; conflict flared, efficiency remained low, and some members left.

(b) The *representative group* was given a hand in the change to the extent that after a preliminary meeting of explanation, representatives were given appropriate training and subsequently trained fellow members. The group was co-operative and submissive and efficiency rose rapidly.

(c) The *total participation group* also had a preliminary meeting, but all members then took part in the design and standard-setting for the new job. The group recovered its efficiency rating very rapidly, and to a level much higher than before the change, without conflict or resignations.

(d) The *non-participative members* were later re-grouped and followed the total participation procedure - with the beneficial results of the latter. Coch and French concluded that it was not the people or personality factors that mattered, but the *way in which change was implemented.*

Acceptance

6.7 It takes time for changes to get accepted, in other words the 'Refreeze' steps. Conner and Patterson (1981) identified three phases and eight stages in the process of accepting change by the people affected.

Phase 1: Preparation phase

Stage 1	Contact	First knowledge that a change is 'in the air'
Stage 2	Awareness	Knowledge that change will happen

Phase 2: Acceptance phase

Stage 3	Understanding	Gaining an understanding of the nature and purpose of the change
Stage 4	Positive perception	Developing a positive view towards the change, and accepting the need for it

Phase 3: Commitment phase

Stage 5	Installation	The change becomes operational
Stage 6	Adoption	The change has been in force for long enough and its value has become apparent
Stage 7	Institutionalisation	The change has been in for long enough to become 'routine' and the 'norm'
Stage 8	Internalisation	Individuals are highly committed to the change because it is now congruent with their personal interests, goals and value systems.

6.8 Conner and Patterson argued that **commitment** to change is necessary for its successful implementation.

(a) Getting commitment is **expensive**, and calls for an investment of time, effort and money - eg providing information, involving subordinates in the planning and implementation process, rewarding them for their participation etc.

(b) Strategies for commitment ought to be developed. For any change, management needs to decide how far through the eight stages the acceptance process needs to go. Some changes can stop at Stage 5; other must go to Stage 7 or Stage 8, otherwise the benefits of the change will be lost.

6.9 Section summary

- The scope, manner and pace of change can cause problems.
- Participation can be valuable in winning over support, but coercion can be necessary and effective too.
- User involvement is needed in information systems projects.

7 MANAGING CONFLICT

Constructive and destructive conflict

7.1 Organisations are political systems within which there is **competition** for scarce resources and unequal influence. Competition can be healthy as it can:

(a) Set standards, by establishing best performance through comparison.
(b) Motivate individuals to better efforts.

7.2 In order to be fruitful, competition must be:

(a) Perceived to be **open**, rather than closed. ('Closed' competition is a win-lose, or 'zero-sum' situation, where one party's gain will be another party's loss. 'Open' competition exists where all participants can increase their gains - for example productivity bargaining.)

(b) Seen to be fair, and the determinants of success are within the competitors' control. If these preconditions are not met, competition may again degenerate into conflict.

Causes, symptoms and tactics of conflict

7.3 **Causes of conflict**

(a) **Differences in the objectives** of different groups or individuals.

(b) **Scarcity of resources.**

(c) **Interdependence of two departments** on a task. They have to work together but may do so ineffectively.

(d) **Disputes about the boundaries of authority.**

(i) The technostructure may attempt to encroach on the roles or 'territory' of line managers and usurp some of their authority.

(ii) One department might start **empire building** and try to take over the work previously done by another department.

(e) **Personal differences,** as regards goals, attitudes and feelings, are also bound to crop up. This is especially true in **differentiated organisations**, where people employed in the different sub-units are very different.

7.4 **Symptoms of conflict**

(a) Poor communications, in all 'directions'

(b) Interpersonal friction

(c) Inter-group rivalry and jealousy

(d) Low morale and frustration

(e) Widespread use of arbitration, appeals to higher authority, and inflexible attitudes towards change.

7.5 **The tactics of conflict**

(a) **Withholding information** from another.

(b) **Distorting information.** This will enable the group or manager presenting the information to get their own way more easily.

(c) **Empire building**. A group (especially a specialist group such as accounting) which considers its influence to be neglected might seek to **impose rules, procedures,** restrictions or official requirements on other groups, in order to bolster up their own importance.

(d) **Informal organisation.** A manager might seek to by-pass formal channels of communication and decision-making by establishing informal contacts and friendships with people in a position of importance.

(e) **Fault-finding** in the work of other departments: department X might duplicate the work of department Y - hoping to prove department Y 'wrong' - and then report the fact to senior management.

Managerial response to conflict

7.6 **Management responses to the handling of conflict** (not all of which are effective).

Response	Comment
Denial/withdrawal	'Sweeping it under the carpet'. If the conflict is very trivial, it may indeed blow over without an issue being made of it, but if the causes are not identified, the conflict may grow to unmanageable proportions.
Suppression	'Smoothing over', to preserve working relationships despite minor conflicts. As Hunt remarks, however: 'Some cracks cannot be papered over'.
Dominance	The application of power or influence to settle the conflict. The disadvantage of this is that it creates all the lingering resentment and hostility of 'win-lose' situations.
Compromise	Bargaining, negotiating, conciliating. To some extent, this will be inevitable in any organisation made up of different individuals. However, individuals tend to exaggerate their positions to allow for compromise, and compromise itself is seen to weaken the value of the decision, perhaps reducing commitment.
Integration/ collaboration	Emphasis must be put on the task, individuals must accept the need to modify their views for its sake, and group effort must be seen to be superior to individual effort.

7.7 Handy suggests two types of strategy which may be used to **turn conflict into competition or argument**, or to manage it in some other acceptable way.

(a) **Environmental ('ecological') strategies** involve creating conditions in which individuals may be better able to interact co-operatively with each other: they are wide-ranging, time-consuming and unpredictable, because of the sheer range of human differences. Such strategies involve:

(i) Agreement of **common objectives**
(ii) Reinforcing the group or **'team' nature** of organisational life, via culture
(iii) Providing **feedback** information on progress
(iv) Providing adequate co-ordination and communication **mechanisms**
(v) Sorting out territorial/role conflicts in the **organisational structure**

(b) **Regulation strategies.** These are directed to control conflict - though in fact they make it so much a part of the formal structure of the organisation that they tend to legitimise and even perpetuate it. Possible methods include:

(i) The provision of **arbitration** to settle disputes.

(ii) The establishment of **detailed rules and procedures** for conduct by employees.

(iii) A liaison/co-ordination officer or **committee.**

(iv) Using **confrontation**, or inter-group meetings, to hammer out differences, especially where territorial conflicts occur.

(v) **Separating** the conflicting individuals/departments.

(vi) **Ignoring the problem,** if it is genuinely likely to 'go away', and there is no point in opening fresh wounds.

Question 3

In the light of the above consider how conflict could arise, what form it would take and how it might be resolved in the following situations.

(a) Two managers who share a secretary have documents to be typed.

(b) One worker finds out that another worker who does the same job as he does is paid a higher wage.

(c) A company's electricians find out that a group of engineers have been receiving training in electrical work.

(d) Department A stops for lunch at 12.30 while Department B stops at 1 o'clock. Occasionally the canteen runs out of puddings for Department B workers.

(e) The Northern Region and Southern Region sales teams are continually trying to better each others results, and the capacity of production to cope with the increase in sales is becoming overstretched.

Changes and external stakeholders

7.8 The company's relationship with its stakeholders and other aspects of its boundaries with the environment has been presented so far as a passive and reactive process. Management 'respond' to stakeholder demands. However there can be a number of conflicts in the relationship.

7.9 Management (and other internal stakeholders) are in possession of a lot more information about the company than any other group. Management are therefore in a position to **mould the expectations** of some stakeholder groups, to direct their demands in certain directions. In other words, management can 'craft' stakeholder expectations in a similar way to that in which they might 'craft' strategy. Here are some examples.

(a) Customer expectations can be 'crafted' by **clever marketing**. Also, the power of customers can be reduced by product differentiation, erecting barriers to entry, raising switching costs and so forth.

(b) Suppliers and distributors can be managed in a number of ways. Drawing them into a **closer operating relationship** (eg joint product development, just-in-time systems) can be a way of managing the relationship and controlling their influence.

(c) The public and the government can be **'managed' by advertising, public relations,** lobbying, and pre-empting legislation. Supermarkets, for example, sometimes promote healthy eating rather than protest about it.

(d) Some companies deliberately **cultivate good relations with members of the investment community** (eg pension fund managers, analysts working for securities firms).

8 NEGOTIATION

8.1 A negotiation is a special kind of interpersonal interaction between two or more parties.

KEY TERM

Alan Fowler *(Negotiation Skills and Strategies)* defines a **negotiation** as: 'a process of interaction by which two or more parties who consider they need to be jointly involved in an outcome, but who initially have different objectives seek by the use of argument and persuasion to resolve their differences in order to achieve a mutually acceptable solution'.

Managers cannot always *impose* change, especially if the other side has rights. Negotiation is often a better way of proceeding.

(a) '**Negotiation** implies acceptance by both parties that **agreement** between them is required (or is **desirable**) before a decision can be implemented.'

(b) 'Consultation implies a **willingness** by one party **to listen** to the views of the other, while reserving the right to make a final decision, whether or not the final party is in agreement.' Asking someone's views or advice should **not** be construed as a willingness to give that person a 'say' in your decision. The other person may have an interest in the outcome, and may use the situation to **muscle in**.

8.2 The implications of this definition are as these.

(a) **Two parties**. Each believes the other's involvement is necessary to reach some desired outcome. There is some common interest which puts the parties in contact.

(b) Although their **interest in the outcome is shared,** the parties begin the negotiation with a **different set of objectives** which prevent, initially, the achievement of the outcome.

(c) All the parties **prefer negotiation to other ways of resolving differences** (such as coercion or arbitration).

(d) Each party considers that the other will be prepared to modify its initial position.

   (i) In theory each party wants the *other* to change.
   (ii) In practice all must be ready to compromise.

(e) Even when the ideal result cannot be achieved, **all participants hope for a result which is acceptable.** In other words, the result will be **better than no negotiation**.

(f) Each participant has a **degree of power** over the others. Power, if you remember, comes in a variety of forms. (Negative power for example is the power to impede a settlement.)

   (i) If one of the parties has no power, there is no point in negotiation.

   (ii) The power may be real, imaginary or indirect (ie related to issues not covered by the negotiation).

   (iii) Sometimes the personnel involved in the negotiation do not have the power to bring about agreement, or to implement it.

(g) The negotiation process is a process of **face-to-face verbal interchanges**. The actual negotiation is greatly affected by the human element: 'The progress of all types of negotiation is strongly influenced by emotion and attitudes and not just the logic of each party's arguments'.

8.3 **Examples of negotiations**

(a) **Employers and trade unions** negotiate over a **pay and productivity agreement**. Both have an interest in reaching the settlement. The employer wants to avoid industrial action; the employees want to keep their jobs.

(b) A negotiation between **two solicitors** on behalf of their clients to avoid **litigation**.

(c) Negotiation between a **salesperson and purchasing personnel** in a company. The customer wants, or perhaps can be persuaded to want, a product that conforms with a number of needs. The salesperson wishes to make a sale at a profit.

(d) Negotiations between the management of a **company and its auditors** cover the accounting treatment of certain items if these were disputed, the audit report and last, but not least, the fee.

(e) Negotiation between **specialists in the technostructure** ('staff' positions) and **line managers**. Specialists (eg human resource managers) may wish to impose certain solutions on what only **they** see as problems. For example, the personnel director might want to try out a new pay and remuneration system. The line manager may not share this perspective.

(f) Negotiation situations can be part of a **long-term relationship** between the parties. **Compromise** in one negotiation can **create a favour** to be called in at a future date.

8.4 The **tone of the negotiation** can be set at the outset. Some parties enter into negotiation:

(a) With **no** real intention to reach an agreement (but because *not* to negotiate would look bad to outsiders or the negotiation can be a delaying tactic).

(b) With a very adversarial spirit, built up over long periods of mistrust.

(c) Predisposed to reach an agreement and all they want to do is hammer out the detail.

(d) With **individual** goals (eg maintaining a reputation for toughness) which may get in the way of the optimal solution.

The stages of negotiation

8.5 There are three 'stages' in the negotiation process.

- The 'pre-negotiation' or preparation
- The negotiation itself
- The 'post-negotiation' stage (publicising and implementing the agreement)

Pre-negotiation

8.6 The preparation stage involves considering a number of questions.

(a) **What are the real issues?** (The supposed issue under negotiation may *relate* to something else)

(b) **Who should be involved?** Exclusion of some people could be taken to be an insult, whereas inclusion is a recognition of someone's power or right).

8.7 **Weigh up the strengths** of each party to the negotiation.

(a) The **relative authority or capacity** of each party has to make the decision and implement it. If two people are negotiating, one may have ultimate decision-making power but will require consent. The weaker party might want to use some different type of power (eg expert power) to conceal his or her weakness.

(b) The **relative ability** each participant has to use some 'carrot' or 'stick' (*un*related to the matter negotiated) to influence the other (eg the long-term relationship, or some future benefit).

(c) The **strength of the arguments** (in logical, business or financial terms).

(d) The **degree of determination** (as persistence is often rewarded).

8.8 **Determine the objectives** of a negotiation.

(a) The **ideal outcome** (either the best possible in an ideal world, or the best achievable within the bounds of practicality). In considering a best achievable outcome, participants must try and look at the situation from the other party's *point of view* (objectives, assumptions and needs) and with the strength of the other party in mind. Over-optimism is a danger (especially if you believe your case is convincing).

(b) The **expected outcome**.

(c) The **minimum acceptable outcome**, below which it would be better not to have entered negotiation at all. A lack of a fall-back position could mean that, as the best achievable outcome is not possible, the actual agreement reached is unnecessarily disadvantageous. A statement that 'this is our final offer' must mean exactly that.

8.9 In an ideal world both participants will be happy with the outcome (a win/win situation). However, many negotiators see the process as one of competition, and will make completely unreasonable claims which should be rejected out of hand.

8.10 **Assess the case of the other side before the negotiation begins.**

(a) **What outcomes are the other participants looking for?** The **other party's aims** might be easy to discern if, say, a meeting is set up for a specific purpose. Some meetings are packaged as 'general policy' issues, but really relate to specific objectives. Fowler cites an example of a manager whose request to discuss 'equipment procurement policy' was actually a request for a new desk.

(b) **What evidence of fact and logic can they marshal to their cause?** A well researched body of evidence is one of the sources of power in a negotiating situation. This means examining trends related to the issue (eg the going rate of pay in the industry).

(c) **Is there a hidden agenda?** For example, a negotiation on a particular issue may be used as the beginning of a long-term relationship which one participant is keen to secure.

Question 4

The Managing Director and Finance Director of Towering Visions plc are preparing for a negotiation with the General Employees Association about the latter's pay claim. The General Employees Association has been recognised as a 'model union' by some companies. It has pioneered no-strike deals, flexible working, and is favourably disposed to the introduction of advanced work practices, new technology and so forth. The Financial Director has told the Managing Director that it is unlikely that the company will meet its profit targets this year, but that a cut in the wage bill of 1% would do the trick. 'After all, it's only 1% - the union has been co-operative: it has always put the good of the company first'. This idea is presented to the union leader, whose jaw drops in astonishment. This is not the expected response. What do you think has gone wrong?

Answer

The 'good of the company' is a subjective concept. The union would not take the view that because of the company's failure to meet its targets (note that the company is still in profit) the workers' pay should be cut. Clearly the Managing Director and Finance Director have not considered the extent to which this would have to be 'sold' to the workforce, who might regard this idea as an abuse by management of the workers' generally co-operative attitudes.

8.11 **Set the context of meeting**

(a) **Style or tone**: is the negotiation a collaborative (win/win) or aggressive (win/lose) situation? The style can be set by either party. Participants need to plan for both situations.

(b) **Who to involve?** Many negotiations involve teams.

(i) One should act as **leader**, being constructive and positive.

(ii) Another should take a **tougher line**.

(iii) The third member **listens** rather than contributes.

The relative seniority of team members must be assessed so that people of similar status meet each other.

(c) **Pace and timing** can affect the outcome. Procrastination might either weaken the resolve of the other participants or increase their determination to succeed. Proper timing can allow for further deliberation.

(d) **Location** can influence confidence and attitudes. (Holding a meeting on other people's territory implies you are interested in them, and you can make them believe you have made an effort.)

(e) **Seating and refreshments**. Seating can affect style (eg face to face as adversaries or a round table as consensus). Similarly hunger (eg a delayed lunch) can encourage the other side to reach a settlement.

(f) **Documentation.** Neither party might accept the other's written summary of the meeting, so perhaps a verbatim record is useful. However, the only necessary document is a full description of what was agreed.

The negotiation itself

8.12 **Setting the agenda** is important, as this establishes the subject matter well in advance.

(a) 'Talks about talks' are a way of setting the agenda. Agendas must be agreed in advance.

(b) Opening the meeting can set the informal agenda and the style and tone.

(c) An agenda also helps concentrate people's minds.

8.13 During the negotiation, while remembering the **objective is to come to an agreement**:

(a) Concessions should not be made lightly (so the opposition's case should be probed and weakened).

(b) Every opportunity should be taken to **build** up your own position.

8.14 **Expose flaws** in the opposition's argument eg:

- Errors of fact;
- Omissions;
- Unsupported assertions;
- Abuse of statistics;
- Faulty logic;
- Appeals to emotion (eg fairness).

It is **better to ask questions which undermine assertions than flatly deny** those assertions.

8.15 **Strengthening your own case**

(a) **Identifying possible sanctions** (eg strike, job losses) and reminding your opponents of them. Threats do not work, but occasional reminders do.

- Financial sanctions (increased costs)
- Legal sanctions
- Reputation
- Loss of face
- Emotion

(b) **Tactics** include:

- Introduce **new issues** (eg by packaging a number of topics);

- Attach **conditions to concessions** (provided that the condition is introduced before the concession)
- Use emotion (only effective if sincere, and used consciously).

8.16 **Plan the timescale of the meeting.**

(a) Two hours is normally the longest continuous period for effective negotiation.

(b) The ideal duration of a presentation is 15 minutes.

(c) An individual contribution in a discussion should be between two to three minutes long.

(d) Massively long sessions are the exception rather than the rule.

(e) Adjournments can be scheduled for food, but might be called for the sides to review their positions. They give an opportunity for informal talks, away from the bargaining table. They can also stop unconstructive arguments.

8.17 The **search for common ground** (real or imagined) is a better way of **reaching an agreement** than adversarial point-scoring. Fowler believes that negotiators have to rise above their own personal views. He advocates the following technique.

(a) **Listen**. The importance of listening, and asking questions to assess both the content of what is being said and the tone in which it is said.

(b) Occasionally, **humour** (reinforcing initial bonhomie) can reduce tension and encourage a collaborative rather than confrontational mode. But humour is **culture-specific** and can cause offence.

(c) **Read between the lines**. There are a variety of coded messages which might imply a willingness to move on a concession, or the acceptability of some aspects in the package rather than others.

(d) **Highlight the benefits of your proposals** to the opposition. Common interests include:

- The success of the business
- Job security
- Reputation
- Morale
- Avoidance of third-party intervention

8.18 **Move towards an agreement**

(a) **Periodic summaries** of what has been agreed are useful progress markers. They provide a way of ensuring that all sides have understood what has gone on.

(b) **Hypothetical suggestions** introduce proposals without creating a strong commitment.

(c) The other side should be **helped to move** (by not gloating, by under-playing the benefits to your side).

(d) **Avoid loss of face** for yourself and the other party.

(i) Do not adopt a position from which movement will be a humiliating climbdown.

(ii) Be thick-skinned.

(iii) Do not 'trap' the other party, as it will drive them to confrontation.

(e) **Constructive compromise** involves:

(i) Retreating on minor issues in the **cause** of greater ones

(ii) Agreeing on minor issues, as a **precedent** for agreeing on major ones.

8.19 **Breakdown** is always a risk.

(a) Taking unilateral action will affect future working relationships.

(b) A conciliator can be appointed to bring the parties closer to agreement.

(c) Binding arbitration, in which both sides are committed to decisions made by an independent arbitrator, is perhaps the riskiest strategy in this case.

8.20 **Striking the deal (or closing the sale) is the 'point of no return'.**

(a) Close the deal at the right time, when there is a good morale in the meeting and when it is also clear that no further concessions are available.

(b) **Last minute deadlocks** can be broken by:

(i) Linking agreement now to a future benefit.
(ii) A stated willingness to review the matter at a future date.
(iii) Pointing out, quietly, the consequences of not reaching agreement.
(iv) A full explanation as to why no further concessions are available.

(c) **Ensure all points have been included** (eg dates of implementation, definition of terms) in the agreement.

(d) The leader should make a **final summary**, obtain verbal agreement, and ensure it is in writing as soon as possible.

(e) **Avoid fudging issues** (ie using a form of words to gloss over important differences). This leads to confrontation later.

Post-negotiation

8.21 After the negotiation has been concluded:

(a) The **agreement must be publicised and perhaps 'sold'** to those not involved in the negotiations (even if this means that both sides claim 'victory' in what had been a non-adversarial contest).

(b) A programme for **implementation** should be included in the agreement (eg date of commencement, who is to undertake the work).

Particular negotiating situations

8.22 **Negotiations between managers**

(a) **The manager's status.** In superior-subordinate situations, the superior has ultimate decision-making authority.

(i) Senior managers 'should **never underestimate the effect of status differences** on the confidence of junior staff, including those in other departments'.

(ii) Junior managers should not worry too much about status but concentrate on their **expertise and persuasive ability.**

(b) **Connections with sources of power**. The connections managers have with other managers are 'unforeseen' factors in the balance of power in a negotiation.

(c) **Obligations**. Negotiations between managers are determined very much by personal factors, and the quality of their relationships. Bad working relationships can mean a negotiation is a battleground for settling personal scores. Some managers like to **create obligations** outside the negotiation (on the grounds that 'if you scratch my back I'll scratch yours') to influence later negotiations. It is best to avoid such obligations.

(d) **Expertise**. This can be used, particularly by junior managers, to counter the effect of manipulation or seniority. Expertise needs to be projected with an appropriate verbal style. Any mistake in the information you present will undermine your case.

8.23 **Commercial negotiations**

(a) **Either side can split up** and find another buyer/customer. They rarely *have* to reach agreement.

(b) The final deal, if it is a **legally enforceable contract**, will be precise.

(c) The **power is generally in the buyer's favour**. The salesperson must try and overcome this by:

(i) Differentiating the product to make it seem unique.
(ii) Make the buyer feel uneasy about not keeping up to date.

8.24 **Trade unions** in the UK still have an important position in many business environments.

(a) The **personal relationships** between managers and workers' representatives, as they have to work together are important.

(b) **Procedures** enable certain matters to be dealt with quickly, without preliminary discussions, and include:

(i) The levels in the hierarchy at which different issues are discussed
(ii) Who takes part
(iii) Timescales
(iv) Chairing the meeting
(v) Agenda and minutes.

(c) **Precedents**, according to Fowler, have a great influence on negotiations with trade unions. Agreements are binding until an agreed future date, or until new agreements are reached.

8.25 Personal **abilities** a person needs to negotiate well are:

(a) **Knowledge** of how to negotiate, the background to the particular negotiation, and the detail of the subject matter.

(b) **Skill** in assessing the issues, in personal interactions (eg avoid over-personalisation) and in communication.

(c) The right **attitudes** towards the negotiation as a whole (eg welcoming), towards each negotiator and towards the role the person plays in the negotiation.

8.26 Section summary

- A negotiation is not a consultation. Both parties have power, and both want to reach an agreement.
- Preparation includes understanding ideal, expected and base line objectives.
- Both sides should be 'helped to move'.
- The conditions of the negotiations and the personalities of the participants affect the outcome.

9 CHANGING CORPORATE CULTURE

9.1 Any programme of cultural change involves identifying and exposing:

(a) The hidden assumptions of the new culture.

(b) The conflicts hidden in the culture.

(c) Cultural mechanisms for change.

9.2 'Changing a culture to increase a corporation's effectiveness is a hazardous undertaking, says Hampden-Turner. He recommends a number of steps that senior managers, perhaps with the advice of management consultants, should take.

Step 1 **Find the dangers ('locate the black sheep').** In other words, the best way to find out about how a culture works is to violate it, by doing something culturally shocking.

Step 2 **Bring conflicts into the open**. Interviewing and observation are the principal tools of cultural investigation. Interviews identify what people believe as *individuals*, as opposed to what they affirm as *employees*. 'Many corporate cultures greatly reduce the permissible variety of individual expression. The interviewees may be trying to use the interviewer as a messenger.'

Step 3 **Play out corporate dramas**. The manager or consultant then discusses the culture with its members. 'A repressive culture may simply deny that remarks qualifying or criticising it were ever made.' 'A narrow or low context culture may agree that such remarks were made, but treat them as the utterances of private persons, irrelevant to the common task.' This can result in heated, but hopefully constructive argument.

Step 4 **Reinterpret the corporate myths**. Corporate stories passed round to recruits indicates something about competing value systems. Sometimes these corporate myths have to change. Hampden-Turner cites the experiences of Volvo in France. The French sales force considered the cars they were selling to be boring: after a long trip to Sweden, when they were shown around the factories, they changed their views.

Step 5 **Look at symbols, images, rituals.** An example quoted by Hampden-Turner is 'PepsiCo', where every month there is a formal meeting comparing Pepsi's sales with Coca-Cola's. Rituals are used to celebrate achievement, or to mark changes (eg in a merger): 'changing a corporate culture can mean that new symbols, rituals and approaches are devised.'

Step 6 **Create a new learning system**. Cultures filter and exclude information. They need to be modified to accept new types of data.

9.3 The norms in a culture include attitudes toward performance, teamwork, communication, leadership, profitability, staff relations, customer relations, honesty and security, training and innovation. A consistent approach is needed, requiring the following.

(a) Top management commitment.

(b) Modelling behaviour. Managers should practice what they preach.

(c) Support for positive behaviour and confrontation of negative behaviour.

(d) Consistency between the evaluation and reward system and positive behaviour (linking pay to acting on positive norms).

(e) Communication of desired norms.

(f) Recruitment and selection of the 'right' people.

(g) Induction programmes for new employees on the desired norms of behaviour.

(h) Training and skills development.

9.4 Baker warned that: 'changing the distinctive culture of a large, old organisation is enormously difficult and may take years'. Most research has shown that, in a large organisation, shifting the value system or culture can take between three and eight years to bring about. Strong cultures discourage the questioning of their basic assumptions, especially where they have been implemented and reinforced in the recruitment of 'clones'.

9.5 Section summary

- Cultures are hard to change.
- Their assumptions must be exposed and challenged.
- Managers have to lead by example.

10 BRAINWORKS PLC UPDATE

Questions can be found in the Introduction box at the beginning of the chapter.

10.1 *Question 1.* The case study makes little mention of conflict, but it has been bubbling under the surface.

(a) PeoplePower effectively won the battle not to have the UK performance assessment system introduced. A possible reason is that the US, with £3bn out of the group's £4.5bn revenues, is powerful in internal decision-making. With Willard Mann's appointment, the US side has effectively won. Ultimately the 'conflict' will be resolved by the demerger of the firm.

(b) In the office conflict is endemic, partly because of the reward system.

10.2 *Question 2.* It seems evident that a change to the corporate *culture* might be needed. The firm is not reacting to the trends in the employment market, with the demand for longer but fixed term temporary contracts. The information system reflects the need but changes to organisation structure are necessary too. Similarly, changes to the UK's performance reward system might be required.

10.3 *Question 3.* There should be little opposition to the demerger, providing shareholders and bondholders are happy. Internal stakeholders will welcome the change: the merger perhaps was a distraction, caused by Begbie's egomania. The firm is decentralised already.

10.4 *Question 4.* A employee database will change the way work is done. Consultants will no longer jealously guard their clients. They will share them. Have the change management implications been thought through?

Chapter roundup

- **Changes** occur within the environment, goods/services, technology, management organisation structure, and in an organisation's capacity to meet them.
- Management sometimes must **introduce change** to the organisation. A variety of forces will promote or resist the change. **Force field analysis** is a way of identifying these factors.
- The **change process** involves:
  - Determining the need for change
  - Preparing a plan
  - Analysing likely responses
  - Establishing a realistic timetable
  - Communicating the change
  - Implementing and reviewing the change
- It may be necessary to appoint a **change agent** who, with the public support of senior management, must promote the change to managers and workers, and ensure they implement it.
- A change is only one of several sources of **conflict** within an organisation. Some consider conflict to be an aberration; others who see organisations as political battlefields see conflicts of interest as inevitable.
- Managing change and conflict is thus a vitally important management task.
  - **Forces of resistance** to change can be weakened intellectually by destroying their case, politically by undermining their support, or by giving in on non-critical issues and striking a bargain.
  - **Negotiations**, where both parties have an interest in reaching an agreement, are necessary to prevent conflicts of interest becoming disruptive.
  - **Consultation** can succeed in reducing resistance to change.
  - Other conflict management strategies include strategies to reduce the likelihood of conflict occurring in the first place, or procedures (ie arbitration) to regulate it.
- People **resist change** because of uncertainty, fear, lack of confidence, and a sense of dissonance. The success of change can be promoted by taking these factors into account.
- Cultural change is especially difficult.

Quick quiz

1. List five types of change. (see para 1.1)
2. What is the happy family view of conflict? (2.3)
3. Is conflict always a bad thing? (2.8)
4. How does change affect an individual? (3.1)
5. Where does resistance to change come from? (3.3, 3.4)
6. Draft a model of the change process. (4.1)
7. Describe the unfreeze part of the change process. (4.2)
8. What is force field analysis? (5.2)
9. Summarise the research of Coch and French. (6.6, case example)
10. Describe five managerial *responses* to conflict, and two *strategies* to manage conflicts. (7.6, 7.7)
11. What is a negotiation? (8.1)
12. What are the three stages of a negotiation? (8.5)

Question to try	Level	Marks	Time
16	Exam standard	25	45 mins

Chapter 13

PERSONAL MANAGEMENT AND COMMUNICATION SKILLS

Introduction

This chapter deals with **individual management skills**, which you may have to exercise now, or fairly soon, as you will be involved in implementing strategy. Some exam questions ask you what you should do as an individual manager.

A **manager's communication** skills are important for two reasons. Firstly, they enhance the manager's personal effectiveness and hence the manager's career. Secondly, they ensure that the information flow around the organisation is efficient and effective. Personal communication skills are also at a premium in the context of change management, discussed earlier. As far as the examination is concerned, some exam questions expressly ask you to use **report** or briefing paper **format**: this is a good reason for taking to heart the lessons of this chapter. (The June 1994 exam specifically asked for notes for an **oral presentation**.)

Brainworks plc

1 What problems of managing individual staff are relevant to BW?

2 Which communication skills are most important to BW, and which audiences must be addressed?

3 What should BW do about the respondent who was outraged at her treatment by one of BW's staff?

1 ACHIEVING WORK OBJECTIVES

1.1 Managerial work contains a wide variety of activities which have to be fitted in. In many cases, however, especially at the level of supervisory management, the manager's job will have two aspects, a **managerial** and a **technical** aspect. This might be especially true of accountants' jobs.

1.2 A manager in this kind of situation has to:

(a) Plan his or her own work.
(b) Plan subordinates' work.
(c) Deal with requests for advice, decisions and so forth from staff.

1.3 While MBO and related systems identify **what** is to be achieved, the **means** by which it is achieved are up to the individual manager. The manager has two sets of tools to organise work.

(a) The **company's policies**, reporting systems and practices.

(b) The **manager's own ability** to organise the available personnel and resources (not least the manager's own time and the manager's own staff).

1.4 **'Tools' and 'standards' to plan the performance of the work.**

(a) **Policies** are general statements or 'understandings' which provide guidelines for management decision-making. Company policies might be, for example, to:

(i) Offer on-the-job training.

(ii) Promote managers from within the organisation, wherever possible, instead of recruiting managers to senior positions from 'outside'.

(iii) Encourage all recruits to certain jobs within the organisation to work towards obtaining an appropriate professional qualification.

(b) **Procedures** are a chronological sequence of required actions for performing a certain task. The manager personally might set certain work times, rules and procedures. For example, a manager in an accounts department might specify that bank reconciliations have to be completed by the end of each week. The advantages of procedures for routine work are as follows.

(i) **Efficiency.**

(ii) The absence of any need for the exercise of **discretion** in routine tasks.

(iii) **Familiarity**. Staff will find jobs easier to do when they are familiar with established procedures.

(iv) **Standardisation** of work. Certain aspects of the work done may be set by work analysts of the *technostructure.*

(v) **Continuity**. The work will be done the same way even when a different person starts in a job or takes over from the previous holder.

(vi) A written record of required procedures can be kept in a **procedures manual**.

(vii) They reduce the likelihood of **inter-departmental friction**.

(c) A **rule is a specific**, definite course of action that must be taken in a given situation. Unlike a procedure, it does not set out the sequence or chronology of events (but a procedure is a chronological sequence of rules). For example, the following are rules, but not procedures:

(i) Employees in department X are allowed 10 minutes exactly at the end of their shift for clearing up and cleaning their work-bench.

(ii) Employees with access to a telephone must not use the telephone for personal calls.

2 PRIORITISING AND WORK PLANNING 6/96

Exam focus point

In June 1996, you were asked to describe how an overstressed *individual* manager could cope with a heavy workload. You could have mentioned delegation (see Section 3 below) - otherwise you could have applied a common sense approach to time management and prioritisation.

In questions of this type, be sensitive to the role and position in the hierarchy of the main actors in the case study - they may not have the power to do things they want, so *realism* is important for such answers.

2.1 **Work planning** is the establishment of work methods and practices to ensure that predetermined objectives are efficiently met at all levels. Basic steps in work planning are as follows.

(a) The **establishment of priorities** (ie considering tasks in order of importance for the objective concerned), or at least assessing where the resources are most usefully spent.

(b) **Scheduling or timetabling tasks,** and allocating them to different individuals within appropriate time scales (for example, there will be continuous routine work, and arrangement for priority work with short-term deadlines).

(c) **Establishing checks and controls** to ensure that:

(i) priority deadlines are being met and work is not 'falling behind';
(ii) routine tasks are achieving their objectives.

(d) **Contingency plans for unscheduled events.** Nothing goes exactly according to plan, and one feature of good planning is to make arrangements for what should be done if a major upset were to occur, eg if the company's main computer were to break down, or if the major supplier of key raw materials were to go bust.

(e) **Co-ordinating the efforts of individuals.**

(f) **Reviewing and controlling performance.**

2.2 While steps *within* a single task may follow in a logical sequence that could be easily scheduled (eg the stages involved in filing procedures, writing an essay etc) a single task is seldom what is required of an individual in any sort of organisation. Some jobs (eg assembly line worker), are entirely routine, and can be performed one step at a time, but for most people, some kind of planning and judgement will be required.

Assessing where resources are most usefully spent

2.3 The decision as to where scarce resources are deployed might be taken in the strategic plan, if the firm is closely controlled. If, on the other hand, a manager (of a subsidiary company, or an office) is simply given a target, the manager will be responsible for allocating resources between:

(a) **Different routes** to achieve the same objective (eg to increase total profits, sell more, or cut costs etc).

(b) **Competing areas** where total resources are limited.

2.4 **ABC analysis (Pareto analysis)** divides items into three groups.

A	=	very important
B	=	fairly important
C	=	marginally important

(a) The assumption is that only a small proportion of items will be significant. For example a business might have 99 customers who each spend £10 per month and 1 customer who spends £100,000 per month. Pareto's Law assumes that, for sales, approximately 80% of sales volume is accounted for by 20% of the customers.

(b) This means that the manager will be able to:

(i) Concentrate scarce resources on the crucial 20%.

(ii) Devise policies and procedures for the remaining 80%, or to delegate.

Urgency

2.5 Some work is **essential** and has to get done fairly **promptly**: other work can wait a bit if necessary. For example, sending out invoices might be an essential daily task, whereas filing office copies of invoices can usually wait a few days. Essential work has a higher priority than other work.

2.6 A piece of work will be **high priority** in the following cases.

(a) **If it has to be completed by a certain time** (ie a deadline).

(b) **If other tasks depend on it:** if the preparation of a sales invoice, or notes for a meeting, depends on a particular file, the first task may be to send a request for it to the file registry.

(c) **If other people depend on it.** An item being given low priority by one individual or department (eg retrieval or reproduction of a particular document) may hold up the activities of others for whom the processing of the item is high priority.

(d) **If it is important.** There may be a clash of priorities between two urgent tasks, in which case relative consequences should be considered: if an important decision or action rests on a task (eg a report for senior management, or correction of an error in a large customer order) that task should take precedence over, say, the preparation of notes for a meeting, or processing a smaller order.

2.7 **Routine priorities,** or regular peak times (monthly issue of account statements, yearly tax returns etc) can be **planned ahead of time**, and other tasks postponed or redistributed around them.

2.8 **Non-routine** priorities occur when **unexpected demands** are made. Thus planning of work should cover routine scheduled peaks and contingency plans for unscheduled peaks and emergencies.

The timescale of work planning

2.9 Planning for individuals and organisations may be conducted over various 'ranges' of time: long-term, medium-term and short-term. The aids to personal planning which you may use or have contact with tend to allow for four basic time units: year, month, week and day.

Deadlines

2.10 A **deadline** is the end of the longest span of time which may be allotted to a task, ie the last acceptable date for completion. If a meeting is scheduled for a certain date, documents will have to be prepared for an appropriate time beforehand. Deadlines are important - failure to meet them has a 'knock-on' effect on other parts of the organisation, and on other tasks within an individual's duties.

2.11 Diary entries may be made on appropriate days (eg: - 'Production completed?' 'Payment received?' 'Bring forward file x' 'One week left for revision')

2.12 Deadlines and timescales can be incorporated into **network analysis**.

Methodical working

2.13 Employees should work methodically rather than plan each routine task afresh.

(a) Ensure that resources are available, in sufficient supply and good condition. This may involve setting up or adhering to procedures for stock control etc.

(b) Ensure that resources are to hand.

(c) Organise work in **batches**, while relevant files are to hand, machines switched on etc to save time spent in turning from one job to another.

(d) Work to plans, schedules, checklists etc.

(e) Taking advantage of work patterns.

(f) Follow up tasks - see them through.

- Checking on progress of an operation.
- Checking completion when the deadline is reached.
- Checking payments when they fall due.
- Retrieving files relevant to future discussions, meetings, correspondence.

Question 3

Choose a task or event that needs planning. On your own or in a group:

(a) make a checklist;
(b) re-arrange items in order of priority and time sequence;
(c) estimate the time for each activity and schedule it, working back from a deadline;
(d) prepare an action sheet;
(e) draw a chart with columns for time units, and rows for activities;
(f) decide what items may have to be 'brought forward' later and how.

3 PLANNING THE WORK OF YOUR STAFF

Scheduling

3.1 **Scheduling** is where priorities and deadlines are planned and controlled in practice. It timetables a logical sequence of tasks leading up to completion date.

(a) All personnel involved in a task must be given adequate **notice** of work schedules, and the schedules themselves should allow a **realistic time allocation** for each task.

(b) For a schedule laying out long-term operations (eg computerisation of a system, or move of premises) allowance will have to be made for unexpected events in the intervening time, and the timetable regularly revised.

(c) Schedules for individual activities or for major but predictable operations (stocktaking, annual returns, or, on a personal level, scheduling your Christmas shopping) should be easier to adhere closely to, especially if they are based on experience of standard operation times.

3.2 We have seen how a number of activities may have to be undertaken in sequence, with some depending on, or taking priority over others.

(a) **Activity scheduling** provides a list of necessary activities in the order in which they must be completed. You might use this to plan each day's work, or to set up standard procedures for jobs which you undertake regularly.

(b) **Time scheduling** adds to this the time scale for each activity, and is useful for setting deadlines for tasks. The time for each step is estimated. The total time for the task can then be calculated, allowing for some steps which may be undertaken simultaneously by different people or departments.

Work programmes and other aids to planning

3.3 From activity and time schedules, detailed **work programmes** can be designed for jobs which are carried out over a period of time. Some tasks will have to be started well before the deadline, others may be commenced immediately before, others will be done on the day itself. Organising a meeting, for example, may include the following.

(a) Booking accommodation two months before.
(b) Retrieving relevant files one week before.
(c) Preparing and circulating an agenda 2-3 days before.
(d) Checking conference room layout the day before.
(e) Taking minutes on the day.

The same applies to stock ordering in advance of production (based on a schedule of known delivery times), preparing correspondence in advance of posting etc.

3.4 Once time scales are known and final deadlines set, it is possible to produce **job cards, route cards** and **action sheets**.

	Activity	*Days before*	*Date*	*Begun*	*Completed*
1	Request file	6	3.9		
2	Draft report	5	4.9		
3	Type report	3	6.9		
4	Approve report	1	8.9		
5	Signature	1	8.9		
6	Internal messenger	same day	9.9		

3.5 Longer-term schedules may be conveniently judged at a glance using charts, pegboards or year planners, holiday planners, sales targets etc. These can be used to show lengths of time and the relationship between various tasks or timetabled events.

3.6 You might schedule your study or work by means of an action sheet, with start and end times or dates for each part of a deadlined task. You are more likely, however, to keep a general 'schedule' of your routine and non-routine duties, appointments and plans in the form of a *timetable or diary*. Such planning aids are designed to:

(a) Remind people of key dates and times.
(b) Remind you to make necessary advance preparations;
(c) Help you allocate your time: ie no 25-hour days, clashing appointments etc.

Case example

This job can be performed by software such as Microsoft Outlook which makes it possible to book meetings with other people on the network.

Work allocation

3.7 It will be the job of those in authority - at organisational or departmental level - to divide duties and allocate them to available staff and machinery: departmental managers will have an overall understanding of the nature and volume of work to be accomplished, and the resources at their command.

3.8 Planning is essential in this division of labour, because although there are some obvious allocations for example of specialist tasks to specialists (computer programmers, engineering draughtsmen etc), others may be more complicated.

(a) Functions such as filing and reprography may not be centralised, and may not have the attention of a dedicated employee. A small volume of filing may not require a filing clerk for the department: who will do the work, and will it interfere with their other duties?

(b) Peak periods in some tasks may necessitate re-distribution of staff to cope with the work load.

(c) Status and staff attitudes must be considered. Flexibility in reassigning people from one job to another or varying the work they do may be hampered by an employee's perception of his or her own status.

(d) Planning should allow for flexibility in the event of an employee proving unfit for a task, or more able than his present tasks indicate.

(e) Efforts will have to be co-ordinated so that all those involved in a process (eg sales orders) work together as a team or a number of groups.

Delegation of authority

3.9 Managers must delegate some authority because:

(a) There are physical and mental **limitations** to the work load of any individual or group in authority.

(b) Routine or less important decisions are therefore **passed 'down the line'** to subordinates, and the superior is free to concentrate on the more important aspects of the work.

(c) The increasing size and complexity of organisations calls for **specialisation**, both managerial and technical.

3.10 However, by delegating authority to subordinates, the superior takes on the extra tasks of calling the subordinates to account for their decisions and performance, and also of co-ordinating the efforts of different subordinates.

3.11 **Effective delegation**

(a) **Specify the expected performance levels** (the expected results) of the subordinate. These should be fully understood and accepted by the subordinate.

(b) **Assign tasks to the subordinate** who should agree to do them.

(c) **Allocate resources to the subordinate** to enable him to carry out his tasks at the expected level of performance, and authority should be delegated to enable the subordinate to do this job.

(d) **Hold the subordinate responsible** for results obtained (because ultimate responsibility remains with the superior).

(e) Bear in mind the **subordinate's ability and experience**, since it is highly damaging to allocate tasks beyond a subordinate's capabilities;

(f) Maintain **frequent contact** to review the progress made.

Problems of delegation

3.12 In practice, many managers are reluctant to delegate and attempt to do many routine matters themselves in addition to their more important duties. Some common reasons for this are listed below.

(a) **No trust**. A manager may feel that his subordinate will carry out the work badly, and that he himself will ultimately be held responsible for his subordinate's errors.

(b) **Isolation**. Some managers believe that they would lose touch with their department (both work-load and staff) unless they retain some routine tasks.

(c) **Fear**. Seniors are often unwilling to admit that subordinates have developed to the extent that they could perform some of the manager's duties.

3.13 Handy writes of a **'trust-control dilemma'** in a superior-subordinate relationship, in which the sum of trust + control is a constant amount:

$$T + C = Y$$

where T = the trust the superior has in the subordinate, and the trust which the subordinate feels the superior has in him

C = the degree of control exercised by the superior over the subordinate

Y = a constant, unchanging value

Any increase in C leads to an equal decrease in T; that is, if the superior retains more 'control' or authority, the subordinate will immediately recognise that he is being trusted less. If the superior wishes to show more trust in the subordinate, he can only do so by reducing C, that is by delegating more authority.

3.14 **Overcoming the reluctance of managers to delegate**

(a) **Select subordinates of the right 'quality'**, so that superiors will be prepared to trust them more.

(b) Have a system of **open communications**, in which the superior and subordinates freely interchange ideas and information.

(c) **Establish a system of control**. Superiors are reluctant to delegate authority because they retain absolute responsibility for the performance of their subordinates. If an efficient control system is in operation, responsibility and accountability will be monitored at all levels of the management hierarchy, and the 'dangers' of relinquishing authority and control to subordinates are significantly lessened.

(d) **Reward effective delegation** by superiors and the efficient assumption of authority by subordinates. Rewards may be given in terms of pay, promotion, status, official approval etc.

Question 2

How is delegation managed at your work place? How good a delegator are you (or your boss)?

4 COMMUNICATION AND INFORMATION

4.1 Communication in an organisation can serve a number of functions.

- Give information
- Instruction
- Persuasion
- Reinforcement (by encouragement) of existing behaviour
- Establishing relationships
- Publicising needs and requirements

4.2 **Good information** will have the following qualities.

(a) **Relevance to a user's needs**

  (i) **Identifying the user**
  (ii) **Getting the purpose right**
  (iii) **Getting the volume right**

(b) **Accuracy for the user's needs.**

(c) **Inspiring the user's confidence.**

(d) **Timeliness.** Information must be readily available within the time period which makes it useful: ie it must be in the right place at the right time.

(e) **Appropriately communicated.** Information will lose its value if it is not clearly communicated to the user in a suitable format and through a suitable medium.

(f) **Cost effective.** Good information should not cost more than it is worth.

4.3 Information as a concept should not be reduced to formal reporting and official correspondence.

(a) **Hard information.** Formal information is only one segment of information that is relevant.

(b) **Soft information**, on the other hand, refers to mere **subjective** and less tangible aspects of a situation. For example, in warfare, an army's 'morale' is held to be an important contributory factor - all other things being equal - to its success. A statement that 'morale' is high or low is important information, even though it cannot be realistically quantified. Or again, an assessment of another person's *character* - again, hard to quantify - can be a factor in negotiations

The importance of communication in organisations

4.4 **The roles of communication in an organisation**

(a) **Internal.** Providing **information for the planning, co-ordination and control** activities of management.

(b) **External.** Providing information about the organisation and its services (or as an integral part of its services) to people in the outside world.

(c) **Learning.** Encouraging the formulation, swapping and testing of **ideas**.

(d) **Co-ordination** of the activities of all the interdependent sub-systems of the organisation, so that the overall objectives of the organisation are met. Co-ordinatory mechanisms such as committees and project teams depend on communication.

(e) **Fulfilling the needs of employees** for information about their task, the standards expected of them and how their performance measures up to standard. Information is important for learning and development, because 'feedback' is necessary for the change or correction of behaviour.

(f) Creating, developing and maintaining **interpersonal relations** between subordinates, supervisors, peers and also customers and suppliers.

(g) Ensuring effective **linkages** between activities in the **value chain.**

4.5 Effective communication is a two-way process, perhaps best expressed as a cycle. A basic interpretation of the process of communication might be as follows.

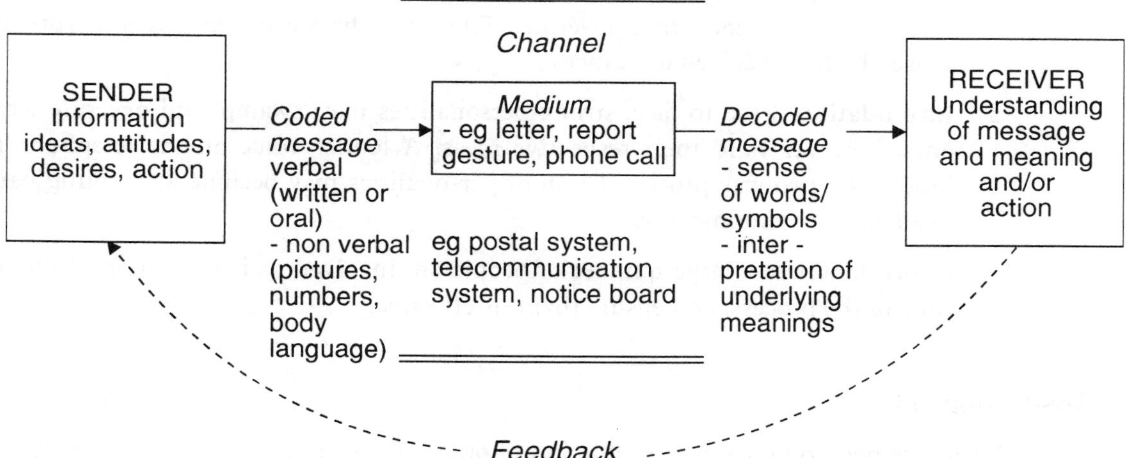

4.6 As illustrated in the above diagram, it is **feedback** that makes communication a two-way process rather than a series of send-receive events. Failure to seek or offer feedback, or ignoring feedback offered, is one of the major problems in communication.

4.7 Feedback takes various forms. In a conversation it can be immediate (eg the changed expression on a person's face). In business it might be delayed.

5 ORAL AND ELECTRONIC COMMUNICATIONS

5.1 **Oral communication** means communication by speech, or word of mouth. Face to face oral media include:

- Conversations
- Interviews
- Meetings
- Public addresses or briefings.

5.2 **Advantages of oral communication**

(a) **Swift and direct**

(b) **Suitable for interactive communication,** the exchange of ideas, opinions, attitudes. Decisions can be arrived at and action taken more swiftly than with a lengthy correspondence, say. All parties present are able to contribute.

(c) **Flexibility**: circumstances and attitudes can be changed more easily, especially since the personality, voice and manner of the parties involved can be employed in persuasion and motivation.

(d) **Instant feedback** is obtainable to overcome doubts or misunderstandings.

(e) **Body language.** Verbal meaning may be reinforced and feedback given by facial expression or bodily gesture.

(f) **Sensitive handling of difficult messages** involving bad news, a reprimand or 'clear the air' discussion.

5.3 **Disadvantages of oral communication**

(a) **Technical noise** (background sounds or bad telephone lines) can interfere with effective transmission.

(b) **Memory is untrustworthy and perceptions differ**. A written confirmation and record of an oral event will be required.

(c) **Less time** is usually available for planning the message's general content, let alone the exact wording. Inferior decisions may be made, because they had to be thought through 'on the spot' in a meeting. Time may be wasted and misinterpretation caused by ill-conceived utterances.

(d) **Intimidation.** Face to face, strong personalities may 'swamp' and overrule weaker ones, however valid their respective ideas. A louder voice on the telephone may hinder the two-way process. Clash of personalities may become a crippling barrier to effective communication.

(e) **Control.** Where a large number of people are involved, it is even more difficult to control the process, and ensure that it is effective.

Body language

5.4 Where we position ourselves in relation to other people, our tone of voice, gestures and facial expressions all communicate something, either deliberately or unconsciously.

5.5 **Control and use of body language** is needed to:

(a) Provide an appropriate 'physical' feedback to the sender of a message (a yawn, applause)

(b) Create a desired impression

(c) Establish a desired atmosphere or conditions (friendly smile)

(d) Reinforce our spoken messages with appropriate indications of how our interest, seriousness and feelings are engaged.

5.6 **Reading other people's body language** helps you to:

(a) Receive **feedback** from a listener and modify the message accordingly.

(b) Recognise people's **real feelings** when their words are constrained by formalities.

(c) Recognise **existing or potential personal problems**.

(d) 'Read' situations in order to modify our own communication and response strategy.

Listening

5.7 **Listening** in the communications model is about **decoding** and **receiving** information. Listening carries much of the burden of communication.

5.8 Many people believe that listening is a natural instinct, rather than a **skill** which can be taught and developed. Effective listening:

(a) Encourages the **sender** to listen effectively to **your** reply.

(b) Reduces the effect of 'noise'.

(c) Resolves problems by encouraging understanding from someone else's viewpoint.

5.9 **Advice for good listening**

(a) **Prepare yourself to listen**. In other words, put yourself in the right frame of mind (ie a readiness to maintain attention). In meetings, be prepared to grasp the main concepts.

(b) **Try to be interested**. Make an effort to analyse the message for its relevance.

(c) **Keep an open mind**. Your own beliefs and prejudices can get in the way of what the other person is actually saying. To understand the message, you must listen exactly to what is being said.

(d) **Keep an ear open for the main ideas**. An awareness of how people generally structure their speech can help the process of understanding. Be able to distinguish between the 'gist' of the argument and supporting evidence.

(e) **Listen critically**. This means trying to assess what the person is saying by identifying any **assumptions**, omissions and biases.

(f) **Avoid distraction**. People have a natural attention curve, high at the beginning and end of an oral message, but sloping off in the middle.

(g) **Take notes,** although note taking can be distracting.

(h) **Wait before interrupting.**

Electronic communication

5.10 Electronic communication imitates some of the features of written communication, and some of the features of oral or face-to-face communication.

Video-conferencing

5.11 Video conferencing has grown in popularity since the Gulf War and with the decreasing cost of technology compared to the cost and inconvenience of flying. It is a meeting conducted over long distance. Each participant shares a room, and interacts with a video broadcast image of the other participants.

Email

5.12 *Electronic mail (EMail)* can be both formal and interactive.

(a) E-mail systems depend on computers being connected with each other.

(b) A person can send a message to another person's **mailbox** (a piece of computer memory) for the recipient to access when convenient.

(c) E-mail is less formal than written memos, but more formal than phone calls. It is very convenient, hence its popularity. However, email can be abused easily so there should be guidelines for its use.

Voice mail

5.13 **Voice mail** is a means of leaving spoken memos, for someone to listen to later. It can be useful as an extension of **paging**, so that a person can leave detailed messages for someone who is absent without the inconvenience of having to write a memorandum or the hazard of leaving a message.

6 WRITTEN COMMUNICATIONS

6.1 A verbal agreement is commonly supplemented by written confirmation - the written communication serves as a permanent formal record of what passed in what might have been a relatively informal manner (eg in a telephone conversation).

6.2 **Advantages of written messages**

(a) They provide a **permanent record** of a transaction or agreement, for confirmation and recollection of details. Evidence may also be necessary in legal affairs.

(b) They provide **confirmation** and clarification of verbal messages, again in case evidence should be needed, but also as an aid to memory.

(c) They are **easily duplicated** and sent out to numerous recipients: this ensures that information, operating instructions etc will be consistent.

(d) They are capable of **relaying complex ideas**, aided by suitable layout and the permanence of the record which allows the recipient to pore over it at length if necessary.

(e) They can be **stored** and later retrieved for reference and analysis as required.

6.3 **Disadvantages of written messages**

(a) **Time**. A written message can take time to produce, and to send (eg by post), if expensive technology is beyond the user's reach. Instant feedback is not available, and so errors in interpretation may not be corrected immediately. Because of the time factor, swift 'interactive' exchanges of opinion, attitude etc are impossible.

(b) **Inflexibility**. Once sent, the message cannot immediately be altered or amended, even though circumstances change, errors are discovered etc. Written communication also tends to come across as formal and impersonal, so in situations requiring greater sensitivity or persuasion, the personal presence or voice of the sender may be more effective.

Reports

6.4 There will be variety in the format and style of a report, depending on what sort of report it is.

(a) **Formal or informal.** Reports can be huge documents with sections, subsections, paras, subparas, indices, appendices etc. A single sheet ordinary memorandum may be sufficient in many contexts. Emphasis should always be placed on the content of the report and its *organisation* - a simple report should not have a complex structure, and *vice versa*.

(b) **Routine** (produced at regular intervals eg budgetary control reports, sales reports or progress reports), **occasional** (eg an accident report or disciplinary report) or specially commissioned for **one-off** planning and decision-making (eg a market research report, or a report on a proposed merger or particular issue).

(c) **Professional** or for a **wider audience** of expert readers. A report prepared for a fellow specialist (eg on issues in accounting), will require a different tone and vocabulary to an article for a club magazine with a non-specialist readership.

6.5 Reports are meant to be **useful**. A business report might be used as:

(a) A permanent record and source of reference

(b) A management tool - a source of information prepared in order to assist in management **decision-making.**

6.6 **Contents of a report**

(a) **Information** retrieved from files or other sources as a basis for management activity.

(b) **Narrative or description** eg of one-off events or procedures, such as a takeover target or the installation of new equipment.

(c) **Analysis** of data and information to render it more useful.

(d) **Evaluation and recommendation,** directly assisting in the decision-making process.

6.7 **Different types of information may be presented in a report.** The value of recognising these different types of information is that it can help to make clear what a report writer is trying to say.

(a) **Descriptive or factual information**. Objective facts and logical, unbiased inferences from them. ('These are the facts'.)

(c) **Instructive information**. This tells the report user how to do something, or what to do. ('This is what we should do'.)

(b) **Dialectical information**. This consists of opinions and ideas, with reasons for why these opinions and ideas have been reached. ('This is what the facts mean'.)

6.8 Report writing is discussed in Section 8 ('Presenting information') of this chapter.

7 OBTAINING AND SUMMARISING INFORMATION 12/94

7.1 Information can be acquired from a number of sources. Sometimes it has to be hunted out; sometimes it is easily available; and sometimes it has to be 'created' from a mass of data, or by research.

Primary or oral sources

7.2 **Primary sources** are the fount of data. If your primary source is a person, rather than a file, you need to:

(a) Assess **who** you need to know (the persons with both the information and the authority to disclose it).

(b) **Persuade** them to part with information or spend time helping you out. The way in which you will obtain information will be influenced by the culture and structure of the organisation.

7.3 These problems can be particularly acute if you are **communicating up the organisation hierarchy**, especially if you are requesting information from another department. You may have to:

(a) Draft a memo requesting the information, and get your superior to sign it.

(b) Get your boss to contact his or her opposite number in the department to ensure that the request will be dealt with.

7.4 In this case it is important that you know:

(a) What questions to ask.

(b) Any 'follow up' questions.

(c) The context and history of the issue (eg if it involves major departmental conflicts).

(d) Any assumptions the information source will have as to what you want to hear.

(e) What your information source *wants* you to hear (in other words, the likely 'spin' or bias impacted to the data).

(f) How to minimise the inconvenience to the other party.

7.5 To check your understanding of the results, it might be necessary to summarise what the person has said, by repeating some of the results or rephrasing slightly. ('So, what you're really saying is ...' .) In other words you should practise some of the oral communication and listening skills identified earlier in this chapter.

7.6 Recording this spoken information can be achieved using a number of different media including notebooks, files, cards and tape recording (which facilitates easy note taking later).

Secondary

7.7 **Secondary sources** of information include reports and articles from within and outside the company. Of increasing value might be other firms' Internet sites. Use of the **World Wide Web** enables easier access to these sites. Sometimes these external sources are sufficient in themselves to provide the data needed. In other cases, they provide essential background material to any brief.

Summarising

7.8 Summarising information, so that its principal features are recorded, is another skill.

(a) **An outline in note form** will be hard for **another** person to understand. Eventually, as the moment it describes loses the vividness of immediate memory, the outline will be hard even for the writer to understand.

(b) **A précis or paragraph summary** is thus important.

(i) **Listen carefully to speeches.** Go through the written material twice: skim-reading first of all helps retention.

(ii) **Take outline notes** or jottings or underline the important facts.

(iii) From notes, write a **rough draft**. Ignore the original source, so as not to quote from it.

(iv) **Check the summary** against the notes and the original to ensure you have:

- Included all the essential points.
- Excluded inessential points (examples, illustrations, quotations).
- Not changed the author's meaning.
- Not introduced any ideas of your own.

(v) The final written précis should be:

- Shorter than the original.
- Concisely written.
- Structured in the same order as the original.
- Edited.

7.9 When writing material from scratch or which summarises or uses a number of secondary sources it you should:

(a) Plan ahead.

(b) Analyse the material in total.

(c) Classify it into logical groups.

(d) Put these 'groups' into a logical order (eg of time, place, importance, complexity, familiarity, cause and effect, the relationship each item has to the overall topic).

8 PRESENTING INFORMATION

8.1 The above considerations naturally inform the whole process of **report writing**. This process involves the following steps, which we shall discuss in turn.

(a) Planning the report
(b) Formatting the report
(c) Report style

Planning the report

8.2 Only people with extremely ordered minds should attempt to prepare a report without planning it first.

8.3 **Factors to consider when planning a report**

(a) Who is the user?
(b) What type of report will be most useful to him/her?
(c) What exactly does he/she need to know, and for what purpose?
(d) How much information is required, how quickly and at what cost?
(e) Do judgements, recommendations etc need to be given, or just information?

8.4 The report plan should indicate:

(a) The **basic objective** of the report - providing the required information in the necessary way. A superior who asks for a 'one off' report should make clear what he/she expects. In the case of routine reports, their purpose and how they should be used ought to be specified in a procedures manual.

(b) The **reasoning required** in the report - particularly if the report is to contain analysis of facts, the line of reasoning should be clear and any assumptions should be stated.

(c) The **sources of information** and techniques used.

(d) The **type of conclusion** required - 'more information needed', 'we can do this, this or this' or 'we must do this'.

(e) The **structure of the report** - including headings, subheadings, tables, figures and appendices.

The report writer and the report user

8.5 The report writer has to communicate information in an **unbiased way**. The report writer knows more about the subject matter of the report than the report user. This information should be communicated impartially, so that the report user can make his/her own judgements. Thus:

(a) Any **assumptions**, evaluations and recommendations by the report writer should be clearly 'signalled' as such.

(b) Points should not be **over-weighted** (or omitted as irrelevant) without honest evaluation of the objectivity of the selection.

(c) Facts and findings should be **balanced** against each other.

(d) A firm **conclusion** should, if possible, be reached. It should be clear how and why it was reached.

8.6 The **needs and abilities of the report user** should be recognised by the report writer.

(a) **Jargon**, technical terms and specialist knowledge should be kept at the level of the user's comprehension.

(b) Simple vocabulary, sentence and paragraph structures should be used for clarity (although the user should not thereby be patronised).

(c) The type and level of **detail** should be kept to what is relevant for the user.

Formatting formal and informal reports

8.7 When a **formal request** is made by a superior for a report to be prepared, eg in a formally worded memorandum or letter, the format and style of the report will obviously have to be formal as well: it will be strictly schematic, using impersonal constructions and avoiding emotive or colloquial expressions.

(a) **Long formal reports** are extensive and high-level. They may run to hundreds of pages and may contain a list of **contents** and index; **summary of findings** (to give the reader an initial idea), strict **sectionalisation** and referencing (to help the reader to 'dip in' to particular points as necessary), supporting **appendices** and list of **sources** (carrying subsidiary material, in order to keep the body of the report as brief as possible) etc.

(b) The **short formal report** is used in formal contexts eg middle management reporting to senior. It should be laid out according to certain basic guidelines. It will be split into logical sections, each referenced and headed appropriately.

8.8 An **informal request** for a report - 'Can you jot down a few ideas for me about ...' or 'Let me know what happens, will you?' - will result in an informal report, in which the structure will be less rigid, and the style slightly more personal (depending on the relationship perceived to exist between the writer and user).

8.9 The **short informal report** is used for less complex and lower level information. You might be asked to prepare such a report for your own direct boss.

8.10 In informal reporting situations within an organisation, the 'short informal report' may well be presented in A4 **memorandum format**, which incorporates title headings and can thereafter be laid out at the writer's discretion.

Case example

Procter and Gamble have a rule that no memo should be more than one side of A4 in length.

Report style

8.11 There are certain stylistic requirements in the writing of reports, formal or informal.

(a) **Objectivity and balance**. Even in a report designed to persuade as well as inform, subjective value-judgements and emotions should be kept out of the content and style as far as possible: bias, if recognised, can undermine the credibility of the report and its recommendations.

   (i) Avoid emotional or otherwise loaded words.

   (ii) Use **impersonal constructions**, rather than 'I', 'we' etc, which carry personal and possibly subjective associations. In other words, first person subjects should be replaced with third person.

   (iii) Avoid colloquialisms and abbreviated forms in formal written English. ('I've', 'don't' etc should be replaced by 'I have' and 'do not'.)

(b) **Ease of understanding**

   (i) Avoid technical language and complex sentence structures for non-technical users.

   (ii) Organise the material logically.

   (iii) Signal or highlight relevant themes by appropriate headings or highlighted for easy scanning.

   (iv) Use the layout of the report to display data clearly and attractively. Figures and diagrams should be used with discretion, highlighting key figures where appropriate.

Writing style

8.12 Style is a vital part of any written communication.

(a) **Reason**. What is to be accomplished and what response is required? If you are applying for a job, for example, your style will need to demonstrate good formal language skills. You will need to sound quietly confident, but not arrogant; willing, even eager, but not desperate; polite and intelligent.

(b) **Recipient**. What type of person is the report aimed at and what is his or her reaction likely to be if the message is expressed in a certain way?

(i) An information leaflet or circular letter to the general public has an undefinable audience. The document's written style should be simple and free from jargon, assumptions etc, yet remain convincing and informative.

(ii) An open letter to employees for a notice board or general circulation has a known audience. The style, depending on the document's purpose, could be more 'friendly' and contain jargon or abbreviations commonly used in the organisation etc.

8.13 Specific **factors about the recipient** which you need to take into account.

(a) **Age.** People's attitudes vary with age and experience.

(b) **Culture**. The personal and corporate background and culture of the recipient may have to be taken into account.

(c) **Education**. Differences in practical, technical and academic education will mean that communication should be expressed as simply and clearly as possible without patronising the recipient.

(d) **Work environment**. People whose jobs are highly specialised - in finance, as much as in medicine or science - often have a language of their own. It is important to recognise when technical language or 'jargon' is being used which the recipient is unlikely to know.

(e) **Context in which document is received.** Obviously the sender has no control over the situation prevailing when the document is received, but as far as possible it should be taken into account. When writing or reporting to a senior, busy person the language and level of detail should be kept to the minimum so that the content is absorbed and understood quickly. Context also has an impact on the level of formality of the document.

(f) **Relationship**. The vocabulary and tone will vary depending on the relationship between sender and recipient - they may be distant acquaintances, trusted colleagues, good friends etc. The degree of warmth and familiarity will depend on this - in a communication between superior and subordinate there will be more formality and distance than in one between two colleagues at the same level.

8.14 From the above analysis, you will see that in written English, style involves conscious choices about the following.

(a) **Vocabulary:** which words should be used (eg colloquialisms or formal)?

(b) **Syntax:** what kind of sentence should be constructed? Simple structures are preferred in business correspondence. Varying structures adds interest.

(c) **Tone:** what reaction is wanted (eg warm and friendly, aloof etc)?

8.15 **Writing reports in the exam: some guidelines**

(a) Remember: **easy marks might be available for presentation.**

(b) **Relate the sections of your report to the structure of the exam question** - examiners find it easier to mark that way.

(c) Be prepared to **state the obvious.**

(d) Some matters can be left to the end - look at the suggested structure offered below.

To: [Name(s)/position(s) of recipients]
From: [Sender - but NEVER use your own name in an exam]
Date:
Subject: [Effectively this will be the title of your report, such as: *Communication Media in A Ltd*]

Contents: [Here you outline the structure of the report. It should help you plan, but if pressed for time, leave until the end. If the worst comes to the worst, leave it out. This is optional, but looks nice. Here is an example.]

1 Terms of reference and work undertaken
2 Executive summary
3 Organisational problems
4 Operational issues
5 Management issues
6 Conclusion and recommendations

1 *Terms of reference and work undertaken*

1.1 [Here is laid out the scope and purpose of the report: what is to be investigated; what information is required, whether recommendations should be made. In the exam, the terms of reference may be given in the question - so don't waste time repeating it - leave this to the end.]

1.2 [You might also describe the work you did, how you collected the data, documents consulted, visits made etc. This gives some indication of the scope of the work that you did, whether it was a detailed investigation or a cursory glance. This information might go in a separate section of a report. Only include it if specifically asked by the question. All the information has been given in the case study.]

2 Executive summary

2.1 [Here you might add a brief summary of your findings and recommendations. If you have run out of time to discuss certain issues fully, at least you can note them here, to show the examiner you have considered them.]

3 [Findings]

3.1 [The remaining sections in the report will depend on the question. if we had followed the table of contents, this section would have been Section 3.]

3.2 [You might like to use numbered paragraphs like this, with subparagraphs organised perhaps like the BPP Study Text. If you end up with too many subparagraphs, the overall structure probably needs redesigning.]

3.3 [The content in this and the following sections should be complete, but concise, and clearly structured in chronological order, order of importance or any other logical relationship.]

4 [More findings]

5 [More findings]

6 Conclusion and recommendations

6.1 [This section allows for a summary of main findings. However, you may not have time for a summary in the exam, but you should at least try to indicate their implications.]

6.2 [If you are required to make recommendations, and not all questions will ask for these, they could come here, referenced, if necessary, to the findings in the earlier section. The recommendations will allow the recipient to make a decision as necessary.]

Oral presentation — 6/94

8.16 Often the accountant has to present information of a financial nature to other financial managers or to managers without an accountant's technical expertise.

8.17 Oral presentation requires a **tighter editing** of material than in a written report. (After all, listeners cannot glance back to earlier notes.) It is also the case that, in a given time, **less information** can be conveyed orally than in a written document.

8.18 **Advantages of oral presentations**

(a) The presentation can be **tailored precisely** to the audience, with the presenter increasing or decreasing speed as appropriate.

(b) It is sometimes **easier to explain** items orally, with the use of suitable graphic assistance.

(c) A lecture can be '**interactive**' in the way that a report is not. In other words the presenter can be asked to say things in 'another way'.

8.19 **Skills in successful oral presentation**

(a) **Clear diction**. Mumbling can make it hard to be heard, and impede the message.

(b) The **material must be mastered** before the lecture. There is little point in simply reading off cards.

(c) It helps occasionally to make **eye-contact** with the listeners.

(d) Complex points should be **recapitulated** in a number of ways.

(e) **Objections should be anticipated** ('if you're wondering why X = Y, I'll come to that in a few moments'), otherwise listeners will be distracted.

8.20 **Use of visual aids**

(a) **Overhead projectors** (eg for graphs, diagrams). Slides can be prepared for these, or alternatively they can be used as a sort of 'blackboard' (eg to write the process of a calculation).

(b) **Slide projectors.** In many corporate presentations (eg at a company's Annual General Meeting) these are used to highlight certain key points.

(c) **Videos** can be used to support a presentation. These allow visual information from outside sites to be brought in to the hall, interviews with third parties to be presented and so forth.

(d) PCs can be used in the presentation. Microsoft Powerpoint is designed for this purpose.

(e) Flipcharts can be used for diagrams, lists etc.

The art of persuasion

8.21 Those most adept at persuasion tend to be sales people whose job is to convince a perhaps sceptical audience to part with money. But even in normal non-selling meetings, their skills can be useful.

8.22 The art of persuasion consists of a number of basic rules.

(a) **Understand the other party's point** of view. In a selling situation this means:

(i) Not just extolling the virtues of a product.
(ii) Detailing how exactly it will satisfy the customer's needs.

(b) **Never underestimate the effect of your own personal style** on the audience. Although 'good listeners' will make an effort to listen to what you have to say, much of what you say will be judged by your appearance and posture.

(c) **Anticipate objections.** If you analyse the case you are trying to make, you can make its strengths seem stronger than they really are, and the weaknesses less so.

(d) **Questions and comments** from the audience, even hostile ones, **are better than silence**. They are feedback information. They might indicate that your message has failed to get across.

(e) Persuasion sometimes can involve **rephrasing your case** in the language of the other party.

9 BRAINWORKS PLC UPDATE

Questions can be found in the Introduction box at the beginning of this chapter.

9.1 *Question 1.* The recruitment consultants in the office face an unpredictable workload, as they have to fit in interviews at odd times for their clients. They cannot plan far ahead. There may be seasonal peaks (eg after university graduation). Scheduling and planning are relevant to the job.

9.2 *Question 2.* BW's staff need to be good listeners - as they will spend a lot of time interviewing - and good talkers to convince their business clients that they have the right candidates.

9.3 *Question 3.* At the very least, a senior member of staff should offer a written apology. A suitable gift (eg a bottle of champagne) might help.

Chapter roundup

- **Work objectives** can be achieved through the establishment of policies and procedures.
- **Work planning** involves establishing priorities, scheduling and resource allocation. Work programmes and activity schedules are useful in the planning of human resources.
- Managers must plan their own time, so that the firm gains most benefit from it.
- **Information** can be **hard** (facts, statistics) or **soft** (feelings, attitudes). Soft information can be useful in interpersonal situations.
- **Good information** should be relevant, correct, timely and cost effective.
- **Communication** is essential in planning and controlling operations and in co-ordinating them. It is also necessary in influencing and persuading people.
- **Oral communication** has the advantages of immediacy. However, memory and interpersonal factors make it much more susceptible to 'noise' not related to the issue discussed. Good listening skills are vital for successful oral communication.
- **Written communications** have the value of permanence and clarity, but are sometimes inflexible.
- Information in a report can be descriptive, instructive and dialectical. **All reports should be written with the user in mind.**

Quick quiz

1 What are the components of a supervisory job? (see para 1.1)
2 Distinguish between policies and procedures. (1.4)
3 Describe work planning. (2.1)
4 When will high priority be given to a piece of work? (2.6)
5 Distinguish between time scheduling and activity scheduling. (3.2)
6 Why do managers fail to delegate? (3.12)
7 What is good information? (4.2)
8 What role does communication play in organisations? (4.4)
9 What are the advantages of oral communication? (5.2)
10 What are the advantages of written communication? (6.3)
11 What types of information are presented in a report? (6.7)
12 Describe an approach to summarising information. (7.8)
13 What factors about the recipient should you take into account when drafting a report? (8.13)
14 What are the advantages of oral presentations? (8.18)

Question to try	Level	Marks	Time
17	Exam standard	25	45 mins

Part D
Maintaining competitive advantage

Chapter 14

MARKETING CONCEPTS

Chapter topic list		Syllabus reference
1	The marketing concept	2(d)(i)
2	The marketing orientated organisation	1(c)(vii), 2(d)(i)
3	Marketing and non profit making organisations	2(d)(i)
4	Identifying market trends	1(b)(ii), 2(d)(i)
5	Segmenting the market	2(d)(ii)
6	Buyer behaviour	2(d)(ii)
7	Marketing research	2(d)(ii)
8	Brainworks plc update	

Introduction

Although **marketing** in many organisations is synonymous with advertising, the **marketing concept** in an organisation requires the identification and satisfaction of customer needs at a profit. Awareness of the customer has to filter back through the value chain to the **whole organisation**.

Analysing what customers require is the essential feature of marketing. The role of market **segmentation** can enable a firm to pursue focus strategies. Marketers also need to understand how **buying decisions** are actually taken. **Marketing research** can identify likely segments, as well as suggest ideas for possible product differentiation.

Brainworks plc

1 What are the problems in applying the marketing concept in BW?

2 What do you consider the value of BW's approach to market segmentation?

1 THE MARKETING CONCEPT 12/95, 6/96

KEY TERM

Marketing is 'the management process which identifies, anticipates and supplies customer requirements efficiently and profitably' (The Chartered Institute of Marketing).

1.1 Marketing thus involves two stages: **analysis** of customer needs, and **satisfaction** of them.

1.2 The marketing process should therefore **begin with the customer**.

(a) **Identify customers' needs** and wants.

(b) **Anticipate changes** in these needs and wants.

(c) **Satisfy the customer's needs** and wants with products or services offered on the market at a price the customer is prepared to pay.

If we add that the provision of goods and services should be done by making efficient use of a firm's resources in order to make a profit, this 'customer orientation' in the marketing process is apparent in the definition in paragraph 1.1(a) above.

1.3 Companies must make a distinction between the **customer** and the **consumer or user**.

KEY TERMS

(a) The **customer** is the person or organisation *buying* the product or service.

(b) The **consumer** or **user** is the person who receives the benefit of the product or service, and the product is not commercially processed any further.

For example, within a household, the **customer** for cat food is the cat's owner. However, the **consumer** of the cat food will be the cat (and no-one else we hope!).

Marketing philosophies

1.4 Some firms may be **product orientated**, others production orientated and yet others **sales orientated**, although a firm should be **marketing orientated** to be successful in the longer term.

Stage	Philosophy	Emphasis
Stage 1: scarcity Demand exceeds supply: a seller's market	Managers are centred on needs of operations: **production orientated**.	The organisation could grow be more successful by **producing more**, so managers concentrate on processes, operations, seeking ways to make more effective use of inputs: an inward looking focus.
Stage 2: affluence Output and new competitors increase. Demand and supply become more equal.	Sales orientated: managers seek to ensure their output is taken up by available customers. A **sales orientation.**	Production is now fine - but there are no longer queues of unsatisfied customers. Managers now turn their attention to advertising and selling to 'push' finished goods at customers
Stage 3: consumer societies Output continues to grow. Supply exceeds demand - a buyer's market	To survive, managers must be sure they satisfy customer needs. A **marketing orientation.**	Emphasis on **market research** to identify and anticipate customer needs before putting scarce resources into production. The **customer now comes before the production** process. Managers are now externally focused.

Stage 4: the future?

Environmental and quality concerns. Emphasis on quality not quantity, the wider interests of society *not* just satisfaction of the individual.	Legal and consumer pressures force firms to consider the long run interest of customers and society *not* just short term mutually profitable exchange. Kotler's *Human Orientation*, or the *societal marketing concept.*	Emphasis becomes broader, encompassing environmental issues and the ethics of business activities. Now managers have needs of society and the customer to satisfy.

The marketing concept

KEY TERM

The **marketing concept** may be defined as 'a management orientation or outlook, that accepts that the key task of the organisation is to determine the needs, wants and values of a target market and to adapt the organisation to delivering the desired satisfaction more effectively and efficiently than its competitors'.

Marketing orientation *Other orientations*

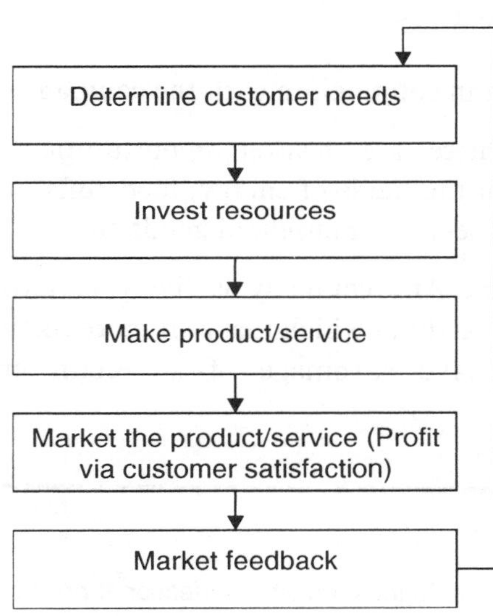

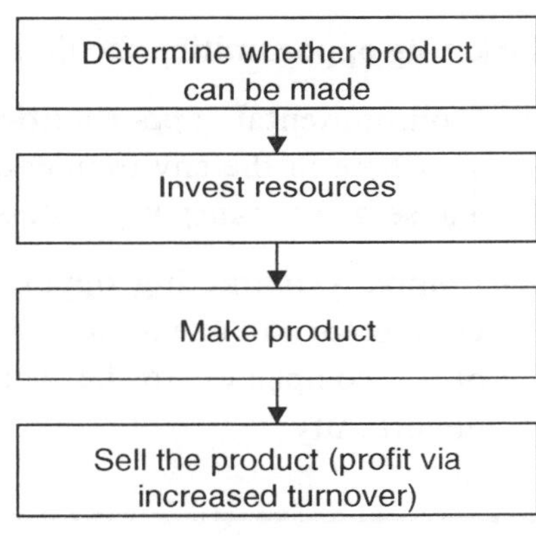

1.5 However, the **needs** of customers are not the same thing as what customers would like to have in an **ideal world**. For example, all airline passengers would **prefer** to fly first class than economy, but cannot afford it. Customer needs are translated into effective demand, if they are backed up by money. In practice, customers accept a compromise based on price and performance.

1.6 Moreover, the customer is not buying a **thing with features** but a **package of benefits**.

Case example

A customer need is for *recorded music,* to be played as and when the customer likes. This need has been satisfied by:

- Wax drums
- Vinyl records - 78, 45, 33 rpm
- Tapes, and digital compact cassette
- Compact discs
- Mini-disks

- The Internet: music can be sent in digital form over the telephone wire, to be stored in a computer. The point is: customers buy the benefit not the technology.

1.7 The **use** of a product may be more than would be suggested by its utilitarian value.

Case example

Trainers, while designed for sports, have been used as fashion accessories. This is the 'value' of trainers, not their use in sporting activities. Nike, the brand leader, designs its trainers for sports. However, the chances are that trainers' role as a fashion item may be subverted by the new fashion for 'heavy' or industrial shoes.

The importance of developing a market orientation in strategic planning

1.8 The marketing concept is concerned with products and markets, and so is at the heart of the strategic planning process: Ansoff's growth vector also deals with the choice of product-market strategies - developing new products and new markets that will fill the 'profit gap'. A marketing orientation should help planners to identify more successfully what products or markets, by meeting perceived customer needs, would earn good profits for the organisation. **Strategic marketing** is concerned with the development and implementation of marketing plans, for both the long term and short term, which should enable a firm to achieve its objectives and goals.

1.9 **Marketing opportunities** should be seen in conjunction with the company's objectives.

(a) **Environmental opportunities**. These are market opportunities which exist anywhere in the environment, eg in the fields of energy, foodstuffs, medical goods and services, transport, professional services, household goods etc.

(b) **Company marketing opportunities**. Any company is likely to have **distinctive competence** in one or more areas of activity which makes it more likely than (most) other companies to be able to take advantage of a certain environmental opportunity.

Question 1

'We take it as axiomatic that customers want the highest quality, perfection if possible - price is not an issue. We don't want to waste money on market research: we know what customers want.'

Is this a marketing orientation?

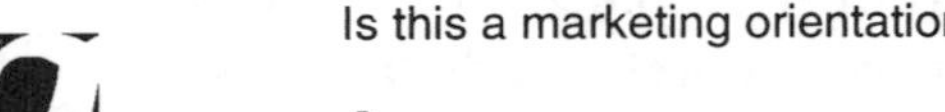

Answer

No. Customers' needs should not be taken for granted.

Exam focus point

Marketing has featured in the 50 mark scenario (December 1995) and was also the subject of a 25 mark question in June 1996, in which a small firm of accountants had to adopt a marketing orientation.

1.10 Section summary

- Marketing is the identification and satisfaction of customer needs at a profit.
- The marketing orientation focuses organisational attention on the customer.

2 THE MARKETING ORIENTATED ORGANISATION

2.1 The marketing orientation is a philosophy of a business. Therefore it **cannot be restricted** to the people in the marketing department.

2.2 Typically, **marketing personnel** are responsible for:

(a) Researching customers' needs
(b) Assisting in the design of the product
(c) Suggesting a suitable pricing strategy
(d) Promotion: advertising, public relations etc
(e) Distribution: identifying how the product should be distributed
(f) Customer service: specifying service levels

2.3 These activities also involve other departments. In effect, the marketing department in a marketing orientated firm should:

- Champion the customer in the organisation
- Promote the organisation to the customer

2.4 **Involvement of other business functions in marketing**

Department	Activity
Finance	Credit terms
	Dealing with customers – invoicing payment
Production	Product manufacture; delivery times; quality
Human resources	Customer care *training*

Internal marketing

2.5 **Internal marketing** may be adopted by some departments. An **information systems department** may try to 'market' its services by:

(a) Researching and analysing what user departments actually want (eg **when** information is required, the **format** in which it is presented and the type of advice and training given about departmental uses of information technology).

(b) Involving users in any systems development projects (a requirement of many information system methodologies).

(c) Meeting 'customer' needs as far as possible.

(d) Charging for its services (if information technology is not treated simply as a corporate overhead) to allocate possibly scarce resources.

Societal marketing

2.6 Kotler suggested that a **societal marketing** concept should replace the marketing concept as a philosophy for the future. 'The societal marketing concept is a management orientation that holds that the key task of the organisation is to determine the needs and wants of target markets and to adapt the organisation to delivering the desired satisfactions more effectively and efficiently than its competitors in a way that **preserves** or enhances the **consumers' and society's well-being**.'

2.7 Societal marketing is likely to receive an increasing emphasis in the future, and no doubt you are well aware of the emergence of 'green' consumer products.

2.8 Section summary

- Marketing should be adopted by all departments.
- Other departments of the organisation are treated as internal customers.
- Marketing considerations can be incorporated in social responsibility.

3 MARKETING AND NON PROFIT MAKING ORGANISATIONS 6/94

Exam focus

You may be given an examination question which asks about the relevance of the marketing approach or the marketing concept for the management of a government department or non profit making organisation, such as a charity, a club, or a public service such as a library or hospital.

3.1 Non profit making organisations (NPMOs) might adopt a **marketing orientation** to achieve their objectives more effectively. Let us take the example of charities.

(a) **Identifying customer needs**. Although NPMOs are not profit-making, they still provide goods/services of some kind. Charities can thus identify the needs of people who will benefit from their activities.

(b) **Satisfying needs**. Marketers can help devise ways by which needs are satisfied. (Many charities are constrained by resources.)

3.2 **Marketing techniques** are also used by non profit making organisations, especially in **fundraising activities**.

(a) Identifying the most likely donors might involve **segmenting** the market.

(b) Planning **advertising and media campaigns** to persuade target donors to pay up.

(c) Trying to drum up sponsoring support.

3.3 The supply of donor funds is limited, so charities have to **compete** for funds with other charities.

3.4 Many non profit making organisations have **complex objectives** which they must satisfy with limited resources.

Question 2

What would be the effects of introducing a marketing approach to a charity?

Answer

(a) The reasons for the organisation's existence should be expressed in terms of the consumer or client.

(b) Marketing research should be used to find out:

(i) who needs help, and in what ways, and how satisfactory is the current help provided;

(ii) where funds should be raised, and what the best approaches should be;

(iii) which political figures are susceptible to 'lobbying' and how such lobbying should best be conducted.

(c) 'Target markets' would be identified for charitable acts, fund-raising and influencing.

(d) The charity might also wish to promote an image to the public, perhaps by means of public relations work.

(e) The management of the charity will be aware that they are in competition for funds with other charities, and in competition with other ways of spending money in trying to obtain funds from the public. It should organise its 'sales and marketing' systems to raise funds in the most effective way. (Some years ago the Band Aid charity recognised the potential of telemarketing - ie telephone 'selling' - to raise funds for its Sports Aid fund-raising campaign.)

4 IDENTIFYING MARKET TRENDS

4.1 As part of the marketing audit, the current markets must be investigated. Marketing seeks to ensure profitable sales, and so current sales and markets can be reviewed, to see:

- If sales can be 'grown' successfully in present markets
- The possibility of growth in new markets, if expansion is considered
- Projections for new products

4.2 Here is an example.

	Year	*19X5/X6*	*19X6/X7*	*19X7/X8*	*19X8/X9*
a	Total market (units)	100,000,000	140,000,000	170,000,000	180,000,000
b	Market share	5%	8%	10%	9%
c	Sales volume (units)	5,000,000	11,200,000	17,000,000	16,200,000
d	Average sales price	£4.0	£4.4	£5.0	£6.0
e	Average variable cost	£2.0	£2.3	£3.0	£3.6
f	Unit contribution	£2.0	£2.1	£2.0	£2.4
		£'000	£'000	£'000	£'000
g	Total sales revenue	20,000	49,280	85,000	97,200
h	Total contribution	10,000	23,520	34,000	38,880
i	Production overhead	1,000	3,500	6,000	7,500
j	Selling costs	2,000	2,500	5,000	6,000
k	Advertising	1,500	3,000	5,000	6,000
l	Distribution	1,500	3,000	5,000	7,500
m	Other marketing costs	1,000	2,000	4,000	5,000
n	Profit	3,000	9,520	9,000	6,880

4.3 From information about the product background, it might be possible to estimate the future trend of the total market and the market share of the company's own product, and to relate the trend in profitability to turnover, contribution and overhead allocations.

Sales and profit projections

4.4 Preparing a sales budget effectively begins with **forecasts** - of sales given a variety of possible product prices and costs for each selling activity.

(a) An **estimate of sales** in the overall budget period (analysed as required, by product, range, type of outlet etc) and sub-divided into budgetary control periods.

(b) A **stated price policy** which will stimulate this sales demand.

(c) An **estimate of the selling costs** (analysed into functions) needed to achieve the level of sales at the given prices.

It is common to begin with a sales and profits projection which assumes no change in the current marketing strategy for the product.

4.5 If there is no change in the marketing strategy for a particular product it ought to be possible to project future sales and profits using linear or multiple regression analysis techniques or possibly simpler analysis techniques.

4.6 In the example in paragraph 4.2, a 'simple' technique for projecting future profitability of the product might be to apply judgement and common sense (ie guesswork) to the historical figures in order to predict the future. To make a forecast for 19X9/Y0, the following assumptions could be made.

(a) Total market. Might increase to, say 190,000,000 units
(b) Market share. Assumed to remain 9%.
(c) Sales volume (9% of 190,000,000) 17,100,000 units
(d) Average sales price - assume inflation-increase of, say, 5%.
(£6 × £1.05) - £6.30 per unit
(e) Average variable cost - also assume increase of 5%
(3.6 × £1.05) - £3.78 per unit
(f) Unit contribution £2.52 per unit

			£'000
(g)	Total sales revenue	(17.1m × £6.3)	107,730
(h)	Total contribution	(17.1m ×£2.52)	43,092
(i)	Production overheads, say		7,900
(j)	Selling costs, say		6,300
(k)	Advertising (high increase expected, say)		7,000
(l)	Distribution, say		8,000
(m)	Other marketing costs, say		5,500
(n)	Profit		8,392

4.7 If this analysis were realistic, it might well be concluded that the product is a cash cow in a maturing market, and marketing plans would presumably be formulated for the product to try to ensure that the sales target of 17.1m units, and the sales price and marketing costs targets are achievable.

5 SEGMENTING THE MARKET

5.1 A market is not a mass, homogeneous group of customers, each wanting an identical product.

(a) Every market consists of **potential buyers with different needs**, and different buying behaviour. These different customers may be **grouped into segments**, with common needs and preferences, who perhaps react to 'market stimuli' in much the same way.

(b) A **different marketing approach** will be taken by an organisation **for each market segment**.

(c) Segmentation is essential for **focus strategies**.

KEY TERM

Market segmentation is 'the subdividing of a market into distinct and increasingly homogeneous subgroups of customers, where any subgroup can conceivably be selected as a target market to be met with a distinct marketing mix'.

5.2 **Reasons for segmenting markets.**

(a) **Focus strategy:** a firm can build itself a niche. A segment is a group of customers whose special needs can be catered for in a focus strategy.

(b) **More money:** by catering specifically for segments and satisfying their needs better, customers will probably spend more than if they were offered a single product.

(c) **Convenience:** a firm cannot be all things to all people. In Chapter 1 we suggested that firms have to choose how to compete and who to serve - if only to survive in the face of competition.

The bases for segmentation

5.3 An important initial marketing task is the **identification of segments** within the market. One basis will not be appropriate in every market, and sometimes two or more bases might be valid at the same time. One basis or 'segmentation variable' might be 'superior' to another in a hierarchy of variables. For example, market segments may exist on the basis of sex; sub-segments may then be age-group within sex.

5.4 **Typical market segments**

- **Geographical area:** commercial radio stations may compete with national radio stations by broadcasting items of local interest.
- **End use:** paper used in offices will vary in quality depending on whether it is used for formal letters and reports, informal working or for typewriter carbon copies.
- **Age:** a useful age division might be 0 - 3 years, 4 - 6 years, 7 - 11, 12 - 19, 20 - 34, 35 - 49, 50 - 64 and over 64.
- **Sex.** There are different magazines for men and women. The gay community might be a segment in its own right for some products.
- **Family size or family life cycle:** eg young and single, young and married with no children, married with one, two or more children, older and single, older and married with one, two or more children.
- **Income:** eg the market for housing.
- **Occupation:** eg the market for men's suits might be segmented according to occupation.
- **Education.** Segmentation by education may be relevant to the marketing of newspapers.
- **Religion or religious sect.** This form of segmentation may be important for marketing by charities.
- **Ethnic origin:** eg the market for certain hair products.
- **Nationality:** eg the market for food.
- **Social class.** Socio-economic groupings appear to provide reliable indicators of different consumer attitudes and needs for a wide range of products.
- **Life style.** Differences in personality, activities, interests and opinions etc might be condensed into a few categories of life style. It may therefore be possible to segment a market according to these life-style categories (eg second hand or new motor cars).

- **Buyer behaviour:** eg the usage rate of the product by the buyer, whether purchase will be on impulse, customer loyalty, the sensitivity of the consumer to marketing mix factors, ie price, quality and sales promotion.
- **Geodemographic segmentation** is more sophisticated than geographical segmentation, as it identifies the precise social and economic profiles (eg car ownership, unemployment rates etc) of people living in areas in the country (eg 'white-collar' workers, better-off multi-ethnic areas).

5.5 Segmentation can also be applied to an **industrial market.**

- The **nature of the customer's business**. An accountant may choose to specialise in the accounts of retail businesses, and a firm of solicitors may specialise in conveyancing work for property development companies.
- **Size**
- **Location**
- **Industry:** components manufacturers specialise in the industries of the firms to which they supply components. In the motor car industry, there are companies which specialise in the manufacture of car components, possibly for a single firm.

Case example

'Generation X'

A segment is a group of customers who might behave in a particular way. In February 1997, *Marketing Business* identified 'Generation X'. This indicates how buyer behaviour and segmental analysis can be related.

'New consumers, Generation X, call them what you will, youth in the 1990s are a cynical and disillusioned bunch. They eschew eighties-style consumerism, laugh in the face of brands which try to woo them and yet paradoxically remain loyal to brands they deem cool. Tap into this illusive but hugely influential demographic and you are onto a winner. Get it wrong and you will miss a golden opportunity.

In 1991 a novel was published called Generation X. It was by an American - Douglas Copeland - and therefore prone to exaggerated generational claims (the country's favourite pastime since the 1960s). But it touched a nerve: today's young adults, it suggested, were terminally disillusioned and cynical. Unemployed and underexploited, they were wasting away in Mc-jobs, serving burgers instead of bettering themselves. They were the first generation in America to realise that they would not enjoy a higher standard of living than their parents.

Bleak stuff. Whether or not Generation X was fact or fiction, its supposed attributes are certainly an important aspect of today's young consumer. However, the apocalyptic tone is not so accurate.

While young consumers have metamorphosed considerably in recent years, they remain very much consumers. Their cynicism and knowingness cannot be ignored, but it should not be taken as a sign that they have rejected capitalism lock, stock and barrel. Targeting them means recognising their outlook as more than just a passing fad. Marketers must first acknowledge certain fundamental changes which have affected all consumer behaviour, and which will become increasingly part of the mainstream as this generation ages.

First people became brand literate. Then, in the 1980s they became advertising-literate, very much into badges and conspicuous consumption. Now, in the 1990s, they have become marketing-literate.

"The single most important element of our whole media targeting is attitude, says Simon Soothill, brand manager of top tequila brand Jose Cuervo. His on-trade, activity centres on the 25-34 age group, who "don't want to be sold to and expect to see very dynamic advertising. We try to find ways of talking to them that they find relevant and involving." Soothill believes this age group has younger tastes than in previous generations.

Just as age is no longer the all-powerful defining factor of consumer behaviour, so gender is not the great divider it once was. This magazine has already commented in detail on the blurring of gender boundaries among younger consumers, as exemplified by the Calvin Klein campaigns.

Marketers climbing the corporate ladder are also managing to find new ways of talking to today's young - and tomorrow's mainstream - consumer.

New Solutions emphasises that while young consumers can be said to have some homogenous characteristics, it is not enough to define them by age alone. The concept of the teenager is now looking quite staid and indeed rather 1950s.'

Testing segment validity

5.6 A market segment will only be valid if it is **worth designing and developing a unique marketing mix** for that specific segment.

Question	Comment
Can the segment be measured?	It might be possible to conceive of a market segment, but it is not necessarily easy to measure it. For example, for a segment based on people with a conservative outlook on life, can conservatism of outlook be measured by market research?
Is the segment big enough?	There has to be a large enough potential market to be profitable.
Can the segment be reached?	There has to be a way of getting to the potential customers via the organisation's promotion and distribution channels.
Do segments respond differently?	If two or more segments are identified by marketing planners but each segment responds in the same way to a marketing mix, the segments are effectively one and the same and there is no point in distinguishing them from each other.

Question 3

Identify the market segments served by your employer.

Positioning

5.7 **Product positioning** is how a product relates to others on offer (eg higher quality/higher price) and the differences that customers perceive there to be. Marketers devise a suitable position for a product to appeal to a particular segment.

5.8 It is not always possible to identify a market segment where there is no direct competitor, and a marketing problem for the firm will be the creation of some form of product differentiation (real or imagined) in the marketing mix of the product. 'Competitive positioning requires the firm to develop a general idea of what kind of offer to make to the target market in relation to competitors' offers.' (Kotler).

5.9 Theodore Levitt gave a useful commentary on **market positioning** in the case of banks.

'... no bank can be the best bank for all customers. A bank must choose. It must examine its opportunities and 'take a position' in a market. Positioning goes beyond image-making. The image-making bank seeks to cultivate an image in the customer's mind as a large, friendly or efficient bank .... Yet the customer may see the competing banks as basically alike .... Positioning is an attempt to distinguish the bank from its competitors along real dimensions in order to be the preferred bank to certain segments of the market. Positioning aims to help customers know the real differences between competing banks so that they can match themselves to the bank that can be of most value to them.'

Even in high-street banking, there can be differences in service according to cost (ie the cost of services), availability of cash card machines and personal loans, hours of opening etc.

5.10 One simple perceptual **map** that can be used is to plot brands or **competing products** in terms of two key characteristics such as price and quality.

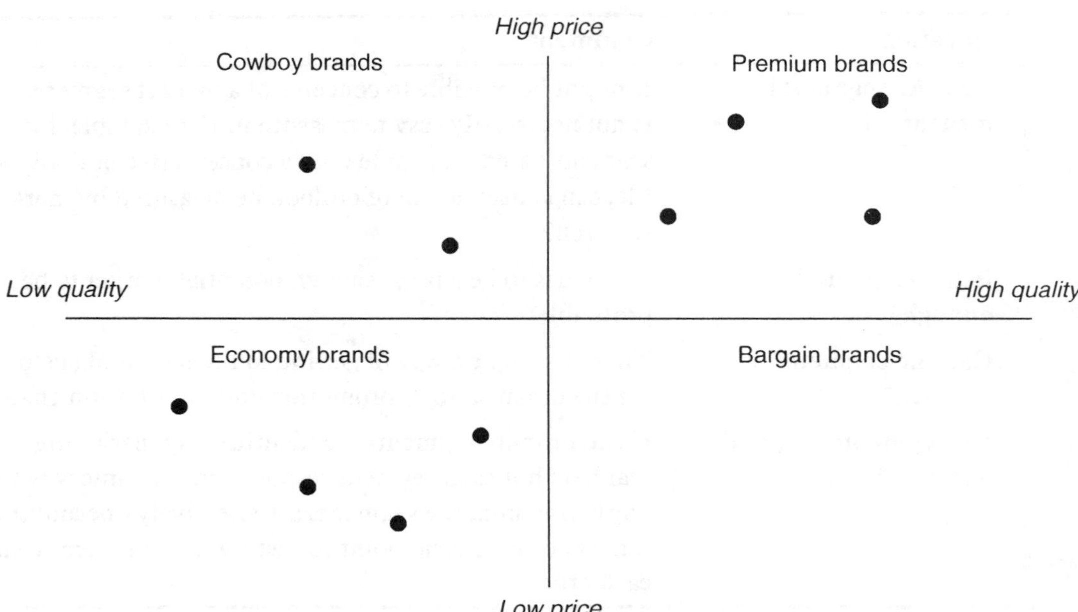

5.11 A perceptual map of market positioning can be used to identify **gaps in the market**. This example might suggest that there could be potential in the market for a low-price high-quality 'bargain brand'. A company that carries out such an analysis might decide to conduct further research to find out whether there is scope in the market for a new product which would be targeted at a market position where there are few or no rivals. (A firm successfully pursuing **cost leadership** might be in a good position to offer a **bargain brand**.)

5.12 Section summary

- Segmentation is the grouping of potential customers according to their common needs.
- A distinct marketing approach can be adopted for each segment.
- Positioning compares one product with another.

6 BUYER BEHAVIOUR 6/96

6.1 Goods are usually divided into two broad categories.

KEY TERMS

(a) **Consumer goods:** these are goods made for the ultimate **household consumer** and they are in such a form that they can be used by the consumer **without the need for any further commercial processing.**

(b) **Industrial goods:** these are goods which are used to make other goods or to render services. They are goods which are not consumer goods.

Customer behaviour in the consumer market

6.2 Once the needs of the segment have been identified, further analysis will be done as to how the segment can be induced to buy. Buyer behaviour is the process whereby customers identify a need and take a purchase decision.

Question 4

Why do some countries ban advertising directed solely at children?

Answer

- Some claim that children are easily manipulated by advertising messages
- 'Pester power' is a force to be reckoned with!

The buying process

6.3 The psychological **process of buying** is as follows.

Step 1 The consumer has an unconscious or conscious **need**, but is unaware of any product which would satisfy that need.

Step 2 The consumer then becomes **aware** of the product.

Step 3 If this awareness suggests that the product might satisfy his need, the consumer will show an **interest** and will wish to obtain more information about the product.

Step 4 The customer will **evaluate** this information, and this may create a **preference** for the product.

6.4 A buying decision might be taken entirely by one person. However, the buying process might be influenced by several different individuals. For example, a family's holiday destination is unlikely to be decided by one person alone.

6.5 The buying decision is not simply a result of a psychological process. It is also the **outcome of an interaction** between the **buyer**, the **seller**, the **product** and the **situation**.

Factor	Comment
Buyer	People's characteristics and experiences influence their buying decisions. Marketing managers may nevertheless be able to make generalisations about different types of consumer.
Seller	The characteristics of the seller will affect the consumer's decision to buy or not buy, because the seller will give an impression of the quality of the firm's after sales service, its experience in the field, its reliability and 'friendliness' etc.
Product	Management can control the characteristics of the goods sold by their organisation (eg quality, durability, price, design features etc).
Situation	The circumstances under which the decision to buy or not to buy is taken. Some aspects might be subject to management control (eg whether the products are available in supermarkets). Other factors may be outside the control of management (eg the weather, or discussions with a friend who has some opinions about the product).

Psychological influences on demand

6.6 **Psychological influences which affect consumer buying behaviour**

(a) **Motivation.** This is discussed in the context of work in Chapter 18. Motivation theories also apply to buying decisions.

(b) **Attitudes.** Some writers have suggested that a buyer's attitude towards a product is an important element in the buying decision. However, there is no empirical evidence to link a favourable attitude directly with consumer purchases.

(c) **Experience** of the type of product.

(d) **Loyalty**. A consumer may demonstrate a loyalty towards a particular company's goods or to a brand, or even to a particular shop or retail chain. Although it is an important phenomenon, it may well be outside the sphere of management influence or control. However **loyalty**, or even just **inertia**, is quite an important factor in the sale of financial services.

(e) **Personality**. Inevitably, a consumer's buying behaviour will be influenced by his or her personality. Kotler identified seven broad personality variables.

- Compulsiveness (compulsive, non-compulsive)
- Gregariousness (extrovert, introvert)
- Autonomy (dependent, independent)
- Conservatism
- Authoritarianism (authoritarian, democratic)
- Leadership (leader, follower)
- Ambitiousness (high-achiever, low-achiever).

(f) **Group influences**. An individual will also be influenced by other people in the groups to which he or she belongs (eg people at work).

Socio-economic influences on demand

6.7 Consumers' buying decisions will be influenced by a variety of social economic and cultural factors.

(a) The **size of population**. The total potential market demand for products will be determined to a considerable extent by the size of the population.

(b) The **family decision-making units**. A widely accepted classification of consumer 'units' which make buying decisions is based on the family situation of the consumer.

(c) **Regional preferences.**

(d) **Culture**. Consumer behaviour in Britain will differ from comparable behaviour in, say, Argentina or Japan.

(e) **Social class**. The most well-known socio-economic groupings in Britain are by occupation (rather than income).

(f) **Life style**. Levy (1964) wrote that 'marketing is a process of providing customers with parts of a potential mosaic from which they, as artists of their own lifestyle, can pick and choose to develop the composition that for the time seems the best'.

The consumer's motivation mix

6.8 **Customer behaviour** is therefore determined by **economic, psychological** and **sociological considerations**. The reasons for buying a product or their relative importance may vary from person to person, or product to product. These reasons make up the **motivation mix** of the customer. The considerations which constitute the motivation mix allow for very wide variations in what customers will buy.

6.9 Complex models of buyer behaviour have been developed to take account of these influences on purchase decisions. These include the Howard Sheth model.

Exam focus point

The June 1996 exam asked you to describe the differences between 'consumer' and 'business to business' marketing.

Buyer behaviour in industrial markets

6.10 Business-to-business markets are:

- More demarcated than the consumer market (eg just look in the Yellow Pages).
- 'Rational' in that customers should not buy beyond economic need.
- Easier to forecast than the consumer market.

The decision-making unit (DMU)

6.11 The decision-making unit (DMU) is a term used to describe the person or people who actually **take the decision** to buy a good or service.

KEY TERM

The **DMU** is defined in marketing management as a group of people containing every person who has some influence (positive or negative) at one or more stages in the purchasing process.

6.12 **People in the DMU**

(a) **Employees or managers** in sales and production might make recommendations about what type of supplies should be purchased.

(b) **Superiors** might authorise the recommendations of a junior buying manager.

(c) **Colleagues.** In large organisations, there will be several buying managers, who might work independently, but might also work closely together, either formally or informally.

(d) **Technical staff and engineers** provide specifications for component purchases.

(e) **Accountants** might be able to set a limit on the price the organisation will pay.

(f) The **board of directors** might approve major items.

(g) **User departments** are also involved.

(h) **Previous strategic or buying decisions** may constrain choices: the information technology strategy may require, say, that all computers should run Windows 97.

Factors in the motivation mix of industrial buyers

6.13 The motivation of industrial buyers is supposedly more rational than that of the domestic consumer.

Motive	Comment
Quality	Even where quality standards are imposed by an outside body (eg the British Standards Institution) or by customer specification, there can be some variation in the quality of goods of competing manufacturers.
Price	The economic value of industrial goods to the buyer depends on the price which the buyer can obtain for the product the buyer produces. Where profit margins in the final market are under pressure, the buyer of industrial goods will probably make price the main purchasing motivation. A supplier can reduce prices or help in other ways (by increasing quality, thereby reducing the usage cost to the customer).
Budgetary control	This will influence the purchaser's buying activities, and the buying department may look further afield (perhaps abroad) for potential suppliers to obtain a better price or quality of goods.
Fear of breakdown	Where a customer has a highly organised and costly production system, he will clearly want to avoid a breakdown in the system, due to a faulty machine or running out of stocks of materials.
Credit	The importance of credit could vary with the financial size of the buyer, but customers should always be attempting to obtain the best credit terms they can get.

6.14 **Types of buying situation**

Situation	Comment
Routinised buyer behaviour	Habitual buying where the buyer knows the offering, the item is frequently purchased, and the buyer has well developed supplier preferences. Deviation from habit behaviour is likely to be influenced by price and availability considerations.
Limited problem solving	The purchase of a new or unfamiliar product/service but where the suppliers are known and the product is in a familiar class of products - for instance a new type of packaging material.
Extensive problem solving	The purchase of unfamiliar products from unfamiliar suppliers. This is time-consuming.

6.15 Webster and Wind see **organisational buyer behaviour** as being influenced by:

(a) The **individual** characteristics of the members of the DMU.

(b) The relationships between members of the DMU. For example, a **gatekeeper controls the flow of information** about the purchase. This role can be senior or junior.

7 MARKETING RESEARCH

7.1 Marketing managers, like all other managers, need information for planning and control. The **marketing information system** (MKIS) is a part of an organisation's overall management information system (MIS).

7.2 Many marketing decisions are taken on a continuous basis (eg decisions are taken on various aspects of the marketing mix - sales, advertising, sales promotion at least annually). A continuous plan of information is also required for control purposes. A marketing information system, normally part of the management information system, meets these needs.

(a) **Internal reports (and accounts) systems**

(i) Results data
(ii) Measures of current performance
(iii) Sales, costs, stock information
(iv) Possible areas for improvement (including timeliness, availability and distribution of reports)

(b) **Marketing intelligence system**

(i) **Happenings data** (eg what competitors are doing)
(ii) Information on developments in the environment
(iii) It involves scanning and the dissemination of a wide range of intelligence
(iv) Possible areas of improvement

(c) **Marketing research system** contains specific studies of marketing problems, opportunities and effectiveness.

(d) **Analytical marketing system.** This uses models to explain, predict and improve marketing processes. Models may be descriptive, decisional, verbal, graphical or mathematical.

All subsystems should be interactive.

Case example

Daewoo

Daewoo has been a significant marketing success story in the UK in recent years. Daewoo does not differentiate on product, rather on service. The following extracts come from an article in *Marketing Business* (March 1997).

'For the marketing director of Daewoo, customer feedback informs all of his decisions. Daewoo launched on the back of extensive research, as Farrell explains. "Before we launched, we did an enormous amount of research to develop our strategy. We used a direct response television and press campaign inviting people to tell us what they thought of the car trade. That brought an enormous response - 200,000 people contacted us. We then sent a detailed questionnaire to 30 per cent of these and to that mailing we had a 60 per cent response."

Daewoo's USP is service and in order to deliver top service, the research never ever stops. "We are continuously doing quality tracking," says Farrell. "Every three months, we phone 200 recent buyers to ask them about their experience of our service and whether they have found any faults with the car. This is a 35-minute conversation. Then, after a year, we phone another sample."

"In the second half of each year we do 10,000 telephone interviews to people who have ordered cars but have yet to take delivery, so the experience is fresh in their minds, and then we contact them after delivery." In fact, customers are interviewed at every stage of their dealings with Daewoo - within 48 hours of having their car serviced, for instance, to find out how it went and whether the courtesy car was satisfactory.

And it is not just customers that are approached. To get a complete picture, Daewoo also interviews those who walk out of the showroom without buying. Research on this scale is a vital part of the company's strategic development but the results have a big impact on individuals as well - Daewoo staff do not work on commission but are rewarded as a result of customer feedback. Constant monitoring means that Daewoo can respond rapidly.

But what about the hassle for customers of being called up by Daewoo on a regular basis? "Our owners can be called more than once," agrees Farrell, "but that is no problem because they have bought into what we are doing. We have never had anyone put the phone down on us. It also serves a commercial purpose because by talking to them, they can become more loyal." '

7.3 The sources of marketing data will vary from organisation to organisation, but are both internal and external, including information provided by marketing research.

KEY TERM

Marketing research has been defined by the Chartered Institute of Marketing as the 'objective gathering, recording and analysing of all facts about problems relating to the transfer and sales of goods and services from producer to consumer or user'.

7.4 **The scope of marketing research**

Area	Items
Market research	• Analysis of the market potential for existing products • Forecasting likely demand for new products • Sales forecasting for all products • Study of market trends • Study of the characteristics of the market • Analysis of market shares
Product research	• Customer acceptance of proposed new products • Comparative studies between competitive products • Studies into packaging and design • Forecasting new uses for existing products • Test marketing • Research into the development of a product line (range)

Area	Items
Price research	• Analysis of elasticities of demand • Analysis of costs and contribution or profit margins • The effect of changes in credit policy on demand • Customer perceptions of price (and quality)
Promotion research	• Motivation research for advertising and sales promotion effectiveness • Analysing the effectiveness of advertising on sales demand • Analysing the effectiveness of individual aspects of advertising (copy, use of media etc) • Establishing sales territories • Analysing the effectiveness of salesmen • Analysing the effectiveness of other sales promotion methods
Distribution research	• The location and design of distribution centres • The analysis of packaging for transportation and shelving • Dealer supply requirements • Dealer advertising requirements • The cost of different methods of transportation and warehousing

Marketing research procedure

7.5 Marketing research involves the following five stages of work.

Step 1 **Definition of the problem.** The marketing problem which management wishes to resolve must be properly defined.

Step 2 **Design of the research.** Once the research team knows what problem it must help to resolve, it will establish the type of data (secondary or primary), the collection method to be used (postal questionnaire, personal interview), the selection of a research agency (if appropriate) and if a sample is to be taken, the design of the sample. Any questions put to respondents must be carefully designed.

Step 3 **Collection of the data.**

Step 4 **Analysis of the data.**

Step 5 **Presentation of a report** which should then lead to a management marketing decision.

The sources of marketing research information

7.6 Marketing research data can be either primary data or secondary data.

KEY TERMS

Primary data is information collected specifically for the study under consideration. **Secondary data** is 'data neither collected directly by the user nor specifically for the user, often under conditions that are not well known to the user' (American Marketing Association). The collection of secondary data for marketing research is sometimes known as **desk research.**

7.7 **Desk research** involves collecting data from the following sources.

(a) **Records inside the firm**, gathered by another department or section for a different purpose to the research task in hand.

(b) Published information from **external sources**, such as:

(i) Publications of market research agencies, such as the Nielsen Index
(ii) Government statistics (eg Social Trends)
(iii) Publications of trade associations
(iv) Professional and specialist journals
(v) The Press
(vi) The Internet

Field research and primary data

7.8 **Field research is the collection of primary data** may be carried out in a number of areas, notably customers, advertising, product, packaging and distribution. Techniques involved in the collection and analysis of primary data are:

- Experimentation
- Sampling
- Piloting
- Observation
- Questionnaires
- Consumer panels
- Trade audits, such as retail audits
- Pre-tests
- Post-tests
- Attitude scales and methods of analysis

Experimentation

7.9 In a **controlled experiment,** a controlled research environment is established and selected stimuli are then introduced. To the extent that 'outside' factors can be eliminated from the environment (ie depending on the degree to which a controlled environment is established) the observed effects can be measured and related to each stimulus. Controlled experiments have been used to find the best advertising campaign, the best price level, the best incentive scheme, the best sales training method, etc.

Sampling

7.10 In marketing research for consumer goods, it will be impossible to obtain data from *every* consumer in the market. A **sample provides an estimate of the characteristics of the entire 'population'**. The accuracy of the sample will depend on:

(a) How the sample is taken.
(b) The amount of variability in the population.
(c) The size of the sample.

The larger the sample, the greater the likelihood that the sample will provide an accurate reflection of the population as a whole.

7.11 To make a truly **random sample** we need a **sampling frame**. This is a list of every member of the target 'population'. If we wished to obtain a sample of opinions among people eligible to vote in an election, a sampling frame would be provided by the Electoral Register.

7.12 **Non-random sampling** is used to save money and increase practicability. The main methods of non-random sampling are as follows.

Method	Comment
Systematic sampling	Select every **nth item** after a **random start**. For example, if it was decided to select a sample of 20 from a population of 800, then every 40th (800 ÷ 20) item after a random start in the first 40 should be selected.
Stratified sampling	Divide the population into strata, and weight accordingly may conform to a consumer characteristic or a market segment. For example, a manufacturer of machine equipment may know that 40% of its sales come from one industry A, 30% from another industry. A stratified sample would aim to obtain 40% of its respondents from industry A, 30% from B.
Multistage sampling	The country is divided into a number of areas and a small sample of these is selected at random. Each of the areas selected is subdivided into smaller units and again, a small number of these is selected at random. This process is repeated as many times as necessary.
Quota sampling	Investigators are told to **interview all the people they meet** up to a certain quota. This problem of bias is partially overcome by subdividing the quota into different types of people (eg on the basis of age, sex and social class).
Cluster sampling	This is similar on the surface to multi-stage sampling, but the statistical justification is different.

Methods of obtaining data

7.13 **Observation** can be used as a means of obtaining sample data where quantitative data is required. For example, if data is needed about the volume of traffic passing along a road at a certain time of day, observers (either people or recording equipment) can be placed so as to count the traffic as it passes by. Observation can also be used to study consumer behaviour, although this is usually within a controlled experiment.

7.14 **Questionnaires** (eg over the phone, postal replies, street interviews) provides a quick, cheap method of conducting a survey, provided that:

- The questions are unambiguous
- People return them, so that the sample is not biased
- Respondents answer truthfully

7.15 **Consumer panels** consist of a representative cross-section of consumers who have agreed to give information about their attitudes or buying habits (through personal visits or mail questionnaires) at regular intervals of time. Consumer panels with personal visits are called home audit panels and panels which send data by post are called diary panels. For example, a panel of households might keep a purchase diary of the goods they have bought, and submit this diary regularly to the market research company. Panels might be established for a long term or short term period.

7.16 **Trade audits** are carried out among panels of wholesalers and retailers, and the term 'retail audits' refers to panels of retailers only. A research firm sends 'auditors' to selected outlets at regular intervals to count stock and deliveries, thus enabling an estimate of throughput to be made. **Retail audits** provide continuous monitoring of retail activity.

(a) Changes in retail sales provide an early warning of problems the manufacturer may soon have to expect in ex-factory sales.

(b) They indicate long-term trends in the market place, thus providing helpful information for strategic marketing planning.

(c) In the shorter term, they may indicate the need for changes in pricing policy, sales promotion or advertising, distribution policy, package design or product design.

Pre-testing and post testing

7.17 Marketing research may be carried out both before, during and after the marketing decision is implemented. Research for an advertising campaign attempts to measure both the communication effect and the sales effect of advertisements.

(a) **Pre-testing**

(i) Before the advertisement copy is finalised, motivational research may be carried out on a sample of potential customers.

(ii) Laboratory tests have been carried out to measure the physiological reactions of people watching advertisements (eg heart beat, blood pressure, dilation of the pupil of the eye, perspiration). Such tests measure the arousal power or attention-drawing power of an advertisement, but cannot measure its effectiveness in communicating the message.

(iii) Ratings tests involve asking a panel of target consumers to look at alternative advertisements and to given them ratings (marks out of ten etc) for attention-drawing power, clarity, emotional appeal, stimulus to buy etc.

(b) **Post-testing.** During an advertising campaign, the effectiveness of the campaign can be measured by means of movements in sales volume, consumer opinion research etc. Most post-testing researches into the communication effect of advertisements in the following way.

(i) Recall tests ask the interviewee to remember, unaided, advertisements which have been seen before the interview.

(ii) Recognition tests involve giving the interviewee some reminder of an advertisement, and testing his/her recognition of it

Question 3

How would you go about the market research for:

(a) A new type of tank;
(b) A new type of teapot?

Answer

(a) Desk research, followed by direct approaches to likely buyers.
(b) Desk research, then sample-based consumer research.

7.18 Section summary

- A marketing information system is a source of intelligence.
- Marketing research covers all aspects of marketing activities. Market research is more restricted in scope.
- Primary research collects data for a specific study. Secondary research collects background data.

8 BRAINWORKS PLC UPDATE

Questions can be found in the Introduction box at the beginning of this chapter.

8.1 *Question 1*. BW has two customer groups: the individuals who use its services to find work, and the employers who ask BW to find them suitable candidates. Ideally, BW should be able to satisfy **both** customer groups - but which is more important? In the current job market, for most skills, the employers hold the upper hand - but if BW wants to satisfy them, it has to attract the right applicants. The marketing concept can highlight attention on the needs of these different customer groups.

8.2 *Question 2*. BW has structured its operations around segments.

(a) Segmentation by area - **most** people do not want to move house when they find a job. This is true of the temporary job market, so BW(UK)'s area offices make some sense for potential recruits, but not for employers.

(b) Segmentation by temporary/permanent work. BW has subsidiaries dealing with permanent staff, for each of the main business areas, and divisions for temporary staff. However, does this arrangement reflect the real needs of its customers, who might want permanent positions, but may put up with temporary appointments for the time being? Currently, they would be shifted between BW(UK)'s divisional and subsidiaries, who employ different personnel. This segment perhaps is more apparent than real.

Chapter roundup

- **Marketing** is the identification of **customer needs** and their satisfaction at a profit. A **marketing orientation** involves identifying needs rather than making products and expecting people to buy them (production orientation) or selling them aggressively (selling orientation).
- **Non profit organisations** use marketing to find out the needs of users and beneficiaries, and to target fund raising exercises on likely donors.
- Marketing analysis involves predicting **demand for products and services**. Market **segmentation** is a way of analysing the market. A **segment** is a homogeneous group of customers who can be offered a distinctive marketing mix. Identified segments must be tested to see if they can be reached.
- **Buyer behaviour** is a term used to describe why people (or firms) buy goods and services. The buying decision frequently involves several individuals (the decision making unit).
- **Marketing research** can be **secondary (desk)** or **primary** (samples, questionnaires etc). Secondary research involves analysing data (eg census information) not specifically collected by the marketer. Primary research is more focused on customer attitudes to particular product or service issues.

Quick quiz

1 Distinguish between production, selling and marketing orientations. (see para 1.4,)
2 What is the societal marketing concept? (2.6)
3 What would be the effects of the introduction of the marketing orientation to a charity? (3.4)
4 What is segmentation? (5.1)
5 List ways of segmenting a market (5.4, 5.5)
6 Describe the buying process for consumers. (6.3)
7 List the psychological influences on demand for a product (6.6)
8 What is a DMU? (6.11)
9 What are the components of an MKIS? (7.2)
10 Outline the five stages of a marketing research programme. (7.5)

Question to try	Level	Marks	Time
18	Introductory	n/a	30 mins

Notes

Chapter 15

DEPLOYING THE MARKETING MIX

Chapter topic list		Syllabus reference
1	The marketing mix	2(d)(i), (iii)
2	New product development	2(d)(ii), (iv)
3	Brands	2(d)(i), (iii)
4	Domestic and international marketing	1(a)(iv), 2(d)(iv)
5	Modes of entry to overseas markets	2(d)(i)
6	Services and customer care	2(d)(i)
7	Marketing plans	2(d)(i)
8	Brainworks plc update	

Introduction

The previous chapter outlined some of the overall concepts of marketing. In this chapter, we describe the **marketing mix**, which is what the firm offers to potential customers and how it reaches them. A different mix can be applied to different stages of the product life cycle - revisit Chapter 6 which introduces this issue. Marketing considerations are, of course, relevant to the development of **new products**. Marketing also involves creating and sustaining **brands.**

International operations (Section 5) provide peculiar difficulties for the marketer, owing to the differing legal and cultural environments of the target markets. Although trade is becoming freer and markets are opening up, firms still have to present a credible marketing mix tailored to each market. The choice of a **mode of entry** to an international market can be a strong factor in the success of the firm's efforts in international marketing.

Special considerations apply to the marketing of **services.**

Brainworks plc

1 To what extent can BW offer a new product/service to its markets?

1 THE MARKETING MIX

1.1 The marketing function aims to satisfy customer needs profitability through an appropriate **marketing mix.**

KEY TERM

Marketing mix: 'the set of controllable variables and their levels that the firm uses to influence the target market'. These are product, price, place and promotion and are sometimes known as the 4 Ps.

1.2 The 'design' of the marketing mix will be decided on the basis of management intuition and judgement, together with information provided by marketing research (eg of the image of the product in the eyes of the customer, and the reasons which make customers buy a particular product).

1.3 **Elements in the marketing mix partly act as substitutes for each other** and they must be **integrated.** This is so the product can be positioned in the market to appeal to the customer. For example, a firm can raise the selling price of its products if it also raises product quality or advertising expenditure. Equally, a firm can perhaps reduce its sales promotion expenditure if it is successful in achieving a wider range and larger numbers of sales outlets for its product, etc.

Case example

Cat food wars

Pedigree Petfoods owns Whiskas, for many years the UK brand leader in cat food. Spillers' brand Felix was 'a minor player in a mature market: it faced the threat of delisting (by the major supermarkets), which wanted to give greater space to the more profitable cat treat and own label sectors'.

Felix responded to this threat by advertising in 1989. Between 1989 and 1996:

	1989	*1996*
Brand awareness	29%	57%
Volume share	6.7%	25.4%

By some calculations, £17m of advertising generated £108m increase in sales. By some measures, Felix outsold Whiskas in March 1996. Four elements contributed to Felix's success.

(a) *Product.* 'Palatability' - apparently cats liked it.

(b) *Price.* Keen pricing.

(c) *Promotion.* Advertising which emphasised cats' 'rogue-ish' nature and were less 'clinical' and idealised than *Whiskas* ads. 'The rational and idealised approach of competitors' advertising didn't reflect what most cat owners really appreciated about their pets'. Spillers made a little advertising go a long way.

(d) Felix had fewer lines, and was less confusing for shoppers.

Competitor response

In Autumn 1996, Whiskas was relaunched with TV advertising, the 'added cat-isfaction' slogan, new packaging and new product formulation. The re-launch cost £8m but, according to Marketing Week (November 22 1996), sales of Whiskas were static three months after the relaunch.

There are about 7.23m cats in the UK.

Although the cat food market may be fairly mature, recent evidence suggests that in the UK at least, cats are overtaking dogs in popularity and suitability as pets, especially for households where both partners work. Cats are seen as 'low maintenance'. Long-term growth might be expected from the market.

However, the Whiskas relaunch leaves some questions for Spillers. Will Spillers invest more to sustain its brands in the long term? Pedigree has done so: 'dominance and brand building being the key words in its lexicon'.

Product

1.4 The product element of the marketing mix is what is being sold, whether it be widgets, power stations, haircuts, holidays or financial advice. (But remember that the customer is buying the benefits that the product brings.) Product issues in the marketing mix will include such factors as:

- Design (size, shape)
- Features
- Quality and reliability
- After-sales service (if necessary)
- Packaging

1.5 **Issues related to products**

(a) The **core product** is the most basic description of the product - a car is a means of personal transport. The **actual product** is the car itself, with all its physical features such as a powerful engine, comfortable seats and a sun roof. The **augmented product** is the car plus the benefits which come with it, such as delivery, servicing, warranties and credit facilities for buyers.

Case example

Barclays has launched its Additions bank account. As well as normal transaction processing, the account offers life assurance, a free will-writing service, an overdraft and other benefits, in return for a monthly fee.

(b) The **product range** consists of two dimensions.

(i) **Width**. A car maker may have products in all parts, known as segments, of the market: luxury cars, family cars, small cheap cars, and so on.

(ii) **Depth**. It may then offer a wide variety of options within each segment - a choice of engines, colours, accessories and so on.

(c) **Benefits offered to the customer.** Customers differ in their attitudes towards new products and the benefits they offer.

Place

1.6 'Place' deals with how the product is distributed, and how it reaches its customers. We discussed aspects of distribution from an operational perspective in Chapter 8.

(a) **Channel**. Where are products sold? In supermarkets, corner shops? Which sales outlets will be chosen?

(b) **Logistics.** The location of warehouses and efficiency of the distribution system is also important. A customer might have to wait a long time if the warehouse is far away. Arguably, the **speed of delivery** is an important issue in 'place'.

Case example

The selling of motor insurance in the UK has been revolutionised by Direct Line insurance, which sells over the phone, rather than through a network of high street brokers. Others have copied this approach.

1.7 A firm can distribute the product itself (direct distribution) or distribute it through intermediary organisations such as retailers, brokers etc. Key issues are:

- **Product push**: the firm directs its efforts to distributors to get them to stock the product.
- **Customer pull**: the firm persuades consumers to demand the product from retailers and distributors, effectively pulling the product through the chain.

1.8 **In favour of direct distribution**

(a) The need **to demonstrate** a technical product (especially in the sale of industrial goods).

(b) **Lethargic intermediaries**. Wholesalers and retailers will try to sell all the products they handle, and will not favour one manufacturer's products.

(c) **No intermediaries might be available to sell the product.**

(d) **High intermediary profit margins** affect the final sale price to customers.

(e) A **small market** with only a few target customers may make direct selling **cheap** (and a dealer network impracticable).

(f) Direct selling maintains **good relations with end-users** and helps obtain feedback (ie market research information).

1.9 **In favour of using intermediaries**

(a) **Cheaper.**

(b) Financial resources can be more profitably employed elsewhere.

(c) A **lack of retailing 'know-how'** and expertise.

(d) A **lack of a sufficiently wide assortment** of products to sell. Retailers obtain a wide variety of products from many different manufacturers and put them all on sale in one store.

(e) Other channels of distribution are more able to deal with orders for **assortments** of products, and to break bulk.

(f) A **wide geographical market** area makes the costs of direct selling very high.

(g) **No other way** of reaching the consumer.

1.10 **Making the choice** between direct and indirect distribution.

(a) **Economic factors:** the most profitable method will differ according to circumstances.

(b) **Control:** the more intermediate stages in the channel, the less will be the extent of control which the manufacturer can exercise over selling to the customer.

(c) **Adaptive:** a manufacturer might wish to adapt its channels to changing circumstances. Long-term contracts with a distributor or agent, or long-term supply arrangements with a major retail group might take away the scope for flexibility and change, and a manufacturer might prefer to avoid these, and go for direct selling instead.

Promotion

1.11 Many of the actual activities of the marketing department are related to **promotion**. Promotion is the element of the mix over which the marketing department generally has most control. A useful mnemonic is AIDA which summarises the aims of promotion, which are to:

(a) arouse **Attention**
(b) generate **Interest**
(c) inspire **Desire**
(d) initiate **Action** (ie buy the product)

1.12 Promotion in the marketing mix includes all marketing communications which let the public know of the product or service. Promotion includes:

- Advertising (newspapers, billboards, TV radio)
- Sales promotion (eg special displays in particular stores)
- Direct selling by sales personnel.
- Public relations

'Above the line': advertising

1.13 Advertising draws **new products** to the public's attention and **reminds the public** that older products exist.

(a) A firm will ask an **agency** to design advertisements for it. It is 'positive' communication to a larger market and the advert will be seen by many people.

(b) The marketing department, in liaison with an agency, will start a **campaign**, a period of intensive advertising, particularly in launching a new product.

(c) The agency will probably determine the choice of **medium** (eg local and national newspapers, terrestrial and satellite TV, direct mail).

(d) Advertising conveys **limited information**. By promoting an image, it may offer a type of emotional satisfaction from the product.

1.14 **Media** include TV, posters, newspapers and radio. Firms try to increase the effectiveness of their advertising efforts by **targeting** them effectively.

(a) **Direct mail** is a useful advertising medium for trying to sell a product to a market segment in which the customer has certain distinguishing characteristics. Banks use direct mail to advertise their various financial services in this way, for example sending out direct mail about gold cards to customers who appear to have an appropriate level of income.

(b) **Internet websites** can also be used - the firm can offer more information than in normal advertising messages.

'Below the line': sales promotion

1.15 **Sales promotions** are essentially **short-term sales techniques** and an advertiser planning a campaign should not be tempted to sacrifice long-term prospects (eg brand image built up through media advertising) in order to spend too much on short-term promotions. Sales promotion can, however, supplement media advertising. Sales promotion activities may be directed at:

(a) People who do not currently use the product or service.

(b) Existing customers (so that they will use the product or service more frequently, or in larger quantities).

(c) People who currently use rival products (to weaken their current brand loyalty).

1.16 **Sales promotion activities**

(a) **Consumer promotions** include free samples, coupon offers (money-off offers), catalogues (for mail order), competitions, free gifts (in exchange for packet tops), exhibitions and demonstrations, and so on. Consumer promotions and advertising act as a 'pull policy' to attract dealer attention by means of consumer demand.

(b) **Retailer or middleman promotions.** As part of a 'push policy' (see paragraph 1.7) include extended credit, merchandising facilities, contests for retailers or shop assistants.

(c) **Sales force promotions** include bonuses, contests between salesmen (based on volumes of sales) and sales motivators - ie gifts linked to sales.

(d) **Industrial promotions** include sales literature and catalogues, special discounts, exhibitions and trade fairs, events (eg invitations to customers to visit the Wimbledon Tennis Championships), trade-in allowances, and so forth.

1.17 **Packaging** has five functions.

(a) Protection of the contents of the package.

(b) Distribution (helping to transfer products from the manufacturer to the consumer).

(c) Selling (the design of the package should help to attract buyers) to the product.

(d) User convenience, as an aid to selling, (eg aerosol cans, handy packs, etc).

(e) To conform to government regulations (eg by printing the product contents of the package).

Personal selling

1.18 The sales force engages in 'personal' selling, as compared with the 'non-personal' selling of advertising and sales promotion activities. The **buyer-seller relationship** is critical, and it is the immediacy of this relationship of face to face selling that helps to 'make a sale'.

1.19 Even in an organisation with a marketing orientated philosophy, there will be a need for a persuasive salesforce, because:

(a) It may not be possible to satisfy a customer's needs exactly.

(b) Customer tastes might have changed since the decisions about designing a product were made.

(c) Customers might need some reassurance that they are getting what they want. This is especially true in industrial goods markets, where buyers purchase goods to exact specifications.

(d) A salesperson might be needed to explain a technically complex product.

1.20 Since the work of the sales force is only one element in the sales mix, **greater dependence on advertising and sales promotion can mean a lesser dependence on direct selling**. At one extreme, direct mail firms do not need any sales force. It is unlikely, however, that salespeople - even shop assistants - could sell without some advertising or sales promotion back-up.

Question 2

What sort of promotion would be most suitable to the following?

(a) A company building railway engines
(b) A company selling toothpaste

Answer

(a) Direct selling and/or consultancy
(b) Advertising (press or TV). Most people use toothpaste, so little advertising would be wasted.

Public relations and corporate communications

1.21 Some organisations have a small public relations department which is responsible for the image of the organisation and its products in the eyes of the general public. An important element of **public relations is free publicity.** Advertising must be paid for: publicity, in contrast, is *not paid for*.

1.22 Publicity can be a useful selling aid, depending on:

(a) The newsworthiness of any item.
(b) Relations between the public relations department and the news media.
(c) The credibility of the publicity.

1.23 It is often relatively cheap in comparison with the cost of advertising.

(a) The need for publicity probably **varies significantly from industry to industry**. The music industry and the tourist trade, for example, rely heavily on publicity to attract customers.

(b) Small industrial firms might restrict their interest in PR and publicity to the locality of its factories and offices (as a local employer, a firm ought to be conscious of its relationship with the local community).

1.24 **Corporate communications** are concerned with influencing the way an organisation behaves and with communicating the benefits of this behaviour to clearly-identified public audiences.

1.25 Market research by MORI has shown that:

(a) Two out of every three people in the UK believe that a company which has a good reputation would not sell poor quality products (this suggests that customers would be more willing to try a new product if it is promoted by a well known corporate name than if it is made by an unknown company).

(b) Nine times out of ten, the better known a company is, the more highly it is regarded.

1.26 Corporate communications might be targeted not only at consumers, but also at:

- The government
- Shareholders (eg in takeover battles)
- Retailers, wholesalers and distributors
- Banks
- Local communities
- Employers

Sponsorship

1.27 **Sponsorship** is now used fairly widely by firms to promote their corporate image. The firm provides funds for a sports organisation (or art exhibition, television programme etc), in return for which the organisation gives publicity to the name of the firm. Sponsorship can be a low-cost method of advertising/promotion, and can therefore be a useful addition to a firm's marketing mix.

Price

1.28 The price element of the marketing mix is the only one which brings in revenue. Factors affecting price include the following.

(a) **Economic influences:** the supply and demand; price and income elasticities.

(b) **Competitors' prices.** Competitors include other firms selling the same type of product, as well as firm selling substitute products. Generally, firms like to avoid price wars.

(c) **Quality connotations.** High price is often taken as being synonymous with quality, so pricing will reflect the a product's image. (Stella Artois lager is marketed in the UK as being 'reassuringly expensive'.)

(d) **Discounts**. These can make the product attractive to distributors.

(e) **Payment terms** (eg offering a period of interest free credit).

(f) **Trade-in allowances.**

(g) The stage in the **product life cycle**. For example, at the introduction stage:

   (i) **Penetration pricing** involves charging a low price to achieve early market share advantages; or

   (ii) **Skimming pricing** involves charging high prices early on to reap the maximum profits.

Case examples

Contrast the marketing mix of these holiday firms. Each has been designed to appeal to a particular *market segment.*

(a) *British Museum Tours.* These are tours with an archaeological or cultural interest, and are accompanied by a leading academic. The tours are expensive and might include destinations such as Iran and Ethiopia. Hotels are the most comfortable available. Advertising is not high profile, and is often directed to those who are already members of the British Museum Society.

(b) *Explore.* This firm offers escorted holidays to small groups, in a variety of locations, which may involve some trekking and camping. Locations include isolated villages in northern Thailand. The firm advertises itself on the basis of 'You'll see more'. The firm advertises in newspapers, but also likes to generate repeat business by word of mouth recommendation. Poster or TV advertising is not used.

(c) *Club 18-30.* Targeted at a specific age group, these promise 'fun' holidays in or around beach resorts. A poster advertising campaign in 1994/5 had to be suspended owing to complaints that posters were too 'raunchy'. Holidays are fairly cheap.

The marketing mix

1.29 The product life cycle (see Chapter 6) has implications for the marketing mix, which will differ according to each stage, as in the diagram opposite.

Phase of the product life cycle

	Introduction	*Growth*	*Maturity*	*Decline*
1 *Products*	Initially, poor quality. Product design and development are a key to success. No standard product and frequent design changes (eg microcomputers in the early 1980s).	Competitors' products have marked quality differences and technical differences. Quality improves. Product reliability may be important.	Products become more standardised and differences between competing products less distinct.	Products even less differentiated. Quality becomes more variable.
2 *Customers*	Initial customers willing to pay high prices. Customers need to be convinced about buying.	Customers increase in number.	Mass market. Market saturation. Repeat-buying of products becomes significant. Brand image also important.	Customers are `sophisticated' buyers of a product they understand well.
3 *Promotion*	High advertising and sales promotion costs. High prices possible.	High advertising costs in absolute terms, but falling as a % of sales. Prices falling.	Markets become segmented. Segmentation and extending the maturity phase of the life cycle can be key strategies.	Less money spent on advertising and sales promotion.
4 *Competition*	Few or no competitors.	More competitors enter the market. Barriers to entry can be important.	Competition at its keenest: on prices, branding, servicing customers, packaging etc.	Competitors gradually exit from the market. Exit barriers can be important.
5 *Profit margins and pricing*	High prices but losses due to high fixed costs.	High prices. High contribution margins, and increasing profit margins. High P/E ratios for quoted companies in the growth market.	Falling prices but good profit margins due to high sales volume. Higher prices in some market segments.	Still low prices but falling profits as sales volume falls, since total contribution falls towards the level of fixed costs. Some increase in prices may occur in
6 *Manufacturing and distribution*	Over-capacity. High production costs. Few distribution channels. High labour skill content in	Under-capacity. Move towards mass production and less reliance on skilled labour. Distribution channels flourish and getting adequate distribution channels is a key to marketing success.	Optimum capacity. Low labour skills. Distribution channels fully developed, but less successful channels might be cut.	Over-capacity because mass production techniques are still used. Distribution channels dwindling.

1.30 Section summary

- The marketing mix is product, place, promotion and price.
- These elements sometimes act as substitutes for each other.
- A product involves features, quality and the benefits the customer gains.
- 'Place' involves logistics and channels of distribution (eg intermediaries).
- 'Promotion' involves all areas of communications from advertising, direct selling, point-of-sale promotions and corporate communications.
- Price is set relative to costs, competition and demand.

2 NEW PRODUCT DEVELOPMENT

2.1 A company with products in the mature or decline stages of the life cycle will seek new products to promise future growth.

2.2 **A new product:**

- Opens up an entirely new market
- Replaces an existing product
- Broadens significantly the market for an existing product.

2.3 **An 'old' product can be 'new'** *if:*

(a) It is introduced to a new market
(b) It is packaged in a different way (qualified)
(c) A different marketing approach is used (qualified).

Any new product must be perceived in terms of customer needs and wants.

Question 4

Can you think of examples of new products and 'new' old products to fit into each of the above categories?

Answer

These suggestions may help.

New product

Entirely new market	Internet 'browsers'
Replacing an existing product	Digital cameras (as opposed to 35mm film)
Broadening the market	Cheap personal computers for home use

'New' old product

In a new market	Guiness stout in South East Asia
New packaging	Toothpaste
New marketing	The RAC has changed its corporate image

2.4 **Degrees of newness**

(a) The **unquestionably new** product features high price, performance problems and patchy distribution.

(b) The **partially new** product performs better than the old ones did.

(c) **Major product changes** involve radical changes to the accepted way of doing things or satisfying customers.

(d) **Minor product changes**, such as styling changes, involves adding extras which give a boost to a product.

2.5 The **mortality rate** of new products is very high. The *Economist Pocket Marketing* describes a museum (in New York) of failed products. These include yoghurt shampoo, deodorant tablets and egg coffee.

2.6 To **reduce the risk of failure** new product ideas should be **screened**.

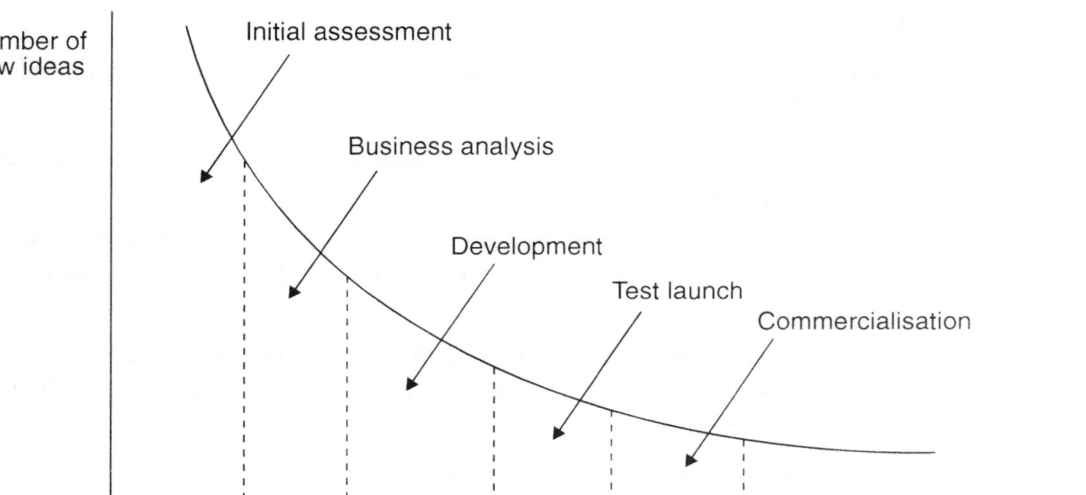

New product development plan

2.7 New products should only be taken to an advanced development stage if they fit the criteria of:

(a) Adequate demand
(b) Compatibility with existing marketing ability
(c) Compatibility with existing production ability

Initial concept testing

2.8 The **concept** for the new product could be **tested** on potential customers to obtain their reactions. But:

- Some new products take 'getting used to'
- People might like something but have better ways of spending money

Business analysis

2.9 A thorough **business analysis** is made for each product idea, projecting future sales and revenues, giving a description of the product so as to provide costs of production, providing estimates of sales promotion and advertising costs, the resources required, profits and ROCE. Other factors such as the product life cycle, and legal restrictions, competitors' reaction etc, must also be evaluated.

2.10 Products which pass the business evaluation will be developed. A timetable and a budget of resources required and of cost must be prepared, so that management control can be applied to the development project.

Development

2.11 Money is invested to produce a **prototype** of the product which can be tried by customers. This process ensures that the product could be produced in sufficient quantities at the right price if it were to be launched. The form which the product test takes will depend very much on the type of product concerned. The test should replicate reality as clearly as possible (eg usage at home, comparison with competitors).

2.12 **Quality** is an important policy consideration. We discuss this in Chapter 16, but some marketing considerations are:

(a) **Customers do not always understand** what they are buying, and tend to judge the quality of an article by its price.

(b) **Quality** should be determined by the expected physical, technological and social **life of the product**.

(i) There is no value in making one part of a product good enough to have a physical life of five years, when the rest of the product will wear out within two years.

(ii) If **technological advances** will make a product obsolescent within a certain number of years, there is little value in producing an article which will last for a longer time.

(iii) If **social tastes** determine the life of a product, the quality required need only be sufficient to cover the period of demand; the quality of fashion clothes, for example, is usually governed by their fashion life.

(c) Quality policy must be carefully integrated with **promotion**, which will have poor success if a product is branded and advertised as having a certain quality which customers then find is not actually true.

Test launch and commercialisation

2.13 **Test marketing** obtains information about how consumers react to the product - will they buy it and, if so, will they buy it again and how frequently?

2.14 Test marketing involves testing a new consumer product in selected areas which are thought to be 'representative' of the total market. This avoids a blind commitment to the costs of a full-scale launch while permitting the collection of market data.

(a) Test marketing enables the company to make sales forecasts, it can also be used to identify flaws in the product or promotional plans.

(b) Test marketing can alert competitors.

2.15 If the test marketing has been successful, the firm will take the necessary steps to commercialise the product/service over the entire market.

Case example

Mondex, a form of digital cash, has been test marketed in Swindon. Other forms of electronic cash are competing with it.

Diffusion and marketing strategy

2.16 Marketers usually want to ensure a rapid **diffusion** or rate of adoption for a new product. This allows them to gain a large share of the market prior to competitors responding.

- A **penetration policy** associated with low introductory pricing and promotions designed to facilitate trial are associated with such a strategy.
- However in some markets, particularly where R & D cost has been high, where the product involves 'new' technology or where it is protected from competition perhaps by patent, a **skimming policy** may be adopted: price is high initially, usually representing very high unit profits and sales can be increased in steps with price reductions, in line with available capacity or competitors responses.

Case example

Companies are using the *Internet* to develop on-line financial services or 'branchless banking'. A leading firm is *Schwab,* a US low-cost stockbroker.

Currently, there are few users: 'but the value of this new breed of customer is considerable. Internet customers at Wells Fargo, the west coast bank, are seven years younger on average than other customers and earn 60% more. These early adopters ... are also active users of financial services'.

2.17 Section summary

- To reduce the likelihood of failure, new product proposals should be subjected to a screening process.
- Penetration or skimming prices can be used once a product is introduced, depending on profit and market share objectives.

3 BRANDS

3.1 **Branding** removes anonymity and gives identification to a company and its goods and services. 'Branding' is actually a very general term covering brand names, designs, trademarks, symbols, a distinctive letterhead, an identifiable shop front or van etc, which may be used to distinguish one organisation's goods and services from another's. ('Trademark' is a legal term covering words and symbols which can be registered and protected.)

KEY TERMS

According to Kotler a **brand** is 'a name, term, sign, symbol or design or combination of them, intended to identify the goods ore services of one seller or group of sellers and to differentiate them from those of competitors'.

Brand equity is the asset that the marketer builds to ensure continuity of satisfaction for the customer and profit for the supplier. The 'asset' consists of consumer attitudes, distribution channels and other relationships.

3.2 **Reasons for branding**

(a) It is a form of **product differentiation**, which make customers readily identify the goods or services and thereby helps to create a customer loyalty to the brand.

(b) The more a product is similar to competing goods, the more branding is necessary to create a **separate product identity**. An example is pet food (eg Whiskas v Felix - see earlier case example).

(c) **Wholesalers and retailers** accept branded goods.

(d) It **facilitates self-selection** of goods in self-service stores and also makes it easier for a manufacturer to obtain display space in shops and stores.

(e) **It reduces the importance of price differentials** between goods.

(f) **Brand loyalty** in customers gives a manufacturer more **control over marketing** strategy and his choice of channels of distribution.

(g) It **eases the task of personal selling** (ie face-to-face selling by sales representatives).

(h) It is supposed to convey **psychic benefits** to the consumer - for example, to be fashionable or to belong to a group.

3.3 Branding strategies

Branding strategy	*Description*	*Implies*
Individual name	Standalone product	Unique
Family branding	The power of the 'family name' to introduce and market new pro-ducts	Image of the family brand across a range of products
Brand extension	New flavours, sizes etc	High consumer loyalty to existing brand
Multi-branding	Different names for similar goods serving similar consumer tastes	Consumers make random pur-chases across brands

(a) **Individual name.** Each product has a unique name. Nestlé uses Buitoni as its brand for pasta, Nescafé as its brand for coffee and so on.

(b) **Family branding.** Kellogg's regularly introduce new breakfast cereals under the 'family name' although the advertisements for each brand are quite distinct.

(c) **Brand extension.** The Mars brand of chocolate bar was extended to Mars ice cream.

(d) **Multi-branding.** Procter & Gamble and Unilever both produce a large number of different brands of soap products. The current trend is to enhance the status of the corporate brand.

3.4 The relevance of branding does not apply equally to all products. The cost of intensive brand advertising to project a brand image nationally may be prohibitively high. Goods or services which are sold in large numbers, on the other hand, promote a brand name by their existence and circulation.

3.5 Where a **brand image promotes an idea of quality**, a customer will be disappointed if his or her experience of a product fails to live up to expectations. **Quality control** is therefore an important element in branding policy. It is especially a problem for **service industries** (eg hotels, airlines, retail stores) where there is less possibility than in a manufacturing industry of detecting and rejecting the work of an operator before it reaches the customer. Bad behaviour by an employee in a face-to-face encounter with a customer will reflect on the entire company and possibly deter the customer from using any of the company's services again.

3.6 Branding is a controversial issue in financial reporting. A brand is sometimes considered as an asset at least for management accounting and decision making purposes - see 'brand equity' defined in the Key Term box above - because it enables the firm to generate higher profits than if the product were unbranded.

3.7 Section summary

- A brand gives a distinct identity to the products/service it sells.
- Some believe a brand image is an intangible asset.

4 DOMESTIC AND INTERNATIONAL MARKETING

4.1 International marketing (IM) refers to the marketing of goods and services in two or more countries.

The reasons for starting to market internationally

4.2 Firms may be pushed into IM by domestic adversity or pulled into IM by attractive opportunities abroad. More specifically, some of the reasons firms enter into IM are these.

(a) **Chance**. An executive may see an opportunity when abroad or the firm may receive chance orders or requests for information from potential foreign potential customers.

(b) **Mature or declining home market**. IM may provide for sales growth since products are often in different stages of the product life cycle in different countries.

(c) **Intense competition** at home sometimes induces firms to seek markets overseas where rivalry is less keen.

(d) **Reduce dependence** on a single domestic market.

(e) **National market is too small:** a large volume is needed either to cover the high costs of plant, equipment, R & D and personnel or to exploit a large potential for economies of scale and/or experience.

(f) **Disposal of discontinued products** since these can be sold abroad without spoiling the home market.

(g) **Favourable opportunities** such as the development of lucrative Middle Eastern markets, marked depreciation in their domestic currency values, corporate tax benefits offered by particular countries and the lowering of import barriers abroad.

4.3 **Some differences between domestic and international marketing**

Factor	Domestic	International
Cultural factors	National price	Diverse national prices
	Usually no language problems	Many language barriers
	Relatively homogeneous market	Fragmented, diverse markets
	'Rules of the game' understood	Rules diverse, changeable and unclear
	Similar purchasing habits	Diverse purchasing habits

Factor	Domestic	International
Economic factors	Uniform financial climate	Variety of financial climates, ranging from very conservative to highly inflationary
	Single currency	Currencies differing in stability and real value
	Stable business environment	Multiple business environments, some unstable
Competitive factors	Data available, usually accurate and easy to collect.	Formidable data collection problems
	Competitors' products, prices, costs and plans usually known	Many more competitors, but little information about their strategies
Legal factors	Relative freedom from govern-ment interference	Involvement in national economic plans
		Government influence on business decisions
	Political factors relatively unimportant	Political factors often significant
Technological factors	Use of standard production and measurement systems	Training of foreign personnel to operate and maintain equipment
		Adaptation of parts and equipment
		Different measuring systems

4.4 **Strategic and tactical issues of IM**

(a) **Strategic issues**

(i) Does the strategic decision to get involved in IM **fit with the company's overall mission and objectives**? Or will 'going international' cause a mis-match between objectives on the one hand and strategic and tactical decisions on the other?

(ii) Does the organisation have (or can it raise) the **resources necessary** to exploit effectively the opportunities overseas?

(b) **Tactical issues**

(i) How can the company get to **understand customers' needs** and preferences in foreign markets?

(ii) Does the company know **how to conduct business** abroad, and deal effectively with foreign nationals?

(iii) Are there **foreign regulations** and associated hidden costs?

(iv) Does the company have the **necessary management skills** and experience?

4.5 **International marketing objectives**

(a) What proportion of total sales will be overseas?

(b) What are the longer term objectives?

(c) Will it enter one, a few, or many markets? **Generally firms should enter fewer** countries when:

(i) Market entry and market control costs are high.

(ii) Product and market communications modification costs are high.
(iii) There is a large market and potential growth in the initial countries chosen.
(iv) Dominant competitors can establish high barriers to entry.

(d) **What types of country** should it enter (in terms of environmental factors, economic development, language used, cultural similarities and so on)? The three major criteria for this decision should be as follows.

(i) Market attractiveness
(ii) Competitive advantage
(iii) Risk

Question 5

Identify *one* product. Try and find out how it is sold in the UK and in another country of your choice. Assess whether undifferentiated or differentiated marketing is being applied.

Standardisation

4.6 Most firms would prefer to sell the same product at the same price through similar distribution channels, using the same means of communication in all its markets. Complete standardisation is rarely possible because of the very **dissimilar marketing environments** encountered in the different markets.

Barriers to standardisation

Environmental variable	*Product*	*Price*	*Distribution*	*Promotion*
Economy	Varied income level	Varied income level	Different retail structures	Media availability
Culture	Consumer tastes and habits	Price negotiating habits	Buying habits	Language and attitude differences
Competition	Nature of existing products	Competitors' objectives, costs and prices	Competitors' monopoly and use of channels	Competitors' budgets, appeals
Law	Product regulation	Price control	Restriction on distribution	Advertising and media restrictions

4.7 A firm's approach to this decision depends to a large extent on its attitude towards internationalisation and its level of involvement in international marketing. There are broadly three types of approach in this context.

Approach	Comment
Ethnocentrism	Overseas operations are viewed as being secondary to domestic operations and are often simply a means of disposing of surpluses. Any plans for overseas markets are developed at home with very little systematic market research overseas. This is the first step into international marketing and involves a centralised strategy.
Polycentrism	Subsidiaries are established, each operating independently with its own plans, objectives and marketing policies on a country by country basis. Adaptation will be at its most extreme with this approach. Polycentrism can be viewed as an evolutionary step and involves a decentralised strategy.
Geocentrism	The organisation views the entire world as a market with standardisation where possible and adaptation where necessary. It is the final evolutionary stage for the multinational organisation and involves an integrated marketing strategy.

4.8 Some **products** are extremely sensitive to the environmental differences which bring about the need for adaptation; others are not at all sensitive to these differences, in which case standardisation is possible. A useful way of analysing products internationally is to place them on a continuum of environmental sensitivity. The greater the environmental sensitivity of a product, the greater the necessity for the company to understand the way in which its products interact with economic, socio-cultural and other environmental variables

Environmentally sensitive	Environmentally insensitive
Adaptation necessary	Standardisation possible
• Fashion clothes • Convenience foods	• Industrial and agricultural products • World market product, eg denim jeans

Global brands

4.9 Some brands are also sensitive to national conditions, whereas some brands are global at least to a degree.

(a) At first sight, Coca-Cola and McDonald's appear genuinely international. However, Coca-Cola advertising has been adapted to the different conditions. McDonald's, too, offer product differentiation in various cases.

(b) The **brand might have a different meaning** in different countries. A commodity in one country is a luxury in others – Stella Artois is marketing as 'reassuringly expensive' in the UK, whereas it is not priced at a premium in Belgium.

(c) Some brands appeal to similar segments – **strategically equivalent segments** in each market so that various makes of trainer or styles of music are **fashion items.** The elderly might be considered a strategically equivalent segment for some problems.

4.10 Section summary

- Firms enter overseas markets because of change, problems at home or attractive markets.

- International marketing has unique problems, particular in relation to standardisation or adaptation of the marketing mix.

5 MODES OF ENTRY TO OVERSEAS MARKETS 6/95

Exam focus point

An easy question in June 1995 asked you to evaluate a suitable mode of entry into a foreign market, comparing joint ventures with acquisitions.

5.1 If an organisation has decided to enter an overseas market, the way it does so is of crucial strategic importance. Broadly, three ways of entering foreign markets can be identified: indirect exports, direct exports and overseas manufacture.

5.2 The most suitable mode of entry varies:

(a) **Among firms in the same industry** (eg a new exporter as opposed to a long-established exporter)

(b) **According to the market** (eg some countries limit imports to protect domestic manufacturers whereas others promote free trade)

(c) **Over time** (eg as some countries become more, or less, hostile to direct inward investment by foreign companies).

5.3 **Choice of mode of entry**

Consideration	Comment
The firm's marketing objectives	These relate to volume, time scale and coverage of market segments. Thus setting up an overseas production facility would be inappropriate if sales are expected to be low in volume, or if the product is only to be on sale for a limited period.
The firm's size	A small firm is less likely than a large one to possess sufficient resources to set up and run a production facility overseas.
Mode availability	A firm might have to use different modes of entry to enter different markets. Some countries only allow a restricted level of imports, but will welcome a firm if it builds manufacturing facilities which provide jobs and limit the outflow of foreign exchange.
Mode quality	In some cases, all modes may be possible in theory, but some are of questionable quality or practicality. The lack of suitably qualified distributors or agents would preclude the export, direct or indirect, of high technology goods needing installation, maintenance and servicing by personnel with specialist technical skills.
Personnel requirements	These vary according to which mode of entry is used. When a firm is unable to recruit suitable staff either at home or overseas, indirect exporting or the use of agents based overseas may be the only realistic option.
Market feedback information	In some cases a firm can receive feedback information about the market and its marketing effort from its sales staff or distribution channels. In these circumstances direct export or joint ventures may be preferred to indirect export.

Learning curve requirements	Firms which intend a heavy future involvement in an overseas market might need to gain the experience that close involvement in an overseas market can bring. This argues against the use of indirect exporting as the mode of entry.
Risks	Some risks, such as political risk or the risk of the expropriation of overseas assets by foreign governments, might discourage firms from using *overseas production* as the mode of entry to overseas markets. Instead, firms might prefer the indirect export mode as it is safer.
Control needs	Production overseas by a wholly owned subsidiary gives a firm absolute control while indirect exporting offers virtually no control to the exporter.

Exporting

5.4 **Exporting** is where goods are made at home but sold abroad. It is the easiest, cheapest and most commonly used route into a new foreign market. Many firms become exporters in an unplanned, haphazard and reactive way, simply by accepting orders from potential customers who happen to be based overseas.

5.5 **Advantages of exporting**

(a) Exporters can concentrate production in a single location, giving economies of scale and consistency of product quality.

(b) Firms lacking experience can try international marketing on a small scale.

(c) Firms can test their international marketing plans and strategies before risking investment in overseas operations.

(d) Exporting minimises operating costs, administrative overheads and personnel requirements.

Indirect exports

5.6 **Indirect exporting** is where a firm's goods are sold abroad by other organisations.

(a) **Export houses** are firms which facilitate exporting on behalf of the producer. The producer gains the benefits of the export house's market knowledge and is normally relieved of the need to finance the export transaction, to suffer the credit risk and to prepare export documentation. Usually the producer has little control over the market and the marketing effort.

(b) **Specialist export management firms** offer a full export management service. In effect, they perform the same functions as an in-house export department but are normally remunerated by way of commission. In other words, exporting work is effectively outsourced with all the advantages and drawbacks outsourcing entails.

(c) **UK buying offices of foreign stores and governments**. Many foreign governments and foreign companies (eg department stores) have buying offices set up permanently in the UK.

(d) **Complementary exporting** ('piggy back exporting') occurs when one producing organisation (the carrier) uses its own established international marketing channels to market (either as distributor, or agent or merchant) the products of another producer (the rider) as well as its own. The carrier earns increased profit from a better use of distribution capacity and can sell a more attractive product range. The rider obtains entry to a market at low cost and low risk.

Direct exports

5.7 **Direct exporting** occurs where the producing organisation itself performs the export tasks rather than using an intermediary. Sales are made directly to customers overseas who may be the wholesalers, retailers or final users.

(a) **Sales to final user**. Typical customers include industrial users, governments or mail order customers.

(b) Strictly speaking an **overseas export agent** or distributor is an overseas firm hired to effect a sales contract between the principal (ie the exporter) and a customer. Agents do not take title to goods; they earn a commission (or profit).

(c) **Company branch offices abroad**. A firm can establish its own office in a foreign market for the purpose of marketing and distribution.

(i) **Advantages**

(1) When sales have reached a certain level, branch offices become more effective than agencies.

(2) The commitment of a producer's own staff should be more effective than those of an agent.

(3) The producer retains complete marketing control.

(4) The producer can acquire better market information.

(5) Customer service should improve.

(ii) **Disadvantages**

(1) Higher investment, overhead and running costs are entailed.
(2) There can be a political risk, particularly expropriation of assets.
(3) The firm will be subject to local employment legislation.

Overseas production

5.8 **Benefits of overseas manufacture**

(a) A **better understanding of customers** in the overseas market.
(b) **Economies of scale** in large markets.
(c) **Production costs are lower** in some countries than at home.
(d) **Lower storage and transportation costs.**
(e) **Overcomes the effects of tariff and non-tariff barriers.**
(f) Manufacture in the overseas market **may help win orders from the public sector.**

Contract manufacture

5.9 **Licensing** is a quite common arrangement as it avoids the cost and hassle of setting up overseas. Licensing was discussed in Chapter 7.

5.10 In the case of **contract manufacture** a firm (the contractor) makes a contract with another firm (the contractee) abroad whereby the contractee manufactures or assembles a product on behalf of the contractor. Contract manufacture is suited to **countries** where the **small size of the market** discourages investment in plant and to **firms** whose main **strengths are in marketing** rather than production.

(a) **Advantages of contract manufacture**

(i) No need to invest in plant overseas.

(ii) Lower risks associated with currency fluctuations.

(iii) Lower risk of asset expropriation is minimised.

(iv) Control of marketing is retained by the contractor.

(vi) Lower transport costs and, sometimes, lower production costs can be obtained.

(b) **Disadvantages of contract manufacture**

(i) Suitable overseas contractee producers cannot always be easily identified.
(ii) The need to train the contractee producer's personnel.
(iii) The contractee producer may eventually become a competitor.
(iv) Quality control problems in manufacturing may arise.

Joint ventures

5.11 Joint ventures are particularly relevant to overseas operations. A joint venture is usually an alternative to seeking to buy or build a wholly owned manufacturing operation abroad and can offer substantial advantages.

(a) Some governments discourage or even prohibit foreign firms setting up independent operations. Instead, they encourage joint ventures with indigenous firms.

(b) A joint venture with an indigenous firm provides local knowledge, quickly.

Wholly owned overseas production

5.12 Establishing and running a production facility in an overseas market demonstrates the fullest commitment to that market. Production capacity can be built from scratch, or, alternatively, an existing firm can be acquired.

(a) **Acquisition**, as a mode of entry, is rapid and offers the benefits of an existing management team, market knowledge and all the other trappings of a 'going concern'.

(b) **Creating new capacity** can be beneficial if there are no likely candidates for takeover, or if acquisition is prohibited by the government.

(i) This entry mode enables the use of the newest production technology.

(ii) The investing company may also be able to start afresh with new forms of managing industrial relations.

5.13 **Advantages**

(a) The firm does **not have to share its profits** with partners of any kind.

(b) The firm does **not have to share or delegate decision-making** and so there are no losses in efficiency arising from inter-firm conflict.

(c) There are **none of the communication problems** that arise in joint ventures, license agreements etc.

(d) The firm is able to operate completely **integrated** international systems.

(e) The firm gains a more **varied experience** from overseas production than from the other arrangements.

5.14 **Disadvantages**

(a) The substantial **investment** funding required prevents some firms from establishing operations overseas.

(b) Suitable **managers**, whether recruited in the overseas market or posted abroad from home, may be **difficult to obtain**.

(c) Some overseas **governments discourage**, and sometimes prohibit, **100% ownership** of an enterprise by a foreign company.

(d) This mode of entry **forgoes the benefits of an overseas partner's market knowledge**, distribution system and other local expertise.

Question 6

You are marketing chocolate for a large UK confectionery firm. The UK style of chocolate is not widely appreciated in Europe. If, however, you wished to expand into European markets, what mode of entry would you use?

Answer

You would probably manufacture overseas, perhaps by buying an overseas company with the expertise and available brands.

5.15 **Section summary**

- Modes of entry are indirect exports, direct exports and overseas production.
- Exports are 'lower risk' but often lower reward than overseas production.

6 SERVICES AND CUSTOMER CARE 6/96

6.1 Many 'products' have in fact a 'service element': remember that a company's *value chain* has 'after sales service' as one of the elements. Service businesses include health care, restaurants, tourism, financial services, education etc. We explore this below.

KEY TERM

Service '... any activity of benefit that one party can offer to another that is essentially intangible and does not result in the ownership of anything. Its production may or may not be tied to a physical product.' (P Kotler, *Social Marketing*)

6.2 **Characteristics of services**

(a) **Intangibility**. Unlike goods (physical products such as confectionery), there are no substantial material or physical aspects to a service. A service cannot be packaged in a bag and carried home, such as a live musical performance (unlike a CD).

(b) **Inseparability**. Many services are 'created' at the same time as they are 'consumed', (eg dental treatment). No service exists until it is actually being experienced/consumed by the person who has bought it.

(c) **Variability.** Many services face the problem of maintaining consistency in the standard of output. It may be hard to attain precise standardisation of the service offered. The quality of the service may depend heavily on:

(i) **Who** (or what) delivers the service.

(ii) Exactly **when** it takes place (booking a holiday using standard procedures may well be quite different on a quiet winter afternoon than on a hectic spring weekend).

(d) **Perishability**. Services cannot be stored. The services of a dentist are purchased for a **period of time**. The service they offer cannot be used 'later'.

(e) **Ownership**. Services differ from consumer goods: they do **not normally result in the transfer of property**. The purchase of a service only confers on the customer access to or a right to use a facility, not ownership.

Exam focus point

Accountancy firms are 'service' businesses - as in the June 1996 exam.

Deploying the marketing mix in services

6.3 Deploying the service marketing mix in services is a rather difficult task.

(a) **Poor service quality on one occasion** (eg lack of punctuality of trains, staff rudeness, a bank's incompetence) is likely to lead to **widespread distrust** of everything the organisation does.

(b) **Complexity.** If the service is intangible offering a complicated future benefit, or is consumed 'on the spot', then attracting customers means promoting an attractive image and ensuring that the service lives up to its reputation, consistently.

(c) **Pricing** of services is often complicated, especially if large numbers of people are involved in providing the service.

(d) **Human resources management** is a key ingredient in the services marketing mix, as so many services are produced and consumed in a specific social context.

6.4 **Service marketing involves three additional 'P's:** people, processes and physical evidence.

People

6.5 The importance of **employees** as an element in the marketing mix is particularly evident in service industries.

(a) If you have had poor service in a shop or restaurant, you may not be willing to go there again. An American retailing firm estimated that there was an identifiable **relationship** between **low staff turnover** and repeat purchases.

(b) Managing front-line workers (eg cabin-crew on aircraft) who are the lowest in the organisational hierarchy but whose behaviour has most effect on customers, is an important task for senior management. It involves corporate culture, job design and motivational issues. People issues include the following.

- Appearance
- Attitude
- Commitment
- Behaviour
- Professionalism
- Skills
- Numbers
- Discretion

Processes

6.6 **Processes** involve the ways in which the marketer's task is achieved. Efficient processes can become a marketing advantage in their own right. For example, if an airline develops a sophisticated ticketing system, it can encourage customers to take connecting flights offered by allied airlines. Efficient processing of purchase orders received from customers can decrease the time it takes to satisfy them. Process issues include:

- Procedures
- Policies
- Mechanisation
- Queuing
- Information
- Capacity levels
- Speed/timing
- Accessibility

Physical evidence

6.7 This is particularly important in service industries, for example where the ambience of a restaurant is important. Logos and uniforms help create a sense of corporate identity.

- **Environment** (eg furnishings, colours, layout, noise levels, smells, ambience)
- **Facilities** (eg vans/vehicles/aeroplanes, equipment/tools, uniforms, paperwork)
- **Tangible evidence** (eg labels, tickets, logos, packaging)

Customer service and customer care

6.8 The idea of **customer service** grew from a focus on 'order-cycle' related activities into a much more general and all-embracing approach which covers activities at the pre-, during- and post-transaction stages.

KEY TERM

Customer care involves '... the management and identification of "**moments of truth**", with the aim of achieving customer satisfaction'.

6.9 These **moments of truth** are **contacts between companies and customers**, where a firm's reputation is at stake.

6.10 Customer care emphasises the importance of attitude, and covers every aspect of customer/supplier relationships. Customer care is aiming to **close the gap** between customers' **expectations** and their **experience**. The service dimension requires a policy, and a set of activities.

6.11 The new focus on the service dimension, whether it is referred to as 'customer care or not, involves a **culture change**. It is a core value for all policymaking and strategic thinking.

6.12 Service levels and TQM (see next chapter), are closely related to each other. Quality programmes, however, cover many topics in addition to those dealing with customers. 'Satisfied customers' are the focus of customer care programmes. The challenge is to maintain this emphasis throughout a quality process. Satisfied customers are likely to be *loyal* customers.

Case example

Heathrow airport

The following example of a customer care programme was described in *People Management* (12 September 1996). Although focused on customer care it describes how marketing considerations go far further than adverts and logos.

'In 1994 Heathrow airport began a grassroots campaign to revolutionise engineers' attitudes to customer service. The project was modelled on an inverted organisational pyramid: the people nearest the customer would develop their own training programme, which managers would follow and support.

At Heathrow, the term 'engineering' covers a number of activities, from the specialised (for instance, aircraft jetty maintenance), to the more routine (plumbing, carpentry, etc).

The engineers' customers include airlines, airport franchises, airport control authorities plus colleagues at Heathrow airport. Representatives of these groups identified the eight key service elements that gave the programme its name: Aces High (standing for ability, communication, etiquette, speed of response, honesty, image, giving a little extra and Heathrow's representatives).

In a series of problem-solving workshops, front-line employees were asked to review their behaviour, customer service attitude and customer relationships against the Aces High elements.

The initial response was mixed. Some engineers rose to the challenge, while others felt they had 'seen it all before and nothing will change'. This reaction, from staff jaded by a series of company initiatives, was not unexpected, but it was a sad indication of how untapped talent can be driven into a rut.

So, while some engineers worked on their standards of behaviour towards customers, a different approach was needed for the cynics. When asked what would convince them of managerial commitment, they came up with a list of the major obstacles to good service. Senior management used these to prepare a statement offering extensive support.

The statement committed *managers* to *eight actions* including loosening the rules on overtime and releasing engineers from having to obtain three quotes before buying equipment. The speed and manner of this support produced an overwhelming response, and the role of engineering customer service representative (a title chosen by the engineers themselves) was born, as a number came forward to help move the programme onward.

The representatives produced a code of conduct; devised and ran special customer service workshops for their customers and contractors; and, most remarkably, composed a customer survey in which engineers were named and assessed by customers for their conduct and service attitude.

As Aces High moves through Heathrow's 14 engineering sections, front-line staff have continued to develop their own approaches to service improvement.

Perhaps the most disappointing problem was some senior managers' lack of responsibility for keeping in touch with customer service representatives.

Resisting the 'quick win' culture at Heathrow has also proved difficult. Productivity has clearly increased. In March 1996, 66 per cent of engineering faults were fixed in less than two hours, compared with 58 per cent a year earlier.

Some of the technicians who came forward to assist as customer service representatives were seen by their managers as lacking either the attitude or the skill for the role. Their involvement has perhaps been one of the most interesting results of using external facilitators who had no preconceptions and judged people on their contribution at the time, not on their history in the organisation.

6.13 Section summary

- Services are intangible, inseparable, variable and perishable.
- The service mix involves people, processes and physical evidence.
- Customer care is becoming a core strategic issue.

7 MARKETING PLANS

7.1 The formulation of a *marketing strategy* to achieve the product-market objectives, will embrace the formulation of a broad strategy and then of more detailed plans for implementing the strategy. A marketing plan interacts with the strategic plan for the firm as follows.

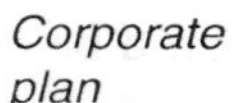

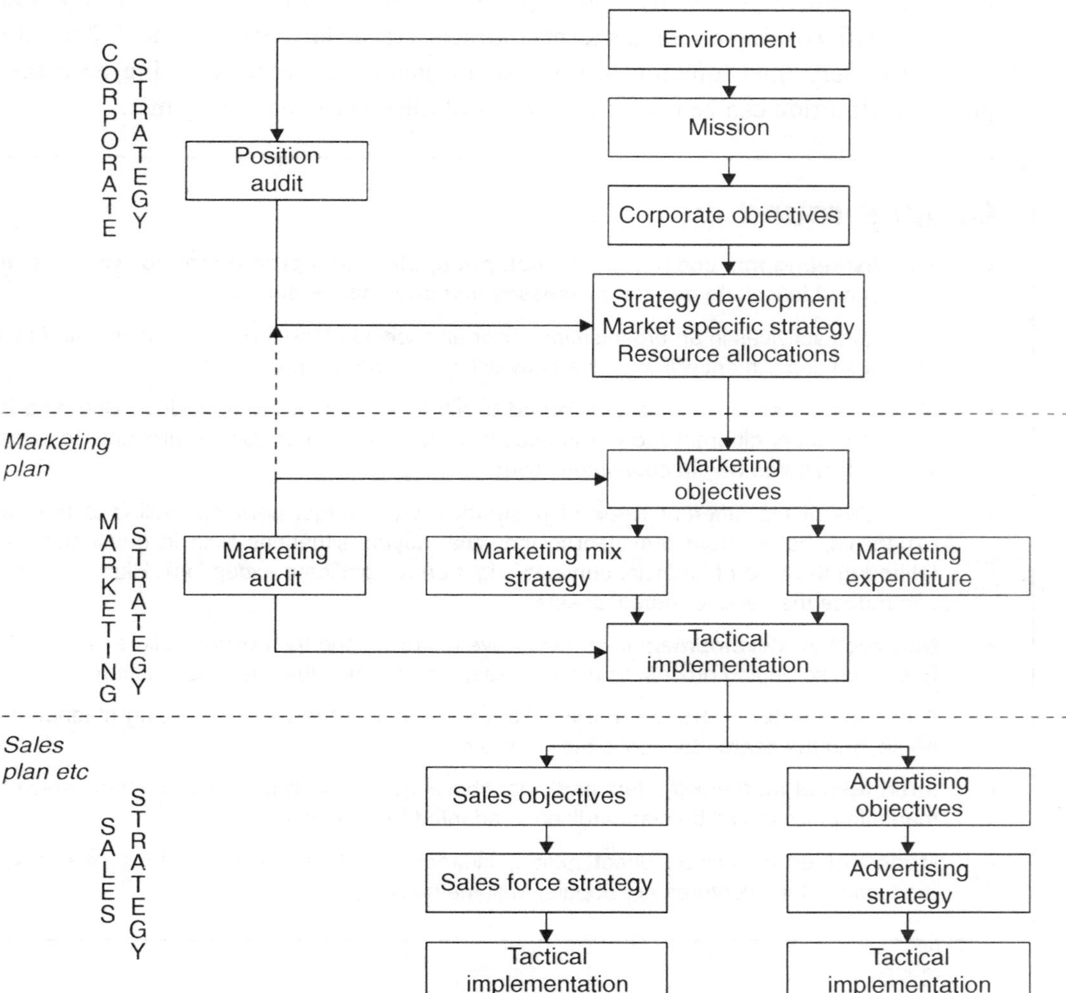

7.2 The marketing plan consists of several inter-related decisions.

(a) **Sales targets***:* these must be set for each product and each sales division (with sub-targets also set for sales regions, sales areas and individual salesmen). Sales targets may be referred to as sales quotas.

(b) The **total marketing budget** must be set.

(c) Given an overall marketing budget, resources (cash) must be allocated between:

- (i) salaries of salesmen;
- (ii) above the line expenditure (advertising);
- (iii) below the line expenditure.

(d) The overall sales target set by top management will incorporate sales price decisions; but within the formulation of the marketing plan there is likely to be some room for manoeuvre and an element of choice in the pricing decision. In other words, top management will decide on a 'rough pricing zone' and a specific price within this zone will be fixed later within the marketing plan.

8 BRAINWORKS PLC UPDATE

Questions can be found in the Introduction box at the beginning of this Chapter.

8.1 *Question 1*. Placing people in jobs would not appear to admit of any radical innovations in the core product or service, but there are a number of augmentations which might be made. For example BW could tempt top notch staff by more generous holiday arrangements. Initiatives taken by its competitors are approaches which could be copied in this area. Furthermore the firm could endeavour to build up long term relationships with the staff working on longer-term contracts. At the farthest extreme, BW might offer to run the personnel function of some small businesses, as outsourcing becomes more popular. Attention can be paid to all aspects of the service marketing mix.

Chapter roundup

- The **marketing mix** comprises **product, price, place** and **promotion**. For **services**, this is extended to include **people, processes** and **physical evidence**.
- Marketing activities in an organisation cover all aspects of the mix, although the staff in the marketing department will have the heaviest involvement in promotion.
- Marketers endeavour to create a **brand** to attract consumers to a product. Branding is a form of product differentiation. It is necessary for a firm to enable its products to appear 'different' in some way in consumers' eyes.
- The roles of the different types of **promotion** vary. Direct personal selling is the most expensive, but is more prevalent in industrial buying situations than in consumer sales (although the sale of financial services might be a significant exception). High advertising can reduce the need for personal sales.
- **New product development** is an expensive exercise, and the costs of failure can be high. Extensive screening processes are necessary to minimise the chances of failure.
- A firm may **enter overseas markets** for any number of reasons, including stagnation at home, and the search for economies of scale.
- **International marketing** offers particular challenges, in particular (the extent to which the marketing mix should be standardised or adapted to local conditions.
- **Modes of entry** include direct export, indirect export and various forms of overseas production. Joint ventures are popular in some markets.

Quick quiz

1. What is the marketing mix? (see para 1.1)
2. What is a product? (1.4)
3. Why might an organisation employ direct distribution? (1.8)
4. List some sales promotion activities. (1.16)
5. What is meant by public relations? (1.21)
6. List the stages in new product development. (2.6)
7. What is a brand? (3.1)
8. Why might a firm contemplate international marketing? (4.2)
9. What sort of products need to be adapted to the overseas market? (4.8)
10. List three modes of entry to overseas markets. (5.1)
11. What considerations should be borne in mind when making a choice of mode of entry? (5.3)
12. What are the characteristics of services? (6.2)
13. List the three additional Ps of service marketing (6.4)

Question to try	Level	Marks	Time
19	Exam standard	25	45 mins
20	Exam standard	25	45 mins

Chapter 16

QUALITY ISSUES

Introduction

Quality is one of the more important management issues to have emerged in recent years, inspired, in part, by the success of Japanese companies in improving the production process. Customers, also, are demanding a higher standard of product design and manufacture.

In the past, quality control was achieved by the **inspection** of finished output. This is now regarded as very wasteful. Instead, quality is viewed as integral to the manufacturing process.

TQM entails a number of changes to the design and manufacturing process, including a culture of **continuous improvement**, techniques to ensure that customer specifications are designed into the product manufacturing process, techniques which minimise defects by reducing and **controlling variations**, and proper systems of **quality assurance** which require better relations with suppliers (Section 3). Introducing TQM sometimes requires a management shakeup.

Although there are **limits** to the role of quality as a source of **competitive advantage,** quality is often necessary to be able to compete at all.

Brainworks plc

1 How might quality be relevant to Brainworks?

1 TRADITIONAL APPROACHES TO QUALITY

Case examples

Siebe, Motorola, General Electric

The case examples below (extracted from a Financial Times article, 24 February 1997) describe how three firms are using quality control to improve performance and save money.

When the UK engineering group Siebe announced recently it was adopting a 'six sigma' programme, the news caused little remark. Quality programmes under the six sigma banner absorb much time and money at such leading US companies as Motorola and General Electric. Siebe's announcement, in fact, was partly a rhetorical flourish: an application to join a world elite of super-efficient manufacturers.

Six sigma means reducing the defects in a process to just over three per million. It is thus a ferociously demanding target. The approach is particularly suited to the high-volume, high-precision electronics industry. For example, a mobile phone such as Motorola produces might contain 400 components. If the company operates to two sigma - 45,000 defects per million - on each part, the cumulative odds of the phone being defective are far too high.

Six sigma is part of a general shift in quality management. Where companies once measured quality by checking the final product, they now aim to control the processes at the outset. In the jargon, they have moved from 'acceptable quality levels' to 'statistical process controls'. Six sigma means tightening up the tolerance on processes to incredible levels.

Six sigma is by no means confined to manufacturing. GE Capital, the financial services division of General Electric, applies it to processes ranging from billing and the tracking of assets to various kinds of customer service.

The real question is whether you can put the right paradigm in place, so the process has fewer moving parts and less things to break down. It's very important to change the process fundamentally. You need to change the whole behaviour of the company, to become more responsive to the customer.

GE Capital surveys its customers regularly - some weekly, some monthly or quarterly, depending on their business - to check its performance.

At Siebe, the same emphasis on the customer crops up immediately. Jim Mueller, president of the company's temperature and appliance controls division, says: "Customer satisfaction is very important for us, especially since we're mostly and OEM [original equipment manufacturer]. Someone else's name goes on the product, so if it fails, someone else gets a bad reputation.

Siebe's adoption of six sigma, he says, follows the introduction of a lean manufacturing programme two years ago. "We had to take inventory out of the system," he says. "When you do that, you have to have reliable processes. So going to six sigma, is part of the lean manufacturing puzzle." Siebe's goal is a 25 per cent reduction in what Mueller calls the cost of quality: money spent on scrap, rework, inspection and warranty.

Six sigma is no good on its own. As Roy David of Arthur D Little says: "You company has to be applying total quality management already, including customer satisfaction, management commitment and employee involvement."

KEY TERM

Quality has been defined by Ken Holmes *(Total Quality Management)* as 'the totality of features and characteristics of a product or service which bears on its ability to meet stated or implied needs.' It is fitness for use.

1.1 **Quality** is concerned with 'fitness for use', and quality management (or control) is about ensuring that products or services meet their planned level of quality and conform to specifications.

(a) Establish standards of quality for a product or service.

(b) Ensure that these required standards of quality are met in a suitably high proportion of cases;

(c) Monitoring actual quality; and

(d) Taking control action when actual quality falls below standard.

1.2 EXAMPLE

The postal service might establish a standard that 90% of first class letters will be delivered on the day after they are posted, and 99% will be delivered within two days of posting. Procedures would have to be established for ensuring that these standards could be met (eg frequency of collections, automated letter sorting, frequency of deliveries and number of staff employed etc). Actual performance could be monitored, perhaps by taking samples from time to time of letters that are posted and delivered. If the quality standard is not being achieved, the management of the postal service could take control action (eg employ more postmen or advertise again the use of postcodes) or reduce the standard of quality of the service being provided.

Traditional approaches to quality

1.3 In the past, quality control meant **inspection** of finished output (or goods inward). Quality was something assured **at the end** of the manufacturing process rather than being considered at the beginning.

1.4 **Problems with 'inspection'**

(a) The **inspection process itself does not 'add value'**. If no defective items were produced, there would be no need for an inspection function.

(b) The **production of substandard products is a waste** of materials and time.

(c) The **inspection department takes up possibly expensive land** and warehousing space.

(d) **Working capital is tied up** in stocks which cannot be sold.

1.5 BS 6143 gives examples of each type of **quality cost.**

(a) **Prevention costs** are the 'cost of any action taken to investigate or reduce defects and failures'.

(i) Quality engineering
(ii) Design/development of quality control equipment and inspection equipment
(iii) Maintenance of quality control equipment and inspection equipment
(iv) Administration of quality control
(v) Training in quality control.

(b) **Appraisal costs** are 'the costs of assessing quality achieved'.

(i) Acceptance testing
(ii) Inspection of goods inwards
(iii) Inspection costs of in-house processing
(iv) Performance testing.

(c) **Internal failure costs** are 'costs arising within the organisation of failing to achieve quality'

(i) Failure analysis
(ii) Re-inspection costs
(iii) Losses from failure of purchased items
(iv) Losses due to lower selling prices for sub-quality goods
(v) Costs of reviewing product specifications after failures.

(d) **External failure costs**. These are 'costs arising outside the manufacturing organisation of failure to achieve specified quality (after *transfer* of ownership to the customer)'.

(i) Administration of customer complaints section
(ii) Costs of customer service section
(iii) Product liability costs
(iv) Cost of repairing products returned from customers

(v) Cost of providing replacement items due to sub-standard products or marketing errors.

1.6 Section summary

- Quality is fitness for use.
- The 'inspection approach' allows for built-in *waste*.
- Quality costs are prevention, appraisal, internal failure and external failure.

2 CONCEPTS IN QUALITY MANAGEMENT

2.1 'Traditionally', writes Holmes, 'quality has been regarded as something which is imparted to a product by the production department of a company...[but]...if a company wishes to ensure that it reliably meets its customers' requirements, *all* parts of the company must be involved in quality.... **Quality management must pervade the whole organisation not just the production function**. Quality management must be **total**.'

2.2 In practice, there are many different ways in which this philosophy can be put into practice, and the gospel of quality has a host of competing interpreters. All too often it is **implemented** as a sop to current fashion, another '**quick fix**'.

Juran: design quality, conformance quality and fitness for use

2.3 Joseph Juran worked with Japanese industrialists in the years immediately after World War II and, with Deming (see below), is credited with increasing Japan's industrial competitiveness.

2.4 Juran was concerned with identifying **specific improvements** for enhancing quality.

(a) The best approach to enhancing quality is to 'identify specific opportunities, evaluate their viability by using conventional methods such as Return on Investment, plan the selected project carefully, monitor their results'.

(b) There is an economic level of quality beyond which it is pointless to strive.

(c) Most quality problems derive from management systems and processes rather than poor workmanship.

2.5 Juran defines quality as 'fitness for use' which in fact includes two elements.

(a) **Quality of design:** the customer satisfactions built into the product.
(b) **Quality of conformance:** a lack of defects in the finished goods.

Question 1

The boss of Acme Umbrellas Ltd believes that customers want robust umbrellas, so he makes one *entirely* out of aluminium apart from some gold decoration. 'It is a bit heavy I suppose', he says, showing an example, 'but it's *perfectly* made, look at the gold pins and look at the perfect, flawless finish. Why don't people want it?'

Answer

The *design quality* is poor, in that it does not meet customer requirements in an *appropriate* way. The umbrella is, however, perfectly made, so its *conformance quality* is *high*.

Crosby: zero defects and right first time

2.6 Philip Crosby (of ITT) is chiefly known for two concepts.

(a) **Zero defects concept**. There should never be any *defects* in a finished product. Some hold it to be an impossible ideal, and invoke the concept of diminishing returns. Alternatively it can be seen as a slogan to employees ('you're paid to get things right').

(b) **Right first time:** a product should not have to be corrected once it is built. It is thus a corollary of the zero defects concept.

2.7 Crosby proposes four standards which flesh out these concepts.

(a) **Quality is conformance** to requirements.
(b) The system for advancing quality is **prevention, not appraisal.**
(c) The **goal should be zero defects.**
(d) The importance of quality is measured by the **cost of not having quality**.

Feigenbaum: quality is everybody's business

2.8 Armand Feigenbaum appended the word 'total' to quality.

(a) He emphasised the relevance of quality issues to all areas of the operations of a business.

(b) Feigenbaum stressed the importance of identifying the **costs of quality**, and the **lack of quality**, to prove that, in economic and accounting terms, **'prevention is better than cure'**.

(c) This involves changing the role of the **quality control function** (which inspected and rejected output) to one in which quality provided an effective system for quality maintenance. A **'planning role'** would involve the design of systems and procedures to reduce the likelihood of sub-optimal production.

Taguchi: design systems and products to reduce variation

2.9 Genichi Taguchi focuses on the importance of functions and activities undertaken **before** the manufacturing process in determining product quality. The aim might be to ensure conformance quality, as identified in paragraph 2.5 above, and implement the 'planning role' in 2.8 above.

2.10 In his **quality-cost model**, Taguchi identifies two aspects of quality.

(a) **Off-line quality control**

(i) Systems design (reflecting appropriate technology).

(ii) Parameter design (it is easier to design a product insensitive to manufacturing variances than to control these variances - in other words, the *robustness* of the product is an issue in the design stage).

(iii) Tolerance design (ie the degree of variation permitted in a process).

(b) **On-line quality control** aims to minimise losses due to variations between items produced. The principle is to weigh the cost of the variation against the cost of correcting the variation. Variations can include, for example, slight differences in:

(i) Weight between identical components.
(ii) Time in producing a service.

2.11 Taguchi developed a mathematical model of loss.

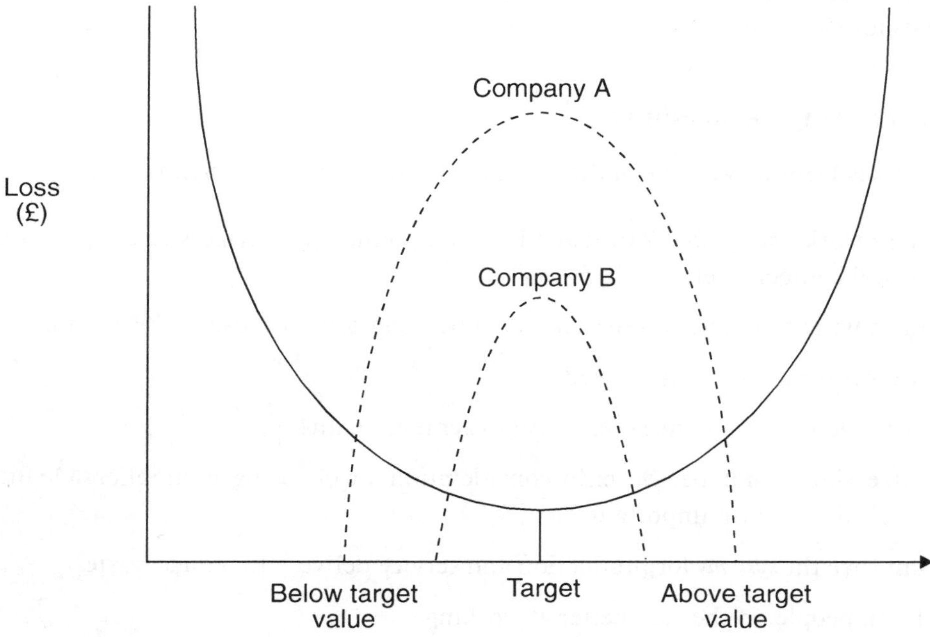

2.12 Loss, in the Taguchi model, refers to 'costs incurred or profits forgone relative to some baseline of performance'. This has two implications.

(a) Loss increases at an increasing rate, the greater the variation. (Loss can be customer dissatisfaction.)

(b) It is important to **reduce variation** within the range. In the diagram, Company A and B reach the same **average** level of performance, but A's performance shows **greater variation, hence greater** losses according to Taguchi's model.

2.13 EXAMPLE

Compare two fast food outlets each selling hamburgers. Both *Gristle Prince* and *Greasy Mike's* sell burgers for £1 each and both outlets aim to serve *each* customer about 90 seconds after the customer has placed an order. Obviously certain times of the day are busier than others, so queues and hence serving times are slightly longer. There are no differences in the quality of the burgers served or in the layout of each shop. Both manage, on *average,* to serve a customer in the target 90 seconds, yet Gristle Prince is beginning to attract more customers. Greasy Mike's employ a quality consultant, who analyses both outlets using a Taguchi model. Here are the consultant's findings.

(a) 100 customers entered *Gristle Prince.* 50 of them were served in *less* than the 90 second target, and 50 of them in more. In fact 50 were served in 80 seconds and fifty in 100 seconds, leading to an average serving time of 90 seconds.

(b) At *Greasy Mike's* on the other hand the story was different. Again 100 customers entered the restaurant.

(i) Ten had to wait five minutes (300 seconds)
(ii) Ten had to wait three minutes (180 seconds)
(iii) Sixty had to wait one minute (60 seconds)
(iv) Twenty had to wait 30 seconds

Again the average service time is 90 seconds.

The result of course is that *Gristle Prince's* service is much more predictable, which is why customers might prefer it. They know they will *never* have to wait more than 100 seconds for their meal.

W Edwards Deming: leadership

2.14 W Edwards Deming was one of the founding fathers of the movement.

2.15 Deming's work *Out of the Crisis* listed fourteen points for managers to adopt to improve quality and competitiveness.

1. Improving products and services must be a constant purpose of the organisation
2. All waste should be eliminated
3. Cease depending on mass *inspection* to achieve quality.
4. Price should not be the only consideration in choosing a supplier. Quality and reliability are also important.
5. Improve the *systems* for production and service delivery to reduce waste.
6. Train people, so they are better at working.
7. *Lead* people.
8. 'Drive out fear'.
9. Break down barriers between staff areas.
10. Get rid of slogans, exhortations, targets. These can be alienating.
11. Get rid of numerical quotas. These encourage the wrong attitude to production. Doing without *targets and goals* might seem bizarre especially in the context of MBO. A short *example* might highlight the meaning of this assertion. Former Communist countries used to measure output as *net material product*. In other words, purely quantitative output targets (eg a number of tractors built) were the basis for measuring production. No attention was paid to quality.
12. Enable people to take pride in their work.
13. Encourage 'education and self improvement for everyone'.
14. Action should be taken to accomplish quality objectives.

Case example

A report in the *Financial Times* compared productivity differences between two aluminium smelting plants in Germany and the UK, each owned by the same company. The German plant had higher productivity. The company's management said that the difference was largely because the German workers were better trained in maintaining the equipment.

Ishikawa: quality circles and employees' responsibilities

2.16 Ishikawa proposed **quality circles** (and the development of a few simple tools for quality improvement). Quality circles are groups of selected workers delegated with the task of analysing the production process, and coming up with ideas to improve it. Success requires a commitment from the circle's membership, and a management willingness to take a back seat.

2.17 Section summary

These ideas can be included in a number of basic principles related to quality management. Its importance which will be fleshed out in the subsequent sections of this chapter.

(a) A **customer first orientation** should ensure design quality.

(b) **Senior management commitment** is necessary to implement certain programmes.

(c) A focus on **continuous improvement** is necessary.

(d) **Employees must be involved** in the improvement process.

(e) **Reductions in variation** can save money.

(f) **Training** is necessary to optimise the production process.

(g) **Statistical methods** of thinking should be used throughout the organisation (especially in process control) to measure and control variation.

(h) **Prevention** is better than detection and cure.

(i) **Suppliers** should be treated as partners.

(j) **Performance measures** should be consistent with overall goals.

(k) Tasks should be **standardised** to minimise variation.

(l) An emphasis on product and service quality should begin in **design**.

(m) **Co-operation** is necessary between all business functions. R & D for example should co-operate with the production function in designing products that can be produced efficiently as well as meet customer requirements.

(n) Awareness of **internal customers**.

(o) Substantial **cultural change** is sometimes necessary.

3 QUALITY ASSURANCE AND STANDARDS 12/94

3.1 The essentials of **quality assurance** are that the *supplier* guarantees the quality of goods supplied and allows the customers' inspectors access while the items are being manufactured. Usually agreed inspection procedures and quality control standards are worked out by customer and supplier between them, and checks are made to ensure that they are being adhered to.

(a) The **customer can eliminate goods inwards inspection** and items can be directed straight to production. This can give large savings in cost and time in flow production, and can facilitate JIT production.

(b) The **supplier produces to the customer's requirement**, thereby reducing rejects and the cost of producing substitutes.

3.2 Suppliers' quality assurance schemes are being used increasingly. One such scheme is BS EN ISO 9000 certification. This is a nationally promoted standard, only awarded after audit and inspection of a company's operations. The standard falls into three parts.

(a) Part 1 covers design manufacture and installation.
(b) Part 2 covers just manufacture and installation.
(c) Part 3 covers inspection and testing.

3.3 The **standard does not dictate the quality of individual goods and services**, but aims to ensure that **quality management systems of a suitable standard are in place**.

(a) The standards 'set out how you can establish, document and maintain an effective quality system which will demonstrate to your customers that you are committed to quality and are able to satisfy their quality needs'.

(b) While it provides feedback about performance, it cannot guarantee that control action is taken. It is 'an indicator of potential, not of achievement'.

3.4 Finally, two other factors should be mentioned.

(a) Certification can be withdrawn, if a firm does not live up to the requirement.

(b) BS EN ISO 9000 increasingly will become a factor in selecting suppliers. Customers wish to avoid the cost of inspecting goods inwards.

Acquiring BS EN ISO 9000

3.5 The diagram on the following page shows the route to acquiring BS EN ISO 9000. An accreditation body will have to be paid for the initial certification process and for regular recertification visits. A number of bodies grant BS EN ISO 9000 certification.

3.6 **Problems with the standard**

(a) The standard is complex and particularly onerous for small firms.

(b) Some feel that it is written in jargon and is incomprehensible to most people apart from management consultants.

(c) It is a time-consuming and expensive process sometimes requiring substantial redesign of the system.

3.7 Section summary

- Quality assurance is when the supplier guarantees a level of quality, thereby reducing the need for inspection.
- BS EN ISO 9000 certifies that a supplier's quality systems are of a certain standard.

4 TOTAL QUALITY MANAGEMENT

KEY TERM

Total quality management (TQM) is 'a culture aimed at continually improving performance in meeting the requirements in all functions of a company'. (Holmes)

'... The total composite product and service characteristics of marketing, engineering, manufacture and maintenance, through which the product and service in use will meet the expectations by the customer' (Fiegenbaum).

'A way of managing a business to ensure complete customer satisfaction internally and externally' (Oakland).

4.1 TQM takes on board many of the principles identified in the previous sections.

BS EN ISO 9000 certification

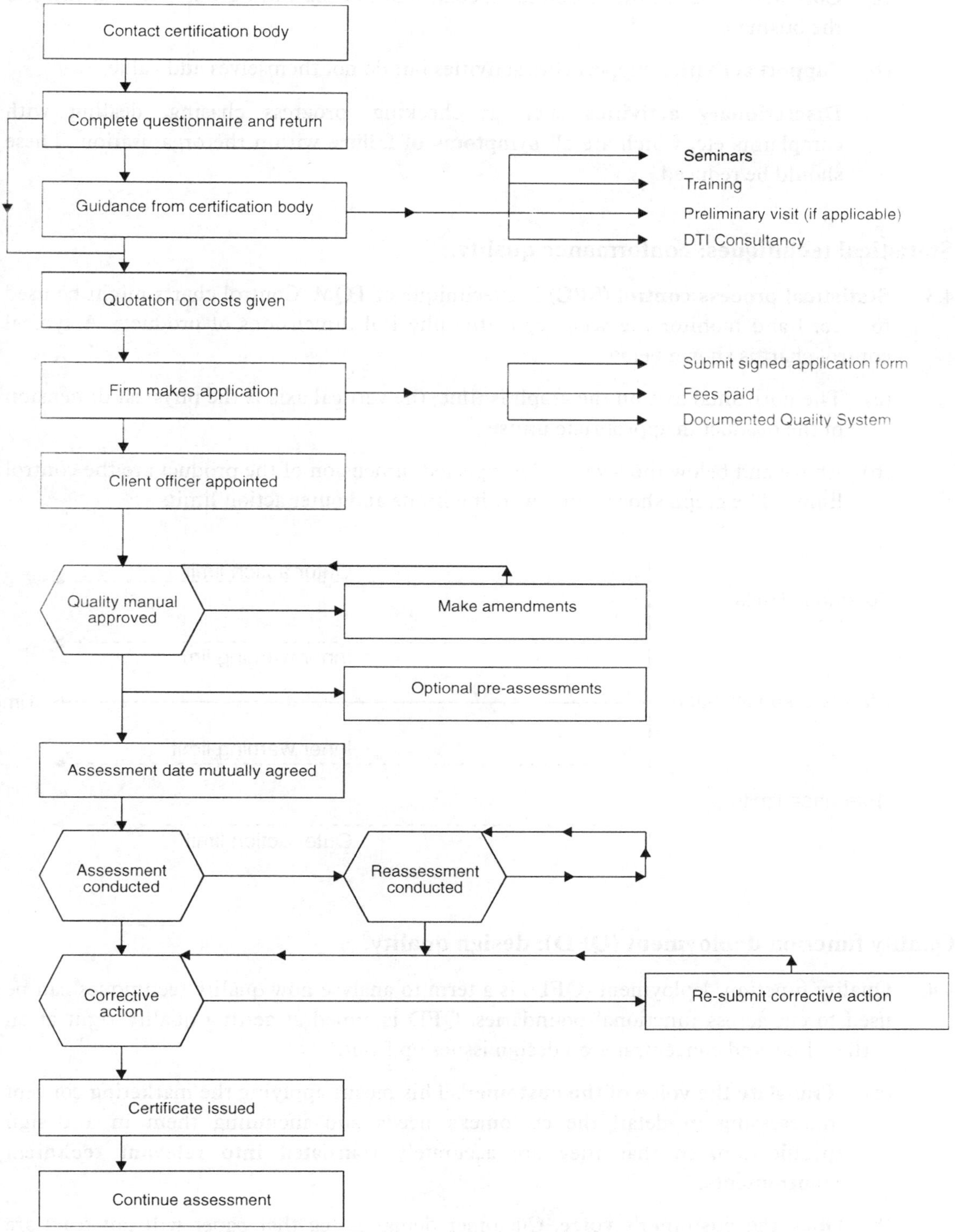

4.2 TQM programmes are aimed at identifying and then reducing/eliminating causes of wasted time and effort.

(a) **Core activities** are the reason for the existence of the work group and add value to the business.

(b) **Support activities** support core activities but do not themselves add value.

(c) **Discretionary activities** such as checking, progress chasing, dealing with complaints etc, which are **all symptoms of failure** within the organisation. These should be reduced.

Statistical techniques: conformance quality.

4.3 **Statistical process control (SPC)** is a technique of TQM. Control charts might be used to record and monitor the accuracy of the physical dimensions of products. A typical control chart is shown below.

(a) The horizontal axis on the graph is time, the vertical axis is the physical dimension of the product in appropriate units.

(b) Above and below the level of the expected dimension of the product are the control limits. The graph shows inner warning limits and outer action limits.

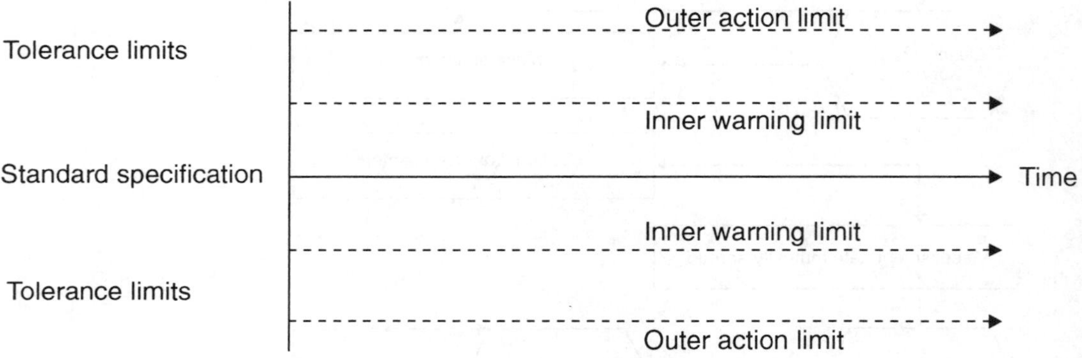

Quality function deployment (QFD): design quality.

4.4 Quality function deployment (QFD) is a term to analyse how quality techniques can be used to cut across functional boundaries. QFD is aimed at getting quality right at an earlier time, and concentrates on design issues up front.

(a) **'Translate the voice of the customer'**. This means applying the marketing concept in assessing in detail the customer's needs and including them in a design specification, so that they are accurately translated **into relevant technical requirements.**

(b) **Obey the customer's voice.** Customer demands (eg that paper will not tear) are converted into quality requirements (paper must be of a minimum thickness). There is a matrix of relationships between customer demand and technical requirements.

Quality characteristics

Customers' demands

	V	W	X	Y	Z
A					
B	○				
C		⊙	△		
D					
E					

⊙ = strong relationship

○ = medium relationship

△ = weak relationship

Customer demand C has a strong relationship to quality characteristic W but a weak one to X.

(i) This matrix can determine where effort should be most expended

(ii) Furthermore, certain customer requirements might contradict each other, so the matrix identifies possible trade offs.

Question 2

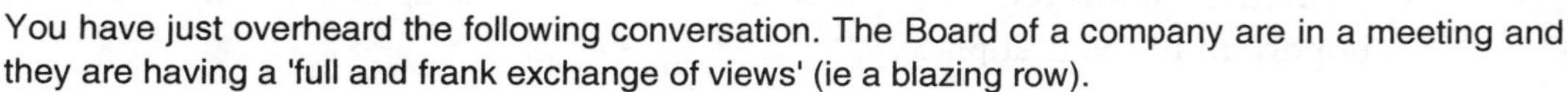

You have just overheard the following conversation. The Board of a company are in a meeting and they are having a 'full and frank exchange of views' (ie a blazing row).

Chairman : Ladies and gentlemen, *please...*

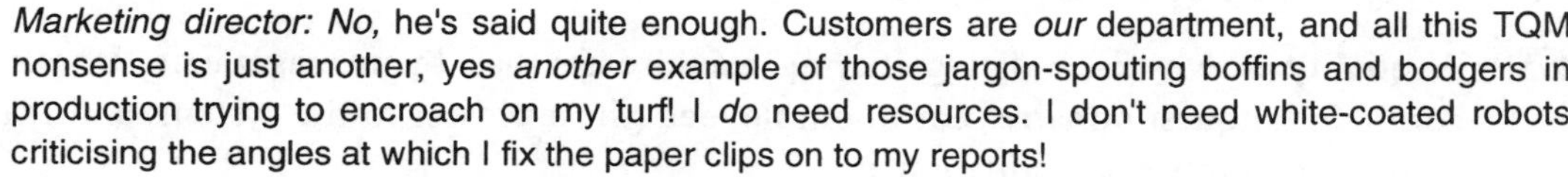

Marketing director: No, he's said quite enough. Customers are *our* department, and all this TQM nonsense is just another, yes *another* example of those jargon-spouting boffins and bodgers in production trying to encroach on my turf! I *do* need resources. I don't need white-coated robots criticising the angles at which I fix the paper clips on to my reports!

Chairman: Ladies and gentlemen, *please...*

Production director: No, she's said quite enough. Marketing people couldn't give *one* hoot, let alone two, about quality and we all know it's quality that sells the goods. Remember, when we had to abandon our solar powered torch? State of the art, state of *the art* that was, and did they try and sell it? Did they?

Chairman: Ladies and gentlemen, *please...'*

Finance director: '*No,* they've both said quite enough. If all we get out of TQM is pointless rows like this, I might as well go back and count some more beans. At least it's *meaningful* and relaxing.

Chairman: Ladies and gentlemen! No, you've all said *quite* enough. I don't think any of you have grasped the point. I'd better get another management consultant in with a better flipchart.

What insights do each of the above characters have into TQM?

Answer

The chairman has got the gist. All of them miss the point as to the nature of TQM. The marketing director has a point in that TQM *does* imply a blurring of functional boundaries, but the marketing director *ought* to be pleased that, if TQM is implemented, the marketing concept will be brought into product design. The production director still has not grasped the concept. His idea of quality is 'technical excellence' not fitness for use. The finance director ought to care, as TQM has meaningful cost implications. The row is not pointless: at least the issue is being discussed, which is a beginning.

Assessing and auditing quality

4.5 Proper quality management depends on information.

KEY TERM

Quality assessment is the 'process of identifying business practices, attitudes, and activities that are either enhancing or inhibiting the achievement of quality improvement' (*Total Quality* Ernst and Young Quality Improvement Consulting Group).

4.6 **Quality assessment exercises**:

(a) **Supply proof** that quality improvement measures are needed.

(b) **Provide a baseline for future measurement**, in other words to make a starting point from which you can measure your progress.

(c) **Build management** support for quality measures, by the power of the evidence collected.

(d) **Convince management**, particularly senior management, that the issue is important in the first place.

Overview of the quality assessment process

4.7 A **quality survey** is a data-gathering exercise for use by management. It can be a confidential questionnaire sent to **employees** (those closest to the system) and it might focus on a number of quality issues.

(a) **Leadership**. Do employees believe that quality is an obviously important consideration for management?

(b) **Quality improvements.** Do managers seek improvements in quality?

(c) To what extent are various **quality techniques** used in the organisation?

(d) Do management recognise and reward **innovatory ideas** in quality improvement activities?

(e) Are employees **accountable** for quality?

Questions range from techniques to management style and work group organisation. It is roughly **subjective**.

4.8 A **quality evidence audit** is then conducted to obtain **observable data related to quality.**

(a) This might include data with which employees are unfamiliar (eg measurements of output variations which have not been measured before).

(b) Benchmark information (eg number of customer complaints) might be collated. Benchmarks can be derived from competitors.

(c) The firm needs to collect the right kind of quality data.

(d) The data from each survey are analysed. Details of barriers to improving quality are conveyed to management. For example, if management secrecy inhibits employee involvement and their commitment to enhancing quality, management should be informed of this fact.

Continuous improvement

4.9 TQM is not a one-off process, but is the **continual examination** and improvement of existing processes.

4.10 Continuous improvement applies both to the finished product, but also to the processes which make it.

(a) A philosophy of continuous improvement **avoids complacency**.

(b) **Customer needs change**, and competitors' performance so a philosophy of continual improvement enables these changes to be taken into account in the normal course of events.

(c) **New technologies or materials** might be developed, enabling cost savings or design improvements.

(d) Rarely do businesses know every possible fact about the production process. Continuous improvement **encourages experimentation** and a scientific approach to production.

(e) It is a way of **tapping employees' knowledge**.

(f) **Reducing variability** is a key issue for quality, if this is assessed on Taguchi's quality-cost model.

(g) Improvement on a continual, step by step basis is **more prudent** in some cases than changing things at one go.

4.11 **Model for improving quality**

Step 1 **Find out the problems** (eg from customer and employees).

Step 2 **Select action targets** from the number of improvement projects identified in *Step 1*, on the basis of cost, safety, importance, feasibility (with current resources).

Step 3 **Collect data** about the problem.

Step 4 **Analyse data** by a variety of techniques to assess common factors behind the data, to tease out any hidden messages the data might contain.

Step 5 **Identify possible causes** (eg using brainstorming sessions). No ideas are ruled out of order.

Step 6 **Plan improvement action.** Significant help might be required.

Step 7 **Monitor the effects of the improvement.**

Step 8 **Communicate the result.**

4.12 Reducing variability often requires improving the process itself, rather than changing the machines or adjusting them.

Total quality and customers (internal and external)

4.13 A **customer orientation** requires the firm to recognise that customers buy products for the benefits they deliver.

4.14 What constitutes a 'quality product or service' must, it seems, be **related to what the customer wants.** Indeed, quality would have no commercial value unless it delivered benefits to the customer. The customer must be the final arbiter of the quality which a product possesses.

4.15 From a strategic point of view, then, **quality is in the eye of the consumer**. If quality is meeting the requirements of the consumer, then it should be recognised that throughout and beyond all enterprises, whatever business they are in, is a series of 'quality chains'.

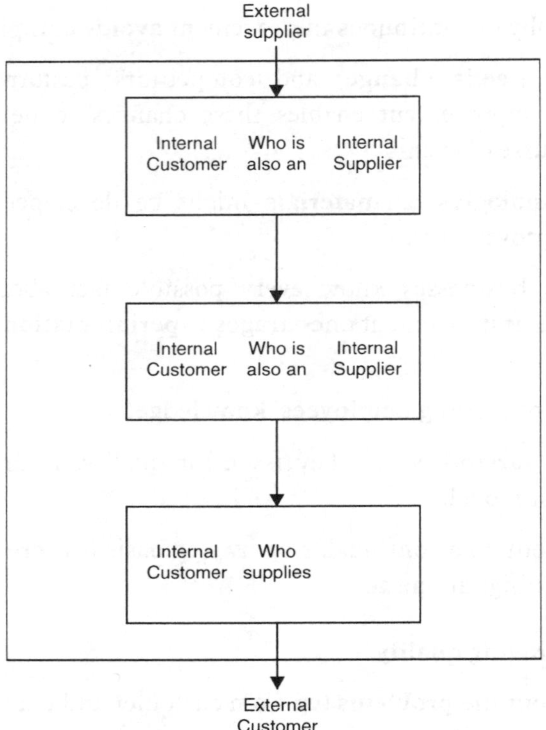

4.16 Oakland argues that meeting customer requirements is the main focus in a search for quality. (If the customer is outside the organisation, then the supplier must seek to set up a marketing activity to gather this information, and to relate the output of their organisation to the needs of the customer.)

4.17 **Internal customers** for services are equally important, but seldom are their requirements investigated. The quality implementation process requires that all the supplier/customer relationships within the **quality chain** should be treated as marketing exercises, and that each customer should be carefully consulted as to their precise requirements from the product or service with which they are to be provided.

4.18 Each link in the chain should prompt the following questions, according to Oakland.

Of customers
• Who are my immediate customers? • What are their true requirements? • How do or can I find out what the requirements are? • How can I measure my ability to meet the requirements? • Do I have the necessary capability to meet the requirements? (If not, then what must change to improve the capability?) • Do I continually meet the requirements? (If not, then what prevents this from happening, when the capability exists?) • How do I monitor changes in the requirements?
Of suppliers
• Who are my immediate suppliers? • What are my true requirements? • How do I communicate my requirements? • Do my suppliers have the capability to measure and meet the requirements? • How do I inform them of changes in the requirements?

4.19 Section summary

- Total quality management involves the whole organisation, and implements zero defects and right first time principles.
- Techniques include statistical process control (conformance quality), and quality function deployment (design quality).
- Quality assessments are fact-finding exercises.
- The purpose is continuous improvement.

5 INTRODUCING TQM: ORGANISATIONAL IMPLICATIONS 12/94

5.1 Introducing TQM involves a significant shake up. TQM involves:

(a) **Giving employees a say** in the process (eg in the **quality survey**) and in getting them to suggest improvements.

(b) **Greater discipline** in the process of production and the establishment of better linkages between the business functions.

(c) **New relationships with suppliers,** which requires them to improve their output quality so that less effort is spent rectifying poor input. Long-term relationships with a small number of suppliers might be preferable to choosing material and sub-components on price.

(d) **Work standardisation** (with techniques perhaps introduced by the technostructure) and **employee commitment**.

(e) **Commitment over the long term.** It will fail if it is seen as just another fad.

(f) **All the organisation,** as the material on quality chains above suggests.

5.2 **Participation** is important in TQM, especially in the process of continual improvement, where workforce views are valued. The management task is to encourage everybody to contribute. **Barriers to participation** include:

(a) An **autocratic chief executive**, who believes he or she is the sole key to the process.

(b) **Individualism,** in which people 'possess' ideas in order to take credit for them rather than share them for mutual benefit.

(c) **Managers, who** see themselves as leaders and directors rather than facilitators and supporters.

(d) Middle managers, who feel their **authority is threatened.**

Case example

Holmes quotes Komatsu's experience in the UK, and cites the comments of Dr Clive Morton: 'the team system was seen as a key factor in a total quality culture, yet the British emphasis on individual development can be very destructive of team working'.

5.3 Morton reported that often the hardest aspects for *managers* to accept are these.

(a) **Social and status barriers** are removed with the removal of office partitions.

(b) **Administrative functions** must now be seen as **supporting** the shop floor.

(c) The **shop floor is the most important** area.

(d) Managers are judged by their **contribution to team spirit**, not 'the virility of their decisions'.

(e) Meetings are used to **gather information**, not to take decisions.

(f) **New personal skills** are needed (eg the ability to listen and communicate).

(g) A manager's role is in **supporting and training, not disciplining and restricting**.

5.4 Holmes believes that managers most suited for a TQM culture will 'understand how people motivate themselves and direct this motivation towards good team results. They are concerned with achieving the goals of the team, supporting the individual members of the team, and keeping the team together'. They will 'ensure time is spent setting objectives, planning, briefing, controlling, evaluating. These activities will be conducted in a participatory or controllable way'.

5.5 A **steering committee** will be set up to introduce TQM. Senior managers will agree specific steps for training. A quality infrastructure of personnel, training systems and quality monitoring systems will then be set in place.

6 QUALITY AND SUSTAINABLE EXCELLENCE

6.1 In Chapter 6 we discussed the concept of excellence. Many excellent companies seem to have pursued operational strategies which seem to bear certain relationships with TQM, in other words:

(a) Close attention to quality.

(b) Closeness to the customer (eg in design).

(c) 'Productivity through people' would seem to be similar to quality strategies which view the worker as a source of ideas.

6.2 'Excellence' was supposed to offer **long-term** success thus gives a strategic role to quality management.

(a) In a **cost leadership strategy**, attention to quality can be seen as a means of improving the efficiency of the total process of design and production, which will have the effect of **reducing costs**.

(i) Taguchi's cost of quality model would indicate that quality cuts losses. High quality is a way of becoming the most efficient producer. A **minimum standard of quality might become a barrier to entry** for particular industries.

(ii) Design improvements can reduce the cost to the buyer (eg supplying metal sheets in the size the buyer wants, so the buyer will not be purchasing waste).

(b) **Differentiation strategies** can also be supported by quality to the extent that:

(i) **Design quality** (ie a design that is particularly good at satisfying the needs of a particular market segment) **can be used to differentiate** a product.

(ii) **Conformance quality** (ie that the product is well made) is a means of differentiation against competitors although it is becoming **less important**.

(iii) The company is able to differentiate its offer, not so much by the design and/or conformance quality of the *end product*, but for some **quality advantage in other activities of the value chain** or in the linkages between them.

6.3 Remember, though, that not all excellent firms have prospered.

Sustainable excellence and quality

6.4 There are limits to the extent to which quality can be a source of **sustainable** competitive advantage.

(a) The **techniques relating to conformance quality can be (and have been) copied.** Conformance quality is a universal language. If everybody speaks it, it will no longer be a source of competitive advantage other than, just possibly, as a barrier to entry. (Remember in Chapter 1, we cited Porter who said that operating excellence, whilst essential, is not the same as strategy.)

(b) **Design quality is still an important source of competitive advantage,** providing it is properly integrated with the demands of customers in the market or market segment. Design quality will thus continue in importance as it is central to differentiation and focus strategies.

7 BRAINWORKS PLC UPDATE

Questions can be found in the Introduction box at the beginning of this chapter.

7.1 *Question 1.* TQM is traditionally associated with manufacturing but it applies to services as well. BW needs to enhance quality for its business clients and the people it interviews.

7.2 *Question 2.* As a service firm BW can:

(a) Set operational standards for service quality (eg follow up every enquiry within a set period).

(b) Obtain and review customer feedback.

Chapter roundup

- **Quality** is the totality of features which bears on a product's ability to meet stated needs.
- **Design quality** includes the degree to which customer satisfactions are built into a product.
- **Conformance quality** is an absence of defects in the finished goods.
- Various writers dealing with quality issues differ in the degree that they believe that a new approach to quality requires changes in culture, in addition to the application of particular techniques.
- Taguchi's quality/cost model is important as it identifies the necessity of **reducing variation** in production processes as a means of reducing losses.
- **Quality assurance** is increasingly demanded of suppliers. Quality assurance standards include BS EN ISO 9000. Certification is granted to companies which have an adequate system of quality assurance.
- **TQM** is a concept which applies quality to the *whole* organisation. Relevant techniques concepts are **statistical process control** (for conformance quality) and **quality function deployment** (for design quality). Important aspects are **continuous improvement**, the fact that production has **employees take part** in controlling and improving quality, **internal marketing** and linking business activities in **quality chains.**
- **Quality assessments** are a management process to identify how quality issues are treated in an organisation. It might involve a survey of employee attitudes followed by the collection of more objective data.
- Conformance quality is easily copied, but certain standards are necessary in order to be able to compete at all.

Quick quiz

1. Define quality. (see para 1.1)
2. Distinguish between design and conformance quality. (2.5)
3. What is meant by 'zero defects' and 'right first time'? (2.6)
4. Describe Taguchi's quality-cost model. (2.10 - 2.11)
5. What are the three parts of BS EN ISO 9000? (3.2)
6. Define TQM. (4.1).
7. Describe statistical quality control charts. (4.3)
8. What is quality function deployment? (4.4)
9. What questions would be asked of employees in a quality survey? (4.7)
10. What are the advantages of continuous improvement? (4.10)
11. How do you establish quality chains? (4.15 - 4.18)
12. Does quality necessarily guarantee competitive advantage? (6.2, 6.4)

Question to try	Level	Marks	Time
21	Exam standard	25	45 mins

Chapter 17

11/2/99

MAINTAINING COMPETITIVE POSITION

Chapter topic list		Syllabus reference
1	Strategic control systems	2(d)(iii)
2	The balanced scorecard and other performance measures	2(d)(iii)
3	Monitoring competitors	2(d)(iii)
4	Responding to competition	2(d)(iii)
5	Tactics in different industry structures	2(c)(iii), 2(d)(iii)
6	Corporate decline	2(d)(iii)
7	Brainworks plc update	

Introduction

Chapters 14 and 15 dealt with the customer. Chapter 16 discussed the importance of product quality in manufacture. This chapter has a focus on competitors.

To monitor its own strategic performance a firm needs to establish a number of performance indicators, relevant to different aspects of the business. Over-reliance on **financial results** alone can mean that managers do not address longer term strategic issues hence measures such as the **balanced scorecard** to redress the emphasis. Other operational **performance indicators** are needed as well.

A firm's competitive advantage is only **relative** to its competitors. In practical terms, a firm cannot choose a competitive strategy in isolation, as competitors can actively respond and change the assumptions on which it was based. The characteristics of each competitor should be examined in a **competitor analysis**, and **responding to them** involves exploiting competences and enacting **ploys** (see Chapter 2) in a number of ways.

Corporate decline is a test of managerial skill, either to turn round an underperforming company or to pull out from a product market area in permanent decline.

Brainworks plc

1 What do you think is the significance for BW of the merger between Diad and Colec? Are they a threat?

2 To what extent is BW an example of corporate decline?

1 STRATEGIC CONTROL SYSTEMS

1.1 Control is the final element of the strategic management process, the review of actual performance in the light of planned performance.

1.2 **Problems with relying solely on budgetary control**

(a) Financial results appear to provide 'proof' that the strategy is working. But it is possible to **overlook important indicators of strategic success.**

(b) Too much emphasis on budgetary control and short-term profit can **disguise strategic problems** from senior managers.

(c) Strategic control measures might **require complicated trade-offs** between current financial performance and longer-term competitive position, and between different desirable ways of building competitive strength.

Gaps and false alarms

1.3 Many firms have spent time measuring the wrong things - the trick is to remove 'false alarms' from performance measures and replace them with measures that fill gaps in coverage.

(a) **False alarms** motivate managers to improve areas where there are **few** benefits to the organisation. A recent *IMD* study of a sample of 92 senior manufacturing executives, suggests that false alarms include:

(i) Concentration on direct costs when most costs are overheads.

(ii) Labour efficiency measures are easily manipulated and ignore labour effectiveness: the task should be to 'work smarter not harder'.

(iii) Machine efficiency: standard hours are irrelevant, as long as the firm has enough capacity.

(b) **Gaps** (important areas which are neglected) include:

(i) New product introduction
(ii) Customer satisfaction
(iii) Employee involvement

(c) **Different measures apply to different industries.** In continuous processes, such as chemicals, 'throughput time' is not important (ie speed of processing) as there will always be buffer stock. However, it is important in consumer electronics.

Strategic control systems

1.4 To encourage the measurement of the 'right' things, firms can institute systems of **strategic control**. The **influences on a strategic control system** are:

(a) The **time-lag** between **strategic control** measures and their conversion into **financial results**.

(b) The **linkages** with the other businesses in a group.

(c) The **risks** the business faces.

(d) The **sources** of competitive advantage.

Goold and Quinn identify two ways in which companies exercise strategic control and review (if they exercise strategic control at all): formal and informal.

1.5 **Formal systems of strategic control**

Step 1 **Strategy review**. Review the progress of strategy.

Step 2 Identify **milestones of performance** (strategic objectives) both quantitative and qualitative (eg market share, quality, innovation, customer satisfaction).

- Milestones are identified **after** the business's **critical success factors** have been outlined.
- Milestones are **short-term steps** towards **long-term goals**.

- Milestones must enable managers to monitor **actions** (eg whether a new product has been launched) and results (the outcome - eg the success of the launch).

Step 3 **Set target achievement levels** (not wholly quantitative).

(i) Targets must be reasonably precise.
(ii) Targets should suggest strategies and tactics.
(iii) **Competitive benchmarks** are targets set **relative to the competition.**

Step 4 **Formal monitoring of the strategic process.** Reporting is less frequent than for financial reporting.

Step 5 **Reward**. For most systems, there is little relationship between the achievement of strategic objectives and the **reward system,** although some companies are beginning to use measures of strategic performance as part of the annual *bonus* calculations.

1.6 Many companies do *not* 'define explicit strategic objectives or milestones that are regularly and formally monitored as part of the ongoing management control process'.

(a) Choosing one objective (eg market share) might encourage managers to ignore or downgrade others (eg profitability).

(b) Informality promotes flexibility.

(c) Openness of communication is necessary.

(d) Finite objectives overlook nuances especially in human resource management. In other words, an objective like 'employee commitment' is necessary for success, but hard to measure quantitatively.

(e) A narrow focus on individual strategic objectives can blind managers to wider issues.

1.7 Informal control does not always work because it enables managers to skate over important strategic issues and choices.

Guidelines for a strategic control system

1.8 The characteristics of strategic control systems can be measured on two axes.

(a) How **formal** is the process?
(b) How many **milestones** are identified for **review**?

1.9 As there is no optimum number of milestones or degree of formality, Goold and Quinn suggest these guidelines.

Guideline	Comment
Linkages	If there are important **linkages** between businesses in a group, the formality of the process should be low, to avoid co-operation being undermined. Arguably, there should be a **large number** of strategic objectives, which would reflect the importance of managing the linkages between the various businesses.
Diversity	If there is a great deal of diversity, it is doubtful whether *any overall* strategic control system is appropriate, especially if the critical success factors for each business are different. Formal processes may not find the right objectives, informal ones may confuse.
Criticality	Firms whose strategic stance depends on decisions which can, if they go wrong, destroy the company as a whole (eg launching a new technology) need strategic control systems which, whether formal or informal, have a **large number of milestones so that emerging problems in any area will be easily and quickly detected**. Where there is high environmental uncertainty, a strategic control process monitors some of the background assumptions.
Change	Fashion-goods manufacturers must respond to relatively high levels of environmental turbulence, and have to react quickly. 'More and more companies see their markets developing in this direction'. If **changes are rapid**, a system of **low formality and few measures** may be appropriate, merely because the control processes must allow decisions to be taken in changed contexts.
Competitive advantage	For control purposes, it is useful to distinguish between two types of business. (i) **Businesses with few sources of competitive advantage**. Control can easily focus on perhaps market share or quality with high formality, or whatever is the main source of success. (ii) **Businesses with many sources of competitive advantage**. Success over a wider number of areas is necessary. In some retailing environments, market share, sales, mix, pricing policy, are all important. The greatest dangers in this sort of business are misdirected effect (focused on inappropriate objectives) and high cost (as it is hard to measure performance).

1.10 EXAMPLE: STRATEGIC CONTROL REPORT

Date: March 19X4
Source: January 19X0 planning document
Mission: Market share

1. *Long-term targets, to be achieved by 19X9*

   (a) X% value of market share
   (b) Y% profitability over the decade

   Status: March 19X4. Market share lower than anticipated, owing to unexpected competition. Profits lower than expected because of loss of scale economies and increased marketing costs.

   Outlook. Profit will be improved thanks to cost-cutting measures. Market share target might be missed.

2. *Assumptions*

   The home market is growing only slowly, and is becoming mature. There are limited opportunities for segmentation.

   Overseas markets are likely to expand by Z% as some are reducing tariffs.

   Status March 19X4. The home market has matured more quickly than expected. Overseas market growth can compensate for this.

3. *Critical success factors*

   Although market share and hence profit are lower than expected, as a result of loss of scale economies, we have become more efficient. Defects per 1,000 have been reduced to 0.3, which allows us to bid for the Japanese contract.

4. *Key tasks*

   - Launch of budget products for overseas markets
   - Setting up of a computerised distribution system to enhance speedy response to demand and to cut warehousing costs
   - Get BS EN ISO 9000 certification

1.11 **Desirable features of strategic performance measures**

Role of measures	Comment
Focus attention on what matters in the long term	Shareholder wealth?
Identify and communicate drivers of success	How the organisation generates shareholder value over the long term.
Support organisational learning	Enable the organisation to improve its performance.
Provide a basis for reward	This is more contentious - but rewards should be based on strategic issues not just performance in any one year.

1.12 Strategic performance measures should be:

- Measureable
- Meaningful
- Defined by the strategy and relevant to it
- Consistently measured
- Re-evaluated regularly
- Acceptable

Compare this with SMART criteria for objectives.

1.13 Some systematic approaches to performance measurement are provided in the next section.

1.14 Section summary

- Strategic control is needed as over-dependence on purely financial measures leads to gaps and false alarms, and ignores long-term features of the business.
- Strategic control systems can be formal or informal, and have any number of measures of performance, depending on the business.

2 THE BALANCED SCORECARD AND OTHER PERFORMANCE MEASURES

2.1 Although financial measurements do not capture all the strategic realities of the business, a failure to attend to the 'numbers' can rapidly lead to a failure of the business, if there is a liquidity crisis. Many successful conglomerates, such as GEC or BTR, take financial issues seriously with detailed plans worked out and targets agreed.

The balanced scorecard

KEY TERM

The **balanced scorecard** is:

'a set of measures that gives top managers a fast but comprehensive view of the business. The balanced scorecard includes financial measures that tell the results of actions already taken. And it complements the financial measures with operational measures on customer satisfaction, internal processes, and the organisation's innovation and improvement activities - operational measure that are the drivers of future financial performance.' (Robert Kaplan, January-February 1992, *Harvard Business Review.*)

2.2 The reason for using such a system is that 'traditional financial accounting measures like return on investment and earnings per share can give misleading signals for continuous improvement and innovation - activities today's competitive environment demands'. The balanced scorecard allows managers to look at the business from **four important perspectives**:

- **Customer**
- **Financial**
- **Internal business**
- **Innovation and learning**

Customer perspective

2.3 **'How do customers see us?'** Given that many company mission statements identify customer satisfaction as a key corporate goal, the balanced scorecard translates this into specific measures. Customer concerns fall into four categories.

(a) **Time**. Lead time is the time it takes a firm to meet customer needs from receiving an order to delivering the product.

(b) **Quality**. Quality measures not only include defect levels - although these should be minimised by TQM - but accuracy in forecasting.

(c) **Performance** of the product. (How often does the photocopier break down?)

(d) **Service.** How long will it take a problem to be rectified? (If the photocopier breaks down, how long will it take the maintenance engineer to arrive?)

2.4 In order to view the firm's performance through customers' eyes, firms hire market researchers to assess how the firm performs. Higher service and quality may cost more at the outset, but savings can be made in the long term.

Internal business perspective

2.5 Findings from the customer's perspective need to be translated into the actions the firm must take to meet these expectations. The **internal business perspective** identifies the **business processes that have the greatest impact on customer satisfaction**, such as quality and employee skills.

(a) Companies should also attempt to identify and measure their **distinctive competences** and the critical technologies they need to ensure continued leadership. Which processes should they excel at?

(b) To achieve these goals, **performance measures must relate to employee behaviour**, to tie in the strategic direction with employee action. This has echoes of MBO.

(c) An information system is necessary to enable executives to measure performance. An **executive information system** enables managers to drill down into lower level information.

Innovation and learning perspective

2.6 The question is '**Can we continue to improve and create value?**' Whilst the customer and internal process perspectives identify the *current* parameters for competitive success, the company needs to learn and to innovate to **satisfy future needs**. This might be one of the hardest items to measure.

(a) How long does it take to develop new products?

(b) How quickly does the firm climb the experience curve to manufacture new products?

(c) What percentage of revenue comes from new products?

(d) How many suggestions are made by staff and are acted upon?

(e) What are staff attitudes? Some firms believe that employee motivation and successful communication are necessary for organisational learning.

(f) Depending on circumstances, the company can identify measures for training and long-term investment.

Continuous improvement measures might also be relevant here.

Financial perspective

2.7 From the financial perspective, the question to be asked is: '**How do we appear to shareholders?**' Financial performance indicators indicate 'whether the company's strategies, implementation, and execution are contributing to bottom line management.'

2.8 Some analysts consider that financial issues take care of themselves, and that they are only the *result* of the customer, internal process, and innovation and learning issues discussed earlier. This view is rather naive for a number of obvious reasons.

(a) Money is a resource, and financial measures will ultimately effect a firm's ability to obtain that resource (eg by raising the firm's cost of capital, if shareholders perceive greater risk).

(b) Well designed financial control systems can actually assist in TQM programmes (eg by identifying variances).

(c) **The balanced scorecard only measures strategy. It does not indicate that the strategy is the right one.** 'A failure to convert improved operational performance into improved financial performance should send executives back to their drawing boards to rethink the company's strategy or its implementation plans.'

Linkages

2.9 **Disappointing results** might result from a **failure to view all the measures as a whole.** For example, increasing productivity means that fewer employees are needed for a given level of output. Excess capacity can be created by quality improvements. However these improvements have to be exploited (eg by increasing sales). The *financial element* of the balanced scorecard 'reminds executives that improved quality, response time, productivity or new products, benefit the company only when they are translated into improved financial results', or if they enable the firm to obtain a sustainable competitive advantage.

2.10 EXAMPLE: A BALANCED SCORECARD

Balanced Scorecard

Financial Perspective

GOALS	MEASURES
Survive	Cash flow
Succeed	Monthly sales growth and operating income by division
Prosper	Increase market share and ROI

Customer Perspective

GOALS	MEASURES
New products	Percentage of sales from new products
Responsive supply	On-time delivery (defined by customer)
Preferred supplier	Share of key accounts' purchases
	Ranking by key accounts
Customer partnership	Number of cooperative engineering efforts

Internal Business Perspective

GOALS	MEASURES
Technology capability	Manufacturing configuration vs competition
Manufacturing excellence	Cycle time
	Unit cost
	Yield
Design productivity	Silicon efficiency
	Engineering efficiency
New product introduction	Actual introduction schedule vs plan

Innovation and Learning Perspective

GOALS	MEASURES
Technology leadership	Time to develop next generation of products
Manufacturing learning	Process time to maturity
Product focus	Percentage of products that equal 80% sales
Time to market	New product introduction vs competition

Financial performance

2.11 Financial performance indicators

Measure	For	Against
Profitability	Easy to calculate and understand.	Ignores the size of the investment.
Return of investment (profit/ capital)	Accounting measure: easy to calculate and understand. Takes size of investment into account. Widely used.	• Ignores risk • Easy to manipulate (eg managers may postpone necessary capital investment to improve ratio) • What are 'assets'? (eg do brands count?) • Only really suited to products in the maturity phase of the life cycle, rather than others which are growing fast.
Residual income	Head office levies an interest charge for the use of asset.	Not related to the size of investment except indirectly

Measure	For	Against
Earnings per share	Relates the firm's performance to needs of its shareholders	Shareholders are more concerned about future expectations; ignores capital growth as a measure of shareholders' wealth
DCF measures	Relates performance to investment appraisal used to take the decision; cash flows rather than accounting profits are better predictors of shareholder wealth	• Practical difficulties in predicting future cash flows of a whole company • Difficulty in separating cash flows for products which share resources

Case example

Chiroscience

Biotechnology firms require heavy upfront development in R&D.

According to the *Financial Times* (29 April 1997):

'*Chiroscience*, one of the UK's largest biotechnology companies, has sharply increased spending and losses in an effort to push its most advanced products to market.

The group yesterday reported a pre-tax loss of £18.7m for the year to February, against £11.6m. Expenses were £27.1m, up 67 per cent on last year's £16.3m. There was net cash and investments of £51.4m. The spending rate was higher than analysts had expected and the shares fell 17½p to 335p.

Costs were rising because the most important drug in development, and anaesthetic levobupivacaine, had entered the final and most expensive medical tests. Mr John Padfield, chief executive, said the trials should be over in time for the drug to be submitted to European medicine regulators by the end of this year.

In the meantime, he said, finances were being bolstered by the rapid growth of the ChiroTech division, which manufactures pharmaceutical ingredients for third parties. ChiroTech sales more than doubled to £9.2m, accounting for most of total revenues of £11.5m (£5).

Mr Padfield said there were opportunities for ChiroTech's non-pharmaceuticals businesses.

2.12 Many firms use profit or investment centre organisation to control the performance of different divisions. A profit centre is where managers are responsible for revenues and costs; an investment centre is a profit centre in which managers have some say in investment decisions. Always keep in mind the following.

(a) Different divisions may offer different risk/return profiles.

(b) Managers will take dysfunctional decisions if these put their performance in a better light.

(c) An economically efficient, fair transfer pricing system must be devised.

(d) There are problems in assessing how shared fixed assets or head office costs should be charged out.

Operating performance: manufacturing

2.13 A number of performance indicators can be used to assess operations. They are particularly relevant to the internal business and customer perspectives of the balanced scorecard. Malcolm Smith (*Management Accounting*, March 1997) identifies four over-arching measures for manufacturing environments.

- Cost: cost behaviour
- Quality: factors inhibiting performance
- Time: bottlenecks, inertia
- Innovation: new product flexibility

Cost

2.14 Possible non-financial or part-financial indicators are as follows.

Area	*Measure*
• Quantity of raw material inputs	Actual v target number
• Equipment productivity	Actual v standard units
• Maintenance efforts	No. of production units lost through maintenance No. of production units lost through failure No. of failures prior to schedule
• Overtime costs	Overtime hours/total hours
• Product complexity	No. of component parts
• Quantity of output	Actual v target completion
• Product obsolescence	% shrinkage
• Employees	% staff turnover
• Employee productivity	direct labour hours per unit
• Customer focus	% service calls; % claims

Quality

2.15 The principal components of quality were discussed in Chapter 10. Integrating quality into a performance measurement system suggests attention to the following items.

Area	*Measure*
• Quality of purchased components	Zero defects
• Equipment failure	Downtime/total time
• Maintenance effort	Breakdown maintenance/total maintenance
• Waste	% defects; % scrap; % rework
• Quality of output	% yield
• Safety	Serious industrial injury rate
• Reliability	% warranty claims
• Quality commitment	% dependence on post-inspection % conformance to quality standards
• Employee morale	% absenteeism
• Leadership impact	% cancelled meetings
• Customer awareness	% repeat orders; number of complaints

Time

2.16 A truly just-in-time system is an ideal to which many manufacturing firms are striving. Time-based competition is also important for new product development, deliveries etc. The accounting focus might be on throughput, bottlenecks, customer feedback and distribution.

Area	*Measure*
• Equipment failure	Time between failures
• Maintenance effort	Time spent on repeat work
• Throughput	Processing time/total time per unit
• Production flexibility	Set-up time
• Availability	% stockouts
• Labour effectiveness	Standard hours achieved/total hours worked
• Customer impact	No. of overdue deliveries Mean delivery delay

Innovation

2.17 Performance indicators for innovation can support the 'innovation and learning' perspective on the balanced scorecard. Some possible suggestions are outlined below.

Area	*Measure*
• The ability to introduce new products	% product obsolescence Number of new products launched Number of patents secured Time to launch new products
• Flexibility to accommodate change	Number of new processes implemented Number of new process modifications
• Reputation for innovation	Media recognition for leadership Expert assessment of competence Demonstrable competitive advantage

Advanced manufacturing technology

2.18 The advent of *advanced manufacturing technology* (AMT) has meant that many organisations will need to modify their performance measures so that the information they provide will be useful in controlling operations in the new manufacturing environment. WCM and JIT methods introduce a new emphasis on performance measurement for control that is based on non-financial rather than financial considerations. Problems are:

- Incorrect use of efficiency measures
- Concentration on maximising output
- Inappropriate use of standard costing
- Over-emphasis on direct labour

Performance measurement in service businesses

2.19 **Types of service organisation**

(a) **Professional services**, for example a management consultancy (or a hairdresser). Such services are characterised as being highly adaptable to individual customer needs, dependent upon staff/customer contact, people-based and relying on short chains of command and highly autonomous employees.

(b) **Mass services**, for example rail travel. These involve little customisation and limited customer contact, they are predominantly equipment-based and require defined tasks and set procedures to be performed with little exercise of judgement.

(c) **Service shops**, for example, a bank. These fall between the above extremes in terms of customisation, customer contact, people/equipment and levels of staff discretion.

Dimensions of performance measurement

2.20 These factors call for a different approach to performance measurement. Performance measures can cover six 'dimensions'.

(a) **Competitive performance**, focusing on factors such as sales growth and market share.

(b) **Financial performance**, concentrating on profitability, liquidity, capital structure and market ratios.

(c) **Quality of service** looks at matters like reliability, courtesy, competence and availability. These can be measured by customer satisfaction surveys.

(d) **Flexibility** is an apt heading for assessing the organisation's ability to deliver at the right speed (you may want a long, slow haircut rather than a fast one), to respond to precise customer specifications, and to cope with fluctuations in demand.

(e) **Resource utilisation** considers how efficiently resources are being utilised. This can be problematic because of the complexity of the inputs to a service and the outputs from it and because some of the inputs are supplied by the customer (he or she brings their own hair to a salon). Many measures are possible, however, for example 'number of customers per hairdresser', 'amount of mousse consumed', 'waiting time to haircutting time' repeat business etc.

(f) **Innovation** is assessed in terms of both the innovation process and the success of individual innovations. Individual innovations can be measured in terms of whether they have improved the organisation's ability to meet the other five performance criteria - have they improved competitiveness, for example? The innovation process can be measured in terms of how much it costs to develop a new service, how effective the process is (that is, how innovative is the organisation, if at all?), and how fast it can develop new services.

Question 1

Draw up a list of performance criteria for a hotel.

Answer

Financial performance: profit and loss per department, variance analysis (eg expenditure on wages, power etc).

Competitive performance: market share (room occupied on a total percentage of rooms available locally); competitor occupancy; competitor prices; bookings; vacant rooms as a proportion of the total attitudes of particular market segments.

Resource utilisation: rooms occupied/rooms available service quality measure: complaints, room checks.

Quality of service: complaints, results of questionnaires (eg percentage of respondents unhappy, satisfied, happy or very happy with the service).

Benchmarking

2.21 **Benchmarking** generally involves comparing your operations to somebody else's.

KEY TERM

Benchmarking

'The establishment, through data gathering, of targets and comparators, through whose use relative levels of performance (and particularly areas of underperformance) can be identified. By the adoption of identified best practices it is hoped that performance will improve. Types of benchmarking include the following.

(a) **Internal benchmarking**, a method of comparing one operating unit or function with another within the same industry.

(b) **Functional benchmarking**, in which internal functions are compared with those of the best external practitioners of those functions, regardless of the industry they are in (also know as operational benchmarking or generic benchmarking).

(c) **Competitive benchmarking**, in which information is gathered about direct competitors, through techniques such as reverse engineering.

(d) **Strategic benchmarking**, a type of competitive benchmarking aimed at strategic action and organisational change.'

Case example

British Airways

British Airways 'used benchmarking since 1987 to help transform itself from a stodgy, state-controlled enterprise to a leading world airline'. Apparently BA staff analysed their own business processes to identify the weakest elements, and then visited other airlines with checklists and questions. Problems are often found to be shared and competitors are willing to pool information in pursuit of solutions.

2.22 **Advantages**

(a) **Position audit**. Benchmarking can **assess a firm's existing position.**

(b) The comparisons are carried out by **the managers who have to live with any changes** implemented as a result of the exercise.

(c) Benchmarking **focuses on improvement in key areas** and sets targets which are challenging but **'achievable'**. What is really achievable can be discovered by examining what others have achieved: managers are thus able to accept that they are not being asked to perform miracles.

(d) The competitive advantages of competitors are effectively negated, if they can be copied. If all firms provide the same standard of quality, it ceases to be a source of competitive advantage.

2.23 **Dangers of benchmarking**

(a) It **implies there is one best way** of doing business - arguably this boils down to the difference between efficiency and effectiveness. A process can be efficient but its output may not be useful. Other measures (eg fiddling with the value chain) may be a better way of securing competitive advantage. (See Chapter 2, on Porter.)

(b) The benchmark may be **yesterday's solution to tomorrow's problem**. For example, a cross-channel ferry company might benchmark its activities (eg speed of turnround at Dover and Calais, cleanliness on ship) against another ferry company, whereas the real competitor is the Channel Tunnel.

(c) It is a **catching-up exercise** rather than the development of anything distinctive. After the benchmarking exercise, the competitor might improve performance in a different way.

(d) It **depends on accurate information** about competitors, in the case of competitor benchmarking, or an **appropriate analogies** in other industries, in the case of process benchmarking.

2.24 To make benchmarking work, it is important to **compare like with like.**

Case example

An article in *Management Accounting* (April 1997) by Ian Malcolm describes benchmarking applied to purchase/sales order processing.

	Best	*Worst*
Accounts payable Number of purchase invoices processed per full-time equivalent (FTE) accounts payable member of staff per annum	50,000	3,000
Accounts receivable Number of remittances processed per FTE remittance-processing staff per annum	750,000	12,000

The article then goes on to describe the *different processes* in which key billing tasks are divided. Clearly, automating some processes enhances efficiency, but also accuracy is important.

Accounts payable (A/P) - process options chart

Process tasks / *Invoice type*	*Receive and sort post*	*Register*	*Authorise*	*Match with order or GRN*	*Code*	*Approve*	*Pay against terms*	*Advise payment*
EDI invoice	Not required	Auto or manual	Auto or manual	Auto or manual	Auto or manual	Auto or manual	Auto or manual	Auto or manual
Self-billed invoice	Not required	Auto	Auto	Not required	Auto or manual	Auto or manual	Auto or manual	Auto or manual
Paper invoice	Manual	Manual	Manual	Auto or manual	Auto or manual	Auto or manual	Auto or manual	Auto or manual
Purchase card	Summary statement and file of receipts	Optional for statement	Pre-determined	Match statement with receipts	Auto or manual	Note required*	Auto	Not required
Cheque or cash paid by service/product recipient	Maintain file of receipts	Summary level only	Pre-determined	Not required	Manual	Not required*	Not required	Not required

*Sample audits are a necessary control to replace the payment-approval process in these cases

Clearly, process failures have to be investigated.

2.25 **Steps in a benchmarking process**

Step 1 Identify items to be benchmarked

Step 2 Identify suitable organisations for comparison

Step 3 Collect data by an appropriate method

Step 4 Determine the current performance gap

Step 5 Project future performance levels

Step 6 Tell people about benchmark findings

Step 7 Establish goals for each business function

Step 8 Develop action plans

Step 9 Implement action plans

Step 10 Re-set benchmarks - to a higher level - to encourage continuous improvement

2.26 Section summary

- The balanced scorecard tracks performance on focus perspectives: customer, internal process, innovation and learning and financial perceptive.
- The balanced scorecard measures strategy, it doesn't say that the strategy is the right one.
- Performance measures for manufacturing cover cost, quality, time and innovation. Service measures include similar type of data (eg resource utilisation), but measurement is by techniques such as customer satisfaction surveys.

3 MONITORING COMPETITORS

Case example

Rolls-Royce

The Americans are unhappy about the way Rolls-Royce is scooping a growing share of jet-engine contracts. At the Paris Air Show earlier this month, Rolls-Royce waltzed off with glittering orders worth $2 billion, while its American competitors sulked.

The good sales run at Rolls-Royce began 18 months ago, when it snatched a huge order to supply Singapore Airlines with engines for its latest twin-engined Boeing 777s. Its hard-nosed American rivals, Pratt & Whitney and General Electric (GE), were prepared to take a loss to land such a prestigious deal. So they assumed Rolls-Royce won the bid by taking an even greater loss.

The Americans suspect Rolls-Royce is still competing unfairly. The problem is they cannot prove it; Rolls-Royce received its last state aid ten years ago, when it was privatised.

Sir Ralph Robins, Rolls-Royce's chairman, rejects accusations of buying market share. He says that the British company's advanced technology means it can run off a range of different-sized engines from one basic model, so dodging the huge development costs (upward of $1 billion) normally associated with each new engine. Rolls-Royce, for example, has five variations of its big Trent class engines that can fit ten aircraft, while GE's sole really large engine fits only the Boeing 777.

Despite their failure to find flagrant subsidy in Rolls-Royce's accounts, Americans in the industry wonder how Rolls-Royce can price so keenly. The answer seems to lie in the structure and the performance criteria of the three companies.

GE is the most successful conglomerate in America, run by Jack Welch, a powerful chairman who insists on a return on sales of around 18%. Pratt & Witney is part of United Technologies, a stodgy, heavy industrial conglomerate. Its 10.6% operating margin is puny by GE standards, but fatter than United Technologies makes in its other divisions, such as Otis lifts. Not only does Rolls-Royce feel quite happy with a return on sales of just over 6%; its conservative accounting policy keeps reported profits low. The British government still retains a 'golden' share in the company, because it makes military equipment, virtually ruling out a hostile takeover.

All this is particularly painful for the Americans, because the jet-engine market is changing. The trend towards more twin-engined aircraft drives up the cost of engine development. So manufacturers such as GE and Pratt need long-term ways to recoup their investment. In America, the antitrust authorities have even allowed the pair to form an alliance to compete with Rolls-Royce to supply an engine for the super-jumbo that Boeing was planning until recently.

They need to do something drastic; both dropped out of recent competitions to supply a stretched Airbus 340 and to develop engines for the double-deck 550-seater that Airbus hopes to launch next year, leaving Rolls-Royce as sole supplier.

(Extracts from *The Economist,* 28 June 1997)

Competitor analysis

3.1 The purpose of analysing competitors is to try and assess what they will do. This will enable the organisation to respond accordingly. Competitive advantage is about **relative** competitive position. Competitors are sometimes used as benchmarks.

3.2 **Aspects of competitor analysis**

(a) What are the **competitor's future goals?**

(b) What **assumptions does the competitor hold** about the industry and its place in it?

(c) **Competitor's current strategy**. How is the competitor competing: on price? by offering a different product? by concentrating on one set of customers?

(d) **What are the competitor's capabilities** (ie its strengths and weaknesses)?

Future goals

3.3 The firm, by reviewing **future goals**, can:

(a) Diagnose the degree of satisfaction the competitor's management feel with the current position.

(b) Predict the competitor's likely response to strategic changes.

3.4 **Useful information about the competitor's (and its SBU's) goals**

(a) What are the business's **stated financial goals**?

(b) What **trade-offs** are made between long-term and short-term objectives?

(c) What is the competitor's **attitude to risk**?

(d) Do **managerial beliefs** (eg that the firm should be a market leader) affect its goals?

(e) **Organisation structure**: what is the relative status of functional areas? For example, do marketing people have more power than finance people?

(f) What **incentive systems** are in place?

(g) What are the **managers** like? Are they divided against each other? Do they favour one particular type of strategy?

(h) To what extent does the business **cross-subsidise** others in the group if the business is part of a group? What is the purpose of the business: to raise money for the group?

Assumptions

3.5 Other questions relate to each competitor's **assumptions** (accurate or otherwise) about:

(a) Itself and its position in the industry.

(b) The industry as a whole (eg does the competitor consider the industry is in decline?)

3.6 Assumptions:

- **Indicate the way** in which the competitor might **react.**
- **Explain biases or blind spots** in the way that the competitor's managers perceive the environment.

3.7 **Useful information about competitor assumptions**

(a) What does a competitor **believe** to be its relative position (in terms of cost, product quality etc) in the industry?

(b) Is there a particularly strong **'emotional' bond** with particular products and markets?

(c) Are there any **cultural or regional differences** that indicate the way managers are likely to respond?

(d) What does the competitor believe about the **future demand** for the industry?

(e) Does the competitor accept the industry's '**conventional wisdom**'?

(f) A **career analysis** of key managers can indicate the possibility of certain strategic choices. An accountant in charge is likely to have different priorities from a marketer.

Current strategy

3.8 Analysing the competitor's current strategy covers:

- Products
- Distribution
- Marketing and selling
- Operations
- Research and engineering
- Overall costs
- Financial strengths
- Organisation
- General managerial skills
- Managerial ability

Capabilities

3.9 Identify the competitor's:

(a) **Core or distinctive competences**

(b) **Ability to expand in a particular market**

- Is the competitor hampered by a lack of production capacity?
- Does it need to raise capital externally?
- Is it capable of adapting to change?
- Can it survive a prolonged battle?

Competitor response profiles

3.10 All these are combined in a **competitor response profile**. This indicates:

(a) The **competitor's vulnerability** to environmental forces, competitors' actions etc, downturn in sales.

(b) **The right 'battleground' on which to fight**. For example, a firm may invade a competitor's position in a weak market, or in a low-priority product range. Japanese companies initially competed in the small car market, before moving to promote luxury models like the Lexus.

3.11 A **competitor intelligence system** needs to be set up.

(a) **Contents**

- Financial statements.
- Information from common customers and suppliers.
- Inspection of a competitor's products.
- Information for former employees.
- Job advertisements.

(b) **Processing**

- The data needs to be compiled, catalogued, for easy access, analysed (eg summarised, ranked by reliability, extrapolating data from financial reports) and communicated to the strategist.

Question 2

Jot down a list of items of information obtained from an environmental analysis of competitors.

Answer

(a) Who are the existing competitors? How much of the market do they hold in each segment of the markets (eg in each particular region or country?

(b) Who are potential competitors? How soon might they enter the market?

(c) How profitable are existing competitors? What is their EPS, dividend yield, ROCE etc?

(d) What do the goals of each competitor appear to be, and what strategies have they adopted so far?

(e) What products/services do they sell? How do they compare with the organisation's own products or services?

(f) How broad is their product line? (eg Are they 'up-market high quality, or down-market low quality, low price and high volume producers?)

(g) What is their distribution network?

(h) What are their skills and weakness in direct selling, advertising, sales promotions, product design etc.

(i) What are their design skills or R & D skills? do they innovate or follow the market leader with new product ideas?

(j) What are their costs of sale and operational capabilities, with respect to:

(i) economies of sale;
(ii) use of advanced technology equipment;
(iii) patents, trademarks, know-how;
(iv) quality control;
(v) location;
(vi) transportation costs;
(vii) labour skills and productivity;
(viii) supply advantages (ie special access to raw materials at a low cost);
(ix) industrial relations and industrial disputes;
(x) reliability in servicing customers.

(k) What are their general managerial capabilities? How do these compare with those of the organisation?

(l) Financial strengths and weaknesses. What is the debt position and financial gearing of each competitor? Do they have easy access to sources of new finance? What proportion of profits do they return in the business in order to finance growth?

(m) How is each competitor organised? How much decentralisation of authority do they allow to operating divisions, and so how flexible or independent can each of the operating divisions be?

(n) Does the competitor have a good spread or portfolio of activities? What is the risk profile of each competitor?

(o) Does any competitor have a special competitive advantage - eg a unique government contract or special access to government authorities?

(p) Does any competitor show signs of changing strategy to increase competition to the market?

The accountant and competitor analysis

3.12 Traditionally, the accounting system has concentrated on analysing the cost structure of the organisation to assess actual performance against the plan, and to correct actual performance or the plan if there is a deficiency. Such a system, while of value, does not assess the key issues that organisations face when developing a strategy.

3.13 However, the accounting system might be less good at identifying those deficiencies in performance arising from competitors' activities. For example, forecast price increases may not be held, because a competitor is charging a lower price. Do you know if:

(a) The competition can genuinely afford lower prices in the long term; or

(b) The competitor is prepared to lose money on a *short term* marketing tactic to gain market share?

Case example

The most notable price wars of recent years in the UK have been in newspapers. The Times massively increased its sales by price cutting, putting the Independent under pressure. Sales of the Times have risen significantly in the three years since the programme started. Revenue might be recouped through higher advertising rates changeable once sales exceed a certain level.

The independent has accused the Times of predatory pricing, but it is unlikely that much will be done about it.

3.14 Clearly the strategic response to such a situation can vary significantly depending on the cost profile of the competitor. Analysing *relative costs*, in strategic management accounting is clearly more important than absolute costs: Ward believes that it took Western firms too long to understand that Japanese firms had *sustainable cost advantages*.

3.15 Furthermore, even if the competitor is not competing on price, despite having a lower cost base, the competitor is:

(a) Under no pressure to raise prices, thus limiting the firm's ability to raise its own
(b) More profitable, and hence can invest more.

Selecting competitors

3.16 **Selecting a competitor** can, paradoxically, be a strategic decision.

(a) Attack 'bad' competitors (who are long-term threats). A bad competitor is intensely committed to the market, faces high exit barriers, has no other business, is highly focused etc.

(b) Maintain relative position vis-à-vis 'good' competitors (who do not represent a long-term threat). Good competitors may not be as committed to the market, may be quite happy for matters to tick over, or do not depend on the market for survival.

3.17 **Strategic benefits of competitors** are:

(a) They increase the possible sources of competitive advantage (eg by enhancing the ability to differentiate by serving unattractive segments).

(b) They improve the industry structure (eg by increasing demand).

(c) They aid market development (eg they share costs, help standardise technologies).

(d) They deter entry by newcomers.

3.18 Section summary

- Competitor responses constrain and influence the activity of a firm.
- 'Choosing' competitors is a strategic decision.
- In analysing competitors, review their goals, assumptions, capabilities and current strategy.

4 RESPONDING TO COMPETITION

4.1 Porter (in *Competitive Advantage*) states that 'the fundamental basis of above-average performance in the long run is **sustainable competitive advantage**' (based on cost or differentiation in the entire market, or a focus strategy concentrating on a few segments).

4.2 Porter believes that a firm gains competitive advantage from **within** an industry. Its **relative position** 'determines whether a firm's profitability is above or below the industry average'. A firm that can position itself well may earn high rates of return even though industry structure is unfavourable and the **average** profitability of the industry is therefore modest.

Competitive responses for cost leadership

4.3 Firms wishing to exploit cost leadership should follow these steps.

Step 1 Identify the activities in the value chain.

Step 2 For each activity identify its size, cost, cost behaviour (indirect/direct).

Step 3 Where possible find competitor comparisons.

Step 4 Identify **cost drivers** which determine the cost of each activity (eg learning curves, capacity utilisation, transport costs, change).

Step 5 Identify cost trends in the industry (eg relative inflation, technological change).

Step 6 Identify cumulative costs for the firm's value activities.

Step 7 Identify the relative cost composition compared with competitors.

4.4 To **sustain cost leadership** and to maintain relative cost position:

- Control cost drivers.
- Redesign the value chain (eg new production processes, chapter distribution)

Competitive responses for differentiation

4.5 Firms pursuing differentiation follow these steps.

Step 1 Identify activities in the value chain: differentiation flows out of doing activities in a different way that customers value (eg inputs - Body Shop's use of rainforest plants).

Step 2 Review customers' value chains: the purpose of differentiation is to ensure that the differentiated product is a unique input to the customer's value chain.

Step 3 Identify **differentiation drivers** (ie how a firm can make its outputs unique). These are:

- Policy choices (with regard to product features, input quality, technology).
- Linkages (eg co-ordination with suppliers and customers).

Step 4 Communicate the differentiation to customer (who may not always understand it).

- '**Use' criteria:** the specific measures a firm takes to enhance the values of the product to the buyer, which might include intangibles such as style, the actual product, delivery systems etc.
- **Signalling criteria** include the firm's reputation, packaging, the company's market share, the 'surface' of a product. Signalling criteria may have little to do with the buyer's **actual** use of the product. Parts of the promotion element of the marketing mix will be to convey signalling criteria (eg branding). A signal could be BS ES ISO 9000 certification, which implies a certain standard of quality.

4.6 **Sustaining differentiation**

(a) Increase the number of sources of differentiation in the value chain (eg product features, delivery systems).

(b) Understand how the product is actually used.

(c) Exploit signalling criteria to reinforce the use criteria.

(d) Exploit non-costly sources of differentiation (eg new packaging).

(e) Change the rules of purchasing (eg by appealing to different people in the **decision making unit).**

(f) Respond to changing buyer or channel circumstances.

(g) Reconfigure the value chain.

Strategic ploys

4.7 Mintzberg describes one meaning of strategy as a 'ploy' or a manoeuvre in a competitive game. Firms devote their attention less at customers perhaps than at competition. Kotler and Singh identified five offensive and six defensive competitive strategies named after military terms - these represent the strategist's generic 'choice set'.

OFFENSIVE STRATEGIES	*DEFENSIVE STRATEGIES*
1 Frontal Attack	1 Position Defence
2 Flank Attack	2 Mobile Defence
3 Encircle Attack	3 Pre-emptive Defence
4 Bypass Attack	4 Flank Position Defence
5 Guerrilla Warfare	5 Counter Offensive Defence
	6 Strategic Withdrawal

(a) Offensive strategies can be effective in challenging market leaders.

(b) Defensive strategies enable firms to stay one step ahead of the competition.

Offence

4.8 Leaders can be vulnerable to attack. Successful attackers, according to Porter, 'all seek to nullify the competitive advantages of the leader while avoiding full scale retaliation'. In other words, the leader is undermined by stealth, rather than attacked with bluster.

4.9 A **challenger** needs:

(a) A sustainable competitive advantage in certain activities (in cost or differentiation).

(b) Proximity in other activities (in other words, the challenger's performance is as good as the leader's).

(c) An impediment to leader retaliation.

4.10 A leader 'stuck in the middle' can be outgunned (but a committed leader can 'force a challenger to bear unacceptable economic and organisational costs'). Also, slow retaliation by a leader can buy a challenger time.

4.11 Here are the main **offensive strategies**.

Strategy	Comment
Frontal attack	This is the direct, head-on attack meeting competitors with the same product line, price, promotion and so on. In principle, to succeed the attacker needs three times the resources as the defender and because the attacker is attacking the enemy's strengths rather than weaknesses, it is generally considered the riskiest and least advised of strategies.
Flanking attack	The aim is to engage competitors in those product markets where they are weak or have *no* presence at all. Its overreaching goal is to **build a position** from which to launch an attack on the major battlefield later without waking 'sleeping giants'. **Segmental flanking** is based on satisfying market needs not being met by competitors', different products or approaches to the market. **Geographic flanking** serves areas in a country or the world with similar products and approaches but where opponents are weak or non-existent.
Encirclement attack	Encirclement involves a **multi-pronged attack** aimed at **diluting the defender's ability to retaliate** in strength. The attacker stands ready to block the competitor no matter which way he turns in the product market.
Bypass attack	This is the most indirect form of competitive strategy as it **avoids confrontation** by moving into new and uncontested fields. Three types of bypass are possible; develop new products, diversify into unrelated products or diversify into new geographical markets.
Guerrilla warfare	Guerrilla attack is less ambitious in scope and involves making **small attacks** in different locations whilst remaining mobile. Such attacks take several forms such as law suits, poaching personnel, interfering with supply networks and so on.

Case examples

e.g.

In the mid-1990s, aviation deregulation in Europe led to the growth of cheap 'no-frills' carriers such as *EasyJet.* No doubt these firms convinced themselves they had identified a new segment. Ever watchful, *BA* decide to launch its own low-cost airline Go competing in the exactly the same segment, head to head. EasyJet responded to the launch by sending four of its staff on Go's first flight to distribute information about EasyJet to Go's first customers.

4.12 **A leader would be discouraged from retaliation** in the following cases.

(a) A **high cost of resources** discourages across the board price cuts.

(b) Different **financial priorities** might shape a competitor's response.

(c) Portfolio **constraints** might mean the competitor is spreading resources on other products (eg on stars, when you are attacking a cash cow).

(d) **Regulatory pressure** (eg if a leader was seen to be abusing a monopoly or near monopoly).

(e) **Blind spots** (ie the leader does not appreciate the significance of the attack, or the leader's information systems for strategic issues are poor).

Defensive strategies

4.13 Market leaders only should play defence in an attempt to hold on to its existing markets in the face of competitive attack.

(a) **Position defence**. This is a static defence of a current position, retaining current product-markets by consolidating resources within existing areas. Dependence on a position defence effectively means that a business is a **sitting target for competition.** Unless a business moves in line with market evolution via product improvement, line extension and product proliferation, it will result in outdated products and lost markets.

Case example

Paper towels

The UK-branded market for paper tissues, toilet paper and similar products is dominated by Kimberly-Clark (K-C). However Procter & Gamble intends to introduce some of its European or American brands to the UK. (*Marketing Week*, 9 April 1998). In the past year, K-C has increased market share of its Andrex brand, as it has been sold on sales promotion for some time. 'K-C has started to behave as a challenger to P & G even though it is a market leader'.

(b) **Mobile defence**. A high degree of mobility prevents the attacker's chances of localising defence and accumulating its forces for a decisive battle. A business should seek market development, product development and diversification to create a stronger base. A mobile defence is often referred to as 'defence in depth' following Levitt's advice in *Marketing Myopia* (1960) to get involved in R&D across the whole range of technology associated with the underlying generic market need.

(c) **Pre-emptive defence**. 'Attack is the best form of defence'. The initiative remains with the company moving first. Pre-emptive defence is launched in a segment where an attack is anticipated.

(d) **Flank position defence**. This is used to occupy a position of potential future importance in order to deny that position to the opponent. Therefore leaders need to develop and hold secondary markets to prevent competitors using them as a spring board into the primary market. For example, Japanese manufacturers used the upper end executive and coupe market to break into the volume car sector.

(e) **Counter-offensive defence**. This is attacking where one is being attacked. There are three types of counter offensive moves; meet the attack head on, attack the flank of the attacker or launch from two sides simultaneously to sever the attack from its base.

Case example

This requires immediate response to any competitor entering a segment or initiating new moves. Heublein's Smirnoff Vodka provides an excellent example of both frontal and flank counter offensive. Wolfschmidt went on the frontal attack by pricing its vodka, of comparable quality, a dollar lower to take market share. Rather than engage in a price war, Heublein raised the price of Smirnoff by one dollar to reinforce the quality brand image and at the same time introduced two new brands, one priced the same as Wolfschmidt and the other one dollar lower.

(f) **Strategic withdrawal.** This is fairly self-explanatory and involves withdrawal from segments perceived as being unattractive for future investment because of a disadvantageous position relative to competitors.

4.14 The above paragraphs have indicated that a great deal of energy goes into dealing with **competitors**. We have seen in Chapter 16 that quality (developed and implemented within the company) is of relative importance depending on the competitor and the firm's choice of generic strategy. Customers assess a firm's performance, simply buying its goods rather than another's, relative to its competitors'. Consequently a customer orientation, TQM etc, must be supplemented by a competitive focus. In short, we are led to Ohmae's strategic triangle. (But remember that **military analogies** are not necessarily the best way to consider business strategies.)

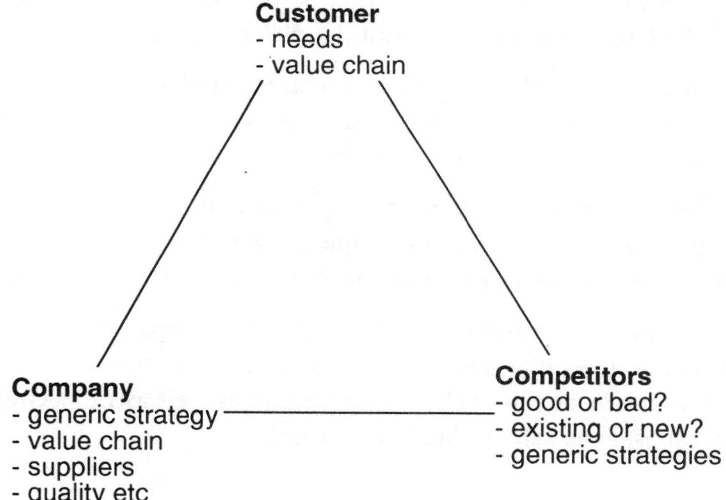

4.15 Section summary

- Activities in the value chain can be analysed to see if they can drive costs or differentiation.
- Direct head-on attack of a market leader is normally unwise in the first instance - better to build a position or attack in a weak spot.

Question 3

You are a prestigious and well established EU based manufacturer of liquid crystal displays (LCDs). You produce LCDs for a wide variety of markets, including makers of pocket calculators, computers and new style TV screens to go along with digital TV. New style screens are soon likely to be your most lucrative product by far. Recently a number of competitors from Eastern Europe have started competing in the high volume low margin pocket calculator LCD market. There is evidence of overcapacity in this market. What defensive tactics might you adopt?

Answer

There is no right answer, but here are some ideas.

(a) Petition the EU to restrict imports of LCDs, say to a maximum *number* imported a year. The disadvantage is that to maximise profits your competitors will attack your lucrative high value business instead. They have low labour costs.

(b) Ignore the competition (but again, they might build up from making a low value product to producing LCDs for your most valuable markets).

(c) Buy one of your competitors, to benefit from its low manufacturing costs, and seek to gain market dominance in Eastern Europe by transferring technology to your new subsidiary.

(d) Compete with them on price, providing you do not damage your own company.

(e) Allow them to slug it out at the low end of the market, by pulling out or providing limited price competition.

(f) Rigorously police them for abuse of your patent rights etc.

5 TACTICS IN DIFFERENT INDUSTRY STRUCTURES

Types of industry structure

5.1 Although the five competitive forces (entry barriers, substitute products, suppliers bargaining power, customers' bargaining power, competitive rivalry) are at work in any industry, the **balance of power within the different industries in a country can vary.**

(a) An industry might be populated by a **large number of small scale competitors.** An example in the UK is hair-dressing: there are few large 'chains' of hairdressers; most hair-dressing salons are independent.

(b) On the other hand an industry might be dominated by a **small number of large competitors**. In the UK, an example is provided by electricity generation which is dominated by a few large companies (eg National Power and Powergen).

(c) There may be a **combination**: a few leading companies may dominate the market, but smaller ones might exist as well. For example, the fast-food industry in the UK features major chains such as McDonald's as well as independent outfits (fish and chip shops, kebab shops, balti houses etc).

Fragmented industries

KEY TERM

A **fragmented industry,** according to Porter is 'populated by a large number of small and medium sized companies.' A fragmented industry is characterised by 'the absence of market leaders with the power to shape industry events.'

5.2 Fragmented industries are common in the retail and services sector, as well as some manufacturing sectors. An industry is fragmented because:

(a) **Barriers to entry are low:** it is easy to set up in business.

(b) There are **few economies of scale** to be had by a large firm.

(c) **Transport cost are high,** so a centralised plant cannot really service a large area efficiently or cheaply.

(d) **Small scale businesses** may be more **flexible** in coping with **erratic demand**.

(e) **Size does not matter.** A large firm in a fragmented industry cannot use its size to get better deals from suppliers.

(f) Being too large might lead to higher **overhead costs**.

(g) **Local image** and reputation are important.

(h) The **market itself might be fragmented,** as buyers may have many different tastes.

(i) The **government** can forbid concentration.

(j) If standards are **enforced locally,** this can encourage fragmentation.

5.3 An industry might be fragmented for only one of those reasons: and if this can be overcome, the whole **industry can be consolidated.**

(a) **New technology** can offer a cheaper way of making something, but it might require an investment of such size that only a large firm could afford it.

(b) A **new standard product** might be preferred to the previous 'custom-made' variety for a number of reasons. Fast food chains such as McDonalds or Spud-u-like offer a consistent standard, and customers might welcome this lowering of the risk of disappointment.

(c) **Identify the cause** of the fragmentation and deal with it. Many big publishing companies have a large number of smaller *imprints*, with their own characteristics.

(d) Some industries consolidate naturally as they **age**.

Concentrated industries

KEY TERM

Concentrated industries are dominated by a small number of large firms, which are able to exercise a significant influence over the market as a whole.

5.4 **Why industries become concentrated**

(a) It is **cheaper to produce in bulk** (ie where there are economies of scale).

(b) **A lot of money needed to stay** in the business. The oil industry is an example. Exploration is often risky and requires high technology.

(c) **Entry barriers are high:** in other words it is hard to set up in business.

(d) The service does not depend uniquely on the skills of a particular individual.

(e) A large firm can benefit from an **integrated distribution** network.

(f) **Customers' needs are fairly standard** in the market.

(g) There are economies of scale in marketing distribution, purchasing etc.

(h) The company has **proprietary product** technology.

5.5 There is nearly always a '**market leader**' who can significantly influence:

(a) The way business is done.
(b) Relationships with sources of supply.
(c) Distribution.

Emerging industries

KEY TERM

An **emerging industry** is a new, or re-formed, industry. It can be created by technological innovation, changes in costs, social and economic changes.

5.6 **Problems with emerging industries**

(a) There is **doubt about the technology** (eg standards).

(b) **Customers' needs are uncertain.**

(c) New industries start with **high costs**, but these fall eventually.

(d) **Newly-formed companies** are in a good position to **enter the industry** (Netscape pioneered the Internet browser, leading to retaliation by Microsoft).

(e) **Ignorance.** Consumers need to be informed about what the industry can offer in order to be interested in new products or services.

(f) Some new industries receive **subsidies.**

(g) **Early barriers** to entry include proprietary technology, access to raw materials and so on.

(h) **Problems** encountered also include:

(i) Competition for raw materials or subcomponents
(ii) Customer confusion
(iii) Obsolescence
(iv) Erratic quality
(v) Scepticism from bankers, investors etc.

5.7 In an emerging market, even the approach to competitors differs. It may be useful to **encourage competition through licensing**. This helps build the market, and in any case, it is rarely feasible to maintain a monopoly. CD technology was developed by Philips and the firm receives licence income when other firms employ it.

5.8 Section summary

- Fragmented industry: many small firms. It might be possible to consolidate them.
- Concentrated industry: large firms, with a strong market leader.
- Emerging industry: special rules apply.

6 CORPORATE DECLINE

6.1 It is easy to rattle off a list of successful companies, and to ascribe to them a whole variety of factors which have fuelled their success. It is less easy, however, to assess precisely those factors which cause industries and companies to fail. Decline has two aspects.

(a) What should a company do to be successful in a **declining industry**, if it cannot realistically withdraw?

(b) How do **corporations 'go bad'** and what can be done to turn them round?

Declining industries

6.2 There are two types of decline, as identified by Kathryn Harrigan.

(a) **Product revitalisation** occurs when the decline is temporary (eg owing to a genuine recession in consumer demand).

(b) **Endgame**. A firm (and the industry) is confronted with substantially lower demand for its products.

Case examples

Since the end of the Cold war, defence budgets being cut, thereby leading to the consolidation of the US defence industry and the beginnings of consolidation in the European defence industry.

6.3 Harrigan researched a number of firms in declining industries and arrived at some interesting conclusions.

(a) In **endgame** conditions, firms which had not competed with each other were drawn into **price wars**. This 'knee-jerk' response should encourage managers to consider their competitive behaviour before the endgame.

(b) The **characteristics of declining industries differ** (eg some have high exit barriers, some are concentrated, others are fragmented), so **different strategies** are appropriate.

(c) The **expectations** of competitors about future demand, and the expectations of their customers about future supplies, can have a powerful **influence** on the nature of the **competitive environment**.

(d) Forecasting techniques can help firms identify the **type** of competitor that will leave the industry and the types most likely to remain.

(e) If the industry is falling to a **substitute product**, then firms should innovate to capture the new technology.

(f) If products become 'commodity-like' (ie differentiation is not all that significant) then **all but the lowest cost competitor will lose market share**. In these conditions a cost leadership strategy is appropriate. On the other hand, it might be a good idea to **differentiate** a product, if this is feasible, to build the security of a niche.

(g) Unless a company has the lowest costs, a strong distribution system relative to competitors, or a 'loyal niche' of customers, it might be **worth selling the business to a competitor** who can make better use of it.

(h) Finally, a firm which is part of a **conglomerate** might be retained because of strategic relationships with other areas of the conglomerate.

Declining companies

6.4 Companies go bankrupt. Their assets are sold. Their former employees find work elsewhere if they are fortunate, or join the dole queues for life if they are not. Stuart Slatter, from an analysis of UK companies during the severe recession of the early 1980s identifies ten **symptoms of corporate decline**.

(a) Declining profitability.

(b) Decreasing sales volume (ie sales revenue adjusted for inflation).

(c) An increase in gearing (debt as a proportion of equity).

(d) A decrease in liquidity, as measured, conventionally, by accounting ratios (eg aged debtors, current ratio etc).

(e) Restrictions on the dividend policy.

(f) Financial engineering (eg changes in accounting policies and periods, delays in publishing accounts, sudden changes in auditors).

(g) 'Top management fear'.

(h) Frequent changes in senior executives.

(i) Falling market share.

(j) Evidence of a lack of planning.

6.5 The severity of any crisis, whose severity for the long term depends on the behaviour of managers. Slatter identifies four stages in the crisis.

Step 1 **Crisis denial**. Managers are complacent, ignore warning signs or do not appreciate their significance. This may result from poor control systems and poor environmental monitoring.

Step 2 **Hidden crisis**. When the signs of crisis appear, managers explain them away, or say that there is nothing they can do. The problem is that if they admit something *is* wrong they will be blamed. If radical change is required, it might adversely affect their position.

Step 3 **Disintegration**. Managers decide that things are amiss and act to do something about them - too little, usually. Moreover, management becomes more autocratic, reducing alternative sources of information.

Step 4 **Collapse**. Slatter says that, in the end, action is impossible. An expectation of failure increases, the most able managers leave, and there are power struggles for the remaining spoils. Eventually, usually after the prompting of a bank, the receiver is called in.

6.6 **Causes of decline and the strategies to deal with them**

Cause	Strategy
Poor management	This should be dealt with by the introduction of **new management** and perhaps **organisation** restructuring (this should only be embarked upon once the new executive knows how the firm *really* works, including its informal organisation).
Poor financial controls	This can be dealt with by new management, financial control systems which are tighter and more relevant, and, perhaps, **decentralisation and delegation** of responsibility to first line management of all aspects **except finance**.
High cost structure	**Cost reduction** is important in improving margins in the long term. New product-market strategies are adopted for the short term (to boost profitability and cash-flow). Growth-orientated strategies (eg as in Ansoff's matrix) are only suitable once survival is assured. A focus strategy (whether cost-focus or differentiation-focus) is perhaps the most appropriate.
Poor marketing	The marketing mix can be redeployed. Slatter believes that the sales force of a crisis-ridden firm is likely to be particularly demotivated.

Cause	Strategy
Competitive weakness	This is countered by cost reduction, improved marketing, asset reduction (eg disposing of subsidiaries, selling redundant fixed assets etc), even acquisition, and of course, a suitable product-market strategy.
Big projects/ acquisitions	Acquisitions can go bad, or there can be a failure of a major project (eg Rolls Royce aerospace once went into receivership because of the cost of developing a particular engine).
Financial policy	Firms might suffer because of high gearing. Arguably many of the firms subject to management buyouts financed by interest-bearing loans are acutely vulnerable. Converting debt to equity and selling assets are ways of dealing with this.

6.7 Companies which recovered did so largely because of the way in which the recovery strategy was implemented.

(a) **Contraction**. As an emergency measure, this requires cost cutting etc.
(b) **Reinvestment** in organisational capability and efficiency.
(c) **Rebuilding** with a concentration on innovation.

6.8 Turning a company round requires an able top management, with the right mix of skills and experience, to stand outside of the culture of the organisation. Substantial changes at the top (eg as at Barings) may be needed, and one of the most important **symbols of a new order is the change of personnel**. The development of an effective top management team requires attention to:

(a) The **context**, both of the industry and of the firm. What resources does the team have to work with?

(b) What is **the ideal management** team given the nature of the crises facing the organisation. For example a firm with poor financial controls may require a team with a financial or systems bias, whereas a firm whose problem was lacklustre products may need a team with a marketing bias.

(c) Against this ideal team, how does the **current team** shape up? New expertise may need to be imported, or a plan may be needed to enhance the capability of the existing team.

6.9 In the context of change and the top management team we can identify specific leadership roles.

(a) **Charismatic leaders** lead by force of personality, which will only be exercised in difficult situations.

(b) **Transformational leaders** not only have charisma, but use it to some purpose.

   (i) To create a new vision for the organisation.
   (ii) To gain acceptance of the new vision.
   (iii) To force through and 'refreeze' the change.

6.10 There are, of course, **corporate governance** issues involved. An overly-powerful leader can be a danger to the good governance of the firm. This is why the Cadbury committee recommended that the **roles of Chairman and Chief Executive should be split.**

(a) The **Chairman**, arguably, should have no day-to-day operating responsibilities but should represent the interests of shareholders, deal with the audit committee and so forth.

(b) The chief executive officer has direct responsibility for the operations of the company.

6.11 The purpose of such arrangements is that:

(a) It avoids **over-concentration** of power

(b) Two senior members offer **different perspectives** on the businesses.

(c) The chairman represents the **shareholders.**

(d) The chairman deals with **key external stakeholders.**

Case example

In *Marketing Week* (April 10 1997), David Benadly described some of the long-term problems facing the Co-op.

'The Co-operative Bank has shown that it can be done. Tesco demonstrates that supermarkets can do it. But whether the 500-strong Co-operative Retail Society grocery chain can carry it off is by no means assured. "It" is nothing less than staging the complete relaunch of a flagging brand, turning round consumer perceptions and giving a real point of difference to rivals.

But speculation about a possible £500m bid for the non-food parts of the Co-operative Wholesale Society and CRS has drawn attention to the group and could put more pressure on Robey (chief executive) to turn things round quickly.

The problems of CRS, a rag-tag portfolio of 500 stores under three different facias - Leo's, Pioneer and Stop & Shop - are profound and difficult. Its market share in the grocery trade has fallen from nearly nine per cent in the late Eighties, to less than six per cent today.

The stores are now being rebranded under two names - the larger stores as Co-operative Pioneer and the convenience stores as Co-operative Local. This move was under way before Robey's arrival. The variation in store sizes and poor location of some stores means different stores offer different ranges, opening hours and standards of service.

Many CRS customers are older and less affluent than those of Sainsbury's and Tesco, so another Robey objective is to make the stores appeal to a broader, more representative, group of customers.

The problems at CRS have been accentuated by the technical advances made by the other multiples in stock replenishment, electronic point of sale, loyalty and customer service. It is not so much what CRS has been doing wrong, but what the competition has been doing right.

Yet CRS, and the Co-operative movement in general, have some important saving graces. Duckworth says: 'The Co-op is one of the best known brands in the UK. It has got latent heritage and there are a lot of things people think are good about the brand - but it has become tarnished in recent years."

But perhaps the most appropriate parallel for what the CRS is trying to do is a similar task carried out by Tesco in the Eighties. The chain also had a downmarket image and its name was synonymous with a 'pile it high, sell it cheap' philosophy.

CRS needs more efficient organisation, and Robey is implementing a new management structure and redefining lines of responsibility and reporting. There is also work to do on product ranges, which are seen as too diffuse. Ranges are decided locally rather than nationally.

While this means local tastes can be targeted accurately, it can lead to confusion in relations with suppliers and in the negotiation of discounts. Part of the new attitude to merchandise and the supply chain at CRS is the introduction of the own-label Co-operative brand.

The strength of the new own-label will go a long way to defining the level of quality of the relaunched CRS.'

Divestment

6.12 Divestment means getting rid of something. In strategic planning terms, it means selling off a part of a firm's operations, or pulling out of certain product-market areas (ie closing down a product line).

(a) **De-growth**. A more common reason is to rationalise a business as a result of a strategic appraisal. A company might decide to concentrate on its 'core' businesses and sell off foreign activities, or to sell off subsidiaries where performance is poor, or where growth prospects are not good.

(b) **Sell off subsidiary companies at a profit,** perhaps as a means of thwarting a takeover bid.

Demergers

6.13 Demergers (unbundling) are the opposite of mergers. The main feature of a demerger is that one corporate entity becomes two or more separate entities. This is now fashionable as the costs of conglomerate diversification became apparent. The central head office function subtracted value rather than added it. In other words the supposed synergies are negative (a '2 + 2 = 3' effect, rather than a '2 + 2 = 5' effect).

6.14 A demerger might feature:

(a) A **management buy-out**. The managers put in some of their own capital, but obtain the rest from venture capital organisations (eg banks), and hope to make a bigger success of the business than the company who is selling it off.

(b) Selling the business intact to a **purchaser** wishing to make the acquisition.

(c) **Splitting the company** in two or more new companies and **floating** them **separately**.

Case example

From the *Financial Times* (21 May 1998)

'*Sutcliffe Speakman*the chemical group, is to sell its two core businesses for £27.7m and return most of the proceeds to shareholders as part of its wide-ranging restructuring effort'. It is to sell its carbons and environmental engineering divisions to Waterlink of the US in order to develop the remaining Samuel Banner chemicals distribution business it acquired in 1996. The group, to be renamed Banner Chemicals, said it would return about half the share capital... to shareholders ... . The rest of the cash would be used to reduce the debt and acquire new chemicals distribution businesses.'

6.15 **Advantages of divestment**

(a) By selling off parts of the business that are not performing as well as others, a firm can concentrate on areas of its business that provide better results.

(b) Selling off a subsidiary will bring in funds that can be invested in other projects.

(c) It might be more profitable to demerge than to expand.

6.16 Section summary

- The industry is in decline, so the firm can choose to retire gracefully (eg by selling assets) or adjust itself to the new conditions.
- Corporate decline can be temporary. A variety of factors - managerial and technical - cause the problem.

7 BRAINWORKS PLC UPDATE

Questions can be found in the Introduction box at the beginning of this chapter.

7.1 *Question 1.* On the surface, the merger between Diad and Colec is not a threat. After all, size in this market does not necessarily denote effectiveness; it may be that they are slavishly copying BW's merger strategy, and will suffer too. BW has the advantage to its clients of being 'the devil you know' - but more worrying is that BW's own employees might defect to assist the new competitor in Europe. Also, once BW (UK) and PeoplePower demerge, BW will be on its own: it still has a large network of offices, but it needs to play to its strengths **operationally**, and put Bill Begbie's grandiose visions to rest.

7.2 *Question 2.* Although BW has problems, it is not in crisis. Thankfully, Begbie's fall has generated a thorough shakeup. Needless to say, matters could be improved, but the firm is beginning to turn itself round. A major unresolved issue is who is to **lead** BW(UK) **after** the demerger with PeoplePower. No-one is mentioned in the case study.

Chapter roundup

- The purpose of **strategic control systems** is to shift management attention away from sole reliance on financial performance indicators towards longer-term strategic milestones which eventually determine financial performance. The **balanced scorecard** is an example of how this might be put into practice.
- **Competitive advantage** results from providing value to customers in a way not provided by competitors. Various **value activities** can drive cost or differentiation strategies. Buyers do not always appreciate the value they are acquiring, so cannot assess a product by this criterion alone. That is why **signalling criteria** (eg as communicated through advertising) are so important.
- Competitive advantage is therefore **relative** and to sustain it firms have to pre-empt the actions of their competitors.
- **Competitor analysis** involves analysing **competitors' goals, assumptions** about the industry and their position in it, their current **strategies** and **capabilities** and their likely **response**. The accountant's analytical techniques are useful in this context. Analysis of a competitor's cost structures indicates the choices available to it; it is possible to use your own firm as a model and adjust accordingly. It is also possible to assess how much competitors spend on marketing.
- A firm's competitors have a **strategic value**, in that they increase sources of competitive advantage, deter newcomers and aid the industry's development.
- The type of competitive strategy adopted varies according to the industry structure and the firm's own position in it. **Fragmented industries** can be consolidated. **Concentrated industries** have a market leader, significantly influencing the way business is done. Emerging industries offer special problems.
- **Defensive tactics** include deterrence and response. **Offensive tactics** can be based on tinkering with the value chain and attacking at the right time.
- **Corporate decline** arises from the decline in the industry and from poor management. It is still possible to make money in declining industries, just as it is possible to **'turn round'** declining companies.

Quick quiz

1 What are gaps and false alarms? (see para 1.3)

2 What influences the strategic control system? (1.4)

3 Describe a formal system of strategic control. (1.5)

4 What is the basic principle behind the balanced scorecard? (2.1)

5 What four perspectives are found on the balanced scorecard? (2.2)

6 List four aspects to competitor analysis. (3.2)

7 What questions would be asked about a competitor's future goals? (3.4)

8 What are the benefits of competitors? (3.16, 3.17)

9 List offensive and defensive strategies. (4.7)

10 What are the components of the strategic triangle? (4.14)

11 What is a fragmented industry? (5.2)

12 What are the symptoms of corporate decline? (6.4)

Question to try	Level	Marks	Time
22	Exam standard	25	45 mins

Part E
Human resources management

Chapter 18

OBTAINING HUMAN RESOURCES

Chapter topic list		Syllabus reference
1	**Personnel and human resources management**	3(a), 3(b)
2	**Business strategies and HRM**	3(a)(iii), (b)(iii)
3	**Assessing human resource needs: personnel planning**	3(a)(i) - (vii), 3(b)
4	**Recruitment**	3(a)(i) - (vii)
5	**Selection**	3(a)(i) - (vii)
6	**Induction**	3(a)(i) - (vii)
7	**Brainworks plc update**	

Introduction

Human resources management is about getting the right employees in the right place at the right time, and ensuring that they work effectively. As opposed to the administrative job of the personnel function, HRM is a set of management techniques designed to get the best out of employees. HRM strategy should derive from the **business strategy**, and HRM plans have to take factors such as labour turnover into account. **Recruitment** processes start with the plan, by identifying the jobs to be done, and then developing profiles of the people to fill them. Interviewing as a **selection** technique should be supplemented by other forms of assessment.

Brainworks plc

1 Identify the strategic role of HRM in BW.

1 PERSONNEL AND HUMAN RESOURCES MANAGEMENT 6/94, 12/94

Personnel management

1.1 The case example below shows some of the issues involved in the management of human resources in an organisation.

Case example

London bus drivers

The pressures faced by recruiters are exemplified by recruiting for the bus industry, here as described in the *Financial Times* (20 August 1997).

'London bus drivers tend not to say in a job for more than a few months. The capital's bus companies are facing the highest levels of **staff turnover** since the 1950s. A combination of the reviving economy and the expanding London bus network means that some bus companies are having to replace up to 40 per cent of drivers a year.

Pay is one issue, shift work is another. A number of bus drivers, for instance, are skilled workers for whom the job was a welcome safety net during the recession of the early 1990s. But the **pay**, at £230 to £300 for a 40 hour week, is not enough to keep them now.

But the bus companies, competing in a deregulated market, are under pressure to **match their services to commuter needs, rather than the body clocks of their drivers.**

The squeeze on numbers of these semi-skilled workers - it takes six weeks to train a bus driver - is now so acute that some bus companies are looking outside London for staff. Go Ahead Group, which owns London General Transport with 1,400 drivers, has launched a scheme to recruit drivers from the provinces.

Some argue that what is really needed is a fundamental change of **culture** at London Transport. This is the authority that puts out to tender the coveted 400 London bus routes. The companies with the lowest cost base scoop the best routes as they require less public subsidy. He estimates that some wages have more than kept pace with inflation over the past five years. "London Transport cannot be surprised that bus drivers are no longer a cheap commodity."

CentreWest, owed by FirstBus, believes that recruiting drivers from outside their local area spells trouble. Instead, it has broadened its **recruitment policy** to include significantly older and younger drivers, as well as more women.

Metroline hopes to keep its drivers by offering the prospect of "virtually a job for life and very high staff share ownership as well as good pension schemes".

Bus bosses agree that the work has got tougher, with congestion now blocking London's roads from 7am to midnight.'

1.2 It is easiest to understand HRM by contrasting it with the traditional model of **personnel management**. Here is a simple diagram.

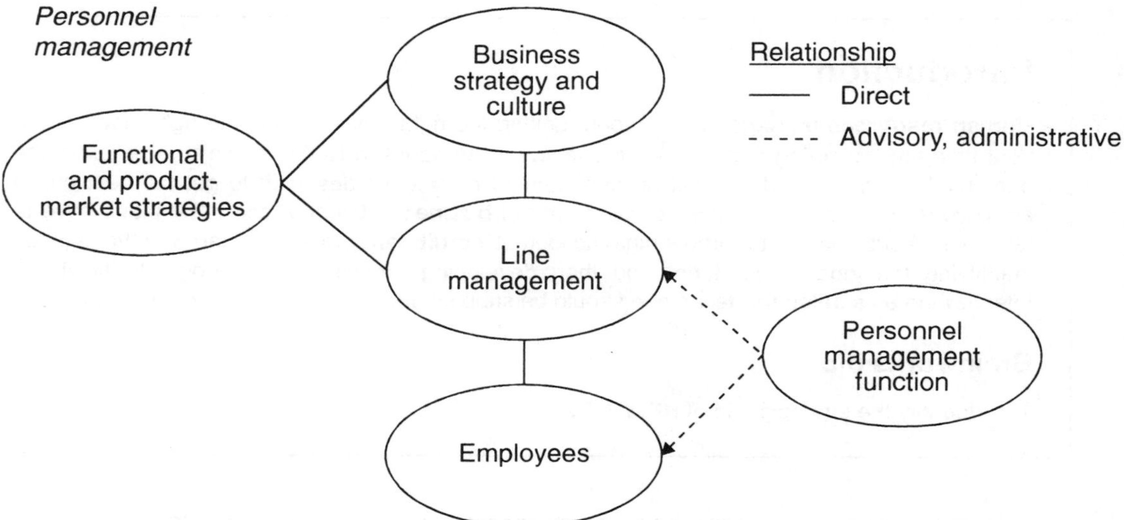

Personnel management is not directly involved in the business strategy. In short, it is essentially task-, activity- or technique-based. Its tasks are:

(a) Setting general and specific **management policy** for employment relationships.

(b) **Administration:** writing job descriptions, visiting the sick, and so on.

(c) **Policing:** ensuring that both management and staff obey the rules and do not abuse the job evaluation scheme, and keeping a watchful eye on absenteeism, sickness and punctuality.

(d) **Collective bargaining** and industrial relations.

(e) **Staffing and organisation:** finding, getting and holding prescribed types and numbers of workers.

(f) **Implementing downsizing** or redundancy programmes.

(g) Aiding the **self-development** of employees at all levels, providing opportunities for personal development and growth as well as requisite skills and experience.

(h) **Reviewing and auditing** manpower and management in the organisation.

Human resources management (HRM)

1.3 **HRM aims to integrate personnel issues with the strategic planning of the business.** The objectives of HRM are directly related to achieving the organisation's goals for growth, competitive gain and improvement of 'bottom line' performance. This is because 'the scarce resource, which is the people resource, is the one that makes the impact at the margin, that makes one firm competitive over another'. HRM has different emphasis to 'mere' personnel management.

KEY TERM

Human resources management (HRM) is 'a strategic and coherent approach to the management of an organisation's most valued assets: the people working there who individually and collectively contribute to the achievement of its objectives for sustainable competitive advantage'. (Armstrong)

1.4 We can expand this statement. HRM deals with the following issues.

(a) It serves the **interests of management,** as opposed to employees.

(b) It suggests a **strategic approach to personnel issues.**

(c) HRM will **tie business mission to HR strategies.**

(d) It implies that **human resource development helps organisations to add value** to products and services.

(e) It deals with gaining **employees' commitment to the organisation's** (or rather, management's) values and goals.

(f) It must be specific enough to provide direction, but at the same time have general principles to help it survive short term fluctuations.

1.5 We can express HRM's strategic viewpoint in a diagram, which you can compare with that in paragraph 1.2.

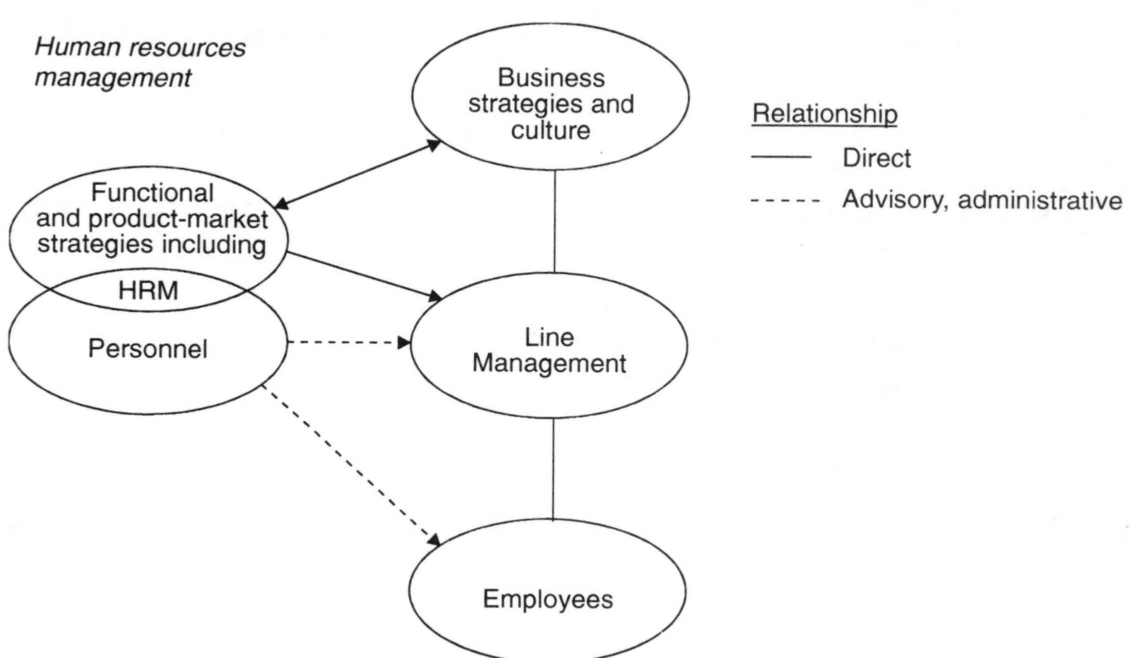

HRM philosophy

EE are asset
strategy & culture are *
commitment

1.6 Underlying HRM is a philosophy or set of values.

Employees are assets

1.7 Employees are **assets** (reminiscent of Peters and Waterman's phrase: 'productivity through people'). HRM believers hold that **competitive advantage** is largely gained by effective use of people. Implications of regarding employees as organisational assets are:

(a) **People are a resource** which needs to be carefully and efficiently managed with overriding concern for organisational objectives.

(b) The organisation needs to **protect its investment**, by retaining, safeguarding and developing its human assets.

(c) **Deterioration in the attitudes and motivation** of employees, increases in labour turnover (followed by costs of hiring and training replacements) are **costs to the company** - even though a 'liquidation' of human assets, brought about by certain managerial styles, may produce short-term increases in profit.

(d) A recently developed concept along these lines is that of **human asset accounting** (the inclusion of human assets in the financial reporting system of the organisation).

Case example

There are difficulties in isolating and measuring human resources, and it is also hard to forecast the time period (and area of business) over which benefits will be received from expenditure on human assets. *Texas Instruments* uses a system which identifies potential replacement costs for groups of people, taking into account the learning time required by the replacement, and the individual's salary during that period.

Strategy and culture are important

1.8 Armstrong believes that every aspect of employee management must be integrated with business management and must reinforce the desired company culture. HRM embodies mission, and monitors its effect.

Commitment

1.9 HRM techniques aims mobilising employee commitment to the cause of management, in the hope that:

(a) The common interests of employer and employed; and
(b) psychological commitment from employees;

will unleash creativity.

Features

1.10 Distinctive features of HRM

Feature	Comment
Top management	Personnel was a staff function of limited impact. Top managers set direction, and so they must be involved in HRM.
Performance and delivery of HRM	Line managers are responsible for implementation of HRM. They do not carry out specialised instructions, but manage within the context of the organisation's HRM strategy.
Strategic fit	The right people in every respect must be chosen.
Cultures and values	HRM tries to inculcate the organisation's values into its employees.
Employee behaviour	HRM seeks to win 'hearts and minds' rather than mere consent to management decisions.
Employee relations	HRM denies that there could be any difference between the goals of organisation and employees (... but what about redundancies?)
Reward systems	These recognise good performance (eg performance related pay systems).

Question 1

Ultraleisure plc is a rapidly growing company involved in the design, building and operation of theme parks and adventure centres. In the UK, the company runs theme parks in Liverpool, Birmingham, Dagenham (South East London) and Dover (expected to benefit hugely as a rival to Disney World from the opening of the Channel Tunnel). In Europe, the company operates large theme parks in Rotterdam, Hamburg and Copenhagen. The company is planning expansion into Eastern Europe, as it considers that land and labour are cheap, and that it will be well positioned to take advantage of the growing market for leisure. You have just had a chat with the Human Resources Manager, the person in charge of the firm's human resources. She is not a Board member but reports directly to the Chief Executive. 'In the past we've hired and fired on an ad hoc basis - there's always a pool of students wanting the job' she says. 'We obviously need skilled technicians to run the rides, so anybody with the right qualifications will do. The students are involved in the retail side, and in guiding customers around, helping them out. Our recruitment policies depend directly on the total number of visitors we expect. We expect a lot of visitors from Northern France to come over to Dover, but I don't really see the need to alter our recruitment policies - we'll just get local people as usual. We haven't quite decided what to do about Eastern Europe. Our research into the local labour market would indicate that many people want a *career* in theme parks - but it's the sort of business where there really aren't that many management positions available. We'll probably have to change our normal policies to cope with long termers'.

Comment on Ultraleisure plc's approach to managing its human resources.

Answer

Ultraleisure plc is in a half way house between personnel management and HRM.

(a) The 'hiring and firing on an ad hoc basis' and the fact that the manager is not considered as important as, say, the Marketing Director, would indicate that the firm had not really adopted HRM. This impression is further supported by the fact that the human resources needs of the Dover Theme park (with its large number of French-speaking visitors) have not been assessed in any coherent way. No mention is made of recruiting people who are bi-lingual.

(b) However, the company is moving *towards* HRM in its dealings with eastern Europe.

HRM in practice: a mixed blessing

1.11 A survey of 2,000 workplaces by Fernie and Metcalf of the London School of Economics (reported in the *Financial Times* April 6 1994) makes interesting reading.

(a) About 20% of the workplaces surveyed employed HRM specialists. Those workplaces had much **worse relations** between management and workers than workplaces which have *no* such arrangement.

(b) **Performance related pay does not improve the climate of relations.** A recent report by the LSE about performance related pay at the Inland Revenue (*Financial Times* 16/6/97) apparently stated that 'two-thirds of Revenue staff were more unwilling to help each other than before'.

(c) **Employee involvement is of limited usefulness.** Team briefings are little use in improving relations. Proper communication has to be a **two-way process: quality circles were a success.**

(d) HRM workplaces treated manual and non-manual employees in a single fashion (eg pensions, same canteen etc). This did not improve the industrial relations climate.

(e) **Union presence could improve relations.** Workplaces with *strong* unions and workplaces *without* unions had better relationships than a workplace with a weak union (recognised only for the purposes of collective bargaining).

1.12 That said, whilst HRM has not improved industrial relations **HRM techniques have had a significant improvement on productivity**.

(a) A comparison of productivity *growth* between 1987 and 1990 indicated that firms employing HRM techniques produced better results.

(b) HRM was 'not a strong differentiating factor for the rate at which people left their employers'. (Staff turnover is lower in firms with strong unions.)

(c) HRM is not a factor determining absenteeism rates.

1.13 To conclude:

> 'Having first removed the caring halo from HRM and its affect on industrial relations, their wider study does put its use in a broader context.
>
> If anything, it shows that the use of human resource management is closer to what the words might suggest - systems or strategies for getting the best and most out of people. The study also suggests that HRM may deliver what management has wanted most - more productive workforces. The notion that it should be viewed in any other light, such as representing a paternalistic approach, would seem misplaced.'

Management

1.14 **HRM are some personnel management compared**

	HRM	Personnel
Purpose of activity	Strategic development of the business-technostructure?	Operations, policies and procedures; crisis management – support staff?
Expertise	Serves the business strategy, and is spread throughout the organisation	A 'professional' specialisation in one department
Drive	The mission of the organisation	Compliance with professional 'good practice' for its own sake

	HRM	Personnel
Responsibility	Everybody's, although the HR department still has an administrative and a 'teaching role'	The personnel department
Employees	Commitment	Consent, compliance with contractual obligations
Work focus	Employee roles in furthering the mission	Job descriptions
Instrument of change	Culture, personal and team developments	Procedures

The HR function

1.15 These difference **exaggerate the real differences in practice** between the two approaches and there are many ways of configuring peronnel/HR activities within the organisation. For example

(a) **Some peronnel activities**, such as developing or maintaining job descriptions, can be outsourced.

(b) The **personnel function** might be:

(i) A **corporate function** at head offices, but some activities are delegated to strategic business units

(ii) A **standalone department**, in which the director is responsible for a variety of personnel activities.

(iii) **Headed by a manager reporting** to another director.

1.16 What do personnel/HR managers do?

Role	Comment
Business partners	Sharing responsibility for the success of the business
Strategists	Contribute to business strategies and formulating personnel strategies to achieve them
Problem solvers	Sorting out strikes, grievances etc
Innovators	Ssuggesting new ways to meet the organisation's needs
Interventionists	crisis prevention and management
Enablers	helping line managers take responsibility
Internal consultants	advising line managers on personnel policies
Service providers	providing internal services for recruitment, redundancy, reward systems and so on to line mangers who are 'clients'
Consistency	ensure fairness and consistency in dealing with people
Guardians of the organisation's values	acting as the 'conscience' of management in dealing with people

1.17 Section summary

- Personnel management was mainly concerned with administration and procedures.
- HRM takes a strategic view, seeing people as a 'resource' or 'asset' to be exploited effectively.

- HRM contributes to, and is derived from, the corporate strategy.
- HRM techniques might improve productivity, but they are not humanitarian.

2 BUSINESS STRATEGIES AND HRM

2.1 Problems in integrating HRM with product-market and business strategies

(a) **Variety**. An organisation with a variety of product-markets has a number of business strategies. **Different approaches to human resources** might be required for each.

(b) **Timescale and change**. If **business strategy changes**, there is a danger that the **HR** strategy **will not change fast enough**. HR strategy involves the internal structure and culture of the organisation, as well as the psychological contract between employer and workers. Cultural change, as we saw in Chapter 12, can take a long time. HRM is often **long-term and large-scale**, but can easily be subverted. A culture change affects everyone, and it is a difficult process.

(c) **Measurability**. HRM is qualitative. Successful HR means recruiting the right people.

2.2 The HR strategy has to be related to the business strategy. Below we show how, using the example of an *airline*: most airlines are trying to become global companies to avoid dependence on one country.

Business strategy	**HR implications**	**Airline example**
What business are we in?	What people do we need?	Air transportation requires pilots, cabin crew, ground crew etc
What products/markets, level of output and competitive strategy, now and in future	Where do we need people what are they expected to do, and how many? Location and size of workforce. Productivity expected and output?	The airline is going global and therefore it needs cabin crew who are skilled in languages and are sensitive to cultural differences.
What is the culture and value system? Is it the right one?	The need to change culture and values	A cultural change programme; recruiting people to fit in with the right value system; attitudinal assessments
Tomorrow's strategies, demands and technologies	Tomorrow's personnel needs must be addressed **now**, because of lead times. New technology requires training in **new skills**	Recruitment, training, cultural education
Critical success factors	How far do these depend on staff?	Service levels in an aircraft depend very much on the staff, so HRM is crucial.

A few more words about some of these issues.

Values

2.3 **Human resource management** recruitment policies emphasise **values.** Michael Armstrong (*Human Resource Management: Strategy and Action*) states that 'HRM places more emphasis than conventional personnel management on finding people whose attitudes and behaviours are likely to be congruent with what management believes to be appropriate and conducive to success'.

2.4 In other words, organisations are concentrating on employees' behaviour and attitudes.

(a) **Service industries** often involve direct personal interaction between an employee and the customer. Employees are ambassadors of the organisation. In a way they are part of 'the product' (eg a troupe of actors in a play).

(b) **New organisational forms** which support autonomous teams and work groups require a **'cultural glue'** to replace direct management control. (Asking employees to have a commitment to quality is an example.)

2.5 The **dangers of recruiting people who fit too neatly** into the firm's culture are these.

(a) The **status quo is maintained** and even when this might be healthy.

(b) Employees become **unthinking clones** of management.

(c) The **lack of cultural flexibility** will mean a reduced ability to respond to the environment. The advantages of 'non-conformists and mavericks' who can buck the system is that, while disruptive at times, they can successfully challenge the conventional wisdom by bringing a different perspective to a problem.

Case example

Some companies tie some of their human resource requirements to the *product life cycle*. Armstrong states that 'Texas Instruments believes that it is necessary to match management style to product life cycle. As a product moves through different phases of its life cycle, different levels of management skills become dominant. It could be disastrous, for instance, to put risk taking entrepreneurs in charge of mature cash flow businesses'.

Question 2

'Productivity through people'. In other words enthusiastic and committed employees are essential for business success. Do you agree?

Answer

Here are a few suggestions. You may have different views. Like any set of ideas which pretends to give businesses an elixir of immortality, the grandiose claims of HRM should be taken with a small pinch of salt. Why?

(a) No matter how good, loyal, committed and enthusiastic the people are, if the basic commercial strategy is wrong, the company will fail.

(b) A strong culture can inhibit the recognition of information that does not conform with its assumptions. Even flexibility may not be enough.

(c) Some organisations can be run without commitment. 'Tapping employees' creativity and insight' might result in disagreement and conflict in some cases.

Case example

Chase Manhattan Bank

The following case example is based on an article in *People Management*, 23 March 1995, by Stephen Martin.

As a major player in global financial markets, Chase Manhattan has operations across the world, covering most geographic markets and product/industry categories. Throughout the 1960s, 1970s and early 1980s, customers were served according to their location or their business sector and the bank flourished. But, during the mid-1980s, something subtle began to happen; customers around the globe were transformed into *global customers*. Assumed boundaries such as the home base, local markets and market segments became less relevant.

The financial needs of customer's around the globe metamorphosed into something beyond the grasp of cosy, locally focused relationships.

Chase, like many of its competitors, suffered during this phase and needed to find a way to focus its extensive resources in unfamiliar terrain ... a much stronger emphasis on developing a clear, differentiated and customer-focused strategy emerged, prompted initially by an early internal paper which addressed the issue of 'What are we good at?' and 'What can we be competitive at?' It asked the question: 'What are our corporate core competences?' This strategic realignment lead to a much clearer understanding of the customer base and a clear determination to focus on their needs.

On the global corporate finance side, a great deal of effort was put into determining what customers were demanding, and this ultimately led to a definition of the competences required in each segment of the market, describing what skills, abilities, traits, behaviours etc, individuals would need to deliver the business strategy.

At the same time, the HR function and senior line managers were taking this opportunity to jointly sponsor a co-ordinated global effort to define the 'supply' side of the equation - what the bank had to offer - and to establish who had what, to what degree they possessed it, where they were, what career history they had, and what degree of mobility they saw for themselves. This information on individual *competences* could then be matched against the 'demand' side of the equation - the data on which customers require what, where, to what degree and so on.

The issue of jobs did not feature on either side of that equation; competences became the new currency, and detailed analysis the new distribution mechanism.

The Chase corporate finance model of competences features many of the categories you would see elsewhere, but the line and HR people involved in the early phases were careful to develop their own strategic definition of areas such as 'team work', 'coaching' and 'selling skills' And, unusually given the wide set of applications envisaged, each competency is defined from a number of perspectives offering distinct definitions, targeted at different applications.

Each individual competency was considered from five different perspectives.

In the Chase model, individuals agree their competences profile (including product, industry and geographic expertise) with their manager, describing what they can offer to client relationships. So rather than seeing themselves and being seen as representing their best-fit job, their unique competences can be matched against clients and integrated with others in to effective teams, empowering them to fulfil the demands of customers rather than jobs.

3 ASSESSING HUMAN RESOURCE NEEDS: PERSONNEL PLANNING

3.1 The human resources plan might arise out of a strategic plan. A human resources plan has to mediate a variety of factors.

(a) **The work to be done will largely result from the business plan**. However, production management might determine how the work will be done. If, for example, the company is introducing new machinery, then the human resource requirements (eg training, possible redundancy, safety measures) need to be thought out.

(b) **The skills base** includes technical skills, interpersonal skills, and management skills. The need for **technical** and **management** skills are obvious enough. **Interpersonal skills** are important, as they deal with the service offered to customers and affect teamwork. Training can include issues of body language (eg eye contact) or how to interpret customer behaviour.

3.2 Unlike machines, materials and money, human resources are hard to predict and control.

(a) **Demand**. Environmental factors (eg government decisions or the state of the markets create uncertainties in the demand for labour.

(b) **Supply**. Factors such as education or the demands of competitors for labour create *uncertainties in the supply* of labour.

(c) **Goals**. Employees as individuals have their own personal goals, and make their own decisions about, for example, whether to undertake further training. When large numbers of individuals are involved, the pattern of behaviour which emerges in response to any change in strategy may be hard to predict.

(d) **Constraints**. Legislation as well as social and ethical values constrain the ways in which human resources are used, controlled, replaced and paid.

3.3 Human resource planning concerns the acquisition, utilisation, improvement and return of an enterprise's human resources'. Human resource planning deals with:

(a) Recruitment
(b) Retention (company loyalty, to retain skills and reduce staff turnover)
(c) Downsizing (reducing staff numbers)
(d) Training and retraining to enhance the skills base

3.4 **The process of human resources planning**

1. STRATEGIC ANALYSIS
- of the environment
- of the organisation's manpower strengths and weaknesses, opportunities and threats
- of the organisation's use of manpower
- of the organisation's objectives

↓

2. FORECASTING
- of internal demand and supply
- of external supply

↓

3. JOB ANALYSIS
- investigating the tasks performed in each job
- identifying the skills required

↓

4. IMPLEMENTATION
- training and developing existing staff
- recruiting required staff

Strategic analysis

3.5 Strategic analysis of where the organisation stands at present and where it wants to be in terms of manpower is the underlying feature of a human resource plan, and should constantly be kept under review.

(a) **The environment**: population and education trends, policies on the employment of women and on pension ages, trends generally in the employment market.

(b) The organisation's HR **strengths, weaknesses, opportunities and threats** need to be analysed so as to identify skills and competence gaps and the level of innovation. Threats may involve competitors 'poaching' staff.

(c) **Human resource utilisation**. An assessment should be made of how effectively the organisation is currently utilising its staff .

(d) **Objectives.** Core and subsidiary corporate objectives should be analysed to identify the manpower implications. New products, technology, sites, 'culture' and structure will all make demands on staff.

3.6 **Timescales** are very important. An immediate gap may prompt instant recruitment while long-term corporate objectives will allow long-term plans for updating existing staff and providing them with the skills required.

Forecasting

3.7 **Estimating demand**. Planning future HR needs requires accurate forecasts of turnover and productivity (eg if fewer staff are required for the same output). The demand can be estimated from:

- New venture details
- New markets (need new staff)
- New products/services
- New technology (new skills)
- Divestments
- Organisational restructuring (eg relocation)
- Cost reduction plans

3.8 **Estimating supply**

(a) **Current workers. A stocks and flows analysis** will define the **internal labour market**. It describes, not just aggregate quantities, but movements in and out of certain grades, by occupation and grade and according to length and service. This can be used in **modelling**.

(b) The **external labour market**. Labour **market research**:

(i) Measures potential employees' awareness of the organisation.

(ii) Helps discern the attitudes of potential employees towards work and the organisation.

(iii) Suggests possible segments for advertising purposes (eg some areas might offer more favourable targets than others).

(iv) Provides demographic analysis of population trends for long-term forecasting.

3.9 A **position survey** compares demand and supply. Discrepancies between them in the numbers required/available, their grade, skills or location can be removed through the application of an integrated manpower strategy.

Closing the gap between demand and supply

3.10 HR strategy requires the integration of *policies* for:

- Pay and conditions of employment
- Promotion
- Recruitment
- Training
- Industrial relations.
- Workforce structure

3.11 Because all these factors are interrelated, an **integrated approach** is necessary.

(a) Job/rate evaluation should be carried out in large companies to avoid unfairness.

(b) The costs of recruitment include intensive training if personnel move quickly between companies and labour turnover is high.

(c) Junior management should be given sufficient training for senior management positions.

(d) In industrial relations, problems may occur because of a lack of communication between unions and management.

3.12 **Tactical plans** can then be made, within this integrated framework, for:

- Pay and productivity bargaining
- Physical conditions of employment
- Management and technical development and career development
- Organisation and job specifications
- Recruitment and redundancies
- Training and retraining
- Manpower costs.

3.13 Shortages or surpluses of labour which emerge in the process of formulating the position survey must be dealt with.

(a) A **shortage** may be met through:

(i) Internal transfers and promotions, training etc
(ii) External recruitment
(iii) Reducing labour turnover, by reviewing possible causes
(iv) Overtime
(v) New equipment and training to improve productivity so reducing the need for more people

(b) A **surplus** may be met by:

(i) Running down manning levels by natural wastage
(ii) Restricting recruitment
(iii) Part-time working
(iv) Redundancies - as a last resort, and with careful planning.

Cost/benefit analysis

3.14 Labour is still a cost, and so a firm should review the *cost* effect of any HR activity, in proportion to the *estimated* benefits derived from it. For any given level of output it compares the costs and benefits of the various options available to a firm.

(a) **Recruitment and/or training**

(i) Recruiting costs (advertisements, fees, management time)
(ii) Training costs (money climbing the learning curve)
(iii) Wages and related costs
(iv) Other costs (eg requirements for factory space)

(b) **Outsourcing** the services or production to outsiders (eg getting a catering firm to run a canteen).

(c) **Buying capital equipment** or altering work processes in other ways to enhance productivity.

(d) Changing the **type of employment** offered.

(i) **Full-time salaried employment or part-time employment**. Part-time employees have been 'cheaper' in the past because they are less likely to be eligible for benefits such as holiday pay or pensions. Recent EU legislation has significantly improved the lot of part-time workers.

(ii) **Temporary or permanent employment**.

3.15 Some firms are dividing their workforce into two sections.

(a) A **core workforce** of permanent full-time staff.

(b) A **peripheral workforce** consisting of:

(i) Part-timers
(ii) Temporary staff, or staff on short-term contracts
(iii) Subcontractors taken on for particular jobs.

3.16 This division was first identified in 1984. However some key issues are these.

(a) Most people look for **secure** employment.

(b) The government intends to give the same employment rights to part-time workers as they do to full-time workers.

(c) Management issues include motivating part-timers to get the best out of them, **co-ordinating** their work and development so that they do not feel like 'second class citizens' in the firm.

The HR plan

3.17 The HR plan is prepared on the basis of personnel requirements, and the implications for productivity and costs. The HR plan breaks down into subsidiary plans.

Plan	Comment
Recruitment plan	Numbers; types of people; when required; recruitment programme.
Training plan	Numbers of trainees required and/or existing staff needing training; training programme.
Redevelopment plan	Programmes for transferring, retraining employees.
Productivity plan	Programmes for improving productivity, or reducing manpower costs; setting productivity targets.
Redundancy plan	Where and when redundancies are to occur; policies for selection and declaration of redundancies; re-development, re-training or re-location of redundant employees; policy on redundancy payments, union consultation etc.
Retention plan	Actions to reduce avoidable labour wastage.

The plan should include budgets, targets and standards. It should allocate responsibilities for implementation and control (reporting, monitoring achievement against plan).

Control over the size of the work force

3.18 Once a personnel plan has been established, regular control reports should be produced.

(a) Actual numbers recruited, leaving and being promoted should be compared with planned numbers. If actual levels seem too high, action can be taken by stopping recruitment temporarily. If levels seem too low recruitment, promotions or retraining activity should be stepped up.

(b) Actual pay, conditions of employment and training should be compared with assumptions in the manpower plan. Do divergences explain any excessive staff turnover?

(c) Periodically the plan itself should be reviewed and brought up to date.

4 RECRUITMENT 12/97

KEY TERMS

(a) **Recruitment** is the part of the process concerned with finding the applicants: it is a 'positive' action by management, going out into the labour market, communicating opportunities and information and generating interest.

(b) **Selection** is the part of the employee recruiting process which involves choosing between applications for jobs: it is largely a 'negative' process, eliminating unsuitable applicants.

4.1 **A systematic approach to recruitment and selection**

Step 1 Detailed personnel planning.

Step 2 Job analysis, so that for any given job there is:

(i) A statement of the component tasks, duties, objectives and standards (*a job description*)

(ii) A specification of the skills, knowledge and qualities required to perform the job (*a job specification*)

(iii) A reworking of the job specification in terms of the kind of person needed to perform the job (*a person specification*).

Step 3 An identification of vacancies, by way of the personnel plan (if vacancies are created by demand for new labour) or requisitions for replacement staff by a department which has 'lost' a current job-holder.

Step 4 Evaluation of the sources of labour, again by way of the personnel plan, which should outline personnel supply and availability, at macro- and micro-levels. Internal and external sources, and media for reaching both, will be considered.

Step 5 Review of applications, assessing the relative merits of broadly suitable candidates.

Step 6 Notifying applicants of the results of the selection process.

Step 7 Preparing employment contracts, induction, training programmes etc.

Job analysis, job design and competences

4.2 Procedures for recruitment should only be carried out in the context of a recruitment policy, whichmight cover issues such as internal/external applications of post, non-discrimination and so forth, courteous processing of applicants, the type of tests favoured.

Exam focus point

The best answered question in December 1997 dealt with recruitment and selection, in the context of a job analysis exercise.

Job analysis

4.3 The management of the organisation needs to analyse the sort of work needed to be done.

KEY TERM

According to Michael Armstrong, **job analysis** is:

'the process of collecting, analysing and setting out information about the content of jobs in order to provide the basis for a job description and data for recruitment, training, job evaluation and performance management. Job analysis concentrates on what job holders are expected to do.'

4.4 The definition shows why job analysis is important - the firm has to know what people are doing in order to recruit effectively. The type of information that might be obtained from a job analysis is listed below.

Type of information	Comments
Purpose of the job	This might seem obvious. As an accountant, you will be expected to analyse, prepare or provide financial information. But this has to be set in the context of the organisation as a whole.
Content of the job	The tasks you are expected to do. If the purpose of the job is to ensure, for example, that people get paid on time, the tasks involve include many activities related to payroll.
Accountabilities	These are the results for which you are responsible. In practice they might be phrased in the same way as a description of a task.
Performance criteria	These are the criteria which measure how good you are at the job. These arer largely taste related.
Responsibility	This denotes the importance of the job. For example, a person running a department and taking decisions involving large amounts of money is more responsible that someone who only does what he or she is told.
Organisational factors	Who does the jobholder report to directly (line manager)?
Developmental factors	Likely promotion paths, if any, career prospects and so forth. Some jobs are 'dead-end' if they lead nowhere.
Environmental factors	Working conditions, security and safety issues, equipment etc.

Case example

Continuing the Chase Manhattan example from earlier in this chapter.

The competency definition and the scale are used to assess to what extent the individual has developed the competency, through seven points ranging from 'minimal knowledge' to 'recognisable ability' (representing a firm professional standard) and up to 'advisory level' (related to the best in the external market). This range is positioned as an external, absolute scale, not an internal relative measure. As such, it is used for individuals (always starting with self-analysis) to agree with their manager their individual competency profile, or for managers to specify the competency demands of given roles or specific job vacancies, or for the business to profile the differing requirements of customers.

It reaches the strategic needs of the organisation at its most macro level, but equally - and vitally, as a prerequisite for a successful corporate agenda - it supports a stream of products which get to the individual's agenda of professional development, career opportunity ad performance-related reward.

Conventionally, people see themselves are hired - and hopefully empowered - to do a job, and increasingly they are also expected to combine in cohesive teams.

Competences

4.5 A more recent approach to job design issues is the development and outlining of competences.

KEY TERM

A person's **competence** is 'a capacity that leads to behaviour that meets the job demands within the parameters of the organisational environment and that, in turn, brings about desired results'. (Boyzatis)

4.6 Some take this further and suggest that a competence embodies the ability to transfer skills and knowledge to new situations within the occupational area.

4.7 There are a number of **different sorts of competences**, according to Armstrong.

(a) **Behavioural/personal** competences: underlying personal characteristics people bring to work (eg interpersonal skills); personal characteristics and behaviour for successful performance, for example, 'ability to relate well to others'. Most jobs require people to be good communicators.

(b) **Work-based/occupational competences** refer to 'expectations of workplace performance and the outputs and standards people in specific roles are expected to obtain'. This approach is used in NVQ systems (see below). They cover what people have to do to achieve the results of the job. For example, a competence of a Certified Accountant includes 'produce financial and other statements and report to management'.

(c) Generic competences can apply to all people in an occupation.

4.8 Many lists of competences, however, confuse:

(a) Areas of work at which people are competent.
(b) Underlying aspects of behaviour.

4.9 **Some competences for managers**

Competence area	Competence
Intellectual	• Strategic perspective • Analytical judgement • Planning and organising
Interpersonal	• Managing staff • Persuasiveness • Assertiveness and decisiveness • Interpersonal sensitivity • Oral communication
Adaptability	
Results	• Initiative • Motivation to achievement • Business sense

These competences can be elaborated by identifying *positive* and *negative* indicators.

Job design

4.10 Mintzberg describes three parameters of job design.

(a) **Job specialisation**

(i) **How many different tasks** are contained in the jobs and how broad and narrow are these tasks? Until recently, there has been a trend towards narrow specialisation, reinforced, perhaps by demarcations laid down by trade unions. On the production line, a worker did the same task all the time. Modern techniques, however, require workers to be **multi-skilled**.

(ii) **To what extent does the worker have control over the work?** At one extreme ('scientific management') the worker has little control over the work. At the other extreme (eg an electrician) the worker controls the task.

(b) **Regulation of behaviour.** Co-ordination requires that organisations formalise behaviour so as to predict and control it.

(c) **Training and indoctrination.**

(i) Training refers to the process by which job related skills are taught.

(ii) Indoctrination is the process by which organisational values are acquired.

Training is relevant to job design, as it deals with the skills the job requires. On the job training, however, is required if the skills are complex, and so learning must be taken into account.

4.11 Belbin (People Management, 6 March 1997) describes a way of **tailoring job design to delayered, team based structures and flexible working systems.**

- Flattened delayered hierarchies lead to greater uncertainty as to how jobs are performed and there is the added problem of **locus of control**.
- Old hierarchies had the merit of clarity in that people knew exactly what was expected of them.

4.12 The authors describe *Workset*, which uses colour coding to classify work and working time into seven types.

1	Blue: tasks the job holder carries out in a prescribed manner to an approved standard
2	Yellow: individual responsibility to meet an objective (results, not means)
3	Green: tasks that vary according to the reactions and needs of others
4	Orange: shared rather than individual responsibility for meeting an objective
5	Grey: work incidental to the job, not relevant to the four core categories
6	White: new or creative undertaking outside normal duties
7	Pink: demands the presence of the job holder but leads to no useful results

4.13 The manager gives an outline of the proportion of time spent on each 'colour' of work. The job holder then briefs the manager on what has actually been done. This highlights differences between managers' and job-holders' **perceptions of jobs**, and indeed different **jobholders had widely different ideas as to what they were supposed** to do. Important issues arise when there is a gap in perception. Underperformance in different kinds of work can be identified, and people can be steered to the sort of work which suits them best.

Job description

KEY TERM

A **job description** sets out the purpose of the job, where it fits in the organisation structure, the context of the job, the accountabilities of the job and the main tasks they have to carry out.

4.14 **Purpose of job description**

Purpose	Comment
Organisational	The job description defines the job's place in the organisational structure
Recruitment	The job description provides information for identifying the sort of person needed (person specification)
Legal	The job description provides the basis for a contract of employment
Performance	Performance objectives can be set around the job description

4.15 **Contents of a job description**

(a) **Job title** (eg Assistant Financial Controller). This indicates the function/department in which the job is performed, and the level of job within that function.

(b) **Reporting to** (eg the Assistant Financial controller reports to the Financial Controller), in other words the person's immediate boss. (No other relationships are suggested here.)

(c) **Subordinates** directly reporting to the job holders.

(d) **Overall purpose** of the job, distinguishing it from other jobs.

(e) **Principal accountabilities or main tasks**

(i) Group the main activities into a number of broad areas.

(ii) Define each activity as a statement of accountability: what the job holder is expected to achieve (eg **tests** new system to ensure they meet agreed systems specifications).

(f) The current fashion for multi-skilled teams means that **flexibility** is sometimes expected.

Alternatives to job descriptions

4.16 **Detailed** job descriptions are perhaps only suited for jobs where the work is largely repetitive and therefore performed by low-grade employees: once the element of **judgement** comes into a job description it becomes a straitjacket. Many of the difficulties that arise where people adhere strictly to the contents of the job description, rather than responding flexibly to task or organisational requirements.

4.17 Perhaps job descriptions should be written in terms of the **outputs and performance levels** expected. Some firms are moving towards **accountability profiles** in which outputs and performance are identified explicitly.

4.18 Armstrong suggests a crucial difference between:

(a) A **job** - a group of tasks.

(b) A **role**. A part played by people in meeting their objectives by working competently and flexibly within the context of the organisation's objectives, structures and processes.

4.19 A **role definition** is wider than a job description. It is less concerned with the details of the job content, but how people interpret the job.

Case example

Guinness

According to *People Management* (11 September 1997) in May 1996 Guinness Brewing Great Britain introduced a new pay system based on competences.

Restrictive job definitions, lengthy job descriptions and a 24-grade structure were replaced by broad role profiles and three pay bands. Roles are now specified in terms of 'need to do' (primary accountabilities), 'need to know' (experience and knowledge requirements) and 'need to be' (levels of competence).

Competences are defined as 'the skill, knowledge and behaviours that need to be applied for effective performance'. There are seven of them, including commitment to results and interpersonal effectiveness. Roles are profiled against each relevant competence and individuals' actual competences are compared with the requirements through the performance management process.

Person specification

4.20 A person specification identifies the **type of person** the organisation should be trying to recruit - their character, aptitudes, educational or other qualifications, aspirations in their career etc. It is an interpretation of the job specification in terms of the kind of person suitable for the job.

Question 3

Do you have a job description? Does it include everything listed in paragraph 5.8? How well do you think it describes what you actually do on a day to day basis? If you do not have a job description, draw one up, and then draw up a job and personnel specification. How well do *you* match?

4.21 A person specification is therefore often used as an all-purpose selection assessment plan for recruiting younger people in fairly large numbers into a fairly junior grade. Research has been carried out into what a personnel specification ought to assess. J *Munro Fraser's Five Point Pattern of Personality* the selector's attention to the candidate's:

- Impact on others
- Acquired knowledge or qualifications
- Innate ability
- Motivation
- Adjustment and emotional balance.

Advertising job vacancies

4.22 After a job description and a personnel specification have been prepared, the organisation should advertise the job vacancy (or vacancies). In many large organisations, the personnel department arranges the advertising, deals with applications and arranges interviews with applicants.

4.23 The job description and personnel specification can be used as guidelines for the wording of any advertisement or careers prospectus pamphlet.

4.24 The choice of advertising medium will depend on:

(a) the cost of using the advertising medium;
(b) the frequency with which the organisation wants to advertise the job vacancy;
(c) its suitability to the target audience.

4.25 **Advertising media for recruitment**

- In-house magazines
- Professional journals
- National newspapers
- Local newspapers
- Local radio
- Job centres
- Recruitment agencies
- Schools careers officers
- University careers officers
- Careers/job fairs
- Open days
- The internet

4.26 Section summary

Before recruiting for an individual position:
- A job analysis defines the tasks and perhaps the individual competences of the job.
- A person specification indicates the type of person wanted.

5 SELECTION

Application forms

5.1 Applicants who reply to job advertisements are usually asked to fill in a job **application form**, or to send a letter giving details about themselves and their previous job experience (**their CV**) and explaining why they think they are qualified to do the job.

5.2 The application form should therefore help the selection officer(s) to **sift through the applicants**, and to reject some at once so as to avoid the time and costs of unnecessary interviews. It should therefore:

(a) **Obtain relevant information** about the applicant and which can be compared with the requirements (education and other qualifications, experience relevant to the job, age, interests even) of the job.

(b) Give the applicant the opportunity to write about himself or herself, his or her career ambitions or why he or she wants the job.

The interview

5.3 The interview is often the deciding factor in whether an applicant gets the job.

5.4 **Aims of the interview**

(a) Finding the best person for the job, through direct assessment.
(b) Giving the applicant the chance to learn about the firm.

5.5 **Preparation.** The interview must be prepared carefully, to make sure that the right questions are asked, and relevant information obtained to give the interviewers what they need to make their selection. The interviewer should study:

(a) The job description and specification, to review the major demands of the job.

(b) The personnel specification, to help the interviewer make relevant assessments of the applicant's character and qualifications.

(c) The application form, to decide on questions or question areas for each applicant.

5.6 **Conduct of the interview**

(a) The layout of the room and the number of interviewers should be planned carefully.

(b) The manner of the interviewers, their tone of voice, and the way their early questions are phrased can all be significant in establishing the tone of the interview.

(c) Questions should be put carefully. The interviewers should not be trying to confuse the candidate, but should be trying to obtain the information they need.

(d) Encourage the candidate to talk.

(e) The candidate should be given the opportunity to ask questions.

5.7 **Limitations of interviews**

(a) **Unreliable assessments**. Interviewers may disagree. A suitable candidate might be rejected or an unsuitable candidate offered a job.

(b) **They fail to provide accurate predictions** of how a person will perform in the job. Research has shown this time and again.

(c) The **interviewers are likely to make errors** of judgement even when they agree about a candidate. These might be any one of the following.

(i) A **halo effect**. This is a tendency for interviewers to make a general judgement about a person based on one single attribute.

(ii) **Contagious bias**. This is a process whereby interviewers change the behaviour of the applicant by suggestion. The wording of questions or non-verbal clues from the interviewer might lead the applicant to tell the interviewers more of what they wanted to hear.

(iii) Interviewers sometimes **stereotype** candidates on the basis of insufficient evidence, eg on the basis of dress, hair style, accent of voice etc.

(iv) **Incorrect assessment** of qualitative factors such as motivation, honesty or integrity. Abstract qualities are very difficult to assess in an interview.

(v) **Logical error**. An interviewer might draw conclusions about a candidate from what he or she says or does when there is no logical justification for those conclusions.

(vi) **Incorrectly used rating scales.** For example, if interviewers are required to rate a candidate on a scale of 1-5 for a number of different attributes, there might be a tendency to mark candidates inconsistently.

5.8 Interviewers should thus be trained to conduct and assess interviews.

Testing

5.9 Tests are used to:

(a) Supplement interviews.
(b) Select applicants for interview.

5.10 **Types of test**

(a) **Psychological tests and personality tests** aim to assess facts about an individual's personality. An individual may be required to answer a long series of questions or score a variety of statements which indicate basic attitude profiles.

(b) **Intelligence tests** measure the applicant's general intellectual ability.

(c) **Proficiency tests** are perhaps the most closely related to an assessor's objectives, because they measure ability to do the **work involved.**

(d) **Aptitude tests** aim to provide information about the candidate's abilities. Aptitude tests can test mental ability (IQ tests, tests in mathematics, general knowledge or use of English) and physical dexterity.

(e) **Psychometric tests** contain features of all of the above. They are selection tests that seek to **quantify** psychological dimensions of job applicants, for example intelligence, personality and motivation. Candidates might be required to answer a list of questions. Those answers are then marked and the candidate is given a score.

Case example

The *Myers-Briggs Type Indicator* is used to categorise people as to whether they are introvert/extrovert, objective/intuitive, logical/emotional, decisive/ hesitant, and so forth. These tests may be used:

(a) in the initial selection of new recruits;
(b) in the allocation of new entrants to different branches of work; and
(c) as part of the process of transfer or promotion.

5.11 **Advantage of tests**

(a) A test can be a sensitive measuring instrument.
(b) Tests are standardised, so that all candidates are assessed by the same yardstick.
(c) Tests always measure the same thing (eg IQ).

5.12 **Disadvantages**

(a) They give a spurious accuracy to complex issues.

(b) They are culturally-specific. Many tests for managers were developed in the US. The culture in the UK and US differ in many respects (eg attitudes to 'hunting').

5.13 The use of **biodata** involves obtaining, analysing and scoring **biographical information** (eg age gender, education, leisure). Items of information are weighted according to their proven ability to predict job performance. A person's biodata is scored and a mark is given. A cut-off score would be a required minimum for the candidate to be considered for further assessment.

5.14 **Group selection methods** might be used by an organisation as the final stage of a selection process for management jobs. They consist of a series of tests, interviews and group situations over a period of two days or so, involving a small number of candidates for a job. Typically, six or eight candidates will be invited to the organisation's premises for two days. After an introductory chat to make the candidates feel at home, they will be given one or two tests, one or two individual interviews, and several group situations in which the candidates are invited to discuss problems together and arrive at solutions as a management team.

(a) **Advantages**

(i) They give the organisation's selectors a longer opportunity to study the candidates.

(ii) They reveal more than application forms, interviews and tests alone about the ability of candidates to persuade others, to negotiate with others, to explain ideas to others and to investigate problems efficiently. These are typical management skills.

(iii) They reveal more about the candidates' personalities - eg stamina, interests, social interaction with others (ability to co-operate and compete etc), intelligence, energy, self-confidence etc.

(iv) They are suitable for selection of potential managers who have little or no previous experience and two days to spare for interviews etc.

(c) **Disadvantages**

(i) Time and cost

(ii) The lack of experience of interviewers/selectors

(iii) The rather false and unreal nature of the group situations in which candidates are expected to participate. Candidates might behave differently in a contrived situation than they would given a real-life problem.

Question 4

'I fluffed the interview, so I haven't got the job!' is a common statement.

Some careers officers give tuition in interview techniques to people looking for jobs. What do you think this says about interviewing, as opposed to testing, as a means of selection?

Answer

If interview techniques are taught, it might imply that, in the absence of any other selection criteria, your success at interview will have more to do with your ability to present yourself in an interview situation than your ability to do the job. On the other hand, an interview is a test of how well you perform under pressure, in an unfamiliar environment and with strangers. This might reflect some of the interpersonal skills required for a job.

References

5.15 It is common to obtain references from the candidate's previous employers and other people the candidate is acquainted with. A reference will tell you little about the candidate: the candidate's friends, unless they have an axe to grind, will hymn his or her praises; the candidate's employer will choose his or her words carefully to avoid legal action for defamation of character. However, a reference does enable an employer to check the basic accuracy of the candidate's CV.

6 INDUCTION

6.1 An applicant who is offered the job and accepts it will have to be introduced to the job. This is the process of induction.

6.2 From the first day at work, a new recruit should be helped to find his or her bearings. There are limits to what any person can pick up in a short time.

6.3 Induction is a continuing process which might last for a few months. This is sometimes referred to as a **probationary period**.

(a) The supervisor must arrange for the recruit's training programme to start.

(b) The recruit will only gradually learn his job through continued on-the-job training.

(c) The person responsible for induction should keep checking up on the new recruit, to make sure that the recruit is settling in well and is learning the ropes.

(d) The senior manager should check on the recruit from time to time (in particular, find out how the training programme is progressing).

7 BRAINWORKS PLC UPDATE

Questions can be found in the Introduction box at the beginning of the Chapter.

7.1 *Question 1.* Human resources is BW's business, so it is obviously of strategic importance.

(a) BW has to understand the human resources needs of its clients, in order to send them the right candidates.

(b) BW depends absolutely on the skills and competences of its recruitment consultants. As a 'people' business, HR issues are not only relevant to the business strategy, but *central* to it. Yet there is no evidence of a strategic approach in the UK. PeoplePower in the US appears to take more care. But BW's main concerns at the moment are organisation and IT, not the core activities of the business.

Chapter roundup

- **Personnel management** in the past was never perceived to have a strategic role, dealing as it did with issues of hiring and firing, industrial relations and so forth.
- **Human resource management (HRM)** is based on the assumption that the management and deployment of staff is a key **strategic** factor in an organisation's competitive performance. HRM requires top management involvement and the promotion of culture and **values**, so that employees' **commitment**, as opposed merely to their consent, is obtained.
- **Resourcing** is about meeting the personnel needs of the organisation. HRM identifies the number of staff needed, the skills needed and the degree to which the staff's personalities and values are suited to the organisation culture
- **Job analysis** determines the requirements for a job. The job's tasks are set out in a job description. A job specification describes the skills or competences required for the job. A **person specification** describes the sort of person suitable for a job.
- Job vacancies are often advertised in a number of ways. Market research is often useful so as to target recruitment efforts effectively. **Recruitment** advertising is still *advertising*, and so is a way in which the organisation shows its face to the world.
- **Interviews** are a widely used selection method. Many firms prefer to use tests as, for large numbers of candidates, they provide a more reliable prediction of performance on the job than interviews. **Tests** can assess intelligence, personality etc. Interviews are flawed because of bias and difficulties people have in interpreting a candidate's behaviour.
- New recruits need time to learn the job and settle in. Many organisations have formal procedures for **induction**.

Quick quiz

1 What was the task of personnel management, in traditional terms? (see para 1.2)
2 Define HRM. (1.3)
3 What are the implications of regarding employees as assets? (1.7)
4 What are the problems in associating HRM with business strategies? (2.1)
5 Why are attitudes and behaviour important in human resources planning? (2.4)
6 What four areas are dealt with by human resources planning? (3.3)
7 List the sources of information about supply of human resources. (3.8)
8 What are the contents of the HR plan? (3.17)
9 Distinguish between recruitment and selection. (4.1)
10 What is a job description? (4.14)
11 Describe J Munro Fraser's Five Point Pattern. (4.21)
12 How would you carry out an interview? (5.5)
13 What are proficiency tests? (5.10)
14 When are group selection tests appropriate? (5.14)

Question to try	Level	Marks	Time
23	Exam-standard	25	45 mins

Chapter 19

MANAGING PERFORMANCE

Chapter topic list		Syllabus reference
1	Performance management: an outline	3(a)(viii)
2	Motivating individuals	3(a)(vii)
3	Creating effective teams	3(b) (i)-(iv)
4	Appraisal and performance management	3(a)(vii), 5(vi)
5	Brainworks plc update	

Introduction

The previous chapter described how the organisation obtains human resources, but HRM places great emphasis on how they are used. This chapter and the next deal with how to get the best out of the people who have been so expensively recruited.

Performance management is an active approach to defining what must be achieved and ensuring it is done. This sets the context for all the motivational, teamworking and appraisal activities in this chapter. The next chapter describes formal steps in which performance can be improved.

Brainworks plc

1 What approaches to motivation are used? Do you think senior managers' view accords with the reality? What are the principal motivating factors for BW's UK employees?

2 How important is teamwork to BW?

3 What might be the importance of appraisal to BW?

1 PERFORMANCE MANAGEMENT: AN OUTLINE

KEY TERM

Performance management is: 'a means of getting better results...by understanding and managing performance within an agreed framework of planned goals, standards and competence requirements. It is a process to establish a shared understanding about what is to be achieved, and an approach to managing and developing people..[so that it]...will be achieved' (Armstrong, Handbook of Personnel Management Practice).

1.1 Armstrong 'unpacks' this definition, and describes some other features of performance management.

Aspect	Comment
Agreed framework of goals, standards and competence requirements	As in MBO, the manager and the employee agree about a standard of performance, goals and the skills needed.
Performance management is a **process**	Managing people's performance is an everyday issue to generate real results. It is not just a system of form filling.
Shared understanding	People need to understand the nature of high levels of performance so they can work towards them.
Approach to **managing and developing** people	(1) How managers work with their teams (2) How team members work with managers and each other. (3) Developing individuals to improve their performance.
Achievement	The aim is to enable people to realise their potential and maximise their contribution to the organisation's well being.
Line management	A performance management system is primarily the concern, not of experts in the personnel/HRM department, but of the mangers responsible for driving the business.
All staff	Everybody is involved in the success of the organisation, so managers must be included in the system.
Specific	As each organisation has unique issues to face, performance management systems cannot really be bought off the peg.
Future-based	Performance management is forward-looking, based on the organisation's future needs and what the individual must do to satisfy them

1.2 The process of performance management

Step 1. From the **business plan**, identify the requirements and competences required to carry it out.

Step 2. Draw up a **performance agreement**, defining the expectations of the individual or team, covering standards of performance, performance indicators and the skills and competences people need.

Step 3. Draw up a **performance and development plan** with the individual. These record the actions needed to improve performance, normally covering development in the current job. They are discussed with job holders and will cover, typically:

- The areas of performance the individual feels in need of development
- What the individual and manager agree is needed to enhance performance
- Development and training initiatives

Step 4. **Manage performance continually throughout the year,** not just at appraisal interviews done to satisfy the personnel department. Managers can review actual performance, with more informal interim reviews at various times of the year.

- High performance is reinforced by praise, recognition, increasing responsibility; low performance results in coaching or counselling
- Work plans are updated as necessary.
- Deal with performance problems, by identifying what they are, establish the reasons for the shortfall, take control action (with adequate resources) and provide feedback

Step 5. Performance review. At a defined period each year, success against the plan is reviewed, but the whole point is to assess what is going to happen in future.

1.3 Organisations are introducing such systems for much the same reason as they pursued management by objectives, in other words to:

- Link the individual's performance with the performance of the organisation
- Indicate where training and development may be necessary

1.4 Success at work is based on a symbiotic relationship between the organisation and the employee. There are many factors which determine the work performance.

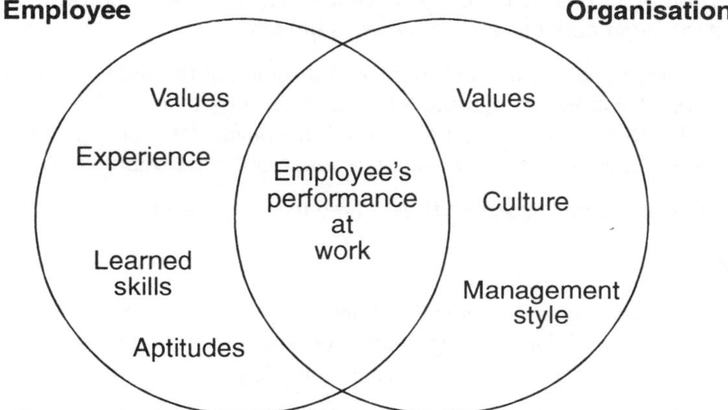

1.5 (a) An employee's **personality and ability** might be **fine for the task** but might **clash with the organisation's culture**. (A person who is a natural bureaucrat will not always fit in a culture where roles are not defined.)

(b) **Work organisation**: is the employee given a suitable job and are the employee's skills appropriately developed?

(c) **Motivation**: can an employee be persuaded to work hard, and well?

2 MOTIVATING INDIVIDUALS

2.1 Managers have basically a crude idea of motivation, or of employees' attitudes to work. Douglas McGregor categorises managers' attitudes into two types. Most fall somewhere between these extremes.

(a) **Theory X**: most people **dislike work and responsibility and will avoid both if possible**. Because of this, most people must be coerced, controlled, directed and/or threatened with punishment to get them to make an adequate effort towards the achievement of the organisation's objectives.

(b) **Theory Y: physical and mental effort into work is as natural as play or rest**. The ordinary person does not inherently dislike work: according to the conditions, it may be a source of satisfaction or punishment. People learn not only to accept but to seek responsibility

2.2 Edgar Schein identified four types of individual and suggests how they might be motivated. (Schein uses 'man' to denote 'person'.)

(a) The **rational-economic man** is primarily motivated by economic incentives.

(b) The **social man** looks for self-fulfilment in social relationships.

(c) The **self-actualising man** is influenced by a wider range of motivations, but is driven realise his own full potential.

(d) The **complex man** represents Schein's own view of people. The motives influencing a particular individual may change from time to time, and their relative importance may also vary, depending on the situation. The complex man will respond to no single managerial strategy, but will consider its appropriateness to circumstances and his own needs.

Question 1

In *Brits at Work*, John Mole (a former manager) describes various work environments which he explored in order to gain a worm's eye view of life in British companies. In this quotation he is talking to a manager about scientists and researchers.

> ' "... but once you've provided them with the money (ie resources to finish research projects) and support (laboratory assistants), what motivates them?" "They motivate themselves, don't they?" There were certainly no material incentives for working in medical research. After a degree and a doctorate ... you might be taken on at the salary I used to pay my secretary!'

Why is the narrator slightly confused? What models of the worker are in conflict here?

Answer

Research scientists perhaps exemplify Theory Y, but even so perhaps the narrator is contrasting *economic man* with *self-actualising man*. For some people the enjoyment of the job itself is satisfaction enough. People will accept less money to pursue an interest.

2.3 In short managers believing in Theory X will brandish the 'stick', supporters of Theory Y will offer the 'carrot'. Note that both describe what managers feel about employees and how employees are motivated. Both are rather crude simplifications. So, to refine them, how are employees motivated?

Question 2

What factors in yourself or your organisation motivate you:

(a) to turn up to work at all?
(b) to do an average day's work?
(c) to 'bust a gut' on a task or for a boss?

Go on - be honest!

Psychological contracts

2.4 Edgar Schein believes that the **roots of motivation** at work can be found in the **psychological contract** an individual has with the organisation. A psychological contract might be thought of as a set of expectations.

(a) The individual expects to derive certain benefits from membership of the organisation and is prepared to expend a certain amount of effort in return.

(b) The organisation expects the individual to fulfil certain requirements and is prepared to offer certain rewards in return.

2.5 Types of **psychological contract**

(a) **Coercive contract**. The individual **considers that he or she is being forced** to contribute his or her efforts and energies **involuntarily**, and that the rewards received in return are inadequate compensation. (An individual might hate the job or be unable to leave; he or she might be forcibly transferred to another job he or she does not like.)

(b) **Calculative contract**. This is accepted **voluntarily** by the individual, who expects to do the job in exchange for a **readily identifiable set of rewards** (for example pay, status, or simply having a job of work to keep occupied).

(c) **Co-operative contract**. The individual voluntarily **identifies his or her goals** with the **organisation** and its goals, so that he/she actively seeks to contribute further to the achievement of those goals.

2.6 The words **motives and motivation** are used to mean:

(a) **Goals or outcomes** that have become desirable for a particular individual. Thus we say that money, power or friendship are motives for doing something.

(b) The **mental process of choosing desired outcomes**, deciding how to go about them and setting in motion the required behaviour.

(c) The **social process** by which the behaviour of an individual is influenced by others. Motivation in this sense apply to the attempts of organisations to get workers to put in more effort.

Motives

2.7 In the most basic terms, an individual has needs which he or she has to satisfy. The means of satisfying these needs are *wants*. For example, an individual's need for power might be crystallised as a want for money and a position of authority.

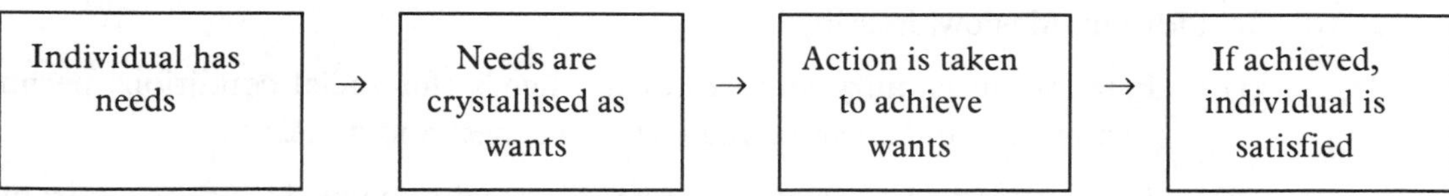

The wants of the individual thus identify the specific outcomes that can be offered as **motives** to act in a certain way. Motivation is then the urge or drive to take action to achieve wants.

2.8 Many theories have tried to explain motivation and why and how people can be motivated.

(a) **Content theories** assume that human beings have a package of motives which they pursue: they have a set of needs or desired outcomes.

(b) **Process theories** explore the process through which outcomes **become** desirable and are pursued by individuals. This approach assumes that people are able to select their goals and choose the paths towards them, by a conscious or unconscious process of calculation.

Content theories

Maslow's hierarchy of needs

2.9 In his motivation theory, Maslow put forward certain propositions about the motivating power of the needs each individual has. (The theory is about motivation in general, not just motivation at work.)

(a) An individual's needs are arranged in a hierarchy. They are satisfied in order, so that basic needs (eg for water) must be satisfied first.

(b) Each level of need is dominant until satisfied. Only then does the next level of need become a motivating factor.

(c) A need which has been satisfied no longer motivates an individual's behaviour. The need for self-actualisation can rarely be satisfied.

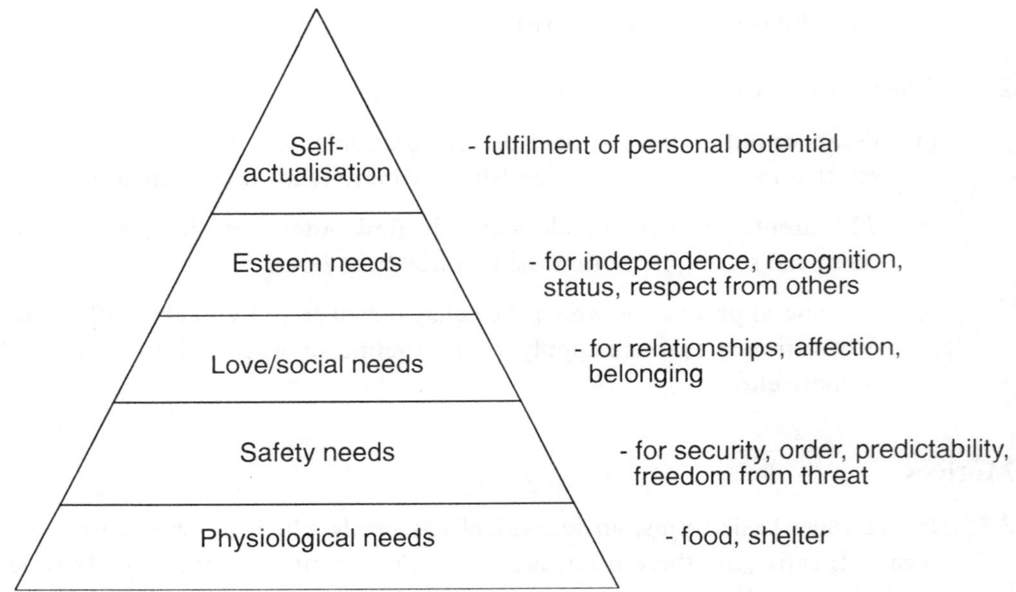

(d) In addition, Maslow described:

(i) Freedom of enquiry and expression needs (for social conditions permitting free speech, and encouraging justice, fairness and honesty);

(ii) Knowledge and understanding needs (to gain knowledge of the environment, to explore, learn).

Question 3

A friend of yours is very fashion conscious. He has just spent £250 on a pair of hi-tech hi-fashion trainers, because the pair he formerly owned were stolen by a rival gang and he has no others. What does this tell you about your friend, in terms of Maslow's hierarchy of needs?

Answer

Quite a lot. Most importantly, however, the story demonstrates that you cannot simply pigeonhole a person's behaviour in a simple way. Your friend's purchase of trainers satisfies several needs.

Physiological needs are satisfied as the trainers provide necessary comfort. *Safety* needs, too, are satisfied as they protect the feet. *Social* needs are satisfied as, arguably, buying fashion products denotes *inclusion* (or desired inclusion) in a group. *Esteem* needs are also satisfied if his trainers are admired, or if the implication of wealth earns him respect.

2.10 **Problems in applying Maslow's theory**

(a) People seek to satisfy **several needs** at the same time.

(b) The **same need may cause different behaviour** in different individuals.

(c) It **ignores the concept of 'deferred gratification'** by which people are prepared to ignore current suffering for the promise of future benefits.

(d) **Empirical verification** of this theory is hard to come by. In a particular test, it revealed it had a bias towards US and UK cultures.

McClelland

2.11 David McClelland also proposes a needs-based theory. It is not as wide ranging as Maslow's in that it does not take Maslow's very basic needs into account. McClelland identified three needs. They are not in any hierarchy.

Affiliation People who need a sense of belonging and membership of a group tend to be concerned with maintaining personal relationships.	*Power* People who need power seek a leadership position to influence and control.	*Achievement* People have a strong desire for success and a fear of failure.

2.12 McClelland argued that:

(a) Top managers have a strong need for power and a low need for affiliation.

(b) Entrepreneurs have a high need for achievement.

(c) It is possible to 'teach' these needs in some cases (by teaching people to think with the right imagery so that they develop the needs).

Herzberg

2.13 Herzberg's two-factor theory identifies **hygiene factors** and **motivator factors**.

(a) **Hygiene factors** are those which, if inadequate, cause **dissatisfaction** with work. They work analogously to sanitation, which minimises threats to health rather than actively promoting 'good health'. They are based on a **need to avoid unpleasantness.** Hygiene factors include:

- Company policy and administration
- Salary
- The quality of supervision
- Interpersonal relations
- Working conditions
- Job security

(b) **Motivator factors** actively create job satisfaction and are effective in motivating an individual to superior performance and effort. They are based on a **need for personal growth.**

- Status (possibly a hygiene factor too)
- Advancement
- Gaining recognition
- Being given responsibility
- Challenging work
- Achievement
- Growth in the job

A lack of motivators at work will encourage employees to concentrate on bad hygiene (real or imagined) such as to demand more pay.

2.14 The job itself, on the other hand, can be interesting and 'exciting'. It can satisfy the desire for a feeling of 'accomplishing something', for responsibility, for professional recognition, for advancement, and the need for self-esteem.

2.15 Herzberg suggested means by which satisfactions could be supplied. Stemming from his fundamental division of motivator and hygiene factors, he encouraged managers to alter the job itself (the type of work done, the nature of tasks, levels of responsibility) rather than the conditions of work.

(a) **Job enrichment:** 'the planned process of up-grading the responsibility, challenge and content of the work'. Typically, this would involve increasing delegation to provide more interesting work and problem-solving at lower levels within an organisation.

(b) **Job enlargement:** although often linked with job enrichment, it is a separate technique and is rather limited in its ability to improve staff motivation. Job enlargement is the process of increasing the number of operations in which a worker is engaged and so moving away from narrow specialisation of work.

(c) **Job rotation:** this is the planned operation of a system whereby staff members exchange positions with the intention of breaking monotony in that work and providing fresh job challenge.

Process theories

Expectancy theory

2.16 **Expectancy theory** (as suggested by Victor Vroom) states that people will decide how much they are going to put into their work, according to two factors.

(a) **Valence**. The value that they place on the outcome (whether the positive value of a reward, or the negative value of a punishment) . Valence is subjective.

(b) **Expectancy**. The strength of their **expectation** that behaving in a certain way will in fact bring about the desired outcome.

Expectancy* x *Valence* = *Force of motivation.

2.17 The theory holds that this is a **conscious decision making process**. Let us examine this in more detail.

(a) If the outcome is worthless (ie has a Valence of 0) then according to Vroom, there will be no motivation. Similar if the **expectation** of the result is 0, there will be no motivation either. Only when both **Expectancy and Valence have positive values** will individual be motivated.

(b) **Expectation** is the individual's **subjective probability**. In other words, people differ in their estimates as to the outcome of an action. If it looks cloudy outside, you may or may not take an umbrella with you, based on your judgement as to whether it will rain. A colleague may have a different judgement, and so arrive at a different decision.

(c) The subjective element of Expectancy and the fact that there is a subjective element in Valence (people will value an outcome differently eg some will value a salary increase more than an extra day's holiday) mean that expectancy theory can account for individual differences in motivation.

(d) **Expectancy theory aims to measure motivation.** As it is based on the assumption that people are to a degree **rational** it aims to be predictive. However, individuals can never have complete knowledge of outcomes nor do they soberly weigh up what they are doing.

Porter and Lawler

2.18 A variant on expectancy theory was provided by Porter and Lawler. Whilst maintaining the crucial distinction between valence (or the perceived value of rewards) and the subjective probability that a given expenditure of effort will achieve it, more elements are added to the model. This is because the revised model aims to predict not just motivation as such but **performance**.

2.19 So as well as valence, expectancy and force of motivation, other variables influencing performance include the following.

(a) **Basic managerial skills** such as the ability to:

(i) Do the job
(ii) Identify jobs which need to be done

(b) The **past record of performance**: this obviously has an impact on *expectancy*, and so can be considered as part of a feedback system.

(c) **Influences on valence** include the differing values of **intrinsic satisfactions** (interest in the job, a sense of accomplishment, enjoyment) and **extrinsic satisfactions** (eg pay etc), as well as the rewards which seem to be *fair*. These satisfactions return to affect valence, again in a feedback system.

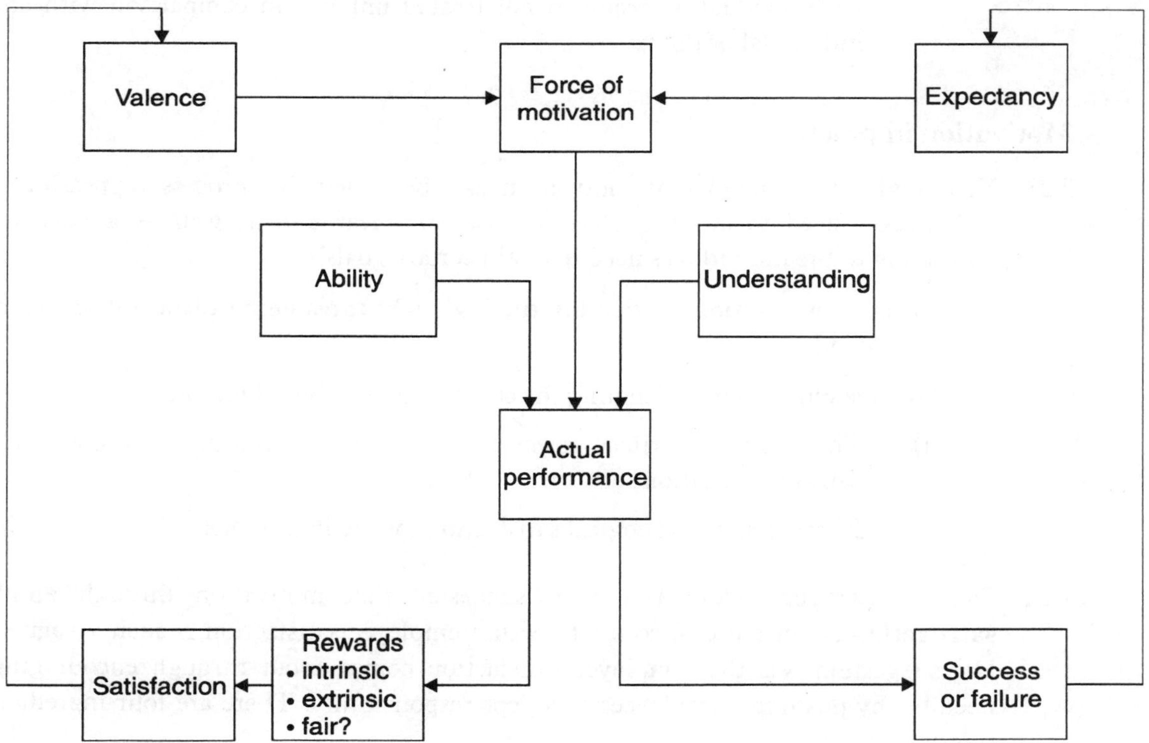

Critiques of motivation: the contingency approach

2.20 A systems and contingency approach to motivation has been developed by a number of writers, notably Kurt Lewin. A systems and contingency approach suggests the following.

(a) The motivation of an individual cannot be seen in isolation, as it depends on the system and environment within which the person operates, the person's work group and the environment.

(b) The motivation of the individual will also depend on both the individual and circumstances.

Social comparison theory

2.21 One aspect of motivation we have not touched is 'fairness'. It is all very well to praise someone for his or her performance, but what if this praise is resented by the individual's colleagues and/or subordinates? To single out one individual for special favour can have a demotivating influence. In other words, comparative evaluation is important.

2.22 In 1951, Festinger suggested that people seek to evaluate their own performance through comparison with other individuals - not by using absolute standards. This can have a number of implications.

(a) It can lead an individual to select a role model for behaviour - someone the individual would like to emulate.

(b) In some companies, comparative performance information can be a strong motivator as can peer reviews and internal competition (eg between sales regions).

(c) It underpins notions of 'fairness' in the work environment.

(i) Unfairness can be demotivating.

(ii) Sexual and racial equality legislation involve the concept of fairness, so that an individual or group in not treated unfairly in comparison with another individual or group.

Motivation in practice

2.23 You might have noted that motivation can be a negative process (appealing to an individual's need to *avoid* unpleasantness, pain, fear etc) as well as a positive one (appealing to the individual's need to attain certain goals).

(a) Negative motivation is wielding the big stick: threatening dismissal or demotion, reprimand.

(b) Positive motivation is dangling the carrot, and may be achieved by:

(i) The offer of extrinsic rewards, such as pay, incentives, promotion, better working conditions etc.

(ii) Internal or psychological satisfaction for the individual.

2.24 Drucker (writing before Herzberg) suggested that motivation through **employee satisfaction** is not a useful concept because employee satisfaction is such a **vague idea**. His suggestion was that employee satisfaction comes about through encouraging - if need be, by pushing - employees to accept responsibility. There are four ingredients to this.

(a) **Careful placement of people in jobs** so that an individual is suited to the role.

(b) **High standards of performance in the job**, so that the employee should be encouraged to expect high standards of performance from himself or herself.

(c) **Providing the worker with feedback control information.** The employee should receive routine information about how well or badly he or she is doing without having to be told by his boss.

(d) **Opportunities for participation in decision making** that will give the employee managerial vision.

Question 4

Carrots and sticks have more sophisticated names nowadays, like 'performance related pay', 'career enhancements', 'worker participation', 'disciplinary action', 'redundancy' and so on. Most days of the week you will find something on subjects such as these in the newspaper. Watch out for news stories along these lines, noting in particular what comments from spokespeople reveal about methods of motivation in the organisations concerned.

2.25 **Improving motivation**

(a) **Incentive schemes.** More pay? For some people (eg piece workers) this might make a difference in encouraging higher output, or for those who are either in financial difficulties or see success in monetary terms. Pay is often a hygiene factor. Incentive schemes have become very popular, with reward tied to the profit of the firm. Problems arise, however.

   (i) They are not always fair, especially when the performance of two people are linked.

   (ii) People might pursue their own goals to the detriment of organisation goals. Such schemes thus inhibit teamwork.

   (iii) They are based on a Theory X mechanistic view, which ignores other ways of motivation.

(b) **Changing the job?**

   (i) **Job enlargement.** The worker might end up doing two boring tasks rather than one.

   (ii) **Job rotation** – switching people between tasks.

   (iii) **Job enrichment** – by extending and deepening responsibilities.

(c) **Fitting the job to the worker**? For example, people with *affiliation* needs can be organised in teams. Many companies now adopt team-based working because it is more effective operationally. Teams are:

- Self managing
- Multi-skilled
- Open, with negotiated production target
- Able to share knowledge

(d) Rewards can be based on **behaviours and attitudes** rather than mere output.

Developments in motivation research

2.26 According to Robert McHenry (*Spurring Stuff*, People Management, 24 July 1997):

(a) Forty years ago, motivation at work tended to be tackled as single-issue psychology. Typical advice was 'people will work harder if you pay them more', or 'people will work harder if you give them more attention'.

(b) A couple of decades later, a long list of single issues had emerged. The fashion then was to classify and combine them in relatively simple ways in order to create a good motivational climate. Perhaps Maslow's or Herzberg's theories are relevant here.

2.27 Recently research has:

(a) Shifted from an external to an **internal perspective** (to how employees **perceive** their job and the working environment).

(b) Explored the **relationships *between* the motivational variables**, to get inside the employee's mind.

2.28 Research by Leigh and Brown in the US identifies two key aspects of the psychological climate.

Psychological safety	Job meaningfulness
• Support: the boss backs you up	• Self-expression
• Role clarity	• Contribution: what you do makes a difference
• Recognition: praise for what you do	• Challenge

2.29 According to the research (Kahn, 1990), these elements can be combined in different ways, into **job involvement**. This is when work is a major **satisfaction** in person's life.

2.30 The research suggests that there are different motivational 'triggers' for different people, and compared salespeople with the HR specialists.

(a) Sales staff

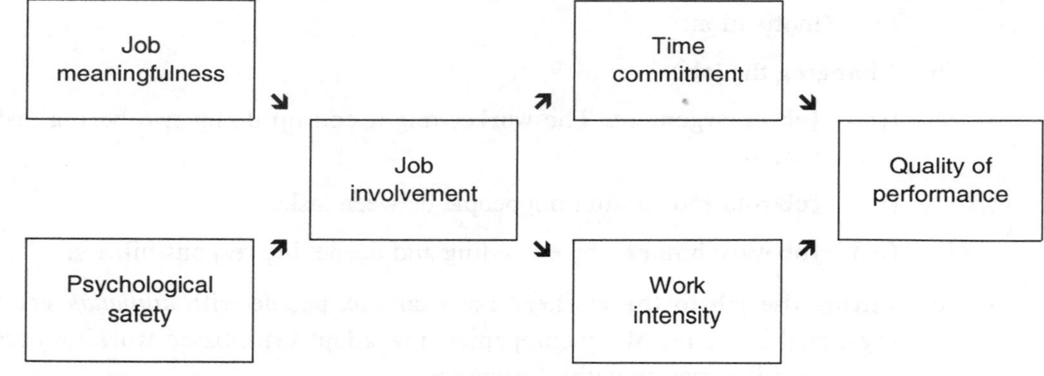

(b) HR specialists

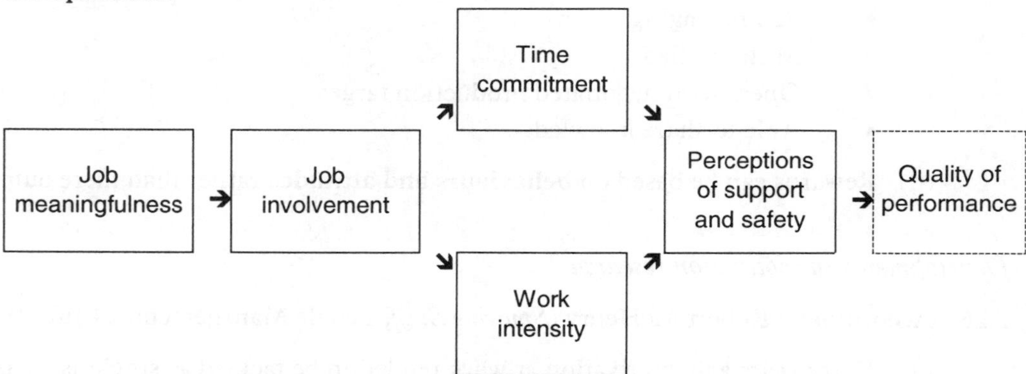

These diagrams suggest that for HR staff, security and safety factors are less important in generating 'involvement' than for sales people.

At the heart of the research are people's **perceptions**. As McHenry says:

'(a) The trigger for HR professionals seems to be the **meaningfulness of their job**. This is defined as **feeling** as if they are a key members of the organisation, and **believing** that they are doing a demanding job that is not taken for granted. Work that offers these qualities encourages involvement, and this leads to the twin effort variables of time commitment and work intensity.

At this point, something even more interesting happens. HR practitioners who are (already) working intensely and committing large amounts of time to their jobs **believe** that they are in a supportive environment that encourages self-expression. This relationship does not work the other way around - that is, if an employer provides support and opportunities for self-expression, it does not lead to greater effort.

(b) Salespeople seem to need these job features **before** they get involved, but HR people seem to **create them for themselves** as a result of working harder.

2.31 McHenry draws some conclusions from the research.

(a) **Perceptions** of the work environment are linked to job and effort. For many people a 'meaningful' climate produces conditions under which involvement flourishes.

(b) 'Distinctions between **intrinsic and extrinsic motivators may become less valuable**, if emphasis is put on employee perceptions, on the train of motivation-related thought, and on the blurred distinction between what is 'reality' and what is created by people in their own minds. That is the true psychology of motivation.'

3 CREATING EFFECTIVE TEAMS

3.1 In your working life, though, you will generally find yourself working as part of a group or **team**; or, if you are a supervisor or a manager, you may direct a team. **A team is more than just a collection of individuals** - it has a specific purpose, a sense of identity and, in a work context, it has a task to perform. First of all, a team is a type of group.

Groups

KEY TERM

A **group** is 'any collection of people who perceive themselves to be a group'. Unlike a random collection of individuals, a group of individuals share a common sense of identity and belonging.

3.2 Groups have certain attributes that a random 'crowd' does not possess.

(a) **A sense of identity**. There are acknowledged boundaries to the group which define who is 'in' and who is 'out', who is 'us' and who is 'them'.

(b) **Loyalty to the group,** and acceptance within the group. This generally expresses itself as conformity or the acceptance of the 'norms' of behaviour and attitudes that bind the group together and exclude others from it.

(c) **Purpose and leadership.** Most groups have an express purpose, whatever field they are in: most will, spontaneously or formally, choose individuals or sub-groups to lead them towards the fulfilment of those goals.

3.3 Any organisation is composed of many groups, with such attributes of their own. People in organisations will be drawn together into groups by:

(a) A **preference for small groups**, where closer relationships can develop
(b) The **need to belong** and to make a contribution that will be noticed and appreciated
(c) **Familiarity:** a shared office or canteen
(d) **Common** rank, specialisms, objectives and interests
(e) The attractiveness of a particular group **activity** (joining an interesting club, say)
(f) **Resources** offered to groups (for example sports facilities)
(g) '**Power**' greater than the individuals could muster (trade union, pressure group)

3.4 A **primary working group** is the immediate social environment of the individual worker, in other words, the people he/she works with most of the time.

3.5 A formal group used for particular objectives in the work place is called a team. Although many people enjoy working in teams, their popularity in the work place arises because of their effectiveness in fulfilling the organisation's work.

Teams

KEY TERM

A **team** is a 'small number of people with complementary skills who are committed to a *common purpose*, performance *goals* and approach for which they hold themselves basically accountable'.

3.6 Teams have these types of role.

Type of role	Comments
Work organisation	Combine skills of different individuals.
	Avoids complex communication between different business functions.
Control	Fear of letting down the team can be a powerful motivator - teams can be used to control the performance and behaviour of individuals.
	Teams can be used to resolve conflict
Knowledge generation	Teams can generate ideas.
Decision-making	Decisions can be evaluated from more than one viewpoint.
	Teams can be set up to investigate new developments.

Teamworking

3.7 The basic work units of organisations have traditionally been specialised functional departments. In more recent times, organisations are adopting small, flexible teams. Teamworking allows work to be shared among a number of individuals, so it get done faster than by individuals working alone, without people:

(a) Losing sight of their 'whole' tasks; or
(b) Having to co-ordinate their efforts through lengthy channels of communication.

3.8 **A team may be called together temporarily**, to achieve **specific task objectives** (**project team**), or may be more or less permanent, with responsibilities for a particular product, product group or stage of the production process (a **product or process team**).

There are two basic approaches to the organisation of team work: multi-skilled teams and multi-disciplinary teams.

Multi-disciplinary teams

3.9 **Multi-disciplinary teams** bring together individuals with **different skills and specialisms**, so that their skills, experience and knowledge can be **pooled** or exchanged. The following chart shows a multi-disciplinary structure, cutting across traditional functional boundaries.

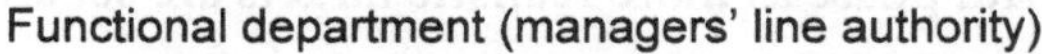

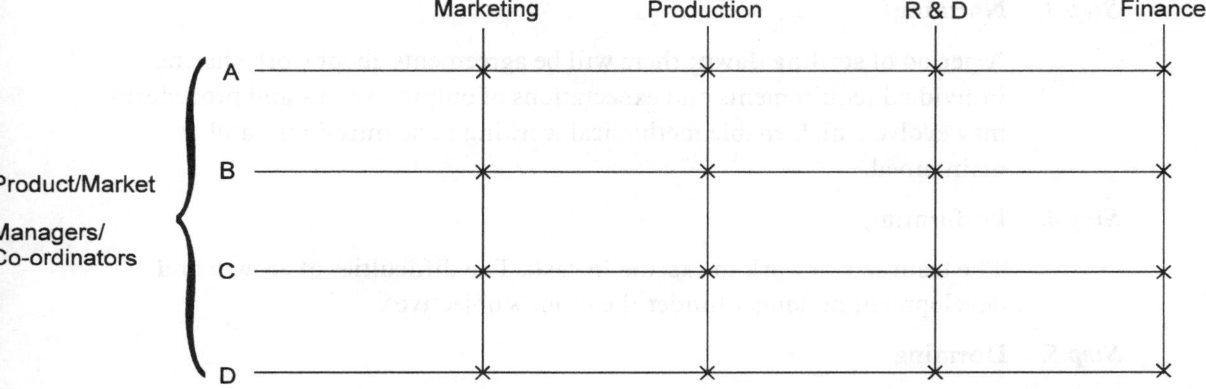

Teamworking of this kind encourages freer and faster communication between disciplines in the organisation, which:

(a) Increases workers' **awareness of their overall objectives** and targets

(b) **Aids co-ordination**

(c) **Helps to generate solutions to problems**, and suggestions for improvements, since a multi-disciplinary team has access to more 'pieces of the jigsaw'.

Multi-skilled teams

3.10 **Multi-skilled teams** bring together a number of **individuals who can perform *any* of the group's tasks** (eg each individual has many skills). These tasks can then be shared out in a more flexible way between group members, according to who is available and best placed to do a given job at the time it is required.

Team development

3.11 Four stages in team development were identified by Tuckman. We have added a fifth at the end.

Step 1. **Forming**

The team is just coming together, and may still be seen as a collection of individuals. Each member wishes to impress his or her **personality** on the group. The individuals will be trying to find out about each other, and about the aims and norms of the team. There will at this stage probably be a **wariness about introducing new ideas**. The **objectives** being pursued may as yet be **unclear** and a leader may not yet have emerged. This period is essential, but may be time wasting: the team as a unit will not be used to being autonomous, and will probably not be an efficient agent in the planning of its activities or the activities of others.

Step 2. **Storming**

This frequently involves more or less open **conflict** between team members. There may be **changes** agreed in the original objectives, procedures and norms established for the group. If the team is developing successfully this may be a fruitful phase as more realistic targets are set and **trust** between the group members increases.

Step 3. **Norming**

A period of **settling down**: there will be agreements about work sharing, individual requirements and expectations of output. Norms and procedures may evolve which enable methodical working to be introduced and maintained.

Step 4. **Performing**

The team sets to work to execute its task. The difficulties of growth and development no longer hinder the group's objectives.

Step 5. **Dorming**

Often, after a team has been performing effectively for a while it becomes complacent. The team goes into a semi-automatic mode of operation, with no fresh energy or attention focused on the task - even if it changes - and with efforts devoted primarily to the maintenance of the team itself.

The ideal team

3.12 Characteristics of the ideal functioning team

(a) Each individual gets the **support** of the team, a sense of identity and belonging which encourages loyalty and hard work on the group's behalf.

(b) Skills, information and ideas are **shared**, so that the team's capabilities are greater than those of the individuals.

(c) **New ideas** can be tested, reactions taken into account and persuasive skills brought into play in group discussion for decision making and problem solving.

(d) Each individual is **encouraged** to participate and contribute and thus becomes personally involved in and committed to the team's activities.

(e) **Goodwill, trust and respect can be built up** between individuals, so that communication is encouraged and potential problems more easily overcome.

Problems with teams

3.13 Unfortunately, team working is rarely such an undiluted success. There are certain constraints involved in working with others.

(a) Awareness of **group norms** and the desire to be acceptable to the group may **restrict individual personality** and flair.

(b) **'Too much discord'**. Conflicting **roles and relationships** (where an individual is a member of more than one group) can cause difficulties in communicating effectively.

(c) **Personality problems,** and will suffer if one member dislikes or distrusts another; is too dominant or so timid that the value of his ideas is lost; or is so negative in attitude that constructive communication is rendered impossible.

(d) **Rigid leadership** and procedures may strangle initiative and creativity in individuals.

(e) **Differences of opinion** and political conflicts of interest are always likely.

(f) **Too much harmony.** Teams work best when there is room for disagreement.

(i) It can become dangerously blinkered to what is going on around it, and may confidently forge ahead in a completely wrong direction. I L Janis describes this as **group think.** The **cosy consensus of the group prevents consideration** of alternatives, constructive criticism or conflict.

(ii) Efforts to paper over differences leads to bland recommendations without meaning.

(g) **Corporate culture and reward systems.** Teams will fail if the company promotes and rewards the individual at the expense of the group.

(h) **Too many meetings.** Teams should not try to do everything together. Not only does this waste time in meetings, but team members are exposed to less diversity of thought.

(i) **Powerlessness.** People will not bother to work in a team or on a task force if its recommendations are ignored.

(j) **Suitability.** Teamworking does not suit all jobs.

Question 3

What might be the strategic impact of group think?

Answer

Group think characterises the behaviour of managers in early situation of corporate decline - see Chapter 17. It also applies to Johnson and Scholes concept of the *recipe*, the tried and trusted formula for success.

Creating an effective work team

3.14 The management problem is how to create effective, efficient work teams. Handy takes a contingency approach to the problem of team effectiveness which is constructed as follows.

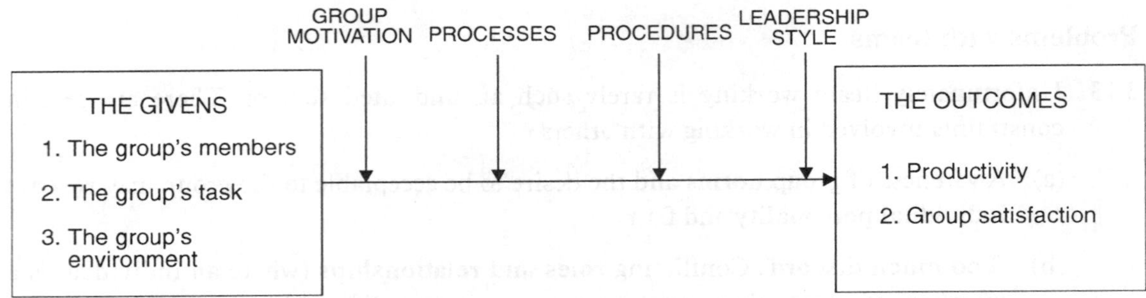

Management can operate on both 'givens' and 'intervening factors' to affect the 'outcomes'.

Givens

3.15 **Group membership will be determined by:**

(a) The personalities and characteristics of the individual *members* of the team,

(b) The *blend* of the individual skills and abilities of its members.

(c) Necessary technical skills

3.16 **Belbin,** in a study of business-game teams at Carnegie Institute of Technology in 1981, drew up a list of the most **effective character-mix** in a team.

Member	Role
Co-ordinator	Presides and co-ordinates; balanced, disciplined, good at working through others.
Shaper	Highly strung, dominant, extrovert, passionate about the task itself, a spur to action.
Plant	Introverted, but intellectually dominant and imaginative; source of ideas and proposals but with disadvantages of introversion.
Monitor-evaluator	Analytically (rather than creatively) intelligent; dissects ideas, spots flaws; possibly aloof, tactless - but necessary.
Resource-investigator	Popular, sociable, extrovert, relaxed; source of new contacts, but not an originator; needs to be made use of.
Implementor	Practical organiser, turning ideas into tasks; scheduling, planning and so on; trustworthy and efficient, but not excited; not a leader, but an administrator.
Team worker	Most concerned with team maintenance - supportive, understanding, diplomatic; popular but uncompetitive - contribution noticed only in absence.
Finisher	Chivvies the team to meet deadlines, attend to details; urgency and follow-through important, though not always popular.

The **specialist** joins the group to offer expert advice when needed.

The task

3.17 The nature of the *task* must have some bearing on how a group should be managed.

(a) **Urgency:** it mat be necessary to dictate how things should be done, rather than spend time encouraging a participatory style of working.

(b) Jobs which are routine, unimportant and undemanding will be insufficient to motivate either individuals or the group as a whole.

The environment

3.18 The team's **environment** relates to factors such as the physical surroundings at work and to inter-group relations.

Intervening factors and outcomes

3.19 With regard to **intervening factors** (processes and procedures), research indicates that a team which tackles its work **systematically** will be more effective than one which lives from hand to mouth, and muddles through.

3.20 **Motivation and leadership style**. High productivity outcomes may be achieved if work is so arranged that satisfaction of individuals' needs coincides with high output. Where teams are, for example, allowed to set their own improvement goals and methods and to measure their own progress towards those goals, it has been observed (by Peters and Waterman among others) that they regularly exceed their targets. The style of *leadership* adopted by the team leader can also affect its outcome. This depends on the circumstances.

3.21 Individuals may bring their own '**hidden agendas**' to groups for satisfaction - goals which may have nothing to do with the declared aims of the team - such as protection of a sub-group, impressing the boss, inter-personal rivalry etc.

Effective teams

3.22 Some teams work more effectively than others, for a variety of reasons, and we can identify ways of evaluating whether a team is effective.

Factor	Quantifiable factors Effective team	Ineffective team
Labour turnover	Low	High
Accident rate	Low	High
Absenteeism	Low	High
Output and productivity	High	Low
Quality of output	High	Low
Individual targets	Achieved	Not achieved
Stoppages and interruptions to the work flow	Low	High (eg because of misunderstandings, disagreements)

Factor	Qualitative factors	Ineffective team
Commitment to targets and organisational goals	High	Low
Understanding of team's work and why it exists	High	Low
Understanding of individual roles	High	Low
Communication between team members	Free and open	Mistrust

Factor	Qualitative factors	Ineffective team
Ideas	Shared for the team's benefit	'Owned' (and hidden) by individuals for their own benefit
Feedback	Constructive criticism	Point scoring, undermining
Problem-solving	Addresses causes	Only looks at symptoms
Interest in work decisions	Active	Passive acceptance
Opinions	Consensus	Imposed solutions
Job satisfaction	High	Low
Motivation in leader's absence	High	'When the cat's away...'

Case example

(Adapted from *People Management* October 1997)

The annual staff survey at *Nationwide Building Society* usually places its customer service teams for mortgages and insurance at mid-table in terms of employee satisfaction. This year the teams are at the top. At the same time their productivity has increased by half, sickness absence has fallen by 75 percent and overtime is down to zero.

In the early 1990s Nationwide began to abandon traditional management hierarchies in the non-retail part of its business. In customer service, they were looking for an approach that would further develop multi-skilling while supporting a flatter structure. Self managed teamworking seemed the obvious answer, as it also addressed issues such as morale and job satisfaction.

They work on the premise that the people who know how best to carry out and improve their own work are the teams themselves. Members have shared authority and responsibility to plan, implement and control how their targets are achieved.

In 1995 the Nationwide began a project in the Northampton administrative centre, revolutionising the basis under which the 12 teams in the mortgage and insurance customer service department operated. They increased the level of training and worked on their decision-making, conflict management and team-building skills. Each team had between nine and 18 members, including a leader, but he or she had a coaching, rather than directing, role.

When work comes in, the team decides who is the most appropriate person to take it on, depending on skills and existing workloads. While teams are encouraged to share recourses with each other when necessary, there is also a competitive element. But this is never allowed to detract from the performance of the department - you are only as good as your worst-performing team.

The results of each team are charted, allowing comparative league tables to be created. Initially, one team finished consistently at the foot of the productivity table. Its members consulted colleagues in the more successful teams and altered their work processes accordingly.

Members compared their sickness and overtime figures with those of other teams, and then took responsibility for controlling these elements. Often this was done using a sense of ownership and pride which, could with peer pressure, reduce the need for managerial intervention.

There are several aspects of implementation to be addressed if self-managed teams are to be successful.

(a) First, there must be clear business reasons for the move.

(b) There also needs to be recognition by all involved parties that self-managed teams are not a quick fix.

(c) Another primary issue is that of 'buy-in' and gaining commitment at all levels, while communicating effectively.

(d) Another important prerequisite is to assess the organisation's existing systems and procedures within which the new teams may have to work.

The value of groups as work units

3.23 **Teams are not the solution to all problems**

(a) Some decisions and tasks are **better reached by individuals working alone** or having the final say.

(b) **Group norms** *may* work to lower effectiveness.

(c) Seeing people as a team - or expecting to work as one - is completely unrealistic in many cases (eg if they work in different countries) and **more formal co-ordination methods** may be necessary.

(d) Groups have been shown to produce **fewer ideas** - though better evaluated - than the individuals of the group working separately. A group will often produce a better solution to a quiz than its best individual, since 'missing pieces' can be added to his or her performance.

3.24 Section summary

- Much work is organised on a team basis
- Team development is forming, storming, norming and performing.
- Teams have a sense of cohesion, against outsiders.
- Effective teams require a mix of people and skills.
- Teams are not suitable for all jobs.

4 APPRAISAL AND PERFORMANCE MANAGEMENT

Appraisal: reviewing past performance to establish the current position.

4.1 The process of appraisal is part of the system of performance management.

KEY TERM

Whilst performance management as a whole is forward looking, the process of **appraisal** is designed to review performance over the past period, with a view to identifying any deficiencies, and improving it in the future.

The purpose of appraisal

4.2 The general purpose of any appraisal system is to improve the efficiency of the organisation by ensuring that the individuals within it are performing to the best of their ability and developing their potential for improvement.

(a) **Reward review**: measuring the extent to which an employee deserves a bonus or pay *increase*.

(b) **Performance review**: for planning and following-up training and development programmes, ie identifying training needs, validating training methods and so on.

(c) **Potential review**, as an aid to planning career development and succession, by attempting to predict the level and type of work the individual will be capable of in the future.

4.3 Objectives of appraisals

(a) Establishing what **the individual has to do** in a job in order that the objectives for the section or department are realised.

(b) Establishing the **key or main results** which the individual will be expected to achieve in the course of his or her work over a period of time.

(c) **Comparing the individual's level of performance against a standard,** to provide a basis for remuneration above the basic pay rate.

(d) Identifying the individual's training and development **needs** in the light of actual **performance.**

(e) Identifying **potential candidates for promotion.**

(f) Identifying **areas of improvement**.

(g) Establishing an **inventory of actual and potential performance** within the undertaking to provide a basis for manpower planning.

(h) Monitoring the undertaking's **initial selection procedures** against the subsequent performance of recruits, relative to the organisation's expectations.

(i) **Improving communication** about work tasks between different levels in the hierarchy.

4.4 The need for appraisal

(a) Managers and supervisors may obtain **random impressions** of subordinates' performance (perhaps from their more noticeable successes and failures), but rarely form a coherent, complete and objective picture.

(b) They may have a fair idea of their subordinates' shortcomings - but may not have devoted **time and attention** to the matter of improvement and development.

(c) Judgements are **easy to make**, but **less easy to justify** in detail, in writing, or to the subject's face.

(d) **Different assessors** may be applying a **different set of criteria,** and varying standards of objectivity and judgement. This undermines the value of appraisal for comparison, as well as its credibility in the eyes of the appraisees.

(e) Unless stimulated to do so, managers rarely give their subordinates adequate **feedback** on their performance.

4.5 Three basic problems

(a) The **formulation and appreciation of desired traits and standards** against which individuals can be consistently and objectively assessed.

(b) **Recording assessments**. Managers should be encouraged to utilise a standard and understood framework, but still allowed to express what they consider important, and without too much form-filling.

(c) **Getting the appraiser and appraisee together,** so that both contribute to the assessment and plans for improvement and/or development.

The process of appraisal

4.6 **A typical appraisal system**

Step 1. **Identification of criteria** for assessment, perhaps based on job analysis, performance standards, person specifications and so on.

Step 2. An **appraisal report** is prepared by the manager. In some systems both the appraisee and appraiser prepare a report: these reports are then compared.

Step 3. An **appraisal interview**, for an exchange of views about the appraisal report, targets for improvement, solutions to problems and so on.

Step 4. **Review of the assessment** by the assessor's own superior, so that the appraisee does not feel subject to one person's prejudices. Formal appeals may be allowed, if necessary to establish the fairness of the procedure.

Step 5. **Action plans** to achieve improvements and changes agreed are prepared and implemented

Step 6. **Follow-up:** monitoring the progress of the action plan.

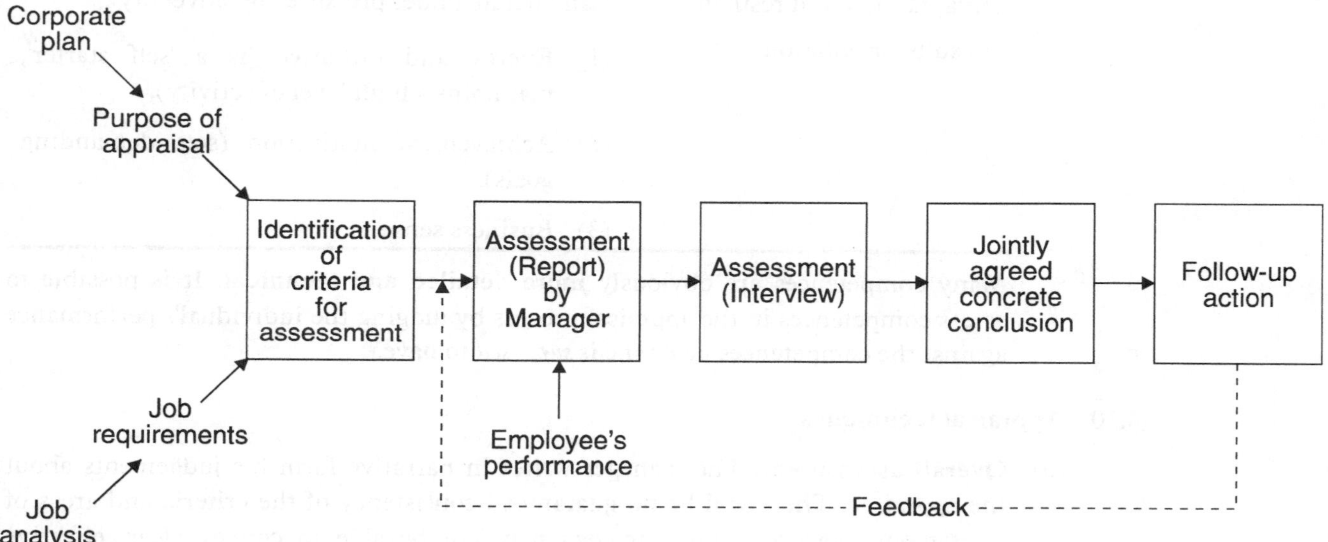

4.7 Most systems provide for appraisals to be recorded, and report forms of various lengths and complexity may be designed.

The appraisal report

What is appraised?

4.8 **Appraisal standard. A common standard** enables people to be compared, but standards should also be related to **meaningful performance criteria**, which take account of the **critical variables in each different job.**

4.9 An **appraisal report** is written before the interview.

(a) Key performance issues relate to the **job description.**

(b) **Personality**: not relevant unless specifically related to performance.

(c) A **competence,** as we have seen, is an observable skill or ability to complete a particular task successfully. It can include the ability to transfer skills and knowledge to new situations. Some competences for **managers and supervisors** might be adapted for appraisal as follows - but they still appear vague.

Management competence	Comment
Intellectual	(1) Ability to see 'the wood for the trees'. (2) Analysis and judgement (eg seeks relevant information, due attention to detail). (3) Planning and organising (eg scheduling and delegating).
Interpersonal	(1) Managing staff (eg leadership style, developing people). (2) Persuasiveness (good in negotiation). (3) Assertiveness and decisiveness. (4) Interpersonal sensitivity (is flexible in dealing with others). (5) Oral communication.
Adaptability and resilience	Can operate under pressure and adversity
Results-orientation	(1) Energy and initiative (is a 'self starter', maintains a high level of activity). (2) Achievement motivation (sets demanding goals). (3) Business sense.

Many competences are obviously **more detailed and technical**. It is possible to assess competences in the appraisal process by judging the individual's performance against the competences he or she is *supposed* to have.

4.10 **Appraisal techniques**

(a) **Overall assessment**. The manager writes in narrative form his judgements about the appraisee. There will be no guaranteed consistency of the criteria and areas of assessment, however, and managers may not be able to convey clear, effective judgements in writing.

(b) **Guided assessment**. Assessors are required to comment on a number of specified characteristics and performance elements, with guidelines as to how terms such as 'application', 'integrity' and 'adaptability' are to be interpreted in the work context. This is more precise, but still rather vague.

(c) **Grading**. Grading adds a comparative frame of reference to the general guidelines, whereby managers are asked to select one of a number of levels or degrees to which the individual in question displays the given characteristic. These are also known as **rating scales**.

Numerical values may be added to ratings to give rating scores. Alternatively a less precise **graphic scale** may be used to indicate general position on a plus/minus scale.

Factor: job knowledge

High ____________√______________ Average ______ Low

(d) **Behavioural incident methods**. These concentrate on **employee behaviour,** which is measured against typical behaviour in each job, as defined by common **critical incidents** of successful and unsuccessful job behaviour reported by managers.

(e) **Results-orientated schemes.** This reviews performance against specific targets and standards of performance **agreed in advance by manager and subordinate together.** The advantages of this are as follows.

   (i) The subordinate is more involved in appraisal because he/she is able to evaluate his/her success or progress in achieving specific, jointly-agreed targets.

   (ii) The manager is therefore relieved, to an extent, of a critic's role, and becomes a counsellor.

   (iii) Learning and motivation theories suggest that clear and known targets are important in modifying and determining behaviour.

   The effectiveness of the scheme will still, however, depend on the **targets set** (are they clearly defined? realistic?) and the **commitment** of both parties to make it work.

Self-appraisals

4.11 Self-appraisals occur when individuals carry out their own self-evaluation as a major input into the appraisal process.

(a) **Advantages**

   (i) It **saves the manager time** as the employee identifies the areas of competence which are relevant to the job and his/her relative strengths in these competences.

   (ii) It offers **increased responsibility** to the individual which may improve motivation.

   (iii) It helps reconcile the goals of the individual and the organisation.

   (iv) In giving the responsibility to an individual, the scheme may offer more **flexibility** in terms of timing, with individuals undertaking ongoing self-evaluation.

(b) **Disadvantage.** People are often not the best judges of their own performance.

4.12 Many schemes combine the two - manager and subordinate fill out a report and compare notes.

Interviews and counselling

4.13 The extent to which any discussion or counselling interview is based on the written appraisal report varies in practice. Some appraisees see the report in advance.

4.14 Maier (*The Appraisal Interview*) identifies three types of approach to appraisal interviews.

(a) **The tell and sell method.** The manager tells the subordinate how he or she has been assessed, and then tries to sell (gain acceptance of) the evaluation and the improvement plan. This requires unusual human relations skills in order to convey constructive criticism in an acceptable manner, and to motivate the appraisee.

(b) **The tell and listen method.** The manager tells the subordinate how he or she has been assessed, and then invites the subordinate to respond. Moreover, this method does not assume that a change in the employee will be the sole key to improvement: the manager may receive helpful feedback about how job design, methods, environment or supervision might be improved.

(c) **The problem-solving approach**. The manager abandons the role of critic altogether, and becomes a counsellor and helper. The discussion is centred not on the assessment, but on the employee's work problems. The employee is encouraged to think solutions through, and to make a commitment to personal improvement.

Follow-up

4.15 After the appraisal interview, the manager may complete the report, with an overall assessment, assessment of potential and/or the jointly-reached conclusion of the interview, with recommendations for follow-up action. The manager should then discuss the report with the counter-signing manager (usually his or her own superior), resolving any problems that have arisen in making the appraisal or report, and agreeing on action to be taken. The report form may then go to the management development adviser, training officer or other relevant people as appropriate for follow-up.

4.16 **Follow-up procedures**

(a) Informing appraisees of the **results** of the appraisal, if this has not been central to the review interview.

(b) **Carrying out agreed actions** on training, promotion and so on.

(c) **Monitoring** the appraisee's progress and checking that he has carried out agreed actions or improvements.

(d) Taking necessary steps to **help the appraisee to attain improvement objectives,** by guidance, providing feedback, upgrading equipment, altering work methods or whatever.

Problems in practice

4.17 In theory, such appraisal schemes may seem very fair to the individual and very worthwhile for the organisation, but in practice the **appraisal system often goes wrong**. L Lockett (in *Effective Performance Management*) suggests some common barriers to appraisal.

Appraisal barriers	Comment
Appraisal as confrontation	Many people dread appraisals, or use them 'as a sort of show down, a good sorting out or a clearing of the air.' (a) There is a lack of agreement on performance levels. (b) The feedback is subjective - in other words the manager is biased, allows personality differences to get in the way of actual performance etc. (c) The feedback is badly delivered. (d) Appraisals are 'based on yesterday's performance not on the whole year'. (e) Disagreement on long-term prospects.
Appraisal as judgement	The appraisal 'is seen as a one-sided process in which the manager acts as judge, jury and counsel for the prosecution'. However, the process of performance management 'needs to be jointly operated in order to retain the commitment and develop the self-awareness of the individual.'

Appraisal barriers	Comment
Appraisal as chat	The other extreme is that the appraisal is a friendly chat 'without ... purpose or outcome ... Many managers, embarrassed by the need to give feedback and set stretching targets, reduce the appraisal to a few mumbled "well dones!" and leave the interview with a briefcase of unresolved issues.'
Appraisal as bureaucracy	Appraisal is a form-filling exercise, to satisfy the personnel department. Its underlying purpose, improving individual and organisational performance, is forgotten.
Appraisal as unfinished business	Appraisal should be part of a continuing process of performance management.
Appraisal as annual event	Many targets set at annual appraisal meetings become irrelevant or out-of-date.

Appraisal and pay

4.18 Another problem is the link between appraisal and **pay**. Many employees consider that the appraisal system should be definitely linked with the reward system, on the ground that extra effort should be rewarded. Although this appears, superficially, a 'common sense' and fair view, there are major drawbacks to it.

(a) **Funds available** for pay rises rarely depend on one individual's performance alone - the whole company has to do well.

(b) **Continuous improvement** is always necessary - many firms have 'to run to stand still'. Continuous improvement should perhaps be expected of employees as part of their work, not rewarded as extra.

(c) In low-inflation environments, **cash pay rises are fairly small.**

(d) **Comparisons between individuals** are hard to make, as many smaller firms cannot afford the rigour of a job evaluation scheme.

(e) Performance management is about a lot more than pay for *past* performance - it is often **forward looking** with regard to future performance.

Appraisal, management expertise and empowerment

4.19 In 4.17 above, we suggested that appraisals could be subverted by managers who were biased, badly briefed or who only looked at yesterday's performance.

4.20 In organisations where **empowerment** is practised and employees are given more responsibility:

(a) Many **managers may not have the time** to keep a sufficiently close eye on individual workers to make a fair judgement.

(b) In some jobs, **managers do not have the technical expertise** to judge an employee's output.

(c) Employees depend on **other people** in the workplace/organisation to be effective - in other words, an individual's results may not be entirely under his/her control.

4.21 **Managers' influence on performance**

A person's performance is often indirectly or directly influenced by the **management style** of the person doing the appraisal. However, given the disparity of power between the manager and the appraisee, key issues may not get raised. (An article in the Harvard Business Review was entitled 'Managing Your Boss': this suggests that an appraiser's own behaviour may be a factor in the appraisee's performance, but that such two-way discussions may not be appreciated.)

4.22 **Personal and interpersonal problems**

(a) Appraisal is often **defensive on the part of the subordinate,** who believes that criticism may mean a low bonus or pay rise, or lost promotion opportunity.

(b) Appraisal is often **defensive on the part of the superior,** who cannot reconcile the role of judge and critic with the human relations aspect of interviewing and management. (S)he may in any case feel uncomfortable about 'playing God' with the employee's future.

(c) The superior might show **conscious or unconscious bias** in the appraisal or may be influenced by rapport (or lack of it) with the interviewee. Systems without clearly defined standard criteria will be particular prone to the subjectivity of the assessor's judgement.

(d) The manager and subordinate may both be **reluctant to devote time and attention to appraisal.** Their experience in the organisation may indicate that the exercise is a waste of time (especially if there is a lot of form-filling) with no relevance to the job, and no reliable follow-up action.

(e) The organisational culture may **simply not take appraisal seriously:** Interviewers are not trained or given time to prepare, appraisees are not encouraged to contribute, or the exercise is perceived as a 'nod' to Human Relations with no practical results.

New approaches to appraisal

Improving the system

4.23 **Evaluating the appraisal scheme**

Criteria	Comment
Relevance	• Does the system have a useful purpose, relevant to the needs of the organisation and the individual? • Is the purpose clearly expressed and widely understood by all concerned, both appraisers and appraisees? • Are the appraisal criteria relevant to the purposes of the system?
Fairness	• Is there reasonable standardisation of criteria and objectivity throughout the organisation? • Is it reasonably objective?

Criteria	Comment
Serious intent	• Are the managers concerned committed to the system - or is it just something the personnel department thrusts upon them? • Who does the interviewing, and are they properly trained in interviewing and assessment techniques? • Is reasonable time and attention given to the interviews - or is it a question of 'getting them over with'? • Is there a genuine demonstrable link between performance and reward or opportunity for development?
Co-operation	• Is the appraisal a participative, problem-solving activity - or a tool of management control? • Is the appraisee given time and encouragement to prepare for the appraisal, so that he can make a constructive contribution? • Does a jointly-agreed, concrete conclusion emerge from the process? • Are appraisals held regularly?
Efficiency	• Does the system seem overly time-consuming compared to the value of its outcome? • Is it difficult and costly to administer?

Upward appraisal

4.24 A notable modern trend, adopted in the UK by companies such as BP and British Airways and others, is **upward appraisal**, whereby employees are not rated by their superiors but by their subordinates. The followers appraise the leader.

4.25 **Advantages of upward appraisal**

(a) Subordinates tend to know their superior better than superiors know their subordinates.

(b) As all subordinates rate their managers statistically, these ratings tend to be more reliable - the more subordinates the better. Instead of the biases of individual managers' ratings, the various ratings of the employees can be converted into a representative view.

(c) Subordinates' ratings have more impact because it is more unusual to receive ratings from subordinates. It is also surprising to bosses because, despite protestations to the contrary, information often flows down organisations more smoothly and comfortably than it flows up. When it flows up it is qualitatively and quantitatively different. It is this difference that makes it valuable.

4.26 **Problems** with the method include fear of reprisals, vindictiveness, and extra form processing. Some bosses in strong positions might refuse to act, even if a consensus of staff suggested that they should change their ways.

Customer appraisal

4.27 In some companies part of the employee's appraisal process must take the form of **feedback from 'customers' (whether internal or external).** This may be taken further into an influence on remuneration (at Rank-Xerox, 30% of a manager's annual bonus is conditional upon satisfactory levels of 'customer' feedback). This is a valuable development in that customers are the best judges of customer service, which the appraisee's boss may not see.

360 degree appraisal

4.28 Taking downwards, upwards and customer appraisals together, some firms have instituted **360 degree appraisal** (or multi-source appraisal) by collecting feedback on an individual's performance from the following sources (outlined by Peter Ward in *People Management*, 9 February 1995).

(a) The person's immediate boss.

(b) People who report to the appraisee, perhaps divided into groups

(c) Co-workers: most people interact with others within an organisation, either as members of a team or as the receivers or providers of services. They can offer useful feedback.

(d) Customers: if sales people know what customers thought of them, they might be able to improve their technique.

(e) The manager personally: all forms of 360 degree appraisal require people to rate themselves. Those 'who see themselves as others see them will get fewer surprises.'

4.29 Sometimes the appraisal results in a counselling session, especially when the result of the appraisals are conflicting. For example, an appraisee's boss may have a quite different view of the appraisee's skills than subordinates.

Assessment centres

4.30 The **assessment centre** approach is used increasingly for the purposes of appraisal. It is particularly useful in the identification of executive or supervisory potential, since it uses simulated but realistic management problems, to give participants opportunities to show potential in the kind of situations to which they would be promoted, but of which they currently have no experience.

4.31 Trained assessors use a variety of games, simulations, tests and group discussions and exercises.

(a) Observed by the assessors, participants may be required to answer questionnaires about their attitudes, complete written tests, prepare speeches and presentations, participate in group role-play exercises, work through simulated supervisory tasks, and undertake self- appraisal and peer-rating.

(b) They are **assessed on a range of factors**, such as assertiveness, energy, initiative and creativity, stress-tolerance, sensitivity, abilities in persuasion, communication, and decision-making.

(c) An assessment report is then compiled from the assessors' observations, test scores and the participant's self-assessment. This is discussed in a feedback counselling interview.

4.32 **Advantages of assessment centres**

- A high degree of acceptability and user confidence.
- Avoidance of single-assessor bias.
- Reliability in predicting potential success (if the system is well-conducted).
- The development of skills in the assessors.
- The assessed individuals get experience of managerial/supervisory situations.

4.33 **Problems in practice**

- Poor specification of the competences against which participants are assessed.
- Exercises bear little relation to the competences being assessed, *or* to the organisation's culture.
- Little or no assessor training and selection.
- Inadequate selection and briefing of candidates.
- Inefficient programming and scheduling of the events.
- Inadequate follow-up action.

Appraisal and the organisation

4.34 'Any appraisal scheme can only be understood within the organisation structure of which it is a part' (Buchanan and Huczynski). Appraisal schemes:

(a) **Reflect the values** an organisation seeks to promote.

(b) Clarify a person's job.

(c) Assess competence.

(d) Assume that feedback improves performance.

(e) Link performance with organisational goals.

(g) They aim to make predictable, and hence in some degree controllable, a person's behaviour, and enable the organisation to encourage that behaviour.

4.35 A problem with many appraisal schemes in practice is that they concentrate exclusively on the **individual subordinate**. In other words they **reinforce hierarchy,** and are perhaps unsuitable to organisations where the relationship between management and workers is **fluid** or participatory. Upward, customer and 360° appraisals address this, but they are not widely adopted.

4.36 Appraisal systems, because they target the individual's performance, concentrate on the **lowest level of performance feedback**. They ignore the organisational and systems context of that performance. (For example, if an army is badly led, no matter how brave the troops, it will be defeated.) Appraisal schemes would seem to regard most **organisation problems** as a function of the **personal characteristics** of its members, rather than the **systemic problem** of its overall design.

4.37 A performance appraisal system is **designed by specialists** in the technostructure and **operated by managers** in the middle line.

Its effectiveness depends on:

(a) The **effort** line managers are prepared to put into the appraisal process.

(b) The **integrity** of line managers.

(c) The **ability** of line managers to do more than just give good appraisals to people who have a similar personality and background.

(d) The congruence between what the organisation **actually wants** and the behaviours it is **prepared to reward.**

4.38 If appraisal systems operate **successfully** as feedback control systems (in other words, if they do alter employees' performance) and identify behaviours to be encouraged, then, assuming organisational success is to some measure based on individual performance, they will influence the success of strategy.

5 BRAINWORKS PLC UPDATE

Questions can be found in the Introduction box at the beginning of this Chapter.

5.1 *Question 1.* As in real life, many techniques of motivation are used. Bill Begbie *appeared* to be interested in the 'social needs' aspect of motivation, in his view of the organisation as 'the big happy family'. However, the existing systems have very much a financial bias, with money as the prime need satisfied. This shows a Theory X view, possibly.

5.2 *Question 2.* The impression is given that, at BW(UK)'s local offices, teamwork is non-existent, with consultants keeping hold of clients and favoured staff. Clients are beginning to notice the competition, however. The rewards system encourages competition between individuals.

5.3 *Question 3.* Appraisal is important for two reasons. Indirectly, BW's business clients expect the right candidates to be sent to them. Directly, it is important in maintaining standards of consulting work, even though it might be hard to achieve.

Chapter roundup

- Managers' views as to what 'motivates' employees vary between **Theory X** (employees are workshy) to **Theory Y** (employees like to work).
- Motivation theory is useful to managers as it exposes in a systematic way why or how people are or can be motivated. Some writers believe that employees' motivation can be raised if the job satisfies their **personal needs**. **Maslow's hierarchy** and **Herzberg's** two-factor theory (hygiene vs motivator factors) are examples.
- The roots of motivation, according to Schein, are found in the **psychological contract** an employee has with an organisation, underpinning basic attitudes to, and expectations of, the organisation and work.
- Others believe that motivation is a **process** in which individuals make partly rational choices based on the desirability of an outcome and the effort required to achieve it. **Expectancy theory** is an example.
- The development of **teamwork skills** is also a function of HRD. Teams go through four stages: forming, storming, norming, and performing. A team's effectiveness is contingent upon the personalities of its members, the task, the environment and the processes and procedures the team uses.
- **Appraisal schemes** exist to **monitor individual performance** in the hope that **feedback** can help **improve** it.
- Appraisal schemes can be subverted if managers (and staff) do not take them seriously, in particular with relation to **bias**.
- Appraisal schemes are part of the **organisation structure**. They work on the assumption that performance failures are the result of personal or communication problems, rather than overall organisation design. New methods of appraisal seek to overcome these problems.

Quick quiz

1. What is performance management? (see para 1.1)
2. What are the steps of performance management? (1.2)
3. Distinguish between Theories X and Y. (2.1)
4. What is meant by rational-economic man and complex man? (2.2)
5. What are the three types of psychological contract? (2.5)
6. List the needs in Maslow's hierarchy? (2.9)
7. Describe expectancy theory (2.16 – 2.17)
8. What is the role of teams in the organisation? (3.6)
9. Distinguish between multi-disciplinary and multi-skilled teams (3.9, 3.10)
10. What are the stages of team development? (3.11)
11. What goes wrong with teams? (3.13)
12. What are the purposes of appraisal? (4.3)
13. Why do organisations need a formal system of appraisal? (4.4)
14. Outline the steps in the appraisal process. (4.6)
15. What is a competence? (4.9)
16. Outline a results-oriented approach to appraisal and its advantages. (4.10)
17. How do appraisal schemes go wrong? (4.17)
18. Why are some firms introducing upwards appraisals? (4.25)
19. What are assessment centres? (4.30)

Question to try	Level	Marks	Time
24	Exam standard	25	45 mins

Chapter 20

IMPROVING PERFORMANCE

	Chapter topic list	Syllabus reference
1	Human resource development and organisational learning	3(b)(i) - (iv)
2	Training and development needs	3(b)(i) - (iv)
3	Training methods	3(b)(i) - (iv)
4	Evaluating training	
5	Career management	3(b)(i) - (iv)
6	Brainworks plc update	

Introduction

One possible result of an employee's annual appraisal is that the employee is sent on a training course, if that is the best way of improving performance. In fact training is one way of enhancing the ability of the organisation to create knowledge which is why the ???? **Training** is widely recognised as a means to render employees efficient and productive, but it is no panacea for bad work organisation, personal incompetence or poor management.

The strategic purpose of training is to raise the overall skills level of the organisation. This is recognised by the **Investors in People** standard.

Many firms like to manage people's **careers**, either to given them a broad experience of the firm as a whole, or to develop specific technical experience in a functional area. The need for training and development encompasses personnel at all levels, the functional manager promoted to a general management position, as well as the new recruit.

Brainworks plc

1 What do you think of BW's training approach for new recruits?

2 What approaches to management training might BW take?

1 HUMAN RESOURCE DEVELOPMENT AND ORGANISATIONAL LEARNING 12/94

1.1 Resourcing an organisation (in HRM jargon) is about building and maintaining the **skills and knowledge base** of the organisation.

KEY TERMS

Human resource development (HRD) is 'enhancing and widening ... skills by training, by helping people to grow within the organisation, and enabling them to make better use of their skills and abilities'.

What is development?

KEY TERMS

Development is 'the growth or realisation of a person's ability and potential through the provision of learning and educational experiences'.

Training is 'the planned and systematic modification of behaviour through learning events, programmes and instruction which enable individuals to achieve the level of knowledge, skills and competence to carry out their work effectively'.

(Armstrong, *Handbook of Personnel Management Practice*)

1.2 **Overall purpose of employee and management development**

(a) **Ensure** the firm meets current and future performance objectives by...
(b) **Continuous improvement** of the performance of individuals and teams, and by...
(c) **Maximising people's** potential for growth (and promotion).

1.3 **Development activities**

- Training, both on and off the job
- Career planning
- Job rotation
- Appraisal (see previous chapter)
- Other learning opportunities

1.4 Organisations often have a **training and development strategy**, based on the overall strategy for the business. We can list the following steps.

Step 1. Identify the skills and competences are needed by the **business plan**
Step 2. Draw up the **development strategy** to show how training and development activities will assist in meeting the targets of the corporate plan.
Step 3. **Implement** the training and development strategy.

The advantage of such an approach is that the training is:

- Relevant
- Problem-based (ie corrects a real lack of skills)
- Action-oriented
- Performance-related

HRD and the organisation

1.5 **Benefits for the organisation of training and development programmes**

Benefit	Comment
Minimise the learning costs of obtaining the skills the organisation needs	Training supports the business strategy.
Lower costs and **increased productivity**, thereby improving performance	Some people suggest that higher levels of training explain the higher productivity of German as opposed to many British manufacturers
Fewer accidents, and better health and safety	EU health and safety directives require a certain level of training. Employees can take employers to court if accidents occur or if unhealthy work practices persist.

Benefit	Comment
Less need for detailed supervision	If people are trained they can get on with the job, and managers can concentrate on other things. Training is an aspect of **empowerment**.
Flexibility	Training ensures that people have the **variety** of skills needed – multi-skilling is only possible if people are properly trained.
Recruitment and succession planning	Training and development attracts new recruits and ensures that the organisation has a supply of suitable managerial and technical staff to take over when people retire.
Change management	Training helps organisations manage change by letting people know why the change is happening and giving them the skills to cope with it.
Corporate culture	(1) Training programmes can be used to build the corporate culture or to direct it in certain ways, by indicating that certain **values** are espoused. (2) Training programmes can **build relationships** between staff and managers in different areas of the business
Motivation	Training programmes can increase commitment to the organisation's goals

1.6 These benefits are real – but training cannot do everything. Training only really covers:

Aspect of performance	Areas covered
Individual	Education; Experience; possibly Personal Circumstances (if successful completion of training is accompanied by a higher salary
Physical and job	Methods of work
Organisational and social	Type of training and supervision

1.7 In other words, training cannot improve performance problems arising out of:

- Bad management
- Poor job design
- Poor equipment, factory layout and work organisation
- Other characteristics of the employee (eg intelligence)
- Motivation – training gives a person the ability but not necessarily the willingness to improve
- Poor recruitment

Training and the individual

1.8 For the individual employee, the benefits of training and development are more clear-cut, and few refuse it if it is offered.

Benefit	Comment
Enhances portfolio of **skills**	Even if not specifically related to the current job, training can be useful in other contexts, and the employee becomes more attractive to employers and more promotable
Psychological benefits	The trainee might feel reassured that he/she is of continuing value to the organisation
Social benefit	People's social needs can be met by training courses – they can also develop networks of contacts
The job	Training can help people do their job better, thereby increasing job satisfaction

Developing skills and knowledge: the learning organisation

1.9 Managers can try to develop the learning organisation. The learning organisation:

(a) Encourages continuous learning and knowledge generation at all levels.
(b) Has the processes to move knowledge around the organisation.
(c) Can transform knowledge into actual behaviour.

The justification for this is that knowledge can be created and exploited. Training is one part of this. We encountered *knowledge management*, another ?? of this issue.

1.10 Let's start with a definition.

KEY TERM

In their book *The Learning Company: A Strategy for Sustainable Development*, Pedler, Burgoyne and Boydell suggest the following might be a good description of a **learning organisation:**

'An organisation that facilitates the learning of all its members *and* continuously transforms itself'.

1.11 The characteristics of the learning organisation are listed below.

Characteristics	Comments
Learning approach to strategy	Experimentation and feedback built into a system. As much information as possible is brought to bear on a problem.
Participative policy making	All 'members' of a learning company have the chance to participate in the learning process.
Informating	This is the use of information not as a control mechanism, but as a resource for the whole organisation to exploit in order to develop new insights.
Formative accounting	Accounting and budgeting systems should be structured to assist learning. Such systems might encourage individuals to act as 'small businesses treating internal users as **customers**'.

Characteristics	Comments
Internal exchange	Internal exchange develops the idea of the **internal customer**. Each unit regards the other units as customers, whose needs must be identified and satisfied, in the context of the company as a whole.
Reward flexibility	In a learning company, there is a flexible approach to reward and remuneration.
Enabling structures	Organisation structures are *temporary* arrangements that must respond to changed conditions and opportunities.
Boundary workers as environmental scanners	In a learning organisation, environmental monitoring is not restricted to specialists or managers. All employees dealing with the boundary should try and monitor the environment.
Inter-company learning	Learn from other firms.
Learning climate	The function of management in a learning organisation is to: • Encourage continuous learning and knowledge around the organisation. • Create processes to move knowledge around the organisation. • Transform knowledge into actual behaviour, products and processes.

1.12 Training has a role in creating the learning organisation.

(a) Training enables skills to be disseminated.
(b) Training courses are an opportunity for people to get together.

A framework for HRD: 'Investors in people'

1.13 The significance of training for TQM programmes is highlighted by the **Investors in People standard**. Award of this standard is managed by Investors in People (UK) Ltd and is co-ordinated by **Training and Enterprise Councils**.

1.14 The aim of the **Investors in People** standard is to promote excellence in the field of human resource development by linking the development of people to the goals and targets of the firm. This involves:

- Plan: a public commitment to develop employees
- Regular review of training and development needs of all employees
- Action to train and develop individuals
- Regular evaluation

1.15 To obtain the standard, the organisation to achieve a satisfactory level of performance in these areas.

Key area	Comment
Planning: a written plan with goals and development targets	• Senior managers make a public commitment • Employees are aware of broad aims of the organisation • Written and flexible plan sets out business goals and targets • Identifies broad development needs • Communication of how human resources will contribute • Where relevant, communication with employee representatives
Review: Regular review of training and development needs, the resources to fulfil them, targets and business objectives	• The written plans identify resources used on training • Training and development needs are reviewed against business objectives • There is a formal review process for assessing people's development needs • Development responsibilities are clearly identified • Managers are *able* to carry out development responsibilities • SMART objectives and standards are set for development actions
Action: Development of staff throughout their employment	• Effective induction of new staff • Develop skills in line with business objectives • All development opportunities should be made available • Employees should be encouraged to identify and meet job-related development • Action is taken to achieve training needs • Managers support trainees
Evaluation: The investment in people should be reviewed to ensure it is effective	• Quantified or measurable targets • Evaluations are effected all levels, the individual, the team, the organisation

1.16 The purpose is to improve performance to world class methods. Abut 20,000 UK companies, employing almost a quarter of the workforce, either have the standard or are committed to achieving it.

'Welfare to Work'

1.17 The government is keen to reduce employment and the 'Welfare to Work' initiative is designed to encourage jobs and training. The government offers a £60 per week job subsidy for six months. Of course, after this, young people will (eventually) receive the minimum wage and the subsidy will end.

Training and performance management

1.18 Training is no panacea for many problems of performance.

(a) It may be inappropriate to problems caused by faulty organisation, layout, methods, equipment, employee selection and placement etc.

(b) Cost, time, inconvenience, apathy and an unrealistic expectations of training in the past may restrict its effectiveness.

(c) Limitations imposed by intelligence, poor motivation and the psychological restrictions of the learning process also restrict its effectiveness.

1.19 Many factors will influence job performance, as demonstrated by the 'wheel' below, and training is only one of these factors. Therefore it is only one of the many methods by which performance can be improved.

Variables affecting job performance

Case examples

Training and IT

A study by the DTI suggests about half of UK companies believe that their employees do not have sufficient understanding of IT to use the technologies to their full competitive advantage. Not surprisingly, then, the study says that a third of UK companies provide no training.

1.20 Section summary

- Human resource development aims to widen the skills base of the organisation by developing people.
- It benefits the organisation and the individual.

2 TRAINING AND DEVELOPMENT NEEDS

The training process in outline

2.1 In order to ensure that training meets the real needs of the organisation, large firms adopt a planned approach to training. This has the following steps.

Step 1. Identify and define the **organisation's training needs**. It may be the case that recruitment might be a better solution to a problem than training

Step 2. **Define the learning required** – in other words, specify the knowledge, skills or competences that have to be acquired. For technical training, this is not difficult: for example all finance department staff will have to become conversant with the new accounting system.

Step 3. **Define training objectives** – what must be learnt and what trainees must be able to do after the training exercise

Step 4. **Plan training programmes** – training and development can be planned in a number of ways, employing a number of techniques, as we shall learn about in Section 3. (Also, people have different approaches to learning, which have to be considered.) This covers:

- Who provides the training
- Where the training takes place
- Divisions of responsibilities between trainers, line managers or team leaders, the individual personally.

Step 5. **Implement the training**

Step 6. **Evaluate** the training: has it been successful in achieving learning objectives

Step 7. Go back to Step 2 if more training is needed.

Training needs analysis

Case example

Training for quality

The British Standards for Quality Systems (BS EN ISO 9000: formerly BS 5750) which many UK organisations are working towards (often at the request of customers, who perceive it to be a 'guarantee' that high standards of quality control are being achieved) includes training requirements. As the following extract shows, the Standard identifies training needs for those organisations registering for assessment, and also shows the importance of a systematic approach to ensure adequate control.

The training, both by specific training to perform assigned tasks and general training to heighten quality awareness and t0 mould attitudes of all personnel in an organisation, is central to the achievement of quality.

The comprehensiveness of such training varies with the complexity of the organisation.

The following steps should be taken:

1 Identifying the way tasks and operations influence quality in total

2 Identifying individuals; training needs against those required for satisfactory performance of the task

3 Planning and carrying out appropriate specific training

4 Planning and organising general quality awareness programmes

5 Recording training and achievement in an easily retrievable form so that records can be updated and taps in training can be readily identified

BSI, 1990

2.2 From the example above, you should see that training needs analysis covers three issues.

Current state	Desired state
Organisation's current results	Desired results, standards
Existing knowledge and skill	Knowledge and skill needed
Individual performance	Required standards

The difference between the two columns is the **training gap**. Training programmes are designed to improve individual performance, thereby improving the performance of the organisation.

2.3 **Training surveys** combine information from a variety of sources to discern what the training needs of the organisation actually are. These sources are:

(a) The **business strategy** at corporate level.

(b) **Appraisal and performance reviews** – the purpose of a performance management system is to improve performance, and training maybe recommended as a remedy.

(c) **Attitude surveys** from employees, asking them what training they think they need or would like.

(d) **Evaluation of existing training** programmes.

(e) **Job analysis** covers:

  (i) Reported difficulties people have in meeting the skills requirement of the job

  (ii) Existing performance weaknesses, of whatever kind, which could be remedied by training

  (iii) Future changes in the job.

  The job analysis can be used to generate a training specification covering the knowledge needed for the job, the skills required to achieve the result, attitudinal changes required.

Setting training objectives

2.4 The **training manager** will have to make an initial investigation into the problem of the gap between job or competence *requirements* and current performance of *competence*.

2.5 If training would improve work performance, training **objectives** can then be defined. They should be clear, specific and related to observable, measurable targets, ideally detailing:

(a) Behaviour - what the trainee should be able to do.
(b) Standard - to what level of performance.
(c) Environment - under what conditions (so that the performance level is realistic).

2.6 EXAMPLE

'At the end of the course the trainee should be able to describe ... or identify ... or distinguish x from y ... or calculate ... or assemble ...' and so on. It is insufficient to define the objectives of training as 'to give trainees a grounding in ...' or 'to encourage trainees in a better appreciation of ...': this offers no target achievement which can be quantifiably measured.

2.7 Training objectives link the identification of training needs with the content, methods and technology of training. Some examples of translating training needs into learning objectives are given in *Personnel Management, A New Approach* by D Torrington and L Hall.

Training needs	Learning objectives
To know more about the Data Protection Act	The employee will be able to answer four out of every five queries about the Data Protection Act without having to search for details.
To establish a better rapport with customers	The employee will immediately attend to a customer unless already engaged with another customers.
	The employee will greet each customer using the customer's name where known.
	The employee will apologise to every customer who has had to wait to be attended to.
To assemble clocks more quickly	The employee will be able to assemble each clock correctly within thirty minutes.

Having identified training needs and objectives, the manager will have to decide on the best way to approach training: there are a number of types and techniques of training, which we will discuss below.

3 METHODS OF DEVELOPMENT AND TRAINING

Incorporating training needs into an individual development programme

KEY TERM

A personal development plan is a 'clear developmental action plan for an individual which incorporates a wide set of developmental opportunities including formal training.'

3.1 The purpose of a personal development plan will vary from:

- Improving performance in the existing job
- Developing skills for future career moves within and outside the organisation.

KEY TERM

Skills: what the individual needs to be able to do if results are to be achieved. Skills are built up progressively by repeated training. They may be manual, intellectual or mental, perceptual or social.

3.2 Preparing a personal development plan involves these steps.

Step 1. Analysis the current position. You could do a personal SWOT (strengths, weaknesses, opportunities, threats) analysis. The supervisor can have an input into this by categorising the skills use of employees on a grid as follows, in a **skills analysis**.

		Performance High	Performance Low
Liking of skills	High	Likes and does well	Likes but doesn't do well
	Low	Dislikes but does well	Dislikes and doesn't do well

The aim is to try to incorporate more of the employees' interests into their actual roles.

Step 2. **Set goals to cover performance in the existing job**, future changes in the current role, moving elsewhere in the organisations, developing specialist expertise. Naturally, such goals should have the characteristic, as far as possible of SMART objectives (ie specific, measurable, attainable, realistic and time-bounded).

Step 3. **Draw up action plan** to achieve the goals, covering the developmental activities listed in paragraph 3.1

Formal training

3.3 **Formal training**

(a) **Internal courses** are run by the organisation's training department or may be provided by external suppliers.

(b) **Types of course**

(i) **Day release**: the employee works in the organisation and on one day per week attends a local college or training centre for theoretical learning.

(ii) **Distance learning, evening classes and correspondence courses**, which make demands on the individual's time outside work. This is commonly used, for example, by typists wishing to develop or 'refresh' shorthand skills.

(iii) **Revision courses** for examinations of professional bodies.

(iv) **Block release** courses which may involve four weeks at a college or training centre followed by a period back at work.

(v) **Sandwich courses,** usually involve six months at college then six months at work, in rotation, for two or three years.

(vi) A **sponsored full-time course** at a university for one or two years.

(c) **Computer-based training** involves interactive training via PC. The typing program, Mavis Beacon, is a good example.

(d) **Techniques** used on the course might include:

(i) Lectures
(ii) Seminars, in which participation is encouraged
(iii) Simulation. For example, you may have been sent on an audit training course.

3.4 **Disadvantages of formal training**

(a) An individual will not benefit from formal training unless he or she **wants to learn**. The individual's superior may need to provide encouragement in this respect.

(b) If the **subject matter** of the training course does not **relate to an individual's job**, the learning will quickly be forgotten.

(c) Individuals may not be able to carry over what they have learned to their own particular job.

On the job training

3.5 **Successful on the job training**

(a) The assignments should have a **specific purpose** from which the trainee can learn and gain experience.

(b) The organisation must **tolerate any mistakes** which the trainee makes. Mistakes are an inevitable part of on the job learning.

(c) The work should **not be too complex**.

3.6 **Methods of on the job training**

(a) **Demonstration/instruction:** show the trainee how to do the job and let them get on with it. It should combine **telling** a person what to do and **showing** them how, using appropriate media. The trainee imitates the instructor, and asks questions.

(b) **Coaching:** the trainee is put under the guidance of an experienced employee who shows the trainee how to do the job.

  (i) **Establish learning targets**. The areas to be learnt should be identified, and specific, realistic goals (eg completion dates, performance standards) stated by agreement with the trainee.

  (ii) **Plan a systematic learning and development programme.** This will ensure regular progress, appropriate stages for consolidation and practice.

  (iii) **Identify opportunities for broadening the trainee's knowledge and experience:** eg by involvement in new projects, placement on inter-departmental committees, suggesting new contacts, or simply extending the job, adding more tasks, greater responsibility etc.

  (iv) **Take into account the strengths and limitations of the trainee** in learning, and take advantage of learning opportunities that suit the trainee's ability, preferred style and goals.

  (v) **Exchange feedback**. The coach will want to know how the trainee sees his or her progress and future. He or she will also need performance information in order to monitor the trainee's progress, adjust the learning programme if necessary, identify further needs which may emerge and plan future development for the trainee.

(c) **Job rotation:** the trainee is given several jobs in succession, to gain experience of a wide range of activities. (Even experienced managers may rotate their jobs, to gain wider experience; this philosophy of job education is commonly applied in the Civil Service, where an employee may expect to move on to another job after a few years.)

(d) **Temporary promotion:** an individual is promoted into his/her superior's position whilst the superior is absent due to illness. This gives the individual a chance to experience the demands of a more senior position.

(e) **'Assistant to' positions:** a junior manager with good potential may be appointed as assistant to the managing director or another executive director. In this way, the individual gains experience of how the organisation is managed 'at the top'.

(f) **Action learning:** a group of managers are brought together to solve a real problem with the help of an 'advisor' who exposes the management process that actually happens.

(g) **Committees:** trainees might be included in the membership of committees, in order to obtain an understanding of inter-departmental relationships.

(h) **Project work**. work on a project with other people can expose the trainee to other parts of the organisation.

Learning styles

3.7 The way in which people learn best will differ according to the type of person. That is, there are **learning styles** which suit different individuals. Peter Honey and Alan Mumford have drawn up a popular classification of four learning styles.

(a) **Theorists**

Theorists seek to understand underlying concepts and to take an intellectual, 'hands-off' approach based on logical argument. They prefer training to be:

(i) Programmed and structured.
(ii) Designed to allow time for analysis.
(iii) Provided by teachers who share his/her preference for concepts and analysis.

Theorists find learning difficult if they have a teacher with a different style (particularly an activist style); material which skims over basic principles; and a programme which is hurried and unstructured.

(b) **Reflectors**

- Observe phenomena, think about them and then choose how to act are called reflectors.
- Need to work at their own pace
- Find learning difficult if forced into a hurried programme with little notice or information.
- Produce carefully thought-out conclusions after research and reflection
- Tend to be fairly slow, non-participative (unless to ask questions) and cautious.

(c) **Activists**

- Deal with practical, active problems and who do not have much patience with theory.
- Require training based on hands-on experience.
- Excited by participation and pressure, such as making presentations and new projects.
- Flexible and optimistic, but tend to rush at something without due preparation, take risks and then get bored.

(d) **Pragmatists**

- Only like to study if they can see its direct link to practical problems - they are not interested in theory for its own sake.
- Good at learning new techniques in on-the-job training which they see as useful improvements.
- Aim is to implement action plans and/or do the task better.
- May discard as being impractical good ideas which only require some development.

The implications for management are that people react to problem situations in different ways and that, in particular, training methods should be tailored to the preferred style of trainees where possible. Moreover, training interventions should ideally be designed to accommodate the preferences of all four styles. This can often be overlooked especially as the majority of training staff are activitists.

The learning cycle

3.8 Another useful model is the **experiential learning cycle** devised by David Kolb. He suggested that classroom-type learning is 'a specialist activity cut off from the real world and unrelated to one's life': a teacher or trainer directs the learning process on behalf of a passive learner. Experiential learning involves **doing**, however, and puts the learners in an active problem-solving role: a form of **self-learning** which encourages the learners to formulate and commit themselves to their own learning objectives.

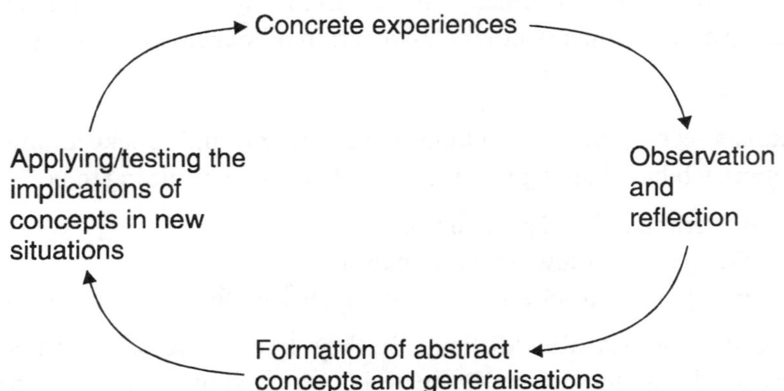

4 EVALUATING TRAINING

KEY TERM

Validation of training means observing the results of the course and measuring whether the training objectives have bee achieved.

Evaluation of training means comparing the actual costs of the scheme against the assessed benefits which are being obtained. If the costs exceed the benefits, the scheme will need to be redesigned or withdrawn.

4.1 **Ways of validating and evaluating a training scheme**

(a) **Trainees' reactions to the experience:** asking the trainees whether they thought the training programme was relevant to their work, and whether they found it useful. This form of monitoring is rather inexact, and it does not allow the training department to measure the results for comparison against the training objective.

(b) **Trainee learning:** measuring what the trainees have learned on the course by means of a *test* at the end of it.

(c) **Changes in job behaviour following training:** studying the subsequent behaviour of the trainees in their jobs, to measure how the training scheme has altered the way they do their work. This is possible where the purpose of the course was to learn a particular skill.

(d) **Organisational change as a result of training:** finding out whether the training has affected the work or behaviour of other employees not on the course - seeing whether there has been a general change in attitudes arising from a new course in, say, computer terminal work. This form of monitoring would probably be reserved for senior managers in the training department.

(e) **Impact of training on organisational goals:** seeing whether the training scheme (and overall programme) has contributed to the overall objectives of the organisation. This too is a form of monitoring reserved for senior management, and would perhaps be discussed at board level in the organisation. It is likely to be the main component of a cost-benefit analysis.

5 CAREER MANAGEMENT

5.1 **Career management** plans the progress of individuals within an organisation from job to job with organisational needs and individual capacity in mind.

KEY TERMS

Career management consists of:

- **Career planning.** This shapes the progression of individuals within an organisation in accordance of the assessment of organisational needs and the performance, potential and preferences of individual member of the enterprise.
- **Management succession planning.** This ensures that as far as possible the organisation has the managers it requires to meet future business needs.

5.2 Career management ensures that:

(a) The organisation has a pool of **managers-in-waiting** (in other words, by training tomorrow's managers). In **flat organisations, this is problematic**, as the jump in responsibility from junior to senior positions is wider than in organisations with extensive hierarchies, and there are few opportunities for promotion.

(b) People **get the right training** so they can develop the right abilities for the job.

(c) People get the **guidance they need** to fulfil their potential.

5.3 **Key issues in career management**

(a) **Internal or external recruitment?**

(i) Promotion from within unless outsiders are necessary
(ii) **Deliberate employment** of outsiders, encouraging wastage
(iii) Shortfalls in demand

(b) **Short term or long-term planning?**

(i) **Short-term**. People are trained and rewarded for current performance and are promoted if they are any good.

(ii) **Long-term planners** develop, according to Armstrong, 'highly structured approaches to career development.'

(iii) **Long-term flexibility**: a half way house between (i) and (ii).

(iv) Each of the above approaches as merit. Clearly, a highly structured approach to career development presupposes a highly structured organisation, in which it is possible to plan for the long term.

(c) **Specialists or generalists**. Specialists are good at what they do and become expert at it. Generalists move into general management. A top-ranking specialist with no management responsibilities may add as much or more value than a manager. Examples include R & D and advertising agencies, where there might be two career paths, rewarding excellent performers without a management role.

5.4 **The process of career planning**

Step 1. **Obtain information** about the organisation's requirements.

Step 2. Obtain details of **individual performance** and aspirations

Step 3. Translate information from Steps 1 and 2 into **career development programmes** for individuals and **management development programmes for the organisation**

Step 4. **Identify competence bands**: what people **need to be able to do** at each level to be given a certain degree of responsibility. This enables people to take control of their own training as they know what to aim for.

Step 5. Give people **counselling** if they need it.

Crossing functional boundaries

5.5 To what extent are careers supposed to **cross functional boundaries**? The models below combine the specialist/generalist distinction with the internal/external recruitment distinction.

(a) *Internal generalists*

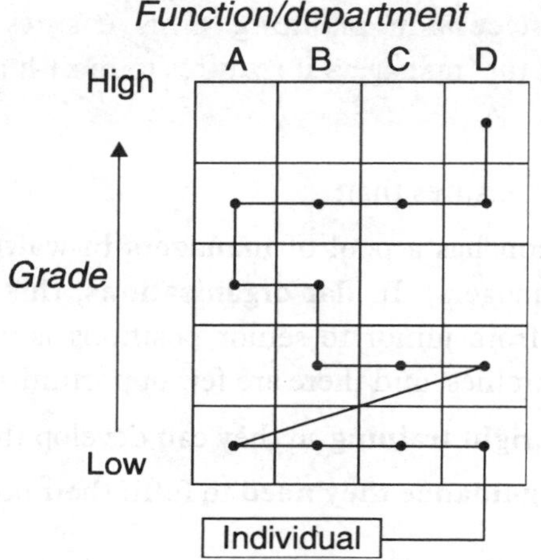

In (a), the individual is given a great degree of experience in different business areas in order to get to know the business. Some Japanese companies, for example, are happy to allocate production executives to marketing departments on their slow way up. Promotion has, in the past, largely been based on seniority. An individual is assessed **on experience**.

(b) *Internal and external specialists*

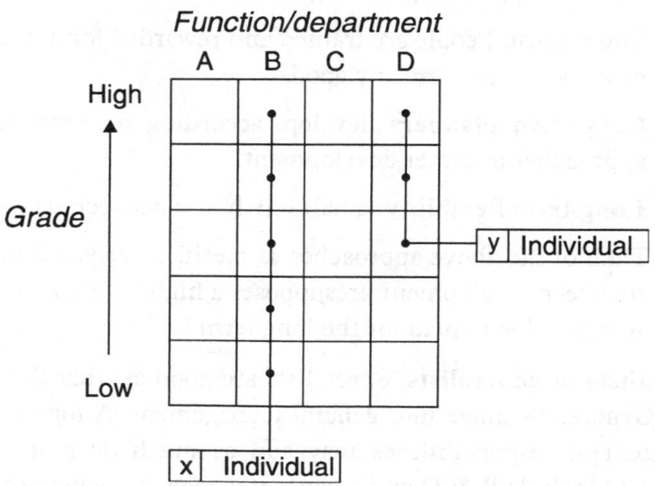

(i) *Individual X*. Promotion is entirely within one business area. This may enhance specialist skills, but create a narrowing of outlook. This line of promotion might be particularly true of professional functions in the technostructure.

(ii) *Individual Y*. This 'fast track' approach also means the outsiders are brought in at fairly high places in the hierarchy.

5.6 Where an organisation's needs are likely to change, it is not always possible to take a too rigid approach to career planning.

Question 2

What sort of career management system do you think is operated in the following cases?

(a) 'People join us at Junior Trainee level. Within one year they are promoted to Senior Trainee, and the year after that Assistant Accountant. Their titles denote the sort of skills and experience they are expected to have. After qualification, they are promoted to Senior Accountant, then Supervisor. Promotion above Supervisor level is not guaranteed, but a successful candidate would certainly reach Manager grade, dealing with larger clients, and running more staff. Exceptional candidates become Partners of the firm'.

(b) 'As a fashion design firm we recruit directly from art schools, but the way the market goes we have to be flexible. People that work with us have to show a willingness to get involved, and a talent for bright ideas which combine flair with a real-world understanding of the people that like our clothes. But the sky's the limit for the talented'.

Answer

(a) Long-range planning at the lower levels, but this tapers off at the higher levels.

(b) The fashion firm combines a policy of recruitment as and when it is needed, with an assumption that people can 'create' their own career structure. People can get on, but this cannot be planned.

5.7 **Career management** issues are especially relevant to professional staff such as **accountants** for a number of reasons.

(a) **They need to retain and develop their technical specialism**. A successful accountant should be able to keep up to date so that his or her knowledge is of continued use to the organisation. An accountant is a member, perhaps, of the organisation's technostructure.

(b) The accountant may view his or her **qualification as a springboard into general management**: in which case the right considerations should be given to easing the path from functional to general management.

The transition from functional to general management

5.8 At some stage in his or her career, a manager will be promoted from a job which is concentrated mainly on functional expertise (eg knowledge of production techniques, personnel techniques, accountancy skills, marketing skills) into a job where the requirement is for broader and more general management skills - eg organising, staffing, controlling, dealing with other departments or organisations, long-term planning and so on.

5.9 **Changes in a manager's job caused by moving from functional to general management**

Issue	Functional manager	General manager
Orientation	• Task orientated - focus on the functional tasks in hand	• Goal orientated - focus on achievement of organisational (and divisional) goals and objectives
Role	• Organiser	• Facilitator - co-ordinating interdepartmental activities; obtaining and allocating resources
Information	• Defined sources • Usually through formal channels	• Poorly defined sources • Often acquired by informal contacts
Goals	• Short term	• Long term

5.10 The transition is **usually accompanied by promotion to a more senior position** in the management hierarchy and therefore the contrast in roles between functional and general management is also found between junior and middle/senior management.

(a) The traditional, **functional structure** tends to keep managers in functional roles until they reach very senior levels and sometimes for their entire careers.

(b) A **divisional structure**, however, gives relatively junior managers experience of general management roles, usually as the chief executive of small business units, at an earlier stage in their careers.

5.11 In addition to the normal problems of switching jobs, the manager taking up a general management post has to deal with an abrupt change in the skills needed to perform the role effectively.

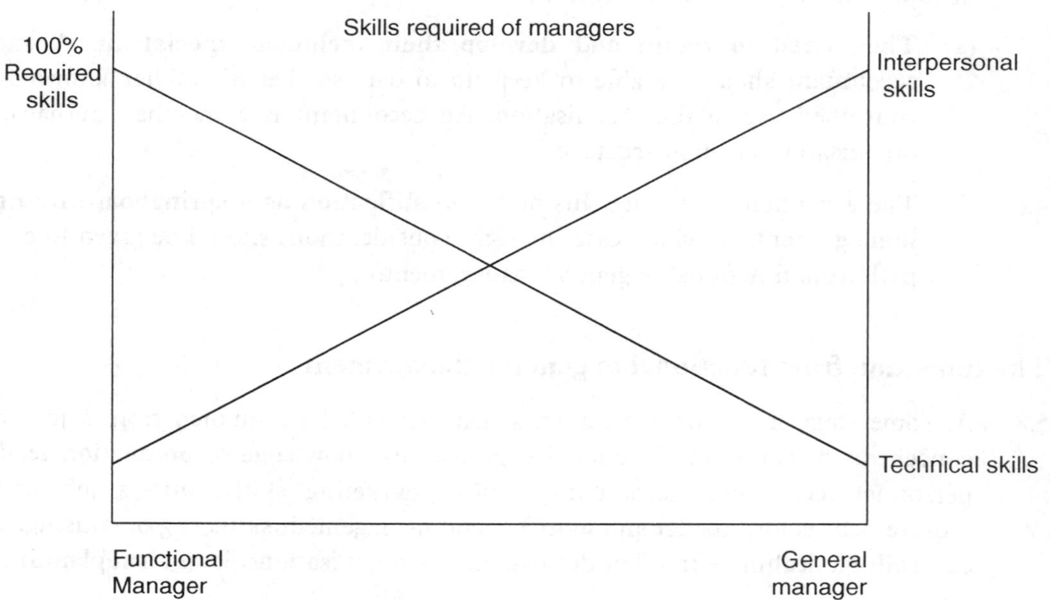

5.12 **Technical skills** are concerned with an ability to cope with large quantities of data and information and to select the appropriate key points to form the basis for decision-taking. **Interpersonal** skills involve inspiring, motivating, leading and controlling people to achieve goals which are often poorly defined. For the general manager, the latter are more important.

The transition curve

5.13 The transition from functional to general manager is a complex process and the time taken to complete the 'learning curve' varies depending on the degree of perceived change. Since a move from functional to general management is often, and correctly, viewed as a major change, transitions of this sort take longer than average to complete. The diagram below shows a typical transition curve.

Transition curve

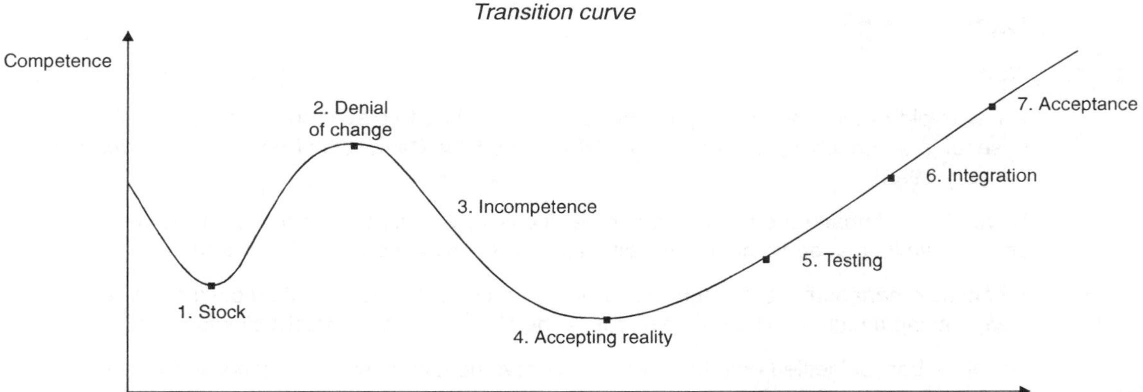

(a) **Stage 1: immobilisation or shock**. A sense of feeling overwhelmed. This occurs because the reality of the new job does not match the person's expectations. The individual stops and tries to understand what is happening. Typical attitudes at this stage are 'did I really want this job?' and 'this isn't the job I expected'.

(b) **Stage 2: denial of change**. There is a reversion to previously successful behaviour. This can be useful if it is temporary, but becomes a handicap if it goes on too long and inappropriate behaviour becomes dominant. Sometimes individuals do remain at this point on the curve indefinitely and this is what is described as the *Peter principle* (promoted to the level of their incompetence). They perform badly because their behaviour is based on their past activities rather than their current ones.

(c) **Stage 3: incompetence.** Awareness that change is necessary accompanied by frustration because the individual finds it difficult to cope with the new situation or relationships. A fall in performance level is common but, despite this, the phase is very important in the transition process since, without the realisation of change, people can never develop new attitudes and patterns of behaviour. Organisations which adopt a 'sink or swim' approach to transition actually hinder the process in that this phase is commonly regarded as the start of 'sinking'. Consequently, individuals are reluctant to share their current experience with others.

(d) **Stage 4: accepting reality**. The reality of the new situation is accepted for the first time. Up to this point managers have been concerned with hanging on to past values, attitudes and behaviours. There is now a preparedness and willingness to experiment with change.

(e) **Stage 5: testing**. Testing new behaviour and approaches. There is a lot of activity and energy as the testing progresses and mistakes are liable to be made. But the experimentation needs to be encouraged since only by doing this can effective approaches be found.

(f) **Stage 6: integration.** This is a reflective period, in which individuals search for meaning in an attempt to understand all the activity, anger and frustration that went before.

(g) **Stage 7: acceptance**. This is the final phase of the transition. Effective new approaches are introduced and the sense of being involved in change disappears. Self-esteem, and performance, rises.

5.14 No two people face and deal with managerial transition in exactly the same way and so the transition curve described above can only be a general model of the process.

5.15 To help with the transition from technical to general management, an organisation should have a **planned management development programme**.

Case example

Novotel

An example of the place management development has to play in the strategy of the firm is in the case of the French hotel group *Novotel* (outlined by David Littlefred, *People Management,* 26 January 1995).

Novotel has embarked on a new 'customer-focus' drive, ' that has seen a relaxation of head office controls, while managers have been given a greater say in how their hotel is run.'

A complex management structure has also added to the problem. Staff, motivated by advancement, were placing a higher value on the needs of their boss than their hotel's clients.

Novotel's bosses settled on a three-phase improvement plan, which began with the launch of a new logo in October 1993, followed by a £5 billion worldwide refurbishment. A staff development programme called 'School of Life' kicked off last year with management assessment centres, and will continue throughout 1995 with self-evaluation and multi-skilling units for other staff.

The company's hotel managers began going through the assessment centres exactly one year ago. These one-day events demand just as much from the training staff as they do from participants, according to Novotel's training manager, Brenda Rosamond.

'You're so deep into it psychologically, it just bombs you out,' she says. 'But we know, in depth, exactly how our managers react to any given situation, and what their strengths and weaknesses are - and so do they. They end up with a very thorough look at themselves.'

As a way of encouraging managers to act more autonomously, the number of management levels has been slashed from about a dozen to five.

'We are measuring their managerial skills and abilities. We believe they would be too tempted to return to their technical skills if we left it in a hotel environment.'

All Novotel's managers worldwide have been assessed against 13 'abilities', divided between four broad areas.

Conceptual skills

(a) Perception
(b) Judgment
(c) Initiative

Applications skills

(a) Decision-making
(b) Implementation of decisions
(c) Organisation and planning

Inspiring skills

(a) Leadership
(b) Delegation
(c) Follow-up and monitoring

Relating skills

(a) Adaptability
(b) Interaction with people
(c) Written communication
(d) Oral communication

Each ability consists of five 'observable key criteria', each one of which is assessed on a points system.

After each assessment, Rosamond compiles a detailed study of each person's performance and development needs, a task which takes about three days per candidate. She awards points based on how participants perform in 13 different areas such as judgement, decision-making, leadership, written communication and perception.

Management education, training and development

KEY TERMS

(a) '**Education** is that process which results in formal qualifications up to and including post-graduate degrees.'

(b) **Training** is 'the formal learning activities which may not lead to qualifications, and which may be received at any time in a working career.' It is designed to equip people to perform effectively in the current work or cope with known changes.

(c) '**Development** is broader again: job experience and learning from other managers, particularly one's immediate superior, are integral parts of the development process.' Arguably it is designed for the future. Development will include features such as:

(i) career planning for individual managers;
(ii) job rotation;
(iii) standing in for the boss while he is away on holiday;
(iv) on-the-job training;
(v) counselling, perhaps by means of regular appraisal reports;
(vi) guidance from superiors or colleagues; and
(vii) education and training.

5.16 **Importance of training and development**

(a) Training and development ensure managers are **ready for promotion** (especially into general management).

(b) Training and development helps **identify suitable candidates** for promotion.

(c) Training and development ensures a **supply of management skills,** with a reduced need to recruit outsiders.

(d) Management development programmes **motivate people**.

Management education

5.17 Designing appropriate in-house courses and encouraging some managers to obtain a professional qualification should be two key features of an education and training programme for managers. Education, for successful students, leads on to a formal qualification.

(a) For managers in the UK, these qualifications include:

(i) Undergraduate business and management degrees.

(ii) Undergraduate degrees in related subjects such as Economics and Accountancy.

(iii) Postgraduate business and management degrees (MBA course).

(iv) The postgraduate Diploma in Management Studies (DMS).

(v) Qualifications from professional bodies.

(b) The time given to managers for education could be provided by:

   (i) A full year off to study for a qualification.

   (ii) Block release to attend study courses or revision courses.

   (iii) Day release, perhaps to attend courses at a local college.

   (iv) Reducing the workload on individuals, to give them time to attend evening classes or study at home.

(c) The employer sometimes pay for time off for studying, textbooks, courses and so on.

Management training

5.18 Formal training which does *not* lead on to a qualification consists mainly of:

(a) Post-experience management courses, provided by training companies or colleges and polytechnics.

(b) In-company management training, using the company's own training staff and/or consultants brought in from outside.

5.19 Training follows on from recruitment and and appraisal.

(a) **Potential managers** can be given **training in management skills**, either on internal courses or on courses with external organisations such as business schools.

(b) **Existing managers** can be given training in **new skills required for their existing job** (eg the technological changes in organisations and the development of computer usage suggest the need for training in computer applications and software for management work).

(c) Existing managers can be given training in the skills required for **higher, general management** (eg with discussions of organisation policy, and lectures given by directors).

Management development

5.20 Management development is the process of improving the effectiveness of an individual manager by developing the necessary skills and understanding of organisational goals. Although management development is in some respects a natural process, the term is generally used to refer to a **conscious policy** within an organisation to provide a programme of individual development.

5.21 Giving an individual time to study the techniques of being a good manager, and any necessary counselling, the individual will realise his full potential. The time required to bring a manager to this potential is *possibly* fairly short.

5.22 The planned nature of management development programmes is shown below.

Management development programme

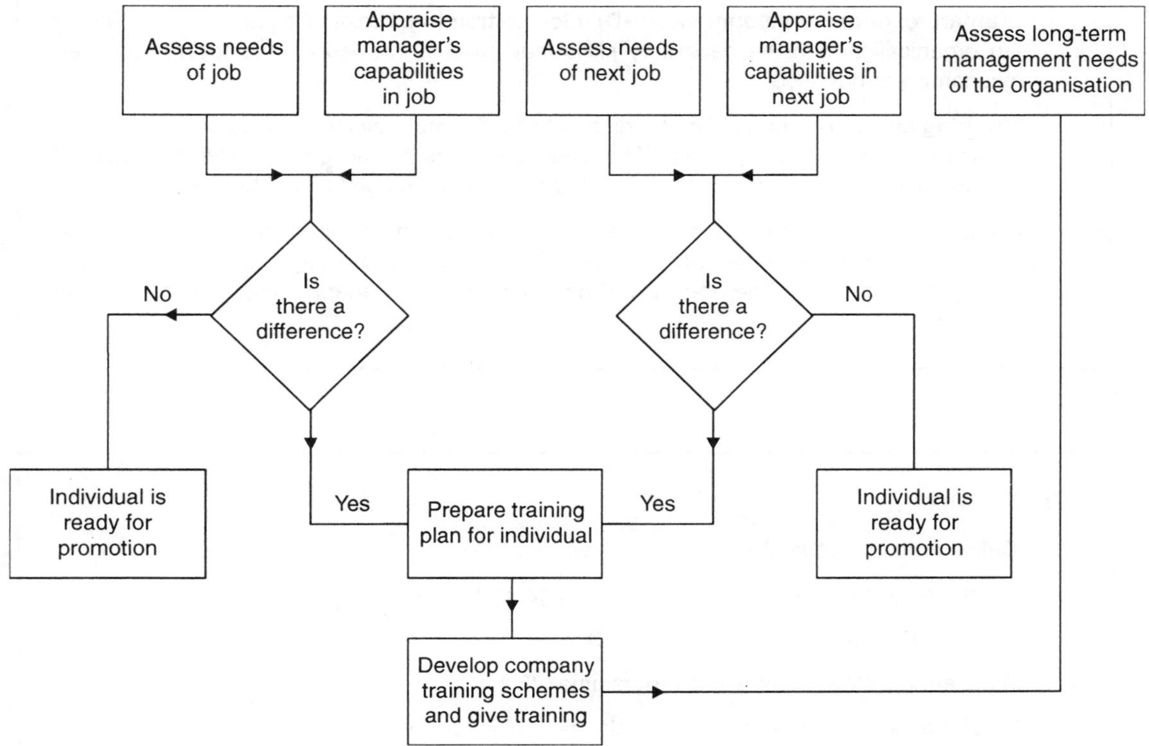

5.23 This diagram brings out the importance of appraisal in a system of development. Although we have been discussing the development of managers, staff appraisal is important for all grades of employees. This is dealt with in Chapter 20.

6 BRAINWORKS PLC UPDATE

Questions can be found in the Introduction box at the beginning of this Chapter.

6.1 *Question 1.* 'On the job' training is probably the best for BW. It gives newcomers real experience of how the organisation works, and it encourages people to learn from observation. The presence of a more experienced 'coach' enables immediate feedback.

6.2 *Question 3.* Little detail is given of management training, perhaps because there is none. BW seems to be a fairly 'flat' organisation, so there may be few development or promotion opportunities.

Chapter roundup

- **Human resource development (HRD)** refers to **training**. Training is one way of providing an organisation with the necessary skills that it needs. It also contributes to improved economic performance.
- **Training** can be **on-the-job** or at a different site. **Formal** training courses are useful if the subject is relevant to the job, and if the course involves interaction with other members of the company. Background knowledge is then imparted through one on the job training.
- **Career management** is a way of planning the development of an individual's jobs and roles throughout his or her working life. Some managers are given a wide experience throughout the firm. The transition from functional to general management can be traumatic.

Quick quiz

1 Define human resource development. (see para 1.1)

2 What are the advantages of training to an organisation? (1.5)

3 What is the learning organisation? (1.10)

4 What are the steps in a training programme? (2.1)

5 What are the steps in a personal development plan? (3.2)

6 Describe the methods of on the job training. (3.6)

7 How can learning theory assist training? (3.7)

8 What is the learning cycle? (2.17)

9 How would you evaluate a training scheme? (4.1)

10 What is career management? (5.1)

11 What are the differences between being a functional and a general manager? (5.9)

Question to try	Level	Marks	Time
25	Exam-standard	25 marks	45 mins

Chapter 21

THE WORK PLACE

Chapter topic list		Syllabus reference
1	General principles	3(a)(ix), (xi)
2	The changing nature of the employment contract	3(a)(ix), (xi)
3	Retirement, resignation and redundancy	3(a)(ix), (xi)
4	Maternity	3(a)(ix), (xi)
5	Discrimination and equal opportunities	3(a)(ix), (xi)
6	Health and safety	3(a)(x), 4(a), (b), (c), (d)
7	The work environment	4(a), (b), (c), (d)
8	Stress	4(a), (b), (c), (d)
9	Brainworks plc update	

Introduction

Employment law is one of the many areas of government regulation of business. The UK has agreed to sign up to the **Social Chapter** which indicates some priorities for employers. Employees have **rights** under their **contracts of employment** and employment **legislation**. **Redundancy** is said to occur when the post the employee fills is no longer available, or when there are fewer jobs to be done than people to do them. Dismissal might be a result of some misconduct. In cases of dispute, the working of a proper system of warnings and reprimands might be seen as evidence of fairness. **Sexual and racial equality** has been advanced in the workplace by a variety of laws and directives (eg these also make it harder for employers to dismiss employees on grounds of pregnancy).

Health and safety practices by firms are governed by their legal environment (eg the 1974 Health and Safety at Work Act and EU directives). Health and safety legislation reflects the **overall environment** of the office or factory (eg ventilation, cleanliness), **fire precautions** etc as well as regulations directly related to **working practices**: employers are therefore advised to have a **safety policy**. Employers can be held liable for injuries at work.

Stress is also an issue in work, and it is more common, contrary to widely held perceptions, in blue collar jobs than managerial work. Maintaining an optimum level of stress, neither too high nor too low, might be seen as a suitable management objective.

Brainworks plc

1 What are the implications of the market research exercise for BW's own employment practices?

2 What do you consider the importance of office buildings to BW?

3 Identify some possible causes of stress for BW staff.

1 GENERAL PRINCIPLES

1.1 Employment conditions and work customs vary from country to country. UK workers tend to work more hours per year than their counterparts in Europe.

Exam focus point

The examiner does not expect a detailed knowledge of UK employment law, but you might want to give some examples. You could use the UK experience as an example of good, even if not best, practice.

The 'Social Chapter'

1.2 The UK government has agreed to sign up to the Social Chapter of the Maastricht Treaty. This outlines in very general terms certain principles which employing organisations in the EU are supposed to adhere to.

Social Charter (incorporated in the Maastricht Treaty as the ***Social Chapter****)*

12 sets of principles covering following areas:	
1	The right to freedom of movement, eg recognition of qualifications.
2	Employment and remuneration, eg fair remuneration, possible minimum wage.
3	Improvement of living and working conditions.
4	Right to social protection - social security.
5	Right to freedom of association and collective bargaining.
6	Right to vocational training.
7	Right of men and women to equal treatment.
8	Right of workers to information, consultation and participation.
9	Right to health protection and safety in the workplace.
10	Protection of children and adolescents.
11	Protection of elderly - pensions.
12	Protection of disabled people.

1.3 The Social Chapter allows for many opt-outs and in practice it is of symbolic rather than practical importance. But it does indicate the priorities employers might consider at work. The Social Chapter is not all new: non-discrimination legislation and health and safety legislation for example, have been in force in the UK for many years.

1.4 Particular areas to watch for over the next few years are:

- **Minimum wage legislation in the UK**. This is due to be implemented from April 1999. Trade Unions want £4 per hour. The CBI would rather no minimum at all, or no more than £3.20. Current suggestions from the Low Pay Commission recommend that the rate be £3.60 per hour, but £3.20 per hour for employees aged between 16 and 18. These are only recommendations at the moment.
- Works councils, with employee representatives for all companies over a certain size.
- The EU's working hours directive (not covered by the Social Chapter) has a slight effect on some working arrangements.
- **The role of unions**. Before 1979, trade unions were a powerful force in the workplace. Since then their power has been eroded through successive Acts of Parliament. The current Labour proposals 'Fairness at work' aim to change the

balance between 'employer' and 'employee' – the emphasis is on improving the rights of the **individual** worker.

(a) Employers (employing over 20 staff) must recognise a union if a majority of the workers are in favour providing that at least 40% of the total work force (not just those who vote) are in favour. (In other words, if only 50% bother to vote and the result is 30:20 in favour of recognition this is not enough for recognition).

(b) Employees are given greater rights to representation in disciplinary procedures. There is no ceiling on compensation for unfair dismissal.

So far, the government is espousing the UK's flexible labour practices as a model for other countries to follow. However, it is likely that its broader social agenda - tackling poverty and exclusion through work - will have an impact. 'Fairness at Work' is a start.

2 THE CHANGING NATURE OF THE EMPLOYMENT CONTRACT

2.1 At the basis of a person's employment with an organisation is the **employment contract**. The legal issues are a mere foundation for the employee's relationship with the organisation. In practice then we can identify the following dimensions of an employee's relationship with the organisation.

(a) A legal contract
(b) A set of expectations about the future

The legal contract

2.2 Once the offer of employment has been confirmed and accepted, the contract of employment can be prepared.

(a) **Fixed term** contracts may be made for a clearly defined period.

(b) Most contracts of employment are **indefinite**: they run until terminated by either party, subject to notice.

2.3 **Contents**

(a) **Express terms:** those specifically agreed upon by the parties, regarding working hours, rates of pay, the nature of the work and so on.

(b) **Implied terms:** those which are not actually stated, but still impose duties and obligations on both parties. They must be well known to all parties concerned. They include common law obligations, such as the employee's duty to perform whatever tasks he or she has undertaken, and the employer's to pay the agreed consideration.

(i) **Employer's obligations**

(1) **Trust:** to behave in a proper and responsible way, and not capriciously (ie not to destroy the relationship of trust and confidence).

(2) **Care:** to provide safe conditions and methods, and compensation for any negligence.

(3) **Provision of work:** (eg for those such as salesmen on commission or specialists for whom idleness might mean loss of skills).

(ii) **Employee's obligations**

(1) **Fidelity:** (eg not to work for competitors).

(2) **Obedience:** to obey any lawful order within the scope of his employment, and without undue risk to himself;

(3) **Care:** to carry out the work reasonably and responsibly.

2.4 **Ending a contract of employment**

(a) **Mutual agreement:** (eg retirement).
(b) **Notice:** (eg resignation, dismissal or redundancy).
(c) **Breach of contract**, entitling the employer to dismiss the employee without notice.
(d) **Frustration** (eg through the death, illness or imprisonment).

2.5 Since 1963, it has been the law that employees should be supplied with a written document or documents containing basic details, or referring to where the information is to be found. The written document is powerful evidence in case of any dispute.

The set of expectations

2.6 In practice, people do not spend a great deal of time worrying about terms and conditions, except when it comes to pay. But there is another sort of contract, which is a set of expectations. After all, why should someone remain loyal to a company, rather than leaving when the next opportunity comes along?

2.7 The reason is that the job comes with a set of expectations about the job. In the past the old 'deal' would have been something along these lines.

(a) The manager gave the company his/her loyalty, competence, functional expertise, and the willingness to go the extra mile for the firm.

(b) In return, the organisation 'offered' security, regular promotions, regular pay rises and care in difficult times.

2.8 However, outsourcing, delayering and downsizing have meant that employers have unilaterally 'broken' the 'contract'.

(a) Job security is felt to be a thing of the past, although the evidence that people are changing jobs frequently is ambiguous.

(b) Prospects of promotion are reduced in delayered organisations.

(c) According to Heriot and Pemberton (*People Management*, 15 June 1995):

'In place of the old deal, organisations now offer constant challenge, and they reward those employees who are eager to meet it. In exchange they expect flexibility, responsibility, accountability and the longest hours in Europe.'

2.9 The 'new' employment contract for managers characteristically embodies these assumptions.

(a) **We will contract for your services** - and you will give of your best so long as the relationship is mutually beneficial.

(b) **Your job may be in jeopardy if circumstances change** - because the organisation will be in jeopardy.

(c) **It isn't enough to do what is required: you must add value** - becoming a contributor rather than a mere player.

(d) **You must grow and develop continuously** - becoming a 'learning person' just as the organisation becomes a 'learning organisation'.

(e) **You must develop skills related to the changing business or organisational needs.**

(f) **You must expect to be paid for performance rather than for simply being there** - promotions will be few, but lateral moves will be many.

(g) **Lifetime careers are no longer the norm** - you may be asked to leave if the 'fit' is no longer right between yourself and the organisation.

2.10 In general terms, Heriot and Pemberton indicate what they think will be the new 'contract' in the 21st century.

The deals of 2005			
Contract	*Individual offers*	*Organisation offers*	*Risks*
Development (core)	Flexibility. Continuous added value. Commitment, not dependence. Innovation.	Security. Employability. Use of skills core to the organisations purpose. Continuous development.	Exploitation of security needs. Life imbalance. Insufficient security to allow for risk-taking. Generality of skills will reduce their external market value.
Autonomy (project)	Ready access to specific skills. Experience gained in wide range of organisations. High performance with low management.	Autonomy to exercise skills. Freedom in how individuals work. Challenge. Experience that increases employability	Performance delivery undermined by: inadequate resources poor management or organisational politics/culture. Constraints on how they work.
Lifestyle (part-time)	Flexibility in matching demand and resourcing. Performance levels to match customer expectations. Performance levels of full-time employees.	Willingness to balance work and other role demands.	Pay and conditions exploitation. Lack of career development.

3 RETIREMENT, RESIGNATION AND REDUNDANCY

Retirement

3.1 Retirement is when someone gives up work and draws a pension.

(a) In the UK, many employees are taking **early retirement** (at 55) perhaps as a result of corporate downsizing, *but* many people still search for work at an older age and there are pressure groups seeking to ban **ageism** in recruitment.

(b) Retirement ages for men and women are being *equalised*.

3.2 Organisations **encourage retirement**, for a number of reasons.

(a) Open promotion opportunities for younger workers.

(b) Early retirement is an alternative to redundancy.

(c) The age structure of an organisation may become unbalanced for future work requirements.

(d) The cost of providing pensions rises according to the age at which the employee joins the pension scheme.

(e) Individual mental and/or physical shortcomings may render an older individual unfit to carry out his or her duties efficiently.

Resignation

3.3 People resign for any number of reasons, personal or occupational. Employees who are particularly valuable should be encouraged to stay. Particular problems the employee has been experiencing (eg salary) may be solvable, though not always in the short term.

3.4 In any case, an exit interview, when the leaver explains his/her decision to go, is a valuable source of information.

3.5 The period of notice required for the employee to leave should be set out in his contract of employment, but some leeway may be negotiated on this.

Question 1

Find out what are the procedures for handling the resignation of an employee in your organisation. Are exit interviews held, and if so, is anything ever done about the problems that may come to light as a result?

Dismissal

3.6 Dismissal includes:

(a) The termination of an employee's contract **by the employer.**

(b) The ending of a fixed-term contract **without renewal** on the same terms.

(c) Termination by the **employee** where the employer's conduct makes him or her entitled to do so (**constructive dismissal**).

3.7 The **statutory minimum** period of notice to be given is determined by the employee's length of continuous service in the employer's service. Longer periods may be written into the contract, at the employer's discretion, and by agreement. Either party may waive his right to notice, or accept payment in lieu of notice. An employee is entitled to a written statement of the **reasons** for dismissal.

Unfair dismissal

3.8 An employee might protest about being dismissed and there are various legal remedies available, subject to the employees' age and employment history. Under employment protection legislation, 1978, the employee has to prove that he has been dismissed. The onus is then on the **employer to prove** that the dismissal was **fair**. Until recently an employee could not sue for unfair dismissal unless he/she had been employed for two years. Current proposals will reduce this period to one year.

3.9 **Dismissal is fair** and justified if the reason for it was one of the following.

(a) **Redundancy** (provided that the selection for redundancy was fair).

(b) **Legal impediment:** the employee could not continue to work in his present position without breaking a legal duty or restriction. (This is fair only if the employee was offered suitable alternative employment.)

(c) **Non-capability:** provided adequate training and warnings had been given.

(d) **Misconduct:** provided warnings suitable to the offence have been given - so the disciplinary procedures of the organisation are vitally important.

(e) **Another 'substantial' reason:** for example, the employee is married to a competitor, or refuses to accept a reorganisation made in the interests of the business and with the agreement of other employees.

3.10 **Unfair dismissal**

(a) Unfair selection for redundancy.

(b) Membership and involvement in a trade union.

(c) Pregnancy.

(d) Trying to enforce the right to itemised pay statements and written details of their employment particulars.

(e) Carrying out certain activities in connection with health and safety at work.

3.11 The Conciliation Officer or Industrial Tribunal to whom a complaint of unfair dismissal is made may order various **remedies**, subject to the circumstances of the case.

(a) **Re-instatement:** giving the employee his old job back.

(b) **Re-engagement:** giving the employee a job comparable to the old one.

(c) **Compensation**. Currently this is:

(i) A **basic award** calculated on the same scale as redundancy pay.

(ii) A **compensatory award** (taking account of the basic award) for any additional loss (earnings, expenses, benefits), as damages for breach of contract.

(iii) A **punitive additional award** if the employer does not comply with an order for re-instatement or re-engagement and does not show that it was impracticable to do so.

The government proposes scrapping the ceiling on compensation for unfair dismissal.

3.12 **Incompetence or misconduct**

(a) **Incompetence** means that the employee has not reached the standard required, although he or she has done what he or she considers his or her best (ie lack of *capability*).

(b) If the employee has deliberately *not* done his best, however, this is **misconduct**.

3.13 The solution to these difficulties lies partly in the hands of the HRM function.

(a) Ensure that **standards of performance and conduct** are set, clearly defined and communicated to all employees.

(b) **Warn** employees where a gap is perceived between standard and performance.

(c) Give a clearly defined and reasonable **period for improvement** - with help and advice where necessary, and clear improvement targets.

(d) Ensure that **disciplinary procedures** and the ultimate consequences of continued failure are made clear.

If such procedures are formulated, the employer will not only feel that the employee has been given every chance to redeem the situation, but will also be in a strong position at a tribunal in rebutting a complaint of unfair dismissal.

Disciplinary procedures

3.14 The use of a disciplinary system can be evidence in certain situations that an employee has not been dismissed unfairly. Types of disciplinary situation include the following.

- Absenteeism
- Poor punctuality
- Poor job performance
- Poor attitudes
- Breaches of safety regulations
- Refusal to obey legitimate instructions

3.15 The initial purpose of discipline should be to improve behaviour. ACAS (the UK's state-funded Advisory Conciliation and Arbitration Service which aims to help settle disputes between management and workers) has issued some guidelines which suggest the following steps.

Step 1 **Informal talk**. If the infraction is of a minor nature and if the employee's record has no previous marks of disciplinary action, an informal, friendly talk will clear up the situation in many cases.

Step 2 **Oral warning or reprimand**. In this type of interview between employee and supervisor, the supervisor emphasises the undesirability of the subordinate's repeated violation, and that ultimately it could lead to serious disciplinary action.

Step 3 **Written or official warning**. A written warning is **formal**, as it becomes a permanent part of the employee's record. Written warnings can serve as evidence in case of grievance procedures.

Step 4 **Disciplinary lay-offs, or suspension**. This course of action result from repeated offences, or if previous steps were of no avail.

Step 5 **Demotion**. Losing pay and status over an extended period of time is a form of constant punishment. This dissatisfaction may easily spread to co-workers, so most enterprises avoid downgrading as a disciplinary measure.

Step 6 **Discharge**. Discharge is a drastic form of disciplinary action, and should be reserved for the most serious offences. For the organisation, it involves waste of a labour resource, the expense of training a new employee, and disruption caused by changing the make-up of the work team. There also may be damage to the morale of the group.

Documentation

3.16 ACAS procedures require that in any form of disciplinary action, it is essential for the supervisor to keep records of what happened and the decision or response made to the situation, since the supervisor may be asked at some future time to justify the action he or she has since taken.

The right to appeal and representation

3.17 ACAS procedures require that the employee should have the opportunity to state his or her case, accompanied by a fellow employee or union representative, and have a right of appeal. The right to appeal against supervisory discipline is available through the various steps of the grievance procedure, if an employee belongs to a labour union. However, this right of appeal should also exist in a comparable manner in any enterprise which does not have a labour union. This right of appeal must be recognised as being a real right and not merely a formality.

3.18 Under the government's 'Fairness at Work' proposals, employees will have the right to representation (eg by a union official) in disciplinary procedures.

ACAS Code of Practice

3.19 A brief summary of the ACAS Code of Practice on disciplinary procedures is given here. Disciplinary and grievance procedures should:

(a) Be in writing (the ACAS code of practice does not extend to informal 'first' warnings).

(b) Specify to whom they apply (all, or only some of the employees?).

(c) Deal speedily with disciplinary matters.

(d) Indicate the forms of disciplinary action which may be taken (such as dismissal, suspension or warning).

(e) Specify the appropriate levels of authority for the exercise of disciplinary actions.

(f) Provide for individuals to be informed of the nature of their alleged misconduct.

(g) Allow individuals to state their case, and to be accompanied by a fellow employee (or union representative).

(h) Ensure that every case is properly investigated before any disciplinary action is taken.

(i) Ensure that employees are informed of the reasons for any penalty they receive.

(j) State that no employee will be dismissed for a first offence, except in cases of gross misconduct.

(k) Provide for a right of appeal, and specify the appeals procedure.

Redundancy

3.20 **Redundancy** is dismissal when:

(a) The employer has ceased to carry on the business *at all* or in the place where the employee was employed.

(b) The requirements of the business for employees to carry out work of a particular kind have ceased or diminished or are expected to.

3.21 Compensation is a legal entitlement, and encourage employees to accept redundancy without damage to industrial relations.

3.22 The employee is not entitled to compensation if:

(a) The employer has made a 'suitable' offer of alternative employment and the employee has unreasonably rejected it.

(b) The employee is of pension age or over, or has less than two years' continuous employment.

(c) The employee's conduct merits dismissal without notice.

There are certain legal minima for compensation offered, based on age and length of service.

Procedure for handling redundancies

3.23 From a purely humane point of view, it is obviously desirable to *consult* with employees or their representatives. Notice of impending redundancies is a legal *duty* for redundancies over a certain number.

3.24 **Softening the blow**

(a) Retirement of staff over the normal retirement age.
(b) Early retirement to staff approaching normal retirement age.
(c) Restrictions on recruitment to reduce the workforce over time by natural wastage.
(d) Dismissal of part-time or short-term contract staff.
(e) Offering retraining and/or redeployment within the organisation.
(f) Seeking voluntary redundancies.

3.25 Where management have to *choose* between individuals doing the same work, they may in addition to the measures in 3.22 above:

(a) Dismiss the less competent.
(b) Require people to 're-apply' for the job.
(c) 'Last in, first out' (LIFO). Newcomers are dismissed before long-serving employees.

3.26 Many large organisations provide benefits in excess of the statutory minimum, with regard to consultation periods, terms, notice periods, counselling and aid with job search, training in job-search skills and so on.

3.27 Many firms provide advice and **outplacement** counselling, to help redundant employees find work elsewhere.

Question 2

Will HRM become increasingly involved in getting rid of people instead of recruiting them?

Answer

(a) John Hunt *(The Shifting Focus of the Personnel Function)* 'In sharp contrast to the search for talent is the dramatic shift in the personnel function from people resourcing to people exiting.'

(b) Pressures on intensive use of manpower, contraction of workforce (plus expansion in unemployment in UK), viz:

(i) competition
(ii) new technology
(iii) recession and decline in world trade.

(c) But it is not necessarily a trend which will continue in future. Technology does not always 'replace' human operation and lead to manpower savings. It also creates jobs.

(d) There are alternatives to redundancy: job-sharing, use of manpower agencies, part-time or temporary assignments, networking.

4 MATERNITY

4.1 Because of increased attention to the implications of equal opportunities and because of the need to recruit more women returnees to the labour force, many organisations are improving their maternity and child care arrangements. A woman is entitled to:

(a) Leave of absence for maternity, return to her own job afterwards, subject to least 21 days' notice in writing of her intention and reconfirmation that she is to return to work.

(b) Return to her old job or suitable alternative after maternity leave (subject to certain qualification requirements), proper notice having been given.

(c) 14 weeks maternity leave, or more subject to employment history.

(d) Time off must for ante-natal care.

(e) Statutory Maternity Pay is payable, subject to certain qualification requirements. Employers recover these benefit payments by deductions from their national insurance payments to the DSS. The EU directive requires that any maternity pay must *at least* equal statutory sick pay.

4.2 Many employers have introduced more generous maternity agreements. It is possible that time off for fathers upon the birth of a child may be allowed - the right exists in some EU countries.

5 DISCRIMINATION AND EQUAL OPPORTUNITIES

Women in employment

5.1 Only in recent decades has there been a widespread challenge to **sex segregation** in employment - the idea that there are 'men's jobs' and 'women's jobs', with only a few genuinely 'unisex' categories of work. Reasons for this discrimination include the following.

(a) Social pressures on the woman to bear and rear children, and on the man to make a lifetime commitment to paid work as the 'breadwinner'. Employers assumed that women's paid work would be short term or interrupted, and that training, development and promotion were wasted.

(b) The nature of earlier industrial work, which was physically heavy: legal restrictions were placed on women's employment in some areas.

(c) Lack of organisation of women at work and influence in trade unions.

(d) The reinforcing of segregation at home and at school.

(e) Career ladders which fail to fast-track women.

(f) Child-bearing and family responsibilities.

Many of these assumptions are being re-examined, and we will look a bit later at some of the measures being taken to remove the barriers to women in employment.

Ethnic minorities in employment

5.2 Unemployment rates differ amongst the various ethnic groups in the UK.

(a) The ethnic minority population is much younger than the population as a whole.
(b) Direct racial discrimination still exists in favour of white labour.
(c) Ethnic minorities are concentrated in certain industrial sectors, occupations.

Other disadvantaged groups

5.3 Two further forms of discrimination specifically legislated against are:

(a) Failure to provide equal opportunities to suitably **qualified disabled persons**.

(b) Non-engagement or dismissal on the grounds of a **conviction for a criminal offence**, once the offender is rehabilitated and his conviction 'spent'.

Ageism

5.4 Finally, there is the issue of age. Most job advertisements specify age limits which make it difficult for older employees to find work. This is perfectly legal, but some groups are seeking to have it outlawed.

Legal rights to equal opportunity

5.5 In Britain, two main Acts have been passed to deal with inequality of opportunity.

(a) The Sex Discrimination Act 1975, outlawing certain types of discrimination on the grounds of sex or marital status.

(b) The Race Relations Act 1976, outlawing certain types of discrimination on grounds of colour, race, nationality, or ethnic or national origin.

In both Acts, the obligation of **non-discrimination applies to all aspects of employment,** including advertisements, recruitment and selection programmes, access to training, promotion, disciplinary procedures, redundancy and dismissal.

5.6 **Types of discrimination**

(a) **Direct discrimination:** one interested group is treated less favourably than another (except for exempted cases). This is illegal.

(b) **Indirect discrimination:** requirements or conditions are imposed, with which a substantial proportion of the interested group could not comply, to their detriment. The employer must, if challenged, justify the conditions on non-racial or non-sexual grounds.

(c) **Positive discrimination** gives give **preference** to a protected person, regardless of comparative suitability and qualification for the job.

(i) British legislation does **not** (except with regard to training) **permit positive discrimination**. In particular, there is no quota scheme (except for registered disabled persons)

(ii) The organisation may, however, set itself **targets** for the number of such persons that they will aim to employ - *if* the required number of *eligible* and *suitably qualified* people can be recruited.

(iii) A number of countries in the world use positive discrimination as an aspect of social policy to correct perceived disadvantage endured by various ethnic and other groups in society. (For example, in India **scheduled castes** are entitled to a proportion of government jobs.)

5.7 Employees can go to the Equal Opportunities tribunal. The publicity (eg the recent case when Goldman Sachs was charged with racial discrimination) can be very worrying.

Equal Pay

5.8 **Equal pay legislation** is intended 'to prevent discrimination as regards terms and conditions of employment between men and women'.

(a) Where there is an element of sex discrimination in a collective agreement, this must be removed.

(b) A women can claim equal pay for work that is 'the same or broadly similar' as the work of a man in the same establishment.

(c) Women have the right to **equal pay** for 'work **of equal value**', so that a woman would no longer have to compare her work with that of a man in the same or broadly similar work, but could establish that her work has equal value to that of a man in the same establishment.

Disability

5.9 Legislation passed in 1944 established a Quota Scheme, whereby any employer of more than 20 people must employ at least 3% (the 'standard percentage') of registered disabled persons, unless he has a permit to engage an able-bodied person instead. Appropriate records must be kept. If an employer fails to keep the quota, each new vacancy must be offered to a disabled person: only if no-one is available can the vacancy be offered to non-disabled applicants.

5.10 In practice, however, public as well as private organisations frequently fail to meet quota requirements - many protected by bulk exemption permits. The Quota Scheme gives priority to disabled applicants with *equal* qualifications, but gives no positive incentives to employers to re-examine job specifications and employ disabled people.

Rehabilitation of Offenders

5.11 **Rehabilitation of Offenders Act 1974.** A conviction for most criminal offences (earning less than 30 months in prison) is 'spent' after a period of time (which varies according to the severity of the offence). After this period, an offender (provided he or she is not a doctor, lawyer, teacher, accountant or police person) is 'rehabilitated' and is not obliged to disclose the nature of his offence or details of his conviction.

Management practice

5.12 The practical implications of the legislation for employers are set out in **Codes of Practice**, issued by the Commission for Racial Equality and the Equal Opportunities Commission. These do not have the force of law, but may be taken into account by Industrial Tribunals, where discrimination cases are brought before them.

5.13 Organisations make minimal efforts to avoid discrimination, paying lip-service to the idea to the extent of claiming 'We are an Equal Opportunities Employer' on advertising literature! To turn such a claim into reality involves:

(a) **Support from the top** of the organisation for the formulation of a practical policy.

(b) A **working party** drawn from - for example - management, unions, minority groups, the HRM department and staff representatives. This group's brief will be to produce a draft Policy and Code of Practice, which will be approved at senior level.

(c) **Action plans and resources** (including staff) in order to implement and monitor the policy, publicise it to staff, arrange training and so on.

(d) **Monitoring.** The numbers of women and ethnic minority staff can easily be monitored:

(i) Entering (and applying to enter) the organisation.

(ii) Leaving the organisation.

(iii) Applying for transfers, promotions or training schemes.

(e) **Positive action:** the process of taking active steps to **encourage** people from disadvantaged groups to apply for jobs and training, and to compete for vacancies. (Note that this is *not* positive discrimination.) Examples might be: using ethnic languages in job advertisements, or implementing training for women in management skills.

5.14 **Implications for recruitment and selection.** There is always a risk that a disappointed job applicant, for example, will attribute his or her lack of success to discrimination, especially if the recruiting organisation's workforce is conspicuously lacking in representatives of the same ethnic minority, sex or group.

(a) **Advertising**

(i) Avoid wording that suggests preference for a particular group.

(ii) Employers must not indicate or imply any 'intention to discriminate'.

(iii) Recruitment literature should state that the organisation is an Equal Opportunities employer.

(iv) The placing of advertisements only where the readership is predominantly of one race or sex is construed as indirect discrimination.

(b) **Recruitment agencies.** Instructions to an agency should not suggest any preference.

(c) **Application forms.** These should include no questions which are not work-related (such as domestic details) and which only one group is asked to complete.

(d) **Interviews**

(i) Any non-work-related question must be asked of *all* interviewees, if any, and even then, some types of question may be construed as discriminatory.

(ii) It may be advisable to have a witness at interviews, or at least to take detailed notes, in the event that a claim of discrimination is made.

(e) **Selection tests.** These must be wholly relevant, and should not favour any particular group. Even personality tests have been shown to favour white male applicants.

(f) **Records.** Reasons for rejection, and interview notes, should be carefully recorded, so that in the event of investigation the details will be available.

Question 3

Find the policy statement of your organisation related to equal opportunities. Is it being carried out in practice? How many women and racial minority groups are represented in your own office in managerial positions? Do you think the position is improving or not?

Ask your personnel or training department, if necessary, about special programmes and opportunities for women in your organisation. What more do you think (a) could and (b) should be done.

5.15 Some employers have begun to address the underlying problems of equal opportunities, with measures such as these.

(a) Putting equal opportunities higher on the agenda by appointing **Equal Opportunities Managers (and even Directors)** reporting directly to the Personnel Director.

(b) **Flexible hours** or part-time work, 'term-time' or annual hours contracts (to allow for school holidays) to help women to combine careers with family responsibilities. Terms and conditions, however, must not be less favourable.

(c) **Career-break** or return-to-work schemes for women.

(d) Training for **women returnees** or women in management to help women to manage their career potential. Assertiveness training may also be offered as part of such an initiative.

(e) **Awareness training** for managers, to encourage them to think about equal opportunity policy.

(f) The provision of **workplace nurseries** for working mothers.

(g) **Positive action** to encourage job and training applications from minority groups.

(h) Alteration of **premises** to accommodate wheelchair users.

Sexual harassment

5.16 **Sexual harassment** may be defined as any **unwanted** conduct with sexual connotations, physical or verbal. Rulings in a number of high profile court cases suggest that sexual harassment is **unlawful sex discrimination**, under the Sex Discrimination Act.

6 HEALTH AND SAFETY

6.1 Maintaining health and safety at work is important for several reasons.

(a) An employer has **legal obligations** under UK and EU law for the health and safety of employees as well as **moral ones**.

(b) Accidents and illness **cost the employer money** (not just legal damages, but operating costs as well).

(c) The company's **image** in the marketplace and society will suffer if its health and safety record is bad.

6.2 The **major legislation in the UK** includes:

(a) Health and Safety at Work Act 1974

(b) Factories Act 1961

(c) Offices, Shops and Railway Premises Act, 1963

(d) Safety Representatives and Safety Committees Regulations 1977 (under the authority of the 1974 Act)

(e) Fire Precautions Act 1971

(f) Regulations implementing EU Directives on Health and Safety.

Management practices

6.3 **Employers' duties**

(a) All systems (work practices) must be safe.

(b) The work environment must be safe and healthy (well-lit, warm, ventilated and hygienic).

(c) All plant and equipment must be kept up to the necessary standard (with guards on machines and so on).

(d) Information, instruction, training and supervision should be directed towards safe working practices.

(e) The safety policy should be clearly communicated to all staff.

Management of Health and Safety at Work Regulations, 1992

6.4 Implementation of the EU directives as (legally enforceable) regulations, means that employers now have the following additional general duties.

(a) They must carry out **risk assessment**, generally in writing, of all work hazards. Assessment should be continuous.

(b) They must **introduce controls** to reduce risks.

(c) They must **assess the risks to anyone else affected by their work activities.**

(d) They must **share hazard and risk information** with other employers, including those on adjoining premises, other site occupiers and all subcontractors coming onto the premises.

(e) They should **revise safety policies** in the light of the above, or initiate safety policies if none were in place previously.

(f) They must **identify employees** who are especially at risk.

(g) They must provide **appropriate training** in safety matters.

(h) They must provide information to employees (including temporary staff) about health and safety.

(i) They must employ competent safety and health advisers.

Safety Representative Regulations 1978

6.5 The Safety Representative Regulations provide for *safety representatives* to be appointed by a recognised trade union, and for *Safety Committees* to be set up at the request of employee representatives, to monitor safety measures and to assist (or 'police') the employer in providing a healthy and safe place of work.

Employees

6.6 The **employee** must:

(a) Take reasonable care of himself / herself and others.

(b) Allow the employer to carry out his or her duties (including enforcing safety rules).

(c) Not interfere intentionally or recklessly with any machinery or equipment.

(d) Inform the employer of any situation which may be a danger (this does not reduce the employer's responsibilities in any way)

(e) Use all equipment properly.

Question 4

What aspects of your own work environment (if any) do you think are:

(a) a hindrance to your work?
(b) a source of dissatisfaction?
(c) a hazard to your health and/or safety?

The Workplace (Health, Safety and Welfare) Regulations, 1992

6.7 These regulations implement the *workplace directive* covering matters that have been statutory requirements for many years in the under UK legislation although in some cases the requirements have been more clearly defined. It covers:

- Equipment (maintenance and fencing)
- Ventilation
- Temperature
- Lighting
- Cleaning and decoration
- Room dimensions and space
- Floors
- Falls or falling objects
- Rest facilities and eating facilities
- Glazing
- Traffic routes
- Doors and gates
- Escalators and travelators
- Sanitary conveniences and washing facilities
- Drinking water
- Clothing

Manual handling and operations regulations (1992)

6.8 The regulations can be summarised as follows.

(a) **Employers' duties**

(i) Avoid situations where employees are involved in materials handling which carries a risk of injury.

(ii) If not avoidable, assess the risk, and keep it as low as possible.

(iii) Ensure employees are trained in using possibly dangerous equipment.

(b) **Employees' duties**

(i) Use equipment properly;
(ii) Inform employers of any defects.

Health and safety (display screen equipment) regulation, 1992

6.9 If you have ever worked for a long period at a VDU you may personally have experienced some discomfort. Back ache, eye strain and stiffness or muscular problems of the neck, shoulders, arms or hands are frequent complaints. RSI (repetitive strain injury) is cited as causing permanent disability in some occupations.

6.10 Following the implementation of the EU directive on workstations any new workstations put into service now have to meet new requirements and existing workstations must be adapted to comply or be replaced by the end of 1996. Those cover VDU screens, glare, radiation, breaks and free eyesight testing.

Accident and safety policies

6.11 **Common causes of injury**

- Slippery or poorly maintained floors.
- Frayed carpets.
- Trailing electric leads.
- Obstacles in gangways.
- Standing on chairs to reach high shelving.
- Staircases used as storage facilities.
- Lifting heavy items without bending properly.
- Removing the safety guard on a machine to free a blockage.

6.12 **The cost of accidents to the employer**

(a) Time lost by the injured employee and other staff.

(b) *The cost* of disruption to operations at work; damage and repairs and modification to the equipment; compensation payments or fines resulting from legal action; increased insurance premiums.

(d) Reduced output from the injured employee on return to work.

(e) The cost of recruiting and training a replacement for the injured worker.

6.13 An employee who is injured as a result of either the **employer's failure to take reasonable care** or a **statutory duty** can **sue**.

(a) An employee **is not deemed to consent to the risk of injury because he or she is aware of the risk**. It is the employer's duty to provide a safe working system.

(b) Employees can become inattentive or careless in doing work which is monotonous or imposes stress. This factor too must be allowed for in the employer's safety precautions.

(c) It is not always a sufficient defence that the employer provided safety equipment and rules: the employer has some duty to encourage if not to insist on its proper use.

(d) Many dangers can be caused by carelessness or other fault of an otherwise competent employee, possibly by his mere thoughtlessness. It is the employer's duty to be watchful and to keep such tendencies in check.

(e) Employees do not work continuously. The employer's duty is to take reasonable care for their safety in all acts which are normally and reasonably incidental to the day's work.

6.14 **Reducing the frequency and severity of accidents**

(a) Developing a **safety consciousness** among staff and workers and encouraging departmental pride in a good safety record.

(b) Developing effective consultative **participation** between management, workers and unions so that safety and health rules can be accepted and followed.

(c) Giving adequate **instruction** in safety rules and measures as part of the training of new and transferred workers, or where working methods or speeds of operation are changed.

(d) **Materials handling should be minimised** and designed as far as possible for safe working and operation.

(e) Ensuring a satisfactory **standard.**

(f) **Good maintenance.**

(g) In general, the appropriate **code of practice** for the industry/work environment should be implemented in full.

(h) **Safety inspections** should be carried out regularly to locate and define faults in the system that allow accidents to occur.

6.15 **Accident reporting systems.** The report is designed to identify problems and indicate corrective action.

(a) Accidents should be reported on an **accident report form.**

(b) **Statistical trends** should be monitored to reveal areas where recurring accidents suggest the need for special investigation, but only more serious incidents will have to be followed-up in depth.

(c) **Follow-up** should be clearly aimed at preventing recurrence - not placing blame.

Fire

6.16 **Main legal rules**

(a) There must be adequate means of escape kept free from obstructions
(b) All doors out of the building must be capable of opening from the inside
(c) All employees should know the fire alarm system
(d) There must be an effective and regularly tested fire alarm system
(e) There must be fire-fighting equipment easily available and in working order.

6.17 **Preventing fires**

The Fire Protection Association (of the UK) suggests the following guidelines for fire prevention and control.

(a) **Fire risks should be identified,** particularly as regards sources of ignition, presence of combustible materials, and the means by which fires can spread.

(b) The **responsibility for fire prevention** should be established.

(c) A **fire officer** should be appointed.

(d) A **fire prevention drill** should be established and practised.

Health and safety policy

6.18 In order to enhance safety awareness, promote good practice and comply with legal obligations, many employers have a **health and safety policy** for their staff. Such a policy might have the following features.

(a) Statement of **principles.**

(b) Detail of **safety procedures.**

(c) **Compliance with the law.**

(d) **Detailed instructions** should be made available as to how to use equipment.

(e) **Training requirements** (eg no person who has not been on a particular training course can use the equipment) should be identified, as part of the context of human resource planning.

(f) Close attention must be paid to **implementation** for the policy to be a success (eg fire extinguishers, for example, can be regularly checked by the local fire brigade).

6.19 Senior managers **must set a good example**. They should:

(a) **Visibly react to breaches** of the policy (eg if the fire doors are blocked open, remove the blockage).

(b) **Ensure that the policy is communicated** to staff (eg memoranda, newsletters).

(c) **Set priorities for operations.** In other words management insistence on higher productivity should not mean the abandonment of safety policies.

(d) **Involve staff in the health and safety process,** through consultation with unions or workplace committees.

Question 5

Get hold of a copy of your organisation's policy statement on health and safety and read it carefully. Are there any points in it that surprise you - or that do not seem to fit with the practice in your office?

What other material on health and safety is easily available in the office? Are health and safety concerns 'high profile'? Are there notices up about these issues, leaflets available, safety officers or meetings?

Case example

Charles Hampden-Turner (in his book *Corporate Culture*) notes that attitudes to safety can be part of a corporate *culture*. He quotes the example of a firm called (for reasons of confidentiality) *Western Oil*.

(a) Western Oil had a bad safety record. 'Initially, safety was totally at odds with the main cultural values of productivity (management's interests) and maintenance of a macho image (the worker's culture) ... Western Oil had a culture which put safety in conflict with other corporate values.' In particular, the problem was with its long-distance truck drivers (who in the US have a culture of solitary independence and self reliance) who drove sometimes recklessly with loads large enough to inundate a small town. The company instituted *Operation Integrity* to improve safety, in a lasting way, changing the policies and drawing on the existing features of the culture but using them in a different way.

(b) The culture had five dilemmas.

(i) *Safety-first vs macho-individualism*. Truckers see themselves as 'fearless pioneers of the unconventional lifestyle ... "Be careful boys!" is hardly a plea likely to go down well with this particular group'. Instead of trying to control the drivers, the firm recommended that they become *road safety consultants* (or design consultants). Their advice was sought on improving the system. This had the advantage that 'by making drivers critics of the system their roles as outsiders were preserved and promoted'. It tried to tap their heroism as promoters of public safety.

(ii) *Safety everywhere vs safety specialists*. Western Oil could have hired more specialist staff. However, instead, the company promoted cross functional safety teams from existing parts of the business, for example, to help in designing depots and thinking of ways to reduce hazards.

(iii) *Safety as cost vs productivity as benefit*. 'If the drivers raced from station to station to win their bonus, accidents were bound to occur ... . The safety engineers rarely spoke to the line manager in charge of the delivery schedules. The unreconciled dilemma between safety and productivity had been evaded at management level and passed down the hierarchy until drivers were subjected to two incompatible injunctions, work fast and work safely.' To deal with this problem, safety would be built into the reward system.

(iv) *Long-term safety vs short-term steering.* The device of recording 'unsafe' acts in operations enabled them to be monitored by cross-functional teams, so that the causes of accidents could be identified and be reduced.

(v) *Personal responsibility vs collective protection.* It was felt that if 'safety' was seen as a form of management policing it would never be accepted. The habit of management 'blaming the victim' had to stop. Instead, if an employee reported another to the safety teams, the person who was reported would be free of *official* sanction. Peer presence was seen to be a better enforcer of safety than the management hierarchy.

6.20 In many companies, considerations of health and safety are not tied up so intimately and obviously with reward systems and other policies. Nor do health and safety issues relate directly to work. However, from this example, we can learn:

(a) the importance of management practice in ensuring safety;
(b) safety (like total quality) is everyone's responsibility;
(c) culture and structures can either enhance or undermine safety policies.

6.21 Copies of legislation are readily available from the government and the Health and Safety Executive. Various companies produce newsletters on the issue to keep managers regularly informed. There is no real excuse for management ignorance in this matter.

6.22 The diagram below shows a systematic approach to health and safety.

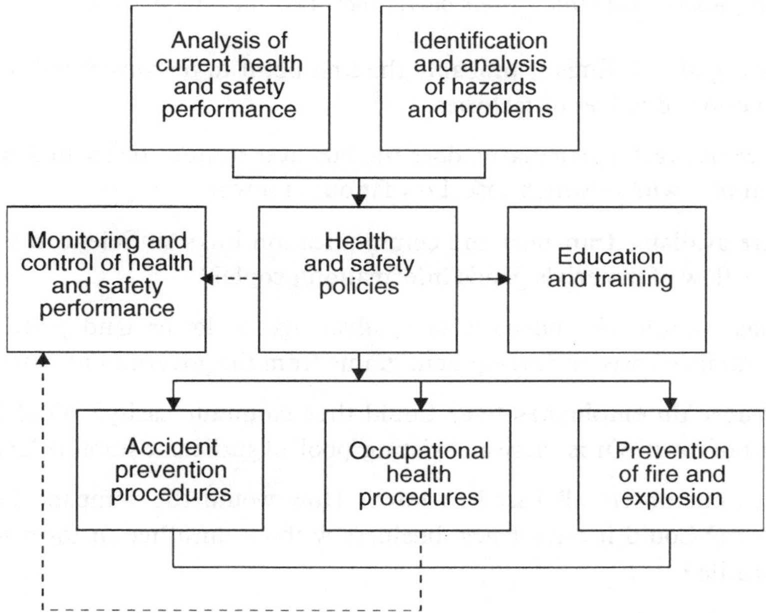

7 THE WORK ENVIRONMENT 6/94

7.1 The office environment is, perhaps, as a 'hygiene' factor. A good working environment will not be able to motivate employees to enhanced performance (beyond the short-term effects of a fresh improvement, perhaps) but shortcomings will be important to them, as a source of *dis*satisfaction.

7.2 Effect of the physical environment on worker morale and/or productivity.

(a) **Health and safety.**

(b) **Employee Performance.** (Certain conditions physically and psychologically enable the worker to perform tasks efficiently, without unnecessary stress, fatigue and other forms of 'interference'.)

(c) **Organisational culture.** The physical environment is an expression of the organisation's self-image to customers/clients and to employees. It can alter the way employees feel about their work and their organisation (is it smart or 'shabby'?). It can also affect the amount of social contact and interaction available to workers: consider the difference between cubicles and open plan offices, for example, in encouraging informal communication ('networking').

(d) **Business performance**

   (i) Does the office project a **positive and attractive image** to potential customers, employees and suppliers.

   (ii) It is **flexible enough** to allow for change and growth, should that be required.

   (iii) Does it make **economical use of space**, equipment and work flows.

   (iv) Does it encourages the **informal communication network** of the organisation for the exchange of information and ideas.

External environment

7.3 The surroundings of a work place include not only the immediate space in which employees carry out their duties, but also the *external environment* in which they may shop, bank, eat, commute and park their cars and the overall design and construction of the complex within which their particular office may be placed.

7.4 The **siting of buildings** is probably the first point to be considered in the acquisition or construction of offices or factories.

(a) **Urban/rural.** Particularly, does the business want to be located in an urban area, or out of town? In which case, how far out of town?

(b) Are available **transport** and communication links sufficient to keep up the in- and out-flow of materials/goods/information/people?

(c) **Cost**. Could the business take advantage of lower land prices, lower rates and insurance costs or development grants from the government outside urban areas?

(d) **Where do employees live**? Could they commute easily? Would they rather move out of town? Or is there an existing 'pool' of sufficient suitable labour in the area?

(e) Are **customers** all based in town? How would the company keep in touch with them? Could it attract new business without an office in town to present a public 'profile'?

(f) **Facilities.** From the point of view of employees and the organisation, the proximity of banks, postal services and transport will be very important. For the employees' well-being, shops, restaurants and perhaps recreation/sports facilities would also be welcome.

(g) **Financial considerations** largely determine the organisation's attitudes to the above factors. The site, size and age of buildings acquired, and whether they are rented, bought or built, will be determined by their cost and will in turn determine such operating costs as insurance and rates, heating and lighting, maintenance and renovation.

Office layout

7.5 **Examples of office layout**

(a) **Small closed offices** linked by corridors have the advantage of privacy, peace and security. Some work requires peace and quiet.

(b) **Open plan offices**. These are arranged like classrooms and lecture halls, to do away with the maze of walls and doors and make better use of the space than small closed offices.

(i) **Advantages**

- Easier supervision
- Freer communication
- Flexible arrangement of furniture and equipment in the available space
- Economies on heating and lighting
- Sharing of equipment, such as photocopiers

(ii) **Disadvantages**

- The soulless arrangement of the desks in ranks
- Lack of privacy
- Distraction from noise and movement
- Loss for managers of the status of a separate office
- Tendency for managers to become unnecessarily involved in routine matters
- Difficulty of satisfying every individual's needs and preferences

(c) **Landscaped offices** are a variation of the open plan system, overcoming some of the latter's problems.

(d) **Hot desking**. Some firms have done away with one desk per employee especially firms where employees have to work 'in the field'. Instead, employees have a locker, and when they intend to be in the office, they phone in to 'book' a desk space. Such firms often provide better communal spaces.

7.6 Work study might be used to determine the best layout for sections in an open plan system, based on the amount of contact usually necessary between each section.

Internal factors

7.7 Poor office design is evidenced in so-called **sick building syndrome** where poor lighting, inefficient air conditioning leads to persistent headaches, colds etc.

(a) **Heating, lighting and ventilation**.

(b) **Noise.** Strangely enough, we do need noise at work - or at least a certain amount of it. Constant loud noise, or intermittent noise at any volume, is distracting and can be reduced by various methods.

(c) **Decor.** A well planned colour scheme, decoration, plants etc can be an important factor in the psychology of work.

(d) **Furniture.** Ergonomics includes the design of office equipment so that, for example, chairs and desks are designed to be comfortable and supportive, and to avoid causing muscular problems.

(e) **Computer networks.** Information technology involves a lot of wiring, and there should be enough **wiring ducts under the floor** to satisfy the organisation's IT needs.

(f) *Cost.* The benefits of the 'perfect' ergonomically-designed office would still have to justify their cost.

Ergonomics

7.8 **Ergonomics** is the scientific study of the demands that can arise from a working environment and the capabilities of people to meet these demands.

(a) Through this research, data is made available to establish *machines* and working conditions which, apart from functioning well, are best suited to the capacities and health requirements of the human body.

(b) Both work study and ergonomics are concerned with 'fitting the job to the worker' and ergonomic data is used in establishing workplace layout.

Management responsibility

7.9 The **office manager** is 'the person in charge of all the office functions of an undertaking or some major part of them'. Mills, Standingford and Appleby *(Modern Office Management)* define the role of the office manager broadly as follows.

(a) Ensuring the efficient and economical use of the office's resources.

(b) Ensuring that sufficient resources are available to meet the company's office requirements.

(c) Preparing budgets and estimates and ensuring procedures are set up to control output and expenditure in the office.

(d) Establish systems and procedures for efficient information provisions for management decision makers.

(e) Arrange recruitment, selection and training.

(f) Ensure effective communications.

(g) Establish systems for health and safety and staff welfare. A fire officer might be appointed.

(h) Maintain the smooth running of the office by clear definition of responsibilities.

7.10 Such a job description is broad. However, in practice some of these tasks will be delegated to technical specialists (eg accounting, personnel and information systems). It is not always clear who is to deal with ergonomic issues: the purchasing department (to make the capital expenditure), the personnel director, or the health and safety officer?

8 STRESS

8.1 **Stress** is the product of demands made on an individual's physical and mental energies:

(a) Demands on an individual's energies may be stimulating (some people work well under pressure) as well as harmful (causing strain).

(b) Many sources of stress are *not* related to work, however. Moving house, bereavement, family change are all sources of stress.

8.2 Stress has sometimes been seen, wrongly, as the exclusive preserve of managerial staff. Any managers are generally less stressed than the people that work for them.

(a) Heavy work and other physical conditions such as heat, noise, dirt or the presence of toxic substances cause stress.

(b) Paced and/or repetitive work causes tress as a result of boredom or monotony.

(c) Tasks characterised primarily by various types of information processing activities and 'decisional complexity', often performed under time constraints (for example at a busy supermarket checkout). In other words, responsibility without authority or some control over the work is stressful.

Symptoms of stress (strain) and methods of coping

8.3 Harmful stress, or 'strain', can be identified by its effects on the individual and his performance. Symptoms usually include the following.

(a) **Nervous tension** sometimes manifested in various physical symptoms - for example skin and digestive disorders.

(b) **Withdrawal**. Unusual quietness and reluctance to communicate, or physical withdrawal by absenteeism, poor time-keeping, or even leaving the organisation.

(c) **Low morale:** low confidence, dissatisfaction, frustration and so on.

(d) **Repression:** in other words refusal to admit the existence of the problem.

8.4 We will look at the causes and control of stress at work, as it relates to:

(a) Insecurity
(b) Management style
(c) Personality variables
(d) Role theory

Insecurity

8.5 Stress may be acute in situations involving uncertainty, and therefore insecurity, together with a sense of responsibility for their outcome. Feelings of job insecurity are perceived to be rife.

(a) A manager may find himself having to initiate change or growth: attempts at innovation may be highly stressful, especially if there is an element of risk. People with high security needs suffer more greatly from the new emphasis on innovation, flexibility and adaptability in organisation cultures.

(b) Career change, end or uncertainty. Worrying about 'burn-out' or redundancy or retirement - or even about ability to cope with promotion - can be a source of stress.

Management style

8.6 Particular management traits that are held responsible by workshop interviewees for causing stress and health problems include the following.

(a) Unpredictability (staff work under constant threat of an outburst).
(b) Destruction of workers' self esteem (making them feel helpless and insecure).
(c) Setting up win/lose situations (turning work relationships into a battle for control).
(d) Providing too much - or too little - stimulation.

8.7 Managers might be guilty of:

(a) Not giving credit where it is due
(b) Failing to communicate policy or involve staff in decisions
(c) Supervising too closely
(d) Not defining duties clearly enough.

The most 'harmful' style of management is said to be *leave alone and zap* - where the employee (frequently young and inexperienced) is given a task, left without guidance, and then 'zapped' with a reprimand or punishment when mistakes are discovered. This simply creates a vicious circle of anxiety and guilt.

Question 3

There must have been times when you have felt frustrated at work and probably when you have suffered from stress (unless you are very lucky). Think of two specific occasions and see if you can identify the causes and recognise the symptoms (as described above). How did you resolve the situation in each case and what help did you have?

Do others around you suffer from stress or frustration? Are you a help or a hindrance to them?

Personality

8.8 People have been divided into two types (first, by Friedman and Rosenheim).

(a) 'Type A' - competitive, 'thrusting', dynamic, impatient, restless, tense, and sensitive to pressure. Their behaviour has been associated by several research studies with a range of unhealthy symptoms (high blood pressure, cholesterol, smoking and drinking).

(b) 'Type B' - 'laid back', patient, calm, etc.

8.9 Type A managers, may feel it acutely, but try to overcome it - with consequent risk to health. Personality traits which might affect one's ability to cope with stress, in either fashion, include the following.

(a) **Sensitivity**. Emotionally sensitive individuals are pressured more by conflict and doubt, which insensitive people are more able to shrug off.

(b) **Flexibility**. Individuals who are seen to give in to pressure tend to invite further pressure from those who seek to influence them: intractable, 'stubborn' individuals may suffer less from this, although, when they are subjected to pressure, they tend to 'snap' rather than 'bend'.

(c) **Interpersonal competence**. The effects of stress may be handled better from a basis of strong, supportive relationships with others.

(d) **Sense of responsibility**. Some individuals have an 'easy come, easy go' outlook - where their own affairs are concerned, as well as those of others that are affected by their actions. Others have a more acute sense of 'owing' other people something, or of their accountability to others for the consequences of their decisions, actions etc.

Locus of control

8.10 An interesting extension to the effect of personality on stress relates to what Taylor and Cooper define as **locus of control**. Control is defined in this context as 'a generalised expectancy concerning the extent to which an individual believes that reinforcements, rewards, or successes are either internally or externally controlled'.

(a) **Internal locus of control:** such a person believes he or she possesses the power and ability to influence the outcome of events. (In other words, such people believe they are in control.)

(b) **External locus of control:** such a person believes that personal power has a minimal effect on events, which are determined by fate, chance, 'Murphy's Law', other people, forces out of their control and so on.

8.11 We can plot locus of control with personality types.

	Type A		
Internal locus of control	'Charismatic' (in control and sociable)	'Hostile' (under pressure)	External locus of control
	'Relaxed' (content, placid)	'Tense' (inhibited and anxious)	
	Type B		

(a) 'Charismatic' people have self-imposed challenges, pressures and deadlines which they enjoy; they are sociable.

(b) 'Hostile': these are victims of pressure, or feel they are; they are 'competitive, expressive and dominant'.

(c) 'Relaxed': such people remain 'detached and emotionally separate from events which would for others constitute anxiety and tension'.

(d) 'Tense': 'over-controlled, seemingly unexpressive and inhibited, these individual appear to be detached, but inside themselves they are seething with anger, hostility aggression and frustration'.

8.12 In this framework 'hostile' and 'tense' people are perhaps more prone to illness.

Role stress

8.13 Several major sources of stress have been identified by **role theory**. A role is a type of behaviour, in relation to others, that the individual displays.

(a) **Role ambiguity** is a situation where an individual is not sure what his role is, or when those around him are not clear what his role is. This may arise for a manager through:

(i) Uncertainty about the responsibilities of his job.
(ii) Uncertainty about other people's expectations of him.
(iii) Lack of clarity about how his performance is evaluated.

(b) **Role conflict** occurs when the individual is called upon to act in several roles at the same time, and they are incompatible - eg the dual roles of a working mother, or a participative manager called upon to administer discipline.

(c) **Role overload** occurs when an individual has too many roles to cope with, and feels out of his depth - eg on moving from a functional to a general management position.

(d) **Role underload** occurs when an individual moves into a role or set of roles which he perceives as being below his capacity (ie out of line with his self-concept).

Delegation may make a manager feel un-needed and insecure. Monotony may be as stressful as constant change and challenge.

Stress and performance

8.14 In *Feeling for the Facts* (*People Management*, 9 January 1997) Rob Briner offers the counter-intuitive view that 'there seems no clear link between stress levels and performance'. The author writes that current thinking as to how people feel about work (and at work) has been reduced to two very narrow concepts, **stress** and **satisfaction**. The underlying assumption is that happier workers are more productive. Hard research evidence suggests that there is 'no strong link between stress, satisfaction and performance...[which also appear to be] largely unrelated to absenteeism'. This does not mean that feelings and behaviour at work are not related, only that simplistic concepts like stress do not explain them. The author describes:

(a) **Moods** - feelings which change relatively slowly.

(b) **Emotions** - more short term and intense than moods eg happiness, anxiety. They can become moods or lead to emotionally laden arguments.

(c) **Emotionally laden judgments** - views about a situation strongly influenced by feeling (eg the type of response given to criticism.

(d) **Thoughts and feelings** about 'feelings' - how to understand how other people feel.

8.15 He suggests a number of approaches. Feelings at work are influenced by:

- What people are actively *trying* to achieve ('stress' and 'satisfaction' are more passive).
- The group/team context.
- The work role.
- Organisational norms and culture.

These underpin employee behaviour, eg absenteeism, conflict resolution, 'organisational citizenship behaviours (eg contributing to the good of the organisation not the individual role) and extra-role behaviours. In each case, these behaviours are affected by specific types of mood.

9 BRAINWORKS PLC UPDATE

Questions can be found in the Introduction box at the beginning of this Chapter.

9.1 *Question 1*. BW is in the employment business. The conduct of its own staff should be above reproach; however, the comment mentioned indicates a problem. The individual concerned might be disciplined for unprofessional conduct. BW must hope that this is an isolated incident rather than indicative of the culture and attitudes prevalent in some offices. Further investigation is needed.

9.2 *Question 2*. Offices are particularly important to BW for a number of reasons.

(a) BW is a provider of services. The *physical* evidence (ie the environment) of the service is an important aspect of it: if interviewees feel welcome and relaxed BW's consultants will do a better job. Corporate image is important.

(b) Location is important too, so that BW is visible and easy to find in major employment centres.

9.3 *Question 3*. We do not know enough about detailed working conditions, but sources of stress might include:

(a) The competitiveness between consultants in each office.
(b) Willard Mann's proposals for change.

Chapter roundup

- Although general in scope, good practice in employment is outlined in the Social Chapter.
- **Exit** from employment takes several forms, voluntary and involuntary. Employees have certain rights and can sue for **unfair dismissal**. A standard **disciplinary scheme** is both fair to the employee and provides evidence that dismissals are not made lightly.
- There are precise rules for **redundancy** and **consultation** is sometimes required. However, selection for redundancy should be taken with the firm's human resources policies in mind.
- **Discrimination of certain types** is illegal on grounds of:
    - **Sex** (including sexual harassment) and marital status
    - Colour, race, nationality and ethnic or national origin
    - Disability
    - Spent convictions
- Employers should note the implications of the Acts for both:
    - **Direct discrimination** - less favourable treatment of a protected group; and
    - **Indirect discrimination** - when requirements or conditions cannot be justified on non-racial grounds and work to the detriment of a protected group.
- Specific legislation (Equal Pay Act 1970) covers the offer of equal pay to a woman as to a man for work for equal and/or similar work.
- The maintenance of health and safety at work is both a moral duty and a legal requirement. Both employers and employees have legal obligations in this respect.
- The main legislation is the **Health and Safety at Work Act**. It has been supplemented by **EU directives**.
- Accidents are costly in terms of lost production, compensation etc. **Accident reporting systems** are necessary to record accidents and to note what action was taken as a result.
- In health and safety matters, **management** can set a good **example**. They can install equipment and institute procedures which encourage safe working.
- The work environment can affect productivity. Good **ergonomics** can reduce discomfort by structuring the work environment and equipment to the demands of human biology.
- The work environment also relates to the extent that individual employees suffer stress - some **stress** can be beneficial: too much can be harmful. Stress arises out of the role, insecurity, personality and management style.

Quick quiz

1. What is the scope of the Social Chapter? (see para 1.2)
2. What is contained in an employment contract? (2.1)
3. How is it changing? (2.10)
4. What procedures should be carried out when an employee resigns from the organisation? (3.4)
5. In what circumstances is an employee 'dismissed' in the sense used in employment protection law? (3.6)
6. What reasons may an employer rely on in seeking to show that a dismissal was fair? (3.9)
7. Suggest some stages of a disciplinary procedure. (3.15)
8. What is meant by redundancy? (3.20)
9. Is positive discrimination permitted under UK law? (5.6)
10. List five possible measures that might support an equal opportunities policy in an organisation. (5.14, 5.15)
11. What is 'sexual harassment'? (5.16)
12. What is the importance of health and safety policies? (6.1)
13. What are employers' duties under health and safety legislation? (6.3 - 6.5)
14. What are common causes of injury at the work place? (6.11)
15. What are the costs of accidents? (6.12)
16. What is the effect of the work environment on performance? (7.2)
17. Describe some types of office layout. (7.5)
18. What is ergonomics? (7.8)
19. What are the causes of stress at work? (8.4)

Question to try	Level	Marks	Time
26	Exam standard	25	45 mins

Question 27 is a 50-mark case study covering many areas of the syllabus. Try it to see how well you have consolidated what you have learned.

Exam question bank

Questions with mark allocations are in the style of full examination questions

1 MEMO ON BUSINESS PLANNING *30 mins*

You are Director of Administration in a functionally organised, £10 million per annum turnover, one product organisation and you have been asked to organise its first business planning exercise.

Write a memorandum for your chief executive outlining the topics which should be covered in the business planning process, and advising him/her on the issue of who should be included in the business planning team.

2 EMPIRE CHEMICALS (25 marks) *45 mins*

> *Tutorial note.* The date in this case is based on the experience of ICI; however, names and certain key details have been changed. You should concentrate on the data in the case study itself, rather than ICI's subsequent history. Remember that Empire Chemicals is a fictitious company, although based on a real one.

Empire Chemicals is one of the UK's largest companies with several divisions including paints, pharmaceuticals, bulk chemicals, and agrochemicals such as fertiliser. The various businesses have different operating and financial interests. The company was formed after World War 1, when several British firms merged in order to compete with large, German chemicals companies.

Empire Chemicals detected three years ago that the financial performance of its paints business was deteriorating. Profits were steady, but its return on capital was falling.

Mr Matthew Black, the main board director responsible for paints, reacted quickly to cut costs. The reward has been that in the declining markets of 1990 and 1991, when sales volumes have fallen six per cent in both periods, profits of the division have been rising, albeit modestly.

Unfortunately, not all the divisions had such foresight. Empire's total profits are falling sharply. Mr Scott Wallace, a chemical industry analyst, says that Empire neglected to keep its costs under control in the buoyant conditions of the late eighties. The worldwide workforce was cut by 50,000 to 175,000 between 1980 and 1985. Mr Wallace says that after the retirement of charismatic chairman, Sir Denis Mack Smith, Empire relaxed its attack on costs.

The impact of the recession on Empire Chemicals was worse than for it rivals, because so many of its operations were bases in the high-inflation economy of the UK. Its labour costs increased more significantly than did the labour costs of USA competitors between 1987 and 1990. Damage was compounded because Empire was surprised by the speed of economic decline. 20,000 jobs are likely to go from the current total of 132,000.

Management controls are 'relatively undisciplined'. This is the legacy of a complicated management structure, which divided financial responsibilities confusingly between territorial and business managers.

Sir Denis Mack Smith created Empire's first globally organised businesses - first a world-wide pharmaceuticals operation and then, in 1984, a global agrochemical division. An increasing number of Empire's operations were set up to operate on an international basis, to meet the trans-national requirements of so many of its clients. However, Sir Denis did not streamline the organisation completely. A parallel power structure, based on geography rather than products, has been kept in place. Up to the end of 1990, considerable responsibility was given to the chief executives of four national companies - in the US, Canada, Australia and India - and another five executives with responsibility for other regions. Any multi-national company must be sensitive to differing requirements of customers and governments in different countries, but there is duplication of accounting and reporting.

A particular danger is that, after a long period of growth, neither the regional executive nor the divisional chief executive want to deliver gloomy news to head office. The autonomy of divisional heads is considerable. Mr Privet, for example, has authority to make capital investments of up to £10m without referring back to the main board. Because Empire is ahead of the pack in running divisions on a global basis, analysts believe that it must be careful not to neglect the differing needs of European, Japanese and US purchasers.

A director points out that only 20% of Empire's business is purely domestic, but the Chairman and main board executives spend a disproportionate amount of time on UK matters. This is partly due to Empire's history as the great British chemical company and to the location of its headquarters, which contains a disproportionate number of staff working on UK issues, by the River Thames. They are in close proximity to the main board and therefore find it easy to attract their attention.

Empire itself has long considered itself virtually bid-proof. It is one of the UK's biggest employers with 53,700 employees in Britain and it spends some 70% of its £679m R & D budget at home. However Cobb Holdings plc has purchased a stake with a view to a takeover.

Despite years of efforts by Empire to refashion itself, which did make it more international and produced a gush of profits when times were good, the company is still spread thinly across an array of separate products and markets ranging from research-intensive products to PVC (which goes to make plastic buckets). Empire has many products, in many different markets. In such a span there are few, if any, synergies.

The company's embattled chairman, Sir Henry Sanderson has had to eat his words about the company being recession-proof. 'When I suggested that I saw no return to the dark days of recession, I was clearly wrong,' he acknowledges.

Clearly, much strategic thinking and acting is required in order to ensure that Empire continues to achieve its group mission and purpose, which is as follows.

'The chemical industry is a major force for the improvement of the quality of life across the world. Empire aims to be the world's leading chemical company, serving customers internationally through the innovative and responsible application of chemistry and related sciences.

Through achievement of our aim, we will enhance the wealth and well-being of our shareholders, our employees, our customers and the communities which we serve and in which we operate. We will do this by:

- Seeking consistent profitable growth
- Providing challenge and opportunity for our employees releasing their skills and creativity
- Achieving a standard of quality and service internationally which our customers recognise as being consistently better then that of any of our competitors
- Operating safely and in harmony with the global environment.'

Required

To what extent do you think strategic planning has succeeded or failed at Empire Chemicals?

3 PLANNING FOR THE FUTURE *30 mins*

Senior management needs to ensure that the organisation responds to changes in the external environment. This can only be achieved by corporate planning.

Discuss.

4 INFORMATION SYSTEMS STRATEGY *30 mins*

Tutorial note. This question asks about IS strategies in general and then applies it to a specific firm.

(a) Many major organisations use formal strategies to identify development priorities for information systems (IS). Discuss the reason for this.

(b) Wimp plc is a USM company. Seven years ago, when the company was still private and employed 50 people, it did not use computers at all. Now, employing 250 people in six different locations, it uses 60 microcomputers, for diverse uses ranging from financial accounts, payroll and stock records to forecasting and financial modelling, budgeting, cash management, statistical analysis, customer analysis, management accounts, personnel records and marketing planning. The use of computers has been built up in a piecemeal fashion, with extra microcomputers being purchased (currently at an average cost of £5,000 with peripheral equipment) as the need has arisen. The company's financial director has often argued in the past that his staff were not using computer technology to its full potential. Two problems which particularly concerned him were:

   (i) the time wasted by computer users, who often had to wait for responses from the computer before they could carry on with their next task;

   (ii) computer users could only do one thing at a time with their computer, when individuals should be quite capable of keeping several tasks on the go at the same time.

The financial director has now made a proposal which he believes would radically improve computer working in his department. He has obtained details of the new range of personal computers. Although they are much more expensive than the current, ageing office PCs currently in use, they provide the advantage of high-speed working with multi-tasking facilities, so that they can carry on several tasks quickly and simultaneously. They can also be linked into networks of other computers, and provide multi-access facilities. He would therefore like to scrap all the 24 PCs currently in use in his department and replace them with about 15 of the new machines. The financial director's proposal has brought his fellow-directors to the realisation that the company has no clear strategy for its acquisition and use of computers, but that it perhaps ought to have one. You have therefore been asked, as management accountant, to make some suggestions to the board on this matter.

For what reasons might it be appropriate for Wimp plc to have an information technology strategy?

5 MISSION STATEMENTS *30 mins*

The managing director of TDM plc has recently returned from a conference entitled 'Strategic planning beyond the '90s'. Whilst at the conference, she attended a session on Corporate Mission Statements. She found the session very interesting but it was rather short. She now has some questions for the accountant.

'What does corporate mission mean? I don't see how it fits in with our strategic planning processes.'

'Where does our mission come from and what areas of corporate life should it cover?'

'Even if we were to develop one of these mission statements, what benefits would the company get from it?'

You are required to prepare a memorandum which answers the managing director's questions.

6 STRATEGIC PLAN FOR CHANGED ENVIRONMENT (25 marks) *45 mins*

BG plc is a defence contractor faced with a changing environment. In the past, all the work done by BG plc was for its own National Government, and it was performed on a 'cost-plus' basis. That is, BG plc was paid on the basis of its costs, plus a profit percentage. The company was exposed to minimal competition.

The existing government believes that the 'cost-plus' system encouraged inefficiency. In the future, BG plc will be require to quote fixed prices for government business. Government defence contracts are being increasingly given to BG plc's foreign competitors, who have been undercutting BG plc's prices. In addition, BG plc is faced with a general contraction of defence expenditure by its home government.

BG plc's existing costing system is aggregated, that is, all overheads are recovered on direct labour cost. BG plc has to have confidence in its costs, in order to get the government orders at an economic price, and to compete internationally.

You are required to state:

(a) what factors would influence BG plc when it formulates a strategic plan to meet the new situation; (12 marks)

(b) what strategic responses are available to BG plc in the new environment; (13 marks)

7 FIREBRIDGE TYRES LTD (25 marks) *45 mins*

Firebridge Tyres Ltd (FTL) is a wholly owned UK subsidiary of Gonzales Tyre Corporation (GTC) of the USA. FTL manufactures and sells tyres under a number of different brand names:

(a) Firespeed, offering high product quality, at a price which offers good value for money;
(b) Freeway, a cheap brand, effectively a standard tyre;
(c) Tufload, for lorries and commercial vehicles.

FTL has good relationships with car firms and distributors.

GTC is rather less focused; not only does it make tyres and some other components, but it also owns a chain of car service centres specialising in minor maintenance matters such as tyre replacement, exhaust fitting, and wheel balancing.

FTL has experienced a fall in sales revenue, partly as a result of competition from overseas producers, in what is effectively a mature market. Moreover, sales of new cars have not been as high as had been hoped, and consumers are more reluctant than before to part with their money.

FTL's managers have had meetings with GTC's managers as to how to revive the fortunes of the company. FTL would like to export to the US and to Asia. GTC has vetoed this suggestion, as FTL's tyres would compete with GTC's. Instead, GTC suggests that FTL imitate GTC's strategy by running a chain of service stations similar to GTC's service stations in the US. GTC feels that vertical integration would offer profits in its own right and provide a distribution network which would reduce the impact of competition from other tyre manufacturers. GTC has no shortage of cash.

You are a strategic consultant to FTL.

Required

(a) What are the principal factors in the external environmental that would influence FTL's strategic choice? (8 marks)

(b) Describe the barriers to entry that FTL might face if it decided to enter the service centre business. (7 marks)

(c) Can FTL's distinctive competences satisfy the critical success factors of the service business? (10 marks)

8 ZETON LTD (25 marks) *45 mins*

Zeton Ltd is an engineering company based in Kuala Lumpur in Malaysia. It has been established for nearly sixty years. The company originally began by supplying components for small machines and war equipment during the second world war. However, since the early seventies it underwent rapid transformation under the founder's son, Tommy Lee. Tommy Lee has diversified the company into supplying automobile components and machine tools to the Malaysian market. The company now employs some 1,000 staff around the city and is well known for the quality of its workmanship. The company operates under three divisions. One division is concerned with the manufacture of automobile parts, a second division with machine tools and a third small division undertakes specific one-off work in engineering and engineering design. The automobile section is by far the biggest and accounts for seventy per cent of the total turnover. The smaller specialist engineering design section is by far the most profitable in terms of the capital employed and it relies a great deal on a senior engineer, Chow Fung, who has been with the company for twenty years.

Recently, the company was invited to send sample component supplies to a German car manufacturer who was keen to set up in Malaysia. These components were needed in eight months' time. However, Mr Lee was concerned that his company may not be able to meet the strict standard imposed by the Germans. The deal would also make sure that 'Zeton Ltd' became known in the west as an important auto component supplier, thus opening up the potential for exports. Lee realised that the export potential was great and that any initiatives would get full backing from the Government. While this was happening, the machine tools division was also showing signs of growth. Recent reforms in Eastern Europe meant that companies in that area were very keen to modernise and develop their old manufacturing bases. Zeton had received enquiries from this area.

Tommy Lee faced a dilemma. He knew that the opportunities that had presented themselves would establish the company on a world wide footing. At the same time he knew that the company was solely under his management as chief executive. Tommy Lee held eighty per cent of the shares. The other directors held ten per cent each. Although the other divisions had managing directors, they relied on him for decision making. The current managing directors were drawn from family members. One was a brother in law and the other a cousin. Their knowledge of the industry and the workings was generally poor. He made these appointments to please his father so that he could be left to run the company as he saw fit. Tommy knew that in order to satisfy the German auto manufacturer he needed to reorganise that division and consider issues of total quality management. His time would be taken up. He needed to delegate to the divisions, but felt uncomfortable in doing this.

The company was at a crossroads. The three divisions were doing well, and potentially could do even better. The systems driving these divisions were old, bureaucratic, and hierarchical. Some of the younger managers and engineers would prefer a more open flexible management structure. Some of them had studied both engineering and management in the UK and the USA and were keen to see changes happening. He knew that these opportunities could not be missed, but how was he going to ensure that they were handled successfully so that the future for Zeton Ltd was even brighter? He knew that he needed to make some harsh decisions and restructure the company within the next few months. He still had time.

Required

(a) What are the key issues facing Zeton Ltd? Give justifications for your priorities. (15 marks)

(b) How should Mr Lee restructure his company, and what leadership skills will he need to exhibit? (10 marks)

9 R PLC: COMPETITIVE USE OF IT (25 marks) *45 mins*

R plc is a large public manufacturing company, which sells its products directly to industrial companies throughout Europe. It manufactures approximately a dozen different products. The products are all based on a similar technology. They range from low-price, high-volume products characterised as 'commodities', to specialised products produced in relatively small quantities and used by high-technology companies. Nearly all R plc's customers will buy several of the products, and use them in their manufacturing processes. The products are bulky: at the cheaper end of the range, transport costs become significant.

Each product is manufactured in a process designed specifically for that product. Raw material represents 75% of the cost of the product. Products are initially produced in bulk, and subsequently cut up to meet customers' orders. Eliminating waste by scheduling the cutting operations to minimise unusable offcuts is one of the keys to success. This requires daily, routine but complex decisions by production management.

Due to the high capital cost of such plants, high capacity utilisation is required for breakeven. The specialised products tend to be made in one plant serving the whole of Europe. Higher volume, lower priced products are produced in more than one plant, located to minimise transport costs. Each plant is at present regarded as an investment centre, although there may be several plants on one site.

Each plant has its own team of management accountants. Copies of all the information they produce are sent to the head office in London, and redistributed to other units. Each plant also has personnel services, maintenance services, and laboratories for quality control.

The marketing function is structured by product. For each product, there is a sales force, consisting of sufficient salespersons, well trained in the technical properties of that product, to visit customers about once a month. Their task is to maximise sales: they gain information on customers' future requirements for both quantity and quality, gain information on competing products, and deal with problems and queries on existing orders.

Only the finance, corporate planning and legal departments are at the head office.

Product and process development is centralised on a product basis, but the facilities and staff are located at one of the production units.

The political changes in eastern Europe have opened up a tremendous opportunity for R plc, as the market potential for its product range is enormous, while few of the products are currently manufactured in eastern Europe. A decision has therefore been taken to increase manufacturing capacity by 10% in each of the next five years. This will require the building of several new plants. The finance director has asked the management accountants to ensure that reporting and control systems are adequate for the planned expansion. The corporate planning department is looking into expanding the planning process accordingly.

Several issues face the chief executive.

(a) Customers regularly complain of being visited by several of R plc's salespersons, each dealing with one product only, whereas many customers may use six or more products. This is particularly irritating if there are queries to be sorted out on one product and a salesperson for another product calls, and is unwilling or unable to help. Some competing companies in the industry have organised their marketing on a customer basis. The complaining customers point out that when representatives of these competitors call, they can deal with matters put to them on any product.

(b) Inefficiencies in the cutting operations, because local managers are not aware of orders in other parts of the company which they could accommodate.

(c) Unnecessary costs are incurred because of the time taken for purchasing officers to become aware of changes in raw material availability and cost. There is also doubt about raw material stock levels and capital tied up in work-in-progress. These seem to vary considerably between similar plants.

(d) Orders are sometimes lost because delivery times from a particular plant are too long, although other plants may have spare capacity for the same product.

(e) Other orders are lost because of the time taken to assess the implications of changed technological specifications by the customer, and implementing such changes.

(f) How to ensure that R plc is able to react quickly to changes in the environment in which it operates.

Required

Advise the chief executive how information technology may be used to gain competitive advantage for R plc if the expansion plans are implemented.

10 WONDERHORSE (50 marks) *90 mins*

Wonderhorse Foods Ltd (WFL) is a fast-growing firm that grew out of the food processing and biotechnology industries. It specialises in new types of foods. The firm has three main activities:

(a) research and development of the 'pharmafood' concept and providing consultancy advice;

(b) manufacture of foods to be sold under supermarkets' own label brands, incorporating pharmafood technology;

(c) manufacture and promotion of its own brands.

The concept of 'pharmafoods' has become an obsession of the co-founder and current chairman, Casey Johns. Pharmafoods are foods manufactured to imitate fatty and sugary junk foods, but, in the manner of artificial sugars, are made of harmless substitutes for these substances. Pharmafoods acquire their nutritional value by having added vitamins, amino acids and other chemicals. Many supermarkets, food manufacturing companies and fast food chains are interested in Wonderhorse's expertise. Although supermarket executives judge that the public is not quite ready for foods which are entirely artificial, they are interested in incorporating some of Wonderhorse's discoveries in existing products. 'Our goal,' says Casey Johns, 'is to enable consumers to consume nothing but twenty burgers and strawberry milkshakes each day for the rest of their lives without increasing their chances of coronary heart disease or stomach cancer. Take the junk out of junk food and add nutrition instead.'

The research side of the business has been successful, with consulting fees providing large one-off cash sums, although these cannot be easily predicted, and patent royalties which provide a steady stream of income.

The food processing side of the business has also been successful and the firm has been deluged with orders for supermarket-brand products, so much so that sales of its own product have begun to suffer slightly, despite increasingly heavy marketing costs. Food processing is inevitably a lower margin business than the consultancy work, but future profits should be generated by high sales volume. Some statistics are provided below.

	19X5	*19X6*	*19X7*
	£'000	£'000	£'000
Fixed assets	1,000	1,250	1,750
Current assets	700	800	850
Current liabilities	500	800	600
Net current assets	1,200	1,250	2,000
Long term loan (8%pa)	n/a	n/a	500
Net assets	1,200	1,250	1,500

	19X5	19X6	19X7
Consultancy revenue	350	200	500
Patent royalties	120	130	140
Total revenue (R&D and consulting)	470	330	640
Profit	141	99	192
(%)	(30%)	(30%)	(30%)
Revenue: supermarket brands	700	750	800
Profit	70	70	72
(%)	(10%)	(9.3%)	(9%)
Revenue: Wonderhorse's brands	400	500	600
Profit	35	40	45
(%)	(8.75%)	(8%)	(7.5%)

Fixed assets consist of the factory, new research sites and equipment. The company takes advantage of SSAP 13 by capitalising some of its research and development expenditure. Capitalised R and D expenditure amounts to £100,000.

The long term loan was taken out as an existing shareholder, a venture capitalist firm, was not willing to increase its exposure unless the firm's founder-directors sold some of their shareholdings.

Principal shareholdings are as follows.

Venture capitalist	40%
Casey Jones, co-founder	30%
Lorna Ranger (in charge of food manufacture)	15%
Alan Quatermass (research and consultancy)	15%

The directors collectively have a rather confused view about how the business is going to go. Casey Johns does have a vision for pharmafoods, which he sees as the food of the future. How this translates into commercial strategy is harder to assess. Both the research and the food manufacturing arm can eat up resources. Naturally, the two directors dealing with those areas have different views as to which they should develop.

Alan Quatermass feels that as the consulting side of the business is the most profitable, the firm should devote all its resources to this side of the business.

Lorna Ranger begs to differ. She argues that eventually the competitors will find ways of imitating the technology once there is a market for it, and that Wonderhorse should develop a distinctive competence not only in design but in manufacture. After all, she says, patents expire in the end. Also, she feels that the manufacturing side will produce a steady inflow of cash. Whilst patent income is also steady, the consultancy fees are too unreliable to keep the venture capitalist happy.

A problem with the food manufacturing arm is its size. The firm aggressively markets itself to supermarkets, but then finds that supermarkets' own brands take away sales of Wonderhorse's own products. Lorna is also concerned, that if the consultancy side gives away too much of the firm's knowledge, the firm's expertise in manufacture will no longer be a source of competitive advantage. However, Wonderhorse is small, and depends on the supermarkets to promote its products. Although profit margins are lower on Wonderhorse's brands than on the supermarket brands, this reflects the fact that supermarket brands do not have to be promoted by Wonderhorse. She feels that increasing the advertising expenditure for Wonderhorse's brands would increase sales by generating public awareness. The increased revenue would cover the costs. Alan Quatermass feels that the manufacturing strategy is fundamentally misconceived: he feels the firm will be at the mercy of supermarkets, and will never be big enough to have real clout.

Casey Johns and the other two founders have invested a great of time and their personal savings in the business. The venture capitalist firm is prepared to take a fairly long term view, but will want to realise its investment in five years time: effectively this means a stock market listing, unless the three directors can find the cash themselves. The evidence suggests that this is not the case.

Required

You have been hired as a management consultant to advise the management team on Wonderhorse's strategic direction.

(a) What other information do you need to conduct an objective assessment of the firm's current situation and future prospects? (12 marks)

(b) Using any analytical tools you feel appropriate, write a report to the shareholders:

(i) assessing the current state of affairs;
(ii) identifying possible strategic options for Wonderhorse;
(iii) suggesting the most suitable strategic option. (38 marks)

11 PAVAN AND GALLIARD (50 marks) *90 mins*

Pavan and Galliard Ltd (PG) is a small but growing chain of shops. From its twelve premises, PG sells jewellery, decorative ornaments and other items, all of which are replicas of designs available in previous centuries. The firm also has a substantial mail-order business, winning orders for its 'heritage' products from the USA and also Japan.

Henry Lawes, managing director and majority shareholder, has until now seen PG primarily as a retailer. However, its relationship with its suppliers is very close. PG employs a number of designers and researchers who draw up product specifications and blueprints. Manufacture is subcontracted to a number of specialist jewellery, metal-work, leather-work and textile firms, as well as individual craftspeople for high value items.

In addition to the main business, PG also arranges for the manufacture of jewellery and accessories for other high street shops. These products do not of course compete with PG's product range, but PG's contacts and reputation amongst its suppliers are helped by this. PG makes a profit of about 10% on this service.

In its head office, PG employs five full-time designers, and a three-person accounts department headed by finance director, Bill Byrd. Each of the twenty shops has a full time manager, and between three and five part-time staff. Henry Lawes likes the informal atmosphere which 'allows us to feel like a family; it's amazing how we all get on. I haven't really thought about what our mission is, but I suppose it is to be *the best in the business*'. Henry deals with the suppliers himself.

Up until now, PG has no real competitors, although similar products are sold on site and by mail order by the National Trust, the British Museum and the Victoria and Albert Museum. Henry has noted that a number of department stores in London have recently begun to sell similar 'heritage' jewellery, under the brand name 'Arcadia'.

For some time, Henry has wanted more control over the manufacturing process. He has heard rumours that the Arcadia range is being produced by one of his subcontractors, John Dowland Jewels (JDJ). When Henry challenges John Dowland (the managing director of JDJ) about this, John replies that he has no alternative in the current climate, but that if PG wishes to buy his business, he will be open to offers. JDJ employs about 100 people. Its machinery is old but still serviceable. A long term agreement with the union is shortly up for renegotiation at the moment. The firm's procedures are in a large looseleaf file, nicknamed 'the book of knowledge'; JDJ is not very profitable currently, but Henry believes this can be improved by making JDJ more efficient. At the moment, 10% of JDJ's turnover comes from PG.

Henry decides to take the opportunity to buy JDJ. He believes it will profitable, and will give him more control over his business's value chain. He will redirect some of the work he subcontracts elsewhere to JDJ.

After negotiations, Henry has agreed to buy JDJ for four times its current level of profits. 50% will be paid on the takeover, the remainder in equal annual instalments over five years. The initial sum will be financed entirely by five-year loan secured on the assets of the company, repayable in equal annual instalments over the life of the loan. The loan repayments and the second tranche of the purchase price will be paid out of the group's cash flows.

Summary financial data is provided below, comparing PG, JDJ as currently run, and what Henry Lawes believes, with the agreement of John Dowland, JDJ could be achieving at the moment if it was better run.

	PG	*JDJ Current*	*JDJ Improved*
	£m	£m	£m
Turnover	7.0	14.0	14.0
Cost of sales	4.5	11.2	10.7
Gross profit	2.5	2.8	3.3
Expenses	1.5	2.1	1.8
Net profit	1.0	0.7	1.5

Fixed assets	1.5	9.5	8.3
Current assets	3.0	1.5	1.5
Current liabilities	0.5	1.0	0.8
Long-term liabilities	1.5	-	-
Net assets	2.5	10.0	9.0

Required

As a management consultant you have been asked for your advice.

(a) Identify and assess the risks, business and financial, of the proposed acquisition. (30 marks)

(b) Advise Henry Lawes whether he should go ahead with the acquisition, in the light of the merits and demerits of acquisition as a method of growth. (10 marks)

(c) Comment on the PG's existing mission statement and design a new one for PG only. How do you think it should change if the acquisition goes ahead? (10 marks)

12 VOYAGE OF A LIFETIME (25 marks) *45 mins*

Voyage of a Lifetime plc (VL) is a firm of travel agents, employing 1500 people in the UK and overseas. In the past, it has operated only as a broker, selling holidays run by package holiday firms. However, the managing directors have decided to go into the holiday business themselves. To avoid competing directly with some of their suppliers, VL will offer a bespoke service to customers who wish to have the flexibility that many package holidays do not have: VL will help customers design their itineraries and will do all necessary bookings as they wait. Each office will have a consultant to deal with such enquiries, and also head office will have a team of consultants to deal with enquiries over the phone and the Internet in real time.

The managing director, Julia Verne, believes that the *critical success factors* underlying this new business will be the following.

(a) The ability to charge a premium price for the service.

(b) The quality of advice offered by the newly trained consultants. They will have to be knowledgeable, experienced and adequately supported.

(c) Continued access to cheap flights, so that the service is profitable.

(d) The ability to make bookings swiftly.

(e) Efficient communications with hotels, transport providers and local agents in the destination countries.

(f) Identification of customer needs for future business.

Julia is well aware that information technology will be a major factor underpinning the success of the new project, and can also be used in the main travel agency business, which is becoming decreasingly profitable.

VL's existing information systems are these.

(a) A mainframe computer sited in head office's computer centre at head office which carries out most of the heavy-duty processing (eg booking, invoicing, payroll, cash book and treasury management, debtors and creditors ledgers). Bookings are processed in real time. Accounting information is batch processed at night.

(b) PCs at each branch, connected over leased lines to the head office mainframe deal with the bookings. Some users have been complaining about the constant delays in the system.

(c) 50% of the costs of the computer centre are charged out to each branch, by the number of bookings. Accounting and treasury processing is just written off as an overhead.

(d) Proposals for equipment and software upgrades are made every year. Most of the time, branches must submit proposals with their annual budget. If rejected in one year, they can be resubmitted to the budget committee.

(e) Information systems are the responsibility of the finance director, although for the new business a comprehensive review is proposed.

You have been employed as a management consultant to advise on the firm's use of IT.

Required

(a) What role do information systems play in VL's existing activities and how will this change in future? Support your answer with reference to appropriate frameworks. (12 marks)

(b) How will VL's information strategy need to change in line with the new strategy for the business? (*Tutorial note*. Detailed technical descriptions of the system configuration are not the subject of this part of the question.) (13 marks)

(25 marks)

13 PRESCIENCE GROUP: VOLUME AND PROFIT (25 marks) *45 mins*

John Ellison, manager of the general products department of the Prescience Group, was trying to decide on an appropriate course of action in the light of his department's failure to meet the previous quarter's targets. It seemed to John that three courses of action were open to him.

(a) He could eliminate his advertising budget for the rest of the year; or
(b) postpone two new appointments to the department; or
(c) reduce raw material purchases.

Each course of action would result in an improvement in his department's ratio of costs to sales. The direct profit would rise.

Following an earlier reorganisation of the group it had been decided to arrive at new targets for the newly created departments using a management by objectives (MBO) approach. First, departments had been encouraged to consult within themselves and individually to formulate an initial set of targets for the coming year. John had begun by asking sales representatives for their views of the year ahead and, in particular, their sales estimates. Simultaneously he requested his marketing team to forecast next year's sales using planning and market forecasting techniques. With his senior staff he considered over a period the discrepancies between the two and arrived at a consensus. The new figures were then shown to the marketing staff and field sales people who commented upon them. John made the final adjustments himself and forwarded the figures to group headquarters.

At group headquarters a problem was emerging. The forecasts from the various departments were unacceptably low in senior management's estimation. Shareholders would be disappointed, as would be the market, with the projected results. It was felt that the departments were not really stretching themselves in the pursuit of excellence. Senior managers met each of the department managers in turn and pressed, in each case, for a more positive approach.

Like most product department managers John Ellison, under pressure, revised upwards his targets for the year.

Now after the first quarter he was in a quandary. By taking any of the three actions previously mentioned he could improve his department's return on assets performance.

John was not certain as to how the group viewed performance within departments. He was unsure how the centre would react to sales targets achieved at the cost of profits or of profit ratios achieved at the cost of sales. He was aware that he was likely to be judged quarter-to-quarter while his own staff would tend to think longer term, ie looking to the year's results.

Required

(a) What are the root causes of the problem?
(b) What would you advise John Ellison to do?

14 COMPUFLEX INTERNATIONAL PLC: ORGANISATION STRUCTURE (25 marks) *45 mins*

Compuflex International plc (CI) was founded in 1980. It hoped to profit from the opportunities available in the fast growing computer industry, by providing hardware and software 'add-ons' for PCs.

In its early days, the firm had a very loose and flat organisational structure. The firm was growing quickly, and a system of project teams with interchangeable members was felt to offer the most suitable way to keep track of changes in market conditions.

CI was unusual in that it practically started life as an international company, with offices in California and London, connected by e-mail. All offices of the firm were early members of the Internet. Furthermore, a company-wide electronic 'bulletin board' was set up to enable staff from around the world to come up with ideas or comment on them. Bennet and Marvell lived in London, whereas Zeno lived near San Francisco. All three of them had responsibilities covering the whole company. One of the firm's earliest successes was the Cyclotron, patented for use on the Apple Macintosh and other machines. The patents underlying Cyclotron formed the basis of a number of related technologies, and products developed from them. The firm also provided software enhancers. For a variety of reasons, the Cyclotron was manufactured in the UK but most of the marketing effort was directed to manufacturers in California. The firm later set up a factory in the US, but also started to manufacture in Taiwan to serve markets in Asia.

The US and UK operations were formed as separate companies, without a clear reporting relationship between them. The UK facility developed markets in Europe, but also significantly contributed to the global business by supplying R and D and other support. In practice, the business units had a lot of local autonomy. This was extended to the Taiwanese operation.

The company prospered in the early 1980s. No thoughts were given to organisation structure as the senior managers were too busy focusing on different investment projects.

However, in 1985, the current loose operation was showing signs of strain, and there were problems co-ordinating activities at higher levels. A central secretariat was set up, with a small corporate staff. Formal roles were assigned to the founders. Bennet took care of special projects, but as Chairman became responsible for overall co-ordination. Zeno's job had a marketing focus. An executive committee was set up, and now includes the three founders and the most senior manager from each of the firm's three regions. The executive committee meets every two months, with meetings lasting over several days. Decisions are not always taken at this meeting, but employees and managers receive details any which have been made at regular meetings held in each area. The executive committee therefore provides the overall direction of the company.

Despite the new central secretariat and the executive committee, the firm is effectively decentralised to the three business areas (California and the US, the UK and Europe, and Taiwan and Asia). However, elements of a matrix approach were introduced in that some managers were supposed to co-ordinate and provide leadership for global functions; for example the regional manager for the US was supposed to look after CI's human resources management policy.

Functional heads from each site met every year to co-ordinate policies and activities. At one such meeting, encouraged by Marvell, the functional heads for finance agreed to generate a budget for CI as a whole, whereas previously none had existed.

As well as the executive committee and functional meetings, other co-ordination mechanisms were employed. *Project teams* were selected from various business functions and areas to oversee and manage the development of new products, from initial development to mass production. *Product management teams* were also developed, to keep an eye on the market for particular products, to assess competitors, to prepare (and translate) manuals, and to arrange advertising.

In 1991, the company conducted another review of its organisation structure. A number of criticisms were made. Most notably, even the founders realised that a company the size of CI, which now had over 1,500 employees spread over the world could not work as efficiently as one which had only 20 employees. The managers of functional heads in each region were not sure who they should report to: their immediate regional manager or the manager with global responsibilities for that function. Furthermore, there had been problems in ensuring consistency of approach and standards in the various project teams. Purchasing and procurement were also problematic. As computers fall in price, manufacturers and assemblers are driving harder bargains, and executive committee has suggested that savings on procurement can help save costs. At present, subcomponent purchasing decisions are made by local managers, although in practice 65% are sourced from the far east. The executive committee wishes to reduce the dependence on this area for supplies.

(a) Briefly describe the types of co-ordination found in an organisation. (8 marks)

(b) Using Mintzberg's approach, how would you say Compuflex's structural configuration has changed since its foundation? (10 marks)

(c) Discuss the possibilities for the design of formal reporting mechanisms in Compuflex. Suggest a design which you think is most appropriate and justify your choice. (*Note.* This part of the question specifically deals with the design of organisation hierarchy, not more general issues of structural configuration.) (7 marks)

15 FLEET WATER SERVICES LTD (25 marks) *45 mins*

Fleet Water Services Ltd (FWSL) has been formed by centralising a number of regional management units of *Fleet Water*, the holding company. FWSL, which provides a variety of technical services, has been formed so that Fleet Water will benefit from economies of scale. FWSL will sell its services to other companies in the water industry, firms in industries such as brewing and chemicals, and public sector organisations such as hospitals. Water is to be priced according to usage. Water firms need to introduce metering technology; user firms are seeking to manage their use of water more effectively, and FWSL is there to help them.

A major issue to be faced relates to information. FWSL requires a strategy for the use of the information resource. FWSL also needs to install new information systems to get up and running; of these, an accounting system is felt to be most urgent.

Required

(a) Outline the senior management structure and the planning process by which FWSL can develop a strategy for information. (10 marks)

(b) FWSL's managers are aware that project management techniques will need to be used in introducing new systems.

(i) What are the distinguishing characteristics of project management and how can its success be defined? (6 marks)

(ii) Describe the project management techniques which can be used to introduce new information systems to FWSL, and to minimise the risk of the project failing to meet its objectives. (9 marks)

16 ANYBOROUGH COUNCIL: REORGANISATION AND REDUNDANCY (25 marks) *45 mins*

You are a recently appointed member of the management team in the chief executive's office of Anyborough Council. Over the past few years - prior to your arrival - Anyborough has experienced radical changes in almost all of its departments and there has been some extensive upheaval. Most of the changes were badly handled and often caused bitter conflict amongst the workforce, including strikes. Relations between management and the trade unions are still extremely strained and you have noticed that a great deal of suspicion remains amongst the staff.

The one area of Anyborough Council which has not experienced much change has been the housing maintenance section. The housing maintenance section is a sub-division of the housing department. The section consists of 37 members of staff of whom five are operations supervisors looking after the skilled maintenance workers. The operations side consists of about 300 skilled building trade craftsmen and about 50 unskilled workers. The whole section is currently situated in a depot close to the centre of Anyborough. The chief executive officer, who personally 'head-hunted' you, has notified you that changes are coming to the housing maintenance section and has asked you to handle the problem. He has suggested that he wants it handled as smoothly as possible and you are therefore in overall charge of the operation. Rumours are already circulating and tension is beginning to build up. Most of the rumours are incorrect for concrete decisions are yet to be taken. There is, for example, no real appreciation as yet as to the likely effects of compulsory competitive tendering (whereby the Council are required by the government to invite tenders on a range of activities from its own departments, other local authorities and public sector companies to ensure the cost effectiveness of its services). However, the rumours are having an adverse effect on staff morale.

The following programme of tentative change is put forward from committee for consideration and is essentially what is required. It is intended that the programme will commence in six months time and will be completed thereafter in two months. You do have some margin of control over the changes although you will have to convince the housing committee of any changes to the programme that you make. The areas on which no change can be made are indicated below; the other areas are negotiable.

(a) The central depot which is currently the home of the housing maintenance section will be vacated and made available for town centre redevelopment. The decision cannot be changed.

(b) The administrative staff will move to another building, which is older and less desirable than the present premises and is situated some five miles away. This decision is final and cannot be changed. It will involve extra travelling for most employees.

(c) The operations side of the housing maintenance section will be moved to two separate sites in the centre of the council housing estates. The workforce will be divided roughly in half, as will the supervisory staff. Again this will involve extra travel for most employees.

(d) The move will involve the immediate loss of five administrative posts and the creation of three new posts under a new job category entitled 'technology assistant'. The new posts will be necessary for the introduction and maintenance of a sophisticated computer based 'management information system'.

(e) There is a strong possibility of a considerable loss of work on the operations side which may subsequently lead to redundancies. This potential loss of jobs will largely be the result of competitive tendering. This is a 'grey' area with so many interdependent factors that it is not possible to forecast its outcome with any certainty.

(f) Your budget will be increased in line with inflation as agreed at a recent Council meeting. However, the chief executive officer has already warned you that the chairman of the housing committee will seek savings in the region of 10% about half way through the year. How these economies will be made is not yet known but they must be expected to have effects upon the workforce.

(g) There is some possibility of surplus labour being absorbed in other departments of the Council. However, the problem here is one of compatible skills.

Required

(a) Make specific proposals on the immediate steps you intend taking prior to the changes commencing.

(b) Outline the manner in which you see the changes taking place and how you will handle them.

(c) What alterations to the proposals would you advise?

17 QUICK TRIP (25 marks) *45 mins*

Having successfully passed your ACCA examinations, you have moved out of accountancy and are working for McKendrick and Co, management consultants. You are a junior member of a team investigating the affairs of Conglomerated Holdings plc (CH), a firm with a number of businesses in basic industries throughout Europe.

McKendrick believes in throwing its employees in at the deep end, and you have been sent to Paris to investigate a plastics plant in the northern suburb of Sceaux. The plant has only been intermittently profitable, with a record of strikes, and a severe fine from the French government after an accident in which a small cloud of toxic chemicals was released into the atmosphere. While such management problems have been sorted out, a fundamental problems remained in bringing the plant to profit. There have been many management changes over the past three years, numerous initiatives to improve performance, the wholesale adoption and abandonment of management by objectives, TQM, empowerment and business process re-engineering. You have been sent on a quick fact finding mission, covering two days, to discover what is going wrong with the firm.

You are at London's Waterloo station waiting for the Eurostar service through the Channel Tunnel. You have just been informed of a technical hitch which will delay the journey for a while.

Required

(a) Set yourself some objectives for the visit, and indicate how you would meet them in the two days allowed to you. (18 marks)

(b) Describe the features of a written report. (7 marks)

18 THE MARKETING CONCEPT

What is the 'marketing concept'? Comment on its relationship to other business orientations.

19 COMPETING UNIVERSITY (25 marks) *45 mins*

PG is a university. It is a 'not for profit-making' organisation. PG earns its income from charging fees to its students, and these are set by central government. PG is not the only university in the market, and there are other educational institutions, whose prices are also controlled by the government. These institutions are competing with each other, as they all search for a bigger market share.

You are required:

(a) to describe the ways in which PG can compete against the other institutions; (10 marks)

(b) to describe how PG can establish the extent to which its users are satisfied with its services; (7 marks)

(c) to describe how PG could measure the effectiveness of its use of resources. (8 marks)

20 CLOCKWORK RADIO (25 marks) *45 mins*

Intertalk Ltd (IL) has invented a new sort of radio which dispenses with the need for batteries or a mains electricity supply: it is powered by clockwork. Once wound up, a small motor provides the current. The radio has to be rewound every twenty minutes.

The designer is aware that the market for the product in the industrialised world is probably limited, but he sees opportunities for the product in poorer countries, especially in areas without electricity and/or where batteries are too expensive for people to buy regularly. Indeed, he was photographed with a recently-elected head of state, who said that the clockwork radio is a marvellous tool for bringing education to isolated areas.

IL needs to plan the manufacture of the product and to decide to how it should approach its overseas markets. The firm sees significant opportunities in Africa, South Asia and Latin America. The directors are undecided whether simply to export or whether to invest in overseas facilities.

Required

(a) The marketing director supports direct investment in overseas facilities, as opposed to other entry modes. Give reasons for his view. (7 marks)

(b) What should you bear in mind if you have to decide between building a factory from scratch or acquiring a local company which already has manufacturing facilities? (9 marks)

(c) What are the disadvantages and advantages to IL of:

(i) a wholly owned subsidiary overseas?
(ii) a joint venture? (9 marks)

21 QUALITY STANDARD (25 marks) *45 mins*

Challenger Sealants plc (CS) is a firm which manufactures specialist adhesives and sealants, many of which are used in high-stress environments, such as aircraft, boats and motor vehicles. The firm also sells sealants to the motor industry and has a reputation for reliability. The company has a haphazard programme of total quality management. There is no doubt that quality has improved, although the TQM programme has not had the financial benefits that were commonly felt to accrue from its introduction.

Viking Cars for many years has been one of CS's major customers. Viking Cars is now owned by Mizoguchi Motor, a Japanese firm.

Viking Cars has received BS EN ISO 9000 (ie BS 5750) accreditation, and has introduced a number of other new management techniques.

The marketing director of CS has received a letter from the chief purchasing officer of Viking Cars. The letter says:

'As part of our policy of building long term relationships with key suppliers and reducing our total number of suppliers, we are notifying suppliers that those who wish to be considered eligible for key supplier status must have BS EN ISO 9000 (formerly BS 5750) accreditation. We regard Challenger as potentially a key supplier, but we are unable to be flexible about the BS EN ISO 9000 requirement as we ourselves are registered for it.'

CS's managing director, Mr Blond, is depressed by the letter. He feels that TQM as a whole has been oversold, and what he knows about external quality standards such as BS 5750 (now BS EN ISO 9000) suggests paying more money to yet more management consultants. As production director, you disagree.

There is no quality manager at CS.

Required

Write a report covering the following issues.

(a) Briefly suggest why might it be in Viking Cars' interests to pursue its policy of reducing the number of suppliers and forcing its suppliers to apply for BS EN ISO 9000 accreditation? (3 marks)

(b) From CS's point of view what are the advantages and disadvantages of accreditation, apart from the obvious fact that failure to obtain it will lose them a major customer? (7 marks)

(c) What is the relationship between BS EN IS0 9000 and TQM? (5 marks)

(d) Draft a plan outlining how CS can obtain accreditation. (10 marks)

22 X & Y ADVERTISING LTD: FUTURE POLICY (25 marks) *45 mins*

X & Y Advertising Ltd produce annual reports, magazines and diaries for churches, charities and other voluntary organisations. The firm offers its services free to such organisations relying on selling advertising space in these publications to meet costs and provide profits. Over the past thirty years the business has grown steadily. The sales force had increased to 60 by the early 1970s, making personal calls on customers. However, as supermarkets ousted small shopkeepers and reurbanisation expanded, direct sales opportunities fell - and it became harder to recruit sales staff. As a result it was decided to convert from direct selling to telephone sales.

With the recession of the late 1970s and early 1980s clients cut back on advertising to save money and the firm's revenue were hit hard. Additionally a strike in the printing end of the business forced up wages. Advertising rates had to be raised substantially and many customers were lost.

The firm took cost saving action. In particular the workforce was reduced from 240 to 180.

X & Y's approach to advertising is geared towards the smaller business advertising in the area in which it is located. 'Rather than having one advertisement at £1,000 we look for 20 at £50 a time.' This creates problems in handling a large number of small accounts. However it has the consolation that there is less risk involved from the point of view of bad debts. The market is looked at from a geographical point of view with local knowledge as an important factor.

Before carrying out a project the company will calculate the total cost involved. A total cost factor would be carried on the printing. The company works on a percentage basis for the advertising revenue, telephone sales cost and administration.

One of the major problems is cash flow. Telesalespersons must be paid weekly whereas the advertisement may not appear for 2-4 months. Also the company must retain sufficient finance to cover the quarterly telephone bills. In an average week the money tied up in securing business is:

	£
Wages	12,000
Telephone costs	6,000
	18,000

In addition payment from customers can take up to 20 weeks.

You are called in as a consultant to advise the company on its future policy and are given the above information.

Required

(a) (i) What are your initial views on the situation?

(ii) How would you structure your approach to this task?

(iii) If no further information was available what would you recommend to the managing director? (15 marks)

(b) It has been suggested that companies could improve the quality of their service to customers (eg delivery times and maintenance back-up) by differentiating between customer groups, and providing a different quality and level of service to each. Discuss the merits and drawbacks of this point of view. Which of Porter's generic strategies underpins it? (10 marks)

23 PERSONNEL MANAGEMENT (25 marks)

45 mins

You have recently been appointed to a management position in a high-technology enterprise that has expanded very rapidly during the last few years. You have quickly discovered that the personnel policies and procedures used in the organisation are haphazard and unsystematic. The administrative, professional, engineering and managerial staff employed by this company all seem to vary greatly in their quality and performance. The few statistics that are available to you also indicate high levels of labour turnover and employee dismissals amongst all grades of staff. You have therefore decided that the establishment of a systematic recruitment and selection policy and procedure is an urgent priority. The implementation of this policy and procedure would require the appointment of appropriate professional staff, and would involve additional administrative, clerical and information technology costs. In making the case for implementation, you should explain the financial benefits to be gained from the operation of a more effective recruitment and selection procedure. You are required to write a report to the managing director. In this report you should:

(a) describe the characteristics of such a recruitment and selection policy and procedure; (15 marks)

(b) make the case for implementing it. (10 marks)

24 DOSEY URETAULD (25 marks)

45 mins

Dosey Uretauld (DU) is a small advertising agency based in central London. The two partners, Dave Dosey and Christine Uretauld, are supported by a creative team of twenty people, seven account managers who look after key clients, a media liaison manager with two staff (who buy advertising space on TV, radio and press), seven account managers who maintain relations with clients, a two-strong accounts department and other office support of seven secretaries and administrators. The agency is known to be innovative and creative.

The partners feel that the agency is just too big to manage in an informal way. Dave took a management textbook away with him on holiday to Thailand and came back with the idea that a staff appraisal scheme should be introduced. He believes that rewards should be related to performance, and wants to use the appraisal scheme as the basis for pay rises, bonuses and other perks. Over the past six months, appraisal interviews have been fitted in somehow.

The two partners, the accountant, the media buyer, the senior account manager and one of the graphic designers are currently discussing strategy for the next year. They are reviewing the salaries budget and subject of the appraisals raised. The following points are made.

(a) Nobody knew what appraisals are for: a bland pep-talk to give people a pat on the back, or a haggling session for more money and perks.

(b) Some members of the 'creative' staff consider appraisals a complete waste of time and have said so. They say that their performance depends on how other members of the team do their work, how well they are briefed and the time they are given.

(c) The partners are rarely in the office so cannot really judge what is going on.

(d) Creative staff feel that appraisals are obviously a low priority for the partners, who fit them in at very short notice when they happen to be in the office.

(e) Some staff say nothing in the appraisal interview. Others whinge.

(f) No follow up action has taken place.

(g) Some feel that an informal system is more realistic in the context of the business.

Required

(a) Describe the role and benefits of appraisal systems. (7 marks)

(b) Describe the process of appraisal. (5 marks)

(c) How should DU manage its appraisal scheme to address the problems outlined? (13 marks)

25 DEVELOPMENT FUNDING (25 marks)

45 mins

Holmes and Watson plc is a firm which provides private security services to businesses and individuals. The managing director, Dinsdale Piranha, sees an opportunity for vast expansion once the UK government starts privatising the prison service in a big way. The company has begun to tender for various public sector contracts, such as escorting remand prisoners to court.

The jobs the firm is being asked to do are becoming bigger and more complex.

Dinsdale Piranha has a fairly uncomplicated view of employees and how they ought to be managed. Staff who do well get more money. Those who do not, leave the company. The carrot and stick is therefore the only approach to motivation that he recognises.

Faced with increased rates of defection by senior employees to competitor companies, his first response was to offer them more money, but he was dismayed to find that they merely quote these increased salaries in negotiations with the new employers. Existing staff who were not offered more were up in arms.

You are a management consultant. Dinsdale Piranha has done you a number of favours in the past and has decided to call them in. 'I don't know what's up with my managerial staff,' he complains. 'They get drowned in cash and perks, and still they want to leave; I can't even entice them with flashier company cars. I can't even recruit any really good people. The best candidates mutter some jargon about staff development. What do they expect when they start work: a nursery school?'

Your investigation of the company, its personnel practices and its human resources development function indicate that a staff development programme, comprising training and management education and a more structured career progression is exactly what the firm needs.

Required

(a) Justify the need for expenditure on a staff development programme, indicating those arguments which are most likely to satisfy Dinsdale Piranha. (10 marks)

(b) 'Human resource management is no different from personnel management.' Discuss in the light of Holmes and Watson plc. (15 marks)

26 NEW OFFICES (25 marks) *45 mins*

Anatomy and Biochemistry Books Ltd (AB) is a small medical publishing company based in Paddington, London, near St Mary's teaching hospital. AB employs eight medical editors specialising in different areas of medicine, and a studio containing a number of graphic artists - 'the cream of their profession' according to managing director Dr Christie - who do the detailed line drawings, with the help of computer graphics. The firm benefits from informal and formal contact with the hospital which is a source of photographs and new research. Most of the in-house editors were former medical students at St Mary's.

For many years, the firm produced huge textbooks, carefully illustrated with line drawings from specimens supplied by the hospital but now Dr Christie wishes to expand into producing CD-ROMs. Although manufacture of the disks will be subcontracted, Dr Christie is keen to develop the capacity for designing CD-ROM material in-house, and to this end he has taken on three former employees of Darling Candy Ltd, a book publisher which has blazed trails in developing CD-ROM publication.

The new arm requires some investment in information technology, and Dr Christie proposes moving three of the existing editorial staff to a spare room, and installing the new recruits in these vacated offices, which would be knocked together.

The reception area doubles as a stationery storage room; the receptionist actually works in the studio. The door to the office is left open permanently.

On their first day at work, the new employees are aghast. The offices they have to inhabit have no windows, apart from a small, slightly leaky skylight. The air conditioning and heating do not work properly, and existing staff wear woollen mittens and import fan heaters to keep out the cold. Some cracks in the windows have been mended with blu-tac. In one of the rooms there is the sound of an unpleasant buzz. Worse, the corridors are badly lit, and it is easy to trip over the large boxes of invoices which litter them.

As far as catering is concerned, a kettle has been supplied.

There are no signs indicating the fire exit. Tapping one of the fire extinguishers reveals that it is empty.

The new CD-ROM team will have a large amount of computer equipment to install. This will require substantial cabling, but the team are wary at laying cables on the floor. The office was built in the

1960s, well before personal computers, and there are doubts as to whether the cabling will fit under the floor.

Dr Christie notices their disquiet and has asked you, as a consultant, for your advice.

A number of new offices are being constructed on nearby sites. An architect friend of Dr Christie has suggested converting a large farmhouse deep in the countryside into offices. It should be big enough to house AB.

AB is financially solvent. It owns the freehold of the office block which it shares with three other companies.

Required

Write a report to Dr Christie:

(a) outlining the legal, safety, security and operational implications of the current office; (10 marks)

(b) suggesting remedial action; (10 marks)

(c) suggesting, and justifying as far as possible, a move to new premises. (5 marks)

27 TRAINS R US (50 marks) *90 mins*

Trains R Us Ltd (TRU) is a private company which has the contract to run railway services in North London. British Rail has been reorganised for privatisation: TRU and other operating companies like it run the trains, lease or buy carriages, engines etc; the track and signalling is maintained by Railtrack, still state-owned (at time of writing). TRU pays access charges to Railtrack to use the rail network.

TRU has the franchise to run the services for fifteen years. During that period, it will receive a guaranteed subsidy from central government to cover part of its costs. TRU will have the freedom to invest and run new services and embark upon innovative marketing campaigns. The bulk of its business is commuter traffic going in and out of central London each day.

TRU is the result of a management buyout by former British Rail managers and employees, supported by a number of venture capitalist firms and a 15 year bank loan. The guaranteed level of subsidy reduces the risk of the investment but, of course, this is no guarantee of a satisfactory return: this is the responsibility of the new team.

The buyout contract allows TRU to take over some of the assets of the line, including office buildings. Responsibility for managing the stations is split. Smaller ones are TRU's responsibility for the 15 years of the contract. The main terminus at Liverpool St is owned and run by Railtrack.

The contract is to be handed over in January 1997. The managers need all the time they can get to prepare themselves for the new challenge. A number of critical issues remain to be dealt with.

(a) Currently the firm has no independent information systems, which makes monitoring and assessing operational and financial performance very difficult to do. They rely on British Rail. New accounting systems are to be introduced, with managers involved in the budgeting process.

(b) There is public hostility to privatisation. Newspapers regularly report the problems people have obtaining accurate ticketing information from competing companies. A consumer pressure group has reported widespread overcharging on some routes. Recently, a major ticketing fraud has been reported. There is also concern that safety standards have been sacrificed in the chaos of change.

(c) Productivity has improved dramatically over the past few years. Compared to some railway systems in Europe, British Rail is financially very efficient, and is sophisticated in getting as much mileage as possible out of its ageing assets. However, the managers are convinced that with the right improvements, productivity can be significantly enhanced further, to American and Japanese levels. Inevitably, this means cutting staff, by about 20%. The workforce is highly unionised. Although the union is opposed to privatisation, it has been willing to negotiate new working practices and agree to voluntary redundancies - for a price. Working practices have been characterised by low basic pay; workers make up for this by extensive overtime.

TRU runs four routes. Two of these have new rolling stock, requiring fewer train operators than the other two.

(d) There is no marketing department. TRU will be competing over some of its routes. The managers see opportunities for joint ventures with local bus firms. Of course, the main competitor is a substitute product, the motor car. About 50% of TRU's regular customers own monthly or annual season tickets.

(e) The past few years has seen some management training in customer care on the railways. However, the managers are concerned that as a service business, higher standards of customer care must be expected, and the culture of the firm must be adjusted as a consequence. This is a particular problem as no one has on the board experience outside the industry. Also, management training has been superficial.

(f) The stations are not always manned, and they are badly lit. Anecdotal evidence suggests that many potential customers are worried about security.

The management team and organisation structure are outlined in the diagram below.

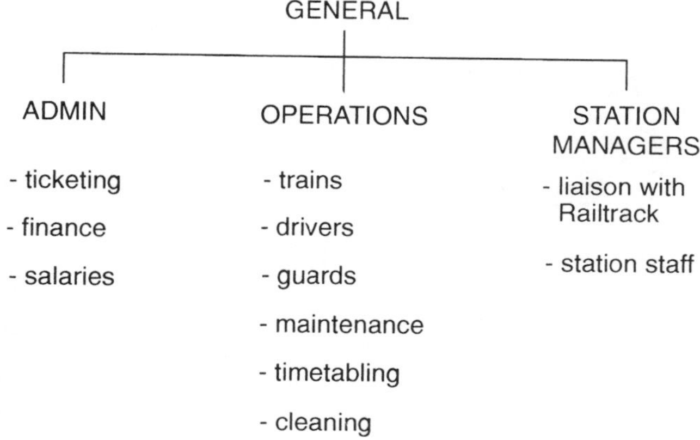

Required

(a) What strategic and operational role should be played by marketing at TRU? What problems exist in introducing a marketing orientation to the firm? (8 marks)

(b) Identify the principal task of marketing personnel at TRU, and suggest ways of incorporating them in TRU's organisation structure. (5 marks)

(c) The finance director has suggested that profit centre organisation be introduced to TRU. He proposes making each of the four routes a profit centre and each station a profit centre.

   (i) Comment critically on the finance director's suggestion. (5 marks)

   (ii) The firm intends to run a training programme for station and route managers, covering profit centre organisation, budgeting and accounting procedures. Draw up a plan indicating the aims and objectives of the training programme, how it will be delivered, and its content. (12 marks)

(d) (i) Explain why organisation culture is important to TRU and indicate the likely changes needed. Note changes to organisation configuration if you consider these relevant. (10 marks)

   (ii) What problems will there be in introducing a new culture and how can these be overcome? (10 marks)

Exam answer bank

1 **MEMO ON BUSINESS PLANNING**

To: Chief Executive
From: Director of Administration
Date: 16/2/19X4
Re: Business Planning

Rationale

To set down effective criteria for improving the business's performance through a process of planning and evaluation.

Objectives

To analyse and evaluate the company's current activity with a view to establishing an effective business plan. Further, to identify the need for involvement in the planning process of all primary managerial functions.

Content of business plans

Business planning involves developing a *strategic direction* of the business over the short (1 year), medium (2-3 years) and long terms (4-7 years). The content of the business plan is described below.

(a) The *organisation's mission*. To what extent have the firm's values changed over time and how should this be reflected in what the firm does?

(b) *Appraisal*. How are both the internal and external environments currently affecting the firm's activities?

   (i) *External*

      (1) Changing customer requirements
      (2) Impact of economic policies
      (3) Influence of competitive forces

   (ii) *Internal*

      (1) Need for staff training and development
      (2) Affect of organisational culture
      (3) Influence of organisational structure

   The environmental appraisal must evidence the use of PEST analysis as a tool of business evaluation. (Simply, what are the main political, economic, social and technical factors affecting the business?)

(c) *Environmental assumptions*. How does the firm see its own approach to what it does, in terms of its current strengths, weaknesses, opportunities and threats? Evidence of the use of SWOT analysis needs to be shown here. An example would be that the firm has expertise and experience in the one product area, yet this may also be a weakness should this product decline (thereby illustrating an opportunity to diversify into a new product or market).

(d) *The establishment of clear objectives* which should be quantified wherever possible. This information needs to be supported with details of the resources required by the organisation (human, capital and physical) to meet its objectives.

(e) The development of clear and appropriate *marketing and promotional mixes*, illustrating how the firm's product will be sold to customers.

(f) The construction of *budgets* and financial performance measures to support the activities of production and marketing and to measure the results of corporate activity.

(g) The development of a system of non-financial performance measures and controls to identify the efficiency and effectiveness of the organisation, eg productivity measurement, performance appraisal, marketing audit.

(h) The construction of a system to enable feedback and review so that market intelligence is able to flow quickly and effectively back to the organisation, enabling the firm to adjust its plans in the light of new information.

Each of the major departments needs to be involved in the business planning process, so this will mean that the senior managers of marketing, production, personnel, purchasing, accounting and research should all contribute to the business plan and oversee its implementation. At an operational level all staff need to feel that they own the strategy of the organisation; they will only be able to feel this if their departments are involved in setting business direction.

The business plan will be developed at senior level but implemented at the operational level, so to be effective all staff must know what is expected of them. This necessitates a hierarchy of objectives and delegated responsibilities so that at each level of the organisation clear performance requirements are identified and sound tactical plans implemented. Also, it is necessary to get the insight of people from a variety of sources so that an overall sense of direction can be given.

The clues to necessary adjustments to the business plan will emerge at the operating level, close to the customer so it is imperative that at this level, personnel are fully involved in both the setting and implementing of the business plan.

A failure to involve all necessary personnel will result in a loss of business direction, staff will become confused about their roles and inefficiencies will start to develop. This can only result eventually in a loss of competitive edge and a loss of customers to other businesses.

2 EMPIRE CHEMICALS

A plan is a consciously intended course of action. Many early books on business strategy supposed that strategy making was *necessarily* a planning process. Often, this involved delegating the task of strategic planning to a separate department. The strategic planning view suggests a formal, rational sequence of processes and decisions. This is highly systematised: arguably it brings a bureaucratic approach to the planning process. Mintzberg argues that while planning is good for programming or organising strategies, it is useless at generating them, in principle and in practice.

Strategic planning at Empire Chemicals

The firm's original foundation after the World War I had a competitive rationale it seems, not necessarily an economic one. Although Empire Chemicals has a large range of businesses, there is always the danger that like any conglomerate business it can lose its sense of direction.

Mission. A mission statement can define the business's values, and also what the business is. Empire Chemicals' mission defines its values, with nods towards shareholders, employees, customers and the public, but it says nothing more than this. Empire includes diverse product-market mixes such as paints, fertiliser and agrochemicals, pharmaceuticals, bulk chemicals. Each of these products has different characteristics. The synergies, between for example paints and pharmaceuticals are hard to see. However, it is probable that profits from bulk chemicals are much more volatile than, say, pharmaceuticals, which perhaps require a higher research base. The business synergies might be financial.

The question 'what business are we in?' is therefore hard to answer, other than in the most general terms. The mission statement therefore evades more than it explains.

Objectives. The mission statement describes consistency of profits as a corporate goal. Profit objectives are almost certainly set for each business, but achieving consistency is perhaps unrealistic.

Position audit, environmental analysis and SWOT analysis. Sir Henry Sanderson's statement that at one time the business had been thought of as recession-proof seems complacent. Each individual business might have conducted such analyses, but as the group operates in so many different environments, it might have been hard to conduct an analysis overall for the group as a whole. The fact that the effects of recession were not anticipated does indicate at group level at least, a failure of analysis.

Strategic choice and implementation. The overall strategic choice for the group as a whole has obviously been made. It functions largely by conglomerate diversification, like Cobb. The admittedly poor cost control, and Cobb's bid, suggests that tactical plans allow for too much corporate flab. Possible economies of scale in accounting and other overheads are avoided.

Success of strategic planning at Empire Chemicals. The only way to judge the success or failure of strategic plans is with hindsight, which is not available to the planners. There are a number of criticisms of strategic planning in general:

(a) that it precludes an opportunistic approach;
(b) that it is never possible to plan out environmental uncertainties;
(c) the planning process becomes an end in itself.

In Empire's case, these criticisms do not necessarily apply.

(a) The past history of the company suggests a freewheeling approach to entering different product-market areas. Freewheeling opportunism has perhaps seduced the company into spreading itself too thinly.

(b) The planning process failed to take the fluctuations of the business cycle into account. The existence of the business cycle is not an uncertainty, although the exact timing and severity of any down turn cannot be predicted. It is hard to see how any major environmental discontinuities have affected Empire. The bid by Cobb, however, could not be predicted. Perhaps the firm regarded itself as secure from any takeover.

(c) Arguably, there is insufficient planning. An internal appraisal would have revealed the excess costs sooner. Bad planning, rather than an excess of planning, would seem to be evident.

3 PLANNING FOR THE FUTURE

> *Tutorial note.* An interesting angle on this answer is the tension that exists between management's need to cope with short term pressures and its need to consider the future.

The rational model

The corporate planning process starts with mission and objectives. Environmental analysis, position audit (internal appraisal) SWOT analysis, strategy generation and evaluation follow on, in a logical sequence. Plans are drawn up on the basis of rational discussion and assessment and are imposed 'top down'. Strategic plans are translated into targets, and then into activity plans.

Problems with the rational planning model

(a) *Strategic plans often fail.* The environment is, or has become, more unstable. The best-laid plans can be invalidated by a new competitor, changes in technology etc. You cannot identify something as a strength until it is tested.

(b) The *information flow* from the environment is often perceived most acutely at operational level. A separate strategic planning department is perhaps less capable of picking up signals from the market then front-line employees.

(c) The model ignores the *'political'* activity within organisations, and the conflicting groups wanting power.

(d) *Detachment.* The people who design the strategy are not those responsible for its implementation. Planning thus becomes divorced from reality.

(e) A planning obsession with particular *performance indicators* can reduce managers' readiness to cope with uncertainty.

(f) *Formulation.* Planning exercises usually occur on a routine, regular basis, whereas the environment is turbulent. Strategic responses have to be made at any time.

An alternative approach: emergent strategies

Although plans fail, there are other sources of strategy: strategy can emerge, as it were, from a consistent *pattern* of behaviour.

(a) *Intended strategies* are plans. Those plans or aspects of plans which are actually realised are called *deliberate strategies.*

(b) *Emergent strategies* are those which develop out of patterns of behaviour. They do not develop from management's explicit control or from planning. The result from operational decisions and their unintended consequences exploiting sudden insights, and develop in the process of business itself, rather than as a separate planning exercise. Mintzberg holds that this is how many business strategies actually developed in practice.

The manager's role in emergent strategies

(a) Sooner or later an emergent strategy will need some conscious direction, perhaps to change its course or to stress some aspects of it over others.

(b) Some emergent strategies may have to be stopped from emerging any more.

(c) Mintzberg uses the metaphor of *crafting strategy* to reconcile management direction with emergent strategy.

(i) The idea of strategy as a craft evokes an idea of 'skill, dedication, perfection, through mastery of detail.' More importantly, forming a strategy and implementing it are 'fluid processes of learning through which creative strategies evolve'.

(ii) Mintzberg uses the image of a potter's wheel. The clay is thrown, and through shaping the clay on the wheel, the potter gives shape to the clay lump through a gradual process. Mintzberg believes this is a good analogy of how strategies are actually developed and managed. The trouble with the long feedback loop is that there is a separation between 'thinking' and 'doing' when it comes to strategy. This has the following result.

(1) A purely deliberate strategy prevents learning (once the formulators have stopped formulating). For example it is hard with deliberate strategies to 'learn from mistakes', or stumble by accident into strategic growth.

(2) A purely emergent strategy defies control. It may in fact be a bad strategy, dysfunctional for the organisation's future health.

(d) Mintzberg mentions the following essential activities in crafting strategies.

(i) Managing stability
(ii) Detecting discontinuity
(iii) Knowing the business
(iv) Managing patterns
(v) Reconciling change and continuity

Planning processes may be relevant to these activities, but Mintzberg doubts whether planning can *create* effective strategies.

4 INFORMATION SYSTEMS STRATEGY

(a) *Reasons for having a formal IS strategy*

Information is now regarded by many organisations as something more than a useful by-product of commercial data processing. Instead, it is seen as a resource of an organisation, like the organisation's pool of human skills, fixed assets, goodwill and so forth. Planning in all these areas is widely regarded as desirable, so that an organisation can adapt to a changing environment.

As information is so critical to an organisation's success, then the provision of information must be an important organisational activity. Just as many organisations have a long-term plan covering sales and markets, production and so forth, so too a long-term plan is needed for information provision.

An organisation's financial investment in information technology is also substantial, especially with the proliferation of computing power around different departments. Moreover, information technology covers areas of management which previously would have been distinct: high volume data processing (a computer department); telecommunications (which may have been a general administrative function); office administration (as microcomputers are bought to replace dedicated word processors, which were themselves purchased to replace typewriters). Many organisations report dissatisfaction with the outcomes of their investments. Some overall direction is therefore required.

A long-term plan, concentrating on the overall performance of the system, stating long-term objectives and goals, and outlining the measures to achieve them, is sometimes called a strategy. Strategies are articulated differently in different organisations. In some circumstances, the organisation's very survival in a hostile economic climate is the long-term goal. The strategy contains the measures to achieve it. In other organisations the goal might be growth in market share. Mission statements are sometimes used to encapsulate an organisation's long-term goals, but these are often too vague or obscure to be anything more than motivational platitudes.

Because information technology is pervasive throughout the business, and can significantly affect the relationship an organisation has with its customers, the IT strategy should be developed within the overall corporate plan. Not only does IT have to compete with other investments (eg other fixed assets) or expenditure programs for resources, but also implementing IT can be very disruptive. Moreover, with the growth of end-user computing, it is important that there is at least some central direction to ensure that the IT resources are used to the best advantage of the organisation. This will not be the case if the organisation is plagued with incompatible hardware and/or software.

A strategy for information systems will therefore be part of the overall organisational strategy and will be geared to meeting organisational objectives. Equally significantly, it demonstrates the importance of IT to senior management and their commitment to it. Finally, it has the function of laying down the plan for managing IT in terms of technical standards and organisational responsibilities.

(b) Why WIMP should have an IS strategy

(i) The total investment in computer equipment is already somewhere up to 60 x £5,000 = £300,000, and in all probability it is still increasing. This is likely to be a large investment for a USM company, and the company ought to have a clear strategy for such a large capital investment.

(ii) Computers should either enable their users to carry out more activities - ie be more effective in their work - or to carry out work more quickly - ie be more efficient. The benefits of greater effectiveness or efficiency should be monitored, and further computerisation ought to be planned if the benefits would justify the costs. In order to establish a procedure for planning computerisation and monitoring its benefits, the company ought to establish a strategy for computerisation within its corporate plan.

(iii) There ought to be guidelines for the useful operational life of computer equipment. The finance director is proposing to scrap 24 existing machines which may or may not have been in operation for a 'commercial' period of time.

(iv) Computer technology is continually changing. The finance director wants to buy the new series of IBM personal computers, but other developments in recent years have been local area networks, multi-access systems for microcomputers, improved off-the-shelf software, and other data transmission services such as facsimile. Technology is likely to continue to develop and improve, and any company which makes extensive use of computers ought to keep developments under review as part of its routine strategic appraisals.

(v) The value of information should be recognised and the company ought to assess the strategic value of having wider access to information, more information on file for accessing, and a common database for all information users.

5 MISSION STATEMENTS

To: Managing Director
From: Anne Accountant
Date: 29 February 19X1
Subject: Mission Statements

Contents: Introduction
Mission statement and strategic planning
Originating a mission statement
The scope of mission statements
The benefits of mission statements

Introduction

A *mission* can be defined as a business's basic function in society. It is often visionary, open-ended and has no time limit for achievement. It is possible however to reach a more expanded definition of mission to include four elements.

(a) *Purpose*. Why does the company exist, or why do its managers and employees feel it exists?

(i) To create wealth for shareholders, who take priority over all other stakeholders.

(ii) To satisfy the needs of all stakeholders (including employees, society at large, for example).

(iii) To reach some higher goal and objective ('the advancement of society' and so forth).

(b) *Strategy*. This provides the commercial logic for the company, and so defines:

(i) the business the company is in;
(ii) the competence and competitive advantages by which it hopes to prosper.

(c) *Policies and standards of behaviour*. Policies and strategy need to be converted into everyday performance. For example, a service industry that wished to be the best in its market must aim for standards of service, in all its operations, which are at least as good as those found in its competitors. In service businesses, this includes simple matters such as politeness to customers, speed at which phone calls are answered, and so forth.

(d) *Values*. These relate to the organisation's culture, and are the basic, perhaps unstated beliefs of the people who work in the organisation. For example, a firm's moral principle might mean not taking on an assignment if it believes the client will not benefit, even though this means lost revenue. An example of this can be found in the standards of professional ethics required of accountants.

A *mission statement* is a document embodying some of the matters noted above. A mission statement might be a short sentence, or a whole page. It is intentionally unquantified and vague, and is sometimes seen as a statement of the guiding priorities that govern a firm's behaviour. Mission statements are rarely changed, as otherwise they have less force, and become mere slogans.

(a) *Purpose*

  (i) The firm's purpose might be described in terms of more than just self interest. A pharmaceutical company might define its corporate mission as 'the well-being of humanity'.

  (ii) The firm's responsibility to its stakeholders.

(b) *Strategy*

  (i) The statement should identify the type of business the firm is engaged in.

  (ii) The statement should perhaps identify the strategy for competitive advantage the firm intends to pursue.

(c) *Values*

  (i) The statement should identify values that link with the firm's purpose.
  (ii) The values should reinforce the corporate strategy.

(d) *Behaviour standards*

  (i) Defined standards of behaviour can serve as benchmarks of performance.
  (ii) Individual employees should be able to apply these standards to their own behaviour.

(e) *Character*

  (i) The statement should reflect the organisation's actual behaviour and culture, or at least its aspirations for improved behaviour and culture.

  (ii) The statement should be easy to read.

Objectives, on the other hand, are the embodiment of a mission statement in a commercial context. They specify the meaning of a mission in a particular period, market, or situation.

Mission statements and strategic planning

The relationship between mission statements and strategic planning is an ambiguous one. In some cases, the mission statement is prepared after the strategic plan is drawn up as a sort of summary of it. However this would only be done if there was a major change in the company's direction.

Whilst the mission inspires corporate objectives, the strategy is a means for fleshing them out. The strategy also provides directions for specific context. The mission statement cannot institute particular strategies but it can indicate priorities. Say an investment company prided itself on investing funds in companies which it regarded as behaving ethically, and its mission statement contains a clause which says that the company is 'to invest clients' funds in companies whose products promote health'. It would be unlikely to invest in tobacco firms, but no indication is given as to which shares to buy, on which stock exchanges, when to sell, what returns to expect, and so forth.

Originating a mission statement

A mission statement originates at the highest levels of the organisation. It is possible that, given a mission statement is meant to inspire as well as direct, a process of consultation with employees should take place to determine what the mission statement should be, or to assess what would be laughed out of courts. A company which declared its commitment to customer service in a mission statement, but whose practices for years had been quite the opposite, would have problems in persuading employees to take it seriously. The fact that the employees were consulted about the current ethos in a formal procedure would make the mission statement more effective. The mission statement would be introduced as part of an attempt to change the culture of the organisation.

The scope of mission statements

All areas of corporate life can be covered by a mission statement. This is because it is broadly based, and as a statement of an organisation's values and objectives, it should affect everyone in the organisation. That means its scope is wide-ranging. If it did not affect everybody in each department, from managing director to clerk, then its power would be lessened, and its purpose poorly satisfied.

For example, if a company's mission highlights the provision of *good quality* products and services, then this does not only include the way in which products are made and services delivered, but the way in which commercial relationships are conducted. Given that a successful business requires, in the long term, good commercial relationships, 'quality' applies to these as well.

The benefits of mission statements

The benefits of mission statement are that they:

(a) describe what the company is about;

(b) provide a guiding philosophy where there are doubts about the direction a company should take, or a decision an individual manager or employee should make;

(c) display the area in which the company is operating;

(d) enable the communication of a common culture throughout the whole organisation;

(e) stimulate debate as to how the mission can be implemented.

6 STRATEGIC PLAN FOR CHANGED ENVIRONMENT

(a) *Factors to be considered when formulating a strategic plan*

BG is in an unhappy position: it is being exposed to new and growing competition in a declining market. Moreover, until now, the market has consisted of but one customer, the government. BG is unlikely to have well developed marketing skills or commercial contacts. Also the costing system used does not encourage operational efficiency.

The strategic plan needs to take the following factors into account.

The environment

The competitive environment is hostile.

(i) There is a declining market.
(ii) There are new competitors.
(iii) Barriers to entry to BG's market segment (government contracts) are being reduced.
(iv) New markets may not be easy to find.

The *political environment* is likely to lead to no long-term increase in defence spending in the home country. It is unlikely that BG can rely on a sort of holding operation until business picks up. The defence business is one peculiarly dependent on government thinking. Other governments may continue to support national champions in arms industries as a means of ensuring domestic security, so while barriers to entry to the home market are being reduced, there is no evidence that this is happening abroad.

The *economic environment* is also likely to be unfavourable in the long term. Talk of a peace dividend in Europe will lead for pressures for reduced spending over the continent. In the US, the budget deficit does not really enable any increase in defence spending in real terms. Governments of countries with sophisticated arms manufacturing industries are likely to be more vigilant over arms exports to troubled areas of the world, or to regimes of dubious political legitimacy. Many poorer countries can no longer afford to import defence equipment: in particular the re-established democracies of Latin America are likely to reduce defence spending as the role of the armed service in society is reduced. As armies fall under civilian control and as military regimes are removed, then the armed services do not have the first tug on a nation's purse strings.

The *technological environment.* High technology weaponry is likely to be popular with governments as such weapons minimise blood shed by their own troops. These are very expensive to produce.

The *competitive environment* is likely to become fiercer, as former Eastern bloc countries export arms to the world market.

BG's own organisation structure and orientation

BG's *reliance on one customer*, in a very cosy relationship, has not prepared it for the rigours of the new competitive situation. It probably has few marketing skills: getting new business perhaps depended on having suitable contacts in the defence ministry. As the company never really had a marketing objective, it would not have enough experience to reorientate itself. At the same time, its contacts with the government might enable it to benefit from government sponsored export drives.

Product range. It is possible that BG's products were made according to detailed government specifications. These specifications might have been laid down for the government's particular defence needs. There is no reason to suppose that other governments will have the same requirements. Moreover, some defence products, especially of a high-tech nature, require that those who operate them have a high degree of technical training. This might not often be available, so the products might be too complex and over specified for some markets.

Accounting systems. The cost-plus system may not be the cause of BG's difficulties, but it will certainly provide no remedies. If BG is losing contracts on grounds of price, this indicates that there is something wrong with the way BG has operated. It may be simply a reflection of size: competing firms might be much larger and so benefit from economies of scale. Or it may be that BG is inefficient, and lacks proper project management skills. Furthermore, it may be that BG's overhead recovery system gives incorrect costing information, thus leading to poor pricing decisions.

Interested parties

BG is a quoted company and so has shareholders to satisfy, in the short and long term. They will expect performance to improve. Otherwise they might sell the share to a bidder.

(b) *Strategic options available to BG*

(i) *Find new markets*. This is not easy, as there is strong competition, and, as mentioned in part (a) of this answer, BG's products may be too advanced or too specialised for many. Also, if it is losing government contracts at home, then there is no reason to suppose that it will be any more successful abroad, unless it can match competitors on price. Moreover, BG has little experience in marketing.

(ii) *Develop new products*. Again, this is easier said than done. Most of BG's work has been on government defence contracts. Product development in this field is expensive, and it is not certain that BG has the necessary marketing skills to identify what would sell. Development of a new product and its failure to sell would probably mean the end of the company.

(iii) *More aggressive pricing*. The company still has strengths in that it is well attuned to the personnel and internal politics of the defence ministry of the home government. In the short term therefore, it can bid competitively for home government contracts at lower margins. Although there is strong competition, BG has still a powerful position with that particular customer.

(iv) *Changing accounting systems* for better cost information. This will support the objective in (iii) above. It is unlikely that overhead absorption by direct labour hours is appropriate in a high-tech company.

(v) *Rationalisation*. BG will have to make itself more efficient in order to survive, and build up margins.

(vi) A long-term strategic option would be to assess any *civilian applications* of its military technology. If its technical expertise involves computer program writing it could set itself up as a specialist software supplier. A UK example has been the development by a defence company of software to provide computerised road maps.

(vii) Declining markets and increasing costs might lead BG to *share its resources* with other companies. This would also be a means of gaining expertise, and building up commercial relationships. The company could set up joint ventures with other defence contractors.

(viii) If BG having reviewed its options fails to come up with a viable plan, or the plans it develops require large amounts of capital it should, in its shareholders' interest, consider selling itself to a larger company prepared to invest in its future. This would preserve jobs and skills, and enable shareholders to invest elsewhere.

7 FIREBRIDGE TYRES LTD

> *Tutorial note.* This is a fairly straightforward question on the environment and how an organisation can ensure environmental fit.

(a) *Main factors in the external environment*

The environment of an organisation is everything outside the boundaries of the organisation. Organisations are by definition open to the environment: it is the source of their inputs; it is the destination of their outputs; and it sets constraints over what the organisation can do. Some argue that the environment is increasingly a source of uncertainty for organisations, and that it is becoming harder to read. The degree of uncertainty it causes results from its complexity and the rate of change.

Hofer and Schendel argue that the very purpose of strategy is to secure some sort of environmental fit. This might be an extreme position, as it implies reaction to the environment rather thaN activity to shape environmental forces. However, any formal strategic planning process takes the environment into account.

As far as the general environment is concerned, we can analyse PEST and competitive factors.

(i) *Political and legal factors*. Firebridge Tyres Ltd (FTL) operates in a stable political environment. Agreements between governments on the single European market and GATT have opened up international markets, not only to FTL but to its competitors: however GTC does not want FTL to increase its exports outside Europe. There is no shortage of car service stations, a fragmented industry, so political interference is unlikely. Local government might determine the siting of certain activities. FTL is indirectly affected by government transport policy, if this affects the demand for and use of cars.

(ii) *Economic factors*. In the UK, tyres must be checked annually, as part of the MOT testing process. The overall level of economic activity determines transport use, which influences wear and tear of tyres. However, in times of hardship, people will be less likely to buy the premium brand range preferring to go for the lower cost Freeway range, cheaper overseas tyres, or even retreads. The general level of prosperity also influences the number of people in the population who use cars; rising incomes and wealth mean rising numbers of cars purchased, hence greater demand for tyres. People will also move to lower cost service options in hard times: FTL does not want a service business lumbered with heavy overheads. The UK market is much smaller than the US: GTC might be unrealistic in assuming that the same formula, which might depend on economies of scale, would work over in the UK.

(iii) *Social factors* influence demand indirectly, via political pressure for legislation or changing patterns of demand. For examples, governments are more concerned with ecological issues. There are disposal problems with used tyres. This might affect what they are made of. Some can be burnt as fuel, but with landfill taxes increasing, recyclable tyres may be preferred. The proposed service business depends on patterns of car use. It may be that many drivers and will prefer a garage.

(iv) *Technological factors*. Tyres are a fairly mature technology, although there are improvements to be made to increase their grip, their longevity, and their recyclability. Any changes in the plastics and materials industry might be relevant. Also, if cars become lighter, lighter tyres will be needed.

The main factor in the environment is competition, which is impinging directly on FTL.

(i) A number of service chains already exist in the UK, but otherwise the industry is fairly fragmented. Competition on price is important, but also on quality. However, FTL needs to assess how the competition will respond.

(ii) The competitive environment can be described using Porter's five forces model (barriers to entry- see below, substitute products, customer bargaining power, supplier bargaining power, competitive rivalry). There are few substitute products, but competitive rivalry is intense. Suppliers have low bargaining power probably.

(b) *Barriers to entry* discourage new competitors to an industry. If they are low, it is easy to set up shop, but hard to discourage other people from doing so too. The main barriers to entry are described below.

(i) *Economies of scale*. For some firms, a barrier to entry is the size of the operation needed to be profitable. Tyres are high volume, low margin products on the whole, and for most cases, the best way to make money is to manufacture in large quantities. A large plant implies high fixed costs and a high breakeven point. There is little evidence that significant economies of scale can be achieved in *servicing*. There are some service chains, but the industry seems fragmented.

(ii) *Product differentiation*. FTL already pursues this strategy by producing different tyres, directed at different segments. In service, differentiation might be achieved on the basis of FTL's brand name, and a promise of service quality. Advertising costs might be considerable, however, to build the brand.

(iii) *Capital requirements*. No new factories need to be built, of course, but FTL will have to acquire leases or freeholds of a number of properties in which to set up its service stations. Many of the prime spots might be taken over by petrol stations. Ideally FTL will be positioned near residential areas or near roads, to make them easy to find. The cost of this depends on the size of the operation that GTC is proposing.

(iv) *Switching costs* are minimal; new customers are easy to find, but hard to keep, unless service quality is better.

(v) *Distribution*. The chain is basically a distribution outlet for FTL's tyres. The importance of choosing the right sites for distributing the service was identified in (iii) above.

(vi) *Existing service* providers know the market, but otherwise they have no special advantages.

Barriers to entry are fairly low. This will make it easy to set up business, but hard to make a profit perhaps, unless some unique lessons can be transferred from GTC, operating in a very different transport infrastructure.

(c) *Distinctive competences and critical success factors*

A distinctive competence is those activities which a firm carries out uniquely or distinctly well. To be an enduring source of competitive advantage, a distinctive competence should be hard to imitate.

Critical success factors, on the other hand, are aspects of a business's performance which are essential to its success. Some of these relate to internal processes, others to the basic infrastructure of the business.

What is FTL's distinctive competence. FTL is a manufacturing business, making what is essentially a commodity products, tyres, with a stab at product differentiation. This competence is not truly distinctive, as there are other tyre manufacturers in the world, but FTL has built up a market presence in Europe. The distinctive competences in such a business might be the ability:

(i) to build a brand which customers recognise;

(ii) to make incremental technical innovations, to encourage new sales;

(iii) to keep costs under control, to support the brand, and to prevent its erosion by competition;

(iv) to win the support of distributors and garages for the tyres, as opposed to competitors.

How do these relate to the service business? A key problem is that services are a very different proposition to products. The critical success factors for the service business might be:

(i) a brand which customers recognise (eg as with McDonald's for hamburgers) and choose, having realistic and satisfied expectations of what it offers;

(ii) a number of well chosen sites for people to choose and access easily, which make the experience not too unpleasant (eg by offering customers a lounge or coffee bar);

(iii) well trained staff who not only know how to change wheels and tyres, and do other repairs but who are able to demonstrate higher standards of customer care;

(iv) to be seen as preferable to the local garage in terms of the processes by which the service is provided.

FTL's existing competences at best cover brand building. It has no experience in choosing and managing properties: US conditions are different, so a transfer of skills between the US and the UK firm may be hard to achieve. FTL runs a manufacturing business; a service business, based on a variety of intangibles such as staff courtesy, is a different proposition. The required cultures of the two businesses might conflict.

The firm might have to spend a lot of money on training, both technically and in terms of customer care. Also money would have to be spent on building the brand. However, GTC should be able to provide some expertise in building the service aspects.

In short, FTL's distinctive competences are not sufficient to make a go of this plan, given the fragmented nature of the industry. GTC may be able to provide some help, but GTC might end up investing more money and making short term losses, rather than the profits it is looking for.

FTL is in a difficult situation, because its managers are tied by the priorities of the US parent.

8 ZETON

Tutorial note. Although the question does not specifically require it, report format often makes your answer easier to mark, especially pertinent in case studies, which generally cover a number of different issues.

This was an interesting question. Zeton's circumstances were described in some detail. Whilst you might have been tempted to use SWOT analysis, this is probably too general an approach to the situation. We have divided our answer into product-market issues, organisational issues and management issues - but remember that part (a) offers only 15 marks, and should take no more than 27 minutes. Moreover, in part (a) don't discuss strategies. Remember also that part (b) contains two distinct issues: organisation structure and leadership.

To: Mr T Lee
From: A Consultant
Date: 7 December 19X5
Subject: Management and organisation issues

Tutorial note. A formal report would have a table of contents and a terms of reference. For exam purposes, these are both icing on the cake, although a table of contents can help you plan your answer.

1 Table of contents: see tutorial note above
2 Terms of reference: see tutorial note above

3 *Key product market issues*

3.1 Malaysian government policy has been to build up a motor sector. The German auto firm is undoubtedly interested in high quality, low cost production to support an expansion into Asian markets.

3.2 Supplying the German investor might require investment in new manufacturing facilities to meet demand, as well as introducing TQM to meet quality targets. It is not clear what resources are available for investment.

3.3 Expanding into Eastern Europe is a highly risky venture for a firm such as Zeton, best put off until the long term. Zeton does not have the management expertise or any experience of running an overseas operation. Furthermore, the government is unlikely to support overseas production, as opposed to exporting.

3.4 If resources are pumped into car components, less will be available for investment in the other divisions, particularly in machine tools. The company may have to focus on one activity.

3.5 Mr Fung is the heart of the bespoke engineering design business. When he retires, what will happen?

4 *Key organisational and management issues*

4.1 *Zeton is primarily a family business.* It will suffer from an insufficiently professional management team. (An example is the Taiwanese computer company Acer.) Already, there are rumblings of discontent amongst the professional engineering staff.

4.2 Any attempt by Mr Lee to professionalise the management would mean displacing his brother-in-law and his cousin, which is difficult for family reasons. They need a role, where they can do no harm.

4.4 Raising money from outside investors will have major consequences for the organisation of the firm.

4.5 Indications are that the hierarchical, centralised nature of the business is not working properly. The younger managers, with wider global experience, clearly have got used to a different organisation structure and culture, more flexible and less rigid.

4.6 TQM is more than a set of production techniques. To be implemented successfully, it requires a change in the approach to management. Some of Mr Lee's younger managers and employees might already be familiar with it.

4.7 Mr Lee is used to taking all the decisions. This cannot work in a TQM culture. Mr Lee's time is a scarce resource and should be used where it most effectively adds value.

5 *Restructuring the company*

5.1 *Ownership.* Does Zeton have the resources to supply the Germans, and, later, to compete in overseas markets? How will it raise capital? By selling shares to outside investors, via the Stock Exchange, Mr Lee will be able to raise capital, and it might reduce the power of family members on the board. However, Mr Lee might also be able to raise money from the government.

5.2 *Establish a clear divisional structure.* The markets for machine tools, auto components and the specialist department are different even though they exploit some manufacturing synergies.

5.3 Divisionalisation will focus management attention on key product market issues, and also it will prevent problems spreading from one division to another. Each division should have its own management committee, which will be responsible for most strategic and operational decisions. Mr Lee will of course chair each committee, but, having made suitable promotions, he will be less involved in operational matters; he will have to learn to delegate.

5.4 *Symbolic roles for the family.* At the same time, assuming the businesses remain in the same company, there will be an executive committee for the holding company, chaired by Mr Lee, the chief decision-maker, and with representatives of each of the divisions. It is here that Mr Lee's family can be dealt with, by offering them a seat on board, giving them symbolic, rather than practical, importance. To cement relationships with customers, Mr Lee might invite, at a later stage, representatives from key customers on the board. However, as a major shareholder, Mr Lee still has most clout.

5.5 The *holding company board* might also be responsible for any central functions or decision-making.

(a) Resource allocation decisions will be made.

(b) A central research and development centre might be established, although product development will be at divisional level. This could be based in Chow Fung's department or it could be centralised, for the benefit of the entire group.

(c) Some other administrative aspects, such as finance, might be controlled on a functional basis, depending on the size of the firm.

5.6 *Mr Lee's own job needs greater focus.* This is an organisation structure issue, as it is about division of labour. Mr Lee will need to maintain good relations with the government and external investors, if any. Also, he will need to ensure that the divisions he has created do not conflict with each other.

5.7 Mr Lee is fortunate that some of his managers have had some management education, by reference to courses done in the UK and the USA. Mr Lee perhaps should build on this, by developing the management roles on a more professional basis.

5.8 As far as work organisation is concerned, the introduction of TQM requires a change to a team-based organisation, in which employees are supposed to contribute expertise. Fortunately, this ties in well with the more flatter structures that the younger managers are supporting, but it might involve a change of culture nevertheless.

6 *Leadership skills*

6.1 At present, Mr Lee is perhaps an authoritarian, patriarchal boss who likes to control the business. As owner of 80% of the shares, people perhaps may be wary of disagreeing with him. However, in the decentralised structure, this approach to management may be hard to sustain, and frustrating for Mr Lee and his managers alike.

6.2 John Kotter (The Leadership Challenge) suggests that whereas management issues involve planning and budgeting, organising and staffing and controlling and problem solving - much of the content of the earlier discussion - leadership requires a different set of skills and a different mindset.

6.3 Leadership skills which, as a senior manager, Mr Lee might consider are these.

(a) Creating a sense of direction for the group as a whole, despite the autonomy given to product divisions.

(b) Communicating his vision of the business to the divisional committees (eg a shred commitment to quality).

(c) Energising, inspiring and motivating.

He already has position power and, presumably, is not afraid to exercise authority.

6.4 If the restructuring suggested above is adopted, and if TQM is introduced, then Mr Lee will also consider:

(a) the management of change;
(b) corporate culture.

Mr Lee is a very powerful figure, and if he wants to encourage initiative in his staff, he will have to lead by example, and be committed to the change process. Little will change, unless he not only takes an interest, but is *seen* to do so.

9 R PLC: COMPETITIVE USE OF IT

Tutorial note. This is a question where you need to apply your theoretical knowledge of competitive advantage to the actual situation of the case study. There are a number of models you could identify: Porter's cost leadership, differentiation and focus is model one example, although we have used McFarlan's grid first of all. However, you should apply these directly to the situation in the case study, by suggesting activities in which IT would be relevant. There are plenty of hints. We have not used formal report format in the answer as this was not requested by the question, but we have identified the recipient of the information.

To: Chief Executive, R plc
From: Management Accountant
Date: 23 May 19X5
Subject: Competitive advantage and IT

IT and competitive strategy

(a) IT should be considered as an aspect of the overall business strategy as IT can have major competitive implications. McFarlan's grid will help us determine the overall importance of IT to R plc's future strategic development.

		Strategic impact of application development portfolio (ie future systems)	
		Low	*High*
Strategic impact of existing systems	*Low*	Support	Turnround
	High	Factory	Strategic

(i) IT has a *support role* for a business where information systems have little relevance to a firm's *existing* or *future* success. This means that:

(1) IT thus requires below average investment;
(2) IT requires little management attention.

(ii) If IT has a *factory role,* this means that its existing IT applications are important. However, *future* IT developments are not anticipated to be critical.

(iii) IT's *strategic role* is where *existing* and *future* developments are at the heart of the company's future success. In fact, the business operation *depends* on IT: without IT it would not exist at all.

(iv) IT's *turnround role* is where *existing* IT is not important, but *future* developments are likely to have a significant impact. In this case, IT is becoming *more* important. Its role and profile in the organisation is being enhanced.

(b) *Role of IT in R plc*

In R plc that IT probably has a *turnround* role, especially with regard to the firm's future expansion, for a number of reasons.

(i) Eastern Europe is both a market and a competitive threat. R plc cannot afford any excess costs, such as the wastage in raw materials arising out of poor communications. With more plants, materials wastage will increase, adding to the costs.

(ii) Poor co-ordination means a loss of customer orders. East European customers need be no more accommodating than our existing customers if we can't deliver.

(iii) At the same time, capacity utilisation at some of the plants is low, which hampers profitability.

The expansion plans will magnify these problems considerably. If more plants are built, communications difficulties will be magnified. Demand is likely to be unpredictable, and the new plants will take some time to come on stream. Flexibility in dealing with the demands of new markets and the problems of building the infrastructure to serve them will make great demands of management.

(c) *Use of IT in R plc's competitive strategy in each of the product-market areas it operates in*

(i) *Bulk area.* R plc needs to minimise materials and transport costs. The commodity products require a *cost leadership strategy*. In other words, like the market for basic silicon chips, profits are reaped through volume, by eliminating waste and ensuring high capacity utilisation.

(1) Each plant should be given MRP technology systems to integrate production and purchasing. Manufacturing resource planning (MRP II) builds on materials requirement planning (MRP I) so that there are no ordering delays.

(2) Basic stock control systems are needed, as the firm has problems identifying levels of stock and work in progress.

Although the production process differs for each product, the underlying technology is similar, and so these should be easy to implement across the company.

(3) R plc needs to create a single *corporate database*, regularly updated, with details of capacity and materials levels.

- This should be available to managers of all plants, so that everyone will know where there is spare capacity, and so that orders can be made up elsewhere in the group if necessary.
- This requires investment perhaps in E-mail or other *corporate communications systems* (eg as offered by BT's Concert system).
- This should be combined with a *logistics management system*, so that customer orders are routed to the nearest appropriate plant.

(ii) The *advanced products* have their own plants. Their specialised nature suggests that they are *customised* or *differentiated products*, even though they may be sold to the same end customer.

(1) In this field, product *innovation* is a key factor, and so investment in computer automated design systems will help in this respect.

(2) IT can also be used in the production equipment itself. Computer numerical control tools offer production flexibility.

(d) The matters in (i) and (ii) above are at the very heart of the firm's *primary activities* (to use the value chain model). *Secondary activities* are also important, and IT can assist here also.

(i) To ensure the business is adequately controlled, especially the new plants, new *management information systems* can be developed, to identify costs and variances and to suggest efficiency gains. Of course, a standard reporting framework will be required for each plant.

(ii) Senior managers can use *executive information systems* to review the workings of the firm as a whole, as well as to drill down into details of the data. Such systems will make it easier to manage the planned expansion without a severe increase in the size and complexity of the head office operation.

10 WONDERHORSE

Tutorial note. You could easily spend a long time answering this case, and exploring various of the issues. The question unpacks into two main areas: your information needs as a management consultant and the tools you have available, and practical recommendations despite the lack of information (as identified in part (a)). Do not speculate overmuch, and as far as possible base your recommendations in (b) on the information offered in the case. The case contains many strategic planning issues, from overall objectives to detailed commercial strategy. Be sure to keep to the time available.

You may have chosen other tools such as the ones available. PEST analysis might have been suggested as a result of Part (a). However, a key issue of the case is the urgency of the strategy decision, in which competitive strategy, product-market strategy and the need to raise money are all related. For a similar reason, you might have quoted the marketing mix - but the question was only indirectly about marketing.

(a) *Information needed to conduct an objective assessment of the firm's current situation and future prospects*

This can be conveniently analysed into the external and external appraisals.

Internal appraisal

(i) *Mission.* This answers the question 'what business are we in?'. This is hard to answer at present. Although Casey Johns has a vision for the pharmafoods concept, this does not translate into a business mission for Wonderhorse. Perhaps all three founder-directors should be asked the question. It is almost certain that a mission statement is lacking. The lack of such a document is a significant item of information in itself.

(ii) *Goals and objectives.* Have any goals and objectives been articulated by the management? For example, does the firm have a target rate of return on its activities? If so, how are they set? Are they benchmarked to other firms in the industry?

(iii) *Distinctive competences.* There is some indication that the directors have considered what they are good at, but there are disputes as to how they are to be sustained. Quatermass considers the firm is best at generating ideas. Ranger feels there is a distinctive competence in manufacturing synthetic foods. Which is right? Or are they both right? The consultant will need considerable knowledge of the business and the industry worldwide to reach any sort of assessment.

(iv) *Critical success factors.* How does the business measure its success? Public awareness? Market share? Favourable press publicity? Ranger suggests that success in generating positive cash flow is a critical success factor for other aspects of the business. Has the firm analysed this with any rigour?

(v) Detailed breakdowns of research and development costs, and how these are allocated to products. Details of the patents the firm has taken out, in the UK, the EU and the US. How are they monitored? Are they watertight against copying?

(vi) *Product profitability.* Detailed breakdowns are required of the profitability of the firm's products, as effectively we only have profitability by type of distribution and promotion (supermarket vs Wonderhorse brands) rather than type of product. It may be the case that certain of Wonderhorse's products are more profitable across both distribution methods and overall profitability could be increased by concentrating on the most successful items. However, we are not even provided with a list of the firm's products and brands. What is the reason for the decline in profit margin? Pressure on prices, or increasing costs?

(vii) *Cost structure.* What is the relationship between the firm's fixed and variable costs, and how are these absorbed? High fixed costs would suggest that once breakeven point is reached, profits should increase significantly.

(viii) *Marketing plans and strategies.* What marketing objectives does the firm have, in terms of market share. How does the firm advertise and promote its products.

(ix) What outstanding contracts does the consultancy side of the business have?

(x) How effective are the firm's financial controls, and use of working capital?

(xi) How good is the firm at generating cash.

(xii) How much of the firm's fixed assets are devoted to the different arms of the business. What is the return on investment (as opposed to profitability) of the two businesses. This might give a different picture: the research base could conceivably have a lower ROCE.

External matters

(i) A general environmental analysis might be needed (eg using the PEST framework). In the long term, what are likely social attitudes to pharmafoods? Will the firm be subject to legal regulation?

(ii) How easy will it be for competitors to copy Wonderhorse's products and expertise? How much competition exists overall?

(iii) How will the firm be affected by supermarkets' plans for marketing and sales and distribution? To what extent will Wonderhorse be dominated by its retail customers?

(iv) What are the trends for junk foods and food consumption generally? Is the market mature, in which case little growth can be expected? Or are lifestyles still changing? It is sometimes suggested that the UK is moving towards practices in certain parts of the US, where people are more likely to eat 'on the hoof' than sit down for an evening meal.

(v) What other developments in cheap fast food might there be? (Balti houses are a relatively new invention.) Casey Johns seem fixated on the McDonalds model.

(b) REPORT

To: Shareholders of Wonderhorse Foods Ltd
From: Management Consultant
Date: 27 January 19X8
Subject: Strategic options for Wonderhorse plc

1 *Terms of reference*

1.1 This report offers an overall review of the strategic situation of Wonderhorse Ltd.

1.2 This report also suggests a number of strategic options and offers a tentative recommendation as to which one should be pursued.

2 *The current state of affairs*

2.1 Wonderhorse is perhaps operating in two distinct industries, the scientific consulting side on the one hand and the food manufacturing side on the other.

2.2 *Competitive environment*

(a) *Barriers to entry*: how easy it is for other firms to enter the market? At present we are not sure, but if entry barriers are low, more competition can be expected rather than less. Entry barriers will probably differ between the food manufacturing and the consulting business. For the consulting business, entry barriers will be high.

(b) *Substitute products.* All existing food is a substitute for pharmafoods, so this is not terribly relevant. Nor is it relevant to the consultancy business.

(c) *Bargaining power of suppliers.* No information is given, but it is probable that the firm produces some of its own chemicals anyway. There is no suggestion of high supplier bargaining power.

(d) *Bargaining power of customers.* End-consumers can accept or reject the product. Customers in this instance relate to retailers. They have high bargaining power, when it comes to stocking Wonderhorse's products, but they probably have low bargaining power in the consultancy business.

(e) *Competitive rivalry.* Wonderhorse is in part pitching its own brands against the supermarkets' brands, even though these are manufactured by Wonderhorse. Wonderhorse's customers are also competitors.

2.3 *Product portfolio.* The Boston matrix analyses the characteristics of products in different market situations. How far is the market growing and what is the market share? Rising stars have a high share of a high growth market, questions marks a low share of a high growth market. Cash cows have a high share of a low growth market, dogs a low share.

Wonderhorse's position is unusual. Pharmafoods is a new concept, and Wonderhorse is *creating* the market. The rising sales revenues and lack of competition in basic manufacture (as opposed to competition between retailer brands and Wonderhorse's own brands) suggest a rising star or at least a question mark. At the same time, this rising star already seems to be generating positive cash flows. However, as pharmafoods compete with other foodstuffs as *substitutes*, prices are likely to be set by reference to these substitutes which makes enormous profits hard to achieve. The consulting business appears to be a rising star.

This model is relevant in that it suggests different cash generation capabilities, but it is possible that it does not fit Wonderhorse's situation very well.

2.4 *Product market strategy.* The Ansoff model is a technique for determining future strategy, based on the arrangement of new and/or existing products in new and/or existing markets. Introducing new products to new markets is the most risky option.

However, its relevance to Wonderhorse is that it might suggest new strategic options, such as selling to fast food outlets, which is, indeed something that has been considered. The firm's research arm is developing new products, but the important thing to realise is that all these products share the same technology. The firm is perhaps too small to start exporting, although it might consider doing so in future. It is unlikely that the consultancy side of the business can diversify.

The Ansoff matrix provides a long term framework for assessing the firm's direction of growth.

2.5 There are evident *synergies* between the two businesses, in particular the input of the research unit into the food manufacturing businesses. However, are the synergies such to justify the continued aggregation of the two businesses? The fact that they grew out of the same resource base should not obscure their very different characteristics.

2.6 In effect there are two *value chains* in Wonderhorse, although they intersect around the research and consulting side of the business. In the consulting business, research and development is a primary activity, as this is what customers are in fact buying. In the manufacturing business, the research and development arm is a support activity, although an absolutely vital one. This might explain the differing perspectives of Quatermass and Ranger.

Does the existence of two value chains cause operational confusion, or are the linkages exploited efficiently? For example, are Wonderhorse's consultancy customers introduced to the factory division?

2.7 The research and consulting side of the business is profitable, with no less than a 30% margin. An increasing amount of this derives from patent royalties. Patent royalties provide a steady source of income during the life of the patent. This income can be invested in other activities or new projects. However, the income of the research and consulting arm is still. To survive at all, this part of the business needs investment in R and D and continual upgrading of the research base to maintain the competitive advantage.

2.8 The food manufacturing business is much more stable in revenue growth. In absolute terms, profits increased from £105k in 19X5 to £110K in 19X6 and to £117k in 19X7. Revenue increased faster than this.

2.9 It is reasonable to anticipate that the market will grow, once customers become used to the concept of pharmafoods. There are slightly conflicting approaches to promoting the product, whether through supermarkets' own brands or independently. At present there is no choice. Sales are still low and the supermarket route is currently more profitable.

3 *Financial resources problems*

3.1 The two businesses inevitably will compete for resources. This is another area of difficulty.

3.2 The business has an expanded asset base, although the impact of capitalising research and development expenditure must be discounted. However, the shareholders' unwillingness to provide any more money is forcing the business to rely on bank finance.

3.3 There is a limit to the amount of money a bank is prepared to lend, especially to a new business such as this. The long term loan, at 10%, indicates a fairly high gearing. The rate of interest is still substantially less than the rate of return for the business as a whole. [*Tutorial note.* Unfortunately, we do not have individual rates of return for the two different businesses, as we have no idea as to the split of the fixed assets between them.]

3.4 It is likely that the business is going to require increased financial resources:

(i) to fund new research;
(ii) to expand new manufacturing capacity;
(iii) to invest in brands and promotion.

This has to be financed from somewhere. The bank is unlikely to contribute more and the venture capitalist does not wish to expand his investment.

3.5 In competitive terms, the consultancy business is the stronger for the time being, although in the long term, major chemicals, biotechnology and pharmaceutical companies might try and invade the market.

3.6 Thus the over-riding consideration in the medium term is to ensure adequate funding for both sides of the business so that both can develop, and so that the venture capitalist firm can cash in its investment.

3.7 Such funding can be achieved by full or partial stock market listing. There are several ways by which this can be achieved for the business as a whole, for example:

(i) simply sell a proportion of the shares in the business as it stands. The venture capitalist will sell 40% and pocket the rest. The other directors can sell a proportion of their shareholdings, to invest money in the business;

(ii) issue new shares, which will dilute the proportionate holding of the directors.

3.8 Restructure and float off part of the business. One of the business areas could be given a separate legal status and could be sold off. The food manufacturer would be the best candidate, as it offers steady earnings growth and its earnings are likely to be less volatile.

4 *Competitive strategy*

4.1 The two businesses face different problems.

4.2 At present, it is probably inappropriate to apply Porter's analysis to the *consultancy* group. Basic research and subcontracted product development depends on insights which cannot easily be replicated. At the moment, Wonderhorse seems the only participant in this market anyway. Their task must be to develop their expertise, and maximise their patent income, as a source of funds for research. As yet they do not need a competitive strategy

4.3 In the long term, the firm might face consultancy competition from a variety of sources, such as universities, desperate for private sector finance to add to their public sector grants. There, the firm will probably have to decide exactly what kind of research, development and consultancy it wants to do: a product differentiation strategy might be chosen.

4.4 A variety of opportunities exist for the *food manufacturing* arm:

(i) abandon the own brands and become a supplier of pharmafoods to supermarkets and other retailers only;

(ii) invest in new technology to spend on its own brands, supported by targeted advertising at existing segments.

4.5 In the market for food as whole, Wonderhorse's manufacturing arm is pursuing a *differentiation* strategy. It can turn this into a differentiation-focus strategy by advertising at particular segments (eg slimmers) or by allying itself with slimming organisations.

5 *Conclusion*

5.1 As far as selecting an appropriate strategy for the firm, the following is tentatively recommended.

(a) Split the firm into two distinct groups, and divide the assets between them.

(b) Float the food manufacturing business as soon as practicable, to enable it to raise money to invest in new capacity. There is nothing to stop the same personnel from being involved in both companies.

(c) Invest in its own brands. The danger of relying exclusively on retailers is they are too powerful, whereas if Wonderhorse establishes its own brand identity, it will be able to command premium prices.

(d) The research and consultancy arm should continue on its current course, until the competitive situation changes. It might expand into related areas, such as product design, and might also consider investing in market research to target its efforts more precisely. It may also consider licensing some of its discoveries, so as to build the market for the pharmafood concept. This will indireclty help the manufacturing business, as a major supplier to the market.

5.2 A major issue to be faced is the attitudes of the directors, who will almost certainly require a continued involvement in the business.

11 PAVAN AND GALLIARD

Tutorial note. This is a wide ranging question, in which the necessary disciplines of exam technique are of crucial importance. Part (a)(i) should have taken you just over fifty minutes. Parts (a)(ii) and (b) should *each* have taken you about 18 minutes. This question also asks you to use techniques learnt in your other ACCA studies. You should make use of the financial data provided - you are training for an accountancy qualification after all. However, don't spend all you time on this simply because you feel more comfortable with numbers; you are required to take a strategic perspective as well.

(a) *Risks of Pavan and Galliard (PG) buying John Dowland Jewels (JDJ)*

PG is an informal business, which seems characterised by a simple or entrepreneurial structure (Mintzberg), with a person or Zeus culture. Henry Lawes has a clear theory of his business, which he sees as retailing, although this is not articulated in any coherent mission statement (see part (c) below). It is also surprising that he has chosen to diversify, when there appears to be ample room for expanding with the existing product-market mix.

Furthermore, the acquisition of JDJ seems an example of a freewheeling opportunistic approach to strategy formation. This does not bode well for the future, given the risks that this strategy entails. In this case, there are two types of risk: business risks relate to the overall strategy of diversification by vertical integration, and the financial risks relating to this particular acquisition.

Business risks

There are risks in diversification as such, and the method by which this is achieved, acquisition.

(i) Diversification is the expansion into new industries and/or new product-markets. The proposed acquisition is an example of related diversification, in that there connections between the two businesses. PG is seeking to become its own supplier, by vertical integration: the purpose of vertical integration might be to reduce supplier bargaining power, to strengthen relationships, to win higher profits and to pursue differentiation more effectively. Do these apply in this case?

(1) *Attitudes of existing suppliers.* PG already has substantial bargaining power over its suppliers, and already has good relationships with them. Taking over JDJ will mean it will take custom away from other suppliers. It will not have the effect of reducing competition from the Arcadia brand, as barriers to entry are low.

(2) PG already pursues a successful differentiation strategy. If it reduces the number of suppliers it might be over-concentrating its expertise; some of its suppliers may have particular skills of their own, which the firm will be sacrificing, just in order to keep JDJ working to full capacity. It will therefore be losing the flexibility it once had.

(3) For many firms, diversification is seen to be a more risky strategy than market penetration, market development or product development. There is no evidence that these other directions of growth have been fully explored by Henry Lawes.

(ii) *Culture and structure*. The two firms have very different cultures. PG is a person or task culture, possibly, with what Henry Lawes refers to as a family atmosphere. This is very different from JDJ which appears to be run as a machine bureaucracy, with books full of procedures, rather surprising given the craft nature of the business. Although the two business units are unlikely to merge, Henry Lawes' management responsibilities are likely to become confused. The firms will no longer operate at arms length, and cultural differences will exacerbate communication problems, especially if PG's team of designers is going to be more closely involved in operations at JDJ.

(iii) *Change management*. Henry Lawes suggests that JDJ's profitability can be more than doubled, from £0.7m to £1.5m, entirely through cost cutting. Is this realistic? We are not told how this is to be achieved. Perhaps redundancies are envisaged, or employing more part timers. However, there is no evidence that a proper programme of change management has been planned.

(iv) *JDJ's existing customers*. We are not told how much of JDJ's turnover is with PG's few competitors (Arcadia), but turnover of £14m must be maintained.

(v) *Size*. PG has between 90 and 130 staff. JDJ has about 100 staff. The size of the business in human resources terms has been doubled overnight. Turnover and cost of sales have tripled, and the asset base is much larger.

(vi) Who will run JDJ when John Dowland resigns? There is a problem of *management succession*. The recruit will be responsible for improving the business. Not everyone will want this task.

(vii) *Technology*. JDJ has ageing but serviceable technology. Oddly, assets employed appear to be lower in Henry Lawes' projection than is currently the case. New machinery will probably be needed.

Financial risks

Some calculations below indicate some of the implications of the acquisition.

(i) ROCE. Currently PG has a ROCE of 40% (£1.0m/£2.5m), or 25% if adjusted for the long-term liability. JDJ's current ROCE is 7%, and might be improved to around 16% (£1.5m/£9m). The ROCE of the entire group, before interest payments are taken into account and taking into account the most optimistic projections, is likely to be 21% or 20%. After interest payments, however, the situation does appear worse. Loan interest (50% • 7 • £0.7m • 8%) will be about £196,000 in the *first* year, which will reduce profit and ROCE.

We can also query the wisdom of a fixed interest loan in this case. It does give the advantage of certainty, but interest rates may well fall further.

This ignores the possibility that more sums will have to be raised to finance new investment.

(ii) *Cash flow* is more serious. The combined business must be able not only to repay the interest both to the bank and to John Dowland but the initial loan. The annual sum required to repay the *capital* borrowed over 15 years will be £4.9m/5 years is £980,000.

The average annual interest payment over the life of the loan will be £196,000/2 = £98,000. On average therefore, the firm will have to find £1m in cash each year. Is this feasible?

(iii) *Gearing* will increase. At least £6.4m (£4.9m + £1.5m which PG already owes) will be owed at the outset of the merger. Assuming that JDJ is currently ungeared, the combined net assets of the group (before long term liabilities) of £13m (on Henry's projections) will be supported financed by borrowings of £6.4m or 49%. This might be considered high.

(iv) *Fixed assets*. Henry projects a reduction in the value of fixed assets employed in JDJ. We are not told why this is the case. It may be that some will be sold, or scrapped. On the other hand this may be an example of financial engineering, revaluing the assets downwards. Or again, perhaps new equipment can be acquired more cheaply.

Currently, JDJ's asset turnover is 1.47, but on Henry's projection, this will increase to 1.68, suggesting greater efficiency in their use.

In short, one financial risk appears to be that Henry's projections and other matters mentioned in the case are not consistent. This is worrying given that PG is going to embark on such a strategically significant venture.

(v) The price for the business seems rather high at £4.9m, given the current levels of profits. Perhaps John Dowland has given Henry too rosy a picture of JDJ's future; after all, why hasn't John Dowland initiated the necessary changes himself? It is possible, however, that assets will be sold to raise cash - but JDJ's main asset, the factory, cannot be sold, as it is security for the bank loan.

(b) *Should acquisition be the method of growth?*

As has already been suggested in part (a), diversification is one of four directions of growth, and acquisition is one method of achieving it. There are severe doubts as to whether diversification is the right strategy, in the first place, but the question specifically relates to acquisition as opposed to organic growth.

Acquisition and conglomerate diversification were very popular in the 1960s, but have since fallen out of favour, as more and more companies demerge and seek to define core businesses and core competences.

The benefits of diversification by acquisition need to be high to offset the risks associated with it. Ansoff suggests that many of the advantages of acquisitions can be achieved by management synergy. The supposed benefits of conglomerates such as Hanson Trust have been assumed to be that new management can squeeze extra value out of the businesses. The acquired company can be improved with extra resources and better management (as suggested in Certified Accountant, October 1994).

However, to succeed, an acquisition should demonstrate the following.

(i) A common thread with the acquiring business (eg stable technology, mature markets). Although there is vertical integration, the two businesses are very different.

(ii) The possibility to add value: JDJ can probably be improved, but at a price.

(iii) The management skills to turn the business round. This is clearly lacking, as there is no change management programme and PG has no experience of manufacturing. Moreover, JDJ's owner is quitting the business.

In short, the strategy would appear ill advised.

(c) *Mission statement*

Mission describes the organisation's basic function in society, in terms of the products and services it produces for its clients. From a strategic point of view it answers to questions: what is our business and what should it be? Mission is also an aspect of the culture of the organisation.

Ideally, mission should include the following.

(i) The organisation's purpose, and the identity of the people for whom it exists;
(ii) The organisation's competences
(iii) Ways of competing
(iv) Principles of business

The mission as articulated by Henry Lawes is not really a statement of mission at all: 'to be the best' at best indicates a commitment to excellent performance, but it indicates none of the other factors that a mission statement is supposed to have.

A better mission statement for PG (assuming it does not go ahead with the acquisition) might be as follows.

'PG aims to be the leading supplier of top quality heritage giftware. To this end, we will:

- use authentic designs
- purchase from the most skilled suppliers, with whom we aim to build up long-term relationships
- sell to customers worldwide who value this premium product through a variety of distribution channels
- offer a rewarding working environment for employees'.

The mission statement will change with the acquisition. The references to suppliers will be deleted, and its scope will change to that of a manufacturing business. Reference might also need to be made to other important stakeholders such as the bank.

12 VOYAGE OF A LIFETIME

Tutorial note. In part (a) don't simply list the IT frameworks that you know. They need to be relevant to the question. In part (b) you should indicate the relationship between IT and business strategy.

(a) *The role of information*

Information technology can be of strategic importance to an organisation because of its:

(i) costs;
(ii) criticality to organisational success;
(iii) use as a strategic weapon;
(iv) macro-economic role in reshaping entire industries;
(v) effect on management levels;
(vi) stakeholder involvement;
(vii) technical impact;
(viii) revolutionary effect on information use within the organisation.

This more than anything else is a justification for examining Voyage of a Lifetime's (VL's) use of IT from a strategic point of view.

In many organisation's, the use of IT has changed over time and with IT's increasing technical sophistication and cheapness. Applying Nolan's stage hypotheses would indicate that VL is past the initiation and contagion stages, and is in the control stage, with IT being controlled from head office and the subject of established budgetary and procurement procedures. Its origins are suggested by the fact that it is the finance director's responsibility, rather than that of a steering committee.

Julia's awareness of the potential strategic importance of IT, however, and the future developments outlined indicate that VL is moving, or needs to move, to the integration or data administration stage, where IT is seen to be integral to business issues, and is seen as a resource. However, this does not indicate how important IT should be. Two useful models can suggest IT's existing and future strategic roles.

IT's existing role can be mapped on McFarlan's grid, which relates the strategic impact of existing systems and the strategic impact of future systems.

(i) Up until now, IT has had a support or perhaps a factory role in that it dealt with basic accounting and invoice processing, although IT has become very important in processing bookings.

(ii) The new business opportunity suggests that IT will be even more important, in that it will move centre stage to the effective and basic provision of the firm's business. It will not simply process transactions previously agreed, but will be a vital link in servicing customers, and will be essential if VL is to provide bespoke holidays successfully: IT is more than administration, but at the heart of the service.

An assessment of its strategic importance can be gauged by using Porter and Millar's information intensity matrix. This is a *scoping model*, which suggests how IT can be exploited for competitive advantage. It maps how much information exists in the product and how much in the value chain.

We must first identify VL's product - in fact VL is providing a service, in which information is a crucial component. VL needs up to date accurate information about flight details, prices and availability, hotels to stay, exchange rates. The information embedded in the total service is not as high as that in a newspaper say, but it is higher than, say, in cement. A lot of the service VL will provide consists of information enabling the customer to make informed choices.

As far as VL's value chain is concerned, how it provides the service is intimately connected with the information it actually gives. It cannot offer information if this is not entered to the system and processed in some way for it to be use. The information content of the value chain is also high.

This indicates that VL's use of IT for the new strategy is of strategic importance.

(b) *Information strategies*

The centrality of IT to the success of the business indicates that IT and business strategies need to be designed together, and that IT issues should be specifically related to the business strategy. For example, complementing the corporate SWOT analysis there could be an IT SWOT identifying the strengths and weaknesses of existing systems and their impact on the business, and the opportunities and threats offered by systems developments elsewhere. IT can increase productivity or reduce costs, and a firm might find its generic competitive strategy invalidated by developments in IT.

We are helped in that Julia Verne has given us a list of critical success factors (CSFs) which will determine the success of the new strategy. The premium pricing policy suggests that Julia is pursuing a product differentiation strategy when it comes to this service.

The use of CSFs in IT strategy formation, to translate business into IT imperatives works as follows.

(i) Identify business objectives - increased profits by tapping customers' demand for more freedom in arranging their holidays.

(ii) Identify CSFs. These have already been given. The quality of advice is mentioned, as is the need to book swiftly.

(iii) Identify information systems to support CSFs. In this case, a large and flexible database is needed to offer the information. Modern computer systems can provide top-quality graphics, and so the capacity for summoning pictorial data (eg of the hotels) as well as timetabling information will be needed. An on-line communications network and an *internet* site are also needed.

The application must be seamless to the consultants who use it and user-friendly. Basically, this means that VL will have to build on its existing strengths to ensure that it maintains its competitive advantage by the following.

(i) Ensuring proper training in the system.

(ii) Ensuring the right technological decisions are taken.

(iii) Changing the method of accounting for IT: people should be encouraged to make use of the system, not penalised for it, and so charging per booking as at present might be counterproductive. It is possible that IT will have to be written off as a corporate overhead.

(iv) Ensuring the firm's top managers support and understand the need for:

(1) a strategy for information systems;
(2) the technology which implements them;
(3) the management of information systems developments.

13 PRESCIENCE GROUP: VOLUME AND PROFIT

(a) *The root causes of the problem*

Ellison's situation has two fundamental causes:

(i) poor management techniques by senior management;
(ii) conflicting, or at least badly designed, objectives.

It is not apparent that the departments were involved in the decision to introduce management by objectives at all. If any new management technique is to work, then it has to have the support of the people implementing it, otherwise it becomes a sort of 'quick fix'.

Furthermore, it is not clear whether MBO was properly implemented. In theory it is supposed to integrate broader organisational strategy with short term objectives. This does not seem to have been the case in Prescience Group. Senior management should have been involved at the start with developing the group's strategy. It thus appears that senior management has a present view as to what is required, rather than what is actually achievable.

Senior management are thus operating another system of a more traditional nature, on top of the MBO system which is supposed to be introduced below.

The MBO system actually introduced appears also to be flawed in certain key respects. It seems poorly defined, in that there should not really be a conflict between objectives. All should point in the same direction. Currently, performance objectives seem similar to budgetary control measures. Neither is it clear that the critical success factors or key result areas have been properly identified. There should not be the conflict between any objectives, and the objectives should not be mutually contradictory.

Also, some of the key factors in implementing MBO have not been adhered to.

(i) Each manager's targeted performance *should* be derived from the target achievements of the business as a whole.

(ii) A manager's results must be measured in terms of contributions to the business as a whole.

(iii) Each manager must know what the targets of performance are (and we see that Ellison is confused).

(iv) Managers should be able to identify policies in case of difficulties (ie guides to making decisions which are in keeping with corporate objectives), but Ellison has no guidance to help him out of his dilemma.

(v) At the end of every quarter, it should be possible to assess and revise the plans (so Ellison's targets should be reassessed and revised with his superiors, and so he should not be facing this decision alone).

(vi) The time horizons and objectives of the different businesses have the effect of confusing both Ellison and his subordinates. After all, Ellison's staff work on a year-by-year basis, presumably after comparing seasonal trends, whereas senior management are more interested in quarterly results.

Other additional features of MBO appear to be missing. Does Ellison have a job improvement plan, for example? How seriously have the unit objectives been drawn up?

Finally, it is not clear that a key results analysis has been prepared.

As well as the problems of implementing MBO, there are also problems with the decision Ellison has to make and his rather unusual set of choices.

(b) Shareholders, in the short term, are concerned with profit. Therefore in theory Ellison should not have to choose between the options of sales growth or profit. The main advantage of sales growth is that it is a way of ensuring market share. Perhaps this is one of the objectives that Ellison has to satisfy.

However, Ellison's three choices look rather poor in themselves.

(i) *Cutting advertising expenditure.* This will certainly reduce costs, but it may also have the effect of reducing sales and market share, to the company's disadvantage for the rest of the year. Customers will be confused. Whether this is a viable option should depend on how much others are willing to spend on advertising, and the state of competition. It may be that the advertising expenditure could be used more efficiently, however.

(ii) *Cutting raw materials purchases.* If the division is overproducing, then a useful short term measure would be to run down stocks. After all, the sales targets are not being met at current prices. If the company has been producing to meet a *forecast* sales demand in excess of what has actually been sold, then it is likely to have an excess of unsold stock which can be sold.

(iii) *Cutting recruitment.* If this means staff can be deployed more efficiently, then this policy could be adopted. Again, this might be a palliative which might have adverse consequences later on in the year.

It is not clear the extent to which the business is a seasonal one. Cutting back in these areas now may damage the business's seasonal performance.

Perhaps Ellison would be best advised, then, to put his case to the senior managers. In particular, he should:

(i) ask for clarification as to his objectives when they contradict each other;

(ii) get senior management to accept responsibility for the actions that he is about to take;

(iii) suggest a quarterly review of objectives, as outlined in the MBO guidelines for implementation.

14 COMPUFLEX INTERNATIONAL PLC: ORGANISATION STRUCTURE

(a) Mintzberg lists the following ways in which work can be co-ordinated.

(i) *Mutual adjustment* co-ordinates work by informal communication. 'Work rests in the hands of the doers'. This is used for the most simple work, and the most complicated: simple, because it is an obvious mechanism for small groups (eg two canoeists); complex as in some tasks it is impossible to plan ahead if the value of the task itself is uncertain. For example, thousands of specialists may not know what needs to be done on a research project if the outcome is uncertain. They cannot predict in advance what will be discovered, and so will adjust their activities in the light of new information.

(ii) *Direct supervision* achieves co-ordination by having one person responsible for the work of others. This person issues instructions and monitors performance. The division of labour is sharp.

(iii) *Standardisation of work processes* occurs if the contents of work are 'specified or programmed' (eg the assembly instruction for a child's toy). This bears some relationship to scientific management.

(iv) *Standardisation of outputs.* Outputs in this instance can mean a set level of profits (or level of performance) but the work process itself is not designed or programmed.

(v) *Standardisation by skills and knowledge* co-ordinates work by specifying the kind of training to perform the work. An example is a hospital. Doctors are trained in the necessary skills before being let loose on the patients.

The importance of these co-ordinating mechanisms, Mintzberg says, is that the relative complexity of the work affects the chosen method of co-ordination.

(b) Structural configuration

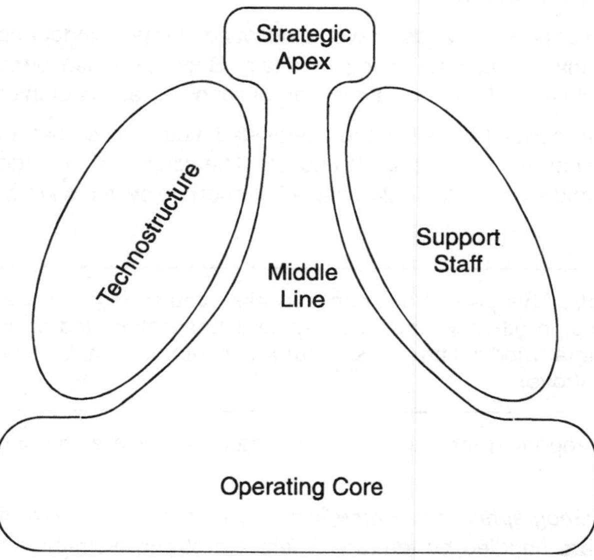

Mintzberg's theory of structural configurations suggests that any organisation is made of five components:

(i) the operating core, where work is done;

(ii) the strategic apex;

(iii) the middle line, between strategic apex and operating core;

(iv) the technostructure which standardises work processes, and designs and proceduralises the work of others;

(v) the support staff, such as PR, legal department, even R and D, who facilitate the organisation's functioning and environmental relationships in a number of ways, but outside the work process.

Each of these components exerts a pull to a particular type of organisation structure. Five structural configurations are: the professional bureaucracy (operating core), the simple structure (strategic apex), the divisional form (middle line), the machine bureaucracy (technostructure) and the adhocracy (support staff). These structural configurations represent ideal types, and most real organisations contain elements of all of them. The example of

Compuflex also shows that organisation configuration need not be static, and that it will change according to the needs of the environment, size and the work.

In its early days, Compuflex employed about twenty staff. The firm's structure was flat, suggesting a non-existent or minimal middle line. The loose structure suggests that the work was not sufficiently routine for some of the forms of co-ordination suggested by Mintzberg. Work was probably co-ordinated by a combination of mutual adjustment, between UK and US operations, as well as in individual project teams, and direct supervision. It has the features of an adhocracy as well, with the project team approach.

By 1985, co-ordination was regarded as a problem. After the formation of the executive committee, the firm has a number of features.

(i) A more powerful strategic apex to co-ordinate the firm's disparate activities, rather than set rigorous targets for them.

(ii) A loose divisional form. The relationship between apex and the UK, US and Asian arms is not too distinct. The period has seen the growth of a middle line. The apex would not take day to day responsibility for the manufacture of the Cyclotron. Mintzberg suggests that many divisional forms are arranged as a collections of machine bureaucracies.

From being primarily a project based organisation, the firm has a manufacturing capability. Presumably this will be co-ordinated like many factories elsewhere, with a technostructure setting standards and a uniformity of approach. However, not all of Compuflex's activities can be described in this way.

That said, co-ordination is still achieved by mutual adjustment in some instances, with the regular meetings of functional heads to sort out problems of mutual benefit. However these meetings establish standards and rules, and so suggest an incipient bureaucracy.

(iii) Support services have developed largely independently of the rest, providing advertising and writing manuals. Such expertise perhaps needs to be drawn more closely into the main decision-making processes of the business.

A consequence of the suggested flotation is that the firm will have to report to shareholders in the UK and US. The volume of management information will increase, and it is inevitable that financial reporting systems will be standardised.

(c)

> *Tutorial note.* This part of the question asks you to discuss the design of formal reporting mechanisms, in other words hierarchy, divisionalisation and so forth. It does not ask you to draw a diagram indicating the structural configuration in Mintzberg's terms which we have discussed above.

Formal reporting mechanisms and organisation hierarchy can be designed on a number of bases.

(i) *Geographic area.* Some authority is retained at head office, but day to day operations are handled by territory. There are strong elements of this approach in Compuflex's current way of working.

(ii) *Function.* Functional organisation divides workers into departments or units based on specialist activities. The functions are co-ordinated centrally. There are currently some elements of functional organisation, as each function has a global manager in charge.

(iii) *Brand or product.* The case mentions that there are product management teams, recruited from over the company who are responsible for keeping an eye on the market for certain products. However, this is some way from product departmentation, whereby a product manager for a division is given authority over production and marketing of a product, and, if the division is independent, will be responsible for management accounting also.

It is clear that the main basis of Compuflex's organisation will continue to be geographical, because of the need to remain close to its local markets. That said, each region does slightly different things and therefore is important globally. A lot of the firm's R and D takes place in Europe. Functional activities have to be co-ordinated, and there is evidence that cost pressures will force the firm to seek economies of scale, for example, in purchasing and procurement. Cross-area and cross-functional co-ordination is achieved by project and product management teams. Given that each area carries out a variety of activities, product organisation may cause the firm to miss out on local marketing nuances.

Clearly, any organisation structure will be a compromise between and organisation structure which recognises local flexibility, and one which takes advantage of global company-wide realities.

Two suggestions are offered below.

(i) *Global matrix organisation.*

This exists in embryo, in that functional managers in the regions do not know who to report to, their regional boss or the functional boss. A formal matrix structure would define responsibilities precisely. This would also enable a centralised procurement policy to be introduced, but this would be administered by the regions. A matrix organisation is inevitably bureaucratic, but this might be a price worth paying.

(ii) *Hybrid design*

Most organisations are structured with a mix of centrally administered functions and some other form of organisation. For example, human resources management may be managed centrally, whereas, a product organisation can be developed for production and marketing. A hybrid design would also be suitable, given it would mean relatively minor adjustments to the existing set-up, and would clarify such ambiguities as exist. There would be a number of central functions such as finance, with marketing and production matters organised on an area basis, as now. There will still be some functional co-ordination. The success of this requires effective communication at senior levels.

15 FLEET WATER SERVICES LTD

(a) *Management and planning process for developing a strategy for information at Fleet Water Services Ltd (FWSL)*

Management

In organisations where information is a key resource, and where information systems and technologies have a strategic importance, information technology needs to be considered at a suitable strategic level in the firm. Not doing so, managers might:

(i) miss opportunities offered by IT;
(ii) have an unrealistic idea as to what is possible;
(iii) make uninformed decisions which have long term drawbacks.

There are a two main ways of ensuring IT considered at board level.

(i) Make information the responsibility of one of the functional directors (eg the finance director). There is a danger that the wider uses of IT may not be appreciated (eg the finance director might appreciate IT's administrative importance, but not its impact on competitive strategy).

(ii) Appoint a director of information systems with specific responsibility for IT. Anybody appointed to a board of directors should be able to take a strategic viewpoint, and not be beholden to professional specialists in the technostructure. An alternative would be to appoint an information manager reporting directly to the managing director.

In FWSL, either approach would be valid.

(i) The accounting system appears the most urgent, so initially at least, IT might be the responsibility of the finance director.

(ii) On the other hand, there is a good case for appointing an information systems specialist, in case the role of IT is enhanced. For example, information may be required in the metering technology. The company is new, and the technical aspects of the task might be quite demanding.

Planning processes

Once the management structure of IT has been decided, the firm needs to do the following.

(i) Incorporate issues relating to information and IT in the strategic planning process. Just as there might be a marketing SWOT contributing to the to overall corporate SWOT, so too there can be an IT SWOT, in which specific strengths, weaknesses, opportunities and threats can be identified.

(ii) The contribution that information and information technology make to the firm's distinctive competence can also be assessed, both currently and in future (using a framework such as McFarlan's grid). The value chain is a useful model to assess this.

(iii) Identify the critical success factors of the business as a whole, in the light of corporate objectives, and identify how information and information technology can support these critical success factors. These CSFs might be generic to the industry or just to the firm. FWSL is a new firm, and profitability and cash flow is essential; the accounting system, which will facilitate invoicing is therefore quite important for the business's health (and maintaining appropriate accounting records is a legal requirement).

(iv) Once CSFs and the information to support them have been identified, appropriate strategies can be developed and implemented.

The *information systems (IS) strategy* is the 'long-term directional plan...seen to be business-led, demand-oriented and concerned to exploit IT either to support business strategies or create new strategic options'. An IS strategy therefore deals with the integration of an organisation's information requirements and information systems planning with its long-term overall goals (customer service etc). IS strategy is formulated at the level of business where specific customer needs etc can be delineated. It deals with what applications should be developed, and where resources should be deployed.

The *information technology (IT) strategy* provides a framework for the analysis and design of the technological infrastructure of an organisation. For example, this might involve guidelines for makes of computers purchased (eg must support open systems) and so forth. This strategy basically indicates how the information systems strategies will be implemented.

The *information management (IM) strategy* refers to the basic approach an organisation has to the management of its information systems, including:

(1) planning IS developments;

(2) organisational environment of IS (eg the role of the information director;

(3) control (eg cost control);

(4) technology (eg systems development methodologies case, program development tools).

(b) (i) *Project management*

Project management is directed at an end. It is not directed at maintaining or improving a continuous activity. It thus has a limited objective within a limited time span. All projects involve, according to Dennis Lock, the 'projection of ideas and activities into new endeavours. No project can ever be exactly the same as anything which has gone before.' The steps and tasks leading to completion can never be described accurately in advance. Therefore, according to Lock, 'the job of project management is to foresee as many dangers as possible, and to plan, organise and control activities so that they are avoided.'

There are therefore some special management problems.

(1) The work is carried out by a team of people usually assembled for one project, who must be able to communicate effectively and immediately with each other.

(2) There can be many novel *expected* problems, each one of which should be resolved by careful design and planning prior to commencement of work.

(3) There can be many novel *unexpected* problems, particularly with a project working at the limits of existing and new technologies. There should be mechanisms within the project to enable these problems to be resolved during the time span of the project without detriment to the objective, the cost or the time span.

(4) There is normally no benefit until the work is finished. The 'lead in' time to this can cause a strain on the eventual recipient who feels deprived until the benefit is achieved (even though in many cases it is a major improvement on existing activities) and who is also faced with increasing expenditure for no immediate benefit.

(5) Contributions made by specialists are of differing importance at each stage. Assembling a team working towards the one objective is made difficult due to the

tendency of specialists to regard their contribution as always being more important than other people's and not understanding the inter-relationship between their various specialities in the context of the project.

(6) If the project involves several parties with different interests in the outcome, there might be disputes between them.

(ii) *Project management techniques*

The objectives of project management are these.

(1) *Defining the project.* The project has a task which it must achieve. A technique for making this clear is the specification prepared by or with the client; constantly changing client specifications can increase the cost of the project and lead to its failure. This defines the scope of the project.

(2) *Quality* (in the sense of conformance to client specifications, and any appropriate safeguards). The result of the project should achieve what it is supposed to do. Some information systems methodologies have a series of steps which specifically relate to ones which have gone before, right back to the specification.

To ensure the right level of quality is achieved, a systems project will require specific documentation to ensure there have been no short cuts taken. Tests should be carried out and fully documented. For greatest benefit, the quality controls over the project should relate to BS EN ISO 9000. This will also give additional assurance to the client.

(3) *Budget* and (4) *timescale* (deadlines) can be dealt with together. In order to plan the project effectively, a number of techniques are used. *Work breakdown structure* is an approach which determines the tasks needed to complete the project, which are then broken down into sub-tasks. These can then by mapped on Gantt charts, or even on critical path networks, to find the optimal allocation of resources to activities. Some activities can be crashed or shortened by throwing more resources at them; of course playing around with the critical path in this way might have the effect of increasing the cost of the project. Other activities might be less urgent, depending on the critical path. Estimating the timescale is quite important; for many commercial contracts there are penalties for late delivery.

Some of the cost aspects relate to the work breakdown structure, in that costs can be ascribed to the resources used by each activity. Generally speaking, estimates are prepared, based on the work breakdown structure. A standard costing system might be relevant here.

A further issue to be considered is that of *risk*. There is the risk that the project will be late or over budget. This can be managed by ensuring that the specification is as accurate as possible. Effective project management should minimise the risk. Insurance might compensate for some of the immediate financial problems.

In other cases, a project may have to be over-specified with fail-safe mechanisms. In other cases risks can be dealt with by means of contingency plans. Some firms have back-up computer systems if an application is judged to be critical.

16 ANYBOROUGH COUNCIL: REORGANISATION AND REDUNDANCY

(a) *Specific proposals on steps to be taken prior to change*

(i) *Draw up a plan.* This might be easier said than done, as there will be a whole variety of different activities which have to be co-ordinated.

(ii) *Issues a series of statements* to the workforce as soon as possible, indicating what is likely to occur, as the existence of rumours is likely to make matters worse. However, at this stage it is best not to be too specific, as it might make things hard to negotiate later.

It is important to untangle the various issues involved, as some will require different approaches.

(i) The relocation itself must be planned, to minimise the inconvenience and to continue.

(ii) The introduction of the new management information system needs to be planned in detail.

(iii) Personnel issues need to be sorted out, particularly the relocation, the redundancies, and the impact of compulsory competitive tendering.

In fact both the redundancies and the relocation will have to be handled with a certain degree of sensitivity. Both might require consultation with the relevant trade unions. There might be several representing different kinds of workers.

Each of the issues above will have its own dynamic, demands and objectives. The difficult part will be to integrate them together to ensure that normal service is not interrupted.

This is particularly necessary if the risk of strike action is to be avoided.

The following will be matters to consider when dealing with the personnel issues.

(i) Publicise the likely changes, and indicate the options that are available.

(ii) Enter into discussions with workers' representatives immediately.

(iii) Matters to negotiate include the possibility of compulsory competitive tendering. Most of the unions will be well acquainted with the fact that this is government policy. The case is to assess whether the efficiency standards can be reached so that the existing workforce can be a competitor.

(iv) On a more specific note, the minimum requirements of the plan do involve redundancy. This is something which the workers' representatives are certain to be interested in, to ensure that employees, many of whom might find it hard to find jobs elsewhere, are fairly treated.

To ensure harmonious settlement of these items, the possibility of voluntary redundancies might first be considered. It is possible that many workers nearing retirement will take these terms.

However, there should be a back up in case not enough people resign *voluntarily*. Some can be found jobs elsewhere within the council, but these may not be of equal status. Alternatively, some members of staff might by happy to consider job share arrangements.

(v) *New offices.* There is unlikely to be any compensation for the redeployment, or staff might be given a one-off payment, especially for those who have to travel further, and spend more on bus or train fares, or petrol.

(vi) On a practical note, there should be a timetable for moving section by section. As far as possible, the work of the department should not be interrupted.

(b) *Implementing the changes*

Assuming that there are no personnel problems such as strikes or go-slows - and this is a big assumption - then the changes would be implemented in a phased way.

Some of the steps of implementing change are those mentioned above. The change agent has to ensure that he or she has won at least the consent, if enthusiasm is too much to hope for, of the people most affected by it.

This propaganda exercise is important. As the changes are more or less inevitable, there may not be a great deal that can be negotiated for. If they are presented to the work force as a fait accompli, the change agent can *still* offer the workforce some say by negotiating at the margin. Negotiable items can include extra allowances for travelling and so forth, and redundancy terms. These should be sorted out before the change is implemented. It would also help to have some further options already available.

The order in which the changes take place is most important.

(i) The new building should be ready to receive the new occupants.

This does not mean that all the necessary refurbishment has been done. Rather, that the refurbishment exercise is in planned stages (eg one floor at a time), so groups of people can be transferred in batches. This has the advantage that any teething problems with the building can be sorted our early.

Obviously, matters such as telephone connections must be sorted out in advance.

(ii) The new sites must be set up to run the computer system. The changeover to the new system must also be planned. During the period, the three personnel selected to be administrative assistants can be sent on training courses individually. It is probably the case that new and old systems will have to run in parallel for some time. This will enable the change agent to give some sense of security for the short term. On the other hand, the other disruptions may mean that the system should be delayed.

(iii) The move should be planned so that, if compulsory competitive tendering is introduced, it is possible to 'mothball' the sites for some other use.

(iv) The possible introduction of compulsory competitive tendering does put all the changes in jeopardy, as it will have a much greater long term impact. If there are to be so many redundancies, then the offices will be too large, and it will be an expensive and inefficient use of space.

(v) The first people to be moved in should be those sections whose work requires the least contact with the work of other sections. This means that the normal day to day operations of the department are not impeded.

(vi) Special transitional procedures need to be introduced to cover the two sites for the two month period. These can include special mail deliveries or couriers.

(c) *Alterations to proposals*

The basic flaw with the proposals as they now stand is that the issue of compulsory competitive tendering is so vague. This would have the greatest impact on the workings of the department, leading to large scale redundancies if the council's workforce failed to win the contract.

A first proposal then, would be to try and obtain a commitment as to a particular time for its introduction.

Secondly, the workforce should be given time to prepare a bid. It is not perhaps appropriate to expect them to bid when they are in the throes of a move to a new site.

The timescale is almost certainly too short. Three months would be better.

The issue of funding must be sorted out in advance with the chairperson of the housing committee. This is bound to be affected by compulsory competitive tendering, which may have the effect of producing those reductions. There are bound to be some costs involved with the change for it to be effective.

To conclude, then, the change agent could advise the housing committee to put the whole project on ice until the issue of compulsory competitive tendering has been agreed, to avoid the expense of moving. There is also the additional expense of training people in the new computer system. This must be considered, too.

In the probable absence of their agreement, the change agent should get a commitment as to the level of financial resources, and approval of the plans outlined.

17 QUICK TRIP

> *Tutorial note.* This question does not ask for solutions to the problems of the plant at Sceaux, but it deals more with how you would go about finding out problems.

(a) The visit is short, and you are more or less free to set your own agenda. As well as setting your own objectives for the visit, you are asked to say how you would go about them. This should concentrate the mind on whether your objectives are achievable. The basic purpose of the visit is to find out what is going wrong with the firm. This implies a broad brush approach to the firm's problems, with an attempt to find if possible a common factor.

Some objectives of the visit are therefore as follows.

(i) Meet the local management and develop their trust. They are bound to feel suspicious or sceptical. In two days it will be hard to build up a relationship, so your communication and listening skills will be important. If they feel threatened in any way, they are likely to clam up.

(ii) Discuss with them their views of the various management initiatives and why they have failed. There does seem to be an element of the quick fix. There may be specific reasons, however, which can be investigated. Time is limited and so these chats will have to be brief.

(iii) Get an idea of the corporate culture of the plant, employee morale and the views of middle management. If there is a management problem, this will show up. A walk around some areas of the plant might give an overall impression as to how business is done.

(iv) Obtain the main reasons local managers give to the failure to be profitable. They may quote sound reasons (eg old equipment). What they omit might be just as revealing. For example, they might have lost a major customer, but do little to get new business. A concentration on production issues might indicate marketing failures. Most of the techniques tried out have involved concentrating on the internal workings of the business.

(v) Discover, through review of appropriate personnel documentation, the causes of the management changes.

(vi) Review the firm's accounting systems to see if they provide relevant management information. For example, the costing information may lead to bad management decisions. Does the costing system identify waste? What management reports are produced? Who sees them? What control action is taken?

(vii) Review the main customer relationships, and the firm's marketing strategy, if it has one. Does it offer discounts?

(viii) Verify the accuracy of the information held at head office.

(ix) Review supplier relationships. Are discounts taken? How aggressive are negotiations on price and quality.

(x) Obtain broad information as to how the distribution system works.

As the overall problem with the plant is a failure of profitability, it will be easy to be sucked into a forensic examination of the accounting information. However, two days will not really provide enough time, although you should be able to calculate some management ratios, provided you are familiar with French accounting conventions.

However, a concentration on accounts can mean fail to get sight of the larger picture, some of which has already been suggested in the case study documentation.

The methods used will be based on some document review, but sometimes the only way to glean any information is by chatting to key personnel in an informal but attentive way.

(b) *Features of a good written report*

Reports are meant to be *useful.* There should be no such thing as 'information for information's sake' in an efficient organisation: information is stored in files and retrieved for a purpose. The information contained in a business report might be used:

(i) as a permanent record and source of reference; or

(ii) as a management tool - a source of information prepared in order to assist in management decision-making. Often more junior managers do the 'legwork' in obtaining information on a matter and then prepare a report for more senior managers to consider. This saves senior managers' time and ensures that the information on which they base their decision is more objective than if it had all been gathered and used by one person only.

A business report is usually made by someone who is instructed by a superior. Whether the report is 'one-off' or routine, there is an obligation on the part of the manager calling for the report to state the use to which the report will be put. In other words the purpose of the report must be clear to both the report writer and the report user.

In the case of routine reports, their purpose and how they should be used ought to be specified in a procedures manual. One-offs will require terms of reference, explaining the purpose of the report and any restrictions on its scope.

There is also an obligation on the part of the report writer to communicate information in an unbiased way. The report writer knows more about the subject matter of the report than the report user (otherwise there would be no need for the report in the first place). It is important that this information should be communicated impartially, so that the report user can make his own judgements. This means that:

(i) any assumptions, evaluations and recommendations by the report writer should be clearly 'signalled' as such;

(ii) points should not be over-weighted (or omitted as irrelevant) without honest evaluation of the objectivity of the selection;

(iii) facts and findings should be balanced against each other; and

(iv) a firm conclusion should, if possible, be reached. It should be clear how and why it was reached.

The needs and abilities of the report user should be recognised by the report writer.

(i) Jargon, technical terms and specialist knowledge should be kept at the level of the user's comprehension.

(ii) Simple vocabulary, sentence and paragraph structures should be used for clarity (although the user should not thereby be patronised).

(iii) The type and level of detail should be kept to what is relevant for the user.

18 THE MARKETING CONCEPT

The marketing concept has been defined as a 'management orientation or outlook, that accepts that the key task of the organisation is to determine the needs, wants and values of a target market and to adapt the organisation to delivering the desired satisfaction more effectively and efficiently than its competitors'.

In other words, customer needs and the market environment are considered of paramount importance. Since technology, markets, the economy, social attitudes, fashions, the law and so on are all constantly changing, customer needs are likely to change too. The marketing concept is that changing needs and attitudes must be identified, and products or services adapted and developed to satisfy them. Only in this way can a supplier hope to operate successfully and profitably (if the supplier of the goods or service is a profit-making organisation).

Some firms may be *product oriented* and others *sales oriented*, although a firm should be *marketing oriented* to be successful in the longer term.

(a) A product oriented firm is one which believes that if it can make a good quality product at a reasonable price, then customers will inevitably buy it with a minimum of marketing effort by the firm. The firm will probably concentrate on product developments and improvements, and production efficiencies to cut costs. If there is a lack of competition in the market, or a shortage of goods to meet a basic demand, then product orientation should be successful. However, if there is competition and over-supply of a product, demand must be stimulated, and a product-oriented firm will resort to the 'hard-sell' or 'product push' to 'convince' the customer of what he wants.

(b) A sales oriented firm is one which believes that in order to achieve cost efficiencies through large volumes of output, it must invest heavily in sales promotion. This attitude implies a belief that potential customers are by nature sales-resistant and have to be persuaded to buy (or buy more), so that the task of the firm is to develop a strong sales department, with well-trained salesmen. The popular image of a used car salesman or a door-to-door salesman would suggest that sales orientation is unlikely to achieve any long-term satisfaction of customer needs.

The marketing concept should be applied by management because it is the most practical philosophy for achieving any organisation's objective. A profit-making company's objective might be to achieve a growth in profits, earnings per share or return on shareholder funds. By applying the marketing concept to product design the company might hope to make more attractive products, hence to achieve sustained sales growth and so make higher profits.

Another implication of the marketing concept is that an organisation's management should continually be asking 'what business are we in?' This is a question which is fundamental to strategic planning too, and the importance of developing a market orientation to strategic planning is implicit in the marketing concept.

(a) With the product concept and selling concept, an organisation produces a good or service, and then expects to sell it. The nature of the organisation's business is determined by what it has chosen to produce, and there will be a reluctance to change over to producing something different.

(b) With the marketing concept, an organisation commits itself to supplying what customers need. As those needs change, so too must the goods or services which are produced.

If the marketing concept is to be applied successfully, it must be shared by all managers and supervisors in an organisation. 'Marketing is a force which should pervade the entire firm. It must enter into the thinking and behaviour of all decision-makers regardless of their level within the organisation and their functional area' (Boyd and Massy). 'Marketing' in its broader sense covers not just selling, advertising, sales promotion and pricing, but also product design and quality, after sales service, distribution, reliability of delivery dates and in many cases (such as the retailing industry) purchasing supplies. This is because the customers' needs relate to these items as well as more obvious 'marketing' factors such as sales price and how products are promoted.

Another way of expressing the important point made above is: 'most firms have a marketing or sales department, but the marketing concept should be shared by managers in every department'.

It could also be suggested that marketing should aim to maximise customer satisfaction, but within the constraints that all firms have a responsibility to society as a whole and to the environment. Not only is there the idea that 'high gross national product also means high gross national pollution' but also there is a need to make efficient use of the world's scarce and dwindling natural resources.

(a) Some products which consume energy (motor cars, houses) should perhaps make more efficient use of the energy they consume.

(b) It may be possible to extend the useful life of certain products.

(c) Other products might be built smaller, so that they make use of fewer materials (products made using microtechnology).

19 COMPETING UNIVERSITY

> *Tutorial note.* You could just as easily have used the service marketing mix - people, process and physical evidence - as the 4Ps we have chosen to structure the answer.

(a) *Ways in which PG can compete with other institutions*

PG has a limited control over its own cost structure, as university lecturers' salaries are in part determined centrally, and university facilities involve a high degree of relatively fixed costs (eg buildings, laboratories and so forth). PG might also have a limited control over one of its major sources of revenue: the level of tuition fees per student is determined, in the UK, by central government. Central government, through the University Grants Committee, also determines how other government funds to universities are distributed.

Firstly, we must identify what the universities are competing for? In fact, the university is competing in a number of different markets and market segments. We can use the four Ps: product, price, place, promotion.

UK undergraduate students

Product. Generally, the university will be offering an honours degree at the end of a three year course. To compete, the university should identify the popular subjects, or perhaps more profitably offer degree courses in subjects for which there might be a suppressed demand. Alternatively, if the university has recognised strengths in particular fields (eg a first class history faculty) then these can be used as a basis for marketing.

Place. There is not much that PG can do about its location and building. Capital expenditure might be limited and restricted. At best, it can seek the co-operation of a local tourist board, which might be trying to enhance the image of the town generally (eg the repackaging of some declining industrial towns as heritage centres of industrial archaeology).

Price. There is little that can be done here either. Tuition fees are paid by the state. High rents for accommodation might deter students.

Promotion. There are a variety of promotional measures. Some universities (eg Cambridge) are well known. Other universities, which might have equal academic strengths but are less well known, need to alert prospective students to their virtues. Examples are:

(i) prospectuses sent to 6th forms in schools;

(ii) inviting teachers to inspect key departments in the hope that they will recommend the university to pupils;

(iii) having open days at convenient times for prospective students;

(iv) persuading current undergraduates to take students round the campus;

(v) well-publicised ties with local businesses to attract students from the immediate location;

(vi) 'star' academics can give publicity to their department by appearing on television current affairs programs as 'pundits';

(vii) the university might employ the services of a PR consultancy.

Overseas students

Overseas students also study at UK universities. Their fees are paid by their governments or families. As the fees are greater, and the UK university system still has a good reputation, there is a demand from overseas. However, demand can depend on the overall political relationship between the countries involved: if relationships are bad, students will be sent elsewhere. PG is also competing with other universities overseas. The natural market would be countries in the British Commonwealth.

Product. It might be harder to discover the sort of studies which overseas students are particularly keen on. If they are sent by the governments of poor or developing countries, they are likely to be interested in subjects such as engineering or medicine, if the aim of sending them is to bring back skills. If sent independently by their families, then the desired degree course will reflect the social and cultural preoccupations of their parents.

Place. PG will have to convince overseas students even more that the place is the right one for them. In this case, price, another important element in the marketing mix will be important.

Promotion. The co-operation of institutions like the British Council might be helpful. Also, maintaining contact with government agencies for public funds (eg the know-how funds for Eastern Europe) might gain some business.

Research students

Universities exist both to teach and to expand knowledge. A research department is a source of prestige to a university, if it is good, and it encourages the brightest individuals to study at the university. It also commands respect from the fund-granting authorities (such as the Department of Education and Science). However, that sort of reputation is hard to build up from scratch. A research student will be interested chiefly in the facilities available and the academic environment.

Mature students

Students who have worked for some time before choosing to study for a degree have their own special interests and needs. The *product* element must therefore include flexible course design, for those who continue to work. *Price* is likely to be a significant element in the marketing mix, as many mature students are self-financing: some, being slightly older, might already have financial and/or domestic commitments. *Place* can therefore be important: perhaps mature students are likely to choose a local university.

Business sponsorship

Governments are trying to enhance the interconnection between universities and industry. It is held that while the UK is good at pure science and research, exploiting research in developing new and marketable products is less successful. It is held that forcing universities to seek out commercial sponsorship is a way of building up those ties.

From the university's point of view, sponsorship by industry is a way of securing funds which are no longer available from the government. Using the marketing mix, we can identify that the product will partly depend on the amount of money the business is prepared to invest and will partly depend on people: the university is effectively selling the brainpower of its research scientists. The price depends on what the business requires or what the university can persuade the business to fund. Promotion is a matter of publicising the university's facilities and interest to decision makers in the business community.

To summarise therefore, the university must recognise that it is operating in a number of market segments, and weight the marketing mix accordingly.

(b) *Establishing user satisfaction*

The university's product - education - typically takes three years to consume, and so the final judgement can only be made once a student has left. Moreover, given that people's memories of university are often clouded by factors extraneous to the service offered by the university (such as leaving home, the unsupervised company of like minded individuals, independence) asking questions of students who have left might give only vague responses.

The university can, however, ask its students what they think of particular elements of the learning environment offered by the university.

(i) It is relatively easy to assess students' views about basic services such as canteen food (in fact it might be easy to predict) simply by handing out questionnaires, and monitoring complaints.

(ii) Similarly, for services such as the use of libraries, market research would be easy and cheap to conduct. This might lead to changes in opening hours and other operational adjustments. However, as the university will probably have a budget for book acquisition and the salaries of library staff, any large scale changes will be hard to implement.

(iii) Quality of teaching. This is likely to be a contentious area with some academic staff. Universities function both as teaching institutions and research institutions. Brilliant researchers may be poor public speakers and poor communicators at classroom level. The best communicators may have few original ideas. Or perhaps some academics see teaching as a necessary but resented distraction from what they regard as their principal activity, the pursuit of knowledge.

The quality of tuition, however, is something to which students are likely to be very sensitive. From the students' point of view, tuition is one of the main reasons for going to university. For those who have taken time off work, borrowed money, or are paying privately (eg mature students, overseas students), poor tuition is likely to be resented far more than boring food or other privations.

In the university, teaching should be recognised as a skill in its own right. Students might be invited to prepare confidential questionnaires giving their opinions of particular lecturers. Those that do not come up to scratch can be trained to do better, as some communication skills can be taught.

(iv) Quality of research. This can be assessed by the reputation the university builds up amongst the academic community and other interested parties such as industry. Quantitative measures of output (eg number of articles) are not appropriate in such an environment. If the department is besieged with applications from well qualified research students, then that is a sign of quality. Similarly, if industry uses the research department's services and returns for further prospects, that is an indication of success.

Using market research techniques is rather simple minded in such a context. Much of a research department's reputation may rest on the genius of one particular scholar. It would however be possible to monitor what research students felt about the facilities available.

(v) Social utility. While it might be current fashion to regard universities as providers of educational services to students who are consumers, the university's main customer is the state, and through the state, the taxpayer. Education is one of the most important long-term investments a society can make, and the educational standard of students can effect a country's long term economic performance. This effectiveness of the university in this regard is very hard to measure quantitatively. The skills required by today's businesses and social institutions are not necessarily those required by future ones.

(c) *Measuring effectiveness*

A university's resources consists of:

(i) tangible fixed assets such as lecture theatre, halls of residence, laboratories and so forth;

(ii) intangible assets such as reputation, goodwill;

(iii) liquid assets, normally the funds provided by the government;

(iv) spare capacity (during university vacations, some of the university's assets will not be used by students);

(v) personnel (lecturers, administrative staff).

The university is a not-for-profit organisation. This does not mean that the resources can be squandered, or used inefficiently. The ultimate measure of effectiveness of use of resources is something that, perhaps, cannot be measured: have students been well educated for both their personal development and for society's needs?

However it is possible to measure the efficiency with which resources are used to pursue particular objectives. Both quantitative and qualitative measures of performance can be used.

Measures of students satisfaction, as noted in part (b) of this question, are an indication of how well the university is performing its basic task: education. Also, if the university receives increasing numbers of applications, that is an indication of a good reputation.

However, the university operates under resource constraints, which are basically financial. The university has to tie in the success of its primary objective, while minimising the cost of achieving it.

Some measures, therefore, will reflect the university's use of resources in the light of its operations.

(i) Student/lecturer ratio
(ii) Total cost per department
(iii) Total cost per student
(iv) Student cost per department
(v) Course fees received/student cost per course
(vi) Administration costs/total costs
(vii) Cost drivers for administrative costs
(viii) Cost of research for business/sponsorship fees.

The university will wish to spend as little as possible on administration, to maximise resources available for its main objectives: teaching and research. If it does work for business, establishing the costs of this work will help it get some indication as to whether this uses up more resources than it provides.

20 CLOCKWORK RADIO

Tutorial note. Don't conflate all the issues together. Part (a) compares direct investment basically with exporting, whether direct or indirect. Part (b) asks you to decide between building up the business and its facilities from scratch or making a local acquisition. Part (c) asks you to assess the need for a local partner.

(a) *Exporting vs direct investment*

The most suitable mode of entry varies amongst firms in the same industry, according to the market and over time. The markets identified are fairly poor, and are in the process of development. Low cost is therefore important; no other firm as yet produces clockwork radios, and substitute products such as batteries are too expensive.

(i) Exporting is easy and cheap. Its advantages are:

(1) concentration of production in a single location;

(2) avoids the risk of overseas production;

(3) enables testing of international strategies;

(4) takes advantage of the exporting country's skills base which might be higher than in overseas markets;

(5) avoids corporate culture problems.

(ii) Direct investment on the other hand:

(1) avoids barriers to entry caused by tariffs;

(2) in IL's case, offers access to much cheaper labour;

(3) is welcomed by overseas governments, who need not worry about losing foreign exchange;

(4) enables better understanding of the local market;

(5) can reduce some of the risks associated with exchange rate fluctuations;

(6) reduces transport costs;

(7) in IL's case, offers market leadership.

In fact the issue for IL is relatively simple, as it probably only has a research and development facility in the UK. The choice is between manufacturing and sourcing from the UK, or from one of the overseas markets. Although the firm will probably obtain investment finance in the UK, manufacturing abroad is a better bet for both marketing and cost reasons.

(b) *New factory versus acquiring a local firm*

In this case, the general arguments for acquisitions versus organic growth apply.

(i) Building a new factory from scratch:

(1) offers greater control;

(2) will ensure the most up to date production facilities for the price;
(3) involves no previous labour relations history;
(4) offers the opportunity to handpick new staff (eg as Nissan did in the UK)
(5) offers an ideal choice of location;
(6) may attract tax advantages or government funding;
(7) may possibly attract more support.

(ii) Against this, there are major benefits in acquiring local facilities which exist already.

(1) The firm may have useful distribution networks in the target areas. Where communications infrastructure is poor, this might be a deciding factor, as to build new distribution systems my be very expensive.

(2) Production can start very quickly - but there is no competing product at the moment.

(3) Staff may have good knowledge of the local market, and what design features of the product are likely to appeal, and how the product might be marketed successfully.

(4) Some multinationals like to hide behind a local subsidiary, but this is unlikely to be a problem for IL.

(c) *Wholly owned overseas subsidiary or a joint venture.*

We now discuss the legal structure of the enterprise.

(i) *Wholly owned*

The advantages of wholly owned overseas subsidies are as follows.

(1) The firm does not have to share its profits with partners of any kind.

(2) The firm does not have to share or delegate decision making and so there are no losses in efficiency arising from inter-firm conflict.

(3) There are none of the communication problems that arise in joint ventures, license agreements etc.

(4) The firm is able to operate completely integrated international systems.

(5) The firm gains a more varied experience from overseas production than from the other arrangements.

There are also major disadvantages.

(1) The substantial investment funding required prevents some firms from establishing operations overseas.

(2) Suitable managers, whether recruited in the overseas market or posted abroad from home, may be difficult to obtain.

(3) Some overseas governments discourage, and sometimes prohibit, 100% ownership of an enterprise by a foreign company.

(4) This mode of entry forgoes the benefits of an overseas partner's market knowledge, distribution system and other local expertise.

(5) There may be problems repatriating dividends.

(ii) *Joint ventures*

A joint venture is an arrangement where two firms (or more) join forces for manufacturing, financial and marketing purposes and each has a share in both the equity and the management of the business. A joint venture is usually an alternative to seeking to buy or build a wholly owned manufacturing operation abroad and can offer substantial advantages.

(1) Some governments discourage or even prohibit foreign firms setting up independent operations. Instead, they encourage joint ventures with indigenous firms. This is because:

- they are averse to sending precious foreign exchange outside the country;
- joint ventures generally involve a transfer of know-how and technology that benefits the local economy. Joint venturing between outside and local firms is encouraged, for example, in India, Nigeria and Russia.

(2) As the capital outlay is shared, joint ventures are especially attractive to smaller or risk-averse firms, or where new technologies are being researched and developed.

(3) When funds are limited, joint ventures permit coverage of a larger number of countries since each one requires less investment by each participant.

(4) A joint venture can reduce the risk of government intervention as a local firm is involved (eg Club Mediterranée pays much attention to this factor).

(5) Licensing and franchising often give a company income based on turnover, and any profits from cost reductions accrue to the licensee. In a joint venture, the participating enterprises benefit from all sources of profit.

(6) Joint ventures can provide close control over marketing and other operations.

(7) A joint venture with an indigenous firm provides local knowledge, quickly.

The major disadvantage of joint ventures is that there can be major conflicts of interest between the different parties. Disagreements may arise over profit shares, amounts invested, the management of the joint venture, and the marketing strategy. IL might benefit from a joint venture to maximise penetration of the product.

21 QUALITY STANDARD

(a) Reasons for reducing the number of suppliers and requiring them to get quality certification.

(i) Viking wishes to save on administration costs.

(ii) Building up relationships with a smaller number of suppliers will be commercially beneficial in the long run, as communications will be better.

(iii) Suppliers, if promised secure business, will be able to invest more time to improve quality.

(iv) It will be easier for Viking to earn BS EN ISO 9000 certification if its suppliers also have it.

(v) Quality assurance will enable Viking to save money on inspection.

(vi) Modern production systems such as JIT cannot cope with the wasted time and resources in dealing with poor quality inputs.

(b) Advantages and disadvantages to CS

Advantages

(i) BS EN ISO 9000 (and its renamed equivalent) is an internationally recognised standard. It thus communicates certain facts about the firm's production process to potential customers elsewhere in the world.

(ii) It is a useful discipline in that in ensures a rigorous approach to quality and other production issues. The very fact of applying for the standard and the effort necessary might reveal useful improvements in operations. Given that CS's approaches to quality have been haphazard, the accreditation will be a systematic and disciplined review of their procedures.

(iii) Standardised procedures make it easier to understand what goes wrong.

(iv) The quality manual can act as an aid to training.

(v) Hopefully, there will be less defective production, and so, despite the cost of applying for certification, there will be a positive effect on profit.

(vi) As there are standard procedures, there might be less need for direct supervision and unnecessary checking.

(vii) Suppliers are unlikely to impose individual requirements, if the firm can promise to adhere to a standard.

(viii) It will be harder for people to cut corners in their work.

Disadvantages are as follows.

(i) The cost (in consultancy fees)

(ii) The paperwork and bureaucracy on a long term basis

(iii) The fact that certification itself does not guarantee high quality product, only that the quality systems are of a certain standard.

(iv) BS 5750 is probably better at ensuring conformance quality (ie zero defects etc) than design quality, which is as important in meeting customer requirements.

(c) *Quality standards and Total Quality Management*

TQM is 'a culture aimed at continually improving performance in meeting the requirements in all functions of a customer'. It is as much a way of doing business as a set of techniques or procedures.

That said, TQM relies on meticulous observation and recording of the production and significant analytical rigour to ensure that it is successful. TQM does involve bureaucracy, as it is carrying on the Taylorist project of the scientific analysis and improvement of work.

That TQM is a culture of continuous improvement, allied to techniques to ensure a minimum of variation in th production process is shown in the ideas of some of the founders of the movement.

TQM includes such concepts as zero defects and right first time. It is also a culture in which the production workforce has a crucial part to play. A quality survey is one of the necessary tools.

Successful implementation of TQM does not in itself depend on the adoption of an external standard. A company can adopt BS EN ISO 9000 without being committed to the continuous improvement that is at the heart of the TQM culture.

BS EN ISO 9000 does, however, provide the necessary bureaucratic underpinning for an adoption of TQM, as it is systematic and rigorous.

(d) *Outline plan for accreditation*

The diagram on the following page indicates the process of obtaining certification. To this we can add:

(i) the necessity for the firm to specify standards which will be incorporated in a manual, which is verified;

(ii) the communication of its success in achieving BS EN ISO 9000 to existing and potential customers.

22 X & Y ADVERTISING LTD: FUTURE POLICY

> *Tutorial note.* You could respond to the case in one of two ways, either concluding that the business had no redeeming features or that it had been showing some signs of improvement. Part (a) should encourage an analysis of the problems into short and long terms. In part (c), remember that you are dealing with a small business, and that without solution to the short term problems, there would be no long term to worry about at all.

(a) (i) Initial analysis of the business

The company has two types of problem. Firstly is the strategic problem about the future of the business. Secondly is the operational problem related to the way the business is run, in particular cash flow.

Strategic problem

The strategic strengths of the business are its local knowledge and experience, its acquaintanceship with local charity and voluntary organisations, and its reputation. There seems to be little competition in the market for this type of product and service, and so X & Y advertising has unique access to its market niche. To voluntary organisations it offers a free service, and presumably has considerable experience in so doing. It also has a well developed list of contacts for its services.

Its strategic weaknesses relate to the changes in the business environment, particularly in the decline in local shops as consumer spending habits favour supermarkets. Another weakness is that, whilst it is geared to small businesses, its rates are obviously too expensive for many of them.

Strategic opportunities include, perhaps, recapturing those businesses which can no longer afford to advertise elsewhere, through innovative marketing. Perhaps it could make better use of its local knowledge.

Strategic threats include, in both the short and long terms, the operational problems outlined below.

Operational problems

The cost and revenue structure of the company leaves it with cash flow problems. This means that it is not terribly liquid. It could be vulnerable to the failure of a major customer, although, as is pointed out, the firm's targeting of small businesses means that it is not dangerously exposed to any one of them. However, it does mean that any fall off in advertising caused by the recession can have a short term impact.

The wage bill is not very flexible, and for a few months at least the same wages are likely to be paid whatever level of business is achieved. In fact if times are hard, the telephone bill might increase given the greater efforts needed to find new clients.

Cash flow could be a problem, if there was a sudden drop in advertising, but at the moment there is not any sign that this will occur. However, it implies that the business is forced to survive on overdraft or short term borrowings which means that financing working capital is expensive.

(ii) *Approaching the task*

The consultant will need to make a thorough analysis of both the long term strategic issues, and the potential operating difficulties which, with bad luck, could sink the company. Each requires a different approach. It is sometimes said that the long term is a collection of short terms, and so short term measures to stabilise the situation are critical. However, they are not sufficient in themselves to guarantee the company's future.

A consultant would carry out the following tasks.

(1) Review management accounts, if prepared regularly. In an organisation of this size - it employs at least 180 people - there is bound to be some regular accounting information. This, and discussions with management, will indicate the extent of deepening trends on the financial front.

(2) Interview senior management, such as the sales director, to assess what they feel about the problems, and to get some idea as to how they would like to deal with them or if there are any particular factors which they think would cause the problems.

(3) Examine the cost structure of the business, particularly the printing side, to assess whether the rates are reasonable, and whether it is used to full capacity. (If not, there might be scope for subcontracting out the work or making cost savings.)

    (*Tutorial note.* It is not exactly clear whether the printing end of the business is part of X & Y Ltd. This answer assumes that it is.)

(4) Discuss with the bank manager and/or the company's financial director the company's financial payments record, and what the bank manager's intentions are should the situation worsen. The bank manager might be prepared to extend further facilities.

(5) Talk to past and present customers about the services offered, and assess whether a new type of service could be provided. It might be the case that X & Y can sell blocks of advertising space in one lump for several publications for which the client might be willing to pay a certain amount in advance.

    Assess the extent to which advance payment can be made. Discuss the cost of the lengthy payment period with senior management.

(6) Conduct market research by analysing the economic geography of the region, as there might be other types of business which have grown, but which do not advertise in the firm's publications.

(7) Review the firm's publications, and their readership. Assess whether non-local businesses or organisations might be interested in reaching the readership of the publications.

(8) Assess the extent to which the firm's services are known about by the businesses in the region.

(9) Assess the extent to which X & Y can offer similar services outside the area, or perhaps offer a different service within the area.

The efforts therefore will be directed towards seeing what can be done about the current situation, and developing or redirecting the business.

(ii) *Recommendations to the managing director*

(1) The company must investigate ways of securing a greater proportion of its funds up front, to ease the pressure on cash flow and so to save expenditure on overdraft charges. Suggested measures are:

- offering early payment discounts to customers;
- offering bulk deals to customers at cheaper rates, based on the company's future expected publications;
- investigating a deal with a debt factoring company (a debt factor is a business which collects revenue on another's behalf, and gives an advance payment).

(2) In order to reduce cash outgoings, the company should consider:

- closing its printing side if subcontracting would be cheaper as the company is not so much a *printer* as a *publisher*; or
- using the printing side to earn revenue by doing other printing jobs, so that printing is a profit centre in its own right.
- perhaps a proportion of wages could be paid by commission, if is not so already.

(3) Drum up new business by:

- advertising in appropriate trade journals;
- assessing pricing policy for smaller customers who can no longer pay the rates to see if they can be coached back to the service;
- assess whether regions further afield would benefit from the service;
- assess whether certain classes of business are being overlooked in the marketing effort.

(b) A *focus* strategy is a strategy based on identifying and developing market segments, and focusing on being the market leader in a particular segment. 'The strategy rests on the premise that the firm is able to serve its narrow strategic target more effectively or efficiently than competitors who are competing more broadly.' (Porter)

Differentiating between customers means recognising that different customer groups have their own 'motivation mix' and so an organisations should develop a different marketing mix for each customer group. If an organisation tries to service all its customers and sell to them in the same way, the danger will be that all customers will receive a 'lowest common denominator' of service, and that marketing resources will be neither properly targeted nor fully effective.

As an example, order books and waiting lists can differentiate between customers. Some groups of customers might expect immediate service, whereas other group of customers might be prepared to wait several weeks or even months for delivery, without fuss.

Customer expectations might also vary from region to region. For example, customers in London might expect a certain speed and standard of service from suppliers and can choose from a large number of suppliers of the same product in the area. In contrast, in a region where there is only one supplier, customer expectation will be much lower.

Customer differentiation ought to be based on extensive market research into what customers expect and also what competitors can provide. The main merit of differentiation is that organisations should be able to use their limited resources to satisfy customer needs more effectively than if differentiation were not exercised.

The drawbacks to differentiation in customer service standards are:

(i) it is often difficult enough to educate employees into accepting the importance of customer service, and so expecting them to appreciate the value of customer differentiation might be seen to be more difficult;

(ii) there is a danger that if standards of service to one group of customers is allowed to slide, the general standards of service might eventually slip too.

23 PERSONNEL MANAGEMENT

To: Managing Director
From: A Newbodd

Date: X/X/19XX

POLICIES AND PROCEDURES FOR RECRUITMENT AND SELECTION

Contents

1. INTRODUCTION

1.1 This report has been written in response to the company's current personnel performance.

1.2 It assesses the current situation and makes some suggestions for improving it.

2. EXECUTIVE SUMMARY OF FINDINGS

2.1 There is currently no personnel policy worth speaking of. This situation is costly in the long term, and strategically unwise in the long term.

2.2 In order to benefit from the investment in personnel, the company would benefit by:

(a) appointing a personnel manager;
(b) instituting a formal policy and procedures for recruitment;
(c) implementing a review of current staff.

Such proposals are financially justified.

3. CURRENT PERSONNEL PERFORMANCE

3.1 *Staff profile*

There is a mixture of staff. High technology skills are relatively rare, and it takes a while to train them on the company's projects. Staff display different levels of competence.

3.2 The high levels of labour turnover are disruptive, especially if a leaver occupies an important position in a project. Newcomers have to be trained, which takes up time which could be better spent working. The high turnover does not encourage a sense of commitment, and has had an adverse effect on morale.

3.3 There is also resentment, as the better performing staff feel they are carrying others who are less productive.

4. SUGGESTED RECRUITMENT AND SELECTION POLICY

4.1 Firstly a series of objectives should be defined:

(a) a reduced rate of staff turnover;
(b) the establishment of proper job descriptions according to the company's requirements;
(c) the recruitment of suitable personnel.

4.2 Secondly, a management structure should be put in place as, inevitably, there will be a lot of work to do.

(a) A personnel department should be set up under the control of an experience personnel manager. The personnel manager should be given a brief.

(b) Suitable information systems should be provided to collate knowledge of staff, perhaps in an employee database.

4.3 The personnel manager should be given the following brief.

(a) Assess formally the type of jobs the company offers.

(b) Assess the skills needed to fill those jobs.

(c) Draw up a profile of the sort of people the company is looking for in each of the various capacities. This will include professional expertise, and personality.

(d) Draw up guidelines for employee development.

(e) Draw up guidelines for the use of recruitment consultants and outside agencies.

(f) Determine a selection method that is best needed for the diversity of skills the company requires, to give a systematic and objective case for employing a particular candidate.

(g) Design application forms that properly draw out the biographical information from candidates.

(h) Assess reasons (eg through exit interviews) for the current rate of staff turnover.

4.4 It is recommended that the method of selection should be more scientific than currently to date. Interviews are generally a poor predictor of performance in a particular job, so *aptitude tests* and *personality* profiles should be used to ensure:

(a) the candidate's suitability and ability;
(b) that the person will fit into the group.

4.5 The personnel manager should seek actively to promote the company in the relevant job markets, through advertising, and the development of recruitment documentation.

5. THE CASE FOR IMPLEMENTATION

5.1 Clearly introducing such a policy would mean incurring costs, in financial terms, and also a reduction in the autonomy which perhaps some managers have enjoyed in recruiting staff.

5.2 However, a cost benefit analysis which looked at the wider issues would take the following into account.

(a) *Costs of new system*

(i) Salary of a personnel manager and perhaps an assistant at some stage.
(ii) Cost of information technology to support the new personnel function.

(b) *Against these costs must be set the costs of doing nothing*

(i) *Staff turnover:* quantifiable costs. The cost of recruiting a new member of staff is sometimes equivalent to a quarter of their annual salary if recruitment consultants are used. Even a small reduction in staff turnover caused by this policy would probably justify pay for the salary of the personnel manager.

(ii) *Staff turnover:* non-quantifiable costs means disruptions to projects and production, time lost in training, and managerial time lost in advertising and recruiting for new staff. In short this results in lost productivity and output.

(iii) *Boundary management.* The company is not in a position to promise a standard of performance quality with such a rapidly changing staff.

24 DOSEY URETAULD

Tutorial note. A bad appraisal scheme is probably worse than no appraisal scheme at all, if it fails to generate better performance.

(a) *Role and benefits of appraisal scheme*

Dosey Uretauld (DU) is at the cross-roads. The firm is too big for the existing informal appraisal system to be effective. This is because the partners cannot assess everybody; the firm employs specialists from different disciplines; some way has to be found to improve performance.

The general purpose of any staff appraisal system is to improve the efficiency of the organisation by ensuring that the individuals within it are performing to the best of their ability and developing their potential for improvement.

In his book *Human Resource Management* (1988) George Thomason identifies the variety of objectives of appraisals.

(i) Establishing what actions are required of the individual in a job in order that the objectives for the section or department are realised.

(ii) Establishing the key results which the individual will be expected to achieve in the course of his or her work over a period of time.

(iii) Assessing the individual's level of performance against some standard.

(iv) Identifying the individual's needs for training and developing.

(v) Identifying candidates.

(vi) Establishing an inventory of actual and potential performance within the undertaking to provide a basis for manpower planning.

(vii) Improving communication between different levels in the hierarchy.

It may be argued that such deliberate stock-taking is unnecessary, since managers are constantly making informed judgements about their subordinates and (should be) giving their subordinates feedback information from day to day. However, it must be recognised that:

(i) managers may obtain random impressions of subordinates' performance, but rarely form a coherent, complete and objective picture;

(ii) managers may not have devoted time and attention to improving employees performance;

(iii) judgements are easy to make, but less easy to justify in detail;

(vi) different assessors may be applying a different set of criteria;

(v) unless stimulated to do so, managers rarely give their subordinates adequate feedback on their performance.

(b) *Appraisal procedures*

A typical system would therefore involve the following.

(i) Identification of *criteria* for assessment, perhaps based on job analysis, performance standards, person specifications and so on. The basis of appraisal must first be determined. Assessments must be related to a common standard, in order for comparisons to be made between individuals: on the other hand, they should be related to meaningful performance criteria, which take account of the critical variables in each different job. A blanket approach may provide a common standard, but may not offer a significant index for job performance.

(ii) The preparation by the subordinate's manager of an *appraisal report.*

(iii) An *appraisal interview*, for an exchange of views about the results of the assessment, targets for improvement, solutions to problems and so on. There are three types of approach to appraisal interviews.

(1) The *tell and sell method.* The manager tells the subordinate how he or she has been assessed, and then tries to sell (gain acceptance of) the evaluation and the improvement plan. This requires unusual human relation skills in order to convey constructive criticism in an acceptable manner, and to motivate the appraisee.

(2) The *tell and listen method.* The manager tells the subordinate how he or she has been assessed, and then invites the subordinate to respond. The manager therefore son longer dominates the interview throughout, and there is greater opportunity for counselling as opposed to pure direction. Moreover, this method does not assume that a change in the employee will be the sole key to improvement: the manager may receive helpful feedback about how job design, methods, environment or supervision might be improved.

(3) The *problem-solving approach.* The manager abandons the role of critic altogether, and becomes a counsellor and helper. The discussion is centred not on the assessment, but on the employee's work problems. The employee is

encouraged to think solutions through, and to make a commitment to personal improvement.

(iv) Review of the assessment by the assessor's own superior, so that the appraisee does not feel subject to one person's prejudices. Formal appeals may be allowed, if necessary to establish the fairness of the procedure.

(v) The preparation and implementation of *action plans* to achieve improvements and changes agreed.

(vi) *Follow-up*: monitoring the progress of the action plan, to provide feedback to the next appraisal session.

(1) informing employees of the results
(2) carrying out agreed training programmes etc
(3) reviewing performance to see if it has improved, and helping the employees

There may not be a need for standard forms for appraisal - and elaborate form-filling procedures should be avoided - as long as managers understand the nature and extent of what is required, and are motivated to take it seriously. Most systems, however, provide for appraisals to be recorded, and report forms of various lengths and complexity may be designed.

(c) *How Dosey Uretauld should manage its appraisal scheme*

The managers are right be alarmed at the problem. At the moment, the scheme has been introduced in a random and haphazard way. This is probably even worse than the old formal appraisal system, for the simple reason that nobody knows any longer what the rules are, and everybody knows that the appraisal system is being applied inconsistently, and therefore unfairly. They might need guidance from an expert in this area; there will be no shortage of management consultants willing to help them out.

One problem is that the partners are not clear as the objective of the system, and the employees do not really know how to approach appraisals. This is because appraisal schemes are often required to satisfy three sometimes contradictory assessments.

(i) *Reward review* - measuring the extent to which an employee is deserving of a bonus or pay *increase* as compared with his or her peers.

(ii) *Performance review*, for planning and following-up training and development programmes, ie identifying training needs, validating training methods and so on.

(iii) *Potential review*, as an aid to planning career development and succession, by attempting to predict the level and type of work the individual will be capable of in the future.

For the time being, the concentration should be on *performance*. Some firms, where managers can spare the time, offer two interviews, a performance review and a salary review. For the system to work, DU should have consistent and coherent answers to the questions below.

(i) *Relevance*

(1) Is the system relevant to the needs of the organisation and the individual?
(2) Is its purpose clearly expressed and widely understood by all concerned?
(3) Are the appraisal criteria relevant to the purposes of the system?

(ii) *Fairness*

(1) Is there reasonable standardisation of criteria throughout the organisation?
(2) Is there reasonable objectivity?

(iii) *Serious intent*

(1) Are the managers concerned committed to the system and are they prepared to make time available?

(2) Who does the interviewing, and are they properly trained in interviewing and assessment techniques?

(3) Is reasonable time and attention given to the interviews?

(4) Is there a genuine demonstrable link between performance and reward or opportunity for development?

(iv) *Co-operation*

(i) Is the appraisal a participative, problem-solving activity - or a tool of management control?

(ii) Is the appraisee given time and encouragement to prepare for the appraisal, so that he can make a constructive contribution?

(iii) Does a jointly-agreed, concrete conclusion emerge from the process?

(iv) Are appraisals held regularly?

(v) *Efficiency*

(1) Does the system seem overly time-consuming compared to the value of its outcome?

(2) Is it difficult and costly to administer?

25 DEVELOPMENT FUNDING

(a) *Justifying a staff development programme*

In this case, three sets of arguments have to be put forward:

(i) why Dinsdale Piranha's approach to motivation and staff development is misconceived in the first place;

(ii) why a strategic approach to human resources management is necessary, in current business conditions;

(iii) how a programme of staff development can play a role in human resources management.

(i) Problems with existing approach

(1) Although money is an important factor in many career decisions, people are motivated by more than this. Maslow suggested a hierarchy of needs ranging from food etc to self-actualisation. Whilst it is unrealistic to expect work to satisfy all these needs, it may be wise for Dinsdale to listen to what his employees are saying

(2) Herzberg made a distinction between hygiene and motivator factors. Hygiene factors include the basics of pay and conditions, perks and so forth. When unsatisfactory these can demotivate, but on their own they can only rarely generate exceptional commitment.

It is clear from the case that hygiene factors are not a problem. The fact that staff are unmoved by the offers of higher salaries and company cars, and specifically mention staff development, and by implication job satisfaction issues, suggest that motivator factors rather than hygiene factors are the issue. Dinsdale Piranha is trying to deal with motivator factors by offering benefits which deal with the hygiene factors.

The failure of the current approach is also shown in the difficulties the firm is having in recruiting good people; again, staff development is specifically mentioned.

(3) Staff development programmes may have the effect of building loyalty and retaining staff as well as keeping the firm's accumulated expertise in house. Successful organisational learning depends on suitable staff management.

(ii) Dinsdale Piranha also thinks that staff development is not really his problem as a businessman. Instead he seems to regard it as an unreasonable and even eccentric demand of his employees that they should want such a thing. However, this is wrong for a number of reasons.

(1) Holmes and Watson plc is a service industry, par excellence. Its very success in being able to deliver its service depends on its staff. In the long run, success in service industries depends on a suitable policy of involving and developing front line staff. The firm will suffer if the best staff leave, and good staff cannot be recruited.

(2) Many other firms are taking staff development issues seriously, as part of initiatives such as total quality, customer care programmes and so forth.

(3) A number of surveys have revealed that taking a professional approach to the management of employees and their development increases productivity.

(4) Staff development and empowerment would enable Holmes and Watson to dispense with a layer or two of middle management, and hence save money. Cost is likely to be a significant factor in Dinsdale Piranha's outlook.

(5) Any service business is not only competing for customers; it is competing for the right staff.

(iii) The long term success of the firm therefore bears a strong relationship to its use of human resources in a number of areas.

(1) Assessing the firm's demand for manpower as suggested by its overall business strategy

(2) Assessing the overall skills needed by the firm. For example if the firm is going to run private prisons, the type of skills needed are very different than it has hitherto needed.

(3) Assessing the gap between future capacity, and suggesting how this should be filled. This should demonstrate the need for staff development as providing the essential skills the firm needs.

(4) A precise programme of training and staff development can therefore be suggested, tailored to the firm's strategic needs. This exercise alone will show why a strategic approach to HRM is as necessary as a plan for marketing and other business functions etc. The programme will include on the job training, professional courses (eg in the law), management courses etc. It might also present a structured career path, ensuring that employees are given a rounded variety of challenging work experience. This will also identify the most talented recruits.

(5) Of course, this will have to be budgeted, and the increased expenditure on staff retention and training might have to compared to the hidden costs of staff turnover, and the effect of high staff turnover on other service businesses. Real savings will help convince Dinsdale Piranha that the expense is worthwhile.

(b) *The differences between HRM and personnel management*

The main difference between personnel and HRM is that personnel management basically deals with administration, whereas HRM takes a much a more strategic approach. Personnel management is an indirect result of the overall business strategy, whereas HRM suggests that personnel and staffing issues are as vital an ingredient of the business strategy as the strategies for production and marketing.

The traditional view of personnel management has been essentially task-, activity- or technique- based. Dr Dale Yoder of the Graduate School of Business, Stamford University, defines the personnel management function as follows.

(i) Setting general and specific management policy for employment relationships and establishing and maintaining a suitable organisation for leadership and co-operation.

(ii) Collective bargaining.

(iii) Staffing and organisation: finding, getting and holding prescribed types and numbers of workers.

(iv) Aiding the self-development of employees at all levels, providing opportunities for personal development and growth as well as requisite skills and experience.

(v) Incentivating: developing and maintaining the motivation in work.

(vi) Reviewing and auditing manpower and management in the organisation.

(vii) Industrial relations research, carrying out studies designed to explain employment behaviour, and thereby improve manpower management.

In 1968, Crichton (*Personnel Management in Context*) complained that personnel management was often a matter of 'collecting together such odd jobs from management as they are prepared to give up'. Other writers shared this view, notably Peter Drucker, who - while recognising the importance of human resources in the organisation - saw the personnel function of the time as 'a collection of incidental techniques without much internal cohesion'. According to Drucker, the personnel manager saw his role as 'partly a file clerk's job, partly a housekeeping job, partly a social worker's job and partly "fire fighting" to head off union trouble or to settle it' (*The practice of management*).

A more imaginative set of job titles for personnel managers - albeit just as depressing, insofar as they reflect a purely administrative and reactive role for personnel - was suggested by Nick Georgiades (*Personnel Management,* February 1990).

(i) The *administrative handmaiden* (writing job descriptions, visiting the sick, and so on).

(ii) The *policeman* (ensuring that both management and staff obey the rules and do not abuse the job evaluation scheme, and keeping a watchful eye on absenteeism, sickness and punctuality).

(iii) The *toilet flusher* (administering 'downsizing' policies such as cutting staff numbers).

(iv) The *sanitary engineer* (ensuring that there is an awareness of the unsanitary psychological conditions under which many people work).

The status and contribution of the personnel function is still often limited by the image of *fire-fighting*, an essentially reactive and defensive role.

HRM is a fashionable term, which some personnel specialists have seized upon and applied to themselves (whether or not they are in fact doing anything more than personnel administration or manpower planning) in the interests of their status and self-esteem. HRM is not yet being carried out by personnel functions in the majority of organisations, and to some extent, therefore, widespread use of the term is unhelpful. It is rather a case of the 'Emperor's New Clothes'. However, a precise and positive interpretation of HRM centres on the following notions.

(i) Personnel management has been changing in various ways in recent years. Many of its activities have become more complex and sophisticated and, particularly with the accelerating pace of change in the business environment, less narrowly concerned with areas previously thought of as personnel's sole preserve (hiring and firing, training, industrial relations and manpower planning). The personnel function has become centrally concerned with issues of broader relevance to the business and its objectives, such as change management, the introduction of technology, and the implications of falling birthrates and skill shortages for the resourcing of the business.

(ii) Personnel management can and should be integrated with the strategic planning of the business, that is, with management at the broadest and highest level. The objectives of the personnel function can and should be directly related to achieving the organisation's goals for growth, competitive gain and improvement of 'bottom line' performance.

In a survey of twenty top personnel directors (reported in Personnel Management, October 1989) Michael Armstrong identifies the key issues of HRM, with implications for the personnel function of the future.

(i) HRM implies a shift of emphasis in personnel management from the peripheral staff role of the past to mainstream business management.

(ii) The definition of entrepreneurship is the 'shifting of economic resources out of the area of lower and into an area of higher productivity and greater yield' (JB Say), and this is essentially what HRM embodies, in terms of finding, obtaining and developing - getting the best out of - the human resources of the business.

(iii) This implies a close match between corporate objectives and the objectives of the human resource function.

(iv) The integration of personnel and overall corporate objectives firmly establishes personnel as an enabling function.

(v) This 'enabling' role brings us back to the term HRM. A major part of personnel's relatively new-found concern for performance management is the re-orientation towards resourcing in its broadest sense. Personnel's strategic contribution to a business is the definition of relationships between business requirements and organisational and human requirements: the human resourcing of the business is how this works in practice, and includes not only the obtaining of an increasingly scarce resource (people) but the maximisation of their contribution through development, reward, organisational culture, succession planning and so on.

S Tyson and A Fell *(Evaluating the Personnel Function)* suggest four major roles for personnel, which illustrate the shift in emphasis from the odd job to the 'strategic' viewpoint.

(i) To represent the organisation's central value system (or culture).

(ii) To maintain the boundaries of the organisation (its identity and the flow of people in and out of it).

(iii) To provide stability and continuity (through planned succession, flexibility etc).

(iv) To adapt the organisation to change.

Holmes and Watson presumably has had some sort of personnel function before, but it has never been considered of strategic importance.

26 NEW OFFICES

Tutorial note. This answer uses UK health and safety legislation as an example of the legal implications of the type of issues raised by the scenario. The legal situation in the UK is described in the BPP Study Text. However, if you are based outside the UK, you may have preferred to use the laws of your own country. The examiner does not expect a detailed knowledge of UK law. Certain aspects of the scenario might strike you as more relevant than others. For example, is the firm really supposed to supply catering facilities, when, in the centre of London, there are many sandwich bars and fast food restaurants etc where people can buy their lunch. A move to a farmhouse in the middle of nowhere will mean that a canteen probably will need to be provided; but there are other reasons against the move.

REPORT

To: Dr Christie, Anatomy and Biochemistry Books Ltd
From: A Consultant
Date: January 29th 19X5
Subject: Office accommodation

1 *Terms of reference*

1.1 Review Anatomy and Biochemistry Books Ltd's (AB's) existing office accommodation in the light of the legal and operational requirements; suggest remedial action.

1.2 A result of the review suggests that AB should consider moving to new office accommodation, but remain in central London.

2 *Current offices: legal, safety, security and operational implications*

2.1 On a prima facie assessment AB is breaking the law in a number of areas.

2.2 Fire. The Fire Precautions Act 1973 stipulates that:

(a) there must be adequate means of escape which should be free of obstruction;
(b) all doors in a building must be capable of opening from the inside;
(c) employees should know the fire alarm system;
(d) the fire alarm system must be tested regularly;
(e) fire fighting equipment must be in working order.

2.3 AB is clearly in breach of (a), in that the invoice boxes are a hazard, and could be obstruction if say a fire destroyed the lighting system, and people had to escape in the dark. AB is also in breach of (e) in that fire fighting equipment is clearly not working. No information has been provided about the fire alarm and testing.

2.4 The introduction of more information technology, cable etc merely enhances the risk.

2.5 The employer also has a duty under the Health and Safety at Work Act (1974) and the 1993 regulations implementing the EU directives on health and safety.

2.6 The employer's duties under the act are to ensure that:

(a) all systems and work practices must be safe;

(b) the work environment must be safe and healthy (well-lit, warm, ventilated and hygienic).

2.7 The EU *workplace directive* deals with matters that have been statutory requirements for many years in the UK under legislation such as the *Offices, Shops and Railway Premises Act 1963*, although in some cases the requirements have been more clearly defined. The following provisions are made.

(a) *Equipment.* All equipment should be properly maintained.

(b) *Ventilation.* Air should be fresh or purified.

(c) *Temperature.* The temperature must be 'reasonable' inside buildings during working hours. This means not less than 16°C where people are sitting down, or 13°C if they move about to do their work.

(d) *Lighting* should be suitable and sufficient, and natural, if practicable. Windows should be clean and unobstructed.

(e) *Cleaning and decoration.* Floors, walls, ceilings, furniture, furnishings and fittings must be kept clean.

(f) *Room dimensions and space.* Each person should have at least 11 cubic metres of space, ignoring any parts of rooms more than 3.1 metres above the floor or with a headroom of less than 2.0 metres.

(g) *Floors* must be properly constructed and maintained (without holes, not slippery, properly drained and so on).

(h) *Falls or falling objects.* These should be prevented by erecting effective physical safeguards (fences, safety nets, ground rails and so on).

(i) *Glazing.* Windows should be made of safe materials and if they are openable it should be possible to do this safely.

(j) *Traffic routes.* These should have regard to the safety of pedestrians and vehicles alike.

(k) *Doors and gates.* These should be suitably constructed and fitted with any necessary safety devices (especially sliding doors and powered doors and doors opening in either direction).

(l) *Escalators and travelators* should function safely and have readily accessible emergency stop devices.

(m) *Sanitary conveniences* and *washing facilities* must be suitable and sufficient. This means that they should be properly ventilated and lit, properly cleaned and separate for men and women. 'Sufficient' means that undue delay is avoided!

(n) *Drinking water.* An adequate supply should be available with suitable drinking vessels.

(o) *Clothing.* There should be suitable accommodation for outdoor clothing, which should be able to dry out if wet. Facilities for changing clothing should be available where appropriate.

(p) *Rest facilities and eating facilities.* These must be provided unless the employees' workstations are suitable for rest or eating, as is normally the case for offices.

2.8 It is clear that AB is in breach of many of these requirements.

(a) The poor state of the air conditioning system is a problem.
(b) It is possible that insufficient space or natural light is provided.
(c) There is no evidence that a proper risk assessment has been carried out.

2.9 There is a severe risk of accident, arising from the cramped conditions, particularly the obstacles in the gangways. The increased cabling will make this worse, as well as risking damage to the equipment. AB is putting itself at risk of civil legal action from employees so injured.

2.10 Many of the legal issues discussed are relevant to the operational parts of the business.

(a) The risk to safety and health endangers the functioning of the firm. An accident laying a member of staff of work will severely disrupt operations. Similarly the consequences of fire would be catastrophic.

(b) The cramped and unhealthy conditions may not make it easy for staff to give of their best.

(c) The extensive cabling would be safer and more secure under the floor, but this is not possible in the present building.

2.11 The security arrangements, with the door left open to all comers without any effective gatekeeper, leave a lot to be desired. This is especially pertinent with regard to the computer equipment.

3 *Remedies*

3.1 To implement EU directives overall for health and safety requires firms carry out the following.

3.2 Implementation of the EU directives as (legally enforceable) regulations, means that employers now have the following additional general duties (as summarised in the *Administrator*, September 1992).

(a) They must carry out risk assessment, generally in writing, of all work hazards. Assessment should be continuous.

(b) They must introduce controls to reduce risks.

(c) They must assess the risks to anyone else affected by their work activities.

(d) They must share hazard and risk information with other employers, including those on adjoining premises, other site occupiers and all subcontractors coming onto the premises.

(e) They should revise safety policies in the light of the above, or initiate safety policies if none were in place previously.

(f) They must identify employees who are especially at risk.

(g) They must provide fresh and appropriate training in safety matters.

(h) They must provide information to employees (including temps) about health and safety.

(i) They must employ competent safety and health advisers.

3.3 Other specific remedies include the following.

(a) Creation of proper storage space for invoices. Old invoices can be archived by subcontracted firms.

(b) The advice of a professional construction company will need to be sought with regard to the IT network, and the security of the cabling. It may be possible to carry them overhead and down the walls, but, given the state of some of the windows, this could be a hazardous option.

(c) The windows should be repaired. Failing natural light, halogen bulbs should be purchased.

(d) New air conditioning should be installed, if the current system cannot be repaired.

(e) New accommodation should be acquired for new staff.

3.4 Reviewing the existing premises and the operational requirements of the company there is an argument for obtaining new premises. This is outlined in section 4 below.

4 *New premises*

4.1 There are a number of reasons why the firm can consider moving to new premises.

4.2 As the firm owns the freehold of the current office block, it has a large source of funds to finance the move. The firm does not in fact need to buy and equivalent office block; selling the freehold will release funds to acquire new premises. It is unlikely that without substantial refurbishment expenditure, a new tenant would be interested in the current site.

4.3 The advantage of new offices would be as follows.

(a) Adequate space for existing staff, complying with legal requirements.

(b) Proper arrangements to ensure that equipment is secure and safely installed, particularly with regard to cabling.

4.4 The importance of location should not be overlooked.

(a) Moving to the converted farmhouse has some advantages in terms of the site, but against this must be set the severe disruption to employees, who might have to sell their houses, buy new ones, and so forth. The move will be operationally disruptive.

(b) The firm benefits from its close proximity to St Mary's hospital, and the access that this provides to the latest research. Whilst a move to the countryside would not necessarily destroy this, it would make maintaining contacts much more difficult than before.

(c) There is the additional problem that whilst the farmhouse can be converted it was not designed with the requirements of a modern high-tech work environment in mind. This is therefore a severe drawback.

4.5 On balance, if a decision is taken to move, the offices chosen should be near the current premises.

27 TRAINS R US

> *Tutorial note.* This is a wide ranging case study, covering the organisation's structure, culture and systems in the context of change.

(a) *Strategic and operational role to be played by the marketing department*

Marketing involves the identification and satisfaction of customer needs at a profit. It assumes that the customer should be the focus of the business, rather than the product or service being provided: it does not assume that customers will buy what the firm makes, or that aggressive selling is necessarily the best way to profitability over the long term.

One of the implications of the marketing orientation is that a product or service is not a thing with features but a *package of benefits* for the customer, which provides the customer with satisfactions by meeting needs.

The strategic role of marketing is therefore to orientate the firm to meeting customers' needs. Strategic marketing issues relate to market segmentation (as part of a focus strategy), and the development of new products/services to satisfy these needs.

The marketing mix for services covers seven Ps, which indicate its operational role.

(i) Product: this is the basic product/service provided: rail transportation. Unfortunately, TRU does not have complete control over this, as Railtrack owns the railway. However, this relates to the frequency and destination of services, rolling stock and so forth. There is little opportunity to segment here, but expresses can be run etc.

(ii) Price: here the firm can be innovative in issuing season tickets, off peak fares. For many years, fares outside the rush hour have been lower than rush-hour fares. Different tickets might be issued to groups.

(iii) Place: this relates to distribution. Firstly, there is the distribution of the service itself. Obviously this is limited to the railway, but it can also relate to feeding customers on to the railway from other transport modes; arrangements can be set up with local bus companies, so that bus and railway timetables are co-ordinated. Parking facilities might encourage passengers to use the service. Place also refers to the distribution of tickets. A wide range of travel agencies might be employed, or even booking by telephone.

(iv) Promotion relates to letting customers know about the service, eg advertisements in the local press, accurate timetables and prices, telephone help lines.

(v) People: refers to those giving the service, and covers matters such as staff courtesy, customer care.

(vi) Processes indicate how the service is provided, such as ease of access to the network, efficiency of provision.

(vii) Physical evidence relates to the physical environment of the service, as people are put off from using the railways be perceived threats to their security. The trains themselves should be clean and pleasant.

Introducing a marketing orientation might be difficult on account of:

(i) TRU's former public sector monopoly status;

(ii) prior concentration on operational issues;

(iii) the fact that customers use the network as a whole, not just one service provider; common timetabling information might lead customers to choose a competing service.

(b) *Marketing organisation*

In a marketing orientated company, the customer should be at the heart of the firm's decision making, and so marketing considerations are everyone's concern, not just those of the marketing department. However, the activities of the marketing department tend to relate most heavily to advertising and promotion. On operational issues, the operations department and the stations department need to be consulted. The admin department deals with ticketing and pricing, another element of the mix.

The danger of having a separate marketing department is that, as newcomers, they might have little influence over the organisation as a whole. The drawback of ascribing marketing specialists to each individual department is that they would be too junior to have any real effect.

The better option would be to have a separate marketing function, with somebody of sufficient seniority to challenge existing operations and to suggest enhancements. This job will not be easy, if the whole board is made up of experienced personnel from the industry, who might be resistant to new ideas.

(c) (i) *Profit centre.* A profit centre is a part of a business accountable for its costs and revenues, although it has little say over investment. Managers in theory might control costs, sales prices and output volumes; profit is the principal measure of performance.

If taken to extreme, each station manager would have freedom to charge his own prices. However, different ticketing strategies might be acceptable on the different routes, depending on the level of customer demand.

In practice, therefore, only *route managers* can be considered as running genuine profit centres. Profit centre organisation gives them the right to adjust ticket prices where necessary, and some control over costs - but again, some of these costs (eg pay scales) may be fixed centrally.

Much of TRU's revenue comes from a government subsidy: again this is outside anybody's control.

Although not genuine profit centres, measurements of relative profitability can be made for each station. Each station's cost profile may be known; station managers might be given freedom to enhance revenue to the station by renting out retail outlets, or providing other facilities. However, it is unrealistic to treat the stations as separate businesses, as they are merely access points to the network. Station managers have little say over services and how often trains stop. Stations are cost centres rather than profit centres.

What the finance director, is proposing, however, is a performance measurement system which analyses the performance of each of the areas of the business: the cost of one station may exceed the revenues generated from it; or there may be unmet demand elsewhere.

There is certainly scope for new systems which highlight the financial profile of the business, but these should recognise the limited scope of control which some of the managers possess. For example, if the marketing department advertises the railway effectively, more people will be drawn in to use the network, increasing traffic at *all* stations.

The firm as a whole should be able to plan, and station managers may be responsible for spending budgets (eg on refurbishment) efficiently and effectively.

It is likely that a system of charging out *overheads* to cost/profit centres should be devised on some basis to relate them to usage.

(ii) *Training programme*

The training programme might be entitled: *Planning for profit.*

Its aim is to teach managers some of the principles of financial accountability, how these will apply to the areas under their control. There will be separate sessions for route managers and for station managers, given that their tasks and responsibilities are very different.

Training sessions are a good opportunity for people from different areas of the business to mix, and so some of the new marketing staff might be on hand as well. Training also facilitates any necessary changes to corporate culture

The course might last two days, although follow up courses, particularly in the details of the accounting systems, will be needed. The course will be structured as follows.

Day 1

First morning session: introduction of main participants, given by the finance director or another member of the board. Brief description of what they see as TRU's competitive task; although a subsidy is guaranteed for the long term, the firm is a private business, and other sources of revenue must be exploited eg by encouraging people to use the service.

Tea

Second morning session

The focus now is on the financial issues underpinning the business. The need for analysing the performance of each area of the business, from a profit point of view. Profit as a measure of efficiency.

Lunch

First afternoon session. The key features of the type of responsibility centres to be introduced. The degree to which managers over these performance measurement centres will have actual control over costs and revenues, and the degree to which these will be imposed by the centre (eg in determining the basis for allocating the access charges paid to Railtrack). The relationship of the new system to the strategy of the business.

Tea

Question and answer session.

Day two

First morning session: the proposed accounting structure for the group; main centres where profitability will be measured. Importance of cost control and enhancing revenue. Planning operations and budgeting procedures: the need to distinguish between what they would like and the funds available for investment. Timescales. Finance department assistance.

Tea

Second morning session: details of accounting reports and new systems; new hardware and software; perhaps a simulation exercise to be commenced.

Lunch

Afternoon session. Completion of simulation exercise. Details of implementation plans and further training.

Tea

Further questions. Summary of aims of the course, and what should have been achieved (eg understanding the new accounting system).

Ideally, the training will take place in a relaxed atmosphere. The trainers will be supported by a panoply of flipcharts, overhead projectors, slides and so forth. The use of computers for the simulations would be a help.

(d) (i) *The importance of culture*

Peters and Waterman, in their book *In Search of Excellence*, found that the 'dominance and coherence of culture' was an essential feature of the 'excellent' companies they observed. A 'handful of guiding values' was more powerful than manuals, rule books, norms and controls formally imposed (and resisted). They commented: 'If companies do not have strong notions of themselves, as reflected in their values, stories, myths and legends, people's only security comes from where they live on the organisation chart.' Such values might be part of the organisation's mission.

All organisations will generate their own cultures, whether spontaneously or under the guidance of positive managerial strategy. The culture will consist of the following.

(1) *Basic, underlying assumptions* which guide the behaviour of the individuals and groups in the organisation, eg customer orientation, or belief in quality, trust in the organisation to provide rewards, freedom to make decisions, freedom to make mistakes, the value of innovation and initiative at all levels etc.

(2) *Overt beliefs* expressed by the organisation and its members, which can be used to condition (a) above.

(3) *Visible artefacts* - the style of the offices or other premises, dress rules, display of trophies, the degree of informality between superiors and subordinates etc.

A culture is partly self-correcting. Feedback from customers, for example, might help reinforce an organisation's attempts to conform to its culture. (Is it living up to its standards?) Cultures are patterns: Hampden-Turner argues that the way a member of staff treats a customer will be similar to the way in which the member of staff is treated by his or her supervisor. Cultures communicate support, in that they facilitate the sharing of information and experiences. They make members supportive of each other (to the point of reinforcing wishful thinking).

The importance of this is that TRU is going to be *radically* different from its predecessor. Not only is it a lot smaller, but the managers have more freedom to manage the business. People will be less able to hide behind bureaucracy, and one of the features of the new accounting system is that responsibility is devolved downwards.

The need to improve profitability and to ensure the right size will lead to new a new combination of cultures. Under the old system, TRU's culture may perhaps have been a *role culture*, simply because of its size; Handy calls this culture Appollonian, or in Mintzberg's analysis we can say it was a machine bureaucracy.

This change in size more than anything else changes the structural configuration and the culture to support it. Devolving responsibility downwards indicates some of the elements of the professional bureaucracy (where some skills are determined by outside agencies). On the other hand, a task culture might be created if team work is encouraged: in fact team work will be needed if the whole of TRU is to engage upon a marketing orientation focused around the customer.

(ii) *Introducing cultural change*

It is possible to turn large bureaucracies into customer-focused organisations: the example of British Airways is often cited. TRU is a service business, and there are plenty of examples which can be emulated. Perhaps the airline business is a good example. A problem with culture change is that culture is so pervasive.

An organisation's culture is influenced by many factors.

(1) The organisation's *history* (and its founder)

(2) *Recruitment.*

(3) *Leadership and management style.*

(4) *Structure and systems* affect culture as well as strategy.

The railway might have a culture all of its own which will be need to be.

Changing culture involve more than just a change of logos and letterheads, but in the way people relate to each other, and the style of management. Lewin's three-stage model of the change process can be applied to corporate culture.

Unfreeze. In this stage the existing cultural norms can be brought into the open an questioned. An outsider is best able to do this, by intervening to see how the culture works. For example, suppressed conflicts of values can be brought into the open. For example, how are staff supposed to care for customers if they do not have the autonomy to do so? An examination of symbols myths and rituals: for example, are people known by their job titles or by their names?

Change. This will involve identifying the causes of resistance. At present they are likely to be weak, given the turmoil in the railway industry, with a completely new organisational structure, the requirement to adhere to service contracts, and so forth. The small scale of the business also makes a difference. Change can be embedded in:

(1) a mission statement;
(2) top management behaviour;
(3) training for managers and employees;
(4) new working patterns.

The difficulties are that top management have known little other than railways.

Refreezing involves implementing the cultural changes in organisation structure, systems, and training programmes. In particular, behaviour which supports the new culture can be rewarded. Perhaps employees can be offered shares in the new concern.

A consistent approach is needed, requiring:

(1) Top management commitment;

(2) Modelling behaviour - management should be seen to be acting on the new norms themselves, not merely mouthing empty words about change;

(3) Support for positive behaviour and confrontation of negative behaviour;

(4) Consistency between the reward system and positive behaviour .

(5) Communication of desired norms;

(6) Recruitment and selection of the 'right' people;

(7) Induction programmes for new employees on the desired norms of behaviour.;

(8) training and skills development.

Most research has shown that, in a large organisation, shifting the value system or culture can take between three and eight years to bring about. One of the disadvantages of strong cultures is that, as we have seen, they discourage the questioning of their basic assumptions.

Lecturers' question bank

1 COMPETITIVE FORCES

Identify *five* competitive forces in the environment of a firm and discuss the threat posed to the firm by *each* of these forces.

2 BARRIERS TO ENTRY

Discuss the nature and effect of significant 'entry barriers' on the formulation of a strategic plan for a business which is already established in the industry.

3 GENERIC STRATEGIES

Michael Porter suggests that there are three generic strategies for creating and sustaining superior performance. These strategies are:

(a) overall cost leadership;
(b) differentiation;
(c) focus.

Describe *each* of these strategies and indicate how *each will result in* competitive advantage.

4 UNBUNDLING

Until quite recently many firms pursued a policy of conglomerate diversification. This was usually linked with the strategic objective of growth, and often effected by mergers. However, a contrary form of policy has now become popular, that of 'de-merger' or 'unbundling'.

You are required:

(a) to assess the appropriateness of growth as a strategic objective; (6 marks)
(b) to explain why a company might follow a policy of conglomerate diversification; (13 marks)
(c) to explain why a company might follow a policy of demerger. (6 marks)

5 QUALITY CONTROL

Explain and comment on the objectives, techniques and management of quality control in manufacturing or service enterprises.

Illustrate you answer using examples with which you are familiar.

6 SOCIAL RESPONSIBILITY

(a) How would an understanding of the economic and social history of the surrounding community be relevant to the organisation and management of a commercial enterprise?

(b) The senior management of your company has expressed the opinion that there should be social responsibility of managers. What do you understand by this and could you expect this view to be translated into policies and procedures within the organisation?

7 TESTS

(a) Examine the role of tests in the employee selection process.

(b) Briefly identify the types of test which might be appropriate for selecting an accounts clerk. Refer to the limitations of the tests you identify.

(c) Describe the limitations of interviews in the selection process.

8 WORK TEAM

What are the characteristics of an effective work team? Describe briefly one training method by which an effective team can be developed.

9 RESISTANCE TO CHANGE

Commenting about the problem of implementing change in organisations, the nuclear physicist Edward Teller once remarked that 'In all my scientific explorations, the most inert material I have ever discovered is the human mind - with one exception, a group of human minds'. Why, in fact, do people (both as individuals and as members of groups) resist change? What can we learn, from the causes of resistance to change, about how managers should go about introducing change successfully?

10 THE STAGE HYPOTHESIS

(a) Richard Nolan's 'stage hypothesis' identifies the stages through which an organisation engaged in computer development passes.

   (i) Describe the stages through which such an organisation passes.
   (ii) What are the potential benefits of the stage hypothesis? (12 marks)

(b) Your organisation is setting up a steering committee to assist in the planning and control of computer development. Prepare a short report to user department managers which sets out:

   (i) the reasons for having a steering committee;
   (ii) options for organisation and staffing of a steering committee;
   (iii) potential problems which may arise. (8 marks)

11 SYSTEMS DEVELOPMENT PROJECT

Identify and briefly describe the major stages in a computer systems development project.

12 PRESENTING TECHNOLOGY

Senior management in an organisation need to make certain strategic decisions in respect of information technology in the organisation.

They particularly want to know whether the information technology function should be centralised or decentralised, its administrative location in the organisation, and how it should be controlled financially.

Required

As an external consultant engaged by the managing director, your first task is to make a presentation to senior management which:

(a) analyses the arguments for and against centralisation/decentralisation;

(b) explains the various alternatives available for information technology administrative location and financial control.

What would your presentation contain?

List of Key Terms and Index

These are the terms which we have identified throughout the text as being KEY TERMS. You should make sure that you can define what these terms mean; go back to the pages highlighted here if you need to check.

List of key terms

ORDER FORM

To order your ACCA books, you can phone us on 0181 740 2211, email us at publishing@bpp.co.uk, fax this form to 0181 740 1184 or cut this form out and post it to the address below.

To: BPP Publishing Ltd, Aldine House, Aldine Place, London W12 8AW

Tel: 0181-740 2211
Fax: 0181-740 1184

Forenames (Mr / Ms): ______________ Surname: ______________________________

Daytime delivery address: ____

____

Post code: _________________ Date of exam (month/year): _________________

Please send me the following books:	*Price* 6/98 Text £	1/98 Kit £	1/98 Passcards £	*Quantity* Text	Kit	Passcards	*Total* £
Foundation							
The Accounting Framework	18.95	8.95	4.95	....	....	....	....
The Accounting Framework (Int'l)	18.95	8.95*		....	....		....
The Legal Framework	18.95	8.95	4.95	....	....	....	....
Management Information	18.95	8.95	4.95	....	....	....	....
The Organisational Framework	18.95	8.95	4.95	....	....	....	....
Certificate							
Information Analysis	18.95	8.95	4.95	....	....	....	....
The Audit Framework	18.95	8.95	4.95	....	....	....	....
The Audit Framework (Int'l)	18.95	8.95*		....	....		....
The Tax Framework FA 98 (7/98 Text, 8/98 P/c, 8/98 Kit)	18.95	8.95	3.95	....	....	....	....
Managerial Finance	18.95	8.95	4.95	....	....	....	....
Professional							
Information for Control and Decision Making	19.95	9.95	5.95	....	....	....	....
Accounting and Audit Practice A: Accounting	15.95	9.95	5.95	....	....	....	....
Accounting and Audit Practice A: Accounting (Int'l)	15.95	9.95*		....	....		....
Accounting and Audit Practice B: Auditing	13.95			....			....
Accounting and Audit Practice B: Auditing (Int'l)	13.95			....			....
(Kit and Passcards cover both accounting and auditing)							
Tax Planning FA 98 (7/98 Text, 8/98 P/c, 8/98 Kit)	19.95	9.95	5.95	....	....	....	....
Management and Strategy	19.95	9.95	5.95	....	....	....	....
Financial Reporting Environment	19.95	9.95	5.95	....	....	....	....
Financial Reporting Environment (Int'l)	19.95	9.95*		....	....		....
Financial Strategy	19.95	9.95	5.95	....	....	....	....
Postage and packaging:							
UK: Texts £3.00 for first plus £2.00 for each extra				....	....	....	....
Kits and Passcards £2.00 for first plus £1.00 for each extra				....	....	....	....
Europe (inc ROI & CI): Texts £5.00 for first plus £4.00 for each extra				....	....	....	....
Kits and Passcards £2.50 for first plus £1.00 for each extra				....	....	....	....
Rest of the World: Texts £20.00 for first plus £10.00 for each extra				....	....	....	....
Kits and Passcards £15.00 for first plus £8.00 for each extra				....	....	....	....
(Single Kits/Passcards are airmailed. All other parcels are sent by courier and should arrive in not more than six days.)							
						Total	______

*** International Stream Kits will be published in Autumn 1998**

I enclose a cheque for £ _________ or charge to Access/Visa/Switch

Card number | | | | | | | | | | | | | | | | | | | |

Start date (Switch only) _________ **Expiry date** ____________ **Issue no. (Switch only)** ___

Signature ___________________________